In Memory Of

Thomas Swallen 1951

Dedicated by the
Carleton College
Alumni Association

Mind and Its Evolution: A Dual Coding Theoretical Approach

Mind and Its Evolution: A Dual Coding Theoretical Approach

Allan Paivio
University of Western Ontario, Canada

LEA

LAWRENCE ERLBAUM ASSOCIATES, PUBLISHERS

2007   Mahwah, New Jersey   London

Lawrence Erlbaum Associates, Inc., Publishers
10 Industrial Avenue
Mahwah, New Jersey 07430
www.erlbaum.com

Cover design by Kathryn Houghtaling Lacey

Library of Congress Cataloging-in-Publication Data

Paivio, Allan.
   Mind and its evolution : a dual coding theoretical approach / Allan Paivio.
         p.   cm.
Includes bibliographical references and index.

ISBN 978-0-8058-5259-2 — 0-8058-5259-X (cloth)
ISBN 978-0-8058-5260-8 — 0-8058-5260-3 (pbk.)

1. Thought and thinking. 2. Cognition. 3. Mental representation. 4. Dual-coding hypotheses.   I. Title.
BF441.P35   2006
155.7—dc22   2006002506
                                                                         CIP

Printed in the United States of America
10 9 8 7 6 5 4 3 2 1

120806-12760 U8

Contents

Preface

This volume updates the dual coding theory of mind and then extends it to the interpretation of mind evolution. The update is necessary because of new findings from psychological research on memory, thought, language, and other core areas covered by the theory, as well as explosive developments in the cognitive neurosciences. The novel extension of the theory to the analysis of the evolution of mind follows logically from the generally accepted premise that mind evolution proceeded from a primeval nonverbal phase to a recent period that incorporates language as well. Dual coding theory is a natural candidate for the interpretive extension because it deals explicitly with the adaptive functions of the nonverbal and verbal systems in their current form. The challenge here is to show how those adaptive systems might have evolved.

Problematic issues in the extended domain arise from the historical background of the core concepts, mind and evolution. Both are complex and controversial ideas when considered individually and doubly so when combined. Opposition to the concept of mind began with the difficulty of explaining how Cartesian immaterial mind and material body could influence each other. The opposition was reinforced by the behaviorists' rejection of mentalistic ("Ghost-in-the-Machine") ideas in their pursuit of psychology as an objective science of behavior. In what is still the most thorough review of the concept, Philosopher Gilbert Ryle (1949) found both the Cartesian and the behaviorist views of mind to be unacceptable and proposed that the concept be defined essentially in terms of inferences from behavior: "The ascertainment of a person's mental capacities and propensities is an inductive process, an induction to law-like propositions from observed actions and reactions (p. 172)." Ryle nonetheless recognized that there is a logical hazard in using "mind" at all because it is too easy to make such illogical statements as "body and mind interact upon each other." Thus, when logical candor is required, we should speak only of persons doing and undergoing things–which, paradoxically, is essentially the radical behaviorist position on the issue (e.g., Skinner, 1974, pp. 117–118).

The concept regained acceptability in psychology when it was linked operationally to observable activities. Neuropsychologist Donald Hebb said that mind "can only be regarded, for scientific purposes, as activity of the brain" (1949, p. xiv) and used the term freely in that sense (Hebb, 1980). Others used the concept in specific experimental contexts when dealing with such problems as the role of mental imagery in memory and thought. So used, mind is synonymous with cognition, which referred classically to the "faculties" of perception, thought, reason, and memory as distinct from emotion and "volition" (motivation). Today, cognition encompasses all of these and more, including especially language, which not only is a behavioral phenomenon but also something that is "used" in perception, thinking, and memory. Influenced by information theory and computer science, cognitive psychology emerged as the original descriptive framework for the broad domain (Neisser, 1967) and soon spawned an even broader field, the cognitive sciences, now largely dominated by the cognitive neurosciences. The core phenomena of cognition have expanded as well to include emotion and motivation.

However, a unifying theory for the phenomenal domain proved to be elusive. Many hoped that such a theory would emerge from computational models based on programming languages. None of the early versions did "even remote justice to the complexity of human mental processes" (Neisser, 1967, p. 9). Neisser proposed an alternative model based on the notion that cognition consists of acts of construction that make use of whatever stimulus information is available in the situation. He spelled out the implications of that idea for perception and other aspects of cognition but concluded that "no contemporary psychological theory or existing program deals satisfactorily with the constructive nature of the higher mental processes" (Neisser, 1967, p. 300).

Dual coding theory was developing during the "contemporary" phase covered by Neisser's volume and shortly thereafter reached a form complete enough to deal comprehensively with the kinds of mental processes to which he referred. It contributed to the development of cognitive psychology particularly by helping the ostracized concept of imagery to become "scientifically respectable" (Reese, 1970). In its competitive ballpark, however, dual coding was opposed by models that assumed that all cognitive work is carried out by a single mental code, based either on natural language or on the kinds of computational languages that Neisser found wanting. We shall see that variants of the single code approach continue to be influential, although still burdened by the shortcomings of their ancestors.

Turning now to evolution, it also is a complex and controversial idea even in its biological home, and more so in the range of its application to other domains, especially the fuzzy domain of mind. Before Darwin, it was used to describe such inorganic phenomena as evolution of the solar system and of geological formations (Murphy, 1950). The concept continues to be applied widely to all kinds of phenomena that show gradual, orderly changes, ranging from evolution of language to evolution of the universe (Dennett, 1995). Recent evidence justifies such concept stretching, splendidly so in coupling the evolution of life with evolution of the universe in a literal sense, for the essential atomic elements of life are abundant in the traces of the primordial universe (Tyson & Goldsmith, 2004). As Carl Sagan (1980, p. 233) said, "We are all made of starstuff."

Psychology was an early beneficiary of evolutionary thinking, particularly the functionalist movement that was based on the view that mental processes and behaviors are adaptive mechanisms (Murphy, 1950). Comparative psychology emerged from that context, inspired directly as well by the fact that Darwin himself applied evolutionary thinking to comparative psychology in his books, *The Descent of Man* (1882) and *The Expression of the Emotions in Man and Animals* (1873), conveniently available in a Darwin collection edited by J.D. Watson (2005). The concept was extended by Darwin's cousin, Herbert Spencer, to social evolution, which finds a broader base in the modern concept of cultural evolution. In the meantime, Darwinian evolution emerged as the organizing principle in all of biology, becoming more and complex as the domain evolved from the study of species to the molecular basis of their evolution.

The complexities multiply greatly in the lofty domain of mind evolution. A bewildering variety of theories have been proposed by theorists who come from such diverse disciplines as archeology, anthropology, psychology, linguistics, and philosophy. Thus, the theorists begin with different views of evolved mind, vary in the range of phenomena they encompass, and differ in the kind and amount of scientific data they bring to bear on the mind-evolution problem. Given that diversity, it is not surprising that the resulting theories are incomplete in important respects and vary greatly in what aspects of mind they focus on for evolutionary interpretations. The most general limitation is that they are not founded on a comprehensive analysis of basic cognitive mechanisms (e.g., sensorimotor and memory systems) and their adaptive functions in animal and human life. They tend to focus instead on higher order phenomena and processes, such as intelligence, language, consciousness, and mating behavior, which depend on evolution of the basic processes. The following examples illustrate this selective diversity.

The experts on the evolution side of the equation include paleoanthropologists and archeologists, who draw their inferences about human evolution from the remains of bones, stones, and artifacts. Leakey and Lewin (1978) used such clues along with evidence from psychology and other sciences to construct a fascinating story of human origins, family life, intelligence, language, our warlike nature, and more. "The story is, of course, pure fantasy, but we construct it around as many facts and inspired guesses that we can" (Leakey & Lewin, p. 12). More recently, British archeologist Steven Mithen (1996) used similar evidence to speculate about how modern mind evolved as a series of unconnected "intelligence modules" specialized for dealing with social, technical, natural history, and language skills. Mixing of these modules eventually resulted in "cognitive fluidity," which produced the cultural explosion in art, technology, and so on. As for his database, in a subsequent debate on such issues (Donald, Mithen, & Gardner, 1998), Mithen argued that archeology "can go just as far beyond speculation about past behavior as can, say, a cognitive developmental-psychologist when speculating about what might be going on in a child's mind." Psychologist Howard Gardner responded to Mithen's argument by pointing out that archeology must deal with a necessarily scanty record of past events and radical reinterpretations of new findings, whereas psychologists participate in experimentally grounded science that depends on replicable tests of hypotheses carried out with participants available anywhere in the world.

Although relying on experimental evidence, evolutionary psychologists also vary in the scope and selective emphasis of their speculations about mind evolution. Merlin Donald (1991) proposed a progression from primate episodic memory—a capacity for remembering specific events—to human gestural, linguistic, and written forms of cognitive representation. These individual representational stages are the basis for evolution of different cultures in which knowledge is passed on through gestural-imitational modeling, narrative, and writing—the last leading to scientific and philosophical views of the world. These sweeping and fascinating speculations are broadly grounded in observations from psychology and other disciplines, but their theoretical base is eclectic rather than general and unifying.

Other evolutionary psychologists focus on aspects of social-behavior. Geoffrey Miller (2001) argued that sexual selection through mate choice has been as important in mind evolution as has natural selection for survival. Higher order human behaviors such as morality, creativity, art, music, and language evolved as sexual attractors—mental equivalents of a peacock's tail. However defensible this hypothesis might be, it is clear that basic needs for food and shelter must be satisfied before sexual, aesthetic, and other higher order needs can emerge and be expressed (cf. Maslow, 1954), and that satisfaction of those basic needs depends on evolution of the necessary perceptual, memory, and learning skills. Miller took this basic stage for granted in his evolutionary hypothesis but it must be included in a more complete story.

Greenspan and Shanker (2004) proposed a specific social-emotional theory of the origins and development of symbols and their use in thinking. The theory emphasizes the cumulative effects of cultural evolution based on an innate capacity to learn from experience. The most important experience is coregulated emotional communication between infant and its caregivers, through which the infant learns how to predict and respond to adult patterns of behavior. This promotes general pattern recognition skills that can be applied later to problem solving in the physical world as well. The capacity to recognize and produce emotional signals led to the development of symbols, and ultimately, language. This is a bold hypothesis with a welcome emphasis on the roles of emotion and social learning in the ontogenesis and evolution of the hominid mind. From this perspective, however, the hypothesis does not constitute a general theory of mind that can be applied to an even broader range of cognitive phenomena and their evolutionary foundations.

Currently, consciousness and language are the most popular mind evolution topics. The former is especially speculative and intractable, as evidenced by a recent comprehensive review of the subject by Susan Blackmore (2004). The uncertainty that consciousness poses for evolutionary theorists is starkly revealed by her conclusion that "there is no consensus over when consciousness evolved. Proposals range from billions of years ago to only a few thousand" (p. 160). Why the concept is contentious is discussed in this volume in contexts that deal with the place of consciousness in psychology, cognitive neuroscience, evolutionary theories, and dual coding theory.

Language is even more prominent as an evolutionary target. The perspectives range from the view that language dominates mental life to the reverse view that it serves more fundamental nonlinguistic cognitive systems. Its evolution has been interpreted on one hand in terms of natural Darwinian selection working over eons of time, and on the other hand, as an explosive change fueled by a genetic mutation. Researchers from all relevant disciplines contributed to a massive volume

(Harnad, Steklis, & Lancaster, 1976) on the nature of language, its evolution, general cognitive-behavioral precursors, and functional contexts. A subsequent landmark publication by linguist Derek Bickerton (1990) particularly emphasized the dominant role of language as the representational medium of mind and proposed a theory of how it evolved from more primitive representational systems. Others have emphasized very specific precursors, such as gestures and imitation, based on evolution of brain systems among which "mirror neurons" have emerged as the flavor of the decade in cognitive neuroscience.

Cummins and Allen's (1998) edited volume covers mind evolution in general, with chapters on such topics as numerical reasoning, communication, language and thought, social norms, and applications of Darwinian principles to psychology. The broad coverage nonetheless leaves important gaps. For example, memory and perception are barely mentioned despite the attention these topics receive in psychological works on animal cognition. Imagery is notably absent, which isn't surprising because no one has written about how it might have evolved.

In contrast with the others, this approach is based on a general theory of mind that is systematically applicable to all aspects of nonverbal and verbal cognition. Thus, it is well-suited in principle for interpreting evolution of mind from its ancestral nonverbal forms to the time when language began to emerge and develop as a contributing intellectual partner. The subsequent adaptive interplay of the two systems over countless generations of cultural evolution led to the growth of knowledge and skills that now characterize ordinary and extraordinary individuals working in their different domains.

The dual coding approach combines structural and functional viewpoints. The structural side is reflected in assumptions about the multimodal nature of dual coding representations and their complex interconnections. The functional side appears in multiple adaptive roles that are attributed to the dual coding systems. The functional emphasis is notably strong in regard to the nature and evolution of language in particular. By way of contrast, Chomsky (1968) invested his theoretical capital in attempts to uncover the structural essence of language, reasoning that one must understand what language is before one can understand what it does. Those who focus on the evolutionary role of gestures, imitation, mirror neurons, and language genes also are not asking why language began and evolved, but rather how it evolved. The principal function of language as a communication system may be so obvious that evolutionary theorists tend to take it for granted. However, even this function has been questioned. For example, Christiansen and Kirby (2003, p. 305) concluded their informative review of agreements and controversies about language evolution with questions for future research, among which one finds the following: "Is communicative function central to an evolutionary story or an epiphenomenon?"

The communicative function of language was never in doubt in the dual coding context, where human language was defined as a "biological communication system that is specialized for the transmission of meaningful information between and within persons by means of linguistic signs" (Paivio & Begg, 1981, p. 14). That definition is implicitly accepted in this volume. Other theorists also view language from multifaceted functionalist perspectives and I review their contributions where appropriate.

The volume is divided into two general parts that are defined by the title. The first half deals with mind as it is, and the second half, with how it got to be that way. Each half is divided into two parts defined by thematic chapters. Thus, Part I consists of five chapters that present the raison d'être for the dual coding approach, explain its principle assumptions, describe supporting evidence for the adaptive functions of the dual coding systems, and compare it to other theoretical "species" that are the main alternatives to dual coding theory. Part II is the neuropsychological parallel to Part I in that it presents brain evidence for the multimodal verbal and nonverbal brain-systems, and how they contribute to basic adaptive functions. It also examines brain-based common-coding alternatives to dual coding theory, and proposals about how the brain might solve the classical binding problem, namely the integration of parts (shapes, colors, etc.) into objects that are experienced as whole entities.

Part III is about mind evolution, covering background issues related to biological and cultural evolution, comparative psychological analyses of preverbal animal minds, and the origins and evolution of language from simple to complex forms. Here, memory and imagery are viewed as key players in those stages of the evolutionary process. Part IV further extends dual coding theory to the interpretation of the cultural evolution of "peak mind" as reflected in expertise, intelligence, creativity, and the innovative achievements of acknowledged "geniuses" in various domains of arts and science. The volume concludes with evidence based suggestions about nurturing mental growth through applications of dual coding theory in education, psychotherapy, and health.

An epilogue closes the volume with a graphical summary of the dual coding theory of mind evolution from its primeval nonverbal base to a recent period of exponentially-accelerated growth in hominid cognitive power that peaks in modern humans.

ACKNOWLEDGMENTS

Finally, I gratefully acknowledge the encouragement and advice I received from friends and colleagues. I am especially grateful to my wife Dolores Niskanen for her patience during the many years when she thought I was glued to my computer. But then, she understands passion for a calling from her own long career in dance and choreograpy. I am indebted to many colleagues who provided feedback on the content and style of draft chapters. It happens that are also cited in this volume for their scientific contributions to relevant topics. My friend Mark Sadoski, cognitive generalist and literacy research expert at of Texas A & M University, read and commented on all chapters. Wallace Lambert, long ago my graduate supervisor at McGill University, once again was my mentor when he critiqued the first nine chapters. Anders Ericsson (Florida State University) informed me on aspects of the psychology of expertise in its many forms (Chapters 14-17). Colleagues in my own university showed me how I could improve chapters related to their domains of expertise: Bill Roberts and David Sherry on animal memory and cognition (Chapters 10 and 11), Tony Vernon on intelligence (Chapter 16), and Bill Harper on the Einstein section in Chapter 18. Mustaq Khan on applications of DCT principles, especially in psychotherapy (Chapter 19). My daughter Sandra Paivio (University of Windsor) helped me improve my descriptions of research approaches to psychotherapy (Chapter 19). Long time friends Nanci Bell and Paul Worthington, directors and developers of the remedial education programs at Lindamood-Bell Learning Processes (San Luis Obispo, California), commented on early drafts of Chapter 1 and, more recently, aspects of Chapter 19. A number of colleagues in my department (Albert Katz, Richard Harshman, Jim Neufeld) helped me improve the graphical summary of the DCT interpretation of mind evolution that appears in the epilogue and on the cover. The graphic construction of the figure was done by audiovisual technician Rick Cornwall who, along with John Cesarini, prepared camera-ready copies of all illustrations, many of which had been adapted for this volume by my daughter-in-law, graphic artist Laura Paivio.

General editorial guidance and specific improvements in the final manuscript were expertly provided by Chief Editor Lori Stone, Book Production Editor Suzanne Sheppard, and an anonymous copyeditor for Lawrence Erlbaum Associates. I especially want to thank Lawrence Erlbaum, already publisher of other books of mine, for taking on this project. And last but not least, I will forever be grateful to my laptop, without which this book would never have been written.

I
EVOLVED DUAL CODING MIND AND RELATED SPECIES

CHAPTER ONE

Not by Language Alone

In an evolutionary eyeblink our species evolved from "just another primate" into the intellectual superstar of our planet. Life began 4 billion years ago and it took evolution most of the time since then to produce our earliest primate ancestor, the tiny "dawn monkey" (Eosimias) who appeared just 45 million years ago. Some 40 million years later, our hominid line branched off from other primates and gradually evolved into anatomically modern humans capable of making stone tools. That dates back a quarter of a million years, less than 1% of the time span of primate evolution. Then, perhaps a mere 100,000 years ago, our ancestors had developed a primitive language–new evidence of an advanced intellect—and from that time on, traces of assorted tools and other creative expressions of mind proliferated explosively.

Given the concurrent historical advances in language and material artifacts, it is understandable why evolutionists generally attribute the intellectual spurt of humans to the emergence of language. As evolutionary biologist Stephen Jay Gould put it in 1999, "scholars usually assume that speech (or writing) is the quintessential act of human mind ... the centerpiece of our evolutionary distinctiveness from all other creatures" (p. 6)—distinctiveness referring of course to what humans have achieved by means of language and not simply the fact that only humans speak or write. That idea was stated even more explicitly by the linguist Derek Bickerton (1990) in his volume, *Language and Species*: "... language was not only the force that launched us beyond the limits of other species but the necessary (and perhaps even sufficient) prerequisite of both our consciousness and our unique capacities" (p. 4).

I have quite a different view of the language-intellect relation. I accept the obvious truism that language played a critical role in our giant intellectual leap as a species, but language never worked its magic alone and it cannot do so now. Instead, it was always depended on a silent partner that provides it with something to talk about, a general cognitive system that had evolved to a high level before it invited language in as a coplayer in the evolutionary scene. I see language as a benevolent, octopus-like parasite whose tentacles invaded the brain and was empowered by it to survive and thrive to the point where it could contribute something useful to its host.

3

Nonverbal mind and verbal mind thus became interlocked in a synergistic relation that evolved into the nuclear power source of our intellect.

That thesis does not arise out of the blue in response to the linguistic dominance view of the evolution of mind. It had its precedent years ago in a similar reaction to verbal mediational theories of memory and cognition. Such theories and their subsequent abstract (propositional) renditions motivated a research program that evolved into the *dual coding theory* (DCT) of cognition. Chapters 2 and 3 describe the history and evolved theory in sufficient detail to justify its interpretive extension to evolutionary issues. The rest of this chapter reviews and evaluates the language-dominance and other "single-minded" views to provide a contrasting framework and raison d'être for the mental "duality" thesis.

The issues revolve around the concept of thought, for, in commonsense terms, thinking is what the mind does. The question here is, what is the nature of the mental entities and processes that make thinking possible? We turn first to language and then to imagery, abstract "mentalese," and dual coding as answers to that question.

LANGUAGE AND THOUGHT

The language-supremacy view of mind is ancient and tenacious. In the Judeo-Christian tradition, we find its roots in one interpretation of the biblical view of genesis, "in the beginning was the word," according to which God used his preexisting, divine language to create the material universe. Modern parallels have been expressed in terms of the relation between language and thought. The most extreme view is that the two are equivalent. Thus, in the 19th century, psychologist J. Herbart (1891) wrote, "Words used as the signs of thought are so closely connected that it would appear that we think by means of words" (p. 17) and the great pioneer of linguistic science, M. Muller (1892), stated that "Language and thought are inseparable" (p. 385, Vol. 1) and that "thought in the sense, of reasoning is impossible without language" (p. 72; Vol. 2). A bit later, J. B. Watson (1930, p. 238), the father of American Behaviorism, asserted similarly that "What the psychologists have hitherto called thought is in short nothing but talking to ourselves."

More moderate views distinguish between the two concepts but still imply that language somehow dominates or controls thought. The best-known example is the Whorfian hypothesis (developed most fully by Benjamin Lee Whorf in 1956), according to which language is a kind of mold that shapes the way we conceptualize the world, so that speakers of different languages "see" their worlds in different ways. The hypothesis has been extensively investigated and debated, with mixed support, depending on how "thought" is measured. We shall encounter the hypothesis again in various guises in the evolutionary context.

In what sense and degree can language really be equated with thought and credited with our intellectual achievements? The answer depends on how language is defined. You might think that by now we would have a straightforward definition acceptable to all students of language, but this is not the case, and the reasons are related to the complexity of what the term covers. In a comprehensive volume on human cognitive abilities, psychologist-psychometrician John Carroll (1993) referred to the difficulty of summarizing the relation of language abilities to cognitive processes, which he attributed mainly to the fact that "language behavior is enormously complex and diverse, and ... there appear to be a series of somewhat separate factors of language ability, reflecting that complexity and diversity" (p. 194).

Definitions also reflect that complexity and diversity. The broadest definition consists of 16 "design features" proposed by linguist Charles Hockett (1963) to distinguish human language from communication systems of other animals. Those features are discussed later in the context of the origin and evolution of language, but at this point let's just consider the variety of defining characteristics that can be found in any dictionary. Typically, the first definition identifies language with speech—spoken words and the methods of combining them. Another definition refers to functions of speech as a means of expressing and communicating thoughts, emotions, and so on. A third asserts that the words and their combinations must be meaningful and understandable to the language community.

These characteristics, among others, can also be found in definitions adopted by language scientists and scholars. In his popular volume, *Mother Tongue,* science writer Joel Davis (1994) listed definitions proposed by such eminent linguists as Noam Chomsky (e.g., 1957), who referred to language in one context as "a set (finite or infinite) of sentences, each finite in length and constructed out of a finite set of elements" (cited in Davis, 1994, p. 7) and in another context as a vehicle for expressing "indefinitely many thoughts and for reacting appropriately to an indefinite range of new situations" (cited in Davis, 1994, p. 9). The first statement refers to linguistic units and their combination into larger structures; the second, to the functions of language in relation to thought and behavior. (Both statements also allude to the creative potential or productivity of language, its capacity for creating new combinations and expressing new thoughts, which is generally attributed to syntax, a topic on which we focus, in the context of language evolution, in Chapter 13. Also implied in the functional statement is the idea that the units and structures of language must have shared, language-community-wide meanings, which, according to Chomsky and certain other linguists, are represented in a semantic component of the general language system.

The language dominance view of mind is tenable or not, depending on which definition (or characteristic) of language we choose to emphasize. It is surely untenable if we consider only structural units and combinations—that is, the acoustic or articulatory patterns of speech, or the shapes of written language. We know, for example, that actors can memorize and deliver foreign-language passages in a play without understanding what they are saying unless they have also memorized the translations. The words of the language may have no meaning for the actor, although they do for the audience. One can also imagine extending such meaningless language to include some degree of productivity: the actor could memorize sets of nouns, adjectives, verbs, and so on, and insert them into sentence frames according to the grammatical rules of the target language. The actor could thereby arrive at some sense of grammatical appropriateness without any deeper understanding.

A native speaker–listener might recognize that the actor's creations are grammatically correct and find some of them to be sensible whereas others might resemble Chomsky's (1957) famous example of a grammatical but meaningless sentence, "Colorless green ideas sleep furiously" (p. 157), indicating that the actor's speech does not reflect meaningful thought.

We also know from neuropsychological data that the ability to speak does not necessarily reflect a full capacity for dealing with meaning. The neuropsychologist Norman Geschwind (1972) described the case of a woman who survived carbon monoxide poisoning but was left severely brain damaged and demented, unable to think or communicate except for a residual capacity to sing entire songs perfectly clearly and learn to repeat sentences spoken to her, all with no indication that she understood what she sang or repeated. An autopsy later revealed a lesion that isolated a section of the left temporal lobe from the rest of the brain except for connections to the speech motor system. In some less severe language disorders, the affected person might be able to speak relatively clearly while having difficulty understanding speech.

The aforementioned examples and the dictionary criterion that language must be meaningful to the language community raise questions about the nature of the relation between language and meaning. The strong implication of the dictionary definition is that language itself includes the communicated meanings. How might language do that? Some have suggested that the words of a language are composed of bundles of elementary features that include formal characteristics related to sound and pronunciation as well as semantic features that represent linguistic meaning. Such a definition should leave us wondering about the meanings of the semantic features themselves. For example, how do we know the meaning of "animate" when it is used as a defining characteristic of creatures that move—in what form and where in the word is animateness stored? A variant that seems more useful distinguishes between formal units (word patterns, for example) and concepts. Thus we know the word "dog" and we also know the concept of dog, which covers everything we know about dogs to think and talk "meaningfully" about the animal. In some approaches, however, word pattern and concept are collapsed into a super entity called "lexical concept," which is viewed as the basic unit in our "conceptual lexicon" or mental dictionary. By logical extension, all three components—meaning, concept, and word pattern—collapse into macrolanguage units within a "conceptual semantic lexicon," which would include concepts like "animateness."

There must also be some way of organizing and manipulating such mental primitives if they are to be useful in thinking. Grammar provides the means of completing the language-thought circle. Thus linguist Ray Jackendoff (1992) proposed a "grammar of lexical concepts"—that can creatively combine the composite mental primitives into "sentence concepts"—that is, all possible concepts than can be expressed by sentences. We end up with an even more stretched definition of "meaningful language" as a conceptual-semantic-lexical-syntactic system. Such a view gets a strong stamp of authority from Chomskyy's (1995) last version of universal grammar, which he described as a minimalist language model in which all of syntax is "a projection of the lexicon," which means that all syntactic and semantic features of a word are included with the word in the mental lexicon.

The popularity of these extended definitions of the lexicon was clearly revealed in a call for the Second International Conference on The Mental Lexicon which stated that the Conference "is soliciting abstracts for papers and poster positions that bear on the question of how words are represented in the mind (in terms of their phonological, orthographic, morphological, syntactic and semantic properties), how they are linked to one another, and how they are accessed during language use", Obviously, such a rich mental lexicon, if real, could be the power base for meaningful thinking. At the very least, the idea makes it difficult to distinguish between language and thought.

Functional definitions do not equate language with thought but describe it instead as a vehicle for expressing thoughts, feelings, and so on. We are now back to the basic problem of defining the separated components, namely "thought-less language" and "language-less thought." The language side could be handled by restricting its definition to form, namely the patterns of sound and pronunciation associated with speech and the visual patterns of text, much as in Bloomfieldian structural linguistics. Defining language-independent thought is more difficult and the problem has been approached in various ways. One way has been to define nonverbal cognition operationally, in terms of performance on tasks that can be done without using language, such as tests of spatial and other nonverbal abilities that are included in intelligence tests. In that context, the nonverbal performance tests are usually contrasted with verbal tests of intelligence, implying a kind of mental duality as the basis of intelligent thinking, although it is not usually described that way by intelligence testers, as we shall see later in Chapter 16.

We turn to two other approaches that explicitly focus on nonlinguistic modes of thought. The oldest and periodically-revived approach of this kind equates useful thinking with mental imagery. The second interprets thought in terms of the activity of abstract mental representations that do not correspond directly to natural language or imagery but somehow encompass both of these along with any other conceivable expression of thought.

IMAGERY AND THOUGHT

The idea that nonverbal imagery is the dominant medium of thought also has ancient roots. More than 2,000 years ago, Aristotle argued in *De Anima* that the "thinking faculty thinks of its forms in mental pictures" and that "the soul never thinks without a mental picture;" moreover, drawing on an even older imagery memory tradition, he proposed that the images of thought are under voluntary control, that "it is possible to put things before our eyes just as those do who invent mnemonics and construct images" (cited in Yates, 1966, p. 32).

The use of imagery for remembering and thinking continued to be advocated for centuries by religious leaders, educators, and professional mnemonists (memory experts). The practice became controversial and was repeatedly opposed, partly because of the difficulty of constructing and using images that represent abstract words and ideas, and partly (and more vehemently) because it fell victim to religious iconoclasm. The religious opposition was spurred by the fact that imagery became associated with occult traditions. For example, the famous hermetic philosopher Giordano Bruno developed and advocated use of complex memory systems based on magical astrological images (along with more mundane architectural memory "places") to organize all earthly and "heavenly" knowledge within one massive hierarchical memory structure. These systems were at the heart of his religious teachings, which were viewed as heretical and led ultimately to his execution at the stake. This fascinating history of imagery as a concept from both heaven and hell has been told most completely by historian Frances Yates (1966) and more selectively by others (e.g., Paivio, 1971b; Sadoski & Paivio, 2001). We return later to more detailed discussions of Bruno's influence on the memory tradition and educational practice.

The controversy continued into the 20th century largely because behaviorists rejected imagery as a mentalistic notion that lies outside the pale of objective science, reflecting the iconoclasm of the behaviorists' "protestant reformation." The ostracized concept survived anyway and was revitalized by researchers and scholars beginning in the 1960s. The nature and extent of the renewed "cognitive power" of imagery has varied over theoretical treatments. The following are a few examples of views in which imagery dominates as the medium of thought.

Rudolf Arnheim (1969) presented the case for imagery persuasively. He argued that the perceptual shape of language is not indispensable to thought, and that "Purely verbal thinking is the prototype of thoughtless thinking ... it is useful but sterile" (p. 231). What makes language useful are the concepts to which words refer. The concepts themselves are perceptual images and the operations of thought "are the handling of those images" (p. 227). It is important for his argument that the images can vary in abstractness, but "even the most abstract among them ... must be structurally similar (isomorphic) to the pertinent features of the situations for which the thinking shall be valid" (p. 287). Arnheim concretized his arguments by detailed analyses of nonverbal visual thinking in such diverse domains as visual art, mathematics, theoretical models in science, and education. The important general point is that Arnheim's position is precisely the opposite of the language supremacy position described earlier: for him, imagery dominates over language, which accordingly plays a subordinate role in useful thinking, a role in which it serves mainly as a pointer or tag for features that are the focus of imagistic thought.

J. Bronowski (1997) proposed similarly that imagination is the highest kind of thinking that distinguishes us most clearly from other animals, and that "imagination is the manipulation of images in one's head" (p. 26). Nonverbal imagery is implied by the examples he drew from science and art, but the verbal–nonverbal distinction is blurred by the wide meaning he gave the term *image*: It encompasses all signs including words themselves, which he characterized as the most important images for human beings. This broad definition is reminiscent of imagery typologies around the turn of the 20th century, which included not only nonverbal imagery of different sensory modalities, but also verbal processes, subdivided further into visual, auditory, and kinesthetic types of verbal thinkers (Paivio, 1971b, pp. 477–479). Attempts were made to measure individual differences in dominance of the different types of imagery, but not functional differences in thinking that might go on in the different modalities. The same uncertainty applies in the case of Bronowski's broad definition of imagery, and consequently, the role it plays in his interpretation of imagination as the crowning achievement of our species.

The case for imagery has often been argued using examples of individuals who claim to think primarily in imagery. The most famous is Albert Einstein, who reported the following:

> Words or language, as they are written or spoken, do not seem to play any role in my mechanism of thought. The psychical entities which seem to serve as elements in thought are certain signs and more or less clear images which can be voluntarily reproduced and combined ... this combinatory play seems to be the essential feature in productive thought—before there is any connection with logical construction in words or other kinds of signs which can be communicated to others ... conventional words or other signs have to be sought for laboriously only in a second stage, when the mentioned associative play is sufficiently established and can be reproduced at will. (Hadamard, 1945, p. 142)

This self-analysis is consistent with his frequent use of visual analogies to explain difficult theoretical concepts—relativity of motion in rising or falling elevators, an observer riding on a moving train or a beam of light, and so on.

Another instructive example is the animal scientist, Temple Grandin, a gifted autistic woman whose accounts of what it is like to live and cope with that strange and socially-painful cognitive disorder prompted one reviewer to describe her as "the anthropologist from Mars." Her 1995 autobiography begins as follows: "I think in pictures. Words are like a second language to me. I translate both spoken and written words into full-color movies, complete with sound, which I run like a VCR tape in my head. When somebody speaks to me, his words are instantly translated into pictures" (p. 19). She said that she can do that translation easily with concrete nouns, spatial words such as "over" and "under," verbs ("jumping"), and even adverbs that qualify pictureable verbs ("run quickly"), but not abstract language: "Some philosophy books and articles about the cattle futures market are simply incomprehensible. It is much easier for me to understand written text that describes something else that can be easily translated into pictures." (p. 31). (It happens that this is true for everyone, to varying degrees. Chapter 4 describes research that helps explain why it is so.)

What are we to make of such unique individuals as Einstein and Grandin who claim to think in pictures? The introspective evidence clearly suggests that imagery dominates in their thinking, but this does not mean that they think exclusively in the form of nonverbal imagery. For them, language both evokes imagery and expresses imagery; one can be translated into the other. This is true also of visual thinking as described by Arnheim: words somehow select out salient aspects of scenes, paintings, and situations to be imagined; conversely, the images can be described. In all of these analyses, however, imagery is said to be the engine of cognition. This is true also of entire areas of scholarly and scientific enquiry, including especially creative thinking and achievement, about which we have much to say in

Chapter 18. Imaging also figures prominently in our analysis of nonverbal animal cognition and evolution in Chapter 11.

THOUGHT AS ABSTRACT "MENTALESE"

We deal next with a set of related concepts that are rooted in Western philosophy, beginning with Plato's and Aristotle's theories of the origin and nature of knowledge. Plato believed that there is a universe of ideas that exists independent of the world that we know through our senses. These ideas are eternal truths or realities that our souls knew before we were born, realities of which earthly things are mere reflections. We do not need to learn these innate ideas, they are automatically activated (remembered) when we encounter specific examples that match the abstract "forms" that encompass them all—seeing circles and beautiful objects automatically awakens our eternal but latent ideas of "circularity" and "beauty." Thus, in his book of genesis (of mind), Plato might have said, "In the beginning was the Idea."

The essentials of Plato's doctrine carried over into later philosophies, notably Immanuel Kant's transcendental philosophy (Durant, 1926/1953, pp. 266–267) according to which our *a priori* concepts of objects transcends and precedes sense experience. The absolute and necessary general truths that we know must be independent of experience—clear and certain in themselves. He illustrated his argument using the brilliant example of mathematics (especially axiomatic geometry), which he viewed as such necessary and essential knowledge that we cannot conceive of future experience violating it (it would turn out later that not all mathematical knowledge is quite so immutable; that history is reviewed in Chapter 18). These truths derive from the inherent structure of the mind, which he viewed as an active organ that molds and coordinates sensations into ideas—all very Platonic, but with the "inherent structure of mind" replacing Plato's independent world of ideas..

The term *proposition* as used in modern representational theories of mind blends Aristotelian and Platonic sources. The Aristotelian source uses it in premises that are proposed as accepted truths in logical arguments and (later) axiomatic geometry. Thus, by this definition, mental propositions preserve the abstract truth about relations, events, and so on, that is asserted in sentences or represented in perceptual scenes and images. The Platonic source is reflected in the way the concept or its variants enter into different theoretical views. For example, Chomsky has explicitly asserted his nativistic and rationalistic views concerning the acquisition of grammar: we are born with a language-acquisition device that contains abstract universal syntactic knowledge that permits individuals to acquire their native languages with minimal ("impoverished") exposure to them. As we see later (Chapter 13), he has also touched on the evolutionary implications of his views.

Others accept the abstractness and truth-asserting aspects of mental propositions without necessarily committing themselves to Platonic nativism, but nonetheless retain the rationalistic side of Plato's philosophy. Such theories are often called computational theories because they are modeled after modern computers. Computer language is abstract and organized into internally-consistent networks of operational commands that are related only to each other and any deviation from this "airtight" logical structure is a programming error that results in system failure. Computers can be programmed to model "real-world" situations and events provided that the modeled world has an inherent logical structure of its own, or that some aspect of non-logical phenomena can be selected out and programmed in computer language. Thus, computers can be programmed to play chess because the game has logical rules—only certain kinds of moves are permitted. Psychological, meteorological, and other natural phenomena can be simulated computationally because interesting aspects have already been identified empirically and these can be programmed in different sequences, each of which by definition is a computational (formal) model. Such models can be used to predict unknown possibilities in the phenomenal domain; for example, meteorologists use them to predict the weather. The predictions, however, are expressed as probabilities or percentages because weather is probabilistic and not governed by logical "rules." Psychological phenomena are similarly probabilistic and this limits the predictive scope and success of computational models of the phenomena.

Propositions are often embedded in more general mental structures called schemata, frames, and scripts, among others. The parent concept, schema, originated with Kant and was later used in psychological, linguistic, and other analyses that are identified in relevant contexts. The schema concept refers in genereal to representations that capture our general knowledge of objects, situations, and events as perceived or described. Specific instances are recognized, remembered, and understood if they represent possible "instantiations" of a schematic pattern or description. The process is very much as in the Platonic doctrine of Ideas in which specific examples of, say, a circle or a falling tree activate the abstract ideas of a perfect circle or laws of falling bodies (motion), but without the nativism that defined Plato's theory. Modern schema theories are taken to be supported by such evidence as people filling in information that was missing from a perceived scene or a verbal passage they are trying to recall, as if a more complete, stereotypical schema had been activated by the incomplete input.[1]

Propositional and schema concepts have been criticized on the grounds that they are ambiguous and vague, used by some theorists as convenient ways of describing linguistic or perceptual information and by others as "real" representations of such information, presumably located in the brain. As descriptive concepts, they have the same status as a mathematical equation that defines the properties of gravity; as reified concepts, they are analogous to saying that gravity as we know it "is" the equation. Other questions pertain to their scientific usefulness: How can we observe, measure, and manipulate abstract mental propositions? How can we tell whether a specific memory is a plausible "instantiation" of a schema? Or, relatedly, how do we remember specific information from a general schema, which requires us to unpack the schema into its details? How, when, and why do we do that? The vagueness of the concept, perhaps an inevitable consequence of its abstractness, has made it difficult to test predictions based on the concept, and, where this has

---

[1]Schema theories of memory were particularly influenced by the British psychologist Sir Frederick Bartlett, who viewed memories as schematic reconstructions rather than detailed reproductions of experiences (Bartlett. 1932).

been tried, the results have not been convincing. Here, too, we must postpone the evidence until later.

In addition to abstract representations, some hybrid theories include concepts that more directly reflect the properties of concrete situations. The most popular is the mental model as developed by Johnson-Laird (1983). Mental models refer generally to structural analogues of the world, that is, aspects of real-world information pertinent to problem solving. Johnson-Laird's theory includes such models along with mental images and propositional symbol strings that correspond to natural language. Walter Kintsch (e.g., 1998) and his collaborators have used a similar concept, the situation model (functionally like a mental image but more abstract), along with propositions and verbatim sentence representations in a theory of language comprehension. These theories distinguish between linguistic and nonlinguistic information, but they nonetheless rely heavily on propositional terms to describe the mental codes. For example, in Johnson-Laird's approach, verbatim sentences become mental propositions, and in Kintsch's approach, situational models and sentence representations are ultimately reduced to abstract propositional descriptions. All of this is tantamount to saying that such realities as sentences and pictures (or mental images) are represented in our minds in a form analogous to computer language. Such alternative views of mind are described more fully in Chapter 5.

GENERAL EVALUATION OF MONISTIC INTERPRETATIONS OF THOUGHT

The three general approaches just reviewed are attempts to explain thinking primarily in terms of processes associated with a single concept—language, imagery, or abstract mentalese of some kind. All can be viewed as varieties of psychological monism analogous to classical philosophical monism, the search for a single substance or principle that could explain the "multitude of appearances" of objects and events in the universe. The approach can work only if the diversity and complexity of the universe are incorporated by fiat into the monistic concept. This has been attempted in the psychological domain by (a) stretching the concept of language to include meaning along with linguistic form, (b) restricting imagery to a limited (although broad) cognitive domain, and (c) defining the varieties of abstract mentalese so that they cover all substances and principles that comprise thought. Difficulties arise, however, when one tries to predict and explain performance in cognitive tasks in terms of such monistic concepts, and to explain the evolutionary origins and development of the substantive base of the concepts—something that becomes increasingly difficult the more abstract the concept, the more removed it is from the observable reality. The dual coding approach was intended to avoid such difficulties.

DUAL CODING: A THUMBNAIL SKETCH

The empirical development of dual coding theory and its current form are described in the next two chapters. Here I simply outline the general features that distinguish it from all of the aforementioned approaches to cognition. As its name suggests, the theory is based on the assumption that thinking involves the activity of two distinct cognitive subsystems, a verbal system specialized for dealing directly with language and a nonverbal system specialized for dealing with nonlinguistic objects and events. At another level of analysis, it is a multimodal theory, because both systems are assumed to be composed of modality-specific (visual, auditory, etc.) representational units and structures that are internal isomorphs of the perceptual and behavioral characteristics of "words and things" rather than abstractions of them. The representations are connected to sensory input and response output systems as well as to each other so that they can function independently or cooperatively to mediate nonverbal and verbal behavior. The representational activity may or may not be experienced consciously as imagery and inner speech.

The theory means that both systems are generally involved even in language phenomena. The verbal system is a necessary player in all "language games" but it is sufficient in only a few. In the most interesting and meaningful ones, it draws on the rich knowledge base and gamesmanship of the nonverbal imagery system. Conversely, the nonverbal system cannot play language games on its own, but it can play complex nonverbal solitaire. The verbal system dominates in some tasks and the imagery system in others. Thinking is this variable pattern of the interplay of the two systems. Precisely how this occurs and what it implies for the evolution of mind are central themes in subsequent chapters.

VARIETIES OF DUALISM

This final section puts dual coding in the context of other conceptually related distinctions, none of which are quite like the dualism that characterizes this theory. This overview rules out one variant and shows how others are related to my version.

Mind–Body Dualism

This was a great philosophical debate. Descartes essentially defined the problem by distinguishing sharply between two universal "substances," matter (body included) and nonmaterial mind, the latter manifesting itself in consciousness and pure thought. There is a puzzle here at least as a word game, but I will not play it because it is scientifically irrelevant. Simply put, there is no way we can get a hold on immaterial mind so that we can study its effects on material body, and vice versa. The only practical scientific alternatives are to ignore the problem altogether or to adopt materialistic monism at least as a working hypothesis in which we assume that consciousness awareness in perception and imagery is a reactive property of the brain rather than something with an independent existence "out there." This view may not be satisfactory philosophically but it is necessary as a scientific attitude.

Conscious and Unconscious Mind

We cannot avoid the problem of consciousness, however, because it arises again in contrast with the idea of an unconscious or subconscious mind. Freud was its most famous proponent but the distinction was made earlier by Plato and others. It also emerged out of the era, beginning in the late 19th century, when psychology was defined as the study of consciousness using introspective reports of imagery and other subjective experiences as they occurred during performance of reaction time tasks. One result that helped seal the fate of the introspective approach was that participants often responded appropriately without experiencing imagery or any other form of conscious thought, leading to the apparent paradox of "imageless thought." The paradox was partly resolved by later experiments which showed that a good deal of conscious thinking went on during the early stages of a novel task but diminished as the task was repeated. More recently, researchers have distinguished between automatic and control processes as defined by tasks that can be done automatically ("unconsciously") and ones that depend on processes under conscious control. Another specific example is the distinction between implicit memory, in which there is no awareness of prior events that have influenced performance on some task, and explicit memory, which refers to our "ordinary" conscious memory for objects and events we have experienced.

The development of dual coding theory was influenced by the imageless thought controversy and research on individual differences in imagery. Following Galton's pioneering study in the late 1890s, imagery was measured by questionnaires that asked people about the vividness of their memory images. The result was that reported vividness was unrelated to memory performance: Vivid imagers remembered no better than fuzzy imagers. It is now known that imagery vividness does predict performance in other cognitive tasks (more about that later), but the failures in memory research coupled with the failure of introspective psychology persuaded me not to put my money exclusively on reported vividness as the best approach to research on imagery effects. I relied instead on objective measures supplemented by introspective reports of imagery and verbal thinking. Moreover, I assumed that the underlying systems could be effective in some situations without necessarily "spilling over" into conscious awareness, and, in any case, that introspecting about our conscious experiences does not reveal how the systems do their work in memory and other cognitive tasks. Such understanding is best achieved using controlled experiments and objective procedures for measuring and manipulating thought processes. The concept of consciousness nonetheless remains relevant to later topics because it has increasingly become a widespread and speculative "cottage industry," more for philosophers and scientists in other fields than for psychologists, perhaps because psychologists became especially aware of the "will-o'-the-wisp" nature of the phenomenon and the dead ends that have plagued attempts to investigate it. More is said later, however, because consciousness is a universal human experience and even evolutionary theorists speculate about its origins and functions.

Left Brain–Right Brain

Dual coding mind is not equivalent to the functional distinctions between the left and right cerebral hemispheres, although the concepts are related. At one time, it was trendy to describe the left hemisphere as the source of language and rational thought, and the right hemisphere as the source of imagery and intuitive thought. It is now known that the picture is more complex. It is still true that the left hemisphere controls speech and dominates in comprehension and other language tasks, and that the right hemisphere dominates in certain tasks involving nonverbal information, such as rotating or otherwise manipulating objects "in the mind's eye." Up to a point, however, the speechless right hemisphere can recognize and comprehend language and the language-dominant left hemisphere can generate mental images. In brief, both hemispheres are differentially involved in both verbal and nonverbal thinking and behavior. The neuropsychological details are discussed after dual coding has been explained as a psychological theory.

Logical Dual Coding

Thinkers since ancient times have "known about" dual coding in the sense that they speculated about the relations between words and things. During the Renaissance, influences from imagery mnemonics systems and formal logic brought words and things together in a "new logic" that was intended to mirror the structure of the world. It entailed "a belief in the perfect correspondence between words (*termini*) and things (*res*), between logic and ontology" (Rossi, 2000, p. 61). This view, which I refer to here as logical dual coding, is at least implicit even in the abstract computational theories of mind as described earlier. The computer is a logical machine that can model reality only by assuming a perfect correspondence between computer language and aspects of a phenomenal domain. DCT assumes instead that the relations between words and things are one to many, in both directions, and that (for example) naming things and imaging to words are probabilistic and modifiable. This difference between logical and psychological dual coding has far-reaching implications that show up in various contexts throughout this volume.

CHAPTER TWO

Justification for the
Theoretical Approach

This chapter justifies the dual coding theoretical approach to cognition and its evolution on logical and factual grounds. The concept of verbal–nonverbal duality is the focus of the arguments. The duality seems obvious on commonsense and evolutionary grounds. We live in a world of nonverbal objects and events on the one hand and language on the other. They are fundamentally different "substances" that exist out there and in our minds. We recognize the differences but are aware at the same time of an underlying single-mindedness that makes it easy to assume that, deep down, we think about words and things in the same way. Commonsense therefore justifies a monistic view of mind just as readily as a dual-coding view. An evolutionary argument by itself leads to the same impasse. Evolutionists would agree that nonverbal cognition must have evolved long before language but they can (and do) attribute the shift to the evolution of an abstract system that captures the old nonverbal mind in the computational network of the new. The following philosophical, historical, and empirical arguments provide the initial justification for taking a dual coding theoretical approach to mind and its evolution.

PHILOSOPHICAL JUSTIFICATION

There has been a long-standing tension between empiricist and rationalist philosophies of science that happen to overlap with the distinction between dual coding and monistic views of mind. Dual coding research began in an era when philosophical positivism and operationism dominated method and theory in experimental psychology. Influenced by that climate, I explicitly adopted the empirical method of convergent operations, in which the unobservable mental processes of the evolving theory were grounded in different classes of experimental and measurement procedures. These were compared and contrasted with procedures linked to alternative

16

theories, so that different hypotheses and predictions could be tested by the classical method of strong inference (Platt, 1964).

Underlying the operational approach was an empiricist philosophy of science aptly expressed in different ways by a scientist and a philosopher. The scientist was James B. Conant (1947), a renowned organic chemist and former president of Harvard University, who sought to educate nonscientists about the nature of "normal" science in a book entitled, *On Understanding Science*. He defined science as the *"progressive development of conceptual schemes arising from experiment and observation and leading to new experiments and observations"* (Conant, p. 37, 139). Thus, he viewed science as an iterative inductive and deductive process in which explanatory theories are built on a foundation of empirical observations and earlier theories—or, more often, the rubble of earlier theories, good and bad. As I now see it through my rear-view mirror, Conant's definition neatly describes the steps by which dual coding theory evolved from an informal observation through a series of hypotheses and experimental tests to the integrative theory.

Closely related to Conant's views is a philosophical attitude about the goals of science that is captured by what philosopher B. C. Van Fraassen called *constructive empiricism*, according to which "Science aims to give us theories which are empirically adequate: and acceptance of a theory involves a belief only that it is empirically adequate" (1980, p. 12). Empirically adequate means that the theory "saves the phenomena," that what it has to say about observable things and events in the world is true. He proposed this view when rationalist-empiricist debates concerning the nature of science were at their peak. My empiricist commitment similarly reflected my reaction to rationalistic psychological explanations of cognitive phenomena, based on monistic propositional (and usually computational) views of mind as already defined in Chapter 1.

The rationalist-empiricist debate and the dual coding commitment to constructive empiricism came together explicitly in psychological research on a central issue in those debates, namely the distinction between observational and theoretical scientific language (Clark & Paivio, 1989). The study illustrates the long reach of DCT and it is described later after the details of the theory, the basic evidence supporting it, and its evolutionary extensions are in place.

Philosophy is also relevant to our evolutionary theme. Evolutionary ideas have always raised profound philosophical issues and debates. Daniel C. Dennett (1995), one of the leading evolutionary scholars, put it as follows in his volume, *Darwin's Dangerous Idea*:

> The Darwinian Revolution is both a scientific and a philosophical revolution, and neither revolution could have occurred without the other ... it was the philosophical prejudices of the scientists, more than their lack of scientific evidence, that prevented them from seeing how the theory could actually work, but those philosophical prejudices ... were too deeply entrenched to be dislodged by mere philosophical brilliance. It took an irresistible parade of hard-won scientific facts to force thinkers to take seriously the weird new outlook that Darwin proposed. (p. 21).

The thinkers, of course, included philosophers as well as scientists, as evidenced by the contributions of Dennett and other philosophers to the debates. They have been especially engaged in issues related to cognitive evolution, as illustrated by the fact that almost half the contributors to a volume on the evolution of mind (Cummins & Allen, 1998) are from departments of philosophy. Hence their specific relevance in this context.

HISTORICAL JUSTIFICATION

Dual coding theory is rooted in two intellectual traditions that entail different and often conflicting views of the nature of memory and thought, one based on imagery and the other on language. The recorded history in the Western world began in ancient Greece. Mnemosyne was the Greek goddess of memory and mother of the nine Muses, the goddesses that presided over the fine arts and sciences. Evidently the Greeks believed that memory is the power source of all human intellectual activities—appropriately so, for without memory there can be no thought and therefore no art or science. Dual coding theory recapitulates those mythical origins in the sense that it began with the study of human memory and expanded from that to other cognitive phenomena. Moreover, the research program was influenced specifically by an imagery memory tradition that originated and flourished in Greece and by a verbal memory tradition that arose initially as a reaction to imagery. Finally, memory is a recurrent theme in this volume because it is obviously a product of evolution, and, less obviously, a major force that drove cognitive evolution. Because of memory's linchpin role in the origins and development of dual coding theory, let us examine the memory tradition in some detail.

The use of imagery as a memory aid undoubtedly originated in the dim and distant past when culturally important information was passed orally from one generation to the next by bards and priests. Historical records, however, identify a Greek poet and orator, Simonides of Ceos (circa 500 BC), as the inventor of the most influential imagery mnemonic technique of all time (Paivio, 1971b; Sadoski & Paivio, 2001; Yates, 1966). The oft-told story of the discovery bears repeating because, however mythical the details, they allude to a dual coding interpretation that has not been mentioned by the historians. Simonides was chanting a lyric poem at a banquet when he was called out by a messenger. During his absence, the roof of the banquet hall fell in, crushing and mangling the guests so that they could not be identified. Simonides remembered the places where they had been sitting and could show the relatives the remains of their dead. On the basis of this experience, Simonides formulated a memory technique in which he stressed the importance of orderly arrangement as an aid to memory, and how this could be achieved through images of localities or places, and images of the facts or things to be remembered.

Note especially that Simonides used memory images of the actual banquet setting to recall the guests and their locations and from that image identify the dead, presumably by name. Thus the sequence of dual coding was from the concrete setting to nonverbal imagery to language. Simonides generalized from his experience to other memory situations and thereby invented the "method of loci". This was a creative leap of imagination like many in the history of intellectual achievement, which we analyze in detail later.

The method evolved over generations with some variants, like the original, using images of real locations, such as the rooms of a familiar house, for storing images of things in memory. The natural organization of the places was eventually supplemented by numbering them so that the things could be easily retrieved by an orderly mental search of the locations in which they had been placed. This evolved into use of imaginary places that were constructed from linguistic cues. Whether the mnemonic images were derived from real or imaginary places, however, language increasingly became an important part of the applications of the technique. Greek and Roman orators used it for remembering the points of long speeches, prompting memory using the rhetorical cues "in the first place …, in the second place," and so on, as reminders of the loci and the things stored in them. For example, the Roman orator Quintilian suggested imagining an anchor in the "forecourt" as the cue for discussion of naval warfare as the first topic. Orators also sought ways of remembering the exact wording by means of images, perhaps of shorthand forms (*notae*). Over subsequent centuries, variants of the technique spread into ecclesiastical and educational settings. In one form or other, it has survived right up to the present day.

Professional mnemonists developed simpler versions in which images of numerically-ordered objects served as memory places, metaphorically described as hooks or pegs on which to "hang" the items to be remembered. The best known of these today was invented in the 19th century. It is a convenient technique because it uses picturable words that rhyme with numbers (e.g., one-bun, two-shoe, three-tree, etc.) as the memory pegs. I describe it in detail later because it influenced the initial development of DCT. Modern research has confirmed that the rhyme mnemonic and related techniques really do work as well as their advocates have claimed. Additionally, the research unravelled the effective components of the techniques and with those discoveries came an awareness that imagery mnemonics were based on implicit theoretical assumptions that differed quite radically from those that guided traditional verbal memory research.

The verbal tradition began as a reaction to the method of loci. Quintilian objected to the technique on the grounds that using images to remember the wording of long speeches would overload memory and that it is difficult in any case to find images for abstract notions and function words. He therefore advocated the use of rote memorization coupled with images of the pages on which speeches were written. Later St. Augustine, who wrote extensively on memory and generally accepted imagery as the basis of memory, also observed that he could not find images for abstract ideas in his memory places. However, it was Quintilian's objections and recommendations that became especially influential during the iconoclasm of the Protestant Reformation when imagery mnemonics were ostracized because they were tainted by their association with occult traditions, and because "lively images" (recommended by mnemonists) supposedly aroused "depraved carnal affections" and were therefore impious! Verbal memory systems were promoted instead and one developed by the French dialectician Peter Ramus became a preferred alternative in the 16th century. In this method, a general topic is progressively divided into more specific levels by a series of dichotomous branchings and the topic is learned by studying this hierarchical Ramian epitome. In more subtle forms, it remains an accepted part of educational practice to this day (Sadoski & Paivio, 2001).

A long associative memory tradition went along in parallel with the oratorical and educational memory practices. The tradition began with Aristotle's "laws of association" and reached its peak with the British empiricist philosophers in the 18th and 19th centuries. In general, the tradition was neutral with respect to the imagery-verbal debate because the emphasis was on association of ideas and analysis of the conditions under which one idea suggests another. The prevailing notion was that ideas follow one after the other (knife-fork-spoon-cup-saucer ...). The associationists were quite aware of the imagery-verbal distinction and differences in the nature of associations. For example, James Mill distinguished between the successive ideas that link words in a prayer and the simultaneous or synchronous ideas in which the idea of the sun reminds you of the sun and the sky together. The Scottish philosopher William Hamilton particularly emphasized the integrated nature of clusters of ideas and the capacity of one member of the cluster to redintegrate (remind one of) the whole cluster at once.[2] James Mill (see Mandler & Mandler, 1964) synthesized all of this classical associationism in a treatise that has a thoroughly modern ring, anticipating the associative mechanisms that were experimentally confirmed and elaborated more than a century later.

The modern era of the verbal memory tradition evolved selectively from the associative background. The era began "officially" in 1885 with the publication of a volume by Hermann Ebbinghaus (1964; translation), in which he reported his experiments on rote learning and memory. He focussed on the formation of sequential associations between items using a serial learning task in which each item serves as the cue for the next item in a list. In this regard, he followed the traditional emphasis on successive association rather than the Hamiltonian emphasis on integration-redintegration. To eliminate the effect of natural associations that resulted from prior learning, he invented the nonsense syllable. Thus armed, he conducted a long series of meticulous experiments in which he served as his own subject. His work set the stage for generations of researchers who specialized in the study of verbal learning and memory.

In addition to extending Ebbinghaus's findings and interpretations in various ways, the researchers noticed that nonsense syllables were not entirely meaningless for they tended to remind one of real words, some more readily than others (for example, *jaq* is more word-like than is *vaq*). Accordingly, they began to measure and study the effects of meaningfulness on memory, defining meaningfulness in terms of the ease with which syllables and words evoke other words

---

[2]The distinction between successive (or sequential) and synchronous associations and the concept of integration are key components of dual-coding memory theory and I will elaborate on them later in that context.

as associates. Not too surprisingly, among other less-predictable results, it turned out that more meaningful syllables were easier to learn and remember than less meaningful ones.

The research promptly moved beyond rote memory to the effects of thought processes on memory. What do people think about when they are memorizing a list of syllables or words, and how do these thought processes affect performance? These intervening processes came to be called memory mediators and they too were initially interpreted as being verbal in nature—verbal mediators, or natural language mediators, that the memorizers spontaneously used as memory aids or were supplied and manipulated by the experimenter so that their effects could be systematically studied. For example, one experiment made use of such associative chains as Soldier-Sailor-*Navy*. Word association norms show that Soldier frequently elicits Sailor as an associate, which elicits Navy, but Soldier rarely elicits Navy. Nevertheless, it was shown that Sailor provides an implicit bridge from Soldier to Navy in that participants who first learn nonsense syllable-word pairs such as ZUG-Soldier subsequently find it easier to learn ZUG-Navy than participants who first learned ZUG paired with a word that is not part of the chain. Thus, in the example, the assumed mediator was "Sailor." We need not plunge deeper into these paradigms (descriptions of relevant research can be found in Paivio, 1971b). The relevant point here is that both rote memory and "thoughtful" memory research reflected the language-dominance view of mind discussed in the last chapter and the traditional associationist emphasis on successive associations.

The narrowing perspective of the verbal approach not only followed from the rote verbal memory tradition but was additionally reinforced by the behaviorist manifesto: Words are objective and open to scientific study whereas images are subjective and hence outside the domain of psychology as a behavioral science. That distinction, however, was false when it came to implicit verbal mediators, for they too are internal events, just as "mental" and inferential as images, and thus needing objective procedures to reveal how they operate in memory and cognitive tasks.

It seems odd in retrospect that the imagery and verbal traditions remained conceptually separated for more than 2,500 years. Memory theorists and practitioners during the imagery tradition certainly recognized that memory involves words as well as images but their roles were seen as separate, either one or the other being lauded for its particular mnemonic virtues—or damned for its vices, at least in the case of imagery, for only its shortcomings were emphasized by the Roman orator Quintilian, and only imagery came later to be viewed by the Protestant and behaviorist iconoclasts as the concept from hell.[3] Without such attitudinal impediments, the critics might instead have found a more conciliatory way of dealing with the yin and yang of imagery and language, one in which they are not viewed as competitors but rather as cooperative forces that contribute in different ways to affect memory performance,

---

[3]The iconoclasm associated with behaviorist psychology might have had its roots at least partly in religious iconoclasm. According to biographer Kerry W. Buckley (1989), John Watson, the founder of behaviorism, was raised by a ne'er-do-well father and a devout Baptist mother who fervently prayed that her son John would "receive the call to preach the

and indeed all aspects of cognition. In any case, the dual coding research program was the first systematic attempt to bridge the gap. We shall see that the research has taken us a long way toward a rapprochement—not all the way, for some researchers still seek monistic interpretations of various phenomena that seem to implicate the two codes.

EMPIRICAL JUSTIFICATION

The shift from two solitudes to cooperative dual coding began as follows. In 1950, I took a public speaking course in which we were taught the rhyme mnemonic technique that descended from the method of loci. The instructor asked us to name 20 objects in the meeting room, with a brief pause between each. A student recorded the words and their numerical order. We then called out the numbers in random order and the instructor immediately recalled the associated words and even pointed to the students who had suggested them. We were mightily impressed. The instructor assured us that the memory feat was easy and that she would teach us to do likewise.

Here's how we did it: We first memorized a list of rhyming number-word pairs—one-bun, two-shoe, three-tree, four-door, five-hive, six-sticks, and so on, up to 20-horn of plenty—an easy task because of the rhyming relations. We then used the rhyme as an aid for remembering a list of items by combining mental images of a bun, shoe, and so forth, with images suggested by the memory targets. As an illustrative minilist, take pencil, chair, and lamp as words to be remembered and visualize a pencil as, say, a filler inside a hamburger bun, a chair with a leg stuck in a shoe, and a lamp as a decoration on a Christmas tree. Now, start with the numbers one, two, three in any order and you find that they easily remind you of the rhyming peg-words bun, shoe, tree, which in turn prompt you to remember the compound images you constructed. It is then a simple matter to retrieve the memory targets by a verbal read-out of the novel parts of the images. Anyone can easily master the full rhyme mnemonic.

The rhyme mnemonic experience began to influence my scientific thinking and a few years later became the impetus for a research program that resulted in a dual coding memory theory, and eventually, a general theory of cognition. It is easy to

---

Gospel ... The bewildering contrast in the characters of Watson's parents set up reverberations that echoed throughout his life. As an adult, he oscillated between poles of conformity and iconoclasm" (p. 4). He eventually abandoned religion but he may have retained vestiges of its iconoclastic views of idols of the church and magical images. If so, it was certainly coupled with a behaviorist strategy. In a letter to Bertrand Russell he confessed that he deliberately concealed inconsistencies in his behavioristic treatment of images because he wanted to avoid dealing with them until he had persuaded psychologists to abandon their old mentalistic views (Buckley, 1989, p. 149). Further influences on Watson's "strange reversal" concerning the existence of mental images have been documented by Thomas (1989).

see how this could happen: the technique involves a chain of dual coding events in which words are changed to nonverbal images and images back to words, apparently with potent memory benefits. The processes were gradually extended by a series of analogical steps to other memory tasks and beyond. Thus, it's fair to say metaphorically that the rhyme mnemonic contained the kernel that grew into DCT when nourished by facts arising from systematic research.

The research program that eventuated in a more complete theory began unsystematically a few years after my initial experience with the rhyme mnemonic. I was taking an experimental psychology course as a part-time credit to qualify for the graduate psychology program at McGill. The course required an independent experiment. I was discussing some possibilities with the instructor, Professor Wallace Lambert, whose research focussed on second-language learning and bilingualism. He was curious about the fact that adjectives and nouns are typically used in the adjective–noun order in English (e.g., red, white, and blue flag*)*, whereas the noun–adjective order is usual in French (e.g., drapeau bleu, blanc, rouge). Would this habitual difference be reflected in the ease of learning the two sequences by Anglophones and Francophones? I proposed investigating the question using serial learning of lists containing sets of nouns and qualifying adjectives (essentially novel phrases) presented in either adjective–noun or noun–adjective order. Moreover, I suggested that the question could be answered using only English lists and English-dominant speakers because contrasting predictions are justified. The language-habits view clearly implies that the adjective–noun order should be easier than the noun–adjective order for English speakers. My experience with the rhyme mnemonic suggested the reverse: The retrieval cues (memory pegs) in the mnemonic are concrete nouns—bun, shoe, tree, door, hive, and so forth. By analogy with that technique, nouns might turn out to be better pegs for storing and retrieving qualifying adjectives than adjectives would be for nouns—a possibility not suggested by the language-habits hypothesis.

The results clearly supported the analogical extension of the rhyme mnemonic: the sequential lists were learned in fewer trials when the word groups were presented in the atypical noun–adjective order than when they were presented in the typical adjective–noun order. In the published report (Lambert & Paivio, 1956), we referred to the nouns as particularly efficient *conceptual pegs* for retrieving adjectival modifiers. This would turn out to be a felicitous and productive rephrasing of the memory-peg metaphor in subsequent experiments in which the conceptual-peg hypothesis became part of the increasingly complex structure of dual coding memory theory—a structure that was to include the verbal associative mechanisms that were the theoretical basis of the disconfirmed language-habit prediction in the aforementioned experiment.

The conceptual peg story comes back full circle to Simonides's invention of the method of loci based on his recollection of the people who sat around a real banquet table. He saw in this experience the importance of the "orderly arrangement" of memory places as an aid to recall by means of images. Concreteness was taken for granted as the necessary basis of imagery by Simonides as it was by later practitioners of the method of loci, perhaps until Quintilian pointed out the difficulty of imaging abstract notions. Even so, no one compared concrete loci with purely abstract verbal arrangements, not even when the Ramist verbal branching tree diagrams became the method of choice among Protestant educators. The importance of concreteness remained similarly implicit in the various memory peg or hook systems developed by professional mnemonists. Simply put, for more than two millenia, no one varied concreteness or imagery to determine whether they were effective in the way suggested by the prescriptive formulae of the teachers and practitioners of the memory art. Of course, the advocates were not scientists, and in any case, the experimental method had not been applied to human memory.

Concreteness was similarly assumed to be crucial in the rhyme mnemonic technique and in its analogical extension to the noun–adjective order experiment in 1956. Moreover, imagery as the basis of the conceptual-peg effect also remained implicit in that experiment. The change from the earlier history is that the experimental method was applied for the first time to test an implication of an extension of the method of loci and compare this with an implication of a hypothesis coming from the verbal tradition. Just a few years later, these variables began to be systematically investigated with guidance from a "mature" conceptual peg hypothesis that generated specific experiments and predictions. That hypothesis became a part of a broader theory that extended to other memory phenomena and beyond that to cognition in general—expanded further in this volume to the evolution of cognition.

The next chapter presents the principles of DCT, followed by a chapter on the adaptive functions of the cognitive mechanisms described in the theory—functions that must have operated as well to promote our survival and evolution as a species in the distant past. That and all of the other topics covered in this volume depend on how well DCT can describe and explain the nature of modern mind.

CHAPTER THREE

Basic Principles of Dual Coding Theory

DCT developed through research in which experimental procedures and hypotheses were progressively modified and extended to new cognitive domains. For example, the rhyme mnemonic technique evolved into standard laboratory tasks that isolated its effective components, and further extensions led to more general dual coding interpretations of memory and other cognitive phenomena. The survivors of this conceptual evolution consist of a series of interrelated assumptions and hypotheses that define DCT (e.g., Paivio, 1971b, 1986, 1991a, 1991b; Sadoski & Paivio, 2001), This chapter offers an updated version of the theory and its empirical implications. Detailed discussion of the relevant research is postponed to the next chapter, where the emphasis is on aspects that are especially pertinent to interpretations of cognitive evolution.

In what follows, I build up to the presentation of DCT by first discussing general assumptions that are the basis of the theory and entail issues that are relevant to all cognitive theories, past and present. Thus I begin with the overriding empiricist attitude concerning the origins of knowledge and then discuss in turn the processes responsible for the growth of knowledge, the relation between knowledge and memory, and the organization of knowledge according to different theorists. All of that provides a context for the detailed account of DCT in the rest of the chapter.

THE EMPIRICIST PRINCIPLE

The most general assumption is that all knowledge derives from perceptual, behavioral, and affective experiences with the world. These experiences become internalized so that cognitive representations and processes are modality-specific and multimodal. Our minds "contain" memory isomorphs of how entities and events look, sound, and feel. Our cognitive skills similarly reflect our behavioral skills, how we learned to interact with people and things. Our knowledge of language and its relation to the world also are modality specific. There are no abstract entities, nonverbal or verbal, in the theory, although abstract functions are routinely carried out by the modality-specific internal entities and processes, just as perception and behavior are used for abstract ends. The abstract functions are especially apparent in the case of language, but those language functions do not require translation into an abstract mentalese of the kind discussed in Chapter 1, and again later. Language itself is abstract enough.

This empiricist principle assumes innate contributions to cognition. The functional brain is a result of biological evolution and is thereby constrained in how it accumulates and uses environmental information. Roger Shepard (1984) traced these ecological constraints to limitations on our perceptions and cognitions imposed by physical geometry, motion, time, and distance—properties of the physical world to which internal representations resonate. The ecological constraints and affordances (what the environment allows organisms to do) apply to all creatures, each having different sensory, memory, and behavioral capacities because of the environmental niches in which they have evolved. In addition, it is now common wisdom that all aspects of human nature are products of the interaction of genes and environment (e.g., Ridley, 2003b). This applies to such basic attributes of mind as intelligence and the learning mechanisms that determine the acquired content of mind. All that is assumed here and is discussed as necessary in relevant contexts.

GROWTH OF KNOWLEDGE

Learning and memory processes account for the cumulative growth of knowledge. These are bootstrapping processes because knowledge consists of learned memories that raise themselves to new levels as they grow. The bootstrapping goes by many names: stimulus and response generalization, learning to learn, memory elaboration of the products of the learning experiences, and ultimately, the metamorphosis of all that into what psychologists call metamemory and metacognition: (a) knowledge about the nature of memory and how we think, (b) knowledge that can be used as a feedforward mechanism to accelerate its own growth, and (c) knowledge that draws increasingly on the cooperative activity of language and nonverbal cognitive systems.

The learning experiences that lead to growth of knowledge have been studied experimentally for more than a century. Attention has shifted from behavioral learning to the formation of internal representations that mediate the learned behavior and are the basis of knowledge and thought. The main types of learning include classical and operant conditioning, stimulus–stimulus (sensory) conditioning, and perceptual or observational learning (including imitation). Classical conditioning is familiar to everyone from Pavlov's experiments in which a hungry dog learned to salivate to the sound of a bell that had previously been associated with food. In operant conditioning, an animal learns responses that have been followed by reward. In sensory conditioning and perceptual learning, knowledge is acquired just by observing objects, events, and relations among them. For example, a young infant looks at a novel objects for some time. After repeated presentations the infant habituates or "gets used to" the stimulus and spends less time looking at it. The behavioral change implies that a mental representation of the stimulus has been formed so that it is recognized and becomes familiar. The infant "knows" the stimulus and differentiates it from others. Early developmental changes in brain activity also are consistent with the view that mere exposure to objects can initiate the growth of mental representations necessary for knowledge (Chapter 7). Importantly, the observed "objects" and acquired knowledge include other people and their actions, which the developing infant learns to imitate and respond to in ways that are socially relevant (cf. Bandura, 1986).

Some of the acquired knowledge is experienced as imagery. We are born with the capacity to image, but its role in the growth of knowledge can be improved by training. Research evidence as early as the 1940s showed that mental images can be conditioned. For example, a person hears a tone while experiencing a specific odor, and subsequently reports smelling the odor when presented the tone all by itself. Young children and animals can't tell us whether they experience imagery, but they behave as if they do. Such behavior has prompted cognitive learning theorists to interpret classical and operant conditioning as being mediated by internal representations that function like images. Pavlov's dogs salivated to a tone because it elicited an image of food. Hungry rats press the bar in a Skinner box when a light is on because they image the food that will follow the bar press (a specific mentalistic rendering of vicarious trial-and-error learning). Infants spend less time looking at an object they have seen before because a glance is sufficient to activate an image of the object. The interesting conceptual shift here is that imagery as a product of learning came to be viewed as a process that mediates learning.

KNOWLEDGE IS MEMORY

Memory has been said to be the mother of all wisdom (Aeschylus). To appreciate this, we need only think of the demented (mindless) personalities of advanced Alzheimer's patients or the restricted lives of people with injuries to memory-related brain areas. Such patients can deal up to a point with what is perceptually present. For example, Martin M. became a prisoner of the present after a crucial part of his brain was surgically removed to control his epilepsy (for a nontechnical review, see Hilts, 1995). He could read and write, converse about objects and events in his room, remember who he was, recall in some vague way significant people and events before his surgery; he even tried to infer answers to questions about forgotten events from clues in the conversation. However, all of these capacities were limited to a narrow window of time. He read the same magazine over and over without ever remembering that he had read it before. If the researcher who had repeatedly tested him left the room and returned a few minutes later, Martin M. greeted her as if they were meeting for the first time. He could not remember the location of the testing room or even the bathroom he had just used. And he could not anticipate future events, which depends on remembering what happened in the past under similar circumstances. Thus, unable to remember what happened moments ago or anticipate the future, he had lost the capacity for adaptive thinking. Even his ability to deal, after a fashion, with the present, was dependent on a kind of memory (discussed later) that was not destroyed by the surgery.

Given the essential role of memory in cognition, it follows that memory was crucial as well in the evolution of mind. I argue later for a causal connection in which memory pulled itself up by its own evolutionary bootstraps along with the other elements of the cognitive ensemble of which it is a part, much as in the ontogenetic bootstrapping of cognitive growth described earlier. This is a unique emphasis, generally absent from recent books on cognitive evolution (Donald, 1991, is an exception). The lacunae mean that the evolutionary significance of memory has been either underestimated or taken for granted. In any case, it is a useful preparation to review the varieties of memory before dealing with such issues.

Memory is a many-splendored thing, a complex set of psychological phenomena that have not been defined with full agreement even by the scientific experts in the field. Classification schemes include a half-dozen or more "species." The earliest distinction was between short-term memory and long-term memory, which usually refers to something experienced at most a few minutes ago as compared to an earlier experience, so long ago that it can be said to "reside" in a kind of "permastore" (Bahrick, 1984). One view of the distinction is that short-term memory is a temporary holding place from which memories get moved over to a more capacious and permanent secondary store by means of rehearsal and other processes. Verbal rehearsal was extended to the idea of visual rehearsal (Posner, Boies, Eichelman, & Taylor, 1969) and both were incorporated into the concept of working memory, especially by the British psychologist Alan Baddeley (1986). Verbal rehearsal and the acoustic feedback from it permits information to be maintained for use in some other task. Similarly, visual imagery can function as a "sketch pad" for holding information to be worked on by other cognitive mechanisms.

Cutting across the aforementioned is a well-known distinction between episodic, semantic, and procedural memory (e.g., Tulving, 1983). Episodic memory refers to memories of events we remember having experienced at a specific time and place, including stimuli used in experimental tests of memory. The related concept of autobiographical memory (e.g., C. P. Thompson et al., 1998) includes the additional criterion that memory comes with the sense of reliving the event. Semantic memory refers to long-term factual knowledge about language and the world it relates to, knowledge we must have acquired through learning but can't recall the time or place. For example, we are unable to pinpoint when and where we learned most of the words we know. When we can, it would be classed as episodic memory in Tulving's scheme. Procedural memory refers to memory for skills, such as how to tie shoelaces, which are like semantic memory in that the learning trials usually are forgotten.

A related distinguishing feature is that episodic memories by definition are derived from single experiences, whereas motor skills and semantic knowledge improve with repetition. We did not learn to tie our shoelaces fluently in one trial and we did not learn the various meanings and uses of words without hearing and using them in various contexts. The learning episodes blur over time, although we might just remember the first time we tried to tie our shoelaces or heard a particular word and wondered about its meaning. For example, I remember approximately when and where I heard the word "satisfaction" in the context of the expression "Curiosity killed a cat and satisfaction brought it back." I interpreted this to mean that, if my cat were killed, I would be sad and this would bring it back to life!

Episodic and semantic memory come up so often in later contexts that it is important, before moving on, to touch on theoretical controversies concerning the distinction. Tulving maintains that, although the two systems share common properties, they are distinct and that episodic memory is an extension of semantic memory in both phylogenetic and ontogenetic evolution. Other students of memory (e.g., Hintzman, 1984; McKoon, Ratcliff, & Dell, 1986) have argued instead for a single memory system in which characteristics that define semantic memory emerge from memories for highly frequent and varied episodic experiences. The focus of the controversy changed after Tulving began to associate episodic memory with the concept of "autonoetic consciousness," one's awareness of having experienced an event at a particular time and place (e.g., Tulving, 1985, 2005). It is this "self-conscious" episodic memory system that presumably evolved recently and is uniquely human. The earlier semantic memory allowed other animals to acquire adaptive knowledge of the world without having episodic memory in the autonoetic sense. Ontogenetically, too, this system lags behind and is dependent on the development of semantic memory. Tulving has made a good case for this new view of memory but important issues remain unresolved, many arising directly from its complete dependence on the slippery concept of consciousness as the defining feature of episodic memory. A particularly contentious claim is that the sense of past and future time depends on autonoetic consciousness and is therefore lacking in other animals and children. Such issues and how they fit into the dual coding framework are discussed further in appropriate contexts.

A number of other memory types and distinctions are also relevant to later discussions. One is the contrast between explicit and implicit memory, where "explicit" refers to conscious memories and "implicit" to apparently-forgotten events that nonetheless influence current behavior when "primed" by relevant cues. For example, the word stem "MO" can prompt the response "motor," even when the person does not remember having seen the word earlier. Another addition to the memory typology is a perceptually based representational system (PRS) proposed by Schacter and Tulving (e.g., 1994), which includes component systems for representing visual word forms, auditory word forms, and information about the form and structure of objects. We see that similar representations have long been part of of DCT, with the important difference that the PRS is linked to abstract entities and processes that are shunned in DCT. Thus, Tulving and Schacter assume on one hand that the PRS is constructed from (abstract) structural descriptions, and on the other hand that the PRS "does not 'know' anything about what words mean or what objects are used for. Meaningful associations and concepts are handled by semantic memory, which cooperates closely with PRS" (Schacter, 1996, p. 184). This is quite unlike DCT, in which all memory and other cognitive functions derive from the individual properties and interplay of modality-specific representations.

Also relevant to DCT is the distinction between memory for information from external sources and information from internal sources (Johnson & Raye, 1981; Paivio, 1975a). For example, an external source memory is one's recollection of a recent party one attended. A comparable internal source memory would be one's recollection of a dream about such a party. In the rhyme-mnemonic technique introduced in Chapter 2, the list of 20 items to be remembered come from an external (perceptual) source but the memorized rhyme and the images that are used as memory aids come from internal sources, which are themselves based on either episodic or semantic memory or both. For example, the bun-pencil image for the first item in our memory list might be the memory image of an actual pencil we saw earlier, which we imagine inside a bun that we actually had for lunch. Or both could be constructed from long-term verbal and nonverbal memories of innumerable pencils and buns. It is interesting at this point just to mention that external events (pictures and printed words) are usually remembered better than internal events (mental pictures and words). A related finding is that rated qualities of memories for real events contain more sensory and contextual information than memories for imagined events (Johnson, Hashtroudi, & Lindsey, 1993). The idea of memories embedded in memories entails puzzles that are addressed more fully later.

Finally, cutting across all of the aforementioned categories are further differences that are defined by the tasks used to test memory: memory for items, associations between items, or the sequential order of items; memory as measured by recall or recognition tests with or without prompting by retrieval cues; and various combinations of these. The empirical distinctions are crucial to tests of the memory implications of DCT as reviewed in the next chapter.

ORGANIZATION OF KNOWLEDGE

All of the preceding discussion implies that knowledge is organized. The nature of the organization has long been a major issue in analyses of memory and thought. We encountered it in relation to Simonides's mnemonic method of loci and the Ramian hierarchical knowledge tree. It has philosophical roots in empiricist and rationalist approaches to epistemology. Reflecting such origins, most modern psychological approaches can be classified as semantic memory theories or schema theories of knowledge structure.

Theories of semantic memory structure generally deal with organization of concepts rather than organization of knowledge within individuals, although the two can be combined. Collins and Loftus (1975) proposed an influential theory of semantic memory in terms of connections between abstract conceptual nodes organized in a logical hierarchical manner. For example, the concept node "things" divides into living and nonliving things, living things into plants and animals, each unpacking into general subcategories, and more specific ones grouped by such properties as color (cf. the Ramian branching tree, Chapter 2). Specific concepts are activated by words, and the activity spreads automatically over regions of the network. Various neuropsychological theories (discussed in Chapter 7) extend the approach to individual differences by partitioning semantic memory into specific domains suggested by patterns of functional loss due to focal brain damage. Cree and McCrae (2003) comprehensively summarized and compared such approaches, and presented their own categorization scheme based on analyses of a large, empirically defined set of descriptive features of concrete nouns (names of categories of things) and how the categories map onto effects of damage to different brain regions.

As mentioned in Chapter 1, schema theories are abstract and rational views of knowledge structure. They have their origin in Plato's theory of ideas and Kant's transcendentalism in which the explanation of knowledge lies outside of the content of (transcends) any particular experience. Modern schema theories also are abstract but generally less nativistic. The most influential is the Piagetian concept of schema (Piaget, 1952), a sensory-motor cognitive structure acquired through interaction with people and things. The developing schemas guide those interactions increasingly effectively by assimilating new information that alters the schematic structure. The change is said to be accommodative, a better fit for new behavioral demands as the child matures. The Piagetian schema concept is part of his elaborate developmental theory. Other schema theories are related to specific domains such as memory, comprehension, and behavioral patterns (motor schemas). The shortcomings of the schema concept were listed in Chapter 1 and are considered again in specific contexts. For now, the most important general point is that the knowledge base of DCT is assumed to be more specific in modality and organization than suggested by the abstract framework of schema theory.

The following is a more suitable precedent for DCT. Nineteenth century psychologist Johann Friedrich Herbart presented an elaborate associative theory of knowledge structure under the term *apperceptive mass* (e.g., see Murphy, 1950, pp. 52–54). The concept expands on the term apperception (*Vorstellung*, translating roughly to idea, concept, presentation, representation) that had been much discussed earlier by Leibnitz and others. The apperceptive mass refers to all of the assimilated past experiences that we use when we perceive something new. The greater the amount of accumulated and organized experience in the mind, the easier it is to learn and assimilate a new idea into that apperceptive mass (the cognitive bootstrapping already mentioned). Take the professional wine-taster trying to place a new flavor: because he has so often tasted a variety of different flavors, he has a large organized mental reservoir of tastes into which he can fit the new wine and describe its similarities to others and its distinctiveness.

The concept was criticized by William James (among others) on the grounds that its meaning is too broad, covering the sum total of associative effects that are dependent on a person's entire stock of ideas, character, habits, memory, educations, previous experience, and momentary moods. Nevertheless, it greatly influenced educational goals and practices well into the 20th century because it suggested so directly that, in teaching, new material should be related to the old. It also anticipated similar ideas that remain influential. The most obvious is the Piagetian schema concept, with its specific emphasis on assimilating new information into a schema so that its functional organization is modified. Other related notions include associative fields and conceptual spheres in early structural-linguistic theories of meaning (see Paivio & Begg, 1981; Ullmann, 1962) and semantic memory structure, as already discussed.

The apperceptive mass idea can be viewed from the DCT perspective as divided into regions or domains that vary in richness according to the nature and variety of the antecedent experiences. The important difference is that DCT interprets the domains specifically in terms of interconnected verbal and nonverbal representations that can be accessed, compared, and used for whatever purpose is relevant in a given situation. Experiential differences result in individual differences in the development of particular domains of the apperceptive mass, with some domains being relatively more verbal and others more nonverbal in content. The following examples illustrate the analytic possibilities.

A variant of the word association test requires participants to write different associations to a vertically repeated stimulus word. Developed as a measure of associative meaningfulness (see Chapter 2), it was adapted by Bousfield and Samborski (1955) to determine whether the meaningfulness of words that refer to different interests or values is related to individual differences in such values as measured by a standard test . They found that meaningfulness scores correlated significantly with religious and theoretical values. For example, the higher the individuals' scores on religion, the more associations they produced to such stimulus words as church and prayer. This can be taken as evidence of domain-specific associative structures that resulted from experiences with religious language.

Paivio and Steeves (1967) showed further that the value-related structures include imagery. Specifically, ratings of how easily words evoke imagery correlated significantly with personal value ratings of words related to religious, theoretical, aesthetic, and economic domains: the higher the value score for a word in a given domain, the higher its imagery rating. This implies that the strength of the connections between words and images is determined by their relevance to one's personal interests or values. The important point here is that the word association and imagery data provide evidence for differentiated regions within the representational (apperceptive) domains, which consist of mixtures of verbal associative and imagery structures and processes, all derived from frequency of experience with value-related words and things. The domains contain the long-term memory information that allows them to be activated by words and other retrieval cues. The DCT that follows shortly can be viewed in part as an interpretation of those apperceptive domains. Later, in Section IV of this book, we return to the concept in discussing expert knowledge, skills, creativity, and intelligence in terms of the richness of relevant apperceptive domains interpreted according to DCT.

Before turning to a full description of DCT, let us summarize how it differs from older and current theories of knowledge. The most general difference is that many others assume that knowledge structures and processes are abstract and amodal whereas DCT holds that all knowledge is modality specific. Some semantic memory theories agree that knowledge is modality specific and contains verbal and nonverbal information, but they do not address differences in the way information might be organized in the two systems and how they cooperate in specific tasks. Additionally, DCT explicitly assumes that knowledge is made up of different kinds of memories. All knowledge derives from perception of specific episodes, both verbal and nonverbal, and behaviors related to them. Thus, knowledge consists of episodic and procedural memories. Innumerable encounters with specific words might become blurred and forgotten and we are left with the impression that we simply know the words and their meanings in some abstract, schematic sense. But much of the knowledge remains episodic: asked about cars, we might first think about different episodes involving our present car or the many we have owned over the years. Although this has not been systematically studied (except by such novelists as Proust, who wrote extensively about his auto-biographical "rememberance of things past"), all of us can recall an indefinitely-large number of events involving specific people, objects, and actions. The memory base is continually changing and expanding to assimilate such episodes into an increasingly differentiated organizational structure. Much of the content becomes episode-free and general, as in semantic, implicit, procedural, and schematic memories, but much also remains tied to events that we explicitly remember. The following sections describe this dynamic memory-based knowledge structure in terms of dual coding concepts.

DUAL CODING THEORY

The theory elaborates on the idea (already outlined in Chapter 1 (p. x) that cognition involves the cooperative activity of two functionally independent but interconnected systems, a nonverbal system specialized for dealing with nonlinguistic objects and events, and a verbal system specialized for dealing directly with language. The structural units and interconnections are modeled in Fig. 3.1 (from Paivio, 1986). I unpack this overview into detailed explanations of (a) verbal and nonverbal symbolic systems that cut across sensorimotor systems, (b) the representational units of each system, (c) connections and activation processes within and between systems, (d) organizational and transformational processes, and (e) conscious versus unconscious processes.

Symbolic and Sensorimotor Systems

The importance of the verbal–nonverbal distinction in DCT stems from the fundamentally different ways in which the two systems symbolize reality. The nonverbal system does so relatively directly in somewhat the same way as a sound film

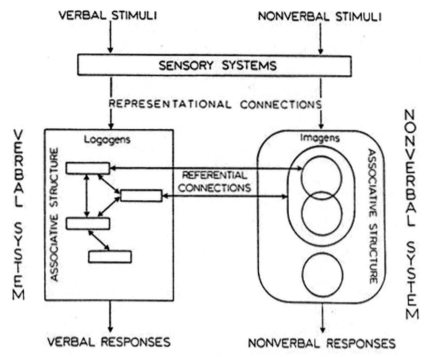

FIGURE 3.1 Structural model of dual coding theory showing the representational units and their referential and associative interconnections. The referentially unconnected units correspond to abstract-word logogens and "nameless" imagens, respectively. [Adapted from Fig 4.1, p. 67, of Mental Representations: A Dual Coding Approach, by Allan Paivio, copyright 1986/1990 by Oxford University Press, Inc. Used by permission.]

represents visual and auditory aspects of dynamic real-world events—"somewhat," because audiovisual media do not include the other modalities by which we know the world. The verbal system symbolizes reality indirectly using language symbols that name static and dynamic aspects of reality according to the conventions of language users. The Greek poet Simonides, already familiar from Chapter 2 as the father of imagery mnemonics, wrote that "words are the images of things," but this is misleading except in a metaphorical sense. Our words can "hold the mirror up to nature" (Shakespeare), but the symbolic mirror itself is our nonverbal representational system.

There also are ambiguous symbol systems such as deaf signing and the writing systems used in China, Japan, and Korea (Egyptian hieroglyphics was a forerunner of all of these), which include iconic or picture-like symbols as well as ones that stand only for language sounds. In such cases, nonverbal representations are embedded within a general communication system, although not mixed as closely as they are in

Rebus where, for example, the word "cry" is represented by the letters "CR" followed by a picture of an eye, or as closely as nonarbitrary gestures accompany speech in ordinary communication (McNeill, 1992), which is discussed further later.

The sensorimotor aspect of the theory means that verbal and nonverbal symbolic representations are composed of specific sensory and motor components. The relation between the symbolic and sensorimotor dimensions is conceptually orthogonal, as shown by the observable stimuli and responses listed in Table 3.1, which correspond to internal representations assumed to be similarly modality specific. This means that objects and words can be visual, auditory, haptic (known by active touch), or motor patterns involved in drawing, writing, and signing. The orthogonal relation is incomplete in that tastes, smells, and emotions are directly represented only on the nonverbal side—that is, we have no language-like symbols that are constructed from these modalities. However, we must have connections between internal representations of words and gustatory, olfactory, and emotional systems so that we can name tastes, smells, and emotions and to some extent image such experiences given the names. The memory representations of these experiences are theoretically uncertain, hence the vague wording here. In the case of emotion, Table 3.1 refers to "felt emotions" rather than images of emotions. One can imagine emotional situations that can arouse feelings of anger, fear, and so on. These are real feelings of varying intensity, not "images" of feelings. The issues at least will be clearer when we discuss activation processes.[4]

The orthogonal model has psychological implications in that a change in symbolic modality can affect behavior when sensory modality is held constant, and vice versa. For example, pictures are easier to remember than their printed names (e.g., a picture of a fireman's hat versus the words FIREMAN'S HAT), which entails a nonverbal–verbal functional contrast within the visual modality. In other tasks, auditory words are processed more effectively than visual words, a sensory contrast within the verbal symbolic modality. Chapters 4 and 7 show that the model systematically organizes important classes of psychological and neuropsychological phenomena.[5]

---

[4]Music and dance also are important nonverbal symbolic forms because they are ancient in origin, present in other species, and universal across societies although not across individuals. They are not representational in the same sense as imagery (drawings) or language. We perform, compose, and we think about music and dance, but not with them. There are parallels between the sequential patterning of language and the written notational systems for music and dance choreography, but they do not stand for anything outside of themselves. Of course, here too we can point to ambiguous cases such as the imitative acoustic patterning of Rimsky-Korsakov's "The flight of the bumble bee" or a sexy dance, but these are representational only in the same limited sense as onomatopoeia in language. They nonetheless entail high level skills that will be discussed in Chapter 15.

[5]The model is necessary for a rigorous portrayal of dual coding theory. The most common description is that the theory contrasts visual and verbal codes, which is a diagonal contrast between a sensory modality and a symbolic modality. I did this myself in the title of a theoretical chapter on "The relationship between verbal and perceptual codes" (Paivio, 1978), as though verbal codes are somehow not perceptual! Such short-cuts are usually understood to mean nonverbal visual imagery versus verbal (usually auditory-motor) representations, but still, they are imprecise and sometimes confusing.

TABLE 3.1

Orthogonal Relation Between Symbolic Systems and Sensorimotor
Systems of Dual Coding Theory With Examples of Modality-Specific
Information Represented in Each System.

Sensorimotor Systems	*Symbolic Systems*	
	Verbal	Nonverbal
Visual	Visual language	Visual Objects
Auditory	Auditory language	Environmental sounds
Haptic	Braille, handwriting	"Feel" of objects
Gustation	—	Taste memories
Olfaction	—	Smell memories
Emotion	—	Felt emotions

Note. Empty cells indicate absence of verbal representations in these modalities.

Representational Units

All theories have structural and functional units. Behaviorist psychology has stimulus-response (S-R) associations and operant acts. Cognitive psychology and neuroscience use internal representations that correspond to perceptual objects and organized behavior patterns. All are memory traces of one kind or another, so they could be called engrams, a concept introduced by Richard Semon and popularized by Lashley. The most famous neuropsychological representational unit is the Hebbian neural cell assembly. The single neuron is being increasingly seen as an information-rich representational unit. Such concepts are discussed in appropriate contexts. Here we focus on ones specifically related to nonverbal imagery and language.

The earliest historical antecedent to dual coding units appeared in the classical associationism of the British empiricists, from John Locke to James Mill (relevant selections are reprinted in Mandler & Mandler, 1964). All held that simple ideas (viewed as originating from elementary sensations) get organized into complex ideas in a hierarchical manner, so that already-formed complex ideas can combine to form more complex ones that function as units. The basic process is summation of what has been associated in experience, but to this Locke added a voluntary source, namely, the power of the mind to put together simple ideas that were not united in experience. With this he added a mysterious integrative or binding mechanism to associationism, a mystery that has not been solved. Integration is an important organizational process in DCT (as in other theories), and accordingly, it comes up again in different contexts. Why it is a puzzle is addressed in Chapter 9.

Hartley and Mill distinguished between synchronic and successive association involving simple ideas or components of complex ideas, which result from corresponding orders of occurrence of sensations from objects and events. "Thus the sight of part of a large building suggests the idea of the rest instantaneously, and the sound of the words which begin a familiar sentence, brings the remaining part to our memories in order, the association of the parts being synchronous in the first case, and successive in the last" (Hartley, 1749, quoted on p. 76 in Mandler & Mandler, 1964). Backward recall of a sentence is difficult because the sensations have been less often experienced in that order. We shall see that the synchronous-successive distinction does yoeman's work in DCT, and persists as well in such contexts as information processing, neuropsychology, and theories of intelligence.[6]

Imagery theorists around the turn of the 20th century used the term *image* to describe inner speech as well as consciously-experienced nonverbal images. Neurolinguistic pioneers (e.g., Wernicke, discussed further in Chapter 6) referred to the neural substrate for words as word images. Cognitive language theorists refer to word representations as lexical units and the entire internal dictionary as the mental lexicon. Early on, I adopted the terms *logogen* and *imagen* to distinguish the "dormant" verbal and nonverbal representational units from their consciously experienced verbal and nonverbal images and their behavioral expressions.

The Logogen Family

The logogen concept was introduced by psychologist John Morton (1969). I incorporated it into DCT as a succinct alternative to verbal representation. Logogen comes from Latin and Greek terms that translate into word generator, which in Morton's theory refers to a representation that accounts for word recognition when activated. Morton first viewed the logogen as an abstract entity but empirical evidence compelled him to postulate modality-specific (e.g., auditory and visual) logogens as well as input and output logogens (Morton, 1979). Logogens in DCT also come in auditory, visual, motor, and haptic modalities. They are activated and used in all language phenomena, including recognition, memory, production, and verbal aspects of thought in general. The logogen can be thought of as a variant of the widely used concept of lexical representation.

The DCT logogen reflects the internal organization and variable size of language units as perceived and produced. Analytically, they are sequential hierarchical structures in which larger units are composed of different combinations of smaller units. This corresponds to the standard componential analysis of words in structural linguistics. Psychological and neuropsychological studies indicate that parts as small as

---

[6]Other speculations in British associationism also anticipated modern theoretical ideas: parts may be lost in complexes (James Mill's famous son, John Stuart Mill, referred to this transformation as mental chemistry), which forecast the Gestalt slogan that the whole is greater than the sum of the parts; ideas are formed in the same sensory systems in which they are received; and miniature vibrations ("vibratiuncles") in sensory and motor nerves are the physiological substrate of ideas (Hartley's forerunner to modern neuropsychological representations).

phonemes have functional reality that shows up in such phenomena as perceptual and memory confusions and speech errors. The syllable in particular seems to have privileged status as a language unit (Paivio & Begg, 1981, p. 127; for its possible role in speech evolution, see MacNeillege) 1998. As a result of reading instruction and experience, literate people presumably have a large stock of syllable-level logogens as separate units, a syllable lexicon as it were. Unlike words and larger units, however, syllables do not stand alone as functional units. They are meaningful only in an intraverbal or grammatical sense as parts of word-level logogens, although some short words (e.g., cat) consist of one (free) syllable.

The dictionary word is the modal logogen unit in terms of its length. We use thousands of different words in speech, listening, reading, and writing, with variants for different languages, scripts, and so on. How much of our use is based on generative and recoding processes rather than separate word units is a continuing issue in language sciences. For example, how much and under what circumstances do we get meaning directly from printed words when we read, as compared to getting it indirectly by recoding the print into inner speech? The answer is that skilled readers probably do both (e.g., see Sadoski & Paivio, 2001, 2004), but all readers with normal vision must at least be able to recognize the visual patterns of words or word parts to read. They have visual logogens that are activated by print. Blind readers of Braille presumably rely on analogous tactile logogens.

The DCT logogen, however, goes beyond the word level to include stock phrases, idioms, and sequences as long as memorized poems, plays, bibles, and oral histories; anything that is remembered as a chunk. Such extensions strain the logogen concept but do not violate the definition. A memorized poem must "exist" mentally as a verbal representational unit. It is not generated anew each time we say it in the way we generate conversational speech (which is peppered with over-learned expressions of all sizes, but arranged to suit the occasion). What is the modality of such a "poetic logogen?" In DCT, it is an extended motor *logogen* constructed by verbal rehearsal. Already established word-level motor logogens are bound together by motor neurons into longer sequentially-integrated structures (sequential integration meaning that processing is sequentially constrained—it's difficult to pronounce words or poems backwards without specific practice). We cannot store poem-length visual strings or auditory sequences as integrated units. When we hear or read a familiar poem, we recognize it because we simultaneously say it to ourselves. This analysis capitalizes on the large role of motor processes in dual coding and other theories of language and cognition, as we shall see in later sections and chapters.

The term logogen raises the question of meaning. We saw in Chapter 1 that certain linguistic theories assume that lexical representations are semantically meaningful. Logogens in DCT are not. They derive their meaning from their connections to other verbal or nonverbal representations. Meaning is contextual. Logogens are meaningful in themselves only in that they have some degree of recognizability and availability for use in appropriate contexts. The contexts are mentally activated via different kinds of connections that are described following analysis of the DCT imagen.

The Imagen Family

I first used the term imagen (Paivio, 1978d) to refer to representational units that give rise to the conscious (reportable) imagery when activated. Imagens also are used in perceptual recognition, memory, drawing, and other kinds of cognitive processing of nonverbal objects. They come in different modalities, so that we have visual imagens, auditory imagens (representing environmental sounds), haptic imagens that permit us to identify felt objects, and motor imagens that guide drawing, gestures, and organized nonverbal behavioral patterns generally. The individual modalities can be distinguished functionally (Chapter 7) but all engage motor activity (e.g., eye movements generally accompany visual imaging of complex objects). Thus, functionally, imagens are a family of sensorimotor representations. Analogous concepts in the psychological literature include *iconogen* (Attneave, 1974), *pictogen* (Morton, 1979; Seymour, 1973), and *geon* (Biederman, 1987), all of which refer specifically to visual representations. Attneave also considered the possibility that visual images are stored in a picture-like form but preferred the notion that they are stored as language-like reversible descriptions from which images can be generated. The elements of such representations have a word-like status which "has the function of a *logogen*, looked at one way, [but] may also have the function of an *iconogen*, looked at the other" (Attneave 1974, p. 498). The DCT imagen does not have that ambiguous conceptual status.

The geon concept in particular is more abstract than the visual imagen in DCT. In Biederman's (1987) componential theory, objects are assumed to be composed of simple geometric shapes such as triangles, cylinders, cones, and "bricks," and identification of an object or visual scene begins with activation of these geons. The hierarchical character of the DCT visual imagen accommodates different levels of parts and wholes of objects and scenes, as described later. Moreover, the imagen pool must include more abstract geometric forms ("geons") by virtue of experience with triangles, squares, circles, lines, crescent shapes, and all the rest.

Another cousin of the DCT imagen is Barsalou's (1999, p. 586) concept of cognitive *simulators* (organized perceptual symbols) that can construct specific simulations of an entity or event, analogous to mental imagery. The simulator is one of the principle constructs in Barsalou's general theory of perceptual symbol systems, which is similar to DCT in certain respects but not in others. The similarities and differences are discussed in Chapter 5, along with other theoretical alternatives to DCT.

Functionally, visual and haptic imagens are organized into synchronous hierarchies or nested sets so that, for example, we see or image faces consisting of eyes, ears, lips, nose, and so forth, each of which is composed of still smaller parts—pupils, lobes, nostrils—and so on for any familiar object or scene. The organization is synchronous in the sense that all of the parts are available simultaneously for processing, although not accessible all at once. We can focus on parts in imagery, as in perception, by scanning the available pattern. The scanning is not sequentially constrained, and so, it can go on in any order. In contrast, as we have seen, language units are organized sequentially or linearly into larger units (e.g., syllables into words) and verbal processing is constrained by that structure in listening, reading, and speaking.

It is said that images have analog properties whereas language representations do not. The intention here is that images bear a nonarbitrary relation to perceptual objects and scenes whereas the relation is arbitrary in the case of language units. But logogens, too, are analog representations in that their sensorimotor structure maps onto the structure of words in a nonarbitrary way. A better distinction is that images (hence imagens) vary continuously in shape, size, and other properties whereas language units at any level are structurally discrete, differing from other units by distinct steps. This structural difference is blurred in monistic propositional theories of cognitive representation because they assume that both language and imagery are generated from abstract descriptions and rules that have no structural resemblance to what they generate. The difficulties with such theories were mentioned in Chapter 1 and are discussed more fully later. Here the point is that DCT imagens and logogens are modality-specific internal structures that map onto the sensorimotor attributes of objects and words.

The question of number, size, and variety arises for imagens as much as for logogens. The size of our imagen pool is enormous and it does increase all the time. For example, we must have multiple face imagens corresponding to all the faces we know and can imagine or recognize from more than one perspective. Moreover, we presumably have a subset of more abstract, generic, or protypical face imagens resulting from experiences with face drawings, caricatures, and so on. Multiply this by all the different kinds of objects we have experienced in different modalities and from different viewpoints, and we must conclude that imagens number in the millions. This would be true of any exemplar theory of cognitive representation, which is why some theorists have tried to solve this apparent cognitive overload problem in terms of a limited set of abstract features that are combined and recombined to generate different object patterns. Variants of the principle have been used in analysis-by-synthesis models of pattern recognition, neural cell assembly models, and generative grammars, all of which make use of computational logic.

I have argued (Paivio, 1986, p. 49) that such computational models have no advantage over exemplar models. In face recognition, for example, the computational program would need a list of feature values for shapes, sizes, and colors of eyes, hair, nose, and so forth, along with construction rules that specify how the features are put together in every face we know. Add to that the indefinitely large and continuous nature of object-filled scenes we can recognize and image. For example, when I visualize my cottage from the perspective of the driveway, I immediately "see" the lake, hills, and trees beyond in an expanding scene that I can scan in either direction. The seamless quality of such experiences implies a functionally continuous underlying imagen structure, a theoretical puzzle that is especially difficult to conceptualize in terms of features and combinatory rules. The issue is discussed further in the context of neural representational models in Chapter 9.

Exemplars also leave us with the problem of identifying the well-spring of novel sentences, bizarre dreams, inventions, and creative works in the arts and sciences.

Generative principles must be at work. We touch on the problem in various contexts and highlight it in the analysis of creativity in Chapter 17.

Connecting Pathways and Activation Processes

The representational units are dormant until they are activated. Activation occurs via pathways that connect representational units to the external world and to each other. The connections are structural and the activity is a patterned energy flow. Taken together, representational units, interconnections, and activation patterns constitute dual coding functional systems as a whole. All are based on neural structures and processes, but they were originally defined in DCT by psychological methods and are so described here, with neuropsychological hints that are fully developed in Chapter 7.

The conceptual scheme began as an analysis of levels or types of meaning based on verbal and imagery reactions to words and things (Paivio, 1971b), which remains a useful point of departure for this analysis. Three levels of meaning— representational, referential, and associative—were proposed. Representational meaning implies that an imagen or logogen corresponding to a verbal stimulus or an object is available for further processing. Availability is indexed by familiarity or recognition responses to the stimulus. Referential meaning derives from the relations between words and their referents, internalized as associations between logogens and imagens. The defining operations included measures of the nameability of objects and the image-evoking value of verbal stimuli. Associative meaning refers to within-system associations between logogens and between imagens. Verbal associative meaning can be tapped by traditional measures of verbal associations. Analogous but less systematic measures of nonverbal associations appear among tests of nonverbal abilities and in specific experimental contexts.

Here, we turn the analytic approach around so that meaning is interpreted as the activation of internal representations via direct and indirect pathways from sensory systems. Thus, representational meaning is conceptualized as relatively direct activation of imagens by objects and logogens by words. Referential meaning is defined as indirect activation of internal representations via cross-system connections between imagens and logogens. Associative meaning involves indirect activation via within-system connections between logogens or between imagens. The analysis also allows for a dual coding definition of the meaning of concept for language-competent humans according to which a concept is the juxtaposition of a logogen and referentially related imagens or associatively related logogens. Conceptualization accordingly entails referential and verbal-associative activity (note that, by this definition, activity of the nonverbal imagen system alone is not conceptualization; the latter always includes logogens as part of the associative activity).[7] The following sections expand on this structural and processing description.

---

[7]The term concept has been theoretically and operationally defined in various ways, all of which are related to categorization behavior, that is, grouping sets of objects or words together according to their perceptual or functional similarity. The process has been studied

The general structural model (see Fig. 3.1) shows the direct connections from sensory systems to the verbal and nonverbal representational systems, indirect connections across and within the two systems, and connections to response systems. The connections are between specific imagens and logogens, as well as between emotional and other nonverbal systems that are not represented directly as imagens. The figure also schematizes the hierarchical nested-set structure of imagens and the sequential associative structure of logogens. An expanded model would also show that all connections are one-to-many, so that pathways from a given sensory stimulus (e.g., object or word) fan out to different representational candidates, as do pathways from an internal representation to others in the same or other system. This means that activation of any particular connection and terminal representation is probabilistic rather than automatic. Which target repesentation is activated on a given occasion depends on a number of factors that are disussed in the following sections.

Direct Perceptual Activation

This level corresponds to meaningful perception. The implied question about what might constitute "meaningless" perception has been addressed historically in terms of the distinction between sensation and perception, the Gestalt psychologists' concern with primitive form perception, and (most recently) early perception, that is, the information that is available in just-detectable stimuli, before "higher-order" processing can affect performance. I discussed such issues and the then-available evidence in Imagery and Verbal Processes (Paivio, 1971b). A relevant conclusion was that stimulus meaning does not affect perception when the response depends only on what is directly available from the stimulus and not on memory. For example, simple classification of stimuli as "same" or "different" is unaffected even by familiarity when both stimuli are simultaneously in view. Here we are more concerned with perception that does involve activation of memory representations.

Activation at this level is initiated directly by verbal or nonverbal stimuli and moves along relatively-direct pathways (via intermediate sensory processing stations) to target logogens and imagens. The activation corresponds to perceptual recognition, which has long been interpreted as requiring some kind of match between a sensory pattern and a corresponding memory representation (the so-called Höffding step, after the 19th Century German psychologist who first insisted on the necessity

---

in many species (see Chapter 11), which means that a concept need not be related to language-for example, pigeons can learn to peck triangles for food regardless of their size, shape, or color. Stimulus generalization defined by a common response of any kind is the operational indicator of a concept in such cases. The dual coding definition applies to the wide range of human conceptual activity that does involve language and I will discuss it again in that context in Chapter 4. I will also rely on that definition in the analysis of scientific theories in Chapter 18.

of such a process). The analysis applies to dynamic as well as static entities. For example, biological motion can be recognized in a pattern of moving dots (Johanssen, 1973), implying that the memory representation includes the movement pattern itself. Measures of stimulus familiarity are operational indicators that such perceptual memory "templates," static or dynamic, are available and accessible. We know this because familiarity is the best predictor of how easily a stimulus can be recognized when presented very briefly or fuzzily. Recognition is probabilistic and depends on a similarity match between the stimulus and an internal representation "selected" from multiple candidates: the sensory pattern "homes in" on the most similar imagen or logogen.

The preceding analysis raises classical issues concerning the definition of similarity and its role in stimulus generalization and discrimination. In conditioning literature, generalization is measured by changes in response amplitude or probability when the stimulus is varied on some dimension, such as the pitch of a tone. However, the range of effective variation can be greatly increased by training procedures, so that quite different stimuli become functionally equivalent. Conversely, the effective range of stimulus variation can be narrowed by discrimination training in which a response is rewarded only when it occurs to stimuli that do not differ by more than a certain amount from each other. Under natural learning conditions, the range of generalization and discrimination depend on the learning history of the individual.

Numerous perceptual phenomena reflect the development and activation of stimulus-matching internal representations. For example, repeated brief presentations of printed words in an unfamiliar language results in an increasingly clear percept (Hershenson & Haber, 1965; summarized in Paivio, 1971b, pp. 120–123), suggesting accessibility to an "organized cognitive structure"—a visual logogen in DCT terms. Figural closure tests similarly reveal activation of imagens or logogens. Figure 3.2 shows an example that most readers will readily identify as a sailing ship (some might even identify it as the Bluenose II, the famous ship used as the picture on the Canadian dime). The interpretation that closure entails imagen activation is strengthened by the fact that performance on closure tests correlates with performance on other tests explicitly used to measure imagery ability (e.g., Ernest, 1980). Comparable tests of completion of fragmented visual and spoken words similarly serve as operational indicators of the reality and availability of logogens. Clear evidence for both types of representations is that prior study of pictures primes (facilitates) subsequent recognition of fragmented pictures but not fragmented words, and conversely, study of words primes recognition of fragmented words but not fragmented pictures (Weldon & Roediger, 1987, Experiment 4). Ambiguous figures first seen as one object and then another are further evidence that underlying memory representations drive the oscillating perceptual experiences. Hebb (1972, p. 235) explicitly interpreted the phenomenon as evidence for activation of different neural cell assemblies, which are further discussed in Chapters 7 and 9.

FIGURE 3.2   Recognition of this fragmented picture is evidence of imagen activation.

Cross-System Connections and Processes

Figure 3.1 shows the interconnections that enable verbal and nonverbal systems to activate each other and function separately or cooperatively in all cognitive tasks. Such cross-system activation occurs whenever we name an object or form an image to its name. The activation is indirect because the object or name must first be identified, entailing direct activation of an imagen or a logogen, which then activates a representation in the other system (e.g., Johnson, Paivio, & Clark, 1996). Motor systems would also be activated in overt acts of reference such as saying or writing the name on the verbal side and drawing (or pointing to) the imaged object on the nonverbal side. Once initiated, reciprocal back-and-forth referential activity can go on entirely "in our minds" as we talk to ourselves and picture what we are ruminating about during ordinary thinking. Simple as it might seem, indirect (referential) activation is a complex process that engages multiple connecting pathways that work in both directions. For example, pathways fan out from the logogen for the word *ship* to imagens representing different types of ships, and conversely, a particular ship imagen connects to logogens for alternative ship names that vary in generality and type—ship, schooner, frigate, liner, the Queen Mary, you name it. The connections in each direction vary in number, individual strength, and other properties that determine the probability that a particular pathway will be activated in a given situation. In brief, the referential cross-over is probabilistic and optional rather than automatic and obligatory.

Which path is activated in our ship example depends on long-term and recent experiences with ships and their names as well as contextual stimuli. The word ship might prompt a naval officer to image a battleship (part of a special knowledge domain). In this context, you might image (re-image) the schooner you detected and named in the closure test mentioned earlier. Such variables can affect referential performance in different ways, depending on the task and individual differences in people. For example, alternative connections can compete with each other and interfere with the speed of "finding" a particular name or image; on the other hand, many connections make it easier for activity to spread to different words and images and thereby aid memory search and other thought processes. Such complexities arise from the way the bidirectional referential processing systems developed and factors that control their activity.

The interconnections obviously result from early experiences with concrete objects and their names. The first words learned by children are object-words (Anglin, 1977). Children first learn to look at objects named by others and then learn to name them, aided by a prelearned capacity to imitate ("echo") speech. The fact that a child will look for and find a named object shows that mental representations of name and object are available and that these are activated by the name and other cues in the situation. Reciprocal pathways between multiple exemplars of objects and names are formed when parents discuss things that are present in the situation (encouraging naming by the child) and in their absence (thus prompting memory images) during vocabulary learning. Generalization and discrimination processes operate at this level much as they do in the case of direct perceptual activation. Infants as young as 18 months have been shown to have functional object-name interconnections (Baker & Poulin-Dubois, 1998).

A study by Paivio, Clark, Digdon, and Bons (1989) illustrates the nature of the capacity for reciprocal naming and imaging. We measured the time it took university students to name pictures of familiar objects and form images to their printed names. We were interested in the correlations between naming and imaging time for referentially related stimuli as well as correlations with the complexity, familiarity, age of acquisition, and other theoretically relevant properties of the pictures and names. We found that the average reaction times for naming and imaging individual stimuli correlated .71, suggesting substantial but imperfect bidirectionality of connections and processes, as expected from the hypothesis that referential experiences are often but not always bidirectional. The unidirectional responses correlated with different variables. Naming time correlated strongly with the number of alternative names given by the group to individual pictures (the greater the number the slower the naming time for the picture), consistent with the idea of multiple activation pathways from imagens to their alternative mental names, which in this situation competed for expression. Imaging time correlated similarly with a measure of the number of alternative images elicited by each picture name—the more alternative images the slower the reaction time.

Reaction times also correlated with characteristics of individual words and pictures. For example, the more familiar the names and the earlier they were learned, the faster they occurred as responses to their referent pictures; and the more complex the pictured objects, the more slowly they were named. Such effects presumably reflect perceptual and response processes associated with logogens and imagens independent of the connections between them.

The experiment just describe included only pictured objects and their highly concrete labels. However, different kinds, modalities, and attributes of objects also have names, as do nonverbal emotions, tastes, and smells. On the verbal side, abstract words such as *truth, love,* and *democracy* have no direct referents but they evoke images. We can also image to adjectives, verbs, and other word classes. Such variables implicate various degrees and kinds of associative processing that is analyzed more fully in the next section.

When varied, concreteness–abstractness is the strongest predictor of imagery reactions to words and larger language units. In a sample of 925 nouns (Paivio, Yuille, & Madigan,1968), concreteness as measured by ratings of the directness with which the words refer to concrete objects correlated .83 with ratings of the ease with which the words evoke visual, auditory, or other modalities of imagery. Concreteness also correlated substantially with reaction time to image to the words (Paivio, 1968b), and similar correlations have been obtained by others. Theoretically, then, word concreteness reflects the directness of connections from a logogen to a related imagens. The connections are most direct for object labels (e.g., *horse*) and least direct for highly abstract words (*truth*). Imaging to the latter requires grounding of the abstract term in a concrete instance, which entails intermediate links through word associations and illustrative images rather than images of referent objects. For example, *religion* might activate *church* first as a verbal associate and then as an image of a church.

The interpretation follows from the acquisition history of words that vary in concreteness. Whereas object names are learned in relation to the objects themselves, the learning of abstract words depends on prior learning of concrete words and thus on intraverbal associative contexts. The evolution from concrete to abstract language has often been described by students of language, not only in relation to individual language development but also the historical progression of language, as discussed later in Chapter 13. The issue is relevant as well to such topics as scientific thinking and the nature of scientific theories (Chapter 18), which include various mixes of concrete and abstract language.

Adjectives, verbs, and other classes of words also vary in rated imagery, but their average imagery value is far lower than that of concrete nouns and comparable to that of abstract nouns (Paivio, 1971b, p. 80). This too would be expected because such words lack direct referents and are instantiated as properties of many kinds of objects. For example, *running* might be concretized as an image of a sprinter approaching the finishing line (cf. Werner & Kaplan, 1963, cited in Paivio, 1971b, pp. 23–24). Colors are abstract attributes of things but they can be separately represented as color patches and easily named and imaged. Geometric forms can be defined verbally as abstract mathematical entities, but they are grounded in perceptual shapes with names that evoke shape images. Pictograms and such invented analogs as Blissymbols also concretize abstract concepts. Such effects are discussed later in relevant contexts.

The analysis of referential processing is more complicated in the case of tastes, smells, and emotions with respect to both naming and imaging. We have large vocabularies in each of these areas because, in addition to names for a relatively small number of elementary sensations or feelings, names of their situational and behavioral correlates are also included in the repertoire. In the case of taste, for example, we have taste buds that respond to sweet, sour, salty, and bitter substances but we can identify specific foods from characteristic tastes that combine many of these basic qualities. We can say that the taste of lemon juice is more sour than that of orange juice, but we can also identify the specific fruit as lemon and orange. The names for odors likewise are mostly the names of the sources—coffee, a rose, burning wood (or meat), feces, and so forth. Taste, smell, and haptic feel all contribute to naming food in the mouth. The naming repertoire in this sensory domain is nicely illustrated by a model of vocabulary intended to add precision to wine tasting. Enology scientist Ann Noble used psychophysical research to develop a three-tiered "aroma wheel" (e.g., Noble et al., 1987), as depicted in Fig. 3.3. The wheel moves from very general terms in the center (e.g., earthy, chemical, fruity) to more specific spokes (e.g., moldy, sulphur, berry) to a rim of very precise odors (e.g., moldy cork, garlic, raspberry). Wine aromas are judged for their match relative to aromas of standards made up of, say, a teaspoon of orange juice or a mix of different fruit in a neutral liquid, and a selection of terms that best describe the wine. The standard wheel includes more than 100 taste-aroma terms of the different levels of generality. The point for us is the demonstration that referential naming even in this heady domain is based on concrete substances.

Like taste and smell, emotion is a subjective experience that includes situational correlates and is associated as well with characteristic behavioral (especially facial) expressions. Only a few basic emotional experiences have been proposed in the long history of speculation and research on the subject—typically no more than three bipolar dimensions (e.g., pleasant–unpleasant, excited–calm, tense–relaxed), and sometimes fewer, usually just pleasant and unpleasant. Recently it has been suggested (Lazarus, 1982; Schacter & Singer, 1962) that there is only an intensity dimension of physiological arousal, and that more specific nameable emotions are identified on the basis of situational cues. We say we feel love, happiness, anger, or fear because of differences in the arousing situation. An alternative view (e.g., Zajonc, 1985) is that we differentiate many emotions on the basis of physiological correlates alone, including feedback from facial muscles that contract in different patterns to different emotions. I return to such issues in subsequent chapters. The point at the moment is that our repertoire of labels for our own felt emotions stem jointly from relatively few bodily changes and a great many more situations in which the emotions occur.

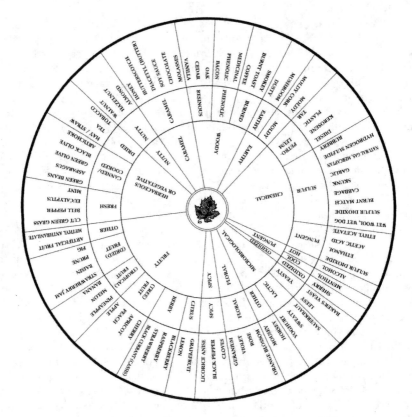

FIGURE 3.3   The Wine Aroma Wheel. Copyright 1990 A. C. Noble
www.winearomawheel.com Reproduced with permission.

We have a large repertoire of names for facial expressions of emotion, both as seen in others and produced by ourselves in response to the names. Moreover, consistent with Darwin's (1873) claim that facial expressions are universal indicators of certain basic emotions, we tend to agree on their names. For example, Paul Ekman (1973), a leading researcher in this area, found high correlations among participants within five different cultures in the names they gave (in their respective languages) to expressions of happiness, disgust, surprise, sadness, anger, and fear. A remarkable demonstration of this capacity is that actors can learn to produce distinct facial expressions to more than 400 emotion names, and participants can learn to name the expressions (Baron-Cohen, 2003). Examples are joy, disgust, sadness, surprise, wonder, and disappointment. This discriminative referential processing capacity reflects the adaptive significance of learning to read emotions in others, a kind of mind reading that presumably has its roots deep in the evolution of nonverbal cognition (Chapter 11).

The reverse referential process of imaging to words that refer to tastes, odors, and emotions primarily entails imaging objects or situations associated with those subjective experiences. Asked to image a sour taste, a pleasant odor, and sadness, I might first picture a lemon, a rose, and a "dear departed" friend. Then I might salivate (a motor component of "lemon in the mouth" imagery), sniff and perhaps get a vague scent of a rose, and feel sad as I think of the friend. I seem not to have images of the taste, smell, and emotional experience independent of the imaged objects.

Taste, olfaction, and emotion are linked especially closely to adaptive motivational mechanisms that have neural representations in particular regions of the brain. Accordingly, we consider them again in subsequent chapters on adaptive functions of dual coding, neuropsychological correlates, and evolutionary contexts.

Perception and Imagery Compared. The discussion thus far implies that perception and imagery engage similar representations and similar processing systems. The main difference, so it seems, is that the activation of representations is direct in the case of perception and indirect in the case of imagery. This interpretation has been proposed by many theorists over the years (e.g., Paivio, 1971b). One kind of behavioral evidence was that participants could not distinguish between their mental image of a banana and a faint projection of such an object (Perky, 1910). Stronger evidence was that perception and imagery can interfere with each other. We know that it's hard to pay attention to what we see when we are daydreaming, and conversely, that we can't daydream while attending to a visual task. Experimental evidence confirms that the interference is modality specific, so that detection of visual signals is hindered more by visual imagery than by auditory imagery, and auditory perception is hindered more by auditory than visual imagery (Segal & Fusella, 1970). Recently, De Beni and Moé (2003) showed that participants using a visual imagery strategy recalled orally presented text passages better than written ones whereas participants using verbal rehearsal recalled the written presentation better than the oral one. We shall see later that the relation between perception and imagery remains a hot research topic in cognitive psychology and neuropsychology.

Despite the overlap, however, it is unlikely that exactly the same representations are activated in perception as in imagery because the pathways and activation processes are different. We could say that we draw from different subsets of imagens or logogens in the two cases, or use different distinguishing labels (e.g., iconogen and pictogen were introduced specifically to account for perceptual recognition). To use an earlier example, a ship seen in the distance "homes in on" a relatively small set of similar ship imagens and a particular imagen is activated when the ship gets close enough to be identified. When asked to picture a ship in our minds, we have a larger imagen pool to draw from and it takes more time before a particular imagen is activated and we can report a conscious image (which could also involve constructive processes of some kind—more about that later). The size of the representational pool and the availability of particular representations depend on the breadth, depth, and recency of one's experience with the perceptual domain—in this case, our knowledge of ships. Perception and imagery converge only in the case of iconic memory, a perceptual, image-like trace that persists very briefly after a stimulus has been glimpsed (Neisser, 1967, p. 20). However, a single glance may not be enough to create a stable imagen or logogen.

Within-System Connections and Processes

We turn to associative links within nonverbal and verbal systems (see Fig. 3.1). On the nonverbal side, we have the "tight" synchronous associations that bind parts into integrated objects (e.g., nose, eyes, and mouth into a face), objects into perceived or imagined scenes (dwellings, trees, and a lake into a summer cottage scene), and associations across the different sensory modalities of such multimodal objects as telephones. Motor processes play a role in the formation and processing of some associations (e.g., scenes must be scanned because they can't be viewed or imaged at a glance), but not necessarily in others (e.g., the associations between the appearance, sound, and feel of a telephone are formed simply by being experienced together). Theoretically, all entail associations between imagens. On the verbal side, we have the classical example of word–word associations of different degrees of complexity, expressed overtly in speech or writing, or internally as silent speech. Theoretically, these involve sequential associations between motor logogens (e.g., saying knife-fork-spoon), but cross-modal associations are involved when, for example, the stimulus is a printed word and the response a spoken word.

The analysis implies that integration of parts into wholes is a special case of association. Gestalt psychologists had maintained, however, that the concepts are distinct because an integrated form is more than the sum of the parts. A square made up of rows of "X"s is perceived as a new entity, not as a conjunction of "X"s and squareness. The perception is immediate and not dependent on learning. The alternative view is that associative experience can integrate separate parts into higher order perceptual or memory units (Paivio, 1971b, pp. 279–280). Perceptual fragmentation (reviewed in Paivio, 1971b, pp. 99–105) provides one kind of supporting evidence.

Under conditions of reduced stimulation, objects show perceptual instability characterized by the disappearance and intermittent reappearance of the object or some portion of it. This occurs, for example, when luminous figures are viewed under reduced illumination (McKinney, 1963). Tees and More (1967) used the technique to study the effect of associative experience on the development of compound representations. Participants were repeatedly presented digit strings in which a critical pair (e.g., 85) was periodically embedded. The result was that the target pair began to disappear together when presented along with a third stimulus in the test situation. The extent to which the two operated together was a linear function of the frequency of previous joint occurrences. Thus, repeated associative pairing resulted in a compound representation in which the pair functioned as an integrated unit. Later (Chapter 7), we review neuropsychological evidence for the gestalt view that the integration effect is more than the sum of the associated parts.

Intermodal associations. Associations that cross different sensorimotor modalities are familiar from everyday experience. We translate visual patterns into auditory motor patterns when we read aloud and can sense the inner voice even when we read silently. Conversely, we can listen to a story and simultaneously track the printed text. We translate into a haptic-motor pattern when we take notes in a lecture. Such recoding processes seem so automatic that some theorists suggest that all are mediated by an abstract, amodal interlingua. Dual coding and some other theories assume that all recodings are between modality-specific representations, whose joint activation becomes increasingly automatic with repeated associative experience, "automatic" meaning highly probable but not certain. Even experienced readers sometimes make mistakes when reading aloud. We shall see later that different kinds of recoding processes can be disrupted by specific brain lesions.

Nonverbal intermodal recoding is equally familiar. We hear a siren, ringing, splashing, barking, or a bird song, and we visualize a fire engine, telephone, waves, a dog, or a bird. The recoding is so likely that it is generally taken for granted, but it does not have to happen, and when it does, the associated visual image varies from time to time. Even more compelling are mental translations between felt shape and visual images of objects, investigated in studies of the speed with which objects experienced in one modality can be recognized in the other (e.g., Johnson, Paivio, & Clark, 1989). Here, too, the translation seems so automatic that some theorists propose a supermodal system for representing both visual and haptic shapes of objects. The alternative, favored in DCT, is rapid intermodal transfer. Behavioral and neuropsychological evidence is presented in later chapters.

The distinction between synchronous and sequential associations has already been discussed in relation to the internal structure of imagens and logogens. It applies as well to associations between representations that have been experienced together but not consistently enough to function as a compound unit, such as a face or a word. Recall that the distinction has its roots in British associationism (an image of the sun simultaneously includes the sky whereas the words of a prayer are remembered successively). It has reappeared in Luria's (1973) neuropsychological theory as simultaneous versus successive synthesis of parts into wholes and was imported into information processing psychology as the contrast between parallel and serial processing.

The dual coding emphasis has been on processing constraints: verbal sequences are sequentially constrained (it is hard to recite the alphabet backwards without practice) but processing of remembered scenes is not similarly constrained. The latter is subject instead to spatial constraints in that the image must be scanned, and, as Kosslyn (1980) has shown for memory images of recently-viewed scenes, it takes longer to get from one object to another the farther apart they are in the image. Similar scanning effects have been obtained for images constructed from verbal descriptions (e.g., Denis & Zimmer, 1992).

An important conceptual distinction is that the information in spatial images is simultaneously available but not simultaneously accessible for processing. I can describe my living room in any order from a memory image—the image is available all at once for sequentially unconstrained processing—but the parts can't be accessed simultaneously because of limitations in visual (perceptual as well as image) span and in motor output systems. Even a clever octopus could not "point to" more than eight objects at once!

A simple experiment (Paivio, 1986, pp. 198–201) concretized the synchronous-sequential contrast. Participants were asked either to image two-dimensional capital letters such as **L** and count the number of inner and outer corners from the image, or they imaged visual words with matching numbers of letters (e.g., MOTHER) and read off the letters from the image. Importantly, they were asked to count corners both clockwise and counterclockwise, and name letters forward and backward from the images. The relevant results were that corner counting speed was unaffected by processing order whereas letters were named much more slowly backward than forward. One can be confident that the sequential constraints applied to the visual images of the words because participants also did the same tasks perceptually by counting corners of block letters or reading off the letters of visual words; in this case, backward letter naming was as fast as forward naming.

Forward and backward readout time from imaged words are equally fast only for words no more than three letters in length (Weber & Harnish, 1974). This is a functional limitation on visual logogens activated by associative cues (e.g., the spoken word as the cue for imaging MOTHER in the experiment just described). The directional-sequential constraint applies even when strings of letters are briefly flashed to both visual fields—letters glimpsed in the left field are reported more accurately than those in the right, perhaps reflecting implicit left-to-right postexposure scanning activity acquired when learning to read (Heron, cited in Paivio, 1971b, pp. 108–109). Alternatively, the imagery and perceptual-memory effects might have resulted from recoding visual letter patterns into motor logogens, which also is sequentially constrained. This argument parallels that made earlier in regard to length limitations on auditory logogens—our memorized poems are stored as motor sequences rather than as auditory streams or visual texts.

We have focused thus far on the associative structural and processing characteristics that differentiate verbal and nonverbal systems. Each system, however, relies on both synchronic and sequential processing. Such nonverbal activities as walking, dancing, figure skating, gymnastics, and any number of such everyday skilled activities as tying shoelaces and eating with a knife and fork (or chopsticks) require coordination of movement sequences going on at the same time in different parts of the body. Moreover, many of the sequences fit into a spatial frame that must be taken into account all at once. Similarly, production of phonemes, the minimal functional units of speech, entails synchronous activity of the larynx, tongue, lips, and so forth, which is why the phoneme is sometimes described as a simultaneous bundle of distinctive (articulatory) features. Hearing and producing language also involve prosodic events—stress, pitch, and other changes—that go on simultaneously at certain points in the verbal sequence. The articulatory muscles exquisitely control the sequence of events from chest to lips to produce speech, much of the activity going on at the same time in different places.

TRANSFORMATIONAL PROCESSES

The activated representations are sometimes experienced as static entities, like snapshots of faces and scenes, but most of the time they are dynamic and change-able, reflecting the activities and affordances of objects and situations. We experi-ence both the "flights and perchings of thought," as William James put it. The dynamic aspects can all be described as *transformations* that are implemented by (or just occur) in both dual coding systems, following the constraints imposed by the organization of nonverbal and verbal structures and the processes that operate on them. They derive from observations of autonomous changes in dynamic objects and events, or changes that occur when we manipulate objects. They accordingly involve motor processes that are residues of the original perceptual activity and behavioral manipulations.

Nonverbal transformations operate on spatial and sensory properties of objects and events. As manifested in imagery, the spatial transformations include mental rotations on any plane, and changes in size, shape, and relative position of objects. All are imagined movements of different kinds–kinematic images of objects that move and change form (animals, clouds, cars), or movements imposed by an inner "agent" as when we imagine ourselves playing chess, or putting a pencil inside a bun using the rhyme mnemonic described earlier. The most-often studied class of transformation is mental rotation, first in psychometric tests of individual differences in spatial ability and later experimentally in the famous experiments by Roger Shepard, which gave us quantitative information on how fast mental images can be rotated. The following event illustrates the phenomenon in everyday terms. When my youngest daughter was about 7 age, I asked her to picture a "big" letter N in her mind. When she said she had it, I asked her to tilt it over on its side and asked, "Now what do you see?" "I see a Z," she promptly replied, which means that she must have rotated the imaged letter 90 degrees. Roger Shepard invented experimental methods for determining the speed of such mental rotations (experiments with dif-ferent collaborators are summarized in Shepard & Cooper, 1982). In one experiment (Shepard & Metzler, 1971), participants compared a block diagram with another view of the same diagram or with another diagram. The same diagram differed sys-tematically from the target in terms of how it would look if rotated through differ-ent degrees. The relevant finding for these purposes was that the time to make a "same" decision increased as the rotational distance between stimuli increased, as if participants mentally rotated the target to the same orientation as the comparison figure to make the judgment.

One version of the task is particularly interesting here because it explicitly involved verbal-imaginal dual coding. Cooper and Shepard (1973, Exp. II) asked their participants to image a letter or a number and then rotate the image through a series of 45-degree angles clockwise to the verbal cues "up," "tip," "down" (i.e., image the letter upright, tipped 45 degrees, 90 degrees), and so on, prior to the presentation of a variably-oriented perceptual test stimulus that was to be identified as a normal or a mirror-image version of the target character. The major result was that reaction time for the decisions increased progressively as the difference between the imaged orientation and the presented orientation of the character increased.

The mental rotation task became somewhat of a research cottage industry over the years. Among other findings (summarized in Paivio, 1986, pp. 197–198), the studies provided additional support for the interpretation of mental rotations in terms of dynamic imagery processes, with the important qualification that the processes can include haptic or kinesthetic components. This would be expected from the assumption that the internal transformational skills derive from perceptual-motor experience with manipulating objects. Motor components could be involved in all dynamic functions of imagery, such as effects of action pictures and interactive images in associative memory tasks, a topic that is covered in the next chapter.

Much less research has been done on transformations along sensory dimensions, although they too are familiar in everyday life. Suffice to say that we can imagine an object changing color, a voice changing pitch, a felt object changing form or texture, and so on. These capacities presumably derive from seeing different colored roses, bananas, cars—whatever—and from such activities as drawing objects in different colors; or hearing different voices and changing the pitch of our voice in speech or song. In brief, any transformation and manipulation that has been experienced can be carried out mentally, in different modalities of imagery. Moreover, consistent with the dual coding perspective, those dynamic functions can be done in response to verbal descriptions.

Organizational and transformational processes apply fully to verbal structures. Verbal transformations operate on a sequential frame, imposing changes in temporal order or substitution of new elements for ones that occupy a particular temporal slot. These are familiar as changes in grammatical form when an active is changed into a passive, a positive into a negative, and all the other changes that were formalized in Chomsky's generative grammar theory. Some of these are explicitly described as movement transformations in recent theories (examples are dissected in the context of neural correlates of grammar in Chapter 8). Pitch, stress, and other extralinguistic changes also occur within the verbal sequential frame.

Novelty of Transformations

A striking feature of mental transformations is their novelty and creativity, which occur spontaneously and unexpectedly in bizarre dreams and in ways taken for granted in imaginative thinking and everyday conversations. Imagination is defined as an ability to create new things or ideas or to combine old ones in new forms. It is the stuff of poetry, art, and invention. Transformational and generative grammars are all about the novelty and creativity of ordinary language. How all of this happens or is achieved by the mind is not fully understood, but we do know that experience—familiarity with the elements, dynamic properties, and uses of things—is essential for creative thinking and behavior in every domain. We focus particularly on the experiential basis of creativity in the chapters to come on cognitive evolution and evolved expertise in various fields.

CONSCIOUS AND UNCONSCIOUS PROCESSING

The activation of representations and their transformations is often experienced at a conscious level. However, it has become increasingly clear over more than a century that much cognitive work goes on at an unconscious level, psychologically inaccessible to introspection and verbal description. That is why I relied on other operational indicators and procedures to tap into nonverbal and verbal processes at the outset of dual coding research. In particular, I downgraded vividness as a functional attribute of imagery because measures of vividness had failed to correlate with memory performance. Still, as Chapter 4 shows, I did routinely (and profitably) use verbal reports of imagery and verbal thoughts as an adjunct to the more objective operational procedures, on the assumption that even fuzzy images (or mental words) can mediate memory performance. Recent evidence has moved me to reevaluate my original position on the role of consciousness in DCT.

What remains unchanged is the view that we are generally unaware of inner mental activity. This can be appreciated most clearly if we focus on neuropsychological explanations of cognition: We simply cannot see what is going on in our brains when we are trying to remember something or solve a problem mentally. We can describe some of the conscious products of the activity but often they just happen, as automatically as walking and talking. This is old hat, but a reminder now and then could keep us from slipping into unproductive, introspective, explanatory habits. The surest alternative is the hard observational and experimental work that eventually leads to scientific knowledge.

But what about consciousness itself as an object of study? This, too, has become a cottage industry among neuroscientists and students of mind evolution. There is even a journal devoted to studies of consciousness. Researchers seek psychological and neural correlates of consciousness, which require an independent definition of the phenomenon. David Marks, a leading researcher in the field, proposed a theory of consciousness and imagery that rests on verbal reportability as the ultimate criterion of consciousness. Thus, Marks (1999) asserted the following: "Mental imagery should never be assumed to be present in the consciousness of research participants without corroboration from their verbal reports. Behavioural or physiological indicators can never stand alone as evidence of mental imagery in human consciousness" (p. 576).

It is difficult to know about the general acceptability of Marks's (1999) view because students of consciousness seldom commit themselves to a single operational definition of the concept. For example, the authors of eight chapters in a section on consciousness in the 1995 volume on the cognitive neurosciences edited by Gazzaniga discussed various behavioral and neural correlates of awareness and conscious experience. Verbal reports were sometimes explicitly mentioned but often they were simply implied in descriptions of perceptual and memory tasks that usually require verbal responses. In any case, verbal reports provide the only sure operational definition of consciousness that is independent of the behaviors the concept is supposed to explain. Even then the concept must be independently informative in some sense rather than being a redundant correlate of the behavior otherwise measured.

David Marks's questionnaire on the vividness of conscious imagery turned out to be informative in that sense, which changed my view of vividness as a functional attribute of imagery. Studies have shown that Marks's (1973) imagery vividness questionnaire (VVIQ) reliably predicts performance in a number of perceptual cognitive tasks. A meta-analysis by McKelvie (1995) revealed that the relation is substantial and consistent across findings from different studies. The analysis also showed equally clearly that memory performance did not correlate with VVIQ, which agrees with negative findings from early 20th Century investigations of vividness and memory. We can therefore conclude that vivid images (defined by VVIQ scores or comparable criteria) contribute to performance in cognitive tasks that require attention to detail but not in standard tests of memory.

Are there other measures of consciousness that correlate in a more informative way with memory? Tulving's (1985) description of qualitative differences in consciousness was intended to do just that. He used the term *anoetic consciousness* to refer to procedural memories, like tying shoelaces, where one is aware of what one is doing but the pattern of activity is automatic. Noetic ("knowing") consciousness applies to semantic memory, one's general knowledge of the world. Autonoetic consciousness refers to memories that include awareness that one personally experienced the remembered events at a particular time and place. However, this "noesis scale" simply labels what individuals can say about their memories. The consciousness distinctions are defined in terms of the memory distinctions and vice versa. The memory distinctions can be otherwise defined in terms of experimental procedures but the nature of consciousness ("noesis") is not further clarified by such operational expansions.

Thus consciousness is problematic even when defined in terms of verbal reports. Measured separately, reported vividness of conscious imagery correlates informatively with objective performance on other tasks. Noesis, however, is defined in terms of the memory performance it is supposed to explain. The definition and explanatory role of consciousness become even more problematic when the verbal report criterion is absent. For example, Tulving (2005) argued that autonoetic consciousness is unavailable to other animals, as well as to children younger than 4 years who can't satisfy verbal criteria of autonoetic episodic memory. However, no independent definition of the concept appears in his discussions. In a chapter in the same volume, Katherine Nelson (2005) described a scale of consciousness in terms of cognitive development in children, according to which signs of autonoesis begin to appear at about 4 years of age. The descriptions are informative in regard to the nature of cognition at different ages, but there appears to be no measure of consciousness that is independent of the developmental behavioral changes themselves. Thus, consciousness neither explains nor is explained by the described behavioral changes.

In the next chapter we shall see that, unlike consciousness, both imagery and verbal processes have been defined in ways that are independent of the effects they predict and explain. Consciousness is implicated when participants are asked about their use of imagery and verbal mediators as memory aids, but consciousness alone cannot be used to explain the patterns of separate and joint effects of mental images and mental words because, in that case, both are conscious according to the verbal report criterion. I deal further with issues that implicate variables related to consciousness in the context of neuropsychological correlates in Chapter 7 and then revisit the concept in Chapter 11, where I argue, somewhat paradoxically, that imagery in preverbal children and animals can be defined in terms of objective indicators without relying on verbal reports, although consciousness cannot be so defined.

Complex Processing

This chapter has described the component structures and processes of DCT separately, generally using relatively simple examples. However, real life cognition is more complex, involving continuous interplay between different levels and types of processes (perceptual, referential, associative, transformational, conscious, and unconscious) in response to verbal and nonverbal stimuli. Consider the task of rearranging a living room. If I were in my living room, I might scan the layout and start moving furniture, lamps, vases, and paintings around. More likely I would first imagine how they would look in different places, talking to myself all the while. If I were telling a friend about my intentions over the phone while in the living room, I could scan and describe what I see directly; if elsewhere, I would do so from memory, viewing and scanning the living room from different angles in my mind's eye while discussing possible arrangements. DCT provides a way of describing and conceptualizing such complexities without resorting to abstract entities that only increase the explanatory burden. We discuss the structures and processes in more complex situations when we turn our attention to the adaptive functions of dual coding systems in the next chapter.

CHAPTER FOUR

Adaptive Functions of
Dual Coding Systems

This chapter explains how dual coding systems help us to survive and thrive in everyday life. It is based on strong and consistent effects of variables that justify DCT while challenging other theories of cognition. The review also provides empirical grounds for the interpretation of cognitive evolution in later chapters. The description of these adaptive functions elaborates on the principle of cooperative independence, the idea that the verbal and nonverbal systems, although functionally independent, must coordinate their activities to achieve common goals. This is a version of the truism that the adaptive mind must function in an integrative fashion. DCT provides a principled approach to how this is achieved. Independence means that the systems can be active separately or together. Cooperation is possible because each system can activate the other via their interconnections. Cooperative independence implies (a) additive benefits of verbal and nonverbal activity in some tasks, (b) selective reliance on one system when it is especially relevant to a given task, and (c) switching back and forth between them according to changing task demands. Such cooperative activities of the two multimodal systems usually serve us well, but, under some conditions, one system might not be helpful and could even interfere with the efficiency of the other. All these possibilities are illustrated with research examples. A summary of the methods used to measure and manipulate the internal systems is followed by a review of dual coding contributions to memory, anticipation, evaluation, motivation, problem solving, and communication—viewed here as the basic adaptive functions of mind.

CONVERGENT OPERATIONS AND STRONG INFERENCE

Three classes of independent variables have been used to measure and manipulate dual coding processes in cognitive tasks. These variables are as follows: (a) stimulus materials that differ in imagery value or concreteness and in comparable verbal attributes, (b) task instructions and other procedures designed to prime verbal or nonverbal processing during task performance, and (c) tests of individual differences in verbal and nonverbal abilities. Two or more of these classes of variables were included in some experiments to reveal their interactions. For example, instructions to use imagery or verbal coding strategies were expected to modulate the effects of stimulus concreteness. These procedures were supplemented by participants' introspective reports about their use of verbal and nonverbal modes of thinking during task performance. Note that, as mentioned in the last chapter, such reports implicate consciousness but the reports are obtained separately from the target task and they might or might not correlate with task performance.

The operations are convergent in the sense that they constitute different ways of getting at the same mental processes. These are complex and it is accordingly vital to ensure that the procedures converge on specific structural and functional properties of each code rather than on some undifferentiated or global property. For example, nonverbal imagery varies in sensory modality and other attributes; therefore, different experimental procedures are needed to reveal effects due to the various properties.

The procedures were linked to the method of strong inference whereby dual coding hypotheses and predictions were compared and contrasted with alternative predictions arising from the verbal memory tradition and its propositional descendants. In this way, the "real" explanatory candidate might stand out from the rest.

MEMORY FUNCTIONS

Memory is the most general of the cognitive adaptive functions because all others depend on it—we need to remember the past to evaluate the present, anticipate the future, satisfy our needs, solve problems, and empower language. Moreover, as argued earlier, the representational structures and processes described in DCT are built from memories and serve to promote their own growth. It takes no great leap of imagination to appreciate the extended argument that memory must have been similarly crucial throughout cognitive evolution, with dual coding memory processes becoming increasingly involved as language joined the nonverbal memory base over time. We focus on episodic memory tasks (memory for experimental or "real-life" events) but theoretical interest centers on how task performance relates to dual coding representational structures and processes.

It is important to distinguish episodic memory in this general sense from Tulving's autonoetic (self-aware) episodic memory. The latter concept is largely irrelevant to the main issues in this section. Tulving (2005) would agree, for he wrote that the term *episodic memory* in the new autonoetic sense "does not refer to a particular kind of memory *task*, or a particular kind of *measure* in a task, or a particular kind of stored *information*, or a particular kind of phenomenal *experience*" (p. 9, italics added). The dual coding approach to episodic memory, however, has everything to do with differences in all of those kinds of variables, emanating from the crucial importance of the verbal–nonverbal distinction in experienced and stored information. The development of the theory revealed some of the most dramatic phenomena in the memory literature, phenomena that are excluded from consideration within the new episodic memory system as defined by Tulving's criteria. By drawing attention to the predictive and explanatory power of variables associated with the verbal–nonverbal distinction, dual coding memory theory could even benefit Tulving's theory, particularly those aspects associated with the definition of autonoetic consciousness. This section, however, seeks mainly to justify dual coding memory theory in its own right.

I take up the story where we left it at the end of Chapter 2. We saw that a modern version of the ancient method of loci worked so well that it astonished those who tried it for the first time. We also saw that the conceptual peg hypothesis, derived from imagery mnemonics, correctly predicted noun–adjective word order effects in a verbal learning experiment in which a verbal association hypothesis predicted different results. However, detailed explanations remained speculative. Word concreteness was thought to be important in the mnemonic technique and its extension but had not been directly investigated in relevant tasks. Imagery itself had not been compared with control conditions. These basic questions and others arising from them began to be systematically investigated in the early 1960s. Answers came within a few years but some key issues have been resolved only recently.

The Conceptual Peg Hypothesis and Associative Memory

There are several good reasons for beginning with research motivated by the conceptual peg hypothesis. First, the research revealed some of the most potent variables in everyday memory. Second, the hypothesis turned out to be so successful and productive that its expansion into DCT was inevitable. And third, it has direct implications for cognitive evolution.

Much of everyday memory is associative and redintegrative, consisting of recollections triggered by events that were part of the original experience. The general principle goes back to 19th century Scottish psychologist William Hamilton, who distinguished between integrative and successive associations on the grounds that presenting any part of an integrated set of elements redintegrates (re-institutes) the whole set rather than a sequence of ideas one after the other. A famous literary example of redintegration is in Marcel Proust's monumental novel, *A la Recherche du Temps Perdu* (In Search of Lost Time). I draw on an excerpt in a proust biography (Crucini, 1971, pp. 57–59). Proust's character describes how the taste of a piece of madeleine sponge cake dipped in tea reminded him of the first time he had that taste experience. The recollection was followed immediately by a flood of memories of childhood: home, garden, street, village, people, the pleasures experienced, all of that emerging from a cup of tea. Another familiar example is so-called flash-bulb memory, which refers to the clarity and certainty of our answer to a question like, "Where were you on September 11, 2001?" My recollection consists of vivid images of where I was, what I was doing, and how I heard about the tragic event (my youngest daughter telephoned me at my cottage and told me to turn on the TV).

Such everyday recollections are relevant to the classical mnemonic techniques and the conceptual peg hypothesis introduced in Chapter 2. The recollections entail memories of concrete events activated by concrete cues, either nonverbal (madeleine cake in tea) or verbal (the "9/11" question). Imagery mnemonics incorporate those features; for example, the stimulus cues and (usually) the items to be remembered are concrete in the one-bun, two-shoe rhyme technique. The conceptual peg hypothesis likewise suggested that concreteness and imagery were crucial elements in the noun–adjective order effect, but it implicitly raised questions about both assumptions because concreteness and imagery variables had not been investigated. Their expected effects are explicitly expressed in the following statement of the hypothesis in a review article:

> *The imagery value* [i.e., concreteness] *of both stimulus and response would contribute to the formation of a compound image … evoked by the individual items when they are presented together … On recall trials, however, when the stimulus is presented alone, its imagery value would be particularly important [because] the stimulus member must serve as the cue that reinstitutes* [redintegrates] *the compound image from which the response component can be retrieved and recoded as a word.* (Paivio, 1969, p. 244)[8]

To appreciate the significance of the hypothesis, let's put it into historical perspective. First, from any verbal dominance view of mind and memory, there is no reason to expect concreteness or imagery to be effective unless they engage verbal associative mechanisms (we shall see later in this chapter that the same argument applies to propositions, schemata, and other abstract alternatives to imagery and dual coding memory mechanisms.) It's as if the Proust and "9/11" experiences were transformed into organized verbal associative networks analogous to Ramist tree structures, which then mediated the recollections. This is not mere speculation, for in the early years of my research on concreteness and imagery effects, I was routinely asked, "How do you know it isn't all really verbal [rather than imagery]?" Second, traditional verbal memory researchers held that verbal associative meaningfulness and familiarity were the most effective word attributes in memory tasks. Moreover, they assumed that these variables are more potent when they are varied on the response side of pairs as properties of the words to be recalled rather than as properties of the stimulus cues that serve to remind one of those responses. That assumption

---

[8]Students of memory should note how the conceptual peg hypothesis differs from the somewhat similar encoding specificity principle later proposed by Tulving and Thomson (1973). The similarity is that both state that an effective retrieval cue must be stored with the event to be remembered during encoding. The difference is that encoding specificity makes no reference to the imagery value (concreteness) of the stored information or retrieval cue and thus cannot explain or predict concreteness effects.

stemmed from decades of research that confirmed the response hypothesis, at least in the case of nonsense syllables and unfamiliar words (e.g., Underwood & Schultz, 1960), which is exactly the reverse of the expected effects of concreteness according to the conceptual peg hypothesis. Once again, therefore, we have contrasting predictions from the verbal memory tradition and the imagery-based conceptual peg hypothesis that was inspired by the rhyme mnemonic technique.

The aim of the research program was to isolate the effects of imagery-concreteness by controlling other memory-relevant attributes of words, and then to determine the effects of both imagery and verbal processes in associative memory. On the assumption that imagery is the major effective memory correlate of concreteness, the key predictions were that concreteness of pairs would be generally effective and that, independently considered, concreteness of the word used as the retrieval cue would benefit recall more than concreteness of the response word.

The first systematic conceptual peg experiment (Paivio, 1965a) is described in considerable detail because it is the prototypical paradigm for testing extensions of the hypothesis. Familiar words judged to be concrete or abstract were arranged in lists containing 16 pairs, four of each possible stimulus-response combination of concrete (C) and abstract (A) words. Examples are as follows: *coffee-shoe* (CC), *flower-theory* (CA), *fate-chair* (AC), and *event-duty* (AA). The words were re-paired while retaining the same combinations in different lists to control for idiosyncratic properties of individual words. The participants had four study-test trials in which pairs were first read aloud and then the first word of each pair was presented as the cue for recall of the second. It turned out that there was no interaction over trials and we need only consider the total number of correct responses over the four trials.

The conceptual peg hypothesis predicted that recall scores for the four pair types would decline in the order, CC>CA>AC>AA. Fig. 4.1 (panel A) shows that this is precisely what occurred. Let us examine the relevant features of the pattern. First, the general effect of pair concreteness can be seen by comparing CC and AA recall. The respective recall proportions were .71 and .38, a two-fold advantage for the concrete pairs. This striking difference reflects the simultaneous effects of stimulus and response concreteness on associative recall. Second, the predicted advantage of concreteness on the stimulus side shows up specifically in the much higher recall for CA pairs (e.g., *flower-theory*) than AC pairs (e.g., *fate-chair*). Thus, concrete words were more effective retrieval cues for abstract associates than abstract words were for concrete associates.[9]

---

[9]Statistical confirmation of the stimulus versus response effect requires a comparison of scores for pairs with concrete stimuli (averaging over CC and CA pairs) and pairs with abstract stimuli (AC and AA pairs). The recall proportions were .67 and .41 with concrete and abstract stimuli, respectively; the same comparison on the response side yielded recall proportions of .58 and .50 for concrete and abstract responses. Statistically, the stimulus effect was eight times greater than the response effect of concreteness.

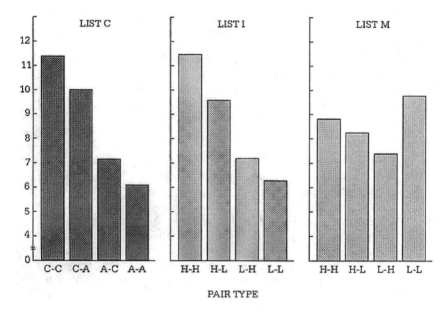

FIGURE 4.1   Paired associate recall scores over four trials as a function of noun concreteness-abstractness (List C), high (H) and low (L) imagery value with verbal associative meaningfulness (M) controlled (List I), and high and low M with imagery value controlled (List M). List C data adapted from Table 1 in Paivio (1965), Abstractness, imagery, and meaningfulness in paired associate learning. *Journal of Verbal Learning and Verbal Behavior*, 4, 32–38. Copyright 1965, with permission from Elsevier. List I and List M data adapted from Figure 1 (p. 431) in Paivio, Smythe, and Yuille (1968). Imagery versus meaningfulness of nouns in paired- associate learning. *Canadian Journal of Psychology*, 22, 427–441. Copyright 1968 Canadian Psychological Association. Reprinted with permission.

An imagery interpretation of the effects was supported by data from a separate group of participants, who rated the concrete words as being much easier to image than the abstract words. However, the concrete words were also higher in verbal associative meaningfulness. I could only argue at the time that meaningfulness was unlikely to be the effective variable because, as mentioned earlier, response meaningfulness was usually related to recall more strongly than stimulus meaningfulness, contrary to the relations observed in this experiment.

To disentangle imagery-concreteness from meaningfulness, the experiment was repeated (Paivio, Smythe, & Yuille, 1968) with new lists in which pairs were constructed using words that are high or low on imagery value but did not differ in meaningfulness. The words were drawn from a large normative word pool.[10] To further test the generality of the effects, the words were presented visually rather than auditorily. As can be seen in panel B of Fig. 4.1, the overall recall pattern was identical to that obtained in the 1965 experiment. Panel C of the figure shows quite a different pattern for meaningfulness, with recall being better for low-meaningful pairs than for the other combinations. The negative effect of meaning-fulness can be explained in terms of interference due to implicit associations an item shares with other items in the list, but the important point here is that verbal asso-ciative meaningfulness cannot account for any part of the effect of word imagery value.

To rule out other possible interpretations of the item imagery effects, another study (Paivio, 1968b) used a long list of words for which separate memory scores were available when they served as stimulus or response members in paired-associate tests. Also included were rated imagery values along with scores on more than 20 different word attributes (e.g., pleasantness, semantic potency, emotional-ity, familiarity, etc.) considered to be potential alternatives to imagery as predictors of memory scores. Correlational analyses showed that recall was related most highly to word imagery, especially when the rated words had served as stimuli (retrieval cues) for response words. Imagery even surpassed rated concreteness despite a high correlation between the two variables. Up to this point, then, the conceptual peg hypothesis was consistently and firmly supported in experiments with word pairs. Not only was the imagery value of words related to recall as predicted but it also turned out to be a stronger predictor than any other language attribute identi-fied up to that time.

Comparable effects of concreteness were subsequently obtained with natural language material extending from phrases to long passages. Sadoski, Goetz, and Fritz (1993) tested memory for two concrete and two abstract factual sentences about each of 10 historical figures. An example of a concrete sentence is as follows: "Georgia O'Keeffe perceived art everywhere—she once purchased a house because she admired the way a black double door was placed in a long, adobe wall". A matching abstract sentence is as follows: "Georgia O'Keeffe's career covers most of the history of modern art in America, and she shares the inner world of reflection with the earliest of modernists". The sentences were equated on familiarity, read-ability, number of syllables, length in words, repetition of content words, and

---

[10]The word pool (Paivio, Yuille, & Madigan, 1968) consisted of 925 nouns on which we had obtained ratings of the ease with which they evoke imagery as well as information on familiarity and meaningfulness (how easily they elicit verbal associates) so that the effects of the different variables could be systematically compared in this and other experiments. The normative pool was later extended to more than 2000 word that included adjectives, verbs, and adverbs as well as nouns, and information on age of word acquisition and other attrib-utes deemed to be relevant to performance in memory and other tasks. Now published (Clark & Paivio, 2004), the extended norms have been used in numerous experiments, some of which will be summarized later in relevant contexts.

number of idea units. Recall was cued by the name of the person in each case. The striking results were that the concrete sentences were recalled more than twice as well as the abstract sentences, both immediately and after 5 days. Similar results were obtained later (Sadoski, Goetz, & Rodriguez, 2000) using matched paragraphs about historical figures and various types of text passages varying in length from 56 to 265 words.

The evocative role of stimulus imagery specified in the conceptual peg hypothesis has also been supported using sentences and passages. For example, R. C. Anderson, Goetz, Pichert, and Halff (1977) found that concrete subject–noun phrases of sentences enhanced recall of the predicate provided that the subject was correctly recognized. The authors suggested that "a concrete phrase makes a good conceptual peg because it is likely to be given a specific, stable coding and because it tends to redintegrate the whole sentence" (p. 142). Sadoski et al. (1993) found that abstract sentences were recalled better when they were preceded by concrete rather than abstract sentences that described the same historical figures, suggesting that the concrete sentences primed concrete interpretations of the abstract ones that followed. Concrete "advance organizers" (functioning as conceptual pegs) similarly assist recall of passages as extensive as textbook chapters (Corkill, Glover, & Bruning, 1988).

We can now conclude more broadly that all predictions from the conceptual peg hypothesis have been consistently supported using language materials ranging from word pairs to long passages. The following details should be noted as well. First, the power of high imagery words as retrieval cues does not depend on their position in the presented pairs. For example, the high imagery word *clock* prompts recall of *justice* just as effectively whether the pair had been presented as *justice-clock* or *clock-justice*. Second, the stimulus imagery effect only appears when the responses consist of meaningful words or nonsense words that readily suggest meaningful words (Paivio & Madigan, 1968). This raises a critical question: How can imagery connect a concrete and an abstract word so that retrieval is easier given the concrete rather than the abstract word as a cue? The theoretical answer is that a concrete word primes a concrete interpretation of its abstract pair mate so that they can be imaged together. Later, when presented alone, the concrete word reactivates the compound image more reliably than does the abstract word. For example, *clock-justice* might be imaged as a frocked judge carrying a clock into a courtroom. The word clock then reminds the memorizer of the image of the clock together with the judge, which is likely to suggest the response word "justice." Justice by itself, however, does not have a definite referent and thus it is likely to evoke other images besides a frocked judge. This need only happen for enough items and people that the concrete-abstract order would be favored on average over the abstract-concrete order.

The interpretation has been supported by various results. One serves to make the point. Begg and Clark (1975) had homonyms with two meanings rated for imagery value when they were presented in the context of sentence fragments that emphasize the different meanings and when they were presented as individual words without contexts. Concreteness of the contexts affected imagery ratings of the words so that words high or low in out-of-context imagery could be inserted in concrete or abstract contexts. Examples are as follows: *play a RECORD* as compared to *set a RECORD* (a high imagery word in concrete and abstract contexts) and *JUSTICE of the peace* versus *love of JUSTICE* (a low imagery word in concrete and abstract contexts). The words were presented in lists with and without the contexts, followed by a recall test. The important results were that (a) high imagery words were remembered better than low imagery words in word lists (the usual result) and (b) words in concrete contexts were remembered better than words in abstract contexts (a new finding). More specifically to the point, it was easier to increase memorability of abstract words (e.g., JUSTICE) by placing them in concrete contexts than it was to reduce memorability of concrete words (e.g., RECORD) by placing them in abstract contexts.

The authors concluded that the free recall test they used "probably represents a conservative test of imagery effects, since the largest effects are observed in cued recall ... especially when the imagery values of the cues are varied" (Begg & Clark, 1975, p. 122). The cued-free recall difference is discussed shortly. The context effects are relevant here because they confirm that concrete words can activate concrete meanings of abstract associates, thereby enhancing cooperative activation of compound images that mediate recall. The results are relevant as well to criticisms of dual coding interpretations of concreteness effects (reviewed in a later section), which are based on the argument that such effects are due to contextual variables rather than imagery evoked by the words. From the Begg and Clark (1975) results, we can anticipate the conclusion that the two variables are not incompatible.

Pictures Versus Words and the Conceptual Peg Hypothesis

Recall that integrated memories in the Proust episode were triggered by concrete things, sponge cake and tea, rather than by words. Such experiences are familiar to us all. Experiments using pictures provide experimental analogues. Pictures arouse images directly and they should therefore be recalled even better than concrete nouns in memory tasks presumed to benefit from imagery. Furthermore, according to the conceptual peg hypothesis, pictures should be especially effective as retrieval cues for other pictures as well as for words. These expectations have been confirmed in numerous experiments with adults and children (summarized in Paivio, 1971b, pp. 255, 271): written verbal recall was much higher for response members of picture pairs than word pairs, and pictures were superior to words as retrieval cues when pictures and words were paired in all four combinations. For example, recall was higher for picture–word pairs than word–word pairs. These are not ho-hum observations because it is not immediately obvious why recall should be better for picture pairs than word pairs in a task in which memory is tested verbally. The one difference from the pattern obtained with concrete and abstract words is that, over different experiments, the picture superiority has been inconsistent on the response side of pairs, so that recall is sometimes higher for picture–word than picture–picture pairs, especially with children as participants (Dilley & Paivio, 1968).

The picture superiority is challenging to contemporary theories of memory and later we return to the issue and also explain the inconsistent finding.

Imagery Instructions and Associative Memory

Instructions to use imagery has been the sine qua non of imagery mnemonic techniques for over 2,500 years. It wasn't until the 1960s that experiments showed that they really "work" by comparing the rhyme mnemonic with control conditions in which recall was simply prompted by neutral cues (e.g., "one" as the cue for recalling "pencil"). Memory in these experiments was much higher for words memorized using imagery than without it (see Paivio, 1971b). In one experiment (Paivio, 1968a), the rhyme mnemonic was compared with a control condition in which the participants also learned the rhyme but were not taught the imagery component. All participants started with the control condition and half then learned the imagery part and used it to learn a second list. The other half learned the second list without imagery. In addition, some participants were taught an abstract word version of the rhyme (e.g., one-fun, two-true, three-free, etc). Figure 4.2 shows that imagery dramatically increased recall. Moreover, the increase was as large when the peg words were abstract as when they were concrete, which contrasts with large advantage for concrete stimuli in the standard paired associates task described earlier. The explanation is that imagery instructions encouraged memorizers to concretize the abstract peg words (e.g., to imagine a party as the context for "one-fun").

As in the case of concreteness effects, however, uncontrolled verbal mediation was an alternative explanation. Early in our research we tried to unravel imagery and verbal contributions by varying concreteness along with imagery and verbal mediation instructions using paired-associate learning rather than the rhyme mnemonic method. The straightforward predictions were that (a) imagery instructions would especially benefit learning of concrete pairs because they are easy to image, and (b) verbal instructions (e.g., "put the word pairs into sentences") would be more helpful with abstract words that are difficult to image. The results of the initial experiment did not support the predictions. We obtained the usual strong effects of concreteness and imagery instructions, but verbal instructions benefited recall as much as did imagery.

A possible explanation was that verbal instructions also encourage use of imagery. This was supported by strategies reported by participants immediately following recall: memorizers instructed to use verbal strategies reported that they also used imagery, especially with concrete pairs. Thus the effects could have been due to imagery or a combination of imagery and verbal mediators—in brief, uncontrolled dual coding. Imagery instructions could also prompt dual coding, but the subjective reports suggested that imagery was the preferred strategy with concrete pairs.

The "elusive interaction" was eventually obtained using improved procedures to control learning strategies (Paivio & Foth, 1970): imagery instructions produced higher recall than verbal instructions with concrete pairs whereas verbal instructions

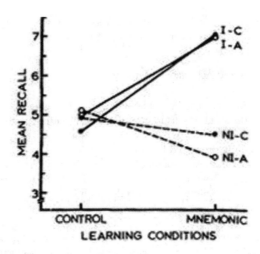

FIGURE 4.2   Mean number of items recalled in ordinal position under control
conditions and under rhyme mnemonic conditions with imagery (I) and
no-imagery (NI) instructions using concrete (C) and abstract (A) peg words.
From Figure 1 (page 78) in Paivio (1968). Effects of imagery instructions
and concreteness of memory pegs in a mnemonic system. Proceedings
of the 76th Annual Convention of the American Psychological Association,
1968. Reprinted with permission of APA, publisher.

had the advantage with abstract pairs. The interaction also showed that the concreteness effect was stronger with imagery than with verbal instructions, suggesting that
imagery instructions selectively primed the use of imagery with concrete pairs whereas
verbal instructions similarly primed the use of verbal strategies with abstract pairs.
Subsequently, Paivio and Yuille (1969) showed that learners abandoned strategies they
were instructed to use if they found them to be ineffective and accordingly switched
to more effective ones over trials (e.g., they changed from imagery to verbal strategies
with abstract pairs). The changes in learning strategies support the dual coding
assumption that nonverbal images are more available and useful with concrete than
abstract material whereas verbal mediators are available and useful with abstract as
well as concrete material. In addition, the students who served as participants were
accustomed to tests in educational settings and thus resorted to whatever strategies
work despite instructions.

   Organizational Structure of Effective Images.   The rhyme mnemonic technique
encourages memorizers to form compound images in which the cues and target
items are integrated in some way—for example, a pencil imaged inside a hot dog
bun. A contrasting arrangement would be bun and pencil visualized side by side,
but not otherwise interacting. Note that the organization in both cases is synchronic
(simultaneous), but the integrative relation is more meaningful in the interactive

image because hot dog buns usually contain fillers. The important implication is that "bun" would be especially effective as a retrieval cue for pencil when they are in an integrated relationship. The implication carries over to the conceptual peg hypothesis as well.

Consistent with the integration hypothesis, Epstein, Rock, and Zuckerman (1960) demonstrated that a pictorially presented pair, such as a hand and a bowl, was easier to learn when the items formed a meaningful unit (a hand in a bowl) than when they appeared as separate units (a hand beside a bowl). Bower (1970) extended the finding by showing that instructions to construct images in which the referents of stimulus and response words are interacting (e.g., picturing a monkey riding a bicycle) resulted in higher cued recall than when the pair members were imaged as separate entities (a monkey beside a bicycle). Begg (1973) took the further step of comparing the two instructions using both cued recall and free recall, in which items studied as pairs were recalled without presenting one member as a reminder. He defined the integration effect in terms of redintegration, that is, the extent to which cuing increases recall relative to free recall of the same word from a pair (e.g., given *hand-bowl*, recalling *bowl* using *hand* as a cue as compared to recalling *bowl* without *hand* as a reminder). He found that recall increased more from free to cued recall when pairs were studied under integrative imagery than separate imagery instructions. We shall see later that the redintegration effect turned out to be decisive in recent experiments that responded to criticisms of dual coding memory theory.

Analogous associative effects also occur when the word units are presented in verbal contexts that provided a relational rather than a nonrelational link (e.g., *hand in bowl* versus *hand and bowl*). Many experiments demonstrated benefits of such grammatical connections with children and adults (Paivio, 1971b, pp. 377–382). Again, such effects could be due directly to the grammatical variable, imagery evoked willy nilly by language, or joint contributions of imagery and verbal processes. To answer such questions, we turn to studies designed to reveal the separate and joint contributions of imagery and verbal codes using free recall tasks, in which recall is not explicitly cued.

CODE ADDITIVITY AND FREE RECALL

Early on free recall was a puzzle for DCT because the task does not explicitly involve retrieval cues or the formation of associations. It is therefore not directly interpretable in terms of the conceptual peg hypothesis. The eventual solution to the puzzle turned out to have important theoretical implications that went beyond the free recall task itself. Our research on the problem began with comparisons of pictures, concrete words, and abstract words, then moved to combined effects of pictures and words and their internal counterparts. Examples of the materials are shown in Fig. 4.3.

It had been known for some time that free verbal recall is higher for pictures than words, and for concrete than abstract words (see Paivio, 1971b, pp. 200–203). Figure 4.4 shows the effect from an experiment that included all three types of

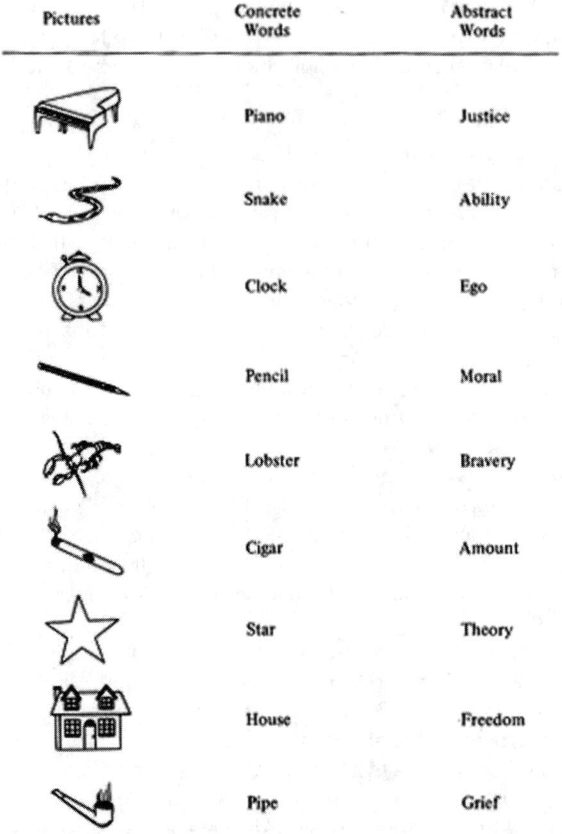

Pictures	Concrete Words	Abstract Words
	Piano	Justice
	Snake	Ability
	Clock	Ego
	Pencil	Moral
	Lobster	Bravery
	Cigar	Amount
	Star	Theory
	House	Freedom
	Pipe	Grief

FIGURE 4.3   Examples of items used in memory experiments that compared effects across pictures, concrete words, and abstract words.

materials. Participants saw long lists of the items presented one at a time briefly and then tried to recall them by writing the words and picture names. Some participants expected the recall test whereas others did not. Those who expected the test recalled more than those who did not but both showed a systematic and large increase from abstract words, to concrete words, to pictures. Prior to the late 1960s, there had been no consistent explanation for the pattern of effects.

A solution was suggested in a study that compared the effects of imagery-concreteness and other variables in free recall and cued recall (Paivio, 1967). The hypothesis was that verbal and nonverbal memory codes are independent and additive in their memory effects (Paivio, 1969). The reasoning with respect to pictures and verbal material is as follows.

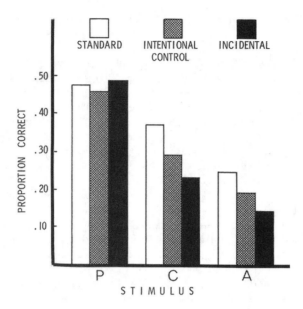

FIGURE 4.4   Free verbal recall of pictures (P), concrete words (C), and abstract words (A) presented under three experimental conditions. Reprinted from Figure 1 (p. 183) in Paivio, A., & Csapo, K. (1973). Picture superiority in free recall: Imagery or dual coding? *Cognitive Psychology, 5*, 176–206. Copyright 1973, with permission from Elsevier.

Memory tasks that require verbal recall induce dual coding of pictures at some stage of the task. Concrete words might be dually coded as well because they can arouse images, but imaging is not essential for their recall. Abstract words are unlikely to evoke nonverbal images, so they will be stored primarily as words. The probability of dual coding would be increased if memorizers also are asked to name pictures or form images to words during study. Dual coding would be expected to augment recall because memorizers could retrieve the name from either the verbal code or the image code if one is forgotten (for example, we can say or write "horse" whether we remember the item as a word or as an image of the animal). The additive effect would be proportional to the probability that such dual coding will actually occur. The benefit would apply to any memory task but it should be clearest in free recall.

The distinction between external and internal memory sources is crucial to the analysis. Pictures and words generate perceptual memory traces directly. Mental images to words and names to pictures are generated indirectly by referential activation of internal imagens and logogens. It is assumed that, whatever their source, the verbal and nonverbal traces are stored independently so that either one or the other, or both, could be remembered, or forgotten. Other assumptions regarding the nature of the memory trace are involved as well but we need not deal with those here (the details can be found in Paivio, 1975a).

This code-additivity hypothesis would explain the overall recall pattern in Fig. 4.4. The pattern shows a further trend that also is consistent with the theory. Participants informed of the memory test would be more likely than those uninformed to use strategies intended to maximize recall. This would especially benefit concrete words because they readily suggest images. Picture recall would be least affected because pictures are likely to be named even when naming is not required during presentation. Figure 4.4 shows a hint of the expected pattern in that readiness to recall benefited concrete words somewhat more than abstract words, and pictures were unaffected by instructions.

Varying the rate of presentation should similarly affect the probability of bimodal coding, and hence, recall. Paivio and Csapo (1969) found that the concreteness effects occurred when items were presented at a slow enough rate that pictures could be silently named and concrete words imaged. The differences vanished when the rate was so fast that participants did not have enough time to name the pictures or image to the words but could still recognize them.

We tested the additivity hypothesis more directly using lists of pictures and words along with procedures designed to ensure single or dual coding (Paivio & Csapo, 1973; Paivio, 1975a). In one experiment, dual coding was perceptually induced for some items by successively presenting a picture and then its printed name (or vice versa), whereas other pictures and words were presented only once. Subsequent recall was expected to be higher for the repeated items by an additive amount relative to recall of the unrepeated pictures and words. We also controlled for benefits of repetition per se by repeating some pictures and some words. Previous research had shown that successive ("massed") repetitions of the same items increased recall by an amount that was less than additive. The reason for this is a matter of theoretical debate, but for our purposes, the result provides a baseline against which to compare dual coding effects. The important result (see Fig. 4.5) was that pictures and words contributed independently and additively to recall. Picture–picture and word–word repetitions also increased recall but only by an amount that was less than additive, as expected from the earlier studies of the effects of successive repetitions of the same item.[11]

Additivity of mental images and words was tested in another experiment by "tagging" these codes onto repeated words. Participants were prompted by the words "image" and "pronounce" either to image to one presentation of a word or to pronounce the word, then reverse the coding on the next presentation, rating the ease of imaging or pronouncing during the interitem interval. The important result (also shown in Fig. 4.5) was that such mental dual coding increased subsequent recall by

---

[11]The recall probability expected for mnemonically independent pictures plus words is computed as follows from the recall probabilities of once-presented items: probability of picture recall plus the probability of word recall minus the product of the two probabilities.

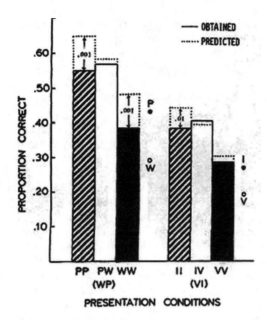

FIGURE 4.5   Correct recall proportions for pictures (P) and words (W) presented once or repeated in the same code (PP, WW) or in a different code (PW, WP) and once-presented or repeated words that were imaged (I) or pronounced (V) on each occasion. The dotted bars indicate that dual-coding (PW/ WP and VI/ IV) augmented recall additively whereas same-code repetitions (PP, WW, II—and VV marginally) increased recall less than additively relative to once presented/coded items. Adapted from Figure 1 (p. 191) in Paivio (1975), Coding distinctions and repetition effects in memory. In G. H. Bower (ed.), *The psychology of learning and motivation, Vol. 9*, New York: Academic Press, pp. 179–214. Copyright 1975, with permission from Elsevier.

an additive amount relative to recall levels for once-presented words that were imaged or pronounced. The benefits of repeated identical coding (that is, pronouncing or imaging to repeated words on each occasion) were less than additive. Other controls showed that the dual coding effect was not due simply to using the different words "image" and "pronounce" as coding cues; what mattered instead was the imagery and verbal coding induced by the different cues.

Image Superiority

A further important aspect of the results was that pictures and images contributed about twice as much as their verbal counterparts to the additive effects, as if an image is worth two verbal codes in memory strength. This is an empirical contribution to dual coding memory theory because such values were unknown prior to the experiments, and no existing memory theory provided a principled basis for predicting a difference. Thus image superiority can be viewed as an addendum to the additivity hypothesis.[12]

UNIFYING DUAL CODING MEMORY THEORY

Ian Begg (1972) provided the basis for unifying the conceptual peg, image integration, and code additivity aspects of dual coding memory theory. Begg reasoned that a concrete phrase such as *white horse* can be remembered as a single integrated image (a white horse), whereas an abstract phrases such as *basic truth* does not activate an image and therefore must be remembered as two words. If so, in free recall, twice as many words should be remembered from concrete phrases as from abstract phrases. In cued recall, moreover, prompting memory by presenting one word from the phrase as a retrieval cue should further augment memory for the other word when the phrase is concrete because the cue (e.g., white) reliably redintegrates the whole image (a white horse). Cuing should be less helpful with abstract phrases because they lack the integrative mechanism provided by imagery.

Several tests and scoring procedures confirmed the expected advantages of concrete over abstract words and phrases in free and cued recall. Figure 4.6 shows the results when participants free recalled (a) word lists, (b) only the nouns or adjectives from the phrases, and (c) whole phrases. Also shown are the results when recall is cued by one word from each phrase. Note that free recall was at least twice as high for concrete than for abstract words and phrases. Furthermore, performance increased sixfold from free to cued recall for concrete phrases but not at all for abstract phrases, confirming the redintegrative effect when a cue presumably accesses an integrated image. Begg's (1972) results thus demonstrated the additive effects of dual coding as well as the retrieval power of concrete cues implied by the conceptual peg hypothesis.

But there's more. It can be seen from Fig. 4.6 that free recall of concrete material (phrases or words from phrases) was more than twice that of abstract material. In phrase recall, for example, the respective proportions were .44 versus .14, a threefold advantage for concrete phrases. This result clearly suggests that imagery

---

[12]Note that image superiority is not a gratuitous ad hoc addition. There are parallel cases in other sciences. In physics, for example, the electrical charge of electrons had to be determined experimentally, following which it was incorporated into theory. In the present case, the additivity hypothesis necessarily implies that verbal and nonverbal codes have some independent mnemonic values but provided no a priori basis for suggesting what those values are. The experiments yielded tentative mnemonic values. New research could suggest other explanations for picture and image superiority, but so far none have "saved the phenomena" better than the dual coding additivity hypothesis with its differential code-strength addendum.

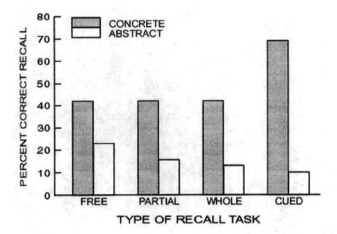

FIGURE 4.6 Percentage of items recalled from lists of concrete or abstract words and phrases under different recall conditions. Adapted from Tables 2, 3, 5, & 6 in Begg (1972). Recall of meaningful phrases. *Journal of Verbal Learning and Verbal Behavior, 11*, 431–439. Copyright 1972, with permission from Elsevier

contributed more than the verbal code to their additive effect, twice as much in the phrase case. Begg's (1972) results are therefore consistent with the image superiority addendum to the additivity hypothesis of dual coding memory theory. He did not test the hypothesis directly because his study was completed well before the code independence-additivity hypothesis had been directly tested and supported in the experiments described earlier. The contribution of imagery cannot be similarly estimated quantitatively from Begg's data, but it is difficult to think of an alternative hypothesis that would account so well for the free recall results. We shall see later, too, that there is no alternative unified theory that can adequately explain the total pattern of free and cued recall.

DUAL CODING AND RECOGNITION MEMORY

Of all the memory tasks, recognition memory may be ecologically the most fundamental, because, to survive, animals must learn to recognize friends from enemies, edible foods from the inedible, and safe places from dangerous ones. It is the simplest memory task because items are presented for study and memory is tested by presenting them again after some delay along with new items. Participants simply indicate whether each test item is old or new (previously encountered in the experimental session or not). A real-life example is the police suspect-lineup that includes foils who look more or less like the suspect in modes of dress and general appearance. The witness might correctly identify the suspect (a "hit"), incorrectly identify a foil in the lineup (a false positive), be uncertain, or reject all of the people.[13] The task differs from perceptual recognition in which participants are tested for the speed and accuracy with which they can identify items, often ones presented under impoverished conditions (e.g., pictures or words that are flashed briefly or disfigured, as described in Chapter 3). Unless the target items are completely novel, however, both tasks depend on the availability and activation of long-term memory representations (imagens or logogens), but recognition memory depends as well on episodic memory traces resulting from the first presentation; detection, as it were, of a change in the mnemonic "strength" of the underlying representations, or the genesis of new copies of them.[14]

Memory and perceptual recognition are similar and dissimilar in other ways as well. Both are ecologically relevant in current and evolutionary contexts. Very early in life and thereafter, we need to recognize significant objects and situations—a mother's face, interesting or dangerous objects, and so on. Our ancestors and other animals similarly had to recognize food, friends, predators, and shelters. The target objects must be distinguished from other similar stimuli. The criteria for discrimination can vary widely. Sometimes it is useful to generalize—for example, to flee from anything that might be a predator—and at other times to discriminate closely: mother's face from others, safe mushrooms from poisonous ones, and so on. In psychological experiments, broad-band discrimination is all that is required when participants are asked to decide whether a picture or word represents a living or nonliving thing, or, when flashed briefly, whether it was a picture or word. Finer discrimination is required when the pictures or words must be specifically identified as a dog, chair, car, and so forth.

The preceding examples all have to do with effects of contextual stimuli on performance. The effects can be positive or negative in both perceptual and memory recognition. Perceptual identification can be primed by temporal context so that a word or picture is recognized more quickly and accurately if it was preceded by another stimulus that is similar or related to it physically, semantically, or associatively. Memory recognition can be similarly primed by a preceding stimulus related in some way to the correct stimulus in a set of alternatives. Negative contextual effects are illustrated by the difficulty of deciding between similar alternatives and

---

[13]The identification decision has enormous consequences in real life. For example, it has been estimated that approximately 4,500 innocent people are convicted each year in the United States because of mistaken eyewitness identification (evidence and corrective measures based on psychological research were reviewed by Yarmey, 2003). The consequences in this example concern the memory target (the accused person) but in most cases it is the memorizer whose welfare depends on his or her decision. So too for other creatures, past and present, as we shall see in Chapter 11.

[14]There has long been a scientific debate concerning trace strength and multiple-trace theories of the increase in memory performance that results from item repetitions. Strength theory states that a single memory trace somehow increases in its capacity to facilitate retrieval of an item, whereas multiple-trace theory states that a new trace is formed each time an item is repeated, thereby increasing the probability of retrieving the item. The issue is not fully resolved. It is logically possible, of course, that both views are correct.

by prior information given, say, in leading (or misleading) questions asked of a witness.

Performance in perceptual and memory tasks are affected differently by the kinds of variables that particularly concern us here. A word's familiarity benefits perceptual identification of briefly flashed words but word concreteness has no effect (e.g., Paivio & O'Neill, 1970). Conversely, concreteness benefits memory recognition but word familiarity sometimes has a negative effect, so that familiar words are recognized less accurately than less familiar ones. This may be because the recognition decision is based on familiarity within the time span of the test situation—that is, the increment in an item's familiarity from study to test, which is larger and more noticeable for unfamiliar items than for familiar ones (this pychophysical analysis was discussed in detail with supporting evidence in Paivio, 1971b, pp. 194–196). Be that as it may, familiarity alone cannot account for powerful effects of dual coding variables on recognition memory.

Experiments have shown that recognition memory is better for pictures than for their concrete noun labels. Especially interesting is the extraordinary level of memory for pictures when long lists are used. For example, an experiment by Roger Shepard (1967) showed that 98.5% of the items from a list of 600 pictures were subsequently recognized correctly. Other experimenters yielded comparably high recognition memory for as many as 10,000 pictures (Standing, 1973). Recognition also is higher for concrete than abstract words, and we have shown experimentally that there is a systematic increase over all three materials, from abstract words, to concrete words, to pictures (e.g., Paivio & Csapo, 1969).

As in recall, the concreteness effects can be explained in terms of a combination of image superiority and dual coding, with the contribution of image superiority perhaps being relatively greater in recognition. The first suggestion of image superiority came from the experiment in which short lists of pictures or words were presented at fast or slow rates (Paivio & Csapo, 1969). Correct recognition responses were higher for pictures than words at the slower rate but not at the faster rate, which prevented picture naming. Even at the fast rate, however, false alarms were lower for pictures than words (i. e., new pictures were correctly recognized as "new") despite the absence of dual coding. The latter advantage of pictures could mean that they are more distinctive as perceptual patterns, or otherwise activate more effective short-term memory traces than words (e.g., Ternes & Yuille, 1972). In addition, however, pictures set up more effective long-term memory traces, as evidenced by the finding that input pictures are recognized much better than words on test trials regardless of whether the test items are pictures or words, as if the test words were translated into pictorial images (Paivio, 1976b, p. 118). The advantage of concrete over abstract words can also be interpreted partly in terms of superiority of the nonverbal image evoked by words over the verbal code. This interpretation is consistent with a suggestion by Standing and Smith (1975) that both pictures and verbal stimuli are encoded in a pictorial or functionally equivalent form in recognition memory tasks; that is, pictures are stored and remembered as images whereas words are transformed into images, which mediate recognition performance. In addition, Standing and Smith found evidence that dual coding contributed to the picture advantage.

My take on the effects was that the items first arouse a memory representation of the items themselves. Then, if a decision is not possible on the basis of that representation, one relies on further verbal or imaginal coding (Paivio, 1976b, p. 128). Part of the picture advantage is due to the initial form-matching process, whereas dual coding contributes relatively more to the advantage of concrete over abstract words. This analysis is generally consistent with more recent dual-process theories which state that recognition memory is based first of all on an assessment of an item's familiarity, and, if that doesn't work, the memorizer tries to remember associated information, such as where the item was previously seen or heard (for a review, see McElree, Dolan, & Jacoby, 1999). In DCT, the associated information stems from dual coding processes.

The recognition memory experiments just described used pictures of diverse categories of common objects that can be easily named and discriminated from each other. The same pattern of results would not be expected with less discriminable stimuli, as in the following experiment in which participants searched through an array of pictures or words to find an item that had been presented as a picture or as a word (Paivio & Begg, 1974). In one condition, the pictures were line drawings of various familiar objects and the words were their printed labels. In another condition, the stimuli were photographs of famous people (movie actors, politicians, sports figures) and their corresponding names. We expected faster search times with picture arrays than word arrays with objects but not with faces as stimuli because faces, like words, share common features that require detailed "reading" to identify a particular item. This would be especially difficult when the target is presented as a name because the generated face image would also have to be detailed. As expected, search times were faster when the array items were object pictures rather than words, and this was so even when the targets were words. However, the pattern differed for faces so that search times were generally slower with face arrays than name arrays, and slowest when the targets were presented as names.

Picture–word memory effects also depend on relevant cognitive abilities. For example, participants in one study (summarized in Paivio, 1971b, pp. 507–508) were categorized as high imagers or low imagers according to scores on spatial ability tests, and compared on recognition memory for pictures and words. High imagers surpassed low imagers with pictures whereas low imagers excelled with words as items. Moreover, recognition errors differed so that the high imagers were more likely to identify a test word as having been presented as a picture, whereas low imagers more often erred by identifying a picture as having been presented as a word.

Errors due to inappropriate verbal coding have been starkly revealed by experiments on recognition of mock criminals by eyewitnesses. Schooler and Engstler–Schooler (1990) showed participants a video of a bank robbery. During a retention interval, half the group were asked to write detailed descriptions of the robber's face whereas the other half completed an unrelated task. The participants then tried to identify the robber's face from an array of eight photographs, one of which was the "criminal." Only about one third of those who wrote descriptions correctly identified the robber's face, as compared to two thirds of those who didn't write descriptions.

The researchers referred to this effect as "verbal overshadowing of visual memories" (p. 36). This was initially interpreted to mean that describing altered the visual memory image of the face, but subsequent studies (reviewed by Bruce Bower, 2003) suggested other explanations, including reliance on word-based operations, poor verbal skills, and verbal blocking of access to perceptual memories that remain intact. Remedies that counteract verbal overshadowing include increasing the delay between description and face identification and encouraging "bare-bones" descriptions rather than detailed ones.

The verbal overshadowing effects can be explained in DCT terms as entailing different patterns of the interplay between verbal and imagery processes. The description itself becomes part of a new memory trace, and is also likely to generate a face image in a piecemeal fashion, one that is "fuzzier" and less holistic than a referent image generated to a familiar name. Skeletal descriptions might generate simpler, less cluttered images. In any case, the verbally generated image could initially compete with the perceptually generated (viewed) face image and then decay more quickly than the latter, much as dreams fade from memory more quickly than perceptions of real events. The descriptions themselves, being imprecise to begin with, might not help distinguish the "criminal" from other faces in the lineup. Individual differences in verbal and imagery skills could qualify the effects in ways already described (further evidence that imagery can mediate false memories is reviewed later). Such DCT interpretations accommodate the alternatives proposed in the current literature on the overshadowing effect. Finally, we should note that, although certain procedures can counteract the negative impact of describing, verbal descriptions have generally not been helpful in remembering faces. This is unlike the usual additive benefit of naming on picture memory.

DUAL CODING AND SEQUENTIAL MEMORY

From the DCTperspective, imagery-related variables were not expected to have the same positive effects in sequential memory tasks as they have in item and associative memory. This follows from the organizational assumptions of DCT: The nonverbal visual imagery system is specialized for synchronous organization of item information rather than sequential organization, which characterizes the verbal system. This implies that the typical positive effects of concreteness and imagery would not occur in "pure" sequential memory tasks. The earliest confirmation was that concrete words were not superior to abstract words in memory span (Brener, 1940), which requires immediate memory for the sequence in which words are presented. Predictions were further supported by the experiments (Paivio & Csapo, 1969) in which pictures, concrete words, and abstract words were presented at a fast rate that did not allow enough time for silent naming of the pictures or imaging to concrete words. The usual picture-concrete word-abstract word ranking in item memory tasks disappeared and tended to be reversed when participants had to recall the items sequentially.

Paivio, Philipchalk, and Rowe (1975) also found that nameable environmental sounds (e.g., whistle, bell) were inferior to their auditorily presented names in serial learning but the sounds were superior to names in free recall, where order did not have to be remembered. We took this to mean that environmental sounds are discrete units that do not share the "auditory streaming" and motor sequencing potential of speech sounds.

There has been some controversy about the dual coding generalization. For example, it was pointed out that the original method of loci, the rhyme mnemonic technique, and other similar imagery techniques are effective for remembering items in their order. However, this is really not an exception to the dual coding generalization because, in all of those techniques, sequential order is encoded in memory by numbered verbal cues (for example, one-bun, two-shoe, and so on) rather than by the images of the things and their locations. Sequential order can also be reconstructed in other imagery techniques, such as generating overlapping pair images from list items, or locating object images at landmarks (houses, etc.) along a familiar route. Some problematic findings remain but the bulk of the evidence is consistent with the hypothesis that the verbal system is superior to the nonverbal memory system in sequential memory for discrete items (Paivio, 1986, pp. 171–175).

SENSORIMOTOR MODALITIES OF MEMORY

Thus far we have discussed imaginal and verbal memories without reference to the fact that both symbolic codes come in visual, auditory, and haptic modalities, and there are nonverbal memories as well for the tastes, smells, and emotions associated with objects. What implications do these specific modalities have for memory performance and the nature of the memory trace? In our early research on the problem, we predicted and found that congenitally blind individuals showed better memory for words of high auditory imagery value (e.g., thunder) than words high in visual imagery (e.g., rainbow) whereas sight individuals showed the reverse pattern (Paivio & Okovita, 1971). Similarly, the signability of words selectively benefits associative learning of the deaf (Conlin & Paivio, 1975). I suggested further (Paivio, 1972) that sensory modalities and symbolic modalities are functionally independent in episodic memory in the manner already described earlier for verbal and nonverbal memories, which implies that different sensory modalities might indeed have additive effects on recall. This has been confirmed (Thompson & Paivio, 1994) by the finding that hearing the sounds and seeing pictures of audiovisual objects (telephone, whistle, etc.) had an additive effect on recall as compared to only seeing or only hearing the stimuli. Repeated sounds or pictures had less than an additive effect. Figure 4.7 shows the results from one of two confirmatory experiments. The recall patterns exactly parallel those described earlier in regard to the memory independence of pictures and visually presented words.

Similar additive effects have been obtained for other modalities. For example, Lyman and McDaniel (1990) found that recognition memory and free verbal recall of odors increased when pictures were presented along with the odors during study; performance increased even further when both names and pictures were presented with the odors. Frick (1984) increased memory span for digits by presenting half the digits auditorily and half visually, suggesting that the two modalities

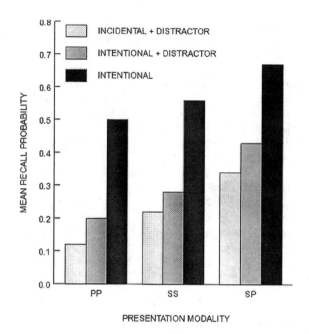

FIGURE 4.7 Data showing higher verbal recall under different recall conditions for environmental sounds followed by pictures (SP) than for items repeated in the same modality (SS or PP). Adapted from Table 1 (p. 386) in Thompson, V. A. & Paivio, A.(1994). Memory for pictures and sounds: Independence of auditory and visual codes. *Canadian Journal of Experimental Psychology, 48*, 380–396. Copyright 1994 Canadian Psychological Association. Reprinted with permission.

contributed independently to memory. Harman, Humphrey, and Goodale (1999) found that active rotation of novel three-dimensional objects resulted in better recognition memory for the objects than passive viewing of the same rotations, suggesting that haptic and visual modalities are mnemonically additive to a significant degree. Viewing and active production similarly have additive effects on memory for movement patterns (see Paivio, 1986, pp. 161–163).

The additivity hypothesis has also been tested for dual-modality imagery by independently varying word attributes (visual and auditory imagery values, imagery and emotional values) and instructions to image in different modalities. The results have been less reliable than in the above perceptual-modality experiments (see Thompson & Paivio, 1994), perhaps because of confounding influences of procedural variables. One is that visual presentation of words might interfere more with visual imagery than with auditory imagery. When exposure time was reduced so that there was less time for visual interference, the expected additive effect occurred in that words high in both visual and auditory imagery were recalled better than words high in only one modality. However, visual and auditory imagery instructions still did not produce additive effects relative to either one alone. A confound here was suggested by the fact that visual images were more likely to be reported by participants instructed to use auditory imagery than vice versa. Thus, uncontrolled dual-coding effects might have occurred in the supposedly single-modality auditory imagery condition. Such explanations for the will-o'-the-wisp independence effect for imagery modalities remain to be further explored, but the general case for functional independence across both symbolic and sensorimotor modalities is buttressed by neuropsychological evidence reviewed in Chapter 7.

CRITIQUES AND REJOINDERS

Criticisms of the dual coding theory of episodic memory have focussed on alternative item attributes that might account for concreteness effects, inconsistent findings, and general theoretical alternatives to dual coding. Many confounding correlates were ruled out by evidence already reviewed, but new ones could be proposed and would need to be similarly evaluated. This section reviews other empirical issues and theoretical alternatives.

Picture–Word Anomalies

Pictures are not always remembered better than words. Some of the exceptions (e.g., the disappearance of the picture advantage at fast presentation rates) were predicted from dual coding principles and others can be explained by the theory. We saw that pictures were not always advantageous as response items in paired associate recall, especially with children (Dilley & Paivio, 1968). In free recall as well, Ducharme and Fraisse (1965) found the usual picture superiority effect with adults whereas children recalled words better than pictures. We suggested that this might be due to labeling difficulties experienced by children. Some direct support comes from an experiment by Cole, Frankel, and Sharp (1971), who found that children in Grades 1 through 8 consistently recalled objects or pictures better than words. The critical difference from the Ducharme and Fraisse study is that Cole et al. explicitly asked the children to name the objects, pictures, or words as they were presented. This means that the objects and pictures were dually encoded whereas the words were repeated in the same code. The dual coding effect was at least additive on the first of five trials in that pictures and objects were recalled more than twice as well as words. This difference diminished over trials but remained substantial throughout. Dual coding theory thus accounts adequately for picture–word reversals in recall. We also see later (Chapter 19) that the theory similarly explains the disappearance of the picture superiority effect when people age.

Next we review a number of general memory theories that have been proposed as explanations of the effects of dual coding variables. All are variants of the idea that some kind of abstract code or process is normally more available to concrete than abstract material, under imagery than other conditions, and so on, and that when this difference is controlled, concreteness-imagery effects of all kinds will vanish.

Processing Depth

In regard to the debate between common and dual coding theorists, John Anderson (1978) suggested that theoretical reliance on picture–word differences was fading because pictures are not necessarily remembered better if words are "deeply encoded." He was alluding to an influential processing-depth theory of memory proposed by Craik and Lockhart (1972). Relevant evidence emerged from an experiment by D'Agostino, O'Neill, and Paivio (1977), which contrasted predictions from a version of processing-depth theory (Craik & Tulving, 1975) and dual coding. The relevant contrast entailed verbal recall of pictures following "shallow" coding (requiring rhyme judgments of the picture names) and "deep" coding (would the name fit into a sentence frame?). Depth theory predicts superior recall under the sentence than the picture condition whereas dual coding does not because both conditions induce dual coding. The results showed equivalent recall under the two conditions, consistent with dual coding and not depth theory. The experiment also failed to support processing depth as an explanation of better memory for concrete than abstract words. A later section on bilingualism (under language functions) describes a bilingual memory experiment that yielded additive effects of bilingual (verbal) dual coding as well as verbal-imaginal dual coding that are consistent with DCT but not processing depth.

Schematic Knowledge Structures

Day and Bellezza (1983) found that concrete unrelated noun pairs were rated lower in imagery than related abstract pairs but the former were nonetheless remembered better than the latter in cued recall. Day and Bellezza concluded that the results contradicted DCT and other imagery theories. Their explanation was in terms of "organized generic knowledge structures" (schemata) based on relations among objects in the physical world rather than their mode of representation in memory" (Day & Bellezza, 1983, pp. 256–257). Paivio, Clark, and Khan (1988) used the same procedure, with one modification, to show that DCT could explain the results. Different groups rated noun pairs on relatedness and compound imagery. In an unexpected cued recall test, the superior recall for concrete unrelated pairs occurred under the imagery but not the relatedness instructions. The Day and Bellezza results thus depended on the mode of representation and not simply generic knowledge about the relations between objects. Further results in our experiment specifically supported predictions from the conceptual peg hypothesis.

Context Availability

This hypothesis states that concrete materials have an advantage in memory and other tasks because contextual information is usually more available for concrete than abstract material (see references in Paivio, Walsh, & Bons, 1994, Sadoski & Paivio, 2001). The hypothesis has failed critical tests. Verbal associative overlap (the number of implicit associations shared by pairs in a list), clearly a kind of contextual variable, was considered and rejected 40 years ago as an explanation of concreteness effects in paired associate learning (Paivio, 1965a). However, proponents of context availability have usually tested the hypothesis using sentences and longer contexts. Sadoski, Goetz, and Avila (1995) supported predictions from dual coding but not context availability theory using carefully constructed concrete and abstract paragraphs. Another argument was that the concreteness effect is specific to mixed lists that include both concrete and abstract material. However, strong concreteness effects were demonstrated using unmixed word lists as long ago as the 1960s across all levels of concreteness (Paivio, 1971b). Going beyond the word level, Sadoski et al. (2000) found much higher recall for concrete than abstract passages presented to different participants.

It was eventually conceded even by erstwhile proponents that context availability is insufficient as an explanation of concreteness effects (Schwanenflugel, Akin, & Luh, 1992). That does not mean, however, that context is irrelevant. Recall, for example, that Begg and Clark (1975) showed that the imagery values of homonyms varied with the concreteness of sentence contexts in which they were presented; moreover, recall of words presented in isolation was a function of their out-of-context imagery levels, whereas recall of words presented in context was a function of contextual imagery. Context can thus influence recall by activating high or low imagery meanings of polysemous words. How this might happen is discussed later under communication functions of dual coding systems. The next section shows that context can also influence recall via verbal associations.

Relational-Distinctiveness Processing Theory

Marschark and Hunt (1989) sought to account for concreteness and imagery effects by a theory which states that, to be remembered, items must be distinguishable and related to each other in such a way that one item can serve effectively as a retrieval cue for another. Imagery evoked by concrete words can make them distinctive and also serve a relational function, but so can other processes unrelated to imagery. The important prediction from the theory is that concreteness effects depend on relational processing of items when they are studied and recalled. In support of the prediction, Marschark and Hunt found that concreteness effects were absent or diminished under conditions in which relational processing was either discouraged or encouraged equally strongly for concrete and abstract words.

My colleagues and I reasoned from previous research and theory that concreteness and relatedness are independent and additive; that is, sets of words can be concrete or abstract and the words within sets can be related or unrelated, and concreteness and relatedness each benefit memory. The experiments used noun–noun pairs (Paivio, et al., 1994) and adjective–noun pairs as well as sentences (Paivio, Khan, & Begg, 2000) that varied in concretenesss and in which the pair members were strongly related or unrelated according to ratings. Following presentation, participants were either asked to free recall the pairs or were presented the first words in each pair as a retrieval cue. We scored recall of response words in the free recall test so that it could be compared with cued recall of responses. Consistent with dual coding predictions, concreteness and pair relatedness had independent and additive effects so that recall was highest for concrete related pairs and progressively lower for concrete unrelated, abstract related, and abstract unrelated pairs. This pattern occurred with both free and cued recall, although, as usual, recall benefited greatly from cuing, suggesting that pairs were integrated (bound together) in memory.

We also measured integration by the degree to which pair members were recalled together, as if they functioned as integrated units. The novel result was that integration scores increased additively with relatedness and concreteness. Importantly, integration was relatively high even for unrelated concrete pairs but low for unrelated abstract pairs. We concluded, therefore, that imagery is sufficient for integrative recall of concrete pairs whereas strong intraverbal relations are necessary for integrative recall of abstract pairs. This resolved what had earlier seemed to be a puzzling finding, namely equivalent integrative recall of abstract and concrete sentences despite higher word recall for the latter (Marschark & Paivio, 1977). The resolution is in terms of the integrative potential of associative connections within the verbal system (a kind of contextual variable alluded to earlier), and thus consistent with the general principles of dual coding theory. The special integrative potential attributed to the imagery system remains intact in that it accounts for significant integration even in the case of unrelated concrete words.

British psychologist John Richardson (2003) independently tested the theoretical alternatives using an experimental design similar to that of Paivio et al. (2000). He varied relatedness by presenting concrete and abstract words in meaningful sentences or in anomalous ones that inhibited relational processing. He found independent effects of concreteness and meaningfulness with "no sign of any interaction either in their effects on recall performance or in their effects on the advantage of cued recall over free recall. These results are consistent with the dual-coding theory of imagery and verbal processes but are not consistent with either of two versions of relational-distinctiveness processing theory" (p. 481). The concreteness effects were especially strong, almost a twofold advantage for concrete words in cued recall and a threefold advantage in free recall. Richardson concluded that, "when taken together, the available research suggests that, after more than 30 years, the dual-coding theory continues to provide a highly successful framework for understanding the effects of concreteness in a wide range of verbal-learning tasks" (p. 504).

It is relevant to note again that it has always been assumed in DCT that concreteness and dual coding processes contribute to item distinctiveness as well as to interitem associations. The distinctive function is paramount when targets must be discriminated from other items in a list, as in recognition memory (discussed earlier). The associative function entails memory benefits arising from links established between items, as in paired-associate learning. Begg (1982) showed that conditions that encourage the formation of "tight" (integrative) associations between items actually increase the difficulty of discriminating correct target items from incorrect ones. Other studies have shown that imagery and dual coding can serve either to associate or differentiate the same items with different effects, depending on the task (e.g., Paivio & Rowe, 1971).

THE DUAL CODING EPISODIC MEMORY TRACE SUMMARIZED

The available evidence justifies the conclusion that the dual coding memory trace consists of a conglomerate of modality-specific verbal and nonverbal information. The information can be activated directly by perceived events (e.g., pictures, environmental sounds, printed words, auditory words, tastes, smells) or indirectly by imagery instructions or properties of words that focus on specific modalities (e.g., their visual or auditory imagery value). The term "conglomerate," like the rock by that name, implies that the components are cemented together so that they can function in an integrated manner, but they can also be separated out of the whole and function independently. This theory shares assumptions with many other multicomponent or multi-attribute theories of the memory trace (Paivio, 1986, p. 141), but differs from all of them in its strong emphasis on the modality specificity of the trace elements and the special importance of the verbal–nonverbal distinction. A review by Estes (2002) shows, for example, that most computational models of recognition memory assume that studied items are stored in memory as arrays of abstract features. Test items also are coded as features patterns that are compared against the stored traces, with the recognition decision depending on the similarity of the match. Estes's own array model differs in that its features "are not treated as abstract entities, but are set into correspondence with perceptual and other properties of the stimuli used as items" (p. 19). This implies that the trace features differ for verbal and nonverbal stimuli, but, without explicit adoption of that assumption along with processing assumptions similar to those of DCT, no memory model can predict such phenomena as the additive effects of different sensorimotor and verbal–nonverbal components.

The modality specificity of the DCT memory trace also distinguishes the theory from the schema approach (Day & Bellezza, 1983, proposed a specific version of it in the study described earlier), which states that memories become less detailed and more abstract and schematic over time. The dual coding view is consistent with Alba and Hasher's (1983) conclusion that the memory representation is far richer and more detailed than would be expected on the basis of schema theory. The most relevant evidence is that memory is far above chance for sensory details (for a recent example, see Magnussen, Greenlee, Aslaksen, & Kildeko, 2003) and that a stimulus complex is stored as separate integrated units rather than as a schematic representation in which the details are lost. In other cases memory affects are better explained by interitem, association than by abstract schemata (Khan & Paivio, 1988).

CONTEMPORARY AND EVOLUTIONARY SIGNIFICANCE
OF DUAL CODING MEMORY EFFECTS

The dual coding effects in cued recall, free recall, and recognition memory have important implications for memory theories and cognitive evolution. The striking picture advantage in all three tasks challenges any theory that emphasizes the dominance of language as a memory code because, from that perspective, recognition and verbal recall should be at least as easy for printed words as for pictures. It can be argued as earlier that pictures have an advantage in recognition because they are perceptually more distinct than words, but that argument does not hold for verbal recall in which input words are silently read and pictures named, either of which, if remembered, can be decoded into the required verbal output. Because decoding is more direct in the case of words, they should be easier to recall than pictures. Linguistic dominance theories also have difficulty explaining why concrete words are recognized and recalled so much better than equally familiar abstract words. The results are puzzling as well when viewed from the perspective of linguistic-dominance views of cognitive evolution: why has evolution left us with such an impoverished memory capacity for abstract language, the purest of linguistic material? DCT provides a consistent explanation of the memory differences, more so than other current alternatives. No one has yet applied Tulving's (2005) autoenoetic-memory theory to dual coding effects, but we already know that it could not account for the effects over tasks and codes because awareness of memory materials and context were either controlled by presentation conditions or it varied unsystematically across subjects and conditions. Whether DCT has anything to say about the absence of self-aware memory in some cases of amnesia (Chapter 8) remains to be seen.

ANTICIPATORY FUNCTIONS OF DUAL CODING SYSTEMS

The capacity to anticipate events is crucial to the well-being and survival of all creatures because it enables them to gear up for appropriate action before an event occurs. Anticipation is based either on long-term memory knowledge of where and when significant events are likely to occur, or episodic memories of recent occurrences. In either case, associations must be formed between the events and the situations in which they occur to learn to respond appropriately in advance. The connection between anticipation and association is implicit in the concept of successive association, where a given event activates an image of what has often followed it or an appropriate response to it. Such anticipatory associations are explicitly studied in paired associate and serial learning tasks using the anticipation method (the appropriate anticipatory response must be produced to a stimulus before the response item appears). Anticipation and expectancy (hereafter I use these words as synonyms) are implicated as well in animal conditioning and learning. Expectancy in particular was a key concept in Tolman's (1948) cognitive theory of learning and behavior. The connection to Tolman's theory is reviewed in detail in Chapter 11. Here I briefly review the roles of imagery and language as anticipatory mechanisms in the general cognitive sense.

David Marks (1999) particularly emphasized the anticipatory function of conscious imagery, arguing that its mnemonic functions are ancillary to its primary function in the selection, rehearsal, and planning of goal directed activity by mentally exploring "possible cycles of action and their consequences before making them physically"

(p. 579). Although agreeing fully with the importance of anticipation, I stress the primacy of the mnemonic function: there can be no planning or anticipating of consequences without memory for what happened before in similar situations. It is notable, too, that Tulving (2005) similarly emphasized the direct connection between memory for past events and anticipation of future ones as a defining feature of autonoetic consciousness. He did not, however, stress the role of imagery in anticipation except for passing references to "imagining" personal happenings in the subjectively felt future. The necessity of memory is apparent in the following examples.

Anticipation has been experimentally demonstrated on a miniscale in the perception of pictures with dynamic and scenic properties. Werner and Kaplan (1963, summarized in Paivio, 1971b, pp. 105–107) investigated the effects of directional properties of pictured objects. For example, when a picture of a bird flying to the left was placed in the objective median plane, observers perceived the bird as displaced in the direction of flight, with the result that the apparent median plane shifted to the right—an anticipatory displacement presumably mediated by memory images of birds in flight. Another finding was that the apparent velocity of pictured objects was affected by their dynamic qualities. For example, when viewed on moving belts, a "running" mouse had to be shown moving at an objectively slower speed than a sitting mouse for the two to be perceived as moving at the same speed. More recently, Freyd (1987) reviewed similar results of experiments on dynamic mental representational of momentum. For example, line drawings of a rectangle were shown successively in different orientations along a possible path of rotation. Participants who were asked to remember the third orientation were less successful in detecting differences between that and the slightly different subsequent (fourth) orientation than the preceding one that differed from the memory target by the same amount. It was as if the observers erred in the direction of the anticipated rotation. Other studies confirmed that the effect represented a shift in memory for the orientation.

Helen Intraub and Richardson (1989) demonstrated a related phenomenon in which participants remember having seen a greater expanse of a pictured scene than was shown. The effect also occurred with imagined scenes "projected" onto outline objects (Intraub, Gottesman, & Bills, 1998) and when regions of three-dimensional scenes were explored haptically by blindfolded participants and by a deaf-and-blind observer (Intraub, 2004). The effects were discussed in terms of anticipatory representations that may facilitate integration of successive views in scene perception. My related interpretation is that the boundary extensions reflect the general adaptive functions of anticipatory imagery, resulting from a lifetime of exploring extended scenes and noticing what is coming up ahead. The representational base presumably consists of spreading activation of a segment of a "scenic imagen pool," cued by the pictures or the referentially related scene descriptions. The phenomena would thus be in the same class as experiencing closure of fragmented pictures, discussed in the last chapter as evidence of imagen activation.

Most directly relevant here is Piaget's pioneering research on the development of anticipatory imagery and object permanence. Piaget and Inhelder (1971) studied anticipatory imagery using tasks that required anticipation of the results of figural transformations. For example, children showed by drawings what kinds of a figure would result when two triangles are joined in a particular way. On average they mastered such tasks at 7 years of age, from which Piaget and Inhelder concluded that anticipatory imagery begins around that time. Investigations of object permanence suggest that anticipatory imagery begins even earlier. Piaget studied ages at which infants behave as if they are looking for an object that disappeared behind a screen or in a container. Such behavior was taken to mean that the infant believed that the object still existed although out of sight. Piaget's observations suggested that object permanence was attained at about 2 years of age. Others have suggested much earlier beginnings (e.g., see the review by Cornell, 1978), associated with experientially determined changes in attentional and memory capacities. For example, 6-month-olds show surprise when they watch an object disappear behind a screen and then see a different object appear on the other side. It is compelling to infer that the infant has begun to develop cognitive representations corresponding to objects (imagens in DCT terms) and that memory images of the objects mediate the surprise and search behavior that occurs when the object is not found or another object appears where the original was anticipated. The relevant point is that Piaget's concepts of anticipatory imagery and object permanence both entail anticipation of changes to or recurrence of remembered figures or objects.

Language obviously plays an important role in anticipation, although usually together with imagery. "What's happening Tuesday?" triggers memory images of what usually happens on Tuesdays, or images induced by earlier conversations about plans for Tuesday, and so on. Language and imagery link past events with anticipated future events and contribute to our sense of the continuity of time. Both codes are engaged in more abstract ways when we plan our activities in the immediate and more distant future using clocks and calendars (cf. Friedman, 1989). The effectiveness of such devices ultimately depends on cumulative nonverbal and verbal memories of diurnal and seasonal changes.

Language-evoked expectancy can also influence reactions in the short term, presumably via imagery in some instances. For example, a story about ships facilitates subsequent perceptual recognition of a fragmented ship (see Paivio, 1986, p. 178). Imagery might be involved but has not been experimentally studied in connection with placebo effects (not always short term), which psychologist Irving Kirsch (1985) interpreted as mediated by response expectancies. These in turn are defined as anticipations of such nonvolitional responses as pain (or reduced pain), vomiting, alertness, and so on. In the typical paradigm, a patient or research participant is given an inert substance and is led to believe that it has physical properties that produce a particular effect. The belief is usually induced by a verbal statement accompanied by a relevant contextual variable. For example, Montgomery and Kirsch (1996) told student participants that they were to be tested for the effects of a new local anesthetic (actually a placebo). Administered from a labeled bottle, the placebo looked and smelled medicinal when applied. The experimenter wore a lab coat and surgical gloves, and time was allowed for the medicine to "work." Pain was applied to a "treated" or untreated finger and the students rated the severity of the pain. The experiment showed the placebo effect but did not distinguish between effects due to the verbal cues and the nonverbal components (placebo odor, lab coat, etc.). Other studies did reveal effects of the latter; for example, placebo "drug" injections are more effective than placebo pills, perhaps because of patients' prior beliefs about the effectiveness of the two modes of drug delivery.

The dual coding relevance is that placebo effects depend on prior verbal and nonverbal experiences with, or knowledge about, the kinds of effects that are to be expected from the real thing. Dual coding processes are implicated even if one uses the concept of "meaning response" as an alternative to expectancy as the explanation of placebo effects (Moerman, 2002). This follows because, in DCT, meaning itself is explained in terms of multimodal verbal and nonverbal responses to objects and situations, as well as to language (discussed later in this chapter). Various research possibilities readily come to mind but we need not pursue them here.

EVALUATIVE FUNCTIONS OF DUAL CODING SYSTEMS

Evaluation is as vital as anticipation to our well being and survival. We constantly choose between objects and actions on the basis of their importance to us. The decisions are based on perceptual properties, verbal information, or just "weighing things in our minds" before making a choice between alternatives. For example, we read a menu but also imagine food alternatives in a restaurant before ordering; we mentally select the shorter of two routes when driving home; or, having forgotten to bring along the worn-out washer, we try to choose one of the appropriate size from a hardware assortment from memory. What kinds of mental entities are being evaluated in such tasks? Are they images, as the examples suggest, or are they simply words, as if we know that a mouse is small and an elephant large because we often describe them in those terms? Or are such judgments based on abstract representations of some kind? How fine are the memory discriminations we are able to make? How similar are they to perceptual judgments of objects on the same dimensions?

Perceptual comparisons have long been used to investigate such questions. They yield smooth psychophysical reaction time (RT) functions so that, for example, we can say which of two lines is longer or shorter more quickly the greater the length difference. By analogy with perceptual comparisons, Moyer (1973) similarly investigated mental comparisons as a problem in memory psychophysics. He showed participants pairs of animal names, asking them to choose the one that was larger in "real life." Some differed greatly in size (e.g., *mouse-cow*) whereas others differed less (e.g., *moose-cow*). The result was that decision RT varied inversely with the size difference: the larger the difference in remembered size the faster the decision. This *symbolic distance effect* was similar to that obtained when people compare perceptual stimuli that differ in size or length. The important point is that the size differences were not perceptually present in the printed words, but rather, had to be represented in some kind of internal perceptual analogs that preserve the size information.

The dual coding interpretation of all this is that the internal analogs are mental images activated by the names. Alternatively, the comparisons could be based on linguistic descriptive habits, related for example to how often we use the words large or small (or the comparatives larger or smaller than) to describe animals. To test such alternatives, I extended Moyer's symbolic comparison task in various ways (Paivio, 1975b). One extension was that I used stimuli that included inanimate objects as well as animals that differed in real-life size according to rating data, and the experimental lists included animal–animal, object–object, and animal–object pairs. Another extension was that the concepts were presented as either words or pictures, the rationale being that pictures activate the memory images more directly than words, and that decisions therefore should be faster with pictures than words even when the pictures do not show the real-life size differences.

The results were as expected from the imagery hypothesis: the decisions were much faster with pictures than words and became progressively faster for both kinds of stimuli as the real-life size difference increased. Further experiments strengthened the imagery interpretation. In one study, the pictured entities were shown so that the perceptual size difference was congruent or incongruent with the real-life size difference. For example, a zebra and a lamp were pictured so that the zebra appeared either smaller or larger than the lamp. The reasoning was that decisions should be relatively slower under the incongruent condition because the perceptual information conflicts with memory information concerning size differences. This Stroop-like conflict should be absent when the sizes of printed words are similarly varied, because both words would have to be read before the images can be activated. The results again were as predicted.

A variant of the congruity–incongruity paradigm provided an even stronger test of the imagery hypothesis: the conflict observed with memory size comparisons should be reversed when observers are asked to decide which of the pictured objects looks farther away. This follows because objects known to be larger appear to be far away when pictured smaller than those known to be small. This prediction, too, was strongly confirmed, as can be seen in Fig. 4.8, which also shows the size comparison results. The contrasting effects obtained with the two kinds of judgments are particularly interesting because they require the observer to take account of visual size information from two sources, one perceptual and the other from visual memory.

Explanations based on verbal and abstract semantic representations are challenged by the effects of the individual manipulations considered separately, and they cannot account at all for the total pattern of effects without post hoc modifications of the hypotheses. The effects follow directly from dual coding assumptions, with particular emphasis in this case on the functional dominance of imagery (the theoretical alternatives are discussed in detail in Paivio, 1986).

The symbolic comparison task was further extended to a variety of concrete and abstract attributes to test the generality of the effects and interpretations. In a time comparison task (Paivio, 1978a), participants saw pairs of digital times, such as 3:20 and 7:50, and were asked to choose the time in which the hour hand and minute hand on an analog clock would form the larger (or smaller) angle. This is a useful variant of the size comparison task because perceptual and symbolic information can be presented in different ways: both times can be presented digitally or as

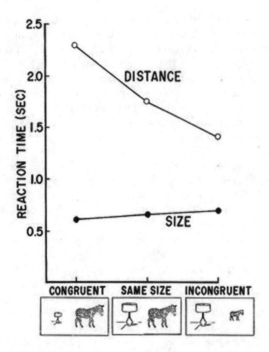

FIGURE 4.8   Mean reaction time for symbolic size and apparent distance comparisons for picture pairs in which the picture size differences are congruent or incongruent with real-life differences. From Paivio, A. (1975). Perceptual comparisons through the mind's eye. *Memory & Cognition, 2,* p. 644. Reprinted with permission of Psychonomic Society, Inc.

analogue clocks; or one can be digital and the other analogue. Dual coding suggests that comparisons should be faster in the mixed condition than in the digital condition because only one digital time need be converted into an imagined analogue clock in the mixed case. Verbal and abstract semantic coding theories suggest instead that the digital–digital condition would be fastest. The results were in fact just as expected from the dual coding analysis.

The clock comparison experiment was repeated in a modified form using angularity-roundness judgments of objects presented as pictures, words, or picture–word pairs. Participants saw pairs of items (e.g., *tomato-goblet, tomato-newspaper*) that differed in roundness according to normative ratings, and they were asked to choose the rounder or more angular of the pair. The results mirrored those obtained with the clocks task in that comparison times were faster with picture–word than word–word pairs, as expected from dual coding. Other variations on these tasks resulted in different patterns of predicted effects, depending on task demands and the imagery or verbal strategies participants were prompted to use (Paivio, 1986, pp. 184–185).

Dual coding ran into some problems of interpretation in this area (Paivio, 1986, pp. 191–196). One was that the symbolic distance effect occurred even with such abstract attributes as pleasantness (e. g., which is more pleasant, a *butterfly* or a *baseball?*), value (which costs more, a *house* or a *ship?*), and the intelligence or ferocity of animals. Moreover, the comparisons for pleasantness and value were faster with pictures than words. How can these be explained in dual coding terms when the information is abstract rather than perceptually concrete? I suggested that such attributes as pleasantness and value, although not correlated with simple perceptual dimensions, are properties of things rather than words, or of learned behavioral and emotional reactions to things. To evaluate such properties, we must first think about (image) the things, and we can do so more quickly from pictures than words. The verbal system can also contribute to the evaluations in various ways, especially by such descriptive habits as how often we say pleasant things about roses and how often we refer to the value of diamonds. Individual differences in cognitive abilities provide evidence on such interpretations, and they are discussed after considering another puzzling finding.

Color is a perceptual attribute of things and therefore should be associated more closely with imagens than logogens. Accordingly, symbolic color comparisons should be faster in response to line drawings of objects than to their printed names. To our surprise, this did not happen: Over several procedural variations (Paivio & te Linde, 1980), comparisons were as fast for words as pictures. This occurred for both brightness (which is darker, a *cucumber* or a *lime?*) and hue (a peach is closer to which color, *orange* or *yellow*?) Moreover, in the case of hue, the reaction times were equal even when the target stimuli were compared to two different color patches, one on each side of a centrally presented object picture or name. Both words and pictures nonetheless yielded the usual symbolic distance effect, so that decision time increased as the difference between the comparison colors on the color circle decreased. Thus, people reacted as if they used a mental rainbow for their comparisons.

We had no explanation for the absence of picture–word differences in the case of color. We noted only that other behavioral and neuropsychological data have independently shown that color is a puzzling attribute, one that closely implicates verbal mechanisms in the processing of long-term memory information about color. The anomaly is no consolation for verbal or abstract coding theorists either, however, because the former would predict a word advantage (faster access to the verbal code) and the latter a picture advantage (faster access to the semantic coding system). We are left with the conclusion that color information about objects is accessed equally quickly via imagery and verbal coding systems. Chapter 7 provides relevant neuropsychological information but no clear resolution.

Individual differences in cognitive abilities bear on the theoretical issues. Many of our experiments included spatial manipulation and other tests presumed to measure relevant imagery abilities as well as fluency and other verbal ability tests on the verbal side. The results (summarized in Paivio, 1980) showed that high imagers were faster than low imagers on comparisons involving concrete attributes (size, digital clock times, angularity-roundness) as well as abstract attributes (pleasantness and value). Verbal abilities were less consistently related to comparison times. A test of abstract verbal reasoning correlated significantly with size and clock comparisons, and another verbal test interacted with imagery so that individuals who scored high on both imagery and verbal tests were fastest on pleasantness comparisons. Of course, the verbal system must be involved in all tasks involving words as stimuli, but there are many different verbal abilities and relevant ones may not have been tapped in some of the aforementioned studies.

An important aspect of the evaluative function not discussed up to this point is that we evaluate other people on all kinds of attributes at least as often as we appraise things, and we learn early in life that we ourselves are constantly being evaluated by others. This has enormous effects on our social behaviors, attitudes, and emotions that will be reviewed in the following section.

MOTIVATIONAL AND EMOTIONAL FUNCTIONS

Motivation and emotion are the forces that drive and guide our adaptive behavior. Motivation refers generally to physiological arousal and goal-oriented aspects of behavior. Most theorists also include qualitative features described as positive or negative affect and different emotions. Goal-oriented behaviors are approach or avoidance responses in regard to objects, situations, and behavioral outcomes that have positive or negative incentive value. A common view is that emotions and goal-oriented reactions are related so that approach and avoidance are mediated by positive and negative affect.

Some emotional-motivational reactions are unlearned or require minimal learning. Fear of falling, for example, appears early in infancy in the absence of prior negative experiences with high places. For the most part, however, we are concerned here with learned motivational reactions to previously neutral stimuli and their relation to verbal and nonverbal representational systems. The dual coding view as already described in Chapter 3 is that affective and emotional reactions are nonverbal by definition and hence are expected to accompany imagery. This association is familiar in nightmares as well as pleasant and unpleasant daydreams. Goal-oriented imagery also appears in the form of daydream fantasies in which one achieves success in love, sports, professional careers, and so on (discussed further in Chapter 15).

Although emotions are directly represented only in the nonverbal system, they also have connections to emotional language so that we can name or describe specific emotions such as joy, fear, and anger, and react in relevant ways to their names. We recognize emotions from facial expressions and when we say that someone looks happy, angry, or sad we demonstrate the referential connections between specific emotional expressions and emotional names. This discriminative referential processing capacity reflects the adaptive significance of learning to read emotions in others, a kind of mind reading that presumably has its roots deep in the evolution of nonverbal cognition (Chapter 11). Of course, we also react emotionally to emotional situations and their descriptions in narratives. The following summarizes the DCT perspective and research on emotion and its motivational consequences.

The basic assumption is that emotional-affective reactions are learned primarily in the context of nonverbal objects and events and thus become connected to nonverbal representations (imagens). Other people are the important nonverbal context in the case of social emotions, which implicates verbal factors in ways that are discussed shortly, but the view remains that affective reactions are generally mediated by imagens with high probability connections to affective systems. This means that language arouses emotions mainly by first activating images of emotional events, as when one reads a horror story. In addition, through conditioning, words themselves acquire generalized affective qualities analogous to referential meaning, in which the referential reaction is a particular emotion. This is clearest in the case of such abstract emotional terms as fear, anger, and joy.

Most of us take the referential relations for granted but some people have difficulty distinguishing their emotions and relating them to emotional terms. The condition is called alexithymia. Autistic people in particular have difficulty reading emotions in others, and Baron-Cohen's development of the large emotional vocabulary and pool of corresponding facial expressions, described in Chapter 3, was motivated by his interest in helping autistics improve their ability to recognize emotions. More generally, there are individual differences in how easily people recognize emotional expression in faces (Martin, Berry, Dobranski, & Horne, 1996).

A further DCT assumption is that an emotion usually follows prior identification of a relevant stimulus or image, although the converse can also occur in the sense that, once aroused, emotions can prime (increase the probability of) relevant imagery and verbal associations. Free-floating anxiety and depression, for example, tend to be accompanied by negative thoughts that are not seen as the immediate causes of the emotions. Evaluation, the adaptive function already discussed, is directly implicated in emotional arousal and its motivational consequences: The situational or cognitive contexts must be evaluated or appraised in some way before one can then react overtly. This view was firmly held by Magda Arnold: "We can like or dislike only something we know. We must see or hear or touch something, remember having done so or imagine it, before we can decide that it is good or bad for us. Sensation must be completed in some form of appraisal before it can lead to action" (Arnold, 1960, p. 33). An alternative interpretation is that a stimulus can arouse a relevant affective response before it is identified (e.g., Zajonc, 1984). A detailed discussion of the alternatives isn't essential for these purposes, although the issue is touched on again in the neuropsychological context (Chapter 8). The important point is that cognitive evaluation is closely associated with emotional arousal.

Predictions based on the dual coding analysis of evaluation and emotion were tested experimentally (Paivio, 1978b). Using the mental comparison task described earlier, participants were asked to decide as quicky as possible which of two stimuli is more pleasant or unpleasant. The stimuli were pictures of objects, concrete nouns,

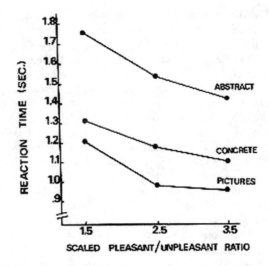

FIGURE 4.9   Mean reaction times for comparisons of pairs of pictures, concrete words, and abstract words as a function of the difference in rated pleasantness-unpleasantness. From Paivio, A. (1978). Mental comparisons involving abstract attributes. *Memory & Cognition, 6*, p. 203. Reprinted with permission of Psychonomic Society, Inc.

or abstract nouns that were preselected to vary equivalently in their rated pleasantness. The predictions from DCT were that pleasantness comparisons would be fastest for pictures (the affectively loaded referents can be seen), next fastest for concrete words (images of the referents can be accessed), and slowest for abstract words (which lack direct access to affective images). In addition, decisions were expected to be faster as the pleasantness difference increased. As can be seen in Fig. 4.9, both predictions were strongly confirmed. This finding provides an important benchmark for a further DCT analysis of the neuropsychology of emotion in Chapter 8.

Effects of Being Evaluated

I turn next to the emotional consequences that result when we ourselves are the objects of evaluation. The problem was investigated in a series of studies (summarized in Paivio, 1965b) that dealt with the roles of evaluation and the individual's reinforcement history in the expression and development of the fear of being observed. This is one of the most common social fears and it has a long evolutionary history in that many species are sensitive to being looked at and behave in various ways to avoid it (Chapter 11). The fear in humans ranges from shyness to stage fright and is evoked by the presence or imagined presence of people who are perceived to be evaluating observers. The research dealt with the measurement and developmental antecedents of audience sensitivity, which refers to the tendency to experience anxiety in the presence or anticipated presence of an audience and thus avoid audience situations. The research also touched on exhibitionism in the sense of "seeking the limelight," which was assumed to reflect the contingencies between being observed, evaluated, and rewarded for one's "performance."

Measures and correlates of audience sensitivity were studied (e.g., Paivio & Lambert, 1959) using (a) questionnaires; (b) stories written to audience-related pictures or verbal cues, and scored for anxiety content; (c) palmar sweating as a psychophysiological stress indicator; and (d) speech hesitations that might reflect anxiety.[15] The relevant outcome for these purposes was that the results justified exploring the developmental hypothesis using questionnaires to measure the audience-oriented traits in children and the evaluative and reinforcing habits of their parents with respect to the children's social behaviors and achievements.

The research was guided by a theory that emphasizes the contingencies between being observed, evaluated, and reinforced for one's behavior. Simply put, one must be seen and evaluated to be praised or criticized (or otherwise rewarded or punished) for what one has done. The contingencies are inevitable, so most people have some tendency to experience audience anxiety and avoid audience situations. The same contingencies associated with rewarding outcomes account for positive reactions to observers, in this case a sense of pride and exhibitionism (showing off) before observers, and an urge to seek the limelight. Ambivalence is perhaps the most common consequence of social judgments that carry "threats of hell and hopes of paradise." Notice, too, that evaluation is a reciprocal process in this context: The audience functions as a potential evaluator and the audience sensitive person in turn perceives and evaluates the audience on its potential to reward or punish.

The notable results from the developmental research (Paivio, 1964) were that children who were favorably evaluated, frequently rewarded, and infrequently punished had lower audience anxiety scores than children who were unfavorably evaluated and frequently punished. The only significant relation with exhibitionism was that children high in exhibitionism were more favorably evaluated than those low in exhibitionism. The causal relations are uncertain in such correlations but they are consistent with the general theory that audience sensitivity and exhibitionism are at least partly determined by evaluation-contingent rewards and punishments.

Audience influence is part of a broader category of social influence related to other people functioning as reinforcers. Other people can also be thought of as sources of information that can be used to attain goals, or as "instruments" that help us attain goals (as in cooperative activity), or as "obstacles" that frustrate our goal-oriented activities. These categories of social influence play an important role in cognitive evolution and are reviewed in detail in that context (Chapter 11).

---

[15]The picture-story test was patterned after the Thematic Apperception Test procedure used by McClelland, Atkinson, Clark, and Lowell (1953) to measure achievement motivation.

This emphasis on audience influence highlights the motivational and emotional effects that result not only from the presence of others as evaluating observers, but also from their imagined and anticipated presence as evoked by pictures, questionnaire items, and verbal cues that refer to speech situations. In brief, the audience-oriented reactions are mediated by the activity of domain-specific dual coding systems.

The studies of pleasantness comparisons and social emotions influenced dual coding analyses of neuropsychological evidence on brain systems involved in emotional experiences and behaviors (Chapter 8). All of that provided the foundation for interpretations of the roles of emotion and motivation in striving for excellence at the highest levels of performance and creative skills (Chapters 14–18).

PROBLEM-SOLVING FUNCTIONS OF DUAL CODING SYSTEMS

Even the simplest of real-life and laboratory tasks involve problem solving that requires complex mixtures of verbal and nonverbal thinking. Take crossword and jigsaw puzzles. By definition, crossword puzzles are primarily verbal tasks that draw on verbal associative knowledge activated by printed verbal cues and structural frames (the number of letters a solution word must have). They also draw on nonverbal meanings suggested by the questions, which might entail imagery of objects or situations that evoke name candidates for the frames. Conversely, jigsaw puzzle solving is primarily nonverbal and draws on perceptual-motor activity and imagery: pieces are searched and compared with slots and tried on for their fit, either by actually moving the pieces or by moving and comparing them mentally.[16] In addition, however, solvers might name shapes or parts of shapes and try to match pieces and slots that way. The same processes occur in assembling barbecues, bookshelves, and anything else that can be purchased in modular form nowadays. Such modules usually come with a picture of the completed assembly, much like a jigsaw puzzle box with the complete scene on the cover, together with instructions on how to assemble the parts, but the assembly could be done from scratch by trial and error. Other problems are more complex: real-life tasks such as fixing a troublesome water pump at the cottage, starting stalled cars, solving surgical complexities, making decisions about departmental or company problems, and so on; or laboratory problems such as "missionaries and cannibals," "Tower of Hanoi," the "two-strings problem," and varieties of syllogistic and conditional reasoning problems.

We can try to unravel the component processes involved in all problem solving. Short-term working memory is required because the elements of the task must be retained for the time needed to compare, manipulate, and organize them mentally. Long-term episodic memory is involved if one draws on previous specific experiences

---

[16]It is theoretically relevant to note that Richardson and Vecchi (2002) developed a jigsaw-puzzle imagery test of visuospatial ability.

with similar tasks. And semantic and procedural memories are essential throughout task performance. Solving riddles depends largely on verbal associative structures according to George Kiss (1975), who used a large associative database to show that the answer to a riddle often appears early among the associates to key words in the riddle. For example, the word "eternity"–the solution to the riddle "I am forever, and yet was never. What am I?"—appears as the sixth most common associate to the key words, "forever" and "never." We shall see later, under language comprehension, that "solving" novel metaphors and proverbs depends similarly on verbal associations along with imagery.

Nonverbal working memory and long-term memory are essential to chess playing, although dual coding is always involved to some degree and becomes essential in blindfolded chess or computer games because the positions and moves are described verbally. Highly skilled players draw especially on long-term visual memory, judging from the common finding that chess masters are no better than average players in memory for random positions of chess pieces but excel when the positions conform to patterns that emerge during chess games (e.g., Simon & Chase, 1973). Thus, the skilled players have a rich repertoire of integrated or chunked sequences of moves stored in long-term or semantic memory. Under some conditions, however, the more skilled players have better memory even for random positions, presumably because they are better at organizing the random positions as a result of their long experience with game situations (Saariluoma, 1991). Chess expertise is considered in more detail from the dual coding perspective in Chapter 15 along with other domains of expert skills and knowledge.

Physical or mental transformations are also required to compare and evaluate relevant aspects of a problem. The manipulations might be done mentally even when parts are perceptually available, so that the outcome can be anticipated and evaluated before it is carried out ("vicarious trial and error"). The mental operations involved have often been described in terms of dynamic or transformational imagery that derives from experience with manipulating and responding to objects. It might come as a surprise to modern cognitivists that B. F. Skinner provided a particularly clear analysis of such "private problem solving" in behavioristic terms using the cube visualization task as an example:

In the following problem ... behavior is usually facilitated by private seeing. "Think of a cube, all six surfaces of which are painted red. Divide the cube into twenty-seven equal cubes by making two horizontal cuts and two sets of vertical cuts each. How many of the resulting cubes will have three faces painted red, how many two, how many one, and how many none?" It is possible to solve this without seeing the cubes in any sense—as by saying to oneself, "A cube has eight corners. A corner is defined as the intersection of three faces of the cube. There will therefore be eight pieces with three painted faces ..." And so on. But the solution is easier if one can actually see the faces. This is easiest in the presence of actual cubes, of course, and even a sketchy drawing will provide useful support, but many people solve the problem visually without visual stimulation [by means of] a mixture of discriminative and manipulative responses. In this example one may *see* the larger cube, *cut* it covertly, *see* their faces, *count* them subvocally, and so on. (Skinner, 1953, p. 273)

Such imagery is implicated in tests of visual-spatial ability. Thurstone (1938) defined this ability factor as facility with spatial and visual imagery. In Guilford's (1967) structure-of-intellect model, such tests (including cube visualization) define what he called "Cognition of figural transformations." They form part of the general nonverbal factors that continue to turn up in all factor analytic studies of intelligence (Chapter 16).

DCT has been applied to other tasks in this broad domain, including spatial problem solving (finding one's way around) using cognitive maps and language, syllogistic reasoning, concept identification, and mental practice effects on motor skills (see Paivio, 1986, pp. 203–209). The relevant research literature has increased rapidly in all these areas since my review. At this point, I mention only cognitive mapping because it has enabled imagery researchers to compare the ability of people to find their way around locations and routes on maps that are perceptually available, remembered from study of seen maps, or created from verbal descriptions of the territory. Moreover, the effects of the different ways of creating cognitive maps can be studied using performance in the mapped territory.

A study by Denis, Pazzaglia, Cornoldi, and Bertolo (1999) investigated many of these aspects of cognitive mapping using verbal descriptions of routes in the city of Venice. Descriptions provided by citizens of Venice were rated for goodness and used to construct skeletal descriptions also judged to be sufficient to guide navigation. Participants unfamiliar with the city were given good or poor descriptions as navigation guides and tested for their actual performance in getting around the city. The important outcome was that the good descriptions (and skeletal descriptions) resulted in better performance than poor descriptions. Additionally, however, participants who used visual memories of landmarks had fewer errors than participants using other strategies even when given descriptions as navigational aids. Overall, the results nicely support the adaptive benefits resulting from the cooperative interplay of dual coding systems. Cognitive mapping and other problem-solving tasks are discussed further in subsequent chapters on the brain, cognitive evolution, and high-level intellectual and performance skills.

COMMUNICATION FUNCTIONS OF DUAL CODING SYSTEMS

Language is the principle means of human communication and it is involved in all dual coding functions described up to this point. We use language to remember the past, anticipate tomorrow, evaluate the good and bad, express our feelings, solve problems, and even use it reflexively to talk and theorize about language itself. Above all, we use it to communicate with each other. Thus language is an adaptive system par excellence. We must bear in mind, however, that it is a symbolic adaptive system that derives its power from its connections to nonverbal representations and response systems that enable us to behave adaptively in response to real challenges. The social context seems to be an exception in that we can use language to influence others to be our providers and defenders, but even that use of language depends on our mutual knowledge of the referents of language, so that others know how to act on our behalf. I expand on the implications of that statement in Chapter 11 when dealing with the social context of evolution. Here, the dual coding lens is on core aspects of language that make it a useful cognitive tool, namely meaning, syntax, comprehension, production, language development, and bilingualism.

Meaning

The concept of *meaning* is so open ended and slippery that whole volumes have been devoted to its definition (e.g., Ogden & Richards's influential classic *The Meaning of Meaning*). It encompasses everything from the meanings of words to the meaning of life. It has been discussed as an evolutionary product that is grounded in biological function (Dennett, 1995, p. 402). The term has been used as if it is some property that resides "out there," in the things and events we observe, much like Platonic ideas or Aristotelian essences. That interpretation persists in the common view that speech and writing have some inherent meaning that one can grasp and send to others on a communicational conveyor belt, a metaphor Reddy (1993) compared with a more recognizable tool-use analogy.

Psychologists' definitions are of the tool-use variety in that meanings are assumed to reside in the mental toolbox of the listener or reader, which is opened up by words and things. The nature of the meaningful tools differ widely across psychological theorists, however, ranging from the covert sensory and motor responses of behaviorists to the abstract features, propositions, and schemata of computational cognitivists. In DCT, the meaning toolbox consists of internal verbal and nonverbal representations and processes that derive from sensorimotor and affective reactions, as already explained. Language and nonverbal objects and events have meaning in the sense that they can activate patterns of such reactions in a probabilistic way depending on the context and the individual's history of experience with words and objects.

The approach capitalizes on the distinction between representational, referential, and associative levels of meaning, described in Chapter 3 with respect to the perceptual, cross-system, and within-system levels of activation of verbal and nonverbal representations. Representational meaning refers to the memory representation activated directly by a word or object in any modality, and is defined by measures of familiarity. Referential meaning reflects connections between the mental representations of words and their referents, and is measured by tests of object naming on the one hand and imaging to names on the other. The connections are one-to-many in both directions: a picture of a dog can elicit different names depending on the context, and the word dog can evoke different images. The number and strength of the connections vary—we have names for many kinds of dog and few names for kinds of giraffe. We also have names for actions, emotions, and sensory experiences and we can respond (or imagine responding) directly to them. For example, we can push when asked to do so in the context of a stalled car, and perhaps salivate to the word "lemon." Direct referential connections are deficient or absent in the case of abstract words, although they might evoke images indirectly by first activating names of exemplars (e.g., religion-church). Finally, associate meaning refers to connections among units within the verbal system or within the nonverbal system, accounting for word associations on the one hand and imagery associations on the other.

The patterns of interconnections differ for concrete and abstract language because they have been learned and used in different contexts (Paivio, 1986, p. 123). Activation can occur and spread in either system, and between systems. The activity patterns will vary with the eliciting context, which implies that the meaning of a unit cannot be fixed but will vary to some extent as the context changes—an old idea that is given a specific interpretation in DCT. We saw an example of the effect of context on imagery value and recall of homonyms in the experiment by Begg and Clark (1975). Many other functional consequences of contextual meaning changes can be found in research on reading (e. g., Sadoski & Paivio, 2001).

Syntax

The interpretation of syntax became especially controversial in language sciences after Chomsky revolutionized linguistics in his 1957 volume, *Syntactic Structures,* and influenced psycholinguistics 2 years later (Chomsky, 1959)] through his critique of Skinner's volume, *Verbal Behavior* (1957). Chomsky's approach has remained controversial in its various revisions, as has his nativist view of the origin of language. We scrutinize that view in Chapter 13. Here we focus on the DCT approach to the nature and development of syntax.

Dual coding stresses the role of the nonverbal perceptual and imagery contexts in syntactic behavior as it does in relation to meaning and associative language phenomena. For example, an early experiment (Paivio, 1971a) showed that imagery value was a better predictor of language memory there was a Chomskyan deep structure variable. Many others have emphasized nonverbal contributions to grammar. The philosopher Ludwig Wittgenstein (Biletzki & Matar, 2003) at one point became excited by his discovery of a picture theory of language. By that he meant that language is isomorphic with the structure of concrete situations and events as represented in pictures. However, there is an important catch here: At the time Wittgenstein developed his picture theory, he held a formal, logical view of language in which the meaning of a sentence is a proposition. Propositions are in turn pictures of objects and their relations. Language is used to express these pictured propositions (note that the theory is a variant of what I referred to as logical dual coding in Chapter 1). Later, Wittgenstein rejected the idea of a formal language that accurately pictures the world, and the picture theory thus became untenable. He moved from that to his famous theory of language as a game with informal rules that govern how people use language to serve their needs as members of a community. Obviously, this pragmatic view of language is acceptable to anyone who sees language first and foremost as a communication system, but it does not require rejection of a more probabilistic (not fixed) "picture" theory in which the essential aspects of a concrete situation can be represented by a picture or mental image and expressed in language. This is the case in modern picture theories of grammar.

Linguist Tom Givón (1989, pp. 94–122) proposed that there is iconicity and isomorphism in grammar in that propositional mental representations of the surface structure of language map onto the concrete world. His analysis applies so thoroughly to various syntactic constructions and the concrete–abstract dimension that it is fully compatible with the DCT of grammar except for the emphasis on the role of imagery in the latter. Case grammars, cognitive linguistics, and other semantically-based systems (e.g., Chafe, 1970; Fauconnier, 1997; Fillmore, 1977; Lakoff, 1977, 1990; Langacker, 1990) also assume that language has experiential correlates or mappings in perceptual scenes, image schemas, and sensory-motor images. Similarly, Rene Thom (1980) developed the concept of "implicit topology" to describe the abstract but isomorphic mapping between language and the perceptual world. Highly relevant as well is David McNeill's (1992) theory of the relations between gestures and language. He proposes essential unity of speech, iconic gestures, and imagery. This relation is increasingly recognized as well in the case of sign languages of the deaf. For example, American Sign Language has been described as "involving an integration of visual imagery and linguistic structure on a scale that no spoken language can equal" (Taub, 2001, p. 1, cited in Marschark, 2005, p. 314). This idea that gestures externalize imagery is reminiscent of the converse Piagetian view (e.g., Piaget & Inhelder, 1971) that imagery is internalized imitation.

Frode Strømnes (1974a) developed an explicit mapping theory in which relational terms (prepositions and comparable morphemic operators) derive their meaning from underlying representational systems or mental models, which differ across language families. To test his theory, Strømnes developed a pictorial realization in which abstract line drawings conveyed the sense of the 12 living cases of Finnish, an inflected language in which relational information is conveyed by morphemic endings of nouns and modifiers. The dynamic relations were shown to Finnish informants in motion pictures in which two entities acted in relation to each other in ways that best represented the meanings of the cases according to Finnish informants (note that this is not a formal definition of the relations). Examples of the pictured cases are shown in Fig. 4.10. A different underlying geometric mental model was similarly developed for Swedish prepositions.

Strømnes describe the Finnish system as a simple topology in which nouns carry more information than verbs, and Swedish (like other Indo-European languages) as a vector system in which verbs carry more information than nouns, The theory was supported, for example, by the finding that verbs were left out relatively more often in Finnish than in Swedish newspaper headlines and in descriptions of the same hockey game by Finnish and Swedish broadcasters (Stromnes, 1974b) These and other implications of the theory for language learning, language behavior, and nonverbal correlates of language are comprehensively reviewed in Strømnes (2006).

Such reality-mapping interpretations of grammar correspond partly to the dual coding view—partly, because the theorists generally incorporate abstract structures of some kind in their analyses whereas DCT relies entirely on modality-specific nonverbal and verbal structures and processes. The following summary draws on

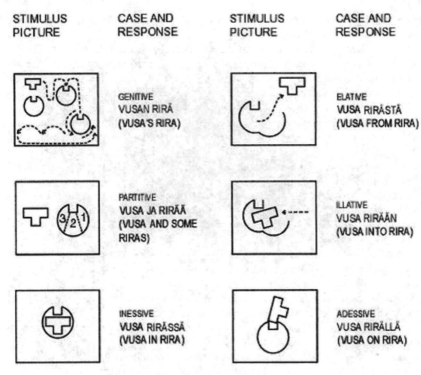

FIGURE 4.10   Examples of pictures used by Strømnes to depict Finnish cases.
The broken lines and arrows depict movement shown directly in the cinematic
version of the pictures. Adapted from Table 1 (pp. 304–305) in Strømnes, F. J.
(1974). No universality of cognitive structures? Two experiments with almost
perfect one-trial learning of translatable operators in a Ural-Altaic and an
Indo-European language. *Scandinavian Journal of Psychology, 15,* 300–309.
Copyright 1974, Blackwell Publishing. Reproduced by permission.

earlier reviews (Paivio, 1986, pp. 215–118; Paivio & Begg, 1981; Sadoski & Paivio,
2001).

To begin with, syntactic behavior includes a substantial component based simply
on associative habits as reflected in stock phrases, idioms, and verbal sequences
defined by association norms. Our ability to generalize by analogy from specific
exemplars to new ones is a kind of associative principal that accounts partly for syntactic productivity. Grammatical class is a case in point: even nonsense words can be
perceived as noun-like or verb-like and "inserted" into familiar sentence frames as in
jabberwocky. Importantly, DCT adds nonverbal perceptual and imaginal context to
the associative mix. Names of things, qualities, actions, and relations all have nonlinguistic situational referents that determine how those names are understood and used

in language contexts (cf. Olson, 1970). A good example is the effect of attentional focus on comprehension of actives and passives. Olson and Filby (1972) found that an active sentence, such as "The car hit the truck", was verified more quickly as true or false with respect to a picture of the event if the participant's attention was drawn to the actor (the car) by a prior picture. Conversely, the passive sentence, "The truck was hit by the car", was verified more quickly than the active if it was preceded by a picture of the receiver of the action (the truck).

Syntactic creativity in sentences and longer constructions can be explained by combinations of all of the aforementioned: generalized associative habits, changing situational contexts, and attentional focus of a speaker or listener. Affirmatives, negatives, interrogatives, passives, and so on, are learned and generalized as constructions because they are appropriate in different verbal and nonverbal contexts. Children in literate societies even learn names for the different constructions, and how to parse and transform sentences in response to the names of the constructions. Abstract discourse becomes possible because the grammatical habits eventually develop functional autonomy, freed to some extent from situational contexts and imagery, and driven largely by intraverbal communicational contexts and associative habits. How this happens is discussed further in a later section on language development.

Comprehension

This sine qua non of receptive language is intimately related to meaning. To be studied, comprehension needs to be operationalized, and, like other psychological concepts, there is no single "true" measure or procedure that can do the job, for there is no all-or-none "click" of comprehension. Instead, there is a set of psychological reactions that vary in kind and degree or "depth" (Mistler-Lachman, 1975), depending on the requirements of the situation. In casual conversations about evolutionary theory, for example, it might be enough just to be familiar with the term and perhaps its association with Darwin. Other situations require a deeper understanding of such concepts as natural selection, the voyage of the Beagle, turtles and birds on the Galapagos Islands, genes, conflicts with creationism, and so on, extending to expert procedural knowledge about how to study fossil records or genetic mechanisms. The upshot is that comprehension has been studied using a variety of procedures that can be collectively called convergent operations. Studies have typically used memory tasks with an emphasis on memory for gist or meaning (itself a complex idea, as we have seen), ratings of comprehensibility, how long it takes to verify a sentence as true or false, and variants of such procedures. The following are some of the most pertinent findings and issues related to the dual coding perspective on comprehension (detailed reviews can be found, e.g., in Paivio, 1986, and Sadoski & Paivio, 2001).

The main theoretical claim is that imagery and verbal processes contribute jointly to the comprehension of concrete language, whereas verbal processes predominate in the case of abstract language. The hypothesis extends the dual coding analysis of levels and types of meaning to include contextual meaning, which is determined partly by grammatical word order as a higher order variant of verbal associative variables, as described earlier. The consequence is that, relative to concrete language, comprehension of abstract language is impoverished because it depends mostly on the verbal patterns and the verbal associations they evoke, whereas comprehension of concrete language is enriched by the addition of imagery to the associative mix.

The following are a sample of findings that support the theory. Concrete sentences and passages are generally easier to understand than abstract ones as measured by a variety of memory tests and other procedures. Imagery is directly implicated because imagery and comprehension reaction times are correlated more highly for concrete than abstract sentences (Paivio & Begg, 1971). Sadoski (1983) found that readers who reported a memory image of the salient climax of a story understood and recalled the story better than those who did not report such an image, as if the image functioned as a conceptual peg that redintegrated the story.

Despite their correlation, however, imagery and comprehension can be teased apart experimentally, and, probably, in real-life language use. We have found that recognition memory is higher for high imagery concrete sentences than for low imagery abstract sentences even when they are carefully matched on ratings of comprehensibility (Kuiper & Paivio, 1977). The relation can even be completely reversed. In the experiment just mentioned, Paivio and Begg (1971) found that comprehension reaction times were generally faster than imagery reaction times even for concrete sentences, but imagery was faster than comprehension in a second experiment that used more complex sentences. The reversal was more dramatic in a study by O'Neill and Paivio (1978), who created anomalous sentences by switching content words from different meaningful sentences, thereby violating semantic and grammatical selection restrictions. Anomalous concrete sentences turned out to be less comprehensible than anomalous abstract sentences (reversing the relation obtained with normal sentences), but concrete sentences were still rated higher in imagery, presumably because they could evoke bizarre images.

The dual coding hypothesis also suggested a unique prediction concerning memory for the gist or general meaning of sentences as compared to memory for the exact wording. Jacqueline Sachs (1967) presented participants with spoken passages followed either immediately or after different amounts of interpolated material by a repetition of one of the spoken sentences. The repetition was identical to the original or changed either semantically or syntactically. Semantic change was achieved, for example, by reversing the subject and object. Syntactic changes were changes in wording that did not affect the meaning of the sentence, such as a change from active to passive or vice versa. The participants were asked to say whether the repeated sentence was changed or identical. The crucial finding was that, after some amount of interpolated discourse, recognition of syntactic change dropped sharply to a near chance level while it remained high for semantic changes. Sachs concluded that the original wording is stored only long enough for comprehension to occur, after which specific wording fades rapidly from memory and memory for the sentence is reconstructed from meaning.

It happened that Sachs's materials were concrete. Begg and Paivio (1969) reasoned that meaning was retained in the form of imagery, which changed sharply with changes such as subject–object reversals. Memory for abstract material depends more on wording and should be affected more by lexical changes than by semantic changes. We repeated Sachs's experiment with the addition of abstract material. The result replicated her findings for concrete sentences but the pattern was reversed for abstract sentences, so that lexical changes were recognized better than semantic changes, exactly as expected from DCT.

Our results were disputed on the grounds that our concrete and abstract sentences were not equated on comprehensibility. Correction was made in the recognition memory experiment (Kuiper & Paivio, 1977) described earlier. The test alternatives for our concrete and abstract sentences included synonyms. We expected synonym errors for both classes because relatedness of any kind interferes with discrimination, but synonym errors should be higher for concrete synonyms (e.g., *woman* confused with *lady*) because of their common referential image than for abstract ones (e.g., *soul, spirit*), which lack a common image. The prediction was confirmed in that, when synonym errors occurred, they were relatively more frequent in the concrete case. However, as already mentioned, overall recognition accuracy was higher for concrete than abstract sentences, presumably because the former elicited memorable images as well as being stored as verbal memory traces.

In sum, the evidence is strong that imagery and verbal processes contribute jointly to language comprehension. When comprehension is assessed using memory tasks, imagery augments memory for nonverbal meaning, or gist, at the expense of some loss of memory for wording.

Language Production

Similar dual coding variables and effects are prominent in spoken or written production (Paivio, 1986, pp. 229–234). The following experiments investigated fluency and other properties of spoken and written definitions of concrete and abstract words. The general dual coding hypothesis was that the availability of imagery would make it easier to define concrete than abstract words. In support of this, Reynolds and Paivio (1968) found that concrete word definitions were longer, were initiated more quickly, had fewer hesitations, and were judged to be qualitatively better than abstract word definitions. The findings were replicated using written definitions (Sadoski, Kealy, Goetz, & Paivio, 1997), with the additional important finding that students reported relatively more use of an imagery strategy to define the concrete words and a verbal strategy with abstract words. Other selective effects of associative, syntactic, and situational variables on language production are described in Paivio (1986).

Language Development

Language concreteness, imagery processes, and verbal mechanisms are intertwined in the dual coding analysis of the development of syntactic knowledge and skill. The initial vocabulary of children is concrete, followed gradually by abstract words (e.g., Anglin, 1977). This sequence is logically inevitable given the definition of concreteness in terms of "object words," which Bertrand Russell (1940) defined "logically, as words having meaning in isolation, and psychologically, as words having been learnt without its being necessary to have previously learnt any other words" (p. 65). All empirical studies have confirmed the developmental sequence and I simply summarize the relation quantitatively using our own correlational data. Age of acquisition of words had been estimated directly from samples, at different ages, of children's vocabularies as well as by rating methods. The direct and rated estimates are highly correlated. For our purposes, we obtained normative ratings of age of acquisition for the large pool of words, which extended earlier norms on concreteness, imagery, and familiarity (Clark & Paivio, 2004). Rated concreteness and age of acquisition correlate –.69, which means that relatively concrete words were judged to have been acquired earlier than more abstract words. The earliest acquired items are such words as *arm, baby, toy, car, candy, mother, tree,* and *flower.* Examples of late-learned ones are *atrocity, banality, bereavement, clemency, deluge,* and *perjury,* as well as relatively infrequent concrete words such as *abbess, bivouac, casement, falconer, opium,* and *vestibule.*

Language development, however, is not a uniform progression from concrete to abstract. Language also becomes increasingly differentiated and specific, moving from words of a middle level of generality ("basic level concepts," Rosch, Mervis, Gray, Johnston, & Boyes-Braem, 1975), such as *dog,* to more specific exemplars (*collie*) and broader categories (*mammal*). The expansion in both directions requires experience with an increasing range of exemplars and language contexts so that there is finer mapping between specific terms and referents and more general associative groupings of referent objects and words under class labels. This entails expansions of associative connections within verbal and nonverbal systems and of referential connections between systems. The contextual learning at this noun level is essential to development of other word classes, including function words that appear relatively early in children's word production and comprehension. The contexts include language structures of increasing size and complexity.

The concrete–abstract sequence is relevant but not enough to explain the development of language structures beyond single words. Two-word utterances classified in terms of pivot grammar (Braine, 1963) or structural meanings (Brown, 1970) are initially concrete inasmuch as they consist of concrete nouns paired with more abstract function words and qualifiers, as well as other concrete nouns that function as qualifiers. Examples are as follows: *that car, hi spoon, more milk, pretty boat,* and *Mommy sock.* This is true as well for longer and syntactically more complex structures involving possession, number, questions, negatives, and so on. The early concreteness at this level is reflected in the materials and procedures used in research studies, which typically involve toys or pictorial referents that can be shown in different relations to each other or in different action sequences.

A classical example is the first systematic experiment that compared ages at which comprehension and production skills emerge. Fraser, Bellugi, and Brown (1963) used sentences and matching pictures presented to children between 37 and 43 months old. Pairs of sentences contrasted on a particular feature. For example, "The girl is cooking" and "The girl is not cooking" contrast on the affirmative–negative feature. The matching pictures showed a girl cooking and a girl doing something else. Both sentences were read aloud to the child. Then, in the comprehension test, one sentence was read and the child was asked to point to the appropriate picture, followed by the same procedure with the other picture. In the production test, the experimenter pointed to one of the pictures and asked the child to name it. The same procedure was followed with other contrasting grammatical features such as singular–plural and subject–object.

The results confirmed the common view that comprehension is easier and begins earlier than production, but modified replications by others showed that the pattern depends on chance factors and how responses are scored (see, e.g., the summary by Paivio & Begg, 1981, pp. 220–221). The question has not been completely resolved but the relevant point here is the use of concrete sentences and referent pictures in studies of grammatical skills in young children. We shall see later (Chapter 8) that such materials also are common in neuropsychological studies of grammar development that implicate dual coding processes.

Development of Syntax. I proposed a DCT analysis of syntax development in 1971 when debates centered on Chomsky's (1965) theory of an innate language acquisition device with an infinite capacity to generate novel grammatical sentences. Behaviorist analyses had lost favor because of Chomsky's criticisms of them and the seductive appeal of his rationalist alternative. Others argued for the centrality of semantics rather than syntax in language development. There were occasional references to imagery as well, but none were foolish enough to put their money on imagery. Having only monopoly money to lose in this speculative game, I put half of it down on imagery:

> The [hypothesis] is that linguistic competence and performance are dependent initially upon a substrate of imagery. Through exposure to concrete objects and events, the infant develops a storehouse of images that represent his knowledge of the world. Language builds upon this foundation and remains interlocked with it, although it also develops a partly autonomous structure of its own ... An infant indicates by his behavior that he recognizes objects before he responds to their names ... Later he can respond appropriately to the name of an object even in its absence (e.g., he may begin to look for it), indicating the emergence of a word-imagery relationship. [Moreover] the developing infant [sees] objects in relation to other objects, and action sequences involving such objects. The events and relations are lawful ... people enter a room through the same door [and] in the same way repeatedly, a bottle is picked up in a predictable way, and so on. In brief, there is a kind of syntax to the observed events, which becomes incorporated into the representational imagery as well. The syntax is elaborated and enriched by the addition of an action component derived from the child's own actions, which have their own patterning or grammar. The child also learns names for events and relations as well as the objects involved in them, which [suggests] that associations have developed between the mental representations of the objects, actions, etc., and

their descriptive names. This basic stage becomes greatly elaborated as function words are acquired and as intraverbal networks expand through usage.
Eventually, abstract verbal skills are attained whereby verbal behavior and verbal understanding are possible at a *relatively* autonomous intraverbal level, i.e.,
free of dependence not only upon a concrete situational context but to some
extent from imagery as well. [Thus] *the theory suggests that the grammars first
learned by children will be "tied to" the syntax of concrete objects and events …
via the medium of imagery … and only later will more abstract grammars
emerge.* (Paivio, 1971b, pp. 437–438, italics added)

The hypothesis focuses on the organizational properties of perceived events, behaviors, and imagery. The language connection is that those properties affect children's
learning of the grammatical patterns that already exist in the language they hear. As
such, the hypothesis is relevant to how our distant ancestors learned whatever
grammatical patterns were present at different stages of language evolution. It says
nothing directly about the role of event perception, behavior, and imagery in the
origins and evolution of the syntactic features of language as those are now
described by "grammarians." I return to that issue in Chapter 13.

It is important to see whether the hypothesis has any support in its ontogenetic
domain. If it does not, there is no point in going on to what is necessarily a completely speculative evolutionary extension. The only relevant evidence I know of
comes from research on the effects of referential contexts on learning foreign languages, miniature artificial languages, and language learning by children who have
learning difficulties. Many of the studies lack essential comparison conditions and
most deal with written language rather than speech. Nonetheless the results are relevant in principle to aspects of the hypothesis. Thus, (a) second language learning
benefits from using referent pictures and images, or from acting out commands in
situational contexts (e.g., reviewed in Paivio, 1983c); and (b) deaf children who had
previously failed to learn to read Finnish were able to do so using demonstrations in
which the various case relations of Finnish grammar were illustrated concretely by
showing, for example, a spoon in a cup to illustrate the Finnish case equivalent of
the preposition "in" (Strømnes & Iivonen, 1985). Negative results have also been
obtained in research involving very simple grammars that pictorial referents either did
not benefit syntax learning or at least had little effect on the manner of learning
(reviewed by Moeser & Bregman, 1973).

The developmental hypothesis was supported most completely by Moeser and
Bregman (1973), who studied the influence of pictorial referents and imagery on
adults' learning of a miniature artificial grammar that was more complex than the
ones used in the prior unsuccessful studies. Thus, phrase structure rules were used
to generate sentences that contained optional elements, embedded phrases, and
relations between items. The words in the language consisted of nonsense syllables
assigned to four classes defined by the shape, orientation, color, and border variation
of forms. Participants in a words-only condition saw only a series of "sentences"
whereas participants in a semantic referent condition saw the same series of

sentences presented along with a picture that the sentence described. A specific example of a correct sentence would be "MIR FET CAS LIM". The corresponding picture would be a tilted red triangle with a double-lined border, followed by a rectangle. Other sentences included additional relational information depicted, for example, by a small triangle above, below, or beside a rectangle.

The participants were presented 80 different sentences varying in length, repeated 40 times, for a total of 3,200 instances of correct sentences. Periodically they were tested with pairs of alternative sentences from which they were to choose the correct one. In a second phase, they were tested for learning of similar sentences that contained new instances of the different word classes, but presented only in verbal contexts without the referents; in addition, they were questioned about their use of visual imagery during this second phase.

The results were striking. Participants in the words-only condition showed essentially no learning in the initial learning phase and in the second phase when they transferred to new sentences. Participants in the syntax correlated referent condition, however, showed excellent learning (far above chance) in both the first phase and in the second phase when they learned new instances in verbal contexts. The visual imagery test showed that the participants did not necessarily have the referent pictures in mind when tested for verbal-contextual learning.

The authors concluded that semantic referents and imagery are necessary for initial learning of syntax. Subsequently, the syntactic class membership of new words can be learned in a purely verbal context, without reference to pictures and sometimes without imagery, using the existing syntactic framework. They noted, too, that the results were consistent with predictions from the dual coding analysis of syntax learning as expressed in the aforementioned quotation. The autonomous intraverbal learning of grammar after the initial imagery-mediated phase presumably is based on a combination of known processes, including responding on the basis of similarity of specific items and grammatical structure to prior instances in episodic memory (e.g., Brooks & Vokey, 1991; Vokey & Higham, 2005), imitation of adult speech, spontaneous rehearsal ("echolalia"), and reinforcement of appropriate speech.

I said that I put half my monopoly money on imagery. After Moeser and Bregman's experiment and concordant analyses by others (e.g., Hebb, Lambert, & Tucker, 1971; Macnamara, 1972; Olson, 1970), I'm now willing to bet real money on the imagery side of the grammar-acquisition hypothesis, with the other half of the money (more or less) going on the verbal side as stated generally in the dual coding hypothesis and interpreted more specifically in terms of empirically supported mechanisms. Discussion of this complex topic is continued in the context of language and the brain (Chapter 8) and evolution of syntax (Chapter 13).

Bilingualism

This is an important theoretical and practical problem because bilingualism (or multilingualism) is the norm in many countries, and in any case, immigrants to a country that uses a different language from their own are faced with the problem

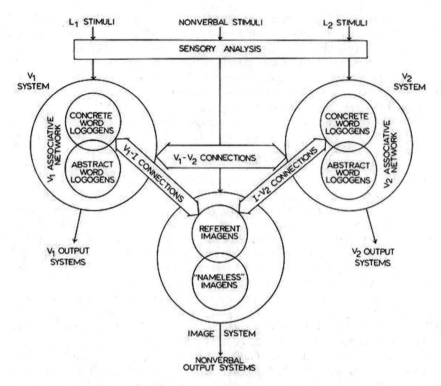

FIGURE 4.11   The bilingual dual coding model showing, for languages L1 and L2, the corresponding verbal systems (V1 and V2), and their connections with each other and with the imagery (I) system. From Figure 1 (p. 391) in Paivio, A., & Desrochers, A. (1980). A dual-coding approach to bilingual memory. Canadian *Journal of Psychology, 34*, 390–401. Copyright 1980 Canadian Psychological Association. Reprinted with permission.

of learning the new one.[17] A bilingual version of DCT has been applied to problems of bilingual memory and second language learning (Paivio, 1986, 1991c; Paivio & Desrochers, 1980). The structure of the theory is modeled in Fig. 4.11.

---

[17]Motivational and cognitive factors are equally important in foreign language learning. For example, Gardner and Lambert (1972) found that measures of positive attitudes and motives regarding French as a second language and measures of language aptitude correlated .37 and .42, respectively, with second-language learning scores. The pattern of results has been replicated and extended in various ways (e.g., Gardner, Tremblay, & Masgoret, 1997), including identifying French language anxiety as a (negative) predictor of French language achievement. The anxiety measure is conceptually similar to the audience anxiety measures discussed earlier, but related specifically to language learning contexts. Further elaboration on the fascinating and extensive research on motivational/attitudinal factors in second language learning is beyond the scope of the present review, which focuses on bilingualism and the cognitive aspects of DCT.

The notable differences from the general DCT model are the separate logogen systems for two languages (L1 and L2) and the direct connections between them. The connections are assumed to be between translation equivalents. The model also shows that concrete word logogens from the two languages are connected to a common imagen system, which is an alternate route for translation of concrete words. The theory specifies further that there could be connections to separate and shared imagens, depending on the way the two languages are learned. Learning the two languages in the same context (e.g., more or less concurrently in the same country) would result in more shared imagens, whereas learning in separate contexts (e.g., at different ages and/or different countries) would result in some differences in referential imagens for L1 and L2. This hypothesis is a DCT interpretation of the distinction between compound and coordinate bilingualism (see Paivio, 1991c). The assumption of direct connections between L1 and l2 has been the most controversial part of the theory, with the alternative being the familiar common coding approach, which in this case states that translation is mediated by common conceptual representations. Numerous implications of the theory and related evidence are reviewed in the cited sources. Here I summarize results concerning bilingual memory and second language learning.

The reasoning in the case of bilingual memory was that translation equivalents such as *horse* and *cheval* are functionally independent and additive for a French–English bilingual. The hypothesis was tested using French–English bilinguals as participants (Paivio & Lambert, 1981). In one experiment, pictures, French words, and English words were flashed one at a time; between items, the participants wrote down the English name of each picture (thereby entailing imaginal-verbal dual coding), translated each French word into English (bilingual dual coding), and copied each English word (monolingual coding). They were then asked unexpectedly to recall the English words they had written down. Participants in a second experiment saw only a series of English words accompanied by cues that prompted them to (a) image to one third of the words (quickly sketching each imaged object), (b) translate one third into French, and (c) copy the remainder. They too were given an unexpected memory test, but in this case, they were asked to recall the English words they had seen during the coding task.

Figure 4.12 shows that recall in both experiments was highest for items in the verbal–nonverbal dual coding condition, next for translated items, and lowest for copied items. What is important here is that the bilingually coded items were recalled about twice as well as the monolingually coded (copied) items, supporting the hypothesis that the two language codes were independent and additive in their joint effect on recall. The further increase with verbal–nonverbal dual coding is strong evidence for the image-superiority addendum to the additivity hypothesis described earlier in the episodic memory section; that is, pictures or images contributed more to recall than did an additional verbal code. The findings directly support for bilingual DCT. The results have been replicated using French–English bilinguals (Vaid, 1988) as well as Japanese–English bilinguals (Taura, 1996).

The aforementioned evidence for verbal dual coding effects does not necessarily mean that imagery was absent in the translation and copy conditions. Because the words were concrete, participants could have imaged spontaneously to some

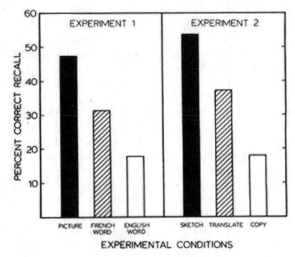

FIGURE 4.12   Incidental free recall scores for English words that bilingual
subjects in Experiment 1 had generated by naming pictures, translating French
words, and copying English words.; and for presented English words that subjects
in Experiment 2 had coded by sketching the referent, translating, or copying.
Reprinted from Figure 1 (p. 536) in Paivio, A. & Lambert, W. E. (1981), "Dual
coding and bilingual memory," *Journal of Verbal Learning and Verbal Behavior,*
20, 532–539. Copyright 1981, with permission of Elsevier.

words, although not as surely as when they were explicitly prompted to image. An
experiment using abstract words (Paivio, Clark, & Lambert, 1988) completed the case
for dual coding: bilingual repetitions using abstract translation equivalents (e.g., truth-
veracité) also showed additive effects, but overall recall was lower than for concrete
translation equivalents, which presumably were more likely also to evoke imagery.
The theory is consistent as well with effects of imagery-based techniques in second
language learning, and specifically, motivated relevant experimental tests. These are
reviewed in Chapter 19 in the context of educational applications of DCT.

A study by Reynolds and Glucksberg (in press) tested predictions from certain discourse models in regard to comprehension of "propositional" and "spatial" bilingual
texts, with supportive results that also turned out to be consistent with bilingual DCT.
The propositional text referred to conditional object relation (e.g., "if models wore a
red shirt, then they would have to wear a green scarf") that presumably depended on
the language of presentation (in this case, Russian or English) for comprehension. The
spatial text referred to visual-spatial relation (e.g., "red dolphins were swimming
behind green dolphins on the right side of a boat") that presumably are represented
visuospatially and thus understood independent of the language of the text. In bilingual DCT terms, the propositional text depends relatively more on processing by the

separate verbal systems of each language whereas the spatial text depended more on processing in a common imagery system accessible to both languages. Reaction times showed that bilinguals answered questions about the propositional text faster if the questions were in the same language as the text they read. However, they performed equally well at answering questions about the spatial text whether the language of the questions and the text they read was the same or different. These language-dependent and language-independent results are as would be expected from the bilingual dual coding model.

This concludes the description of the basic principles of DCT and the adaptive functions of the postulated systems. I have touched on other theories along the way. The next chapter evaluates some of the more prominent theoretical alternatives (including the discourse models alluded to earlier), after which I resume elaborations and extensions of DCT in neuropsychological and evolutionary contexts,

CHAPTER FIVE

Other Representational Species

We are now set to compare DCT with other theoretical family members, some of which have already been mentioned. The species metaphor implies that theories survive and evolve according to their explanatory and predictive fitness—their capacity to save the phenomena in their target domains. This simply restates the constructive-empiricist philosophy of science that guided dual coding research and theory (Chapter 2). The same fitness criteria can be applied to other representational theories. I first summarize the empirical case for DCT as the reference theory, then present examples of three classes of theories that differ more or less from DCT in their representational assumptions and empirical scope. The first alternative class has come to be called embodied cognition because the theories are grounded in the body's interactions with the world. DCT is fully embodied according to that definition. Then I review "disembodied" computational approaches that share the single-code assumption that was the thematic contrast to DCT in the preceding chapters. Finally, I identify hybrid theories that combine features of embodied and disembodied theories in different ways and degrees.

THE EMPIRICAL CASE FOR DCT SUMMARIZED

We saw in the last chapter that DCT focused initially on memory but expanded over the years to accommodate an increasingly broad range of phenomena. Within a decade after the theory began to take shape, it accounted for more than 60 specific empirical facts that could not be explained by any single code theories without the addition of ad hoc assumptions (Paivio, 1983a). The categories of supportive findings, with the number of independent specific effects in parentheses, included (a) imagery-concreteness effects of language on memory and other phenomena (11), (b) picture versus word effects (8), (c) effects of coding instructions (7), (d) symbolic comparison effects (6), perception-imagery functional similarities (8), mental rotations (3), modality-specific interference (6), individual difference effects (3), neuropsychological evidence (4), and subjective report data (3, Paivio, 1983a). A

116

few years later, in a review of my 1986 volume, *Mental Representations*, Lockhart (1987) concluded, that despite reservations, "it is difficult not to concede the book's major point: The available data demand something better than common coding theories have been able to provide. With a deep empirical volley, Paivio's new book places the ball firmly in the other court" (p. 389). The preceding chapter in this volume shows that subsequent volleys by single-code-process competitors, especially in the memory court, have been successfully countered by dual coding experiments. The results of those studies and others in the literature (e.g., functional brain data described in subsequent chapters) further buttress and add to the empirical foundations of multimodal DCT. Let us review and update the comparative empirical–theoretical picture.

EMBODIED REPRESENTATIONS

"There is a movement afoot in cognitive science to grant the body a central role in shaping the mind" wrote Margaret Wilson (2002, p. 625) in her review of theories of embodied cognition, which emphasize the role of sensorimotor systems and their interaction with the environment in shaping cognition, and thereby contrasts with the view of mind as an abstract information processing system. Embodied cognition is recognized generally as old wine in new bottles. Wilson mentioned such notable vintages as Piaget and J. J. Gibson. Older cognitive oenophiles will recognize such labels as the motor theories of thought from the cellar of the late F. J. McGuigan, semantic representations as patterns of internalized response components derived from overt reactions to things (Osgood), and cell assemblies (Hebb) grown from perceptual-motor experience, to name a few. Wilson examined diverse claims by recent proponents of the approach. My aim is to compare DCT with a few conceptual relatives according to shared and distinguishing features.

All of the perceptually-grounded theories of syntax summarized in the preceding chapter are partly related to DCT. These include the cognitive language theories that emphasize the basis of language in nonverbal perceptual scenes, actions, and imagery (e.g., Lackoff, Langacker); McNeill's theory of the relations between language, gestures, and imagery; Strømnes's version of linguistic relativity in which syntactic differences across language families correspond to differences in perceived relations among referent objects; and the highly similar patterns that Denis found between descriptions of perceived and imagined scenes. Still others stress the relation between language and internalized, nonverbal motor activity associated with objects and situations—how language processing is affected by their "affordances" (Glenberg, 1997) or dynamic movement patterns that become part of their meaning, much as in Osgood's theory. These embodied theories nonetheless differ from DCT in that they do not draw on the structural and functional differences between verbal and nonverbal representational systems that lead to predictions and explanations of concreteness–abstractness effects, picture– word differences, and all of the other phenomena that are assumed to result from the separate and cooperative activity of dual coding systems. In addition, many of the theories allude to schema or related abstract notions in the conceptual mix, although without the detailed emphasis we find in the following example of embodied theory.

Barsalou's Perceptual Symbol System Theory

Barsalou (1999) theorized that knowledge is grounded in perceptual symbol (PS) systems derived from perceptual-motor experience. During perception

> association areas in the brain capture bottom-up patterns of activation in sensory-motor areas. Later, in a top-down manner, association areas partially reactivate sensory-motor areas to implement perceptual symbols ... Through the use of selective attention, schematic representations of perceptual components are extracted from experience and stored in memory ... As memories of the same component become organized around a common frame, they implement a simulator that produces limitless simulations of the component ... Once established these simulators implement a basic conceptual system that represents types [and supports] categorization, productivity, propositions, and abstract concepts, thereby implementing a fully functional conceptual system ... while avoiding problems associated with amodal symbol systems (Barsalou, 1999, p. 577).

Barsalou's (1999) theory is obviously similar to DCT in its general emphasis on the sensorimotor origins and multimodal basis of knowledge. The theory also touches on the distinction between verbal and nonverbal representations and their interplay in cognition. Thus, the perceptual simulators become associated with simulators for words, and these simulators can activate each other to produce perceptual simulations (e.g., imagery) or linguistic simulations (e.g., candidates for spoken sentences). The linguistic symbols "index and control simulations to provide humans with a conceptual ability that is the most powerful of any species" (Barsalou, 1999, p. 592). So far so good–the PS simulators correspond functionally to the interconnected and interactive logogens and imagens in DCT. The differences stem from the greater abstractness of representational structures and processes in Barsalou's theory, which (in my view) complicate its explanatory and predictive potential.

Abstraction begins with a schematicity assumption concerning perceptual symbols (the representational units of the theory), which carries through all other hierarchically organized structural and processing levels of the theory. Perceptual symbols result from selective attention to isolated aspects of perceptual information and its storage in long-term memory whereby meaningful, coherent aspects are selected and other aspects are filtered out (Barsalou, 1999, p. 583). This is abstraction in the sense that perceptual detail is taken away, leaving a schematic residue of some kind as the perceptual (memory) symbol. Thus the symbols do not represent "individuals" (specific objects or events) but contain only schematic aspects. They are "componential, not holistic" although, in a reversal of the abstraction process, the symbols "get organized into a simulator that allows the cognitive system to construct specific simulations of an entity or event in its absence (analogous to the simulations that underlie mental imagery)" (Barsalou, 1999, p. 590). For example, color might be removed from a perceived ball, leaving a schematic symbol for the object class, then added back to produce an image of a colored ball. This is a variant of the componential feature approach to cognitive representations already discussed in Chapter 3, and we shall see presently that it entails the same problems.

Abstracting further, "a simulator also contains an underlying frame that integrates perceptual symbols across category instances [and a] potentially infinite set of symbols that can be constructed from the frame" (Barsalou, 1999, p. 586). "Together, a frame and the simulations it produces constitute a simulator" (Barsalou, 1999, p. 590). The evolution of a category frame is illustrated using the hierarchical perceptual symbols for a car to which is added a second car, and so on, resulting in an expandable "car frame". Further symbol compounding results from adding schemata, mental models, and concept to the abstract conceptual mix. Schemata are similar to simulators in that they involve "deep" generative mechanisms that produce an infinite set of (specific) surface images. Mental models are "roughly equivalent" to surface-level simulators. Concepts arise from perceptual input via perceptual symbols and are thus equivalent to simulators in the theory.

There is no quarrel with the idea of a hierarchically organized representational system. As detailed in Chapter 3, DCT imagens also are hierarchical structures, but they reflect their perceptual-motor origins more concretely and directly than their simulator cousins in PS theory. Thus, imagens are not schematic structures from which larger symbol ensembles (frames, categories) are somehow constructed component by component. They are derived directly from perceptions of objects and scenes in which parts are hierarchically organized. In visual imagens, the parts are available but not necessarily accessible simultaneously. We have different imagens for different category exemplars, such as the different cars and car parts we have experienced over the years. Our memory images ("simulations") of them vary in activation probability, detail, and so on, according to recency and frequency of the experience with the individual cars, but they retain their individuality. Theoretically, we do not construct an integrated system of perceptual symbols that constitute a car frame as described by Barsalou (1999), or relatedly, a car concept, although we have learned to draw or describe such schematic cars. In DCT, the symbolic designations are found in the many-to-many referential relations between imagens and logogens that correspond to objects and words. Particular exemplars come to "stand for" categories, and schematic exemplars are created by conventional agreement (e.g., as studied in the science of semiotics). Similarly, new words have been and are being invented to name parts, wholes, or sets of objects.

The essential theoretical difference is that PS representations result from decomposition of perceptual wholes into schematic components, which are then reassembled into holistic entities in long-term memory, whereas DCT representations are isomorphic, holistic copies of modality-specific objects and events. The "proof," as stated in Chapter 3, is that such recognizable entities as faces cannot be constructed piecemeal without models to copy. The stored models would have to be either exemplars of objects and their parts, or features and compositional rules for generating corresponding perceptual models. Accordingly, we need either specific exemplars for every face we can identify and image, or a mind-boggling set of feature-rule descriptions to recognize faces and construct their images bit by bit from modality-specific stuff. DCT adopts the exemplar solution. We see later how the brain might handle the same problem.

Another familiar theoretical construct in PS theory that is not shared with DCT is the "proposition," which, in its classical sense, is the most abstract and amodal of all. Barsalou (1999) used perceptual symbol systems to "implement" propositions and perceptual systems thus become disembodied, or alternatively, propositions become embodied (reified). Barsalou's aim in any case is to redefine propositional functions in terms of the "core properties of perceptual symbol systems." So redefined, the proposition can be construed relative to various situations, including memory, where input items are categorized and encoded propositionally, and established in long-term memory. This redefinition might buttress the proposition as a psychological concept for some, but in my view, it further weakens the embodied status of Barsalou's theory. It certainly distances it from DCT both theoretically and empirically. For example, it is hard to see how propositional encodings could predict or explain the ubiquitous and powerful effects of concreteness and imagery variables in memory tasks.

The dual coding view also relates concepts to images, but only partly. Consider the following study (Katz & Paivio, 1975), in which participants learned to associate nonsense syllable surrogates for concepts with instances of the concepts. The syllables corresponded to concepts that had been rated as easy to image (e.g., a four-footed animal) or difficult to image (e.g., an optical instrument). The main result was that easy to image concepts were attained more readily than difficult to image concepts, and the learning of the easily imaged concepts was further facilitated by instructions to use imagery. These findings support an ancient view (also presumably Barsalou's) that at least some concepts can be represented as images. This would not be the case with abstract concepts such as truth, although they could be illustrated by images (e.g., George Washington and the cherry tree),

The relevant point apropos of Barsalou is that even the images associated with concrete concepts are likely not generated from categorical simulators-frames, or abstract imagens. They are more likely generated from concept names, as in the case of the Katz–Paivio rating procedure for obtaining high- and low-imagery concepts. Of course, concepts can be defined as perceptually derived simulators as they are in Barsalou's theory, but my dual coding preference is to view concrete concepts as juxtapositions of referentially related imagens and logogens, and abstract concepts largely as the relation between the concept name and its verbal associates. Concept is thus related as well to category. Both are abstract in the same sense that the underlying representations can generate many different "simulations" of a concept or a category—many different chair names and images, for example—in a probabilistic fashion.

Kosslyn's Visual Imagery Theory

Stephen Kosslyn (1980, 1994) developed methods for measuring a variety of dynamic functions of visual imagery. The processes were described by analogy with a television set that permits an image to be generated on the (mental) screen and then operated on by processes that scan across the image, zoom in on details, cut from one image to another, rotate the image, and so on. Kosslyn originally intended to develop a formal, computational theory in which images are generated from propositional descriptions and operated on by computer-like commands. I suggested (Paivio, 1986, p. 51) that Kosslyn's experiments show nicely that complex images can be generated from verbal descriptions, which are not conceptually equivalent to propositions even in his approach. More generally, propositions play no essential role in the theory and they were simply assumed for the sake of the computational agenda. Fortunately, the assumption did not constrain the empirical tests and outcomes. Kosslyn subsequently decided that the computer metaphor is an inappropriate basis for a theory of imagery and focused instead on investigating brain correlates of imagery, although he still relies on computational descriptions in that context. The result in any case is the most comprehensive brain-based theory of visual imagery yet proposed. It is not, and was not intended to be, a complete neuropsychological theory that covers language and cognition generally. Relevant aspects of Kosslyn's theoretical and research contributions are discussed in the subsequent chapters on DCT and the brain. The main point in this context is that his theory and research focus on the structural and functional characteristics of nonverbal imagery whereas the dual coding approach always highlights the cooperative interplay of verbal and nonverbal systems.

DISEMBODIED REPRESENTATIONAL THEORIES

Verbal mediation theories evolved into abstract and amodal propositional theories with the emergence of computational models of psychological phenomena in the 1960s. The approach motivated Pylyshyn's (1973) mind's eye critique of imagery. He proposed a propositional alternative that started out as a notational device for describing mental images. This later changed into a reified concept in which the image is "depicted" as a compact descriptive (sentence-like) structure in keeping with Pylyshyn's eventual commitment to a "strong equivalence" (literal) view of the mind as a computational device (for references and discussion, see Paivio, 1986, pp. 45–47). The move to disembodied cognition was complete.

The approach spawned debates but few direct tests of the implications of the descriptive substitute for imagery. Pylyshyn's (1981) only testable alternative to imagery was the hypothesis that participants in imagery experiments have tacit knowledge about the expected results and behave accordingly. The argument is plausible in some instances but not others. For example, it was shown that participants cannot predict the typical outcomes of many imagery experiments (Denis & Carfantan, 1985). When participants can do so, there is no empirical basis for arguing that the tacit knowledge is in the form of abstract computational mentalese. It is more plausible and testable to argue that the knowledge is verbal. Other experiments (Intons-Peterson & Roskos-Ewoldsen, 1989) demonstrated that such sensory-perceptual features of objects as weight, color, and numerosity affect performance based on modality-specific images of those objects in predictable ways. The results could not be easily explained by demand characteristics or tacit knowledge related to the experimental tasks. For example, as in the Denis and Carfantan (1985) study, an independent group uniformly mispredicted the outcome of one experiment. In any case, Pylyshyn never presented positive evidence for his descriptive theory of imagery. Moreover, even the rational arguments he used to defend it are untenable, or so I have argued (Paivio, 1986, pp. 47–51). One of these is the claim that explanatory parsimony is a major advantage of computational theories, which is not compelling for reasons already discussed in relation to Barsalou's componential approach. The one salutary effect of Pylyshyn' s arguments was that they provoked experimental responses which showed that common code theories could neither predict nor explain many imagery and dual coding effects without resorting constantly to post hoc assumptions.

It is relevant to mention that Pylyshyn never explicitly discussed his approach as an alternative to DCT, and he has not responded to empirical or logical appraisals of his position from the dual coding perspective, although he was aware of them from the outset because I was one of the (acknowledged) readers of a prepublication draft of his "mind's eye" article, in which I wrote copious comments and questions. So, too, for the published versions of the critiques (e.g., Paivio, 1977, 1986). Without evidence to the contrary, I assume that Pylyshyn's computational approach simply cannot deal with the facts on which DCT is based. Be that as it may, the so-called "imagery debate" focused on experiments by Stephen Kosslyn and his colleagues. The debate goes on, with Pylyshyn (2003) now characterizing images as abstract internal symbols and arguing that neuroscientific data do not support the parallels between visual imagery and perception that would justify Kosslyn's depictive interpretation of imagery. Kosslyn, Ganis, and Thompson (2005) have responded with counterarguments and further data supporting the depictive view of visual imagery.

Kintsch's Propositional Schema Theory

We have already touched on shortcomings of the schema approach to memory (Chapter 4). The concept has been more generally evaluated and compared to DCT (e.g., Sadoski & Paivio, 2001; Sadoski, Paivio, & Goetz, 1991). Walter Kintsch's evolving schema-based theory of text comprehension can be described as a disembodied DCT. Earlier versions up to 1983 (reviewed in Paivio, 1986, pp. 225–227) showed that highly conventionalized story texts have well-defined, coherent structures when transformed into propositional descriptions. The propositions are organized hierarchically according to degree of overlap (repetition) among propositions, defining the text's referential coherence at different levels. The theory included a situation model that the hearer or reader constructs about the situation denoted by the text. The situational representations can be experienced as imagery, which especially makes the theory similar to DCT. The difference is that the situational model has the same propositional format as the rest of the theory, which means that the experienced imagery must be an epiphenomen because its functional properties are defined by the propositional description. This is yet another example of logical dual coding (Chapter 1), entailing a complete mapping in this case between formal propositions and the imaged situation. This is unlike the probabilistic relations between modality-specific verbal and nonverbal representations in DCT.

I suggested (Paivio, 1986) that Kintsch's model could be recast in dual coding terms by analyzing text coherence in terms of the verbal associative structure of the text (which has precedents in linguistic theories) along with the properties of imagery aroused by the text. Tests of the alternatives were contemplated but not initiated because the earlier models were modified. Later versions (e.g., Kintsch, 1998) were also analyzed and compared with DCT (Sadoski, 1999; Sadoski & Paivio, 2001, pp. 133–135). A major contrast is that the propositional base still cannot explain the powerful role of imagery in the comprehension process, most particularly its contribution to the superior memorability and comprehensibility of concrete over abstract language. The phenomena strain Kintsch's theory just as they strain other propositional theories.

The difference between Kintsch's model and DCT is clearly shown by their treatment of meaning. The two approaches share the assumption that the meaning of a word, sentence, or text is given by the set of relation between it and everything else that is known. However, Kintsch operationalized this idea formally in terms of a high-dimensional semantic space in which words, sentences, and texts are represented as vectors. Meaning is a position in this space, which is defined relative to all other positions that constitute the space (e.g., Kintsch, 2000). Such a semantic space is constructed using a procedure called Latent Semantic Analysis (LSA), a computerized technique developed by Thomas Landauer and his associates (e.g., see Landauer & Dumais, 1997).[18] The measurements are co-occurrences of thousands of different words drawn from thousands of documents. The data and computational program compute semantic distances between words. Kintsch modified the analysis to take account of syntax—specifically, overlap of "semantic neighborhoods" between sentence arguments and predicates. Kintsch found that the model behaved in much the same way as people do (e.g., Glucksberg, 1998) in the interpretations of literal polysemous sentences and metaphors. Later, Kintsch (2004) incorporated propositions, schema, and LSA analysis in an updated model of text comprehension.

An important point to notice is that the LSA approach is entirely verbal, a computational analogue of verbal associative techniques for measuring direct or mediated relation between words. George Kiss's (1975) model, described in the preceding chapter, is an appropriate comparison because it also was based on a large sample of word associations that were used, among other things, to compute similarity between words in terms of their "distribution vectors," that is, patterns of associative overlap. Such techniques can't generate complete theories of meaning or knowledge because they exclude nonverbal knowledge and imagery. They could be used to compare co-occurrences and distribution vectors for concrete and

---

[18]Landauer (1999) explicitly described LSA as a disembodied learning machine, thus justifying its inclusion in the present section.

abstract words. This could yield differences in the verbal-contextual neighborhoods of the two classes of words, but it has already been shown that such contextual differences do not account for the large effects of concreteness on memory and comprehension of verbal materials ranging from phrases to long text passages.

HYBRID REPRESENTATIONAL THEORIES

This class of theories combine aspects of embodied and disembodied theories in different ways and proportions. They are therefore partly like DCT. The exemplars here are mental models, triple-code theories, and an evolutionary model of representational systems that resembles DCT, with a crucial difference.

Mental Models

All cognitive theories are mental models in the dictionary sense of a model as a simplified description of a system, process, and so forth, that is presented as a basis for theoretical or empirical understanding. Theoretical models vary from being concrete and isomorphic with respect to the represented phenomena (e.g., imagery theories) to being very abstract and nonisomorphic (e.g., propositions). DCT is isomorphic in the double sense that the nonverbal and verbal systems mirror the structural and functional properties (affordances) of things and language. The theory is hierarchical in that it includes assumptions and hypotheses that can be represented as specific DCT models.

Johnson-Laird (1983) popularized the concept of mental models. He contrasted his approach with formal theories of inferential thinking according to which deduction is a syntactic process like a formal proof based on propositions. The mental models approach states instead that it is more like a semantic process that searches for counterexamples. Johnson-Laird, Herrmann, and Chaffin (1984) also criticized semantic network accounts of meaning. They argued that network theories, such as the Collins and Loftus (1975) spreading activation model described earlier (Chapter 3), are deficient because they "lack connections to the world. They only provide connections between words ... The meanings of words can only be properly connected to each other if they are properly connected to the world" (Johnson-Laird et al., 1984, p. 313). Mental models provide that connection and in that regard, the approach is similar to DCT. Notably, however, Johnson-Laird (1995) did not reject propositions but treated them as "input to a process that constructs a mental model corresponding to the situation described by the verbal discourse ... akin to one created by perceiving and imagining events instead of merely being told about them" (p. 999).

Mental models could thus be viewed as propositionalized DCT, which leaves us with uncertainty about what propositions are, where they come from, and what they do that differs from verbal statements that generate images of things and situations. And mental models are only "akin" to percepts and images, so what are they? The theory assumes that different numbers and types of models are needed for different deductive reasoning problems (e.g., statements with connectives, quantifiers, or disjunctions). The models generally entail transformation of stated premises into propositional notations from which conclusions can be drawn. Diagrams constructed from statements are especially helpful in some cases. Johnson-Laird's theory has been empirically productive and explanatory. An example is that children in particular find it easier to understand "if-then" sentences when the problem is expressed in terms of specific exemplars rather than more abstract descriptions as in formal logic (Digdon, 1986). The finding clearly is as expected from DCT as well as mental models.

Triple-Code Theories

John Anderson is a prolific and innovative contributor to computational theory and research in cognitive science. Early on, he and Gordon Bower (Anderson & Bower, 1973) proposed a propositional single code theory of human associative memory. Later, Anderson (1978) contrasted propositional and dual coding representations for mental images. Arguing first that propositional and imagery-based theories are not distinguishable because the latter could be expressed in propositional terms and vice versa, he concluded that a distinction could be made in terms of the number of codes that need to be postulated to account for the data. He subsequently opted for a triple coding model (Anderson, 1983) that included nonpropositional phrases and spatial images along with the propositional base that remains the workhorse of his theories.

The difficulty of accounting for modality-specific effects in picture–word studies prompted other cognitive psychologists (e.g., Snodgrass, 1984) to propose three-level models in which the first two levels correspond essentially to the general features of DCT and the third is an abstract, amodal system that could be accessed from either of the two modality-specific systems. The potential advantage is that the surface representations could be used to "save" the same memory phenomena as DCT and in addition the propositional system could account for whatever observations seem unexplainable in dual coding terms. This approach falls short because the more complex theories do not include any principled way of predicting when the common code will be used. It has instead been a "default" function that comes into play if dual coding fails. We shall see in Chapter 9 whether neuropsycholgical evidence can help resolve this common coding issue.

Bickerton's Dual Representational-Systems Model

Linguist Derek Bickerton (1990) proposed what is essentially a dual coding model of representational systems that is the basis of thinking. The model was presented in the context of Bickerton's views on the evolution of language, which makes it especially relevant to this volume, although it was not intended as a psychological theory with testable implications other than a general one that differentiates it from DCT. More about that in a moment, and more later (Chapter 12) about Bickerton's views on the evolution of language.

The model in Fig. 5-1 shows a primary representational system (PRS) and a secondary representational system (SRS) that correspond generally to the nonverbal

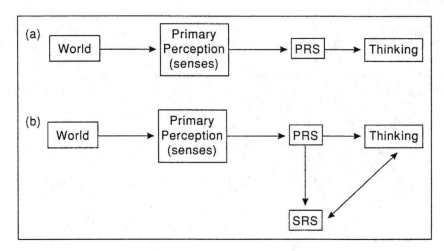

FIGURE 5.1 Bickerton's model of the primary representational system (PRS), secondary representational system (SRS), and their relations to thought. From D. Bickerton (1990). *Language and species*, University of Chicago Press, p. 200. Copyright 1990 The University of Chicago Press. Reprinted by permission.

and verbal representational systems of DCT. The arrows in the model suggest connections from PRS to SRS and from both to thought processes. The text makes it clear that SRS also influences functions of the PRS. I interpret the connections of both systems to thinking as meaning that both contribute to performance in cognitive tasks, as do the nonverbal and verbal systems in DCT. The theories differ, however, in their interpretation of the separate and cooperative roles of the two systems in thinking. Conveniently, Bickerton's (1990) analysis directly implicates imagery:

> ... it is quite conceivable that thought processes conducted entirely in linguistic terms could, before arriving at conscious levels, be translated into imagery. Alternatively, images could simply take the place of words, but they would still have to be organized by syntactic mechanisms. In either case, if the elements of thought, whatever they might be, were not arranged in some type of formal structure in which their relations to one another were lawful and predictable, but instead they were just allowed to swirl around as they pleased, then no serious thought processes could be carried through. Thus, either some mysterious additional way of structuring thought is available, or syntax discharges the function. (p. 200)

Several related points distinguish this view from DCT. First, Bickerton favors a linguistic-dominance interpretation of thought: thinking is disorganized unless controlled by linguistic processes or by some mysterious other process. In DCT, however, nonverbal experience itself is organized and lawful (probabilistically predictable). Language structure reflects that organized perceptual-motor experience, although developing a partly autonomous syntactic capacity of its own (Chapter 4). Second, Bickerton assumes a dependency relation from language to PRS as expressed in imagery, whereas DCT assumes functional independence with a capacity for probabilistic activation in either direction. Finally, Bickerton's linguistic control system is a formal, syntactic mechanism fashioned after a Chomskyan model. This formalization makes the SRS similar to propositional approaches to cognitive representation, which is why Bickerton's model qualifies as a hybrid representational species.

Apropos of the empirical connection, as already mentioned, Bickerton's theory was not intended as a predictive psychological theory. It lacks essential specific assumptions and hypotheses. This is notably so in regard to the overriding cognitive domain of memory, which is not discussed. That aside, Bickerton has important things to say about language evolution, which we evaluate in Chapter 13.

II

DUAL CODING
THEORY AND
THE BRAIN

CHAPTER SIX

Introduction to Dual Coding Theory and the Brain: A Brief History and a Brain Primer

Recent advances in the neurosciences and the theme of this volume call for an updated review of neuropsychological evidence relevant to DCT. Such evidence has always been interesting to the extent that it bears on theoretical assumptions and hypotheses based originally on behavioral data alone. The most obvious example is the verbal–nonverbal distinction that showed up in neuropsychological data before the development of DCT. However, neuropsychology did not reveal the specific functional properties of the two systems, such as their independence and additivity in memory tasks, the integrative mnemonic capacity of nonverbal imagery coupled with the redintegrative power of concrete retrieval cues (the conceptual peg effect), and so on. Neuropsychology alone cannot reveal such capacities unguided by prior behavioral studies, but it can provide independent convergent evidence that might confirm or challenge conclusions from behavioral data. Reciprocally, DCT can be useful to neuropsychology as a systematic framework for analyzing and interpreting the brain-behavior relations that form its empirical domain.

This approach comes with a caveat: in seeking DCT-relevant brain evidence, I do not thereby intend to develop a neuropsychological DCT of mind. Such a theory would require defining all of the dual coding principles and assumptions in neuropsychological terms. We shall see that such a redefinition is not feasible now, for many behavioral predictions and explanations based on DCT have not yet been tested neuropsychologically. It is not even certain that a brain-based theory of mind is possible according to William Uttal's (2005) recent analysis of the empirical and logical problems associated with attempts to bridge the mind-brain gap. Be that as it may, I shall view the brain data mainly as further evidence that might support or challenge one aspect or another of dual coding as a psychological theory of mind.

The analytic review is presented in four chapters, beginning here with a historical sketch of key issues and basic facts about the functional brain that serve as a

131

background for the subsequent chapters. Chapter 7 focuses on brain correlates of the structural and processing assumptions of DCT. Chapter 8 similarly describes neuropsychological observations that map onto the adaptive functions of dual coding systems that were defined behaviorally in Chapter 4. Finally, Chapter 9 explores neuropsychological solutions to two persistent issues—how common-coding alternatives to dual coding systems might be represented, and how the brain binds the parts of perceived and remembered objects into larger wholes.

The discussions continue to be guided by the general empiricist assumption that mental representations retain the modality-specific properties of the experiences from which they are derived. Some neuropsychologists also argue for such specificity whereas others opt for abstract, amodal processes, operating especially at a semantic level of cognition. In brief, the neuropsychological literature recapitulates all of the issues that plagued psychological interpretations of cognitive phenomena. My hope is that the issues will be illuminated if not resolved by a DCT spectral analysis.

HISTORICAL BACKGROUND

The general distinction between verbal and nonverbal processing regions of the brain was supported by default in the late 19th century by observations of language deficits resulting from unilateral brain damage. The most influential person in this regard was the French neurosurgeon, Paul Broca. In 1861, he reported the results of an autopsy on the brain of a man who had lost the ability to speak. Broca discovered a massive lesion in a region of the left hemisphere just anterior to the central fissure. This discovery, along with the finding that comparable injuries to the right hemisphere did not disrupt speech, prompted the conclusion that the left side of the brain is dominant for speech. A decade after Broca's discovery, Karl Wernicke observed a patient with a lesion farther back in the temporal-parietal area of the left hemisphere. The patient could not respond meaningfully to spoken language, although he retained the ability to speak. Wernicke concluded that this particular area was specialized for language comprehension. The left hemisphere thus came to be seen as dominating both expressive and receptive language functions. Furthermore, "The scientific world generalized [the dominance view] to conclude that the left hemisphere was dominant not only for language but for all psychological processes. The right hemisphere was seen as a mere relay station ... an unthinking automaton. From pre-19th century whole-brained creatures, we had become half-brained" (Levy, 1985, p. 38).

Imagery deficits resulting from brain damage were also described as early as 1883 by Jean Martin Charcot, but imagery was generally ignored in neuropsychological discussions of cognition even when the insufficiency of language was recognized. For example, as recently as 1967, in a thorough review of the neurological basis of language, Eric Lenneberg distinguished language from cognition in general but did not even mention imagery as a possible basis for cognition. Instead, he interpreted cognition in terms of activity in systems analogous to Chomskyan linguistic deep structures, for which there was no direct neuropsychological evidence.

Electroencephalographic (EEG) brain-scan research on imagery in the 1940s and other psychophysiological studies in the 1960s did little to change the linguistic bias, perhaps because they did not clearly distinguish imagery from verbal or other cognitive processes. For example, Herbert Simpson and I were hopeful that pupillary reactions could be related to imagery variables in a uniquely informative way. One finding was that the pupil dilated more when participants imaged to abstract than to concrete words (Paivio, 1973; Paivio & Simpson, 1968). Because it was known that dilation reflects cognitive effort, our results confirmed what we already knew from behavioral studies, namely that it is harder to image to abstract than concrete words, but imagery was not thereby distinguished from other effortful cognitive processes.

The neuropsychological path to imagery and dual coding began to open up in the 1960s when Brenda Milner and her associates at the Montreal Neurological Institute discovered that lesions to the right hemisphere (but not the left) selectively impaired performance on such nonverbal tasks as memory for faces and nonsense figures. It was a short step from such findings to the view that nonverbal imagery is controlled primarily by the right hemisphere just as language is apparently controlled by the left. This interpretation received qualified support from subsequent studies (reviewed in detail by Paivio & te Linde, 1982) of how well each hemisphere deals with dual coding variables in perceptual and memory tasks. The left hemisphere continued to dominate when the tasks involved verbal material or verbal processing strategies. Conversely, the right hemisphere tended to be favored when nonverbal material or strategies were used. Among the relevant qualifications were the findings that (a) the left hemisphere as well as the right contribute to performance in some imagery tasks; (b) the usual left hemisphere dominance in word recognition is stronger in the case of abstract than concrete words, as if logogens for the latter are available in both hemispheres; (c) pictures of familiar objects are recognized equally well by both hemispheres and much better by participants with high imagery ability, suggesting that representations necessary for visual imagery are available in both hemispheres; and (d) different areas within each hemisphere are implicated in different effects so that, for example, the temporal lobes and the hippocampus in particular were especially important in memory tasks, and the parietal area of the right hemisphere in mental rotation and other nonverbal cognitive tasks. We shall see in Chapters 7 and 8 that these findings and interpretations have been confirmed and extended over the years.

THE FUNCTIONAL BRAIN

Understanding the factual and interpretive story requires some familiarity with the functional brain and its neural pathways. The following descriptions should be adequate for our purposes (for more details, see, e.g., Gazzaniga's edited volume on cognitive neurosciences, 1995, 2000; Kolb & Whishaw, 2001; and relevant brain entries on the Internet).

Figure 6.1 shows (a) a lateral-surface view of the left cerebral hemisphere, and (b) a medial (front-to-back inside) view of the right hemisphere and central structures of the brain. The labels identify the main functional areas of interest to us. The

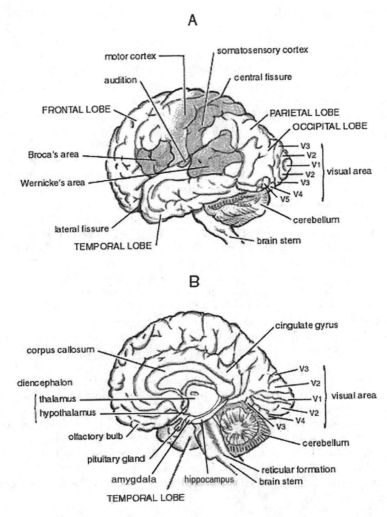

FIGURE 6.1   Lateral view of the left hemisphere (A) and medial view of the right
hemisphere (B) with labeling of general regions involved in cognitive
phenomena. Brain images adapted from Figure 8.17 (p. 293) in B. Kolb and I. Q.
Whishaw (2001), *An introduction to brain and behavior,* New York: Worth
Publishers. Copyright 2001 by W. H. Freeman and Company/Worth Publishers.
Reprinted with permission of the authors and the publisher.

areas of the cerebral cortex are partly demarcated by major fissures or clefts and the
sinuous folds (gyri) between them. The left and right hemispheres are separated by
the longitudinal fissure. The frontal lobe on each side is separated from the parietal

lobe by the central fissure. The temporal lobe is partly separated from the rest of the brain by the Sylvian fissure. The occipital lobe at the back of the brain is less clearly demarcated by anatomical features but is nonetheless functionally distinct. These general areas were further divided into more specific areas on the basis of cellular structure by Korbinian Brodmann early in the 20th century. It is useful, occasionally, to refer to these numbered Brodmann areas, so they are shown in Fig. 7.2 in the context of brain research on imagery.

The cortical regions have primary and secondary sensory and motor areas. The primary cortical areas for vision, audition, and somasthesis (body sensation) have point-to-point projections from their receptors so that the elementary sensory information is organized topographically, or, in the case of audition, tonographically (i.e., tones are represented in different places). The secondary areas organize the information into larger and more functionally meaningful chunks (including divisions into verbal and nonverbal representations within and between hemispheres) that become further elaborated in other areas.

Visual sensory areas are located in the occipital lobe, from where neurons project to parts of the temporal and parietal lobes, and elsewhere. The auditory areas are in the temporal lobes just under the Sylvian fissure and adjoining areas—for example, Wernicke's area for speech reception is just posterior to the primary auditory area in the left hemisphere and a homologous area for music is in the right temporal lobe. The somatosensory areas run down the parietal lobes just behind the central fissure. Each side receives sensory messages from all parts of the body, mostly on the opposite side, including sensations of touch, warmth, cold, and itch from the skin surface; deeper sensations of pressure from below the skin, the muscles, and joints; sensations from the visceral organs; and pain. The mapping is organized topographically in the way depicted by the familiar brain homunculus, with legs represented at the top of the cortex and head and its parts at the bottom.

The motor area is in the frontal lobes just anterior to the central fissure. It is topographically organized with respect to the body in the same way as the somatosensory cortex. The primary motor area sends out motor commands to specific muscles. The secondary motor area integrates neural information from elsewhere in the cortex so that motor commands and responses are organized. For example, Broca's area in the lower part of the motor cortex in the left hemisphere is presumed to organize motor neurons in the face area of the cortex so that they activate the muscles that produce speech. The organizational functions of the secondary motor areas are guided by input from the secondary sensory areas (hence the term *sensorimotor systems*). The sensory-motor connections are especially close in the case of the reciprocal activation of somatosensory and adjacent motor areas, as when we identify objects by active touch. Similarly, identifying an object visually often requires exploratory eye movements that are controlled by the visual contours of the object. Auditory input from speech initiates correlated motor patterns when we repeat what is said—and even if we don't, according to the motor theory of speech perception.

In addition to the aforementioned cortical areas, the medial view in Fig. 6.1 shows other forebrain and midbrain structures with important cognitive and motivational functions. The thalamus is a way station that shunts information from all of the senses (except smell) to the cortex. The superior and inferior colliculi are other way stations (not shown in Fig. 6.1) that relay visual and auditory information to the cortex via different parts of the thalamus. The hypothalamus lying below the thalamus controls hunger and thirst, and plays a part in various motivational and emotional reactions. The hippocampus deep inside the temporal lobe and the adjacent parahippocampal cortex have important functions in emotional and other memories. The amygdala is at the very heart of emotional experiences and reactions. The cingulate cortex along with the amygdala, hippocampus, and hypothalamus are the principal structures that define the limbic system, mainly because of their functional roles in emotion and motivation. Not shown in the figure are the basal ganglia, an important group of forebrain structures just below the neocortex, which have motor functions that include language. Other specific structures and regions are mentioned when we elaborate on what has been outlined here.

All the areas and structures are richly interconnected, many by parallel pathways that enable neural activity to flow in opposite directions between regions. The two hemispheres are connected by a large bundle of fibers called the corpus callosum and by smaller pathways. The length of the pathways varies greatly. They are very short in the case of the tightly correlated sensory and motor systems that control haptic touch. A longer neural bundle called the arcuate fasciculus connects Wernicke's area in the auditory cortex with Broca's area in the motor cortex of the left hemisphere. The classical view was that this pathway conducts messages unidirectionally from Wernicke's to Broca's area. It is now known that there is a bidirectional connection between these areas, probably through the arcuate fasciculus and other cortical and subcortical pathways (Matsumoto, Nair, LaPresto, Najm, Bingaman, Shibaski et al., 2004). A layer of the primary visual cortex sends information along a single axon back to the thalamus to be further processed, and so on. Among other things, as we shall see in Chapter 7, such birectional neural pathways concretize the imagen-logogen referential interconnections that are so crucial to DCT.

PATHWAYS INTO AND OUT OF THE BRAIN

The following summarizes the conventional view of the sensory pathways from receptors to the cortex, the kinds of processing centers and representations encountered along the way, and pathways to response systems. The conventional story provides a useful background for the subsequent dual coding interpretations, and it also raises unresolved issues that are addressed in Chapter 9. The visual system gets the lion's share of the attention.

Visual Pathways

The neuropsychological view is that the brain organizes visual input into neural representations that "stand for" and mediate our reactions to seen or imagined objects and events. How this is done is a mystery story that begins with the retina. The retina creates a raw topographic map of the world from visual information using spatially distributed cone-shaped and rod-shaped receptors that respond to light. Color sensitive cones are clustered at the fovea whereas brightness sensitive rods are distributed throughout the retina. The separate distribution could be thought of as an initial (coarse-grained) level of sensory organization. The rods and cones activate bipolar cells that mediate input to ganglion cells, the axons of which collect together at the optic disk and then leave the eye to form the optic nerve. The ganglion cells consist of large cells and small cells. The large cells (called magno or M cells) receive their input primarily from rods and are sensitive to movement but not color or fine detail. The small (parvo or P cells) receive their input primarily from cones and are sensitive to fine detail as well as color.

The location of objects corresponds to cells activated in different parts of the retina, but the details of shape, color, and movement are not put together in the retina to form the objects we see. Instead, the photosensitive properties and arrangement of cells provide elements for the brain's organization of neurons into structures that are activated when we perceive objects with such properties. Ganglion cells are sensitive to luminance changes so that adjacent cells detect edges of objects. Movement successively stimulates different sets of retinal neurons. On–off responses of different P cells to different wave lengths provide the information for perception of object color further on in the brain.

We follow the retinal information to the brain along the geniculostriate pathway (other pathways are mentioned later). Figure 6.2 shows a top-down view of the divided pathways from the two eyes. The anatomical arrangement in humans is such that all of the information in the right visual field (what is seen to the right of the fixation point) goes to the visual cortex of the left hemisphere and everything seen in the left field goes to the right hemisphere. This occurs because the right field stimulates receptors on the nasal side of the right eye and the lateral side of the left eye, and the neural pathways come together in the left hemisphere. The converse occurs with information from the left visual field. The divided information eventually gets distributed in each hemisphere by crossing over along the bundle of neurons called the corpus callosum and other structures that connect the two sides of the brain. This arrangement is important because it helps explain defects in visual perception and imagery that result from damage to visual structures in one or the other side of the brain. In "split brain" patients, whose corpus callosum has been severed accidentally or surgically (to control intractable epileptic seizures), the visual information remains divided so that each hemisphere receives only (or mostly) the information from the contralateral hemifield, although it takes special tests for a patient to become aware of the deficit. Finally, the anatomical arrangement also permits visual information to activate one hemisphere more strongly than the other even in normal individuals when stimuli are flashed briefly to one visual field or the other. Data relevant to DCT come from all of these sources.

Returning to our journey along the geniculostriate pathway, the lateral geniculate nucleus (LGN) is an intermediate work station located in a dorsal region of the thalamus. All of the P ganglion cells and some of the M ganglion cells go to the LGN, where they produce a transformed retinotopic map. The LGN projects in turn to the primary visual cortex (variously called Brodmann's area 17, striate cortex,

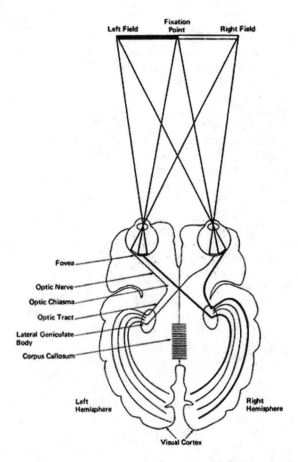

FIGURE 6.2 Classical view of the visual pathways showing complete crossing of the pathways so that all of the visual field to the left of the fixation point stimulates the right visual cortex whereas the right visual field stimulates the left visual cortex.

or V1), which reproduces a retinotopic map of the world.[19] This information is segregated within V1 into color, form, and movement, each represented by neurons that are individually sensitive to the different attributes. The information remains segregated in adjacent visual region V2, where it is represented in different zones. Other regions of the visual cortex send different combinations of information along

---

[19]V1 has six different layers that are conventionally distinguished from different visual areas using Roman numerals. Input comes to layer IV of V1 and then goes to other layers, vertical columns, etc.

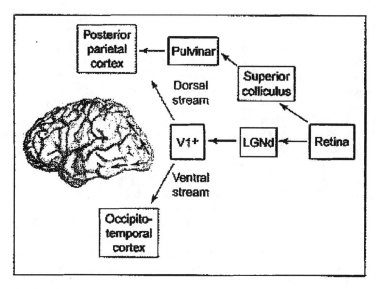

FIGURE 6.3   Schematic representation of the two streams of visual processing in humans. The retina sends projections to the dorsal part of the lateral geniculate cortex in the thalamus (LGNd), which projects in turn to primary visual cortex (V1). Within the cerebral cortex, the two streams arise from early visual areas (V1+). The ventral stream projects to regions in the occipito-temporal cortex, whereas the dorsal stream projects to the posterior parietal cortex. The posterior parietal cortex also receives visual input from the superior colliculus through the pulvinar. On the left, the pathways are shown on the surface of the brain by arrows that indicate a series of complex connections. From Figure 1 (p. 204) in M. A. Goodale and D. A. Westwood (2004), *Current Opinion in Neurobiology, 14*, 203–211. Copyright 2004, with permission from Elsevier.

two different streams (described in the next paragraph) to the temporal and parietal lobes, creating complex information about objects and how to handle them. Thus, the neurons of the inferior (lower) temporal region respond to complex visual stimuli such as faces or hands. Complex objects are represented by the activity of many neurons that combine such features as orientation, size, color, and texture. As if that weren't enough, similar processes occur in individual neurons and their combinations within each of the sensorimotor systems and across systems to give us the seemingly unified multimodal world we know. Relevant neuropsychological data come later in Chapter 7.

As mentioned earlier, there are two neural output pathways, or streams, from the primary visual cortex, a ventral stream going to the temporal lobes and a dorsal stream going to the parietal lobes. The two streams are schematically represented and described in Fig. 6.3. Ungerleider and Mishkin (1982) characterized these as "what" (ventral) and "where" (dorsal) systems, specialized respectively for object and spatial vision. Goodale and Milner (1992; Milner & Goodale, 1995) accepted the object function of the ventral stream but proposed that the dorsal stream is specialized for visually guided action. Thus, "the networks in the ventral stream permit the formation of perceptual and cognitive representations of the enduring characteristics of objects and their relations" (Milner & Goodale, 1995, p. 42), whereas the dorsal stream controls such actions as reaching for and grasping seen objects. The spatial function described by Ungerleider and Mishkin is determined partly by the visuomotor functions of the dorsal stream, because eye movements in particular are needed to locate the positions of objects in space. Moreover, the dorsal and ventral systems may converge and cooperate to provide representations for higher forms of spatial cognition such as "the manipulation of spatial images, thus allowing for the use of spatial maps" (Milner & Goodale, 1995, p. 110). This duplex vision hypothesis has been supported by a variety of behavioral and neuropsychological findings over the years (e.g., see Goodale & Westwood, 2004).

Mishkin and his colleagues modified their original position to take account of visuomotor control as an important function of the dorsal stream (Milner & Goodale, 1995, p. 23). Thus, there is agreement that visual perception includes a functional division between systems for object perception and visuomotor control. This distinction can be included in DCT as an elaboration of the visual sensorimotor system. We have already seen that DCT has always emphasized the role of motor processes in visual processing of scenes and text, as well as in scanning and manipulation of spatial images. The theory was silent on the location of the motor "component" and lacked evidence that it is functionally independent of the visual sensory component. The theory can now be explicit on both questions because of the Goodale–Milner hypothesis and elaborations of it by others. For example, Jeannerod and Jacob (2005) attributed more complex visual-motor processing capacities to the parietal lobe than suggested by the two-visual-systems hypothesis, including perception and imagery of spatial relations among objects, and representation of skilled actions such as use of tools, musical instruments, and sports materials. The next chapter reviews evidence for the relevant functions of the visual systems.

Auditory and Somatosensory Pathways

Sensations from the ears and body are similarly relayed via the thalamus to their primary cortical areas, with subsequent activation of adjacent and more remote areas involved in auditory and haptic perception of meaningful sounds and objects. Thus, there are primary and secondary cortical areas (A1 and A2) for audition such that neural input from speech sounds, for example, first reach A1 in a relatively unanalyzed form and then get analyzed further in the adjacent area A2, especially on the left side (for right-handed people), known as Wernicke's area. Like the visual cortex, the auditory cortex also has two distinct pathways, a temporal pathway for identifying objects by their sound, and a dorsal pathway for directing movement to an object's location.

The somatosensory (or somasthetic) system consists of nerve pathways going from receptors in the skin and deeper body areas to the brain via the spinal cord and important junctions (including the thalamus) along the way. Sensations can be experienced passively, as when one's cheek is touched, but we are more interested in the dynamic haptic perception that enables one to identify objects by manipulating them (Gibson, 1966, p. 100). That clearly entails cyclical sensorimotor activity—sensations arising from the skin and from muscles and joints when an object is manipulated. However, studies of passive and active contact with objects (raised letters) show a similar discriminative capacity by the somatosensory system. Neural activity patterns during tactile perception reveal levels of representation like that in vision and audition, so that an isomorphic representation of a tactile stimulus pattern at the periphery of the somatosensory cortex is transformed into a less isomorphic pattern at "deeper" levels (Johnson, Hsiao, & Twombly. 1995). At some level or levels, the neural patterns become memory representations, for recognition in any modality depends on memory for the pattern.

We are now ready to explore the parallels between the representational and processing distinctions described in DCT and the kinds of functional distinctions that emerge from brain studies. The next chapter deals with issues concerning the nature and brain locations of representational units and structures of different kinds, activation pathways between and within structural systems, transformation of representations, and the status of the concept of consciousness in the cognitive neurosciences. The exploration prepares us for subsequent analyses of the adaptive functions served by dual coding brain systems, and then a final search for modality-free neural representations and solutions to the unsolved neuropsychological binding problem.

CHAPTER SEVEN

The Multimodal Dual Coding Brain

This chapter reviews neuropsychological evidence for the multimodal dual coding structures and processes described in Chapter 3. Because objects and language both come in visual, auditory, and haptic (feelable) modalities, it follows that there must be corresponding modality-specific neural representations that are activated during perception, memory, thought, and communication. Figure 7.1 illustrates this multimodal dual coding model for the concept "telephone"—the word and the object telephone as seen, heard, and felt (including the feel of the object and of movement pattern when one writes the word). The corresponding neural representations presumably are located in different areas of the brain. Also shown are pathways that connect the representations to the perceptual world and to response systems, so that words and telephones "out there" can be recognized and responded to in appropriate ways. As well, there are connecting pathways between the different modalities of verbal and nonverbal representations, so that telephones as seen, heard, or felt can be named, and conversely, their names can evoke images in any modality. A more comprehensive DCT model would also include associative connections between the three sensorimotor modalities of telephone words or objects, and connections to representations for other concepts, so that activity can spread associatively within verbal or nonverbal systems.

An even more complete model would incorporate the purely nonverbal sensorimotor systems for taste, smell, temperature, pain, emotion, and sexual arousal (a complex mix of sensations, emotions, and behaviors controlled by hormones as well as cortical activity). All of these are linked conceptually to motives and needs. We don't think with these nonverbal systems, we think about the needed goals and how to attain them using the cognitive dual coding systems just described. For example, we have a rich vocabulary for describing tastes, smells, and emotions, and imagining them in response to descriptive language (mediated usually by memory images of objects and situations associated with the sensations). There are also neural representational systems for the nonverbal symbolic activities of music and dance, which share some of the rhythmical and prosodic patterns of language and

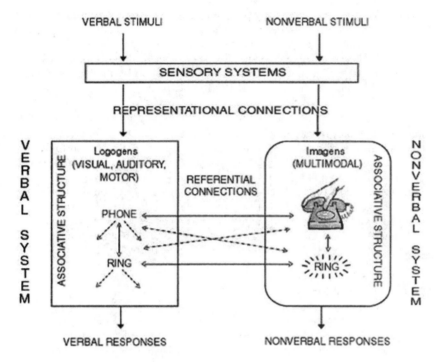

FIGURE 7.1   Depiction of the multimodal dual coding model showing visual, auditory, and haptic logogens and imagens corresponding to the names and sensorimotor properties of the object "telephone."

become connected to it in song and written choreography (again implicating dual coding). We saw behavioral evidence that the systems are functionally independent, across both verbal–nonverbal and sensorimotor dimensions. We consider further evidence for such functional independence from selective deficits that follow localized brain damage and from activation of specific brain regions as revealed by brain scans.

NEURAL REPRESENTATIONAL UNITS

Imagens and logogens are the psychological representational units of the multimodal DCT model. Analogous units, such as engrams, cell assemblies, and brain models, have been proposed by neuroscientists to account for perceptual recognition and memory. The following quotation sums up the neuroscience argument:

'How can we instantly recognize a familar object? Probably because, in the brain, we already have a model of that object which is activated through vision. Similarly, we can quickly comprehend what we hear because the brain is likely to contain a model representing the meanings of the sounds we encounter. And we can probably carry out complex movements so easily and accurately because the cerebellum provides a model of what is to be moved. Such internal models provide an attractive explanation for the brain's subtle cognitive and control mechanisms...' (Ito, 2000, p. 153).

The point here is that such internal models can be viewed as brain correlates of different sensorimotor modalities of imagens and logogens. The difference is that the latter concepts were developed in the context of multimodal DCT and refer to a more comprehensive phenomenal domain than do the neuropsychological equivalents, which are more limited in scope.

In what follows, I first review neuropsychological evidence on the explanatory role of imagens and logogens in both perception and imagery, as well as their multimodal varieties, internal organization, and where they might be "housed" in the brain. Then I describe the network of pathways by which they appear to be activated.

The Imagen Neural Family

According to DCT, imagens are used in both perceptual and imagery tasks. Psychologists have long assumed that visual perception and imagery involve the same systems (early proponents were identified in Paivio, 1971b). This basic idea has ample support from recent neuropsychological studies. For example, psychologist Stephen Kosslyn (1994) used brain scans to identify particular brain regions that are activated in both visual perception and imagery tasks. The matching is incomplete because, for one thing, perception is initiated directly by a stimulus object whereas imagery is aroused indirectly by language and other stimuli. Partial sharing results in interactions of the two kinds of processes, so that prior imaging helps perception more than perception helps imaging in certain tasks, whereas perception helps imaging more than vice versa in other tasks (Michelon & Zachs, 2003). Neuropsychological results confirm such differences by showing that perception and imagery are dissociable. For example, some brain-damaged patients are more impaired in imagery than perception (e.g., Riddoch, 1990) and others show the opposite pattern (e.g., Behrmann, Winokur, & Moscovitch, 1992; Michelon & Biederman, 2003). Brain scan research has shown similarly that auditory perception and auditory imagery are dissociable (Bunzeck, Weustenberg, Lutz, Heinze, & Jancke, 2005).

The dissociations can be explained by assuming that perceptual recognition and imagery entail activation of different sets of neural representations. In perception, an object directly activates an internal representation from a relatively small set by something like a template-matching process whereas in imagery the object name indirectly activates an imagen from an indefinitely-large set of imagens of the same class. The final outcome is determined by contextual cues and recent or remote past experiences with similar objects. We could say that the representations are selected from different sets of imagens, or use different terms such as "iconogen" (Attneave, 1974) or "pictogen" (Morton, 1979) for the object- and picture-activated representations as suggested in Chapter 3. By whatever name, the subtle representational distinction is one hypothesis that could account for the imagery-perception discord.

A salient feature of objects and scenes is their part-whole hierarchical structure. We see pupils within eyes within faces, petals within flowers within fields, and so on. We can identify smaller or larger parts. As explained in Chapter 3, form is essential to part-whole perceptions whereas size is less essential—we can identify a small toy elephant as well as a large one from the shapes of parts or the whole. Color helps but it is embedded within shapes (we do not identify an amorphous patch of yellow as a ripe banana). Changes in movement and shape (as in the sinusoidal wiggle of a snake) characterize some objects, but shape remains essential. Even the perception of biological motion in on and off pattern of points of light depends on the location of the points relative to one other (Johansson, 1973). The hierarchical composition of object form characterizes our imagery as well. In either case, we somehow integrate the parts into larger wholes or disintegrate them into their parts—we can see (or image) the forest or the trees. This means that the underlying representations, the imagens, must have analogous hierarchical structure; or, more accurately stated, a functional structure that allows for integration or dissociation of the seen or imaged parts of wholes.

Earlier we saw evidence from an experiment by Pritchard, Heron, and Hebb (1960) that stabilized retinal images (e.g., of a square) first appear as wholes and then disappear entirely or in part, leaving only disconnected lines. They then reappeared in whole or part. This was consistent with Hebb's theory, according to which neural cell assemblies that represent lines and whole patterns could fatigue and recover. The important point for these purposes is that the results suggest hierarchical neural representations made up of dissociable parts.

More direct evidence comes from perceptual and imagery deficits due to brain damage. Visual object agnosia is a neuropsychological impairment in which patients fail to recognize objects in the visual modality. Particularly relevant is a variant called integrative agnosia (Riddoch & Humphreys, 1987), in which a deficit in object recognition is coupled with a failure in organizational processes (Behrmann & Kimchi, 2003). For example, the patient is unable to detect a simple shape in a pattern background. Oliver Sacks's (1985) famous visual agnosic, "the man who mistook his wife for a hat," seems to fit that diagnostic category at least in the sense that he could not put together a familiar face from the parts.

The agnosias presumably result from damage to ensembles of neurons in particular brain areas. Evidence that the representational unit for visual images may be as small as a single neuron comes from brain stimulation research. Itzhak Fried and his colleagues (Kreiman, Koch, & Fried, 2000) recorded impulses from single neurons using microelectrodes implanted in brains of severe epileptics to find the focus of their seizures. The recordings were taken while the patients viewed pictures of faces, household objects, spatial layouts, cars, animals, food, famous people, and so on. An important aspect of the procedure is that each picture was repeated several times, which, from the DCT perspective, means that quite specific imagens were reinforced. Later, recordings were again obtained when the patients were asked to imagine previously viewed pictures in response to their names. The result was that neurons in various areas of the brain responded selectively while viewing or imaging different pictures. Some neurons responded similarly during vision and imagery of the same pictures (of Mona Lisa, for example), whereas others were activated only during vision and others only during imagery. The authors were especially struck by the selective activation during imagery, presumably reflecting retrieval of picture information from memory, or maintenance of the visual image during imagination.

DCT helps explain the pattern of results. The repetition of each picture during initial viewing resulted in storage of form-specific imagens. Participants were likely to name at least some of the objects to themselves. When later asked to imagine the pictures, the imagen neurons corresponding most closely to those activated during picture naming were most likely to be reactivated by the names alone. Other pictures, however, might have been less reliably named at input and the imagery request would then be likely to activate any old imagen of the named class (one of many cars, for example) from long-term memory, accounting for the instances in which the same neurons apparently were not activated during perception and imagery.

Although it is recognized that populations of neurons are generally involved in cognition, the selective and varied coding of seen and imaged objects is an astonishing feat for individual neurons because it is hard to understand how they could represent a complex object. How do they contribute to the organization of component parts into a whole? This is a puzzling accomplishment feat for neurons even when they work as ensembles. Later, in Chapter 9, we reconsider the standard assumptions about neural coding along neural streams before addressing this neural binding problem in detail. The problem applies not only to dual coding imagens but to logogens as well.

The Logogen Neural family

Recall from Chapter 3 that John Morton introduced the logogen as a single abstract concept that accounted for visual and auditory word recognition, and later expanded it into multimodal forms (Morton, 1979). The same evolution occurred in the case of logogen's conceptual twin, the lexical representational unit. It used to be thought by some that there is a single lexicon (mental dictionary or word store) that could be accessed from speech or print. However, such findings as dissociations of auditory and visual word recognition compelled the conclusion that there must be at least two lexicons (e.g., Coltheart, 2004), although it can still be argued that the functional lexicon is derived from speech and that we can read for meaning only by going through a phonological loop, that is, recoding print as inner speech. Then there is the auditory-motor distinction: We clearly have auditory and motor language systems, but does this justify postulating corresponding logogen systems or lexicons, as opposed to a single auditory-motor phonological system? My early view was that the functional verbal system is auditory-motor in nature (Paivio, 1971b, p. 56). Similarly, and with more empirical justification, Sheila Blumstein (1995) proposed that there is common phonological representation of the sound structure of words that informs both speech production and speech comprehension.

Blumstein's (1995) rationale for a common, abstract lexicon is based on evidence that the classical distinction between Broca's aphasia and Wernicke's aphasia is wrong. The aphasias are not divided neatly into production disorders localized in frontal motor areas and receptive disorders localized in posterior areas. The patterns of aphasic errors suggest instead that the speech production system extends to posterior regions, including the temporal and parietal lobes, and that the speech perception system extends to anterior regions as far forward as the frontal lobe. Hence the argument that production and reception are mediated in part by activation of lexical representations that are phonological in nature, based on phonemic features (inferred from phonemic errors, e.g., "pears" produced or heard as "bears") and syllables (e.g., hearing "auger" as "argue").

Nonetheless, production ultimately requires activation of a motor program corresponding to a word whereas perception requires the initial activation of the primary auditory cortex and superior temporal gyrus (Wernicke's area)—evidence for separate organized representations that define motor and auditory logogens. The loss of ability to read (alexia) following brain damage while retaining the ability to understand speech is evidence that we have distinct visual logogens, although the nature of their neural representation is controversial, as we shall see. There is evidence, too, that spelling is mediated by visual word images (Sadoski & Paivio, 2001, pp. 164–66). For example, children learn spellings of nonsense words such as *tib* significantly faster when they are asked to imagine the correct spellings than when they heard the words spelled (Ehri & Wilce, 1979). And so, it seems that we must have auditory, motor, and visual logogens—and perhaps others related to writing (disturbed in agraphia) and deaf sign language. The term *gestemes,* introduced in the context of human–machine interface systems (e.g., Hundtofte, Hager, & Okamura, 2002), would be an appropriate label for haptic logogens. Perhaps we also have abstract lexical representations of the kind proposed by Blumstein, but alternatively, the abstract functions may fall out of rapid interactions of auditory and motor logogens of different sizes, using bidirectional activating pathways between auditory and motor areas.

Peter Milner's (1999, p. 59 ff) analysis of auditory and response engrams corresponding to words is relevant to the aforementioned issues. His analysis parallels conventional associative accounts, but is expressed in neurological terms. The sound components of the word "cat" must be represented by a pattern of modified synapses. The sequence entails synaptic modifications between neurons so that the phoneme /k/ activates /a/ and inhibits other neurons. The combined aftereffects of /k/ and /a/ then influence the pattern of firing and synaptic change to /t/, facilitating recognition of the entire word. The ability to pronounce the word requires that the sound comes to trigger the corresponding sequence of motor responses. This is facilitated by an inborn tendency for infants to mimic mouth movements and then to mimic those movements and sounds when spoken to. As they babble, babies learn the sensory consequences of their own vocal responses (cf. echolalia as a language learning mechanism in behavioristic accounts). As evidence, Milner noted that users of sign language show increased blood flow, measured by positron emission tomography (PET) scans, in Broca's area when viewing or generating words. Milner's analysis translates readily into a DCT account of the formation of auditory and motor logogens. The correspondence includes his suggestion that the order of occurrence of sound components cannot easily be extracted from the sound sequence alone. The sounds must instead be associated with sequential motor activity.

All of these interpretations of verbal representational units remain neuropsychologically speculative and general. No one has yet seen a logogen, word engram, or lexical representation as directly as electron microscopy has enabled us to see the structure of the gene, the unit of heredity and evolution (discussed further in Chapter 10). Although they are elusive in that specific sense, logogens and imagens serve as names for verbal and nonverbal representations that are activated somewhere in the network of neural pathways as interpreted by DCT.

NEURAL PATHWAYS TO DUAL CODING REPRESENTATIONS

The following sections provide an overall neuropsychological picture of dual coding systems. The model of independent verbal and nonverbal systems that are made up of specific sensorimotor components continues to guide the analytic description. We consider more recent evidence for independent representational units in the context of their locations along different pathways that also are functionally independent. An earlier review (Paivio, 1986, pp. 264–269) summarized some of the evidence available at that time for system independence. For example, processing deficits can be verbal or nonverbal (differentially affecting perception of pictures and printed words) when sensory modality does not change (both are visual in this case), and vice versa; and these independent effects can occur via direct or indirect neural pathways.

The pathways were described in Chapter 3 as different levels or types of interconnections and activation processes. Perceptual activation refers to relatively direct activation of imagens and logogens by nonverbal and verbal stimuli (e.g., pictures or words). The referential level refers to cross-system activation of imagens by logogens, or vice versa. Associative activation refers to indirect activation of representations through connections within each system, nonverbal and verbal. The description needs elaboration to take account of differences in sensory modality as well (e.g., visual and auditory words both can evoke visual images). Ideally, one hopes to find evidence that neatly fits into the structural-processing model. This is difficult because the functional brain structures revealed by brain scans and by patterns of behavioral deficits caused by brain damage generally cut across specific descriptive or diagnostic categories, including those implied by DCT. Despite such difficulties, classical and recent neuropsychological literature contains supportive approximations to the DCT ideal.

As a further orienting reminder, the DCT representations and processes correspond generally to what is conventionally described in terms of semantic memory.

For example, Cree and McRae (2003) mapped categories of knowledge about living and nonliving things as defined by category instances (e.g., cheese is a food, jeep a car) onto category-specific semantic deficits. Semantic dementia is a class of semantic deficits that has been similarly viewed as a window on the structure of semantic memory (Patterson & Hodges, 2000). DCT is partly about semantic memory phenomena as defined in such contexts but it also includes episodic memory information, and its analytic framework is more systematic and specific than most semantic memory models.

Recent neuropsychological studies of semantic memory and meaning have produced masses of data that are remarkably consistent with the basic DCT assumption, namely that cognitive representations and processes retain the modality-specific properties they derived from perceptual-motor experience. For example, reading, producing, or just thinking about names of colors, shapes, actions (or objects that suggest such properties) activate brain regions close to the primary sensory and motor regions that are activated by the real-world attributes and objects (for recent reviews, see, e.g., Cree & McRae, 2003; Martin, Ungerleider, & Haxby, 2000). The DCT analysis describes the direct and indirect neural pathways and representational sites using evidence from brain damage and neuroimaging studies.

Direct Perceptual Activation of Dual Coding Representations

This level refers to relatively direct activation of imagens and logogens by objects and words, respectively. The psychological indicators included judgments of stimulus familiarity and recognition under impoverished exposure conditions (brief presentation, incomplete patterns), which reflect availability and accessibility of imagens and logogens. On the neuropsychological side, damage to the primary sense organs or their afferent nerve pathways completely cut off direct access to already-established representations, or, if occurring early, prevent the formation of representations, in the affected modality. The result is complete or partial blindness, deafness, loss of taste, smell, touch, or temperature sensitivity. Widespread damage to primary cortical areas for the different sensory modalities disrupts activity at that level and interferes with activation of representations downstream. An example in the visual modality is hemianopia: a complete lesion of the primary visual cortex (area V1) on one side results in blindness in the opposite visual field except for some residual low-level capacity that is discussed in a later section. The extent of such effects in any modality depends on how much of the cortical sensory area was damaged.

It is relevant to note in passing that even widespread damage to the primary areas need not preclude indirect activation of already established representations via referential and associative paths. For example, individuals blinded as adults or in late childhood still report experiencing vivid visual imagery. This is not the case with congenitally totally-blind individuals, who have difficulty performing complex visual imagery tasks that cannot easily be done using tactual exploration or imagery in other sensory modalities (Cornoldi, Bertuccelli, Rocchi, & Shrana, 1993).[20] Similarly, after Beethoven became profoundly deaf, he presumably could image music he had previously learned and also create new music in his head (Chapter 18 describes how this could happen). That being said, for the most part, we are interested here in more specific effects of localized lesions downstream from the primary sensory areas.

Direct Pathways to Imagens.   Agnosia ("not knowing") is the relevant diagnostic category for representational level deficits resulting from brain damage, especially because the deficits correspond nicely to normal difficulties in recognizing unfamiliar or degraded inputs. Agnosia usually refers to nonverbal stimulus information, and other terms such as alexia are used to describe comparable verbal impairments. Modality-specific agnosias have been identified for all sense modalities, the most-studied being visual agnosias (e.g., see Farah, 1990).

Visual agnosia encompasses impairments in recognition of visual objects, faces, colors, and more. These usually result from lesions close to the primary visual cortex. Theoretically, we seek effects that can be described as damage to visual imagens or pathways to them from the visual cortex. A good start is visual form agnosia because form or shape is essential for object identification according to mental and perceptual comparisons of objects on various dimensions and other data (Paivio, 1978c).

We immediately find definitional problems about what should be included in this category. Lissauer (1890) translated in Shallice & Jackson, 1988) originally distinguished between apperceptive agnosia, which he called "apperceptive mental blindness" (see Luria, 1973, p. 124), and associative agnosia or "associative mental blindness." He defined apperceptive agnosia as a failure to construct a coherent structural percept of an object, as shown by the inability to draw or identify it. In associative agnosia, however, the person could copy a drawing but not identify it or determine its meaning. The distinction is controversial (e.g., Milner & Goodale, 1995), but it can be interpreted in DCT terms. We can say, for instance, that apperceptive agnosia reflects damage to visual imagens or connections to them from the visual cortex, whereas associative agnosia can be redefined in terms of damaged referential and associative connections to imagens.

The operational definition of visual form agnosia is also problematic because identification is usually by naming or drawing the object (where drawing depends

---

[20]The conclusion holds despite brain scan evidence that the primary visual area is activated in people blind at birth when they generate mental images to verbal instructions. Such evidence was recently presented and the issues discussed by S. Lambert, Sampaio, Mauss, and Scheiber (2004). Their blind subjects reported relying on previous tactile exploration of the animals, toys, or descriptions provided by others in order to generate mental representations of animals to animal names. The authors suggested that the involvement of the visual cortex may reflect early brain plasticity and development of sensory substitution as a result of experience with such tasks as Braille reading.

on motor skill). These problems have, however, been circumvented by procedures that do not require naming. For example, Efron (1969) found that a person with visual form agnosia did poorly on a form matching test and also had profound deficits in copying and identifying drawings of common objects and forms. Thus, deficits in verbal identification and copying can reflect representational- level brain damage.

Another problem is that object agnosia generally encompasses classes of objects and specific objects viewed from different perspectives, implying considerable generalization across exemplars and viewpoints (e.g., Chapters 2 and 5 in Milner & Goodale, 1995). Generality would be expected because the lesions are never so localized that they damage a representation for a specific exemplar, although the psychological evidence makes it clear that we must have such representations given the countless number of different objects we can recognize in different orientations, colors, and so on. Thus, in DCT terms, we must have a visual imagen for every individual object we can identify visually within the range of generalization that defines identification, as discussed in Chapter 3. Just how viewpoint independent such imagens are presumably depends on how often an object has been seen in different positions and contexts, resulting in different representational exemplars in the visual imagen system.

The location of visual imagens along the perceptual pathway presumably varies with size and hierarchical complexity of the perceptual object, as well as color and other properties. Color agnosia, for example, is independent of form agnosia in that objects can be recognized from their shapes without any recognition of color. Agnosia for faces (prosopagnosia) always involves right hemisphere damage, which might be accompanied by more general object agnosia. Moreover, electrophysiological recordings from infrahuman primates have shown that some neurons respond to faces over a wide range of size, color, lighting, and so forth (Milner & Goodale, 1995, p. 61), whereas others respond to one view of a face better than to others. In general, the specificity of the coding response increases as the stimulation site moves away from V1 through other areas of the visual cortex and beyond, areas that respond to more complex visual stimuli such as faces and objects.

Two patients studied by Behrmann and Kimchi (2003) provide a benchmark for relatively "pure" visual object agnosia. Both were impaired in naming objects as well as deciding whether a picture depicted a real object. In contrast, both patients performed normally in naming objects presented to them auditorily or haptically while blindfolded. They could also provide rich definitions of the objects they could not recognize. Thus, the deficit in these patients is restricted to the inability to recognize objects visually, presumably reflecting (in DCT terms) damage to visual imagens, located perhaps in the right inferior temporal lobe (the site of the lesion in one patient, not localizable in the other—a site implicated in object recognition by other data, discussed later). A later section focuses on the inability of these patients to integrate the components of objects into wholes.

A neurological patient extensively studied by A. David Milner and Melvyn Goodale (1995; Goodale, 2000) is particularly informative about distinctions within visual agnosia and their independence from other modalities. The patient, DF, is a woman who, at age 34, suffered irreversible brain damage as a result of near-asphyxiation by carbon monoxide. Her visual system was affected so that she could not recognize the faces of her relatives and friends or identify the visual form of common objects or different geometrical shapes. Her perceptual problems appeared to be largely restricted to form vision in that she could identify colors and easily recognize people from their voices or objects when one was placed in her hands. MRI scans showed that the primary visual cortex was largely spared whereas nearby ventromedial regions of her occipital lobe were particularly compromised.

Curiously, although DF could not copy simple line drawings of objects (e.g., apple, book), she was able to produce reasonable representations when asked to draw the objects from memory. When she was later shown her own drawings, she had no idea what they were. The DCT interpretation is relatively straightforward: the damage was to the visual ventral pathway downstream from the primary visual cortex. The imagen system and referential connections from auditory logogens to the imagens were spared so that DF could imagine and draw the named objects. However, referential connections conducting in the opposite direction, from imagens to motor logogens, were damaged so that DF was unable to name objects or their drawings.

What remains puzzling is DF's inability to recognize a named object even in a forced-choice nonverbal test, despite the fact that she can draw the named object. The puzzle can be resolved by assuming that perceptual identification and imagery entail activation of different sets of representations, as described earlier. In perceptual recognition, form-specific imagens (iconogens or pictogens) are activated directly by objects; in imagery, one of many imagens is activated indirectly (referentially) by words. Only the latter pathway is available to DF. As mentioned earlier and discussed further in the subsequent section on "referential processing," this hypothesis also accounts for other cases of dissociation between imagery and perceptual recognition deficits.

The aforementioned pattern of recognition deficits contrasts with DF's ability to use visual information to guide skilled movements. She

> will reach out and grasp your hand when you first meet her. She is equally adept at reaching out for a door handle … She can walk unassisted across a room or patio, stepping easily over low obstacles and walking around higher ones. Even more amazing is the fact that she can reach out and grasp an object placed in front of her with considerable accuracy and confidence—despite the fact that moments before she was quite unable to identify or describe the same object (Goodale, 2000, p. 370).

The informal observations were confirmed by formal testing. The analysis of DF was an important part of the reasoning that led Milner and Goodale (1995) to propose the distinction between vision for action and vision for perception (see pp. 206–207, this volume), the former associated with the dorsal stream projections to the posterior parietal cortex and the latter, with ventral stream projections to the inferotemporal cortex. Milner and Goodale recognized as well that the two streams interact continually in normal perception.

The idea of two streams is useful but insufficient to capture the complexities of object perception in the visual modality. Of course, it was not intended to account for other modalities by which objects are known, all of which are important to the conceptualization of multimodal imagens and the pathways to them. Nonverbal agnosias and brain scan data have also revealed varieties of visual and other modalities of neural representations in different brain regions. Luria (1973, p. 158) described object agnosias associated with occipito-parietal lesions, suggesting that imagens are housed along both visual streams. Recent neuroimaging studies confirm the importance of the inferotemporal cortex in visual object recognition (hence activation of visual imagens), but different subareas of that region and other temporal cortical areas are implicated as well. For example, Beauchamp, Lee, Haxby, and Martin (2003) summarized studies which have shown that the ventral temporal cortex is especially responsive to complex static objects and that different areas within that region respond to different categories of objects. The latter is one kind of finding that has led some researchers to propose the lower areas of the temporal cortex as the site of semantic memory representations, a complex topic discussed in detail in Chapter 9.

The representation sites broaden out when we consider dynamic objects associated with characteristic motions. The medial temporal lobe is responsive to all kinds of visual motion. Areas anterior and superior to it are differentially sensitive to different types of object motion and biological motion. For example, studies of event-related potentials (ERPs) have shown that the superior temporal sulcus (fissure) is sensitive to details of biological motion as fine as the difference between hands seen as opening or closing. Using functional magnectic resonance imaging (fMRI), Beauchamp et al. (2003) recorded brain responses to different types of complex visual motion. Participants were shown video clips of four kinds of moving stimuli, including humans performing different kinds of whole-body movements (e.g., walking), man-made tools (e.g., hammer) moving with their characteristic natural motion, and both human motion and tool motion shown as moving points of light (cf. Johansson, 1973). The fMRI recordings showed that different regions of the temporal cortex "preferred" (responded most strongly to) the different kinds of displays. For example, middle and inferior temporal regions responded strongly to tool videos and point-light displays, whereas superior temporal regions responded strongly to both types of motion. The responses in the latter case were strongest to the video displays, suggesting that the superior temporal lobe (specifically the sulcus) integrates form, color, and motion. Behavioral data showed that the participants reliably recognized the moving patterns as humans or tools, responding more quickly to the videos than to the point-light displays.

Motor processes involved in manipulating objects entail activation of further brain regions. Lesions of the postcentral somatosensory cortex (secondary zones for kinesthetic and cutaneous sensations, affecting movement control as well) can produce haptic agnosia (also called astereognosis, an inability to recognize objects by feel) without damaging visual form recognition (Luria, 1973, p. 173). Such agnosias implicate tactual-motor representations. Imamizu et al. (2000) showed that another motor control structure, the cerebellum, forms representations of precise movement patterns associated with repeated tool use. Their human participants learned to move a computer mouse (the "tool") so that the cursor followed a randomly moving target on the screen. Concurrent fMRI recordings of their cerebellar activity revealed a corresponding acquired internal model (visuomotor imagen?) of the tool use.

The lesion, neuroimaging, and behavioral evidence permit us to conclude generally that different regions of the brain contain representations that are activated by the static forms and dynamic activities of living and nonliving objects, the haptic affordances associated with the latter, and so forth. The evidence lends itself readily to dual coding interpretations in terms of different kinds of visual and haptic sensorimotor imagens and their activation by direct pathways beginning at primary visual and somatosensory cortices and spreading to adjacent regions in which they are housed. I argue later, however, that the brain data have not caught up with what we know about the representational processes from behavioral data.

There is evidence as well for different kinds of acoustic representations and motor components associated with them. These have been most often studied using speech sounds (thus auditory or auditory-motor logogens), a topic that we explore next along with visual and motor representations for language.

Direct Pathways to Logogens. We have already considered evidence for different modalities of logogens. Here we are interested in their direct activation by different modalities of stimuli, uncontaminated by indirect influences via referential and associative pathways. Luria (1973) described cases of acoustic agnosia (sensory aphasia) associated with local lesions of the left temporal lobe, in which the patient had lost the ability to distinguish between syllables with appositional phonemes (e.g., ba-pa) and made acoustic errors in repeating heard words (e.g., saying kolos instead of golos). These can be described as damage to auditory logogens. So too can classical cases of auditory word comprehension problems resulting from lesions in Wernicke's area, which led to that area being regarded as a crucial site for representation of auditory words. In the visual modality, *alexia* refers generally to an impaired ability to read words without affecting the ability to recognize auditory words. Pure alexia is a specific variant in which writing also remains intact. For example, Toronto novelist Howard Engel woke up one morning to find that he could not read the newspaper (S. Martin, 2002). After some rehabilitation, he "was able to do everything," including write, but he could not read what he had written. I shall discuss this syndrome in some detail because, by definition, it should be the clearest neuropsychological evidence for impaired visual logogens or pathways to them. And yet, its "purity" and the reality of its putative form-specific neural substrate have recently been called into question. Let us review the pro and con evidence for the syndrome and its implications for the neuropsychological reality of visual logogens.

Leff et al. (2001) comprehensively summarized the characteristics of pure alexia and the conceptual issues that have exercised theorists. The syndrome was first described as "alexia without agraphia" in 1892 by the French neurologist, Jules Dejerine, who interpreted it as a disconnection syndrome that isolates the "visual word form system" from the rest of the language zone. It is classically associated with a lesion in the left occipitotemporal area, which often extends to the splenium, a posterior region of the corpus callosum. The deficit pattern might include right hemianopia, which compounds the reading difficulty because it particularly affects perception of letters at the end of a word. The lesion disrupts the "normal" reading system in the left hemisphere so that patients characteristically read words slowly letter by letter in a left to right sequence, until the entire word can be read correctly. The overall reading time thus increases dramatically with word length—as much as 4 or more seconds for each additional letter. By comparison, normal readers can read whole words in less than half a second, with almost no increase with word length up to nine letters.

The main conceptual issues concern the "purity" of the core syndrome and interpretations of the pattern of deficits commonly associated with it. Behrmann, Nelson, and Sekuler (1998) reviewed evidence that pure alexia is associated with general visual perceptual deficits. Difficulties in naming nonverbal stimuli, such as pictures and colors, are most relevant here because they involve the same overt responses as reading and have therefore received much of the critical attention in alexia research. The comparisons are directly pertinent to DCT, according to which naming requires a referential crossover between nonverbal and verbal systems whereas reading does not, so that naming and reading should be functionally independent.

Naming is often reported to be either normal or only mildly impaired in alexics, which implies that naming and alexic reading problems are independent in that they might or might not accompany each other. For example, Leff et al. (2001) reported test data for a participant (A. R.) with pure alexia who could not read text and yet named colors correctly, was in the normal range for picture naming, and showed no evidence of visuoperceptual or visuospatial deficit. They commented further that A. R. and some other pure alexics have normal reaction times when reading numbers, which argues strongly against all patients with pure alexia having a low-level visual impairment.

Direct comparisons of reading and naming latencies in normals and alexics also tell us that naming impairments cannot account for much of the severe reading impairment in pure alexia. It has been known for more than a century that adults name pictures and colors slower than they read their printed names (Johnson, Paivio, & Clark, 1996). The absolute latencies vary over studies but the relative difference between the two reactions remains stable. In one study, for instance, both color naming and color-word reading improved across Grades 1 to 9, yet the difference between the skills remained unchanged (MacLeod, 1991). What happens to the reading-naming latency difference in pure alexia? Given their long reading latencies, the cases that have been described as showing little general naming impairment must be able to name pictures or colors faster than they can read their printed names.

Surprisingly, I was unable to find a direct test of this implication in the literature—perhaps the outcome is just too obvious. In any case, the relevant data are available in a study by Behrmann, Nelson, and Sekuler (1998) on the effect of visual complexity on picture-naming latency by pure alexics and normal control participants. The alexics showed a disproportionate-large increase in naming latency as picture complexity increased, which was consistent with the hypothesis that alexia involves a general visual perceptual deficit. The reading-naming latency difference between the two groups can be estimated from graphically-presented latency data for one alexic female (EL) and two normal control participants. A rough averaging of latencies over word length and picture complexity (and familiarity) yielded the following results. For the normal participants, the average latency for naming printed words was about 500 msec (Fig. 2 in the report) as compared to their picture-naming latency of about 900 msec (Fig. 4 in the report). For EL, however, the reading and naming latencies were about 2,700 msec and 1,050 msec, respectively, thus sharply reversing the difference shown by normals. Five additional alexic participants similarly showed much slower reading than naming times (cf. Figures 5 and 6 in the report). These results and others reported in the literature confirm that pure alexia involves a specific reading deficit that cannot be explained in terms of general visual processing difficulties, which alexics might also manifest to some degree.

The syndrome thus provides evidence for the reality of visual word form representations, or logogens, that are concentrated in the occipito-temporal region of the left hemisphere, as has been classically assumed. We are nonetheless left with questions concerning the exact location and size of the critical area, its other functions, and what other areas might contribute specifically to alexic reading problems. Recent data provide some answers but do not resolve all of these questions.

Functional neuroimaging studies by Cohen and his colleagues (e.g., 2002) suggested that a region of the left midfusiform gyrus is the only area that lies in the occipitotemporal cortex where lesions are associated with pure alexia. The authors accordingly view this region as the "visual word form area" that is activated in normal reading and is the critical lesion site in pure alexia. Price and Devlin (2003) rejected this interpretation for two general reasons. First, pure alexics usually have extensive occipital lesions that make it impossible to localize their word reading deficit to a particular area of the damaged cortex. Second, the area is activated by many tasks besides reading (e.g., naming colors and pictures, reading Braille, repeating auditory words). Such results suggest that the left midfusiform area interacts with other regions so that processing involves the whole set of regions or parts of the set in different tasks. Price and Devlin (2003) concluded that "there is no evidence that visual word form representations are subtended by a single patch of neuronal cortex" (p. 473), and that the neural correlates consist instead of a set of interactive regions that are yet to be identified, although assumed in some current models of normal and alexic reading.

Behrmann, Plaut, and Nelson (1998) had proposed just such an interactive theory to explain both the characteristic slow, letter-by-letter reading of alexics and the fact that they nonetheless respond to lexical and semantic variables earlier than they can name whole words.[21] Their occipital lesion results in a fundamental

---

[21]Behrmann, Plaut, and Nelson (1998) contrasted their theory with one proposed earlier by Coslett and Saffran (1994), which assigns a different role to the two cerebral hemispheres in the contrasting effects-the sequential letter-by-letter output pattern is mediated by the left hemisphere whereas a separate reading mechanism in the right hemisphere is responsible for

peripheral deficit that adversely affects whole word reading. Some information is nonetheless propogated to higher level lexical and semantic representations, a process enhanced by repeated letter-level fixations. These higher level representations then feed back to the letter processing level to support further lexical-semantic activations. They presented new data showing that word imageability and word frequency benefit letter-by-letter processing, especially with longer words. The authors comment that their account accords with parallel distributed connectionist models of reading, which assume that different levels of representations (letter features, visual lexical patterns, semantic features, etc.) in different parts of the neural system are simultaneously activated to support normal reading. Price and Devlin (2003) also noted the similarity between such views and their own proposal that neural substrate of alexia consists of a set of interactive regions.

What conclusions can we draw from the pro and con arguments and evidence in regard to the neuropsychological reality of visual logogens? First, the evidence does not compel one to reject the idea of neural representations that are relatively directly activated by visual word forms as proposed in DCT. The theory does not depend on the assumption that logogens and imagens are neural "patches" located in small areas. However, their epicenters should be in regions close to the sensory systems activated by the modality-specific experiences from which they are derived, as appears to be the case. The representational isomorphs themselves could be distributed or localized neural structures of different sizes—corresponding, for example, to letters, syllables, and words (Chapter 3)—that have been repeatedly activated during reading. Even the parallel distributed models of reading must assume stable patterns of neural activity that are reliably reinstated every time one reads and recognizes a word, regardless of the size of the basic units in the structures, The stable activity patterns require stable structures or, in DCT terms, visual logogens. Pure alexia suggests that such structures, or connections to and from them, are damaged by lesions to the left occipitotemporal junction. However, much needs to be learned about why the area is also implicated in other tasks.

Finally, DCT might help explain the characteristic letter-by-letter reading of pure alexics. By definition, their ability to name and phonemically pronounce letters is retained better than their ability to read words. This means that letter logogens, or pathways from them to motor logogens, are relatively intact—an inference supported by the observation that both letter and word reading are damaged in so-called global alexia, although not in pure alexia. The pure alexic thus uses the connections to the motor logogen system to construct the name sequentially. There is strong evidence for the seriality of phonological encoding in both reading and object naming (Roelops, 2004), within and between syllables and words. Moreover, the representations and processing mechanisms appear to be shared rather than

---

the lexical and semantic effects. For example, the alexic's sensitivity to word imageability is consistent with other evidence (Chapter 7) that the right hemisphere "contains" representations for concrete, high-imagery words. A difficulty for the theory is that different kinds of information must be transferred between hemispheres, but how this happens is unclear, especially when the splenial pathway is damaged.

separate in the two tasks. The DCT view of motor logogens as sequentially-organized hierarchical structures (Chapter 3) is consistent with Roelops's evidence for "output phonological forms" that are processed serially. Here, the concept could perhaps explain the pure alexic's sequential letter-naming strategy for reading words, as well as their relatively spared capacity to access the shared motor logogen system from pictures, which leads us to seek neuropsychological evidence for motor logogens that are independent of other modalities of logogens.

Motor logogens are implicated if a lesion selectively disrupts pronunciation of words, familiar phrases, or longer overlearned sequences. Syntactic production difficulties, such as agrammatism, do not necessarily constitute critical evidence because such patients can utter intact words. Their problem instead suggests disrupted interunit associative or syntactic relations. Luria (1973) reported cases that implicate motor logogens in that the patients show disturbances in smooth pronunciation of polysyllabic words, which require switching from one "articuleme" to another, presumably without any sign of acoustic agnosia for the same words. For example, a patient could pronounce the first syllable, "mu," of the word "mukha," but not the second, "kha,"and so could only say "mu...m...m...mu...ma" (Luria, 1973, p. 185). As would be expected, such disturbances are associated with lesions of the lower zones of the left premotor cortex, where motor logogen are activated prior to actual speech generated by efferent activation of articulatory muscles.

Motor logogens rather than auditory or visual logogens presumably are the representational base for long memorized language chunks such as poems. I am unaware of any evidence of selective disruptions of logogens of such length by brain lesions. What we find is their selective preservation in a few patients. Already mentioned (Chapter 1) is the case of a woman, described by Norman Geschwind (1972), who survived carbon monoxide poisoning but was left severely brain damaged. For 9 years after her accident, the patient could neither speak spontaneously nor understand spoken speech. She could, however, complete well-known expressions so that, if she heard "Roses are red," she would say "Roses are red, violets are blue, sugar is sweet, and so are you." Thus the underlying extended motor logogen must have been intact (as were corresponding auditory logogens activated by hearing "roses are red"). she could also repeat sentences spoken to her and could be taught to sing new songs, suggesting formation of new auditory and motor logogens. Autopsy revealed that her speech area was intact but parietal and temporal lobes were extensively damaged. Thus, the intact motor logogen system was isolated from other systems necessary for comprehension and spontaneous production of speech. In a similar case (Kolb & Whishaw, 2001, p. 341), the patient's singing repertoire was preserved but language was not, suggesting independent logogen systems for speech and song.

There should also be an independent motor-logogen system for writing. Agraphia is the neuropsychological syndrome used to describe disturbances of the ability to write or print letters and familiar words. Dejerine (1892) described agraphia without alexia at the same time that he identified the reverse syndome, alexia without agraphia. However, agraphia is usually associated with acoustic or visual agnosias rather than loss of knowledge of the motor patterns required to write words. Thus, acoustic agraphia involves grapheme-sequencing problems correlated with the phoneme sequencing difficulties in acoustic agnosia as described earlier, and which are associated with lesions of the left temporal lobe (Luria, 1973, p. 141). Optic agraphia similarly accompanies forms of visual-spatial agnosia in reading, which are associated with lesions of the left parieto-occipital region (Luria, 1973, p. 151). A pure form would reflect damage to motor representations that control word writing ("graphemic haptic logogens") without language-related acoustic or visual agnosia. Such cases are difficult to find, but they might yet turn up to round off the evidence for all possible modalities of logogens.

Cross-System Neural Pathways

Neuropsychological evidence for referential processing is especially crucial to DCT, precisely because it involves cross-system activation of logogens by imagens and vice versa, via pathways conducting in opposite directions. The most common psychological tests are object or picture naming on the one hand and imaging to names on the other, but the tests used to identify such syndromes have varied a good deal in the neuropsychological literature and the two directions of referential activity have rarely been studied in the same individuals. We have already encountered the resulting diagnostic complexities in the case of the form-agnosic patient DF, who apparently could image and draw named objects but could not name or otherwise indicate recognition of object drawings, suggesting dissociation of imaging and naming abilities. However, DF's brain damage was too diffuse to permit a precise description of spared and damaged neural systems for referential processing. We also touched on nonverbal-to-verbal referential processing in the analysis of the within-system processing deficit involved in pure alexia and related syndromes, but without any comparison with referential imaging. What other evidence is there on which to draw?

Referential Naming. Anomia is the classic diagnostic category for "pure" naming deficits resulting from localized brain lesions. The trick is to tease apart the different possible sources of the anomia in DCT terms, because anomia could result from damage to imagens, logogens, or the referential connections between them. Only the last of these would qualify as the source of disrupted nonverbal– verbal referential processing, but the source more often is damage to object or language representations.

Luria (1973) described disturbances of object naming associated with lesions of the middle zones of the left temporal lobe (p. 139) and of the parieto-occipital zones of the left hemisphere (pp. 156–60). The former was interpreted as a disruption of the sequential phonemic structure of words so that even prompting with the first syllable did not help the patient produce the name. The parieto-occipital naming disturbance differed in that the patient could immediately produce the appropriate name when prompted by the first syllable. These patients, however, had difficulty identifying and producing object drawings, suggesting that their naming disturbance resulted from a defect in the visual representation of the object. As already discussed, the DCT interpretation is that both of these syndromes are direct perceptual activation problems, possibly entailing deficits to auditory logogens housed in the left temporal area and visual imagens-iconogens in the left parieto- occipital region. More recently, somewhat similar cases of naming disorders and damaged regions of the left hemisphere have been described in terms of independent representations of word form and word meaning (Raff & Caramazza, 1995).

Geschwind and Kaplan (1962, summarized in Geschwind, 1965) reported a case that most clearly suggests naming impairments due to a disconnection of a non-verbal-to-verbal neural pathway. The patient incorrectly named objects placed in the left hand, but afterward could sketch the object with his left hand and select it visually or haptically from a group of objects. These and other tests led to the interpretation that the patient's disturbance was not perceptual in origin (the objects could be identified nonverbally) but more likely resulted from a disconnection of the right hemisphere from the speech area in the left hemisphere. A postmortem revealed an extensive infarct of the corpus callosum which had to be regarded as the cause of this patient's naming disorder. Thus, the corpus callosum is one anatomical site for referential connections that support naming (and probably imaging, although not tested in this patient). Referential pathways must also exist within the left hemisphere, although the evidence is less clear in the case of naming than imaging (discussed later).

A surprising neuropsychological interpretation that implicated both hemispheres emerged from a PET study of neural activity during naming (Etard et al., 2000). Adult men were presented drawings of familiar objects or animals one at a time, which they named aloud or generated a verb semantically related to the object or animal. The brain scans revealed a common network of neural activity for the two tasks extending from the occipito-temporal ventral pathway for object identification to the supplementary motor area (active when an internally driven movement is performed) and precentral gyrus for coordination, planning, and word production. Additionally, naming and verb generation highlighted two different patterns: verb generation specifically implicated Broca's and Wernicke's "semantic language" network, whereas naming did not recruit this network, and instead, activated the primary visual areas (right-hemisphere occipito-temporal and parahippocampal gyri) along with the left anterior temporal region. Thus, naming apparently involved interhemispheric crossover and subsequent processing of the name by the left hemisphere.

Etard et al. (2000) concluded that naming relies on an early-developed language network dedicated to naming overlearned objects. This is consistent with DCT and other views of the infant's earliest language learning (see Chapter 4). What is surprising is their further conclusion (following Locke, 1997) that these word representations are initially housed in the right hemisphere, with the implication from their PET results that adult naming draws on this primary (relatively meaningless) language network. Later the words are housed in the left hemisphere where grammatical and phonological rules can be accessed, presumably accounting for the role of Wernicke's and Broca's areas in the verb generation task.

In DCT terms, the aforementioned analysis would mean two logogen systems, one for early-learned concrete nouns in the right hemisphere, and another for later-acquired word classes (perhaps including abstract nouns) in the left hemisphere. Nothing in DCT rules out such a possibility. In fact, it has long been known that the right-hemisphere has a rich lexicon (e.g., Zaidel, 1978), more for concrete nouns than abstract ones. An alternative interpretation of the PET results is that perceptual and imagery processing of the pictures continued in the right hemisphere during the 4 sec allowed for responding, with a late switch to left-hemisphere motor processing. The verb task, however, created a set for early left-hemisphere associative language processing during each interitem interval, including a search for noun–verb associations. This hypothesis remains speculative in the absence of direct evidence from the Etard et al. (2000) experiment.

Nonverbal-to-verbal referential connections must exist not only for global objects but also for all object parts, modalities, and qualities we can name. It is especially important socially to be able to recognize people by their faces, and to call them by name. Everyone has had embarrassing experiences of not remembering the name of a familiar person, perhaps even a close friend. It seems as if the referential pathway from face imagen to proper name logogen is temporarily blocked. Given the name, however, we immediately recognize it as the correct one. The problem is more severe and long term in cases of face agnosia (prosopagnosia), already mentioned as a representational level defect usually associated with damage to right visual cortical areas, especially the fusiform gyrus located in the ventromedial surface of the temporal and occipital lobe. In those cases, the patient is unable to name the face because he or she does not recognize it, not necessarily because of damage to the referential pathway or the name logogen. Some persons with prosopagnosia, such as patient DF, can identify and name voices of familiar people, thereby providing evidence for a separate (spared) voice-name referential system. A distinct referential system for colors is revealed by dissociations in which colors can be named but visual forms cannot (e.g., DF) and vice versa. Yet another is highlighted by spared ability to name felt objects that cannot be named by sight (DF again), and so on.

The aforementioned is a sample of the neural substrates of naming activity elicited by nonverbal stimuli varying widely in complexity and specificity—generic objects, faces, different modalities of object attributes (color, voice, haptic shape)–all connected to generic object names, proper names, and property names respectively. The list could be expanded to include independent systems for different modalities of naming, revealed, for example, by dissociations between spoken and written picture-naming disorders (see Rapp & Caramazza, 1995), and much more. For these purposes, the point is that they illustrate the many-to-many connections that must exist between imagens for objects, parts, and attributes, and their logogen counterparts. We know this psychologically from our ability to name thousands of objects, parts, colors, shapes, and so forth, often selecting from different possible names in each case. The neuropsychological findings are compatible because they reveal the surprising degree of functional independence of the different levels and kinds of naming ability.

Imaging to words. Here we turn to the issue of imaging referents of words, the verbal-to-nonverbal direction of referential activity. The simplest experimental procedure for studying referential imaging is to ask people to imagine the objects or attributes (e.g., colors) suggested by words and to indicate in some way that they have completed the task. The procedures used in neuropsychological studies are generally more complex because of difficulties in testing patients with brain damage and because some students of imagery tend to focus on image generation as defined within Kosslyn's (1980) computational theory of mental imagery. The generation tasks usually involve imaging to language stimuli but they also include tasks that entail (in DCT terms) associative level processing, such as filling in the colors of line drawings of objects presented as stimuli. There is some uncertainty as well about the theoretical status of the generation concept. For example, Farah (1995, p. 971ff.) questioned "whether image generation is really a distinct and dissociable component from the long- and short-term representational components of imagery," which might be activated by other parts of a visual associative knowledge network rather than a separate generation process.

Referential imaging in DCT is less ambiguous than image generation as defined in the Kosslyn-type studies. Theoretically, referential imaging includes the whole sequence of activation from language stimuli to a criterion response, which indicates that imagery has occurred. The experienced images are by definition generated from imagens (image generators), but the generation process includes all the preceding stages, beginning with verbal stimuli and logogen activation. In addition to generation, various terms have been used over the years (e.g., Paivio, 1971b) to describe the process—image arousal, formation, evocation, elicitation, and activation. These have different connotations. For example, evocation and elicitation put the emphasis on the stimulus as the initiator of the process, as when one refers to the high image-evoking value of concrete words. Image formation implies an active constructive process as when learners construct interactive images to help them remember word pairs. Activation suggests arousal or excitation of "dormant" imagens so that we experience and describe them as conscious images. Image generation, in Kosslyn's (1980) information processing model of visual imagery, refers to this last step, defined as transfer of long-term memory knowledge to a visual buffer which gives it "quasi-perceptual" properties.

Referential imaging is precisely the reverse of referential naming as already described. The neuropsychological indicators of the different steps are reversed as well, involving (a) imaging deficits attributable to damaged name representations, the nonverbal referents of the names, or their connecting pathways; and (b) appropriate neural activation patterns from controlled brain-scan experiments.

The earliest description of an imaging deficit associated with brain damage was presented by Charcot in 1883. As summarized by Goldenberg (1993), "The patient complained of complete loss of his previously very vivid visual imagery ... [he also] had prosopagnosia and pure alexia. These symptoms would point to bilateral tempero-occipital lobe lesions. Loss of imagery was not confined to faces and letters but also concerned objects which the patient could identify in visual perception" (pp. 265–286). Here we have lost imagery for objects the patient could recognize and talk about, suggesting damage either to referential interconnections or to referent imagens in long-term memory. The interpretation is complicated by the face recognition deficit, presumably reflected in naming failures, as well as by alexia and loss of imagery for letters, both of which could reflect damage to visual logogens.

Goldenberg (1993) also summarized an 1892 case of a brain damaged woman who could image objects and topographical relations that she could not recognize when she saw them directly. Thus her pattern of symptoms was the opposite of the Charcot–Bernard case. She also had prosopagnosia but no alexia. Autopsy revealed an extensive occipital and tempero-occipital infarction on the right side as well as a small subcortical lesion on the left side. The symptoms suggest that referential imaging is a left hemisphere function, which remained undamaged in her case.

Few cases of imagery deficits following brain injury were subsequently reported until a clear case was described by Basso, Bisiach, and Lizzatti in 1980. A CT scan indicated that the man had suffered a vascular lesion of the left occipital lobe, with some involvement of structures in the left temporal lobe and possibly the hippocampus. In addition to transient impairments, he had a persistent loss of mental imagery for familiar objects and places—his wife, animals he used to hunt, shops, restaurants—and dreams had completely disappeared. He could, however, report knowledge of things he could not picture: he knew that his wife was small and gray haired, he could enumerate the provinces of Italy, he could say that a pheasant is gallinacean, and so forth. Basso et al. attributed these abilities to retrieval of conceptual information in a propositional format. The DCT interpretation is that verbal associative knowledge was preserved in this patient. What was lost was the referential connection from language to the imagery system. Basso et al. (1980) concluded similarly that the location of the patient's lesion "could lay the conditions for a partial visuo-verbal cleavage" (p. 442).

The conclusions are reinforced by subsequent evidence. Goldenberg (1993) found several patients who were unable to imagine the appearance of objects they could recognize. In all cases where sufficient localizing evidence was available, the lesions were in occipital and tempero-occipital regions on the left side. Farah (1995) concluded similarly on the basis of effects of brain lesions as well as patterns of ERPs in normals that image generation may be a specialized function of the left tempero-occipital region, although she, like Goldenberg, noted that there might be different types of image generation with different hemispheric loci.

A problem with lesion studies is that they may be insensitive to imagery activity in some brain areas. For example, lesions in the primary visual cortex would damage visual perception as well as any visual imagery that comes from early visual experiences. Brain scans and related behavioral data with normal participants avoid that problem. Thompson and Kosslyn (2000) performed meta-analyses on brain-scan results of 37 imagery experiments that used a variety of neuroimaging techniques (e.g., fMRI, PET) to assess brain activation during imagery tasks. The areas of interest, shown in Fig. 7. 2, were the medial occipital cortex (MOC), including V1 and V2; inferior-middle temporal cortex (IT); and the posterior parietal cortex (PP). The tasks involved image generation along with additional processing

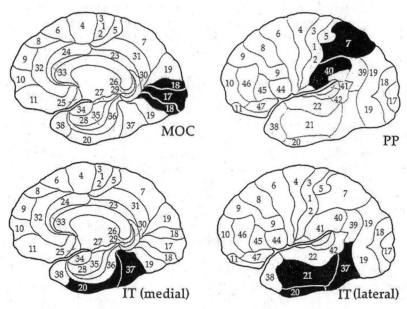

FIGURE 7.2.   Brain regions (black) assumed to be involved in different
stages of imagery generation and processing according to Kosslyn's imagery
theory. The regions are in the medial occipital cortex (MOC), posterior parietal
cortex (PP), and the medial and lateral areas of the inferior temporal lobe (IT).
The numbers identify classical Brodmann areas. From Figure 2 (p. 541) in
W. L. Thompson and S. M.Kosslyn (2000). Neural systems activated during visual
mental imagery: A review and a meta-analysis. In A. W. Toga and J. C. Mazziota
(eds.), *Brain mapping III. The systems*. Academic Press. Copyright 2000, with
permission from Elsevier.

(e.g., image transformation). Kosslyn's (1994) theory of visual imagery processes led
to the prediction that different amounts of activity would show up in the three different regions, depending on task demands. Here the focus is be on those that most
clearly reveal areas activated when verbal cues (hence referential processes) were
used in image generation.

Kosslyn (1994) emphasized the assumption, already discussed earlier, that visual
imagery and perception share the same neural mechanisms. Imagery and perception (especially when we see what we expect to see) involve patterns of activity in
the "visual buffer," including areas V1 and V2 and other nearby topographically
organized areas. The mental images are generated from "descriptions" of objects
and scenes in associative memory. A word or other input sets up processes that

shunt the description to the inferior temporal lobes where a representation of visual properties is activated so strongly that the activation propogates backwards (using backward neural projections) to an area of the visual buffer where an image is formed. Images requiring detailed inspection are formed in MOC (areas V1 and V2). Images requiring less detailed inspection can be formed as far downstream in the ventral system as area IT, thus closer to their memory source. Finally, posterior parietal lobe (PP) areas would be especially activated in such processing as image transformations, discussed in a later section.

The results reviewed by Thompson and Kosslyn (2000) were generally consistent with expectations from the theory. The MOC areas were most strongly activated in imagery tasks requiring high spatial resolution (e.g., visualizing hometown scenes, familiar faces, etc.). Area IT was more activated when the image need not be inspected in detail (e.g., imagery use during recall of concrete words). The authors commented that, "This can be understood if IT stores visual templates, which are used in object recognition. If an image matches a stored representation immediately, and does not require further inspection, the IT areas may be preferentially activated" (p. 556). Note that this corresponds nicely to the DCT view that referential imagery involves a word-activated visual imagen corresponding to the word's referent. Moreover, Thompson and Kosslyn's analysis also accords with the DCT interpretation that images which effectively mediate verbal recall need not be vivid or detailed (Chapter 3). Even a fuzzy image would be sufficient as long as it can be "recognized" as the named object.

Note, too, that the brain scan results essentially confirm the conclusions from the lesion studies that referential imagery is associated with the tempero-occipital areas. Given the essential role of words in activating imagens from long-term memory, we can conclude as well that visual imagens may be housed in the inferior temporal lobe, although they also show up in other locations where they serve memory, motivational, and other adaptive functions (see Chapter 8). Finally, Kosslyn's (1994) theoretical analysis is generally compatible with DCT except that there are specific disagreements (already reviewed in Chapter 5) that stem mostly from his reliance on computational language to describe imagery functions. Thus, in the this context, Kosslyn postulated that images are generated from abstract feature descriptions, for which there is no brain or behavioral evidence and which are paraphrases of the verbal cues actually used in his experiments. I return to this and other issues related to Kosslyn's theory after reviewing the following study.

One of the most remarkable findings from Kosslyn's research program was that the primary visual cortex (V1 or Brodmann's area 17) can be activated in certain imagery tasks. He and his colleagues (1999) started with the accepted fact that V1 and adjacent areas have retinotopic maps of the visual scene. The standard view (Chapter 6) is that V1 neurons respond to object features but do not bind them into representations of objects. Contrary to this interpretation, however, Kosslyn et al. found that V1 is activated when participants imaged visual displays (patterns of stripes) they had previously seen and memorized. The activation was detected by PET scans obtained while subjects compared properties (e.g., length of stripes) with their eyes closed. The role of imagery was confirmed by creating a temporary functional cortical "lesion" by repetitive transcranial magnetic stimulation (rTMS) applied to the skull in a location that targeted medial occipital cortex Area 17 (V1). Relative to a sham control condition, rTMS impaired performance in the imagery task as well as when participants were actually looking at the stimuli. The researchers concluded that early occipital visual cortical areas are used in at least some forms of visual imagery as well as in visual perception. In DCT terms, visual iconogens-imagens useful in perception and imagery are formed in the primary visual cortex. The Kosslyn et al. finding was replicated by Isabelle Klein and her colleagues (2004) using fMRI. Participants viewed horizontally or vertically oriented flashing bow-tie shapes. In the imagery condition, they were cued by a tone to visualize the stimulus they had seen and then press a button when the image was clear. The important result was that imagery globally activated V1. Moreover, the activated pattern closely matched the cortical representation of the horizontal and vertical orientations of the visual field activated when participants actually viewed the perceptual stimuli. I now return to the issues raised by Kosslyn's interpretations. First, although Kosslyn et al. (1999) and Klein et al. (2004) showed that the primary visual cortex was activated when participants were given verbal instructions and verbal or tone cues to generate images of the perceptual patterns they had just studied, there appears to be no evidence thus far that V1 is similarly activated when participants generate images to verbal descriptions alone. For example, Mellet et al. (2000) observed no increased activity in the primary visual area when their participants generated detailed visual images of three-dimensional scenes they constructed from verbal descriptions, although other areas known to be involved in higher order visual processing were activated by the task. Another debatable neuropsychological feature of Kosslyn's theory is the use of neural back-propogation to explain construction of multipart images, which runs into the unsolved neural binding problem: where exactly do such complex images (or the information for their construction) originate and how do they move backward to V1? Such puzzles and further relevant evidence are discussed in detail in Chapter 9.

Within-System Associative Connections and Processes

We deal here with connections and activation processes within the nonverbal system and within the verbal systems. On the nonverbal side we have, for example, the "tight" synchronous associations that bind parts into objects, objects into perceived or imagined scenes, and associations across different sensory modalities of multimodal objects, such as a telephone or a puppy. Motor processes play a role in the formation and processing of some associations (e.g., scenes must be scanned because they can't be viewed or imaged at a glance) but not necessarily in others (e.g., the associations between the appearance, sound, and feel of a telephone are formed simply by being experienced together). Theoretically, all entail associations between imagens. On the verbal side we have the classical example of word–word associations of different degrees of complexity, expressed overtly in speech or writing, or internally as silent speech. Theoretically, these involve sequential associations between motor logogens, but cross-modal associations play a role when, for example, the stimulus is a printed word and the response is a spoken word.

Nonverbal Associations. A key issue here is the relation between association and integration. Traditional associationism proceeded from the assumption that one idea reminds us of another. For Gestalt psychologists, integration implied that separate ideas bind together into a new entity that functions as a whole. A compromise, supported by psychological data reviewed in Chapter 4, was that "sufficient" associative experience can produce functional integration (e.g., Paivio, 1971b, p. 279). Recent neuropsychological evidence further supports the compromise as well as a unique implication of the Gestalt view.

Baker, Behrmann, and Olson (2002) cited studies that show the formation of associations in the inferotemporal cortex of monkeys. For example, prolonged training on a visual paired-associates task resulted in neurons that respond to both members of the pair. In their own experiment, Baker et al. demonstrated the formation of integrated associations in which "the whole is more than the sum of the parts." One implication of this famous Gestalt slogan is that parts should have some kind of superadditive perceptual effect when combined as a whole. Baker et al. observed just such an effect using recordings from single neurons in monkeys. The animals learned to respond separately to the top or bottom part of a configuration and then to the combination of the two parts. The results showed that one neuron responded superadditively to the combination; that is, the amplitude of the neural response to the whole was greater than the sum of the responses to the parts. Such neurons were found in the inferotemporal cortex, the same area along the ventral stream that we have already described as the location of representations for object recognition and imagery in humans. Other studies show disruptions of associative connections between parts of objects and between objects within scenes. These are revealed by different types of visual impairments traceable to brain lesions. We have already been introduced to integrative agnosia, in which the patient has difficulty integrating the elements of a visual display into a whole and (perhaps for that reason) also has difficulty recognizing objects (Behrmann & Kimchi, 2003). We could say that the syndrome involves a breakdown in synchronous associative processing.

The part–whole processing sequence works in both directions, however, and implicates the temporal-parietal junction in both hemispheres. It appears that this region in the right hemisphere is biased to process the parts, whereas the homologous region in the left hemisphere is biased to process the whole. Normally we tend to see the whole before the parts, but this bias can be changed by contextual stimuli so that we focus first on a part. We are, in fact, quite flexible in seeing either the forest or the trees. Not so for patients with lesions in the critical parietal-temporal region. In studies using large letters composed of small letters, Rafal and Robertson (1995) required patients to respond as quickly as possible to either the global target (the large letter) or the local targets (the small letters). Patients with left-hemisphere damage were slower in responding to the local targets (the "parts") and patients with right-hemisphere damage were slower in responding to the global targets (the gestalt whole). Patients with damage in other regions did not show this asymmetry. The asymmetrical processing of hierarchical patterns also shows up in evoked potentials recorded over posterior temporal scalp regions of normal participants. Rafal and Robertson discuss the mechanisms that might be responsible for these and other findings involving hierarchical processing, but the relevant conclusion here is that objects can be processed as wholes or parts using different pathways.

Luria (1973) used the term *simultaneous agnosia* (now sometimes called *simultanagnosia*) to refer to a breakdown of synchronous associations between objects. It is also called Bálint's syndrome, after the Hungarian neurologist who first observed it in 1909 in a patient with bilateral lesions of the anterior regions of the occipital cortex and its boundary with the inferior parietal region. The patient could see only one object at a time and was completely unable to perceive two or more objects simultaneously. Many such cases have been subsequently described (e.g., see Rafal & Robertson, 1995). Such patients are unable to place a dot in the center of a circle because they can only perceive the circle or the pencil point at one time, or join strokes together in writing because, if they see the pencil point they lose the line, or vice versa; they have difficulty in making judgments comparing two objects (which is smaller, longer, closer).

The syndrome is now viewed as a constriction of visual attention to objects. For example, when two colored circles are joined by a line, patients had difficulty reporting two colors because their attention tended to lock onto the dumbbell-like object (Humphreys & Riddoch, 1993). From our perspective, such phenomena imply that the attentional constriction overrides the integrative pull of normal associative processing. The associative pull is revealed by the fact that patients can sometimes process unattended related information. For example, with brief simultaneous presentation of two words or drawings, a patient identified both more often when the two stimuli were semantically related than when they were unrelated (Coslett & Saffran, 1991).

Dissociation of Spatial and Object Imagery.   Earlier we reviewed the important distinction between ventral stream processes for object recognition and dorsal stream processes for location and manipulation of objects. Levine, Warach, and Farah (1985) were the first to demonstrate the same dissociation in visual imagery. They compared two patients, one impaired in object perception and imagery but not in spatial perception and imagery, the other with the reverse pattern of deficits. The patient with selectively impaired object perception found it difficult to recognize and imagine familiar faces, animals, and colors, but performed well on tests of visual-spatial perception and imagery. He also found it difficult to visualize familiar faces, animals, and colors. A CT brain scan showed a temporal lobe lesion extending to the inferior frontal region on the right, and a smaller tempero-occipital lesion on the left—both located in the ventral stream.

The spatially impaired patient, on the other hand, identified common objects or their pictures, and also had good imagery for objects and properties. However, he was impaired on tests of visual-spatial perception and imagery. He had difficulty reaching accurately for objects he had identified, fixating a named object embedded in an array, and describing the spatial relation between two objects. He often got lost in his own house, collided with objects in his path, and needed a companion when he went out. As well, his spatial imagery was severely impaired—he could not say how to get from his house to the grocery store, or from his hospital room to the elevators, and so on. A brain scan revealed bilateral parieto-occipital lesions, placing them within the dorsal visual stream.

Levine et al. (1985) found a large number of published cases that corresponded to the contrasting deficit and brain pathology patterns in their two patients. They concluded that visual agnosia and loss of object and color imagery were due to temporal-occipital damage, whereas visual disorientation with loss of spatial imagery were due to parieto-occipital damage—the ventral "what" and the dorsal "where" (or "how") systems of visual perception and imagery.

Unilateral Visual and Representational neglect. This syndrome refers to a lack of awareness of objects seen in one half of the visual field, which become "visible" if patients shift their gaze so that the same objects are seen in the other visual field. The phenomenon has been studied intensively by Edoardo Bisiach and his colleagues, including a case in which the hemi-neglect showed up in a patient's descriptions of a familiar scene from memory images (Bisiach & Berti, 1989). Kolb and Whishaw (2001, p. 540) described a similar case of a woman who could not recall anything on the left side of her kitchen when she imagined herself standing at the kitchen door. When she imagined herself walking to the other end of the kitchen and turning around she found to her relief that she now knew, could image, what was on that side of the room. Such deficits result from lesions in the parietal lobe, usually on the right side.

Michel Denis and his collaborators (Denis, Beschin, Logie, & Della Sala, 2002) went further and compared neglect patients with control participants on recall of recently presented novel visual layouts and on recall of the same layouts presented only as auditory verbal descriptions. These conditions were contrasted with descriptions of perceived scenes and immediate recall of verbal material. The important result was that the neglect patients showed poorer report of items depicted or described on the left than on the right of each layout. The lateralized error pattern did not show up in the controls, and patients and controls did not differ on immediate verbal memory. One patient showed pure representational neglect, performing at ceiling under the perceptual condition, but making the lateralized errors when scenes were described from memory or from verbal descriptions. Thus, the study showed that representational neglect and perceptual neglect are independent, often co-occurring but sometimes not. In a subsequent study (Della Sala, Logie, Beschin, & Denis, 2004), patients with representational unilateral neglect showed the same pattern of impairment under the aforementioned conditions as well as following mental rotation in which they described the imagined scene from the reverse perspective.

Perceptual neglect and representational neglect have generally been interpreted in terms of some kind of deficit in directing attention to the perceived or imagined hemispace (Della Sala et al., 2004). An alternative view, supported by the results just described, is that representational neglect arises from temporary storage functions of visuo-spatial working memory. In any case, the demonstration of representational neglect of novel scenes presented only as verbal descriptions is strong evidence for referential activation and associative processing of imagens.

Nonverbal Sequential Processing. Thus far we have only considered synchronous associations in which objects or parts are simultaneously available for processing, free from the sequential constraints that characterize verbal processing. However, sequential processing also occurs in the nonverbal system. It is evident that nonverbal neural and behavioral activities consist of chains of actions; they are organized serially over time, and some activities are sequentially constrained. Scanning a scene or an image is serial activity, but one is not constrained to do it in any particular sequence. Walking, however, is sequentially organized in that steps must follow each other smoothly at a certain rhythm or we stumble. The sequences are more complex in the case of such activities as dancing, figure skating, gymnastics, and playing a musical instrument, but the dynamic patterns are sequentially constrained. All such activities are exquisitely programmed in motor and sensorimotor areas of the brain (Kolb & Whishaw, 2001). Lesions in such areas lead to apraxias and movement disturbances of various kinds (Kolb & Whishaw, 2001, p. 393). Sequential processing is, however, especially characteristic of language.

Verbal Sequential Processing. An association between verbal mechanisms and sequential processing was demonstrated by brain lesion and dichotic listening studies in the 1960s and 1970s (see Paivio, 1986, p. 269). The results suggested that the sequential processing capacity of the verbal system derives from a more general temporal processing capacity for which the left hemisphere is somehow specialized. The left-temporal lobe in particular appears to be crucial in the sequential organization of speech, probably through a combination of motor and acoustic control processes (Kimura, 1982).

Verbal and nonverbal sequencing problems also accompany damage to subcortical motor control structures, in particular the basal ganglia, which are always damaged in Broca's aphasia and in Parkinson's disease, among others. The sequencing problem occurs within the smallest linguistic units (phonemes) as well as within longer sequences. When stop consonants such as [p] and [b] occur before vowels, they are differentiated primarily by voice onset time—the time that occurs between the initial burst that results from lip or tongue gestures and the voicing generated by the larynx. Broca's patients are unable to maintain control of the sequences of independent motor acts to produce these sounds and frequently mispronounce them (Lieberman, 2002, p, 43). The sequencing problem in Broca's aphasics extends to difficulties in executing oral, nonspeech, and manual motor sequences (Kimura, 1993). Similar verbal sequential problems occur in advanced stages of Parkinson's disease. The sequencing problem extends to more complex syntactic structures, as is described in Chapter 8 in the context of DCT and neuropsychological language issues.

Cooperative Synchronous and Sequential Processing.   Although stressing the organizational differences, we cannot lose sight of the fact that the operations of each system depend on both synchronic and sequential processing activity. Such nonverbal activities as walking, dancing, figure skating, gymnastics, and any number of everyday skilled activities, from tying one's shoelaces to eating with a knife and fork, require coordination of movement sequences going on at the same time, using different parts of the body. Moreover, many of the sequences fit into a spatial frame that must be taken into account while responding. Similarly, hearing and producing language involves prosodic events—stress, pitch, and other changes—that go on simultaneously at certain points in the verbal sequence. The articulatory muscles control the sequence of events from chest to lips to produce speech, with much of the activity going on concurrently in different places. In the brain, too, sequences of neural activity that control verbal and nonverbal behavior go on simultaneously in different parts of the brain. In fact, neuroscience tells us that the brain is "massively parallel" even in language processing.

Sensory Associations.   The visual forms of objects and written language are often associated with other sensorimotor attributes: the sound, color, and haptic feel of a telephone; the form, feel, odor, taste, and color of a banana; the sound, pronunciation, and haptic writing pattern associated with visual words. These are either simultaneously available in perception as hierarchical gestalts, as in the case of color and texture embedded within form, or periodically associated with form, as in the case of the ring of a telephone and the sound of words read aloud. Moreover, these perceptual attributes can but need not be imaged together.

How do the associated attributes behave neuropsychologically? For example, is there brain evidence that they are functionally independent and additive as hypothesized in DCT, and confirmed by memory effects of visual and auditory attributes of audiovisual objects such as telephones and whistles (Thompson & Paivio, 1994; discussed earlier in Chapter 4)? Some general support for the independence-additivity hypothesis comes from studies in which aphasic patients showed different patterns of impaired and preserved naming (summarized in Paivio & Begg, 1981, pp. 370–371). In one study, aphasics named pictures of "operative" (easily manipulated) objects more easily than "figurative" (not easily manipulated) objects, presumably because the latter were limited to the visual modality. In another study, patients were equally able to name objects on the basis of visual, tactile, olfactory, or auditory cues. In yet another, various sensory modalities of an object contributed additively to the probability of correct naming by aphasics, which is possible only if the different modalities are functionally independent, despite their integrated combination in the object. Recent neuropsychological data confirm the functional independence of object attributes (Cree & McRae, 2003, pp. 11–12). The independence hypothesis, however, needs to be reconciled with bimodal and multimodal regions that have been found in different parts of the brain. For example, several common regions are active bilaterally in both haptic and visual perception of object. Even here, however, there is evidence of some independence in that a lateral occipital area "prefers" visual over haptic stimuli, whereas parietal areas prefer haptic over visual stimuli; moreover, visual imagery apparently contributes to activation of some, but not all, visual cortical areas during haptic perception (Zhang, Weisser, Stilla, Prather, & Sathian, 2004). We shall consider such multimodal phenomena in more detail in Chapter 9 in the context of abstract processing systems as compared to modality-specific systems in the brain.

We have also seen evidence that different verbal sensory modalities are subserved by anatomically separate brain areas. For example, auditory verbal agnosia is associated with left temporal lesions whereas visual verbal agnosia (dyslexia) is associated with left occipitoparietal lesions. Thus, the verbal modalities, too, are independent in the sense that they are neuropsychologically dissociable. Whether they also are functionally additive when the different neural sites are activated concurrently remains to be seen.

TRANSFORMATIONAL PROCESSING

This section deals with the brain correlates of our ability to mentally rotate or alter shapes, change imagined colors, change the order of language components, and the like. We assume that the transformations are governed by the nonverbal and verbal structural and processing constraints already discussed. Thus, nonverbal transformations operate on spatial forms and sensory properties of imagined objects whereas verbal transformations operate on sequential structures (e.g., the various changes to sentences described by Chomsky's generative grammars) as well as such prosodic characteristics as pitch.

Motor processes have always been stressed in the DCT analysis of transformations. Thus, it was suggested that imagery includes "a strong motor component that contributes to its usefulness in transformational thinking" (Paivio. 1971b, p. 149), as reflected in "flights" of thought, construction of interactive images in memory tasks, and so on. Later, this was expressed more specifically in the hypothesis "that all mental transformations engage motor processes that derive originally from active manipulation of the referent objects and observations of perceptual changes in objects as they move or are manipulated by others" (Paivio, 1986, p. 72).

The hypothesis needs two qualifications. First, motor processes are not implicated to the same extent in all types of mental transformations. We shall see that mental rotations in particular involve dynamic activity of neurons in the motor cortex. We would not expect similar activity when imagining moving objects or transformations along sensory dimensions, such as changes in the imagined colors of objects. Second, the idea that mental transformations derive from behavioral acts does not necessarily mean that there is a direct mapping from behavioral manipulations to whatever motor activity is involved in the analogous mental manipulations. The equivalence might instead be between motor imagery and motor intention and preparation (Jeannerod, 1994), which implicates anticipatory imagery in that motor imagery is one way in which a person prepares for a future action in a particular situation (discussed further in Chapter 8).

Mirror neurons may play an important role in such motor processes. These neurons were first discovered in the monkey homolog of Broca's area and functional equivalents were later shown to exist in that area and other brain areas in humans. Such neurons become active both when an object is manipulated and when similar actions are perceived in others (Rizzolatti & Arbib, 1998). They are viewed as action representations that can be used for imitating and "understanding" (e.g., recognizing the consequences of) the actions of others. The concept of mirror neurons has been increasingly stretched and used in interpretations of observation-based acquisition of skills of all kinds, including the idea (discussed in Chapter 12) that speech may have evolved via imitation of grasping and oral movements. The findings that Broca's area becomes active during mental imagery of hand grasping movements and during tasks involving hand-mental rotations (Rizzolatti & Arbib, 1998) provide conceptual links to the dual coding emphasis on motor processes in such phenomena.

Motor processes in imaged transformation have been directly confirmed in the case of mental rotation. Georgopoulos and his collaborators (Georgopoulos, Lurito, Petrides, Schwarts, & Massey, 1989) trained a rhesus monkey to move its arm in a direction perpendicular to and counterclockwise from the direction of a target light that changed its position from trial to trial. The activity of cells in the motor cortex was recorded during performance and the neuronal population vector was computed in successive time intervals during the reaction time. The population vector rotated gradually counterclockwise from the direction of the light to the direction of the movement at a rate that was comparable to (but higher than) mental rotation rates calculated from behavioral data for humans performing mental rotation tasks.

The results supported the interpretation that the directional transformation "was achieved by a counterclockwise rotation of an imagined movement vector. This process was reflected in the gradual change of activity of motor cortical cells..." (Georgopoulos et al., 1989, p. 235). The result is particularly interesting because there is no a priori reason for the neuronal ensemble to rotate at all. That is, the cortical neurons did not rotate to control the arm movement, but rotated instead in anticipation of the movement. The authors noted too that other brain areas are probably involved in such complicated transformations. Thus, brain laterality, lesion, and scanning studies show that right hemisphere frontal and parietal areas are particularly involved in mental rotation tasks, although left hemisphere superiority has also been observed, perhaps because mental rotation is both a temporal and a spatial task that draws on specialized resources of both hemispheres (Corballis, 1982, p. 189).

Less research has been done on neural processes involved in other kinds of transformations. We can image various patterns of motion produced by flying birds, trains, cheetahs chasing a prey, and so on. Logically such experiences could involve "pure" kinematic imagery as if the imagined objects simply pass before the mind's eye, activating motion-detecting neurons in the middle temporal cortex. For example, generating action words to names of such objects as a cart activates a region in the left temporal gyrus just anterior to the area involved in the perception of motion (Martin et al., 2000). However, such imagery might also engage implicit eye movements corresponding to, say, the pursuit eye movements involved in watching a moving object, those controlled partly by the superior colliculus.

Neuropsychological evidence is lacking on the complex mental transformations that are implicated in many tasks that are especially relevant to DCT and other cognitive theories. For example, cube visualization, often used as a test of imagery ability (see Chapter 4), entails imagining slicing a cube into smaller cubes, spreading them apart, "seeing" the colored surfaces, rotating the structure to "view" it from different angles, and so forth. Neuroimaging during the task should reveal neural activity in many brain areas. Another example is the generation of interactive images to verbal instructions, which are known to benefit associative learning but have not been studied using brain scans to reveal neural correlates of the spatial and motor processes presumably involved in the task. The approximations that have been done are reviewed in Chapter 8 in the section on memory functions of imagery and verbal processes.

Transformations in auditory imagery also have not been studied. Especially relevant is our ability to image music played on different instruments, voices of different pitch (a man's, woman's, or child's voice), vocal sounds of different animals, and so on. One could argue that these simply involve auditory memory imagery for sounds we have heard. Alternatively or in addition, the imagery changes might include a substantial contribution derived from motor processes involved in imitating different voices and other sounds, processes that are reflected in the necessary changes in activity of "articulemes" (Luria, 1973, p. 314)—motor logogens in DCT terms.

Related to the aforementioned are the verbal sequential transformations involved in producing and understanding active and passive sentences, and other grammatical transformations. The role of Broca's, Wernicke's, and other language areas of the brain in such transformations are discussed in the next chapter under the heading of language functions of dual coding brain systems.

CONSCIOUS PROCESSING

Consciousness was taken for granted in most of the brain damage and neuroimaging studies reviewed in this chapter. Researchers generally assume that, to respond in some relevant way, participants must be aware of target stimuli and instructions presented to them. The results suggest that different modalities of conscious experience are associated with activity in regions close to the primary cortical areas for the different senses. A large literature deals specifically with neural correlates of conscious experience (e.g., Blackmore, 2004, pp. 226–241; Metzinger, 2000). No consensus has emerged as to what the relations reveal about the causes and nature of consciousness, although the research has revealed specific phenomena that are interesting in their own right.

The first breakthrough into brain correlates of consciousness was the discovery of the arousal system in the midbrain reticular formation. Consciousness was linked to different levels of arousal as indexed by different EEG wave patterns, with an irregular pattern (reflecting irregular firing of neurons in different brain areas) being associated with alert waking states. The arousal system is now known to consist of many different neurochemically controlled systems that affect alertness and attention in interaction with different sensory systems and cognitive tasks. Arousal is discussed further in Chapter 9 as one kind of amodal reaction that could explain certain kinds of common coding effects. It is specifically relevant at this point as the brain-based background for the flood of research that followed the discovery of rapid eyemovement (REM) sleep and its correlation with dreaming (Aserinsky & Kleitman, 1953).

The basic phenomenon is that research participants report many more dreams when awakened during REM sleep than during non-REM sleep. Researchers hoped that this psychophysiological correlate would provide an entree into the nature of consciousness in general, particularly when dreams are compared with waking-state cognition. Hobson and Stickgold (1995) reviewed the research history in the area with emphasis on their own neurocognitive approach, which has enriched our empirical and theoretical understanding of the ways in which dreaming differs from waking consciousness. Unlike waking imagery, dreams have no immediate eliciting stimuli and the dreamer is generally unresponsive to external stimuli. Although relevant presleep experiences can often be identified (Freud certainly thought so), dreams are not ordinary memory images. They involve familiar people and situations but the content is often bizarre. Hobson and Stickgold (1995) analyzed the bizarreness into characteristics of incongruity, discontinuity, and vagueness, viewed generally as different kinds of transformations of objects, people, and scenes as revealed by "narrative graphing" of dream reports. Neuropsychologically analyzed, the bizarreness is due first of all to chaotic internal signals (unconstrained by external input) and second, attempts by higher cortical centers to integrate the signals into the ongoing dream plot (Hobson & Stickgold, 1995, p. 1381). The "higher centers" presumably represent organized information in semantic and episodic memory systems (in DCT terms, imagen and logogen systems). The theoretical analyses focus on attentional mechanisms related to neurotransmitters that alter activation levels in different brain regions, so that "consciousness depends on the chemical microclimate of neuronal networks in the forebrain," the chemicals being secreted by cell bodies located in the brain stem (Hobson & Stickgold 1995, p. 1387).

Other researchers have hoped that some specific brain area might turn out to be especially crucial to consciousness in general, much as Descartes thought that the pineal gland was the seat of the soul. There has been no such discovery and the research accordingly began to focus on correlates of visual awareness in particular. Here, the proposed correlates have ranged from the primary visual cortex (V1) and its vicinity to more distant areas including the thalamus, anterior cingulate, amygdala, and septum, among others. Weiskrantz, Barbur, and Sahraie (1995) favored the primary visual cortex on the basis of the phenomenon of "blindsight" associated with hemianopia, the loss of visual awareness in half the visual field as a result of severe damage to V1 on the opposite side of the brain. Residual information passed on to the higher visual areas via alternative routes nonetheless leaves the hemianope with some ability to discriminate visual information (e.g., direction of movement) without consciously seeing the stimulus.[22] Thus, blindsight suggests that neural activity in V1 is necessary for invoking visual awareness. The evidence is inconclusive, however, because the loss of V1 results in degeneration of cells elsewhere along the visual pathway. Nobel laureate Sir Francis Crick and his collaborator Christof Koch (Crick & Koch,1995), among the most active researchers in this domain, excluded V1 from the correlates, and, on the basis of other empirical evidence, suggested that activity of visual areas directly connected with prefrontal and parietal cortices are crucial to awareness. However, such probing has not yet resulted in a consensus about the neural correlates of "the vivid picture of the world we see in front of our eyes" (Crick, 1994, cited in Blackmore, 2004, p. 231) or, we might add, the picture we see in our mind's eye.

Another idea is that the neural correlate of consciousness consists of nonrandom patterns of activity in widely distributed areas of the brain. Such theories are modern variants of the Gestalt field theory of brain correlates of conscious experience. E. Roy John (2003) has recently updated his version of such a theory, according to which activated information from external sources and from internal memory representations converge to create consciousness. This is achieved through activity in feedback loops between the cortex and the thalamus. which results in "cortico-thalamo-cortical reverberation, binding the fragments [of information from the two sources] into a unified global percept. Sustained reverberation produces a resonating electromagnetic field of synchronized elements … Consciousness is a physical property of this field, producing the subjective awareness of this information" (p. 244).

Two general problems with John's theory immediately come to mind. One is that the cortico-thalamic feedback loop does not solve the binding problem because it does not specify how a "global concept" emerges from the reverberatory cycling of fragments of information. Where is the blueprint for the global concept? It is not found in the thalamus because sensory information is fractionated there and becomes more so as it reaches the primary sensory cortex. The standard theory of the functional brain described in Chapter 6 tells us that fragments of sensory features are combined into larger wholes in areas away from the primary cortex, but how this happens is precisely the binding problem that is discussed in detail in

---

[22]Note that researchers in the 1970s arrived at the same general interpretation of perceptual defence, subception, and other kinds of perception without awareness entirely on the basis of behavioral data. The neural-correlates research permits a more precise, though still tentative, interpretation of the idea of independent systems for conscious and unconscious perceptual phenomena.

Chapter 9. We shall see that neural backpropogation, on which John's theory relies, is the Achilles heel of all proposed binding mechanisms.

The second problem with John's theory is that it implies that different coherent patterns should correlate with different specific states of awareness. There is presently no direct evidence for such correlations. What we have instead is evidence that different modalities of conscious awareness are associated with activity in brain areas that correspond to, or are close to, the primary sensory areas. Moreover, different qualities of conscious experience within modalities can be mapped onto different receptor areas and brain regions. This is especially apparent in the case of pain because it correlates with neural activity in specific regions of the somatosensory cortex corresponding to widely separated body locations of the injury and the felt pain. Moreover, brain scan studies show that larger cortical areas are activated when the pain is more intense. But the extended range of neural correlates within and across sensory modalities has not clarified our understanding of the nature and functions of consciousness any more than the research on correlates of visual awareness has done.

The correlates research has, however, turned up some unusual phenomena that are generally interesting in their own right and relevant to aspects of DCT. I describe some representative examples and then conclude with a dual coding analysis that highlights procedural components common to all of the research on neural correlates of consciousness and in that sense defines the boundaries of the phenomenal domain.

In addition to blindsight, the unusual phenomena include visual illusions, phantom body parts, and sensory transformations. Andrews, Schluppck, Homfray, Matthews, and Blakemer's (2002) reported an especially-informative experiment on reversals of conscious perception of Rubin's vase-faces illusion. This classical illusion involves a black and white drawing in which a central white part can be seen as a vase and its contours on each side as face silhouettes. After a period of viewing, perception begins to oscillate spontaneously between the vase and the faces. While participants were viewing the ambiguous figure, Andrews et al. recorded fMRI activity from areas known to be most active to faces, and areas generally more reactive to inanimate objects. Various controls were used so that stimulus conditions were identical when participants indicated the onset of perception of either faces or vase by pressing one of two buttons. Thus, their responses correlated with changes in their conscious experiences rather than the retinal image. The critical result was that the "face area" of the fusiform gyrus in the right ventral temporal lobe responded most strongly when perceptual awareness shifted from vase to faces. The results pinpointed a cortical face-perception area more precisely than had been possible on the basis of lesion data on prosopagnosia or previous neural imaging studies. We could say that a specific area of the fusiform gyrus "contains" face imagens-iconogens (or Hebbian cell-assemblies) that can be directly activated perceptually by a template-matching process, which competes with vase-imagen activation elsewhere (less precisely localized in this experiment). The authors suggested that ambiguous figures might similarly reveal the role of other sensory areas in the (conscious) resolution of perceptual uncertainty.

The "phantom limb" phenomenon has long been known to neurosurgeons and psychologists (e.g., Melzack, 1992). It refers to the felt presence of an arm, leg, or other body part that has been surgically or accidentally amputated. The experience is especially disturbing because it can include persistent excruciating pain in the missing part. Research aimed at stopping the phantom pain has revealed an extraordinary phenomenon. Ramachandran and Blakeslee (1998) successfully treated certain kinds of phantom-limb pain (especially cramping) using a mirror placed so that the patient sees a reflection of his normal hand where the phantom should be. When the patient moved the real hand the phantom appeared to move and the cramping pain ended. The procedure worked in about half the cases tested. Feedback from movement apparently did the trick.

An analogical extension of the procedure causes normal people to experience touch in a dummy hand (e.g., a rubber glove filled with water). The seated individual rests one hand out of sight alongside the visible dummy hand. The experimenter gently strokes each hand with a paintbrush, and soon the participant begins to feel the sensations in the dummy hand rather than in the real hand (Botvinick & Cohen, 1998). The premotor cortex has recently been identified as the neural correlate of the illusion (Ehrsson, Spence, & Passingham, 2004). The area became active when the participant first experienced the illusion, about 11 sec after the brushstroke started. The authors suggested that the premotor cortex recognizes the body (including the dummy hand) as one's own by accepting information from vision, touch, and proprioception.

Consider next the sensory substitution procedures that seem to restore visual function and awareness in blind individuals (summarized in Blackmore, 2004, pp. 266–268). One procedure uses cameras attached to special lenses to activate an array of vibrators attached to body parts of the blind participant. After some practice, the individual experiences the vibrations as an image out in space and can use them to make spatial judgments. The tongue is especially sensitive as a spatial "scanner" when stimulated by tiny electrodes attached to a video camera. A congenitally blind woman used this attachment to scan her surroundings with her tongue and within a few hours was able to move about, grasp objects, and even catch a tossed ball.

Another procedure converts a video image into a "soundscape" in which changes in pitch and temporal patterning are used to code for left–right and up–down in the image. A woman blinded as an adult mastered the system, and, after many months of practice, began to see depth and detail in the world. Moreover, she insisted that the experience was really visual and that she did not confuse the soundscape with other sounds. Her testimony is persuasive because she presumably could compare her soundscape awareness with remembered visual awareness prior to the accident.

These human experiences are consistent with functional sensory substitution observed in animals with rewired brains. Sharma, Angelucci, and Sur (2000) rerouted visual neurons to the auditory cortex of ferret monkeys, with the result that the auditory cortex began to function as the visual cortex normally does in response to visual stimuli. The crucial difference in this context is that, in humans, the "rewiring" is entirely functional, defined by changes in perceptual performance and the modality of reported sensory awareness.

Dual Coding Theory and the Neural Correlates of Consciousness

The DCT perspective on the scientific study of consciousness becomes especially clear in the neuropsychological context. The general argument is that, in this domain too, the research only reveals correlates of consciousness that are ultimately defined operationally by language. On the one hand, there are the participant's verbal reports of conscious awareness of stimulus objects, images, sensory qualities ("qualia"), feelings, emotions, and so forth., and on the other hand, reactions to instructions to respond in a certain way when a stimulus is perceived or imaged. For example, participants in the Andrews et al. (2002) experiment on Rubin's illusion were told to press one key when they saw the faces, another when they saw the vase. The authors even referred to the key presses as "reports." Dream researchers Hobson and Stickgold (1995) hoped to escape the limitations of verbal reports by relating performance on semantic priming and other tasks to different stages of REM and non-REM sleep from which the participants were awakened for the tests. However, even there the test stimuli and responses were verbal.

The only alternative would be to broaden the behavioral definition to include nonverbal discriminative responding to nonverbal stimuli. We all do this when we assume that people or animals feel pain when they suddenly withdraw from a sharp jab and perhaps scream "in pain" at the same time. Such assumptions are inferences based on our own reactions to stimuli we have learned to call painful. The inference is compelling but not foolproof because one's nonverbal pain response might be feigned. More generally, inferring consciousness from nonverbal behavior means that there would be no boundary conditions on the concept—any discriminative behavior by creatures at any evolutionary level could be said to be mediated by conscious awareness of the effective stimuli. Thus, one could say that a foraging bee is aware of the color of the flower from which it draws nectar. Otherwise we must draw the line on what defines consciousness by some arbitrary behavioral criterion, including (by analogy) equally arbitrary human nonverbal indicators of consciousness. For humans, however, the gold standard for objective measurement of conscious experience is the verbal report. Even pain, which seems so obviously present in a suffering patient, is now widely assessed by the McGill Pain Questionnaire developed by pain scientist Ronald Melzack (1975).

What all that means from the DCT perspective is that consciousness is linked conceptually and operationally to the verbal side of dual coding systems, as activated in referential and associative processing tasks. Studies of the neural correlates of consciousness extend the dual coding connection to patterns of brain activity. Associating consciousness with mental words and images is as common in the neural correlates domain as in psychology generally (recall David Marks's theory of consciousness as discussed in Chapter 3). Crick and Koch (2000), in particular, referred approvingly to linguist Ray Jackendoff's (1987) analysis of consciousness as an intermediate level of sensory computation that operates on words and images. DCT could add precision to such analyses, and it would be a short step to the conclusion that DCT is a theory of consciousness. I have not taken that step because DCT does not equate the functioning of the verbal and imagery systems with conscious processing, although verbal reports are important indicators that those systems mediate performance in memory and other tasks. We see later that separating imagery from consciousness, both conceptually and operationally, becomes essential when the imagery side of DCT is used to interpret the evolution of nonverbal animal minds (Chapter 11).

CHAPTER EIGHT

Adaptive Functions of the Dual Coding Brain

The adaptive functions of dual coding systems were discussed from the psychological perspective in Chapter 4. Recast here in neuropsychological terms, they highlight once again the cooperative independence principle of DCT. Independence means that verbal and nonverbal neural systems can be active separately or conjointly. Cooperation is possible because the neural representations can activate each other via their interconnections. Cooperative independence implies (a) additive benefits of verbal and nonverbal neural activation in some tasks, (b) selective reliance on one system when it is especially relevant to a given task, and (c) switching back and forth between them according to changing task demands. We have seen that such implications have widespread support from psychological research. Relevant neuropsychological evidence is sparser and less systematic, but what is available buttresses aspects of DCT and is interesting in its own right. The following review samples the overlapping domains of memory, anticipation, evaluation, motivation and emotion, problem solving, and communication.

MEMORY

Neuropsychological studies of memory in the 1970s and 1980s focused on the role of the temporal lobes, especially the hippocampus, in episodic memory. This also was the case in dual coding memory research. For example, memory for nonverbal stimuli was selectively impaired by lesions to the right temporal lobe whereas memory for verbal stimuli was more affected by damage to the left temporal lobe (Paivio, 1986; Paivio & te Linde, 1982). Since then, the neural correlates of memory have become more complex and uncertain. The role of the hippocampus in particular became fuzzier than it seemed to be in the early years following the clinical investigations of memory loss after surgical removal of the hippocampus and adjacent regions (e.g., the famous case of patient HM, summarized in Chapter 3). The initial hypothesis was that the hippocampus was the critical storage site for short-term memories, but this changed to the notion that the structure is an important way station that distributes information to other parts of the brain for storage.

Recent evidence has supported the latter view. In a functional brain imaging experiment, Bontempi et al. (1999) mapped regional metabolic activity in the brains of mice tested for retention of a spatial discrimination task. Memory performance was strongly linked to activation of the hippocampal formation shortly after training but, from 5 to 25 days later, its functional contribution diminished and other cortical areas became increasingly active and capable of mediating the retrieval of the learned information. The authors interpreted the results in terms of a consolidation process "accomplished by means of a transitory interaction between the hippocampal formation and the neocortex to establish permanent neo-cortical memory representations" (p. 673). Also consistent with that interpretation, Teng and Squire (1999) reported that an amnesic patient, with extensive bilateral damage to the hippocampus and adjacent structures in the medial temporal lobe, had no memory knowledge of his current neighborhood. He could, however, recall the spatial layout of the region where he grew up but had moved away from more than 50 years ago. He also had intact memory for remote autobiographical episodes. Teng and Squire concluded that "the hippocampus and other structures in the medial temporal lobe are essential for the formation of long-term declarative memories, both spatial and non-spatial, but not for the retrieval of very remote memories, either spatial or non-spatial" (p. 675). Other findings suggest, however, that these medial temporal lobe structures are important for retrieval of remote episodic memory and semantic memory as well (Nadel & Moscovitch, 2001). Thus the memory functions of the hippocampus and related structures remain uncertain.

A different position, based on neurobiological studies of animal behavior and a cellular approach to brain function, is that the hippocampus and other specific brain structures do not play any uniquely important role in learning and memory (Vanderwolf & Cain, 1994). Memory is instead an experience-dependent change in synaptic connectivity that occurs in many different brain systems. Consistent with that interpretation, memory loss has been reported in patients with injury to brain sites as diverse as the temporal lobes, thalamus, frontal lobes, basal forebrain structures, occipital lobes, and rhinal cortex (Vanderwolf & Cain, 1994, pp. 272–273), as well as the cerebellum and amygdala, which are especially involved in procedural and emotional memories, respectively (e.g., Schacter, 1996). The deficit patterns from brain damage thus support a broad multimodal approach to the neuropsychology of autobiographical memory (Greenberg & Rubin, 2003).

Nonetheless, the hippocampus seems to be crucial to some kinds of memories. The evidence has been thoroughly reviewed (Rosenbaum, et al., 2005) in the context of an analysis of the "episodic amnesia " and spared abilities of a brain-damaged patient (K. C.) on whom Tulving (2005) has relied for his theoretical arguments about autonoetic memory. This patient has widespread brain damage but the extent of the damage is greatest to his hippocampus and parahippocampus, which, according to the investigators, could account for his profound impairments on all explicit tests of new learning and memory.

It is directly relevant to DCT that Vanderwolf and Cain, (1994) questioned the conclusion that left-sided hippocampal lesions produce a specific deficit in verbal memory and right-sided lesions produce a specific deficit in nonverbal memory. They nonetheless went on to cite evidence (p. 274) that the poor performance of a temporal-lobe injured patient in various nonverbal learning tasks (e.g., mirror tracing) may be related to a failure to use verbal labels spontaneously. For DCT, this means that pathways to the verbal motor system are somehow affected by temporal lobe injury that concomitantly affects performance on a nonverbal learning task. The temporal lobes and other specific areas are in any case associated with differential memory effects of basic dual coding variables, particularly language concreteness, pictures versus words, and imagery instructions. The evidence comes from brain damage and brain imaging studies.

Neuropsychological Effects of Dual Coding Variables

Dual coding was supported early on by experiments involving the critical variables. For example, Jones-Gotman and Milner (1978) found that right temporal-lobectomy patients were more impaired than left temporal patients in memory for concrete-word pairs learned under imagery instructions, but the two patient groups did equally well in memory for abstract pairs learned under instructions to use sentences to link the pairs. Whitehouse (1981) found that patients with anterior right-hemisphere damage had better recognition memory for words than for pictures of nameable objects, whereas left-hemisphere patients did better with pictures than words. Whitehouse interpreted these and other findings from two experiments to be consistent with predictions from DCT.

Relevant dual coding variables have been investigated in more recent neuropsychological studies. Shayna Rosenbaum and her colleagues (2004) measured K. C.'s visual imagery ability using a variety of tasks such as judgments of shapes of named letters and animal parts, relative sizes of objects, colors of objects, spatial relations of hands on a clock, verification of concrete sentences, and so forth, all of which are deemed to require imagery for their completion according to prior research, much of it reviewed in Chapter 4. It turned out that K. C. showed no deficit on those tasks, and the authors concluded that K. C.'s severely impoverished autobiographic memory cannot be attributed to a generalized visual imagery deficit despite the fact that he has damage to higher order visual cortex along with the severe damage to hippocampal structures. Note, however, that none of the tests required K. C. to use imagery as an aid for remembering episodic information in the way that normal persons did in the early dual coding studies described in Chapter 4. Rosenbaum et al. recognized this possibility, suggesting that a route to episode-specific visual imagery would be disrupted if the hippocampus is needed to access it. The results are interesting from the dual coding perspective because they indicate that K. C. has relatively intact imagens and logogens and access to them via referential pathways. It remains to be seen whether he could be trained to use the available dual coding information effectively as a mnemonic aid.

Brain scan studies with normals have yielded information on the brain areas that are activated by dual coding variables in memory tasks. Brewer' Zhao, Desmond, Glovar, and Gabrieli (1998) used fMRI to scan brain activity while participants studied pictures of everyday scenes, which they later tried to recognize from a new list. Brain activity was higher in both left and right posterior medial temporal lobes and in the right frontal lobe when participants studied pictures they later remembered as compared to pictures they later forgot. In contrast, using a similar procedure with words rather than pictures, Wagner, Schacter, Rotte, Kootstoal, Maril, Dale, et al. (1998) found that the brain activity when participants studied words they later remembered as compared to words they later forgot was greater in left-hemisphere structures, specifically the posterior region of the left medial temporal lobe (parahippocampal gyrus) and in the left frontal lobe. The differential activation of right and left hemisphere areas for subsequently remembered pictures and words is consistent with previous research and with DCT. The activation of bilateral brain areas by pictures but not words is also consistent with the DCT hypothesis (Chapter 3) that pictures are relatively more likely than words to be dually coded, thus benefitting memory performance for the pictures. However, Brewer et al. did not test such a possibility and they did not explicitly relate their results to DCT.

More detailed picture–word effects were reported by Stefan Köhler and his collaborators (Köhler, Moscovitch, Winocur, & McIntosh, 2000) who used PET to examine brain activity when participants studied and subsequently tried to recognize pictures of objects or their printed names. During study, the participants decided whether each of the randomly presented items was a living or nonliving object. During recognition, the participants made yes–no recognition judgments for a mixed sequence of studied items and new distractor items. The recognition items were presented in the studied format (picture–picture or word–word) or in a reversed format (picture–word or word–picture).

The following results are of interest for our purposes. First, the usual superiority of pictures over words in recognition memory occurred when pictures were presented both at encoding and during the recognition test. Second, as in previous studies, right medial temporal lobe (MTL) structures generally showed higher activation to pictures than to words; in addition, two distinct regions in the left anterior and left posterior parahippocampal gyrus showed a differential picture response only at encoding. This means, as in other studies cited by Köhler et al. (2000) that some left MTL structures were co-activated with right MTL structures during picture processing. Third, other left hemisphere regions in the occipital lobe, outside the primary visual cortex, exhibited more activity during encoding of words than of pictures. Finally, Köhler et al. found evidence that converged with data reported by others "which showed that MTL structures are part of a left-lateralized network of regions that supports semantic processes *across* pictures and words" (Köhler et al., 2000, p. 176).

The Köhler et al. results are consistent with DCT in that distinct brain areas were activated by pictures and words. The areas were predominantly in the right hemisphere for pictures and in the left for words. The bilateral activation for pictures during encoding accords with the finding that left and right visual fields are equivalent in picture identification (Paivio & Ernest, 1971), although the encoding tasks differed. The visual-field equivalence for picture identification in our experiment was associated with high imagery ability, so we might guess that bilateral picture encoding in the Köhler et al. experiment was similarly attributable to those participants who happened to have relatively high imagery ability, but no individual difference tests were used in Köhler's experiment. A further argument is that the living–nonliving semantic decision during encoding encouraged dual coding (i.e., participants decided verbally whether a pictured object was living), but again, there is no other evidence for the strong neuropsychological prediction from DCT. Finally, the results suggest a common picture-word processing system in the left medial temporal lobe. I return to this ubiquitous common- coding issue in Chapter 9.

The aforementioned results show patterns of neural activity that are generally consistent with DCT but they do not directly reveal memory effects of imagery or test stronger predictions from the theory, such as additive memory effects of verbal and nonverbal coding that would be reflected in co-activation of different brain regions, integrated imagery effects, and the rest.

Effects of imagery showed up in an fMRI study of recognition memory by Gonsalves et al. (2004). On study trials, participants were shown photos of common objects and concrete nouns to which they were asked to generate visual images. On test trials, they heard equal numbers of words they had seen along with photos, words they had seen without photos, and words that had not been presented at all. The partipants indicated by a key press whether they had viewed a photo of the named object during the study phase. Research interest centered on the fact that participants sometimes claimed they had seen photos of objects they had only imagined. Three cortical areas showed larger responses to words the participants falsely remembered as having been presented with a photo than to words for which these errors did not occur, namely the anterior cingulate, the precuneous region in the medial parietal lobe, and a right inferior parietal area. These are among the areas activated in some but not all studies of word evoked imagery. For example, Thompson and Kosslyn (2000) did not include the anterior cingulate and precuneous in the regions of interest in their meta-analysis of visual imagery studies (Chapter 7), perhaps because they focused more on processes related to Kosslyn's model (e.g., image generation and inspection) than on mnemonic functions of imagery. In any case, the Gonsalves et al. results buttress the conclusion from behavioral studies that imagery can lead to false remembering, along with its beneficial memory effects (see Chapter 4).

Thus far, we have no direct evidence on brain correlates of the joint effects of dual coding variables on memory. A study by Erdfelder (1993) did show how neuropsychological predictions from the independence-additivity hypothesis could be tested but still left unanswered questions. He proposed a statistical "dual-code Markov chain" version of the DCT hypothesis as applied to concrete and abstract words. This formal model assumes that, on memory trials, each item is in one of four mutually exclusive "latent states:" (a) not coded by either the verbal or the imagery system (nocode), (b) coded only by the imagery system (imagcode),

(c) coded only by the verbal system (verbcode), and (d) coded by both systems. Further assumptions specified the probabilities that items would be encoded in the specified states over trials. Parameter estimates based on the model corresponded reasonably well with data obtained from one paired-associate learning experiment using epileptic patients whose seizure activity could be localized in one or the other hemisphere. Compared to healthy controls, epileptics were primarily impaired in encoding of concrete material by the imagery system and in retrieval from the verbal system. There were no major differences between right- hemisphere and left-hemisphere patients, which agrees with some early memory studies of concreteness effects with brain damaged patients (see the historical summary in Chapter 6) and with data showing referential imagery effects associated with the left hemisphere (Chapter 7).

At this time, we await further studies like Erdfelder's, but extended further to other psychologically well-supported DCT memory hypotheses (Chapter 4), such as additive effects of dual sensory coding (e.g., pictures and environmental sounds), integration effects based on imagery and verbal relational processing, and the redintegrative power of high imagery stimuli as retrieval cues (the conceptual peg hypothesis).

ANTICIPATORY FUNCTIONS

Recall from Chapter 4 that mental images enable us to anticipate situations and relevant objects and thereby prepare us to respond to them appropriately. The general importance of this function for animals as well as humans is reflected in such related concepts as expectancy, preparation, intention, and planning. We saw that some researchers now interpret sensory conditioning, classical conditioning, and instrumental conditioning as processes in which a stimulus comes to elicit an image of another stimulus (e.g., a reward), and the image mediates appropriate anticipatory responses. Anticipatory hand-shaping when reaching to grasp an object, even an imagined one, is another example of this basic function, which implicates the dorsal stream and the parietal cortex (Milner & Goodale, 1995). Still another is mental rotation in which the activation pattern of motor neurons in a monkey were found to anticipate the expected position of a stimulus (Georgopoulos et al., 1989). It has also been suggested that the basic evolutionary function of mirror neurons is to simulate actions so that their consequences can be predicted (Stamenov, 2002), which implies motor imagery as discussed in Chapter 7.

What is particularly important is the anticipatory function of spatial imagery, one's ability to imagine the spatial locations of rooms, grocery stores, and other useful places so that one can find them when necessary. We saw the negative consequences of impaired spatial imagery in patients with parieto-occipital damage who could not find their way around in their previously familiar environments. Such examples also show the relation between anticipation and memory in that expected objects, places, and preparatory responses can only be imagined if one remembers them from previous perceptual-motor experiences (cf. Jeannerod, 1994).

The anticipatory function of dual coding systems also overlaps and interacts with evaluative and emotional-motivational functions, thereby engaging neural systems in various parts of the brain. These systems are identified in the following sections.

EVALUATION

Evaluation is a basic adaptive function because perceived, remembered, and expected objects or situations are often appraised for their usefulness or value before one decides how to act. The evaluative roles of imagery and verbal processes were studied behaviorally using mental comparison tasks in which participants decided as quickly as possible which of two symbolically presented items (pictures or words) had more or less of some property, such as size, weight, or monetary value. The research reviewed in Chapter 4 showed that the task is sensitive to fine-grained differences in such remembered properties—for example, the time required to decide which of two named objects is larger (e.g., a cat or a toaster) increases uniformly as the real-life size difference gets smaller. Knowledge about such differences prepares us to respond in appropriate ways when faced with real objects and situations. For instance, we can prepare to use more effort to pick up a shot-put ball than a grapefruit because we know which is heavier.

Perceptual memories of the relevant properties of objects are essential for their evaluation. These memories are represented in different sensorimotor modalities of imagery, and, less finely, in verbal memory. Cortical memory systems are thus involved. For example, neurons of the orbitofrontal cortex receive taste and olfactory inputs perhaps because they are part of a mechanism that evaluates whether a reward is expected (Rolls, 1995, p. 100), thus implicating anticipatory imagery. The anterior cingulate cortex plays a crucial evaluative role in choosing the most suitable response from alternative possibilities, for it is known to be activated in cognitive tasks in which a choice must made between two stimuli (e.g., Badgaiyan & Posner, 1998). Thus, we have to assume that the anterior cingulate cortex is essential in any evaluative comparison task.

The cingulate cortex is part of the limbic system that also includes the amygdala and other structures forming the neural core of emotion and motivation. The limbic system might be generally engaged in symbolic comparisons involving emotionally relevant properties such as the relative pleasantness value of pictured or named objects, which have been investigated using the symbolic comparison task. Consequently, we turn next to such properties and the role of evaluation, imagery, and language in emotion and motivation, including taste and smell as motivational systems.

MOTIVATION AND EMOTION

Motivation deals with goal-oriented behavior, why we do what we do. We seek food, mates, and shelter because they are necessary for our survival. Other goals are means to those necessities or have simply been associated with them through, for example, money, praise, and other secondary incentives that can become more compelling than the primary ones (Maslow, 1954). Motivation includes physiological arousal because energy must be mobilized to attain goals. Positive and negative feelings and emotions are involved because they mediate the direction of goal-oriented behavior—we seek objects and situations that make us feel good and avoid ones that make us feel bad.

Ultimately, all of the sensorimotor and cognitive machinery that have been described are in the service of motivational goals. These include the basic dual coding processes as well as their cognitive functions in memory, anticipation, and so forth. We image and talk about food, homes (shelter), useful objects, people we love or hate, "fun and games," and the purpose of life. In other words, whatever interests us. Later, we categorize and analyze the goals systematically in the biological and social evolutionary context. First, however, we can review the neural basis of motivational and affective-emotional experiences from the dual coding perspective, beginning with taste and smell as intrinsic sensory components activated by the most basic primary goal objects.

Taste and Smell

The chemical senses and affective-emotional systems are linked together by their common association with food, and hence, survival. The systems are connected at the neural level especially through limbic structures. Recall from Chapter 6 that the limbic system is a loosely connected "ring" of cortical and subcortical structures that includes the amygdala, hippocampal formation (the hippocampus plus the parahippocampal cortex adjacent to it, already discussed in relation to memory), hypothalamus, thalamus, cingulate cortex, and the prefrontal cortex. The hypothalamus, for example, has a "hunger center" and a "satiation center" that control and delimit eating, but eating preferences are determined as well by other structures that respond to the taste of food. For example, fMRI recordings show that the pleasant and unpleasant tastes of glucose and salt, respectively, activate the amygdala and the orbitofrontal cortex. Moreover, the positive and negative tastes activate separate areas within both structures, most clearly in the orbitofrontal cortex (O'Doherty, Rolls, Francis, Bowtell, & McGlone, 2001). The connection to affective systems is so close in the case of smell that some neuroscientists include the olfactory cortex as part of the limbic system, with connections to the amygda, hippocampus, prefrontal cortex, the hypothalamus, and other structures. Activation patterns have been found connecting brain areas for taste and smell to areas crucial to language and imagery.

Emotions

The nonverbal status of emotions, like that of tastes and smells, means that they have no verbal counterpart, except by association—we can name or describe specific emotions such as joy, fear, and anger, and react in relevant ways to their names. We recognize emotions from facial expressions and when we say that someone looks happy, angry, or sad, we demonstrate the referential connections between specific emotional expressions and emotional names. The reverse direction of referential activation (implicating imagery as well) is demonstrated by the finding that when participants are told to imagine happy, sad, or angry situations, different patterns of facial muscle activity are produced, which can be measured by electromyography (Schwartz, Fair, Salt, Mandel, & Klerman, 1976). Moreover, as we saw in Chapter 3, actors can reliably produce distinct facial expressions to more than 400 emotion names, and research participants can name the expressions (Baron-Cohen, 2003). This discriminative referential processing capacity reflects the adaptive significance of learning to read emotions in others, a kind of mind reading that presumably has its roots deep in the evolution of nonverbal cognition (see further in Chapter 11). Next, we examine learned emotional and affective reactions and their brain correlates from the dual coding perspective.

Recall from Chapter 4 that affective-emotional reactions are assumed to be learned primarily in the context of nonverbal objects and events, especially including other people, and thereby become connected to nonverbal representations (imagens). In addition, through conditioning, words themselves acquire generalized affective qualities analogous to referential meaning in which the referential reaction is a particular emotion. Emotion usually follows prior identification of a relevant stimulus or image, although the converse can also occur in the sense that, once aroused, emotions can prime (increase the probability of) relevant imagery and verbal associations. Evaluation as discussed in the preceding section is directly implicated in emotional arousal and its motivational consequences: The situational or cognitive contexts must be evaluated or appraised in some manner before one can decide how to react overtly. As we saw in Chapter 4, this assumption that the causal sequence proceeds from stimulus identification to evaluation to emotion is somewhat controversial. The neuropsychological evidence that follows has something to say about the issue but does not resolve it.

The dual coding experiment on emotion comparisons (Chapter 4) provides a context for the neuropsychological analysis. Participants were asked to decide as quicky as possible which of two stimuli is more pleasant or more unpleasant. The stimuli were pictures of objects, concrete nouns, or abstract nouns that were preselected to vary equivalently in their rated pleasantness. In support of the main prediction from DCT, pleasantness comparisons were fastest for pictures (the affectively loaded referents could be seen), next fastest for concrete words (images of the referents could be accessed), and slowest for abstract words (which activated affective images only indirectly). In addition, as expected, decisions were faster as the pleasantness difference increased. A detailed neuropsychological DCT analysis of these and other results follows after a summary of the neural representational base for emotions.

The limbic system is crucial in affect and emotion. The key player is the amygdala (see Fig. 6. 1), an almond-shaped set of nuclei just beneath the surface of the medial part of the temporal lobe, close to the hippocampus. It is best known for its role in emotions such as fear and anger (the behaviors and conscious experiences associated with them), but in that role it must have input from sensory and memory systems, and output to systems involved in emotional reactions. Thus, it has highly processed input from association areas of visual, auditory, and somatosensory cortices, hippocampus, and the frontal lobes, which collectively permit it to recognize objects or situations that could have affective significance. Its crucial role in emotional memory has been revealed by studies in which damage to the amygdala abolishes memory for fear and other emotions without affecting memory for the events that previously elicited the emotions.

The main outputs of the amygdala include stimulation of (a) the hypothalamus, which in turn influences autonomic and hormonal responses associated with emotional arousal; and (b) the prefrontal cortex, which, through memory, connects mood states and conscious emotional responses to positive or negative events. The latter connections, in particular, help explain the role of the amygdala in reacting to and evaluating the affective significance of stimuli. For example, frontal lobotomy as a (now obsolete) treatment for psychosis, cuts the prefrontal cortex from the amygdala, typically leaving the patient with flat affect, lacking in normal emotional reactions to others, unable to comprehend emotion in facial expressions or language, and so on (Arnold, 1960, pp. 108–112; Kolb & Whishaw, 2001, p. 436). Antonio Damasio (1999, cited in Kolb & Whishaw, 2001) proposed a semantic marker hypothesis to explain such effects: People with frontal lobe injury are cut off from the amygda and other neural machinery that underlies emotion, resulting in irrational social and personal decisions. The anterior cingulate cortex also plays a crucial evaluative role in the choice of the most suitable response from alternative possibilities.

Let us see how this neuropsychology relates to the dual coding approach to affect and emotion. The relevant neuropsychological network that connects cognitive and noncognitive aspects of emotion has been reviewed by Halgren and Marinkovic (1995). Electrical stimulation and evoked potential (ERP) experiments have shown that all of the limbic system and many other cortical systems are involved in emotional reactions and experiences. For example, limbic stimulation evokes visceral sensations, emotional feelings, and emotionally symbolic hallucinated images. Relevant ERP components reveal successive stages of face and word encoding that begin in the primary sensory cortex and rapidly arrive at multimodal and limbic structures in all lobes. Emotionally expressive faces evoke different scalp potentials when compared to nonexpressive faces or emotionally significant words. The amygda contributes an emotional evaluation at early stages of event encoding synchronously with cognitive evaluation by the lateral orbitofrontal cortex and the cingulate cortex. An especially relevant study by Damasio et al. (2000) showed that feelings associated with emotional images engaged subcortical as well as cortical brain areas.

The analysis extends directly to the interpretation of the results of the DCT pleasantness comparison experiment. Relevant cortical and limbic areas were presumably involved in the recognition and evaluation of the affective value of pictures and words. The hippocampus and amygdala were primary mediators of viscerosensory emotional responses whereas the frontal lobes and cingulate cortex were the likely areas for comparing and evaluating the affect aroused by the stimuli. The affective experience and its connection to the words "pleasant" and "unpleasant" required interactive processing by verbal cortical systems and nonverbal limbic structures. The following observations suggest further that left and right hemispheres were differentially involved in the effects.

The emphasis on emotion as a nonverbal phenomenon that can be conditioned to language suggests that, like other nonverbal cognitive phenomena, it should be linked more to the right hemisphere than the left. In fact, suggestive evidence of such right hemisphere dominance for emotion was noted as long ago as 1880 by Hughlings-Jackson (Borod, Andelman, Obler, Tweedy, & Welkowitz, 1992). More recent findings support that interpretation in ways that are directly relevant to DCT. Bryden (1982, pp. 126–129) used lateralized presentation of visual and auditory stimuli to show that the right hemisphere is superior to the left in tasks that require participants to match emotional facial expressions, categorize the emotional tone of musical passages, and judge the emotional tone of sentences. Right-hemisphere imagery systems were implicated in a priming study (Ley & Bryden, 1983) in which participants first memorized a list of high imagery or low imagery words that also varied in affective value. The intent of this procedure was to induce the participants to think about emotional material and thereby activate the right hemisphere. The results were that studying the affectively loaded words produced a relative improvement in left-visual field recognition of emotional facial expressions and left-ear recognition of dichotically presented emotional words, both implicating the right hemisphere. Moreover, this right-hemisphere enhancement was greater when the memorized word list used for priming consisted of high imagery words than when it consisted of low imagery words. Ley and Bryden (1983) proposed the following dual coding explanation of their results:

> Study of a high-imagery list of emotional words leads to a representation of the word list that includes not only verbal coding mechanisms that presumably are represented in the left hemisphere, but also imagery-based and affective components that are located in the right hemisphere. Thus ... there is greater activity in the right hemisphere than in the left when either high-imagery or highly emotional words have been presented. This increased right-hemisphere activity makes the right hemisphere more receptive to incoming stimuli, and consequently produces better performance in the left visual field or the left ear, performance better than that which is observed when word lists not having imagery or affective components are studied. (Ley & Bryden, 1983, p. 38)

More recent studies indicated that different areas in the two hemispheres are activated during the arousal and evaluation of emotions evoked by pictures or words. Hariri, Bookheimer, and Mazziotta (2000) used fMRI to record brain activity when participants either matched the affect (anger or fear) of one of two pictured faces to a target picture, or chose one of two labels that best described the emotion of a target face. The results showed that matching expressions was associated with increased activation in the left and right amygdala, the brain's primary emotional response centers. What seems to happen is that labeling these same emotional expressions resulted in increased activation in the right prefrontal cortex, accompanied simultaneously by diminished activity in the amygdala. In brief, the amygdala responded directly to the facial affect whereas the right prefrontal cortex became dominantly active when the emotion was subsequently interpreted. These results suggest that the right hemisphere dominance in the earlier laterality studies of emotion reflected the evaluation stage of the emotional response. The results also justify the neuropsychological analysis of the Paivio (1978b) experiment on pleasantness comparisons of picture pairs, in particular.

The dual coding connection to emotion is even clearer in a recent fMRI study of traumatic memories by Ruth Lanius et al. (2004). Patients suffering from posttraumatic stress syndrome (PTSS), and control participants who also had experienced traumatic events but did not suffer from PTSS, listened to scripts of traumatic events and neutral events they had undergone, and then described the sensations they experienced during recall of the events. Brain activation was recorded during a subsequent quiet (baseline) period and while the participant listened to a repetition of the script. Analysis of the recall reports indicated that the PTSS participants had more emotional imagery content in their recollections than did the control participants. The fMRI data obtained during re-presentation of the traumatic scripts showed that the PTSS group had relatively more activation in right hemisphere areas typically involved in nonverbal cognition (right posterior cingulate gyrus, caudate, parietal lobe, and occipital lobe), whereas the controls had more activation in language-related left hemisphere areas (superior frontal gyrus, anterior cingulate cortex, striatum, parietal lobe, and insula). The authors noted the relation between their findings and the dual coding theory of emotional learning and representation (Paivio, 1986) reviewed in this section.

PROBLEM SOLVING

Many of the tasks and neuropsychological syndromes reviewed in this and the preceding chapter implicate problem solving in the general sense. For example, a person with integrative agnosia would be expected to have difficulty solving problems that require visualizing how parts could be assembled into wholes. Some patients with lesions in the parieto-occipital area have spatial-imagery deficits that are reflected in the difficulty they have in finding their way around their own homes or their neighborhoods. They have forgotten how to solve the problem of orienting themselves even in familiar environments. We focus here on the neural correlates of this cognitive mapping ability because it has great survival value and implicates dual coding processes.

An ecologically-relevant series of experiments involved London taxi drivers who recalled the routes they would take to get to different destinations. The drivers require a 3-year training period in which they have to demonstrate mastery of routes and locations before being licensed to operate taxis in the city. Thus, they are ideal candidates for cognitive mapping research. The general procedure entailed taking brain scans using PET while the drivers imagined and described complex routes around the city. In one experiment (Maguire, Frackowiak, & Frith, 1997), the drivers described such familiar routes and landmarks as Hyde Park Corner, Parliament Square, Queen Victoria Memorial, and so on. Control tasks tapped visual memories that did not include route knowledge. The critical results, for these purposes, were that the drivers gave detailed and accurate memory descriptions of the routes and locations of the London landmarks and that the task activated a network of brain regions that included the right hippocampus. The control tasks activated separate and overlapping regions that did not include the hippocampus.

The researchers did not question their participants about the use of imagery during the task but they did note the association of visual imagery with activation of the parietal region in other spatial memory studies and that the imagery function is "compatible with the requirements of a topographical memory system" (Maguire, et al., p. 7103). Imagery was directly investigated in a PET study of navigation within a complex virtual reality town (Ghaëm et al., 1997). Participants either imagined walking along a segment of a path they had walked the day before or imagined the appearance of a landmark seen from the route. Both tasks activated a network of brain regions that included right- and left-hippocampal areas. In another experiment (Mellet et al., 2002), brain activity was monitored by PET while participants mentally scanned a cognitive map they had constructed from reading a descriptive text. The task activated a parieto-frontal network known to deal with spatial representations, and it also involved Broca's and Wernicke's language areas. These experiments together with the results from taxi drivers clearly implicate spatial problem-solving functions of dual coding brain—areas associated with spatial imagery and memory, together with areas associated with referential processing when maps are described or constructed from a text.

COMMUNICATION FUNCTIONS

Adaptive functions of dual coding language systems were necessarily implicated in neuropsychological studies reviewed so far in this chapter. This section focuses on (a) dual coding brain processes in language comprehension from the word level to sentences, (b) implications of DCT for neurolinguistic studies of syntactic processes in comprehension and production, (c) language development, and (d) bilingualism. The dual coding analyses contrast particularly with monistic verbal and abstract linguistic (propositional, "deep structure") approaches, including traditional neurolinguistic interpretations of the language functions of Broca's and Wernicke's brain areas.

Comprehension and Dual Coding Brain Processes

We have already noted processing differences between left and right hemispheres from experimental studies using lateralized presentation of relevant materials with normal participants and split-brain patients. Thus, when words are flashed to one visual field or the other, concrete and abstract words are recognized equally easily in the right field (hence the left hemisphere), whereas concrete words are often recognized better than abstract words in the left field. This difference suggests stronger bilateral brain representation for concrete than abstract words. Brain scan studies provide more direct evidence of such differences and also reveal anterior–posterior differences in activation patterns within hemispheres.

Concreteness-Imagery Experiments. Experiments by John Kounios, Philip Holcomb, and their colleagues compared neuropsychological predictions from DCT and common coding theories using ERPs to identify cortical regions activated by concrete and abstract words. Interest centered on a component of ERPs known to be sensitive to semantic variables—a negatively-changing component (N400) that peaks about 400 msec after the crucial stimulus event. The research was guided by "the 'spatial distinctiveness principle,'" which assumes that two or more different cognitive systems will tend to be more spatially distinct within the brain than will a single cognitive system" (Holcomb, Kounios, Anderson, & West, 1999, p. 723). From this principle and DCT, they predicted that concrete and abstract materials would be processed by different brain regions rather than a single region as would be predicted from common coding theories.

The results of the experiments supported the general prediction, with some variation in the specific locations of the concrete–abstract differences, depending on procedural details. Kounios and Holcomb's (1994) participants classified nouns as concrete or abstract or distinguished them from nonwords. The main result was that concrete words elicited more ERPs in the N400 range than did abstract words, especially in anterior brain sites and in the right hemisphere. Holcomb et al. (1999) capitalized on a prior finding that N400 is particularly sensitive to semantic anomalies in sentences. They presented participants with concrete and abstract sentences in which the final word was either congruent or incongruent with the prior context (e.g., "Armed robbery implies that the thief used a *weapon* [versus a *rose*]"). Participants judged whether a sentence makes sense. The crucial results were that more N400 ERPs were elicited following anomalous than congruent sentences and by concrete than abstract sentences. Importantly, these variables interacted with electrode site so that the concrete–abstract difference was larger at more anterior sites for anomalous sentences but not congruent sentences. Holcomb et al. concluded that these results (buttressed further by a second experiment) are more consistent with dual coding than context availability theory because the latter predicts only main effects of concreteness and a flat distribution of the N400 across the scalp.

West, O'Rourke, and Holcomb (1998) used concrete and abstract words judged to be imageable along with abstract nonimageable words in sentence processing tasks that did or did not require use of imagery to determine whether the sentence was true or false. For example, to respond appropriately, participants presumably had to image to the sentence, "It is easy to form a mental image of a canoe." However, imagery was not required for another group to decided whether a similar sentence (e.g., "It is common for people to have a canoe") made sense. A further control group simply decided whether a probe letter was present in the final word of the sentence (e.g., "There is a 't' in the word canoe"). There were several notable results. First, the imagery group showed a dramatic increase toward frontal sites in the concrete–abstract difference in the N400 effect. Second, the polarity of the effect actually reversed at occipital sites, so that waveforms to concrete words became more positive than those to abstract words during a 550 to 800 msec time period after stimulus presentation. Third, concreteness and imageability were distinguished in that the concrete–abstract difference at the frontal sites occurred regardless of the word imageability, whereas imageable and nonimageable words differed mostly at posterior regions. The authors concluded that the findings strongly support the dual coding model of mental representation over single code models that reject imagery as a significant symbolic system underlying language.

In the aforementioned experiment, the slower ERP response to word imagery in the occipital cortex may have reflected the time necessary for imagery variables to activate an area known to be involved in imagery effects (Chapter 7). Frymiare et al. (unpublished) sought to determine the earliest time period at which the ERP patterns distinguish concrete words from abstract words. Participants viewed sequentially presented pairs of concrete words, abstract words, and pseudowords. The meaningful word pairs were either semantically related or not according to normative ratings. The first word was seen for 250 msec and "held it in mind" for 2 sec until the second word was presented. A button press indicated whether the pair was semantically related. The crucial result was that concrete and abstract words activated different areas of the brain within 166 to 180 msec after word presentation. Concrete words activated right frontal and right temporal areas more strongly than abstract words, whereas abstract words activated the frontopolar (midfrontal) cortex more strongly than concrete words. The results confirmed the special role of the right hemisphere in processing concrete words for meaning and showed in addition that the concrete–abstract difference occurred earlier than previously shown by any technique. From the DCT viewpoint, the early difference might reflect the initial access to imagens, although useful images are unlikely to be elicited so quickly (< 200 msec). Estimates from behavioral data suggested 600 msec as the threshold for image generation (Paivio, 1971b, p. 76), which is in the ballpark of the N400 and other later ERP waveform peaks for semantic and imagery processes in the West et al. (1998) experiment reviewed earlier. This speculation remains to be confirmed.

An fMRI brain scanning experiment (Binder et al., 2005) provided further clear evidence that distinct brain systems are used for processing concrete and abstract concepts. Their participants were presented concrete words, abstract words, and nonwords and were asked to indicate whether each item was a word or a nonword by pressing one of two keys. The fMRI results showed overlapping but partly distinct patterns of neural activity, such that a bilateral network of association and posterior multimodal cortices were activated during processing of concrete words, whereas a strongly left-lateralized network was activated during processing of abstract words. The authors concluded that the results provide firm evidence for a dual coding model of concrete and abstract concepts.

The above results justify extending DCT interpretations to other brain scan studies in which concreteness and imagery have been varied in sentence comprehension tasks. Using regional blood flow (PET) as a measure of activation, Mellet, Tzourio, Denis, and Mazoyer (1998) found that overlapping but partly distinct patterns of neural activity were elicited when participants imaged while listening to definitions of concrete words as compared to definitions of abstract words. Just, Newman, Keller, McKelney, and Carpenter (2004) used fMRI to study brain activation during more complex comprehension tasks involving sentences that varied in imagery value. Participants read or heard high-imagery sentences (such as "A circle placed at the top of the capital letter v resembles the outline of an ice cream cone") or low-imagery sentences (such as "Horsepower is the unit for measuring the power of engines or motors"). Participants were asked to respond true or false to the sentences. They were also told that, on some trials, they would have to visualize the sentence to answer, and were presented an example of such a sentence. Following are the pertinent results. High imagery sentences resulted in more activation than low imagery sentences in the parietal cortex (particularly the left intraparietal sulcus), whereas low imagery sentences produced more activation of the left temporal cortex. Both regions also showed functional connectivity (co-activation) with frontal regions generally involved in language processing. These generalizations hold for both visual and auditory presentation, although activation patterns were also qualified by modality. For example, the parietal cortex showed a greater difference in functional connectivity between high and low imagery sentences in the auditory condition, whereas the temporal cortex showed a greater difference in connectivity in the visual condition, perhaps because "listening comprehension may be a better modality in which to receive imagery-laden information, whereas the reading comprehension may be a better modality in which to receive abstract information" (Just et al., 2004, p. 122).

The co-activation of parietal and language processing areas in the case of high-imagery sentences suggests a dual coding involvement in the form of verbal-maginal referential processing. The authors interpret the temporal lobe processing of abstract sentences in terms of retrieval and processing of semantic and world knowledge, but a DCT alternative is that the effect simply reflects verbal associative processing. Examination of the low imagery sentences in Appendix A of the Just et al. (2004) article provides suggestive support in that key words in the sentences seem to be strongly associated (e.g., horsepower, measurement, power, engines, motors, in the example given earlier). This interpretation could be checked out by associative ratings, and eventually, brain scan experiments in which associative relatedness is systematically varied within sentences.

A common general outcome from all of the experiments is that, neurologically, regional activation patterns differed for concrete and abstract (or high imagery and low imagery) materials in language comprehension tasks. The following study implicates dual coding because it involved pictorial referents in sentence comprehension.

Sentence-Picture Verification.   Reichle, Carpenter, and Just (2000) used fMRI to study the patterns of cortical activation in participants who differed in verbal and visual-spatial skills according to psychometric tests, and who were given instructions to use either a verbal or a visual strategy in a task in which sentences are verified as true or false relative to pictured scenes. The verbal strategy produced more activation in language-related cortical regions, including Broca's area, whereas the visual-spatial strategy produced more activation in the parietal cortex and other regions that have been implicated in visual-spatial reasoning. These relations were modified by individual differences so that participants with better verbal skills as measured by a reading span test had less activation in Broca's area when they used a verbal strategy than when they used a visual-spatial strategy. Conversely, individuals with better visual-spatial skills as measured by a mental rotation test had less activation in the left parietal cortex when they used the visual-spatial strategy. The pattern of reduced activation was interpreted to mean that skill-compatible strategies helped to minimize cognitive overload. Simply put, the task was easy for brain regions with efficient verbal or nonverbal processing systems when primed by appropriate cues, especially in the context of the dual coding demands of the sentence-picture verification task. Thus, the complex interactive pattern is more consistent with DCT than with abstract coding theories of language comprehension.

Syntax and the Dual Coding Brain

The DCT analysis of syntax in Chapter 4 was motivated by the fact that the adaptive communicative functions of language depend on the way language units are organized. Here, we see how DCT can contribute to the analysis of neural correlates of syntax. Much of the recent work has been done by neurolinguists who view the problem from an intralinguistic theoretical perspective that focuses on the linguistic core of syntax, excluding extralinguistic factors known to contribute independently to communicative competence. These neurolinguistic theories are, therefore, variants of the abstract, single code approach that is the main theoretical contrast to DCT. We see, however, that dual coding neural processes are implicated even in these abstract approaches and they become more apparent in another neurolinguistic approach that emphasizes multimodal contributions to syntax.

When Begg and I reviewed the brain correlates of language more than 30 years ago (Paivio & Begg, 1981), the classic picture was that syntax is associated with Broca's area in the left frontal lobe and semantics is associated with Wernicke's area in the posterior left temporal region. Syntactic aspects were inferred from a breakdown in syntactic relations (agrammatism) in the speech of patients with lesions in Broca's area. Some evidence suggested that agrammatism is associated specifically with impairment in the ability to use grammatical transformational rules, and that comprehension was similarly affected in such patients. It is especially relevant that Caramazza and Zurif (1976) used a sentence-picture matching task to evaluate the comprehension capacities of anterior (Broca's) aphasics and posterior (Wernicke's) aphasics. The sentences had subjects and objects that are either reversible (e.g., "The lion the tiger is chasing is fat") or not reversible (e.g., "The bicycle that the boy is holding is broken"). Sentence-picture pairs were presented in which the correct picture could be chosen on the basis of lexical information or only on the basis of correct syntax. The relevant result was that the Broca's aphasics were 90% accurate on the nonreversible sentences but performed at chance on the reversible sentences. Thus, the agrammatic patients were as impaired in syntactic processing in tests of comprehension as they were in tests of production.

The interpretations have changed as a result of further studies of patients with brain lesions, augmented greatly by brain imaging studies with normal participants. Many more brain areas are now implicated in language processing and the specific role of Broca's area has become controversial. Neurolinguists have hoped that such studies would reveal the neural substrate of Broca's agrammatism and at the same time lead to better neurolinguistic theories of language. We begin with neurolinguistic approaches that have been guided by variants of Chomsky's (1982) "government and binding" theory of syntax. The theories retain the earlier distinction between deep structure and surface structure of language, with changes in the original phrase structure rules and other assumptions that need not be detailed here (an introduction to government and binding theory is conveniently available as an Internet article by Cheryl Black, 1998). Some of these neurolinguistic theories also include revised forms of Fillmore's (1977) case grammar that emphasize different semantic roles (now often called theta roles) of noun phrases in sentences. It is important to remember that all of these theories are entirely intralinguistic in that they deal with relations between language elements even when semantics is involved. For example, in the sentence "The boy kissed the girl," the noun-phrase "The boy" has the theta role of "Agent" relative to the rest of the sentence and not to the situation it describes. As I explain shortly, Fillmore originally adopted a more psychological position on semantic relations than have current theta-role theorists.

Three hypotheses emphasize different aspects of the linguistic approach that are of interest here. Neurolinguist Yozef Grodzinsky (2000) argued that, contrary to the traditional view, most of syntax is not located in Broca's area and its vicinity. For example, although brain scan studies of language processing consistently show activation of Broca's area, it is accompanied by great variation in activation patterns involving other areas. Grodzinsky (2000) suggested that the blurred picture is due to an insufficiently refined view of linguistic structure. He therefore proposed a "new view" that retains the general assumption that syntactic abilities are distinct from other cognitive skills and are represented entirely in the left hemisphere. In this revised view, Broca's area remains important as the "neural home" to a specific transformational component of syntax, namely the movement of sentence phrases that is assumed to occur at the deep structure level of syntactic representation. Thus, in the basic active–passive transformation, the noun phrases presumably change position (e.g., "The girl pushed the boy" "becomes" "The boy was pushed by the girl"). Consistent with this view, Broca's aphasics are severely impaired in sentence-picture comprehension tests involving movement-transformed active–passive sentence contrasts. For example, given "The boy was pushed by the girl", the patients would be equally likely to choose the correct picture or the incorrect one that shows a boy pushing a girl.

Grodzinsky (2000) interpreted such results in terms of a trace-deletion hypothesis coupled with a heuristic default strategy. The hypothesis is based on the idea that grammatical transformations involve moving a structural constituent to another position and substituting in its original place a phonetically silent but syntactically active trace. Thus, in the case of the passive counterpart of "The girl hit the boy," the movement of "the boy" into the subject position leaves its trace in the original position so that the passive is "understood" as something like "The boy the girl hit [the boy]" so that "the boy" retains its thematic role as recipient of the action "hit." The trace deletion hypothesis states that all traces of movement are deleted from the syntactic representation of Broca's aphasics, leaving them confused about who is doing what to whom in noun-role reversible sentences, such as the boy–girl example, thus accounting for the chance performance.

The default strategy is motivated by the conventional assignment of the role of Agent to the initial noun phrase of a sentence, except in passives and some other constructions in English and other languages. Thus, agrammatic Broca's aphasics succeed with active sentences because the default strategy works and they fail on passives because it doesn't work. The strategy assumption is especially contentious but Grodzinsky and his collaborators have amassed considerable support for the hypothesized role of Broca's area in movement transformations in agrammatic aphasics as well as neurolinguistic evidence from brain imaging experiments with normals (e.g., Ben-Shachar, Palti, & Grodzinsky 2004).

Marcia Linebarger and her collaborators (e.g., Linebarger, 1995; Linebarger, Schwartz, & Saffran, 1983) proposed an alternative mapping hypothesis, which is based on the assumption that comprehension entails mapping a syntactic structure (NP, VP, etc.) onto a semantic structure as described by a "theta grid" of thematic roles (Agent, Patient, Instrument, etc.) of noun phrases in sentences with different verbs. The hypothesis is that the process of theta assignment is especially vulnerable to disruption in agrammatics because of the structural complexities of various kinds in all sentences and is exacerbated when syntactic movement is involved.

Yet another interpretation is a double-dependency hypothesis (Mauner, Fromkin, & Cornell, 1993), which states that the agrammatic's deficit allows for at least two alternative deep structure representations where the normal person only has one. To simplify, the "The lion was bitten by the dog" could be read as "The dog was bitten by the lion", because the passive morpheme, en, is associated with both NPs in the underlying representation. The ambiguity results in chance performance, which is also predicted by the trace dependency and the mapping hypothesis in the case of the English passive, but not in the case of some other languages. Beretta et al. (2001) tested the three hypotheses using Korean and Spanish, which have different structural representations of the passive than does English. Only the double dependency hypothesis correctly predicted that structural scrambling would result in chance performance with both active and passive sentences by agrammatic aphasics.

No doubt some hypothesis tweaking will change the pattern of predictive successes in future studies. We can conclude up to this point that linguistic theories generate predictions that are supported by empirical evidence from the performance of aphasics. Broca's area seems to be the locus of specific aspects of syntax which, along with adjacent frontal areas and posterior areas of the cortex, contribute to overall language performance. Here we can ask the following question: which dual coding processes are implicated in these linguistic theories and the empirical tests of their assumptions?

Dual Coding Variables in Neurolinguistic Approaches. The most important DCT implication is that Broca's agrammatism reflects some failure in the beneficial functioning of independent (multimodal) verbal and nonverbal systems rather than a flaw in an abstract syntactic processor of the kind described by linguistic theorists. In DCT, extralinguistic factors influence language via nonverbal–verbal connections. Linguists interpret extralinguistic influences mainly as language-related processes that are outside a formal linguistic theoretical system but some extralinguistic influences are implicitly associated with the semantic component of the linguistic theories. For example, verb roles are metalinguistic names for language meanings that stem originally from actions and functions of perceptual objects. The real-world origins were more explicit in Fillmore's case-grammar forerunner to current thematic theories. Specifically, as mentioned earlier (Chapter 4), Fillmore (1977) asserted that meanings are relativized to scenes, namely, "we choose and understand expressions by having or activating in our minds scenes or images or memories of experiences within which the word or expression has a naming or describing or classifying function" (p. 74).

Fillmore (1977) went on to analyze grammatical-case roles in terms of the kinds of scenes that are evoked by different expressions, emphasizing in particular the various mental perspectives brought into play by different verbs: "Something like a salience hierarchy [of scene elements] determines what gets foregrounded, and something like a case hierarchy determines how the foregrounded nominals are assigned grammatical functions" (p. 80). How all this happens is unanswered in his analysis as it is in current versions of semantic role theory, but Fillmore at least suggested that the answer might be found in the relations between language, scene perception, and behavior (the affordances of objects in scenes), rather than processes operating entirely within the linguistic structures themselves.

Dual coding processes become operationally explicit when neurolinguistic researchers use sentence-picture matching or verification tasks to test hypotheses concerning agrammatism. The task presupposes either that the participant constructs an image to, say, a passive sentence, and tries to match it with a pictured scene; or conversely, verbalizes covertly to the scene and tries to match the read or heard sentence to the generated verbal description—in either case, involving referential processing. Psychological evidence for facilitative interplay in both directions has been available for more than 30 years (Paivio, 1971b), with imagery being favored as the mediating process in the sentence-picture matching task.

The same procedure has also been used informatively in a neurolinguistic study of speech production. Earlier neuroimaging studies had generally involved single words because of control problems associated with brain scans during long utterances. Peter Indefrey et al. (2001) recorded neural activity (PET) during naturally produced speech using a restrictive scene description paradigm. Participants viewed animated scenes containing squares and ellipses in different colors. The scenes were designed to elicit descriptions with different degrees of syntactic encoding. For example, one scene might elicit "The red square launches the blue ellipse." The PET results provided evidence that a region caudally adjacent to Broca's area is involved in the "structuring of individual words into phrases and sentences expressing complex thoughts" (Indefrey et al., p. 5936). The DCT implications are clearly the same here as in the comprehension experiments that used sentence-picture matching tasks. In the aforementioned example, the squares and ellipses activate imagens that in turn activate referentially related motor logogens for shape, color, and movement, which are expressed sequently according to grammatical habits.

Dual coding processes are similarly implicated in remedial applications inspired by the neurolinguistic mapping hypothesis. This mapping therapy focuses on training agrammatic patients to associate syntactic positions with the thematic roles of Agent, Instrument, and so forth, assigned to those positions by given verbs (Linebarger, 1995, p. 87). The procedure entails repeated presentations of a variety of sentences followed by thematically related pictures. Significant improvements in agrammatic comprehension were obtained when this procedure was administered either manually (Schwartz, Saffran, Fink, Myers, & Martin, Ellis & Dean, 1994) or by computer (Crerar, 1996). The applications involve fixed protocols of sentence elements and pictures that can be characterized in dual coding terms as procedures designed to develop referential (mapping) connections between novel sentences and pictures, which apparently generalize to comprehension tests involving different sentences and pictures. In this respect, the procedure is similar to the experimental use of pictures to teach grammars (Moeser & Bregman, 1973; Strømnes, 1974), as described in Chapter 4.

Aphasic agrammatism has also been investigated without pictures using grammaticality judgments of well-formed and deviant sentences (e.g., Shachar et al., 2004). An interesting result was that agrammatics can accurately judge grammaticality of sentences that they cannot comprehend under the sentence-picture matching procedure. For example, they might say that "The boy was kissed by the girl" is grammatical although they cannot choose the appropriate matching picture. The dissociation has been puzzling for linguistic theories (e.g., Linebarger, 1995). What can we make of it from the dual coding perspective? The immediate answer is that some dissociation would be expected from the DCT assumption that verbal and nonverbal systems are functionally independent, although probabilistically interconnected and therefore capable of interplay. This means that grammaticality judgments could be based mainly on the verbal system, with some input from the imagery system especially when participants are asked whether a sentence makes sense. The sentence-picture comparison task, on the other hand, engages the nonverbal system more completely. The different emphases would produce some degree of dissociation in the results of the two tasks. More complete reliance on the verbal system could be achieved by using abstract sentences in grammaticality judgments as they were used in earlier psycholinguistic studies of sentence processing.

Besides the basic DCT "syntactic mechanisms" just described, other psychological processes discussed in Chapter 4 are especially relevant here. One is attentional focus, which is implied in Fillmore's (1977) analysis of the salience of "scene elements." Listeners usually focus first on the surface subject of a sentence because of the perceptual salience of the actor in action scenes described by the sentence, and hence are more dependent on the "default" strategy of mentioning the agent first (cf. Olson & Filby's 1972 analysis of focus in verification of active and passive sentences, as described earlier on). Another relevant process is short-term memory. Broca's patients may be relatively weaker than normals on passives because of working memory limitations (e.g., Shankweiler, Crain, Gorrell, & Tuller, 1989), meaning that they may have forgotten some of the wording by the time they see the pictures, promoting guessing and sometimes reversing the roles of the nouns. It could be argued that Grodzinsky's trace deletion hypothesis is a neurolinguistic paraphrase of selective memory loss for sentence wording that is needed to constrain how the referent picture is read. Interestingly, even Grodzinsky and his collaborators (Ben-Shachar et al., 2004) suggested that the posterior temporal activation they observed in their brain-scan test of the movement transformation hypothesis could reflect maintenance of the moved element in memory.

I conclude this section with a summary of another neurolinguistic approach to syntax, one that is more explicitly compatible with DCT than are the abstract linguistic alternatives we have emphasized thus far. Linguist Philip Lieberman (2002) has long favored a nontraditional approach to the neural basis of language. He rejected the Broca–Wernicke theory and instead emphasized neural circuits that are based on subcortical and neocortical structures throughout the brain, which regulate complex nonverbal behaviors as well as speech and language comprehension. Lieberman especially stressed the subcortical basal ganglia because they are known to help cortically controlled movement patterns run smoothly, and therefore should also perform cognitive (including grammatical) sequential functioning.

Lieberman (2002) cited several kinds of evidence in support of this view. Studies of aphasia have shown that damage to Broca's area alone is insufficient to produce the full syndrome of Broca's aphasia. It must be accompanied also by subcortical dominant-hemisphere damage for the syndrome to appear. On the other hand, subcortical damage that leaves Broca's area intact can result in Broca-like language symptoms. The situation is similar for Wernicke's aphasia in that subcortical structures are often damaged along with Wernicke's area, and premorbid linguistic capability can be recovered after complete destruction of Wernicke's area if the subcortical structures are intact.

Other evidence points to the basal ganglia as the crucial subcortical structures. Brain imaging studies showed that neural circuits involving the prefrontal cortex and basal ganglia are activated when neurologically intact participants perform a picture matching task that required cognitive sequencing over different matching criteria (color, shape, etc.). Lieberman and others have shown that Parkinson's disease, which involves progressive loss of motor control due to damage to the basal ganglia, also is characterized by cognitive and linguistic deficits. These include sentence comprehension difficulties involving particular syntactic constructions. The subcortical neural structures work in concert with cortical regions in linguistic and cognitive tasks as well as in motor control. We see later (Chapter 13) that these structures are also implicated in the evolution of language.

Lieberman (2002) also agreed with the growing body of evidence that sentence processing is lexically driven and that the substrate for the brain's dictionary goes beyond its traditional locus in Wernicke's area and includes areas that code non-verbal knowledge: "When we hear or read a word, neural structures involved in the perception or real-world associations of the word are activated as well as posterior cortical regions adjacent to Wernicke's area" (p. 36). The neural circuits involved cover all of the different sensorimotor modalities we discussed earlier in the context of referential connections and processes. Thus, Lieberman emphasized multi-modal verbal and nonverbal neural representations and processes in all aspects of language, including syntax, which, in this domain, agree with the assumptions of DCT.

Results from studies of language learning after early brain injury by Elizabeth Bates and her colleagues (reviewed in Dick et al., 2005) are consistent with Lieberman's conclusions. The most telling observation is the great plasticity of the brain in regard to language and other functions. For example, comparisons of children with early onset focal lesions and adults with later damage show that the children perform in the low-normal range on tests of language comprehension and production, whereas the brain-damaged adults were massively impaired in the language tasks, relative to healthy age-matched controls. Moreover, in stark contrast to the typical adult pattern of greater deficits following left-hemisphere damage, there was no difference in the performance of children with left hemisphere damage and children with right hemisphere damage. Other studies showed that aphasic patients were impaired to the same extent in comprehending language and environmental sounds, and impaired as well in processing visual stimuli. Lesion sites also overlapped in these cases, suggesting that language has considerable links to nonlinguistic skills and the sensorimotor substrates that allow language to be perceived and produced. These results, like those reviewed by Lieberman, challenge neurolinguistic theories that are based primarily on adult lesion and brain-scan studies.

Language Development

The DCT of language acquisition (Paivio, 1971b, 1986; Paivio & Begg, 1981) was originally proposed as a reaction to the nativistic theory that became prominent in the 1960s. The approach, described in Chapter 4, followed naturally from the priority of concrete nonverbal experience in the development of nonverbal and verbal cognitive systems and the behaviors related to them. Recall that, according to this view, language development builds on a nonverbal cognitive base, including imagery, derived from perceptual-motor experience with relations among objects, events, and behaviors. Everyone assumed that vocabulary develops in that context, so that it is initially highly concrete and later includes abstract words. The more novel assumption was that syntax also arises from the nonverbal base, with grammatical terms and sentence structures mapping onto static and dynamic relations between animate and inanimate objects. Later, syntax becomes more autonomous, and intraverbal bootstrapping further promotes development of syntactic skills on the basis of language experience alone. The initial dependence on nonverbal experience and the later intraverbal autonomy of syntax learning was specifically supported by Moeser and Bregman's (1973) experiments described in Chapter 4.

A nativistic bias remains prominent (e.g., Pinker, Stromswald), but increasing numbers of language researchers argue that syntactic skills are learned and that the learning is based on general motor skills. The contrasting positions also dominate debates about language evolution (Chapter 13). However, the relevant issue here is the neuropsychological status of the DCT view of language acquisition. Lieberman's (2002) review presents broad and detailed support for the foundation of language in nonverbal experience, including especially its relation to such sequential behaviors as walking, and semantically, to the modality-specific properties of referent objects. The review by Dick et al. (2005) supports the same conclusion. Neither review mentions the functional role of imagery in such relations, but the necessary basis for imagery is there. The neural basis for the hypothesized shift from nonverbal dependence to relative functional autonomy of intraverbal experience in syntax learning is also absent in these otherwise-thorough surveys and analyses. Brain scans and other means are available to test both aspects of DCT using natural and artificial languages.

Bilingualism

In Chapter 4, we considered the functional advantages of bilingualism from the perspective of the bilingual dual coding model. The general argument was that the benefits of the interplay of verbal and nonverbal systems would be augmented by having an additional language, especially if the two languages are functionally independent, although interconnected, as stated in bilingual DCT. The hypothesis was supported by additive memory effects of bilingual coding in the case of both concrete and abstract words, enhanced further, as expected, by pictures in a Blissymbols analog (described in Chapter 19) of the bilingual experiment. What would be relevant in the this context is evidence that a bilingual's two languages have some kind of separate representation in the brain, thereby facilitating independent functioning. Motivated by various theories, students of bilingualism have long sought such evidence. The initial hypothesis was that the two languages might be represented in separate hemispheres, at least to some degree and for some bilinguals. The hypothesis was not supported by several decades of research reviewed by Vaid and Hall (1991). An updated review (Hull & Vaid, 2005) concluded that early bilinguals (by age 6) tend to exhibit bilateral activation whereas late bilinguas show left hemisphere dominance overall.

Recent studies by Ellen Bialystok and her collaborators provide some evidence for additive cognitive benefits of knowing two languages and also point to the importance of specific brain regions in the effects. Bialystock, Craik, Klein, and Viswanathan (2004) compared matched groups of monolinguals and bilinguals (who varied in age from 30 to 88) in a reaction time task that requires choosing between competing options. It turned out that bilinguals were faster than monolinguals on the task at all ages. Furthermore, after age 60, bilinguals showed a slower rate of decline in performance than monolinguals. A subsequent study (Bialystok et al., 2005) used a brain scanning procedure (magneto-encephalography, MEG) with adults to determine the neural correlates of the bilingual advantage. The results showed that bilinguals and monolinguals used different subsets of frontal regions of the brain during task performance. Bilinguals showed faster reaction times with greater activity in the left prefrontal cortex and anterior cingulate cortex, whereas monolinguals showed faster reaction times with activation in middle frontal regions. Bialystok et al. (2005) interpreted the results in terms of developmental "exercise" of the frontal regions of the brain because bilinguals have to use them more for the executive functions involved in planning, staying focused, and avoiding distractions in communication situations. Speaking a second language, they argued, creates physical changes in the brain by increasing blood flow and oxygen in the working areas. The neuropsychological implications of the cooperative roles of the imagery system and the bilingual verbal systems remain to be investigated by such means.

CHAPTER NINE

Brain Teasers: Common Codes
and Neural Binding

This final neuropsychological chapter focuses on two issues that are relevant to DCT and challenging to cognitive neuroscience. The first concerns the neuropsychological case for amodal cognitive representations as an alternative (or addition) to the modality-specific representations that were carefully examined in the preceding chapters. The second relates to the old gestalt integration issue that has come to be known in the neurosciences as the binding problem—where and how the brain binds elementary sensorimotor features into meaningful, multimodal percepts and images.

AMODAL CODES AND PROCESSES

This issue dominated debates on imagery and DCT research in the 1970s and 1980s and has become increasingly prominent in neuropsychological literature. Throughout the preceding chapters we examined much evidence for modality-specific neural representations and processes. Here I focus on the revitalized common coding alternative. It appears in many guises, the most general being semantic dementia, and more specific ones such as abstract neural coding of lexical units, sensory integration areas, and multimodal neurons.[23] All implicate processes in the association cortex located in the frontal, temporal, and parietal lobes rather than processes in the primary sensory and motor cortical areas. Both kinds of processes

---

[23]The abstract concept of schema also does yeoman's service at multiple levels of analysis in a comprehensive structural and functional approach to neural organization presented by Arbib and Erdi (2000). I will not review their applications of the concept in detail because they entail the conceptual and empirical problems already reviewed in psychological contexts (e.g., Chapters 1 and 5), especially the problem of instantiation of abstract entities and processes. The problem was pointed out in several peer commentaries on Arbib and

are mediated by the thalamus. The primary sensory cortex receives input from regions of the thalamus that receive information from the sense organs, whereas the association cortex receives its information from regions of the thalamus that receive their input from other areas of the cortex. The information in the association areas has already been processed in the primary sensory areas and represents complex knowledge about objects, events, and behaviors (Kolb & Whishaw, 2001, pp. 534–542). At least some of that complex knowledge has been interpreted in common coding terms. As a specific example, recall from the last chapter that Stefan Köhler (2000) and his collaborators found that encoding and remembering pictures and words activated different regions of the hippocampal area, and also engaged structures in an association area (the medial temporal lobe of the left hemisphere) that are part of a "network of regions that supports semantic processes *across* pictures and words" (p. 176). The common-coding hypothesis is highlighted more generally in the following context.

Semantic Dementia

This neuropsychological syndrome is generally described as a selective disorder of semantic memory, entailing loss of long-term memory knowledge (both verbal and nonverbal) about meanings of words, attributes that define living and nonliving things, and "facts" of all kinds. Semantic memory is viewed as a separate cognitive subsystem that is represented particularly in the inferotemporal regions of one or both temporal lobes. Semantic dementia results from degeneration of this brain system, usually caused by neurodegenerative diseases. The most common and persistent deficit is anomia, which extends to impaired word comprehension as the disease progresses. Other deficits are described later. The capacities that are spared include episodic memory for relatively recent events, phonological and syntactic aspects of language, nonverbal problem solving, and visual-spatial ability.

Semantic dementia has increasingly become a "window on the structure and organization of semantic memory" (Patterson & Hodges, 2000, p. 383).Patterson and Hodges (2000) asked whether semantic memory is one or several systems, more specifically, "are there separate verbal and visual (or sensory) central semantic systems?" (p. 326). They identified some of the major players in both camps and "tend to side with theorists who argue for one central semantic system ... rather than those who propose separate, modality-specific semantic systems" (p. 327).

DCT obviously belongs more with the latter theories than the former, but it differs from both in specific ways, especially in the ways as phrased by Patterson and

---

Erdi (2000). For example, A. Clark (2000) suggested that "what really counts is the unknown process by which the right stuff (schemas) get recruited at the right time to meet higher-level demands (p. 537)." Edelman (p. 539) stated that "attempting to explain the function of a system by saying that it employs schemata is like explaining how a computer program fulfills its function by saying that it employs subroutines...(p. 539)." Even Arbib and Erdi (2000, p. 532) ended up by suggesting that schemas may themselves be viewed as metaphors, which I take to mean that schemas serve expository rather than explanatory functions in theoretical analyses.

Hodges (2000). First, to repeat what has been said earlier, the DCT distinction is not between verbal and visual (or other sensory) systems but rather, between verbal and nonverbal symbolic systems, both of which come in the relevant sensorimotor modalities described in the orthogonal model. Second, those distinctions apply to both episodic and semantic memory information in that memory for specific (autobiographical) episodes and for general facts, names, perceptual properties, and affordances of things are either verbal or nonverbal (or both), and in either case of some specific sensorimotor modality. Thus, even assuming a neurologically distinct "central semantic system" that is selectively damaged in semantic aphasia, everything that it controls consists of interconnected representations that are either verbal or nonverbal and modality specific as defined operationally by stimulus, response, and task variables. Each of these has been described psychologically in Chapter 3 and neuropsychologically in the preceding two chapters.

What then is the empirical case for one (amodal) central semantic system? Patterson and Hodges (2000) offered the following arguments and evidence. They stated first of all that none of the cases of semantic dementia they have studied demonstrated a striking dissociation between different modalities of input or output. On the face of it, this statement seems inconsistent with the semantically relevant selective deficits (e.g., anomia versus loss of object imagery) reviewed in Chapter 7. The rejoinder might be that modality-specific deficits can occur independently but they are relevant to the definition of semantic dementia only when they are part of a syndrome (accompany other deficits) associated with damage to the inferotemporal gyri of one or both temporal lobes. In any case, the authors stated their hope that the few exceptions described by other researchers "will find an adequate explanation in the notion that a single distributed system does not entail identical performance for different modalities" (p. 327).

Patterson and Hodges (2000) then buttressed their single-system argument with evidence from two studies. Lambon Ralph et al. (1999) compared semantic performance for words versus pictures in two conditions. In the first, patients gave definitions of pictured objects and (separately) their spoken names. They found "highly significant concordance" between definitions to pictures and words in how well they defined the core concept.Patterson and Hodges took this as better support for the single-system theory than for separate verbal and visual semantic systems because they assumed that the latter predicts no striking item-specific similarity between word versus picture conditions. Recall, however, that DCT predicts at least some noticeable similarity because concrete words derive their referential meaning from the objects they name, and both verbal and nonverbal codes might be activated by the task. Thus, the patients might covertly name the pictures and image to the words as they try to define them. When such dual coding occurs, it would produce similar definitions to words and pictures.

The theoretical differences are starkly revealed by the authors' analysis of the further observation that the number of definitions containing no appropriate semantic information was greater for words than pictures. They saw this as possible support for a multisystems interpretation that visual semantics were preserved, but countered this with the argument that objects and words differ in how they map onto the central concept—there is a systematic relation among many of the sensory features of an object and its meaning, but the phonological forms of words bear a purely arbitrary relation to their meaning. Thus, when conceptual knowledge is degraded, the patient should be able to provide some appropriate information to a picture but draw a blank to its name. The same argument would extend to image-mediated definitions if we assume that imagery capacity is degraded along with "conceptual knowledge." There is some evidence of imagery loss associated with semantic dementia (e.g., Moscovitch & Nadel, 1999, p. 89). In any case, patients with semantic dementia would not always image to words, and, when they do not, their attempts at defining would suffer from lack of imagery support.

Concreteness–Abstractness Effects. Sarah Breedin and her collaborators (Breedin, Saffran, & Coslett, 1994) reported an unusual concreteness effect in a person (DM) diagnosed as having progressive semantic dementia on the basis of a battery of psychological tests and brain scans that showed atrophic changes in the inferior temporal lobes, particularly on the left side. The relevant finding was that DM performed better with abstract words than concrete words on semantic tasks in which concrete words usually have the advantage—word definitions, word-picture matching, and synonymity judgments. The authors suggested that these reversals of the concreteness effect are not predicted by DCT, at least without further elaboration.

I agree that these particular results would not have been predicted from DCT, or from any other theory for that matter. However, the unexpected reversal (which also turned up in earlier studies cited by Breedin et al., 1994) can be explained by DCT given earlier precedents and the pattern of deficits and spared abilities in semantic dementia. Recall that concrete words are not always advantageous in cognitive tasks and that some of these exceptions were predicted from DCT. For example, no concreteness advantage was expected (or obtained) in identification of briefly presented words because a word must be identified before it can evoke imagery (Paivio & O'Neill, 1970). The usual memory advantage for concrete words vanished as expected when words were presented sequentially at such a fast rate that participants had no time to image to the words. Abstract and concrete words also do not differ in immediate sequential memory tasks, presumably because the task depends primarily on the verbal system. Directly relevant to this issue are Richardson and Barry's (1985) findings that patients with minor closed head injuries showed a specific deficit in recall of concrete words, but the usual concreteness advantage was restored when the patients were instructed to use imagery to remember the word lists. The results were interpreted in dual coding terms to mean that the head injuries impaired spontaneous use of imagery as a memory aid, which nonetheless could be primed by the imagery instructions.

The concreteness effect has even been reversed under some conditions. O'Neill and Paivio (1978) had participants provide ratings of imagery, comprehensibility, and sensibleness for normal concrete or abstract sentences, as well as anomalous sentences that were constructed by arbitrarily substituting content words from one sentence to another. The substitutions produced rating decrements on all dimensions but the decrements were greater for concrete than abstract sentences. Second, comprehensibility and sensibleness were higher for concrete than for abstract normal sentences, but the difference was completely reversed when sentences were highly anomalous. Imagery ratings, however, remained higher for concrete than abstract sentences even when they were anomalous. Finally, in an incidental free recall task following the ratings and a subsequent intentional recall task, recall of content words and of whole sentences was much higher for concrete than abstract materials whether sensible or anomalous.

We interpreted our results against the background of the view that concreteness effects on language processing are mediated by imagery,and the hypothesis that concrete words are more restricted than abstract words in how they can be combined in sentences. The meaningful concatenation of concrete words "is to a considerable extent limited by the constraints governing how their referent objects might relate to one another [whereas] the referent world of abstract things does not seem ... to exert such compelling restrictions ... a difference that is presumably represented in the cognitive structures of concrete and abstract concepts" (O'Neill & Paivio, 1978, p. 15). The cognitive structures of concrete words include their referential connections to object representations (imagens), associative relations among concrete word representations, and relations among referent imagens, any of which would be disrupted by violating selection restrictions in sentences.The cognitive structure of abstract words is based largely on intraverbal associative relations, with more overlap across different words than in the case of concrete associates. Thus, violating selection restrictions would be less damaging to comprehension of abstract words. Imagery ratings and recall were not similarly affected because concrete words could still evoke individual images or relationally bizarre compound images, which benefitted recall in our study as they have done in others.

The extension of the aforementioned results to the concrete–abstract reversals with patient DM is that disruption of normal imagery processes reduced performance in tasks such as defining words, which normally benefit from use of imagery. The damage could have affected the structural integrity of imagens as well as their referential connections to logogens. Abstract words suffered less or not at all because their verbal associative structures were largely intact. How does this compare with the analysis by Breedin and her collaborators? They suggested that, of the theories they considered, "Dual Coding Theory is the most compatible with the account of DM's impairment that we will offer here" (Breedin et al., 1994, p. 649). I suggest that their account differs from DCT only in that they do not refer to imagery in their interpretation of the representation and processing of concrete words. Otherwise the accounts are identical. I compare the salient aspects of the two accounts and then justify the inclusion of imagery in the DCT explanation.

Breedin et al. (1994) "assume that perceptual (or, more broadly, sensorimotor) attributes are of particular importance in the representation of concrete concepts, and that disruption of these facets of word meaning is a core feature of their semantic impairment" (p. 645). These attributes include visual-geometric form in the case of many concepts, and "DM has either lost these geometric structures or the ability to access these structures" (p. 649). The parallel DCT interpretation is in terms of loss of imagen structures or access to them via referential interconnections.

Linguistic-relational aspects of semantic representation are more important in the case of abstract words, and, in the case of DM, these aspects "are better preserved than perceptual-attribute domains, giving rise to a relative advantage for abstract words (p. 652). The DCT equivalent is that abstract word meaning is based largely on internal verbal associative (logogen–logogen) relations, which remained relatively intact in DM.

The parallels extend to the development of concrete and abstract word meanings. Whereas concrete concepts are acquired through their relation to "entities in the physical world ... knowledge of abstract concepts seems to be acquired in the context of language, with little or no direct physical support" (Breedin et al., 1994, p. 650). They are exposed to multiple sentence contexts and thus become flexible in fitting into many different sentence contexts and adapting their meaning to them. In DCT terms, the intraverbal contextual variety results in greater associative overlap among abstract than concrete words, which O'Neill and I (O'Neill & Paivio, 1978) invoked to account for the observation that violating selection restrictions had less effect on comprehensibilty of abstract than concrete sentences.

Breedin et al. (1994) found that DM particularly suffered damage to perceptual components of word meaning (e.g., living things more than nonliving things). The finding is consistent with DCT but it is uncertain whether imagery was affected because it was not directly tested. More direct evidence is available from a patient studied by Ogden (1993, cited in Moscovitch & Nadel, 1999). Among other deficits, the patient had loss of visual imagery associated with inferotemporal damage, the cortical site of semantic dementia. Assuming that DM also had an imagery deficit, his semantic dementia and associated concrete–abstract processing reversals can be interpreted remarkably well in terms of DCT.

More generally, DM is relevant to the controversy about the nature of the representations that are the basis of semantic memory and semantic dementia. Breedin et al. (1994) referred to qualitative differences in the origins and functional characteristics of representations underlying concrete and abstract concepts, thus favoring modality-specific rather than modality-free representations. Whether their interpretation and DCT differ in some respects, both rely on modality-specific representations to explain semantic dementia.

MODALITY-INDEPENDENT BRAIN SYSTEMS

Next we consider evidence for common coding functions of neural ensembles and single neurons. How do these functions relate to the psychological concept of abstract, amodal representational systems? Such systems were proposed as alternatives to modality-specific ones precisely because they purportedly could do the same cognitive work as multiple-coding systems. For example, a modality-free semantic memory system must be able to mediate decisions about specific characteristics of living and nonliving things equally well from pictures or words. Such a system presumably recodes modality-specific information into abstract conceptual codes that we know only from names given to the original modality-specific properties. The evidence for abstract codes comes from similar behavioral outcomes when the critical information is present in different modalities (e.g., pictures and words). I concluded that the relevant behavioral and neuropsychological phenomena are better explained by modality-specific than common coding theories.[24]

We can now ask whether common coding theorists can take comfort from modality-independent brain systems that are known to exist. These include, first, the nonspecific subcortical arousal system (or systems), and second, multimodal cells that are found in many brain regions, where they respond to different modalities in some integrative fashion. I argue that such mechanisms, by themselves, do not provide the kind of modality-specific information that common coding theorists envisaged, although they interact in cognitively significant ways with modality specific systems. In addition, we shall see that modality-specific systems can function in ways that give the appearance of a common code at work.

The Arousal System

This is the most general of the nonspecific systems. It was originally identified as a network of cells in the brain stem, called the ascending reticular activating system (see Fig. 6.1), which is turned on by such nonspecific stimulus attributes as intensity and salience. The level of activity in the whole system was thought to be the result of a pooling of excitation from all sensory modalities. The arousal system played an important theoretical role for Hebb (1972), for whom "cell- assemblies ... do not

---

[24]Plaut (2002) argued for a theory of semantic organization that constitutes a middle ground between the multiple (modality-specific) and the unitary (amodal) accounts. Internal semantic representations are assumed to develop under the pressure of learning to mediate between multiple input and output modalities in performing various tasks. Plaut simulated such a system computationally as a distributed connectionist model that has "a bias on learning that favours short connections, leading to a graded degree of modality-specific functional specialization" (p. 603). Simulated lesions produced results consistent with deficits in optic aphasia. Plaut recognized the limitations of the simulation but argued that it tested fundamental principles that account for modality-specific effects and at the same time retain the parsimony of unitary semantic systems. In my view, however, the approach has fundamental limitations that cannot be corrected by connectionist or other computational models already alluded to in earlier chapters. To mention a few, it is difficult first of all to see how the model is more parsimonious than "pure" modality-specific approaches because all the input-output distinctions people can make must be built into the semantic system. For example, differences in connection length can't account for memory for parts of objects. Second, the conceptual knowledge in the system is essentially verbal in the sense that it is based on computational descriptions derived from language. It excludes direct input from perceptual objects and representations in the form of multimodal imagery. Third, it would have to incorporate modality-specific representational and functional distinctions into semantic memory in order to account for additive effects of verbal-nonverbal codes, sensory codes, modality specific interference, perception-imagery similarities, and so on. Accordingly, I seek a different kind of answer to the common-coding challenge to modality specificity.

function unless the arousal system is providing a kind of general summation to all the cortical synapses" (pp. 174–175).

The underlying system is now known to consist of a number of different arousal systems, each with some degree of functional specificity. The differentiation is based on neurochemical pathways arising from components at different levels of the reticular formation (Robbins & Everitt, 1995). Specific functions are affected by these systems because they project to different cortical areas and modulate information processing at their destinations. They do so especially by affecting alertness, orienting responses, and attention, which can in turn influence performance on specific tasks. In many situations, two or more of these systems are simultaneously active in varying degrees to optimize processing of modality-specific information. For example, experimental manipulation of these chemically defined arousal systems by selective drugs has been shown to affect such psychological phenomena as signal detection, conditioning, discrimination learning, memory consolidation, and organization of sequential behavior. However, the modulating arousal systems themselves do not "contain" the modality-specific information necessary for controlled responding in the various tasks.

Arousal and modality-specific contributions to performance are difficult to tease apart conceptually in the case of the decision-making functions attributed to an executive-control neural network in theories of attention such as that of Michael Posner and his colleagues (e.g., Posner & Rothbart, 2004). For example, in conflict situations such as the Stroop task, responding to (say) the red tint of the printed word "blue" entails conflict that is stressful and physiologically arousing. The arousal helps maintain attention to the tint and the color word but does not explain the response choice. The purported executive control system (e.g., anterior cingulate and prefrontal cortex) can only help control the selective responding by incorporating modality-specific sensory information arising from the color word, the color, and the task instructions used in Stroop experiments. The point is directly relevant to DCT because physiological arousal as measured by the galvanic skin response (GSR) and pupillary dilation is higher during processing of abstract than concrete words, but the arousal difference does not explain concreteness effects on imagery reaction time (Paivio & Simpson, 1968), or on memory (Paivio, 1971b, p. 267). Those effects and the dozens of others reviewed in earlier chapters are explainable in terms of the modality-specific processes related to DCT but not by amodal processes related to arousal, except as modulators of the modality-specific effects. Can the following common coding systems provide a better basis for explaining at least some DCT-relevant effects?

Multimodal Systems

There are multimodal neurons in the amygdala and superior colliculus, and bimodal (visual-tactile) neurons found in three interconnected brain regions. We have already seen the crucial role of the amygdala in emotion. It fills that role as a multisensory receiving system with outputs to numerous systems implicated in emotional experiences and behaviors. It receives inputs from all of the sensory systems and many of its neurons are multimodal in that they respond to more than one modality. Some in fact respond to sight, sound, touch, taste, and smell, creating "a rather complex image of the sensory world" (Kolb & Whishaw, 2001, p. 419). In addition, different regions of the amygdala have afferents from neurotransmitter systems in the reticular formation (Bloom, 1995). The sensory and neurochemical inputs have separate and convergent output effects on the hypothalamus, brain stem, and cortical regions that influence general and specific emotional experiences and behaviors. These include general mood states such as vague feelings of anxiety, fear conditioned to specific stimuli, learned associations between objects and primary reinforcers such as taste and smell, and so on. A specific example of a combined effect is that a group of neurons in the amygdala respond primarily to faces, conveying information about the identity and emotional expressions of individuals (Rolls, 1995), which in turn mediates emotional reactions to them. The relevant point here is that the amygdala functions as a common coding system because it mediates the same general kinds of positive and negative emotional and behavioral reactions to any number of specific objects and situations, or their memory images as evoked by pictures or words.

The superior colliculus is a part of the tectum, a midbrain structure that receives input from the eyes and projects to a region of the thalamus called the pulvinar. Separate parts of the pulvinar project to the parietal and temporal lobes. Most relevant for these purposes is the fact that deep layers of the superior colliculus contain an especially dense concentration of multisensory neurons that combine visual, auditory, and somatosensory information from the same source to produce a focus of neural activity (Stein, Wallace, & Meredith, 1995). Thus, neural responses to an effective unimodal (e.g., visual) stimulus could be enhanced when it is combined with a stimulus from another modality (e.g., auditory), or the combination could be inhibitory, depending on such variables as the spatial and temporal relations between the two stimuli. Consider just the "spatial rule:" if the visual and auditory stimulus originate from the same source (e.g., a mouse seen and heard by a cat), the effect is enhancement of the neural response. The increase is in fact more than an additive combination of the two stimuli. If the events are separated in space, however, there is no enhancement and one stimulus could even inhibit the neural response to the other, depending on what part of the receptive field of the former is activated. Such effects arise from the degree of convergence on a multisensory neuron of the input from the separate modalities.

Once again, the important point is that the functional effects of these multisensory neurons are nonspecific. Their output modifies attentional and orienting responses to stimuli in much the same way as the neurochemically defined arousal systems modulate reactions to the specific sensory stimuli that initiate their activity. These multimodal sensory neurons of the superior colliculus, like those in the amygdala, have general common coding functions rather than specific ones involved in object identification.

Bimodal neurons that respond to both visual and tactile stimuli are found in the frontal lobe (inferior area 6), the parietal lobe (area 7b), and the putamen of the basal ganglia. The three areas are interconnected and may form a distributed system for representing nearby extrapersonal spaces according to Michael Graziano and Charles Gross (1995). They found that bimodal neurons responded to gentle touch on the face and hands of monkeys. Many of the same cells responded to bars of light moving near the animal's face or hands. The cells also respond when the animal moves its face and hands. Thus the cells in all three regions are somatotopically organized, forming an egocentric map in which objects are located with respect to the body: "The visual space near the animal is represented as if it were a gelatinous medium surrounding the body that deforms whenever the head rotates or the limbs move. Such a map would give the location of the visual stimulus with respect to the body surface, in somatotopic coordinates" (Graziano & Gross, 1995, p. 1031). The relevant point here is that the bimodal system is specialized for representing the location of objects and not the identity of individual objects.

In summary, there are multimodal neurons in various brain areas that mediate emotional, arousal, and orienting responses to more than one stimulus modality. They are common coding systems that signal the location of an object, enhance its identification, and mediate approach or avoidance depending on whether the emotional response is positive or negative. They do not "identify" the specific object, although they could help other cortical systems do so by drawing attention to it.

Interactive-Parallel Coding

The close relation between vision and touch bears on the common coding issue without requiring us to consider the role of bimodal neurons. Recall from earlier discussions that J. J. Gibson (1966) particularly emphasized the functional similarity between vision and touch as channels of information pickup in that they provide the same information and phenomenal experience concerning spatial and surface properties of objects. The commonality presumably arises from "covariant inputs" derived from visual and haptic exploration of objects. At issue here is the nature of the representational system that develops from such correlated experience. Specifically, do the two modalities remain separate but become increasingly interactive so that information from one co-activates functionally-equivalent information in the other? Or, does the correlated experience (or adaptive evolutionary changes for that matter) result in a common coding system in which visual and haptic information about the same object is represented in the form of, say, abstract spatial features?

We have seen (Chapter 4) that studies of transfer of training from vision to touch and the reverse provided evidence that the two modalities do indeed provide common perceptual information, but that information seemed to be modality-specific rather than abstract in form. The relevant finding was that form-discrimination learning showed stronger positive transfer from vision to touch than vice versa, suggesting that the transfer was mediated by visual memory of the prior stimulus. It was a short step to the interpretation, supported by questionnaires and other measures (Johnson, Paivio, & Clark, 1989), that visual imagery is the mediating mechanism.

It has been similarly argued neuropsychologically that the haptic system uses visual information to construct a representation of an object. James et al. (2002) explored the issue using fMRI to measure the effects of cross-modal haptic-to-visual priming on brain activation. Participants studied three-dimensional novel clay objects either visually or haptically before entering the scanner. During scanning, the participants viewed some of the same objects (the viewing was "primed" by the prescan experience) and they also viewed or haptically explored nonprimed objects (ones they had not explored prior to the brain-scanning phase).

There were two interesting results. First, visual and haptic exploration of nonprimed objects produced activation in several brain areas, including overlapping activation in an area of the visual cortex. Second, viewing either visually primed or haptically primed objects produced more activation than viewing nonprimed objects in occipital areas. It is especially notable that haptic exploration of novel objects produced activation, not only in the somatosensory cortex, but also in areas of the visual cortex associated with visual processing; and moreover, that previous haptic experience enhanced activation in those visual areas. In considering interpretations of these effects, note that they do not involve areas that contain bimodal visual–tactile neurons.

James et al. (2002) evaluated the visual imagery interpretation of the cross-modal priming arising from prior studies in which imagery was directly investigated. They rejected imagery for several reasons: first, the argument by Easton, Greene, and Srinivas (1997) that haptic recognition of three-dimensional objects occurs so quickly that visual imagery could not be the mediating factor; second, the finding by Amedi et al. (2001) that visually imagining objects produced much less activity in the lateral occipital cortex than did haptic exploration of the same objects; and third, their own observation that the different tasks they used produced equivalent activation in medial and lateral occipital areas. James et al. accordingly opted for the alternative hypothesis that the cross-modal effects are mediated by a common system (or systems) for object representation associated with the ventral visual pathway.

It can be argued, however, that conscious imagery played a role at some processing level prior to and even during the brain scanning period. First, there was plenty of time for imaging during exploration (3 sec or more per object) and scanning (two seconds viewing time plus a 12-sec intertrial interval). Moreover, the fMRI activation response curves for lateral and medial occipital areas peaked more than 5 see after stimulus onset (Fig. 4 in James et al., 2002). Second, according to studies of cross-modal form discrimination mentioned earlier, people readily image visually to felt objects, a tendency that could have been augmented in the James et al. (2002) study because participants experienced both visual–visual and haptic–visual priming conditions. Thus, any haptically activated images would be likely to "resemble" the perceptual images experienced during visual exploration. Finally, the negative results of Amedi et al. (2001) are not conclusive evidence against an imagery interpretation because imagery processes were initiated by verbal cues in their object imaging condition whereas any imagery that occurred in the haptic exploration task was evoked by the feel of the objects. The different cues presumably activated different neural pathways and representations.

The above account suggests that haptically activated images converged on and summated with the visually activated patterns in the critical occipital areas. Alternatively, the representational activity could consist of a continuous interaction between separate but correlated haptic and visual activities in common neural locations. This is a specific neural interpretation of the dual coding hypothesis, namely, that independent representations can cooperate to yield summative effects, as in the case of memory for audiovisual objects experienced or imagined in the two modalities.

Centered Versus Parallel Brain

The different interpretations of cross-modal priming and other phenomena discussed in this section fit nicely into Marcel Kinsbourne's (1995) analysis of the distinction between centered and parallel models of the brain. Originating in the mid-19th century, the centered-brain model "postulates continuing convergence within the brain substance, in service of multimodal integration into [perceptual] objects … This hierarchical serial organization culminates in some ill-specified space, the consciousness module, where the by now elaborately preprocessed information reaches consciousness" (p. 1323) and is acted on via a reverse sequence of messages down the hierarchy. Kinsbourne found little to recommend this model in any subarea of neuropsychology. A centered cortical neuroanatomy is not to be found. Neurophysiology and neuropsychology have found no separate point at which information represented at two (or more) points becomes integrated, no merger of separate information processing streams, no centered locus of activation across consciously performed tasks.

The contrasting model assumes instead that the brain processes information in parallel, with lateral interaction of unrelated neural processors so that activating one processor exerts priming or interfering effects on other systems. Such effects are predictable from Kinsbourne's (1995) functional cerebral distance principle, according to which neural binding (discussed further later) occurs at a distance, probably by means of repetitive interaction between complementary representations (p. 1324). How all of this might work is only incompletely specified but it is consistent with a parallel neuronal architecture, bidirectionality of corticocortical connections, and synchronous neural firing at widely dispersed brain areas. Kinsbourne suggested that there is a dominant focus of patterned neuronal activity that underlies the phenomenal experience of focused consciousness, which, when disrupted by brain lesions, produces unilateral spatial neglect and other syndromes of selective unawareness that we have already discussed (Chapter 7).

THE BINDING PROBLEM

Kinsbourne's (1995) description of neural binding at a distance brings us to the most important general issue that has been lurking in the background throughout our discussions of representations and interconnections: How do two or more neurons get bound together so that they represent complex perceptual objects that we experience as units? Alternatively, can single neurons do the job? The issue is an old one in psychology that appeared as the part-whole issue in Gestalt psychology and as conditioning phenomena in behavioral psychology. The latter is succinctly illustrated by Sheffield's (1961) example of how seeing, feeling, peeling, smelling, and tasting an orange integrates the elements into a unified multimodal perceptual concept. The logogen and imagen units of DCT also are tightly bound sequential and spatial structures. At the conscious level, separate imaged objects can be bonded together into a functionally integrated compound image. Most of us can easily image red, blue, or yellow triangles, Volkswagons, or whatever. We know a great deal about the variables that control binding as defined psychologically. Much less is known about how neural binding occurs, but the problem has increasingly engaged the interests of neuroscientists of all stripes, as evidenced, for example, by a series of review articles published in the journal, *Neuron,* in 1999. There, binding is viewed as "one of the most puzzling and fascinating issues that the brain and cognitive sciences have ever faced" (Roskies, 1999, p. 9).

The complexities of binding stand out in the neuropsychological context. This section identifies the main issues and the (thus far unsuccessful) attempts to solve them. The familiar police "identikit" illustrates the main facets of the problem. The kit consists of typical facial features shown on transparent strips or on a computer. The pieces are assembled by the police artist into a picture of the suspect according to a witness's description. The process is componential and generative. The identikit artist is the composer and the witness provides a model of the suspect in the form of a memory description. The artist tries out different combinations of head shape, hair color and style, eye color and spacing, and so forth. The witness compares the products against the memory model and provides corrective feedback. This procedure eventually results in a face construction that is taken as an acceptable match to the witness's internal model (the accuracy of the match to the actual suspect is another matter—see Chapter 4).

The components in the example are concrete parts of a larger object but they could be of any size and level of abstractness. In computational models, they become completely abstract descriptive features. In this context, the ultimate units are neural ensembles or individual neurons that resonate to different sensory properties of objects. Somewhere along the ventral and dorsal visual pathways, for example, "color, form, and movement information is put together to produce a rich, unified visual world made up of complex objects, such as faces and paintings, and complex visual-motor skills, such as catching a ball" (Kolb & Whishaw, 2001, p. 294). How this happens is the binding problem as applied to the visuomotor system, which is our main focus initially.

The binding problem includes an economy constraint that arises because the brain's resources, vast though they be, are limited. How can the brain accommodate the seemingly unlimited number of attribute combinations that get bound together to form the things we perceive and know? As summarized by Barlow (1995), the problem exists even if everything were represented in individual neurons: although it might be reasonable to postulate "yellowness cells" and even "Volkswagen cells," one surely can't have cells for every possible adjective–noun combination (p. 421). The problem is not removed by postulating stable representations for complex objects made up of neuronal ensembles. There is too much stuff for the brain to handle, say the critics. And so some propose instead that the brain uses a large but manageable number of elementary features and rules of combination to synthesize the representations each time the target object is seen, much as in identikit face assembly.

I argued (Paivio, 1986, p. 49) that such computational models have no advantage over exemplar models. In face recognition, for example, the computational program would need a list of feature values for shapes, sizes, and colors of eyes, hair, nose, and so forth, along with construction rules that specify how the modality-specific features are put together in every face we know—indeed, every viewing angle from which we can identify the face. Would such feature or rule descriptions take less brain space than multiple exemplars of every face?

However binding is achieved by the brain, the economy constraint might not be a crucial limitation. Rado and Scott (1996) reviewed two different approaches to estimating the number of complex (bound) memory units in the brain. One was an estimate of the number of complex cell assemblies of the kind described in Hebb's (1949) cell assembly theory and the other was the number of stable attractors ("basins" of convergent neural activity) based on a model of the neocortex. Both approaches yielded an estimate of about a billion, the number of seconds in 30 years. Rado and Scott reasoned that this is a conservative estimate of the number of recallable stable memories the brain could store in that time, and therefore, that the binding problem is resolved in a simple and satisfying way. This problem, however, is secondary to the main problem of how the brain actually does the binding.

The problem arises because of the standard view, detailed in Chapter 6, of how information reaches the brain. A summary at this point reveals the source of the problem. A visual scene is organized into dynamic, multimodal objects when it reaches the eye. A topographical (or more abstract topological) map is projected to the primary visual cortex (V1) and nearby areas (e.g., areas V3–V5 of the extrastriate cortex). However, the bound attributes of objects in the scene are taken apart on the way to the brain so that V1 only has component neurons sensitive to line orientation, color (wave length),movement, and combinations of orientation and movement. There is organization here in that different kinds of detectors are arranged into columns that run through the six different layers of V1, so that "blobs" of color-sensitive neurons are inserted between columns of orientation sensitive neurons, separately for the two eyes (Kolb & Whishaw, 2001, p. 308). This arrangement permits V1 to process the different kinds of information concurrently but the processing stops short of binding the components into perceptual objects. That begins instead in regionTE of the temporal lobes down the ventral stream from V1, where we find the neurons that respond to complex stimuli such as faces and hands. Here, an object is represented by a combination of neurons that respond to various characteristics such as orientation, size, color, and texture. Importantly, in the monkey at least, the sensitivity of these neurons is changed by experience so that, for example, some fire maximally to shapes that had been followed by reward.

The puzzle is that, according to this standard story, the object-specific combinations are constructed from less organized V1 stuff. The construction, however, requires a model of the original object or scene as well as a composer, as in the identikit analogy. The object in the scene has been decomposed, so the brain's composer must somehow "look back" at the object or bootstrap its construction from bits and pieces of information. Either way it's a puzzle that has confronted all theorists in the neurosciences.

D. O. Hebb (1949) was the first neuropsychologist to describe the binding problem and propose an alternative solution in terms of cell assembly theory. His hypothesis involved activity-related changes at the synapse. This "Hebb synapse" was a fruitful proposal that has been investigated by experimental and theoretical neuroscientists without retaining his model of reverberatory circuits (for recent reviews, see Kolb, 2003, Milner, 2003, Hinton, 2003; Sejnowski, 2003). Details of the evolving Hebb synapse or cell-assembly are not essential for our purposes, so I focus instead on his solution to the binding problem because it is reflected in one form or other in subsequent explanations by neuroscientists.

The first level of binding in the Hebbian cell-assembly model is the association between neurons that results in a "simple" assembly in the visual system (Hebb, 1949). This process begins with neural activity in Brodmann area 17 (V1) that converges on neurons in the adjacent peristriate area 18 (V2), where the organized assembly gets formed. Higher level binding entails association between different assemblies (in peristiate and more remote cortical areas), which are linked by one or more neurons they have come to share. Later, Hebb (1968) extended the analysis to imagery: initiated and guided by external cues, visual imagery consists of activation of perceptual assemblies (of different levels of complexity) by each other.

Hebb (1949) recognized the heavy demand made on the brain by the large number of neurons required for even a simple perception or image. His solution was combinatorial: the same neurons may enter temporarily into different subassemblies which in turn can enter into one higher order assembly or another. Thus, many more active organizations of neuron groups (ideas or images) are possible than the total number of neurons in the brain. This was the precursor to overlapping neural ensembles and feature combining models generally. We have already seen that this economy criterion may not be a problem for the brain's resources and we need not discuss it further at this point.

Hebb's (1949) pioneering effort did not solve the binding problem. Hebb assumed that visual cell assemblies are developed in extrastriate cortex and association areas, not in the primary visual cortex. Neurons in the latter respond to elements such as lines and corners, which are put together into assemblies corresponding to, say, triangles. Eye movements tracing the contours of the triangle are essential for the development of the assembly—one could say that the eye movements controlled by sensory stimulation are the first representational binding mechanism. However, only the elements of the triangle go to the primary visual cortex; they are put together elsewhere. What triangle model does the brain use for the construction when the sensory model has been decomposed? The extrastriate areas cannot look back at the original stimulus to see how successful they were in assembling the parts. Hebb (1949, pp. 70–72) recognized the problem and essentially proposed a solution in terms of backpropagation by neurons from area 18 (V2) to start the assembly construction, but this would still require a model that does not exist in area 17 (V1) and is not yet constructed in adjacent areas.

Consider next neo-Hebbian attempts to solve neural binding. Computer scientist Geoffrey Hinton (2003) discussed how Hebb learning rules can be used to implement error-driven learning in neural networks. Modelers have tried to use backpropogation of errors to construct training signals for intermediate "hidden layers" of multilayered neural networks. But such learning "requires a teacher to specify the right answer and it is hard to see how the neurons could implement the backpropogation required by multilayer versions" (Hinton, 2003, p. 10)—a network version of the problem that remained unsolved in Hebb's (1949) original cell-assembly approach.

Hinton's (2003) neural network alternative requires the brain to construct a model of sensory input data so that the model matches the input. Errors in the model are treated as changes in the output of a neuron that do not correspond to the input. The changes are corrected by means of backpropogation of signals using backward connections between neurons that injects the neuron with additional activation that corrects the error component in the input signal. Hinton hopes that this kind of neural servo-mechanism might help to make Hebb rules work, "but what really happens at a synapse and why remains a mystery" (p. 12). The mystery deepens when we ask how far back the backpropogation must go to find the correct layer of synaptic connections in the real brain—where is the "right answer" if not in the sensory input itself? [25]

Binding By Single Neurons

Individual neurons can function as binding machines. A neuron has many dendrites with synaptic connections to other neurons—hundreds or thousands of connections, depending on the type of neuron. The neuron's cell body selectively processes the information and passes it on to other neurons. A complex neuron could thus collect feature information from dendrites and bind them into a spatial pattern that responds

---

[25]Hinton (2003) pointed out that the neural network model is similar to psychological analysis-by-synthesis models of pattern recognition. As applied to speech perception (see Neisser, 1967, pp. 193–198) analysis-by-synthesis assumes that a listener in a noisy situation generates hypotheses (makes educated guesses) about the content of an unclear message and selects the one that seems to be the best fit on the basis of contextual information. To do so, the listener uses phonetic and other rules to construct possible acoustic inputs in a selective ("strategic") manner. The approach has been applied to visual pattern recognition and other domains. The same problem arises as in the case of the neural network version: the perceiver must have internal pattern models (e.g., rule-based feature descriptions) of sentences or other patterns in order to synthesize plausible candidates to be compared against impoverished input. In computer simulations, they are put in the computer's memory by a programmer. Human perceivers must learn and store such patterns in memory, so we are back to the binding problem once again-how are the patterns constructed in the first place and how are they used later as "hypotheses" to be compared against impoverished input?

selectively to faces or other complex forms. Alternatively or additionally, different patterns could be represented by different temporal firing patterns across synapses. Chapter 7 described a relevant study by Kreiman et al. (2000), who recorded impulses from single neurons using microelectrodes implanted in the brains of severe epileptics to find the focus of their seizures. The recordings were taken while the patients viewed pictures of faces, household objects, spatial layouts, cars, animals, food, famous people, and so on. Later, recordings were again obtained when the patients were asked to imagine previously viewed pictures. Neurons were found in various areas of the brain (hippocampus, amygdala, parahippocampal gyrus …) that responded selectively when the pictures were viewed or imaged. Some neurons responded similarly during vision and imagery of the same pictures, whereas others were activated only during vision, and others only during imagery. The authors were especially struck by the selective activation during imagery, presumably reflecting retrieval of picture information from memory (involving the medial temporal lobe) or maintenance of the visual image during imagination.

The selective and varied coding of seen and imaged objects is a remarkable feat for individual neurons, although it is recognized that populations of such neurons (and other less selective ones) are usually involved in cognition. Barlow (1995) discussed coding by cardinal cells (presumably the neurons from which Kreiman et al., 2000, recorded would qualify as such) and ensemble neuronal coding in a type of cell-assembly described by Abeles (1982, cited in Barlow, 1995 pp. 423–424) as a synfire group—a synchronously firing group of cortical neurons that can fire the next group in a chain.[26] Barlow concluded that both types of encoding are used by the brain, but that a single neuron is capable of perceptual discrimination using evidence from other neurons. But how exactly does asingle neuron know how to combine all this input so that it represents sensible objects? What and where is the model that maps physical events onto a cognitive neuron? And so, the general binding problem persists in the case of single neurons as it does in the case of neural ensembles.

The solution to the problem seems to require a holistic representational system early in the neural stream, between sensory input and cognitive brain representations farther downstream. Three visual phenomena suggest tantalizing possibilities. One is iconic memory, which refers to the initial trace of visual sensory input first demonstrated experimentally by George Sperling (1960). Using a partial-report technique, he showed that as many as nine letters could be accurately reported after they had been flashed too briefly to be scanned. Sperling's pioneering study and many subsequent ones showed that a transient holistic trace persisted for a second or so after presentation. During that period, information could be read from the trace as if the stimulus were still present. The transient trace had the properties of a visual image, a rich representation of a visual scene that can be quickly wiped out or overwritten by any change in the scene (Becker, Pashier, & Anstis, 2000). It has

---

[26]Laubach, Wessberg, and Nicolelis (2000) showed that behavior outcomes in a motor learning task could be predicted from three measures of neuronal ensemble activity: average firing rate, temporal patterns of firing, and correlated firing.

been proposed that this iconic memory trace could be the basis on which more persistent short-term and long-term memory traces in the brain are constructed, although no one has yet proposed how this might happen. The overwriting problem suggests that iconic snapshots would be progressively erased or at least "fused" by changes in the scene. Additionally, there is the mystery of the location and neural mechanism of the iconic memory system itself. Perhaps it consists of pre-attentive persistence of retinal neural activity without object coding, or perhaps it explicitly includes many items in the scene (Becker et al., 2000, p. 285). The latter seems to be required on the basis of the empirical results on the phenomenon as well as on logical grounds. In any case, iconic memory offers at best only a glimmer of hope in regard to the binding problem because the brain systems that construct more enduring representations would have to look back to the retina for their blueprints.

Visual binding is more directly revealed by the following variant of perceptual persistence: A fragmented line drawing of an object that cannot be seen against a background of random lines becomes instantly recognizable if it moves relative to the background; after the motion stops, the percept persists briefly before fading into the background. Brain scans using fMRI (e.g., Large, Aldcroft, & Vilis, 2005) have shown correlated persistence of brain activity that starts at V1 and peaks at the lateral occipital cortex. This has been taken as evidence that binding into a global percept is an emerging property of the ventral visual processing stream. For this to happen, however, V1 would have to have resources at least to begin the organizational process that is completed further downstream.

Let us start with the accepted fact that V1 and adjacent areas have retinotopic maps of the visual scene. The standard view, already discussed, is that orientation, color, and motion detectors are organized in columns, presumably in different locations. They are not yet bound into holistic representation of objects, even their form. However, contrary to this interpretation, as already described in Chapter 7, Kosslyn et al. (1999) found evidence that Area 17 (V1) is activated when participants imaged visual displays (patterns of stripes) they had previously memorized, and Klein et al. (2004) obtained similar results using more object-like bow-tie shapes. The conclusion was that early occipital cortical areas are used in some forms of visual imagery. In DCT terms, visual iconogens-imagens useful in perception and imagery were formed in the primary visual cortex.

The question here is whether such V1 neural representations can be either (a) copied and relayed to adjacent and more distant brain regions known to be activated in the kinds of perceptual and imagery tasks reviewed earlier, or (b) used to kick-start the construction of such neural assemblies by backpropagation servo mechanisms just discussed. The question cannot be answered on the basis of the V1 imagery effect. We especially need to know more about it's scope and limitations. For example, could V1 imagery be demonstrated when participants recall the patterns a day or so after study (that is, from long-term memory)? Can the effect be extended to patterns of curved lines, different colors, or multimodal novel objects? How can we explain the referential connections that must be established between the imagery instructions and the V1 patterns they activate during the imagery task;

that is, how do the instructions do their work in V1? The full impact of the V1 imagery effect for binding problem and other representational issues, including those related to DCT, depend on answers to such questions.

Binding in Other Modalities

All of the issues discussed in the context of binding in the visual system apply to other sensorimotor modalities and combinations of modalities, verbal and nonverbal. For example, auditory logogens and their conceptual equivalents entail binding of lower order units into sequential structures of different lengths. We saw earlier that the auditory sequence corresponding to a recognizable word is not assembled in the primary auditory cortex (A1) but rather in A2 or adjacent areas. Thus, the auditory sequence that we categorize as a word must somehow be constructed from a meaningless sound sequence that leaves only a transient trace in A1. Neisser (1967) called this trace echoic memory by analogy with iconic visual memory. He also recognized that echoic memory would not be useful in speech recognition and language learning if it were too short: "Some persistence of the echo would greatly facilitate the retrospective analysis of what has been heard" (p. 201).

Such persistence was in fact demonstrated by Lu, Wiliamson, and Kaufman (1992) in the form of auditory sensory memory in primary auditory cortex (A1) as measured by magnetoencephalography, which predicted the psychophysically determined duration of the remembered loudness of a tone. The same approach had shown earlier that the neuronal activation trace persisted in association cortex several seconds longer than in the primary cortex (cited in Lu et al., 1992, p. 1668). Assuming that similar persistence occurs with auditory words, the results suggest that the information necessary for sequential binding is available in A1 and radiates to the association cortex. The DCT analysis suggests further that longer sequences are somehow tied together further on in the motor logogen system, the internal spinner of linguistic yarn.

I end with research evidence that suggests neural binding across the verbal and nonverbal systems of DCT. Prabhakaran, Narayanan, Zhao, and Gabrieli (2000) used fMRI to identify brain areas that are preferentially involved in integrating verbal and spatial information in short-term (working) memory. The information consisted of four consonants and four spatial locations. Recognition memory was tested for (a) isolated verbal or spatial information alone, (b) both presented simultaneously in an integrated format in which the letters were displayed in different locations, and (c) an unintegrated format in which letters and locations were separated in the displays. Thus, the design combines features of dual coding memory experiments (Chapter 4) that tested for memory effects of integrated versus separate picture pairs and word pairs, and possible additive effects of pictures and words. Prabhakaran et al. assessed recognition memory speed and accuracy by presenting a single probe letter or a location 5 sec after the display, and requiring the participant to indicate as quickly as possible whether either appeared in the display.

The reaction time and accuracy results showed that the individual verbal and spatial conditions were generally easier than their combined presentation conditions.

This means that there was no additive (beneficial) memory effect of jointly presented verbal and nonverbal information, which contrasts with the additive effects of pictures and words in the earlier dual coding experiments. At the same time, however, memory was better for integrated letter-location pairs than for unintegrated pairs. Thus, verbal and nonverbal information did combine in a functionally integrated manner that was untested in the earlier dual coding memory experiments.

The fMRI results yielded clear brain-site differences in activation patterns. Maintenance of integrated information in memory resulted in greater activity than maintenance of unintegrated information in the rightfrontal cortex, specifically the right middle and superior frontal gyri. Maintenance of unintegrated information relative to integrated information resulted in greater activity in posterior brain areas, including bilateral parietal, temporal, and cerebellar regions. Prabhakaran et al. (2000) concluded that prefrontal activation in the integration condition of their study may reflect one solution to the binding problem in the human brain. This would be remarkable from the DCT perspective because it implies binding across verbal and nonverbal (spatial) representations.

The results and conclusions raise a number of questions relevant to DCT. First, spatial locations are nonverbal but they are not items in the same sense that pictures are nonverbal counterparts of their names. Thus, the letter-location results cannot be generalized to other dual coding variables. Second, the brain scans do not suggest binding of verbal and spatial information in a single location. The volume of the brain area activated by integrated information, although much smaller than for unintegrated information, is substantial (4,368 cubic mm) and encompasses thousands of neurons. This suggests that binding occurred by interaction of two kinds of information at a distance, as described by Kinsbourne (1995), an interpretation strengthened by the fact that the integrative activity involved different frontal gyri (bulges), namely right middle and frontal gyri (Prabhakaran et al., 2000, p. 87). In brief, the integration effect could have been achieved (the binding problem "solved") by rapid cross-talk between separate neural ensembles for representing letters and spatial locations. That the right frontal cortex is specialized for this function among other kinds of problem solving activity is interesting from the neuropsychological perspective. The evidence also encourages further research designed to reveal independent and integrative functioning of different combinations of multimodal dual coding systems located in various brain areas.

To summarize, this chapter has reviewed issues concerning amodal, common coding processes in the brain and the related problem of binding separate units of information into holistic representations—major puzzles in regard to the nature of the evolved mind. Both issues are relevant as well to the evolution of mind because they arise from properties of the environment that impact on the organism. We must have resources to attend to and be energized by many different kinds of stimulus events before mobilizing specific responses to them. Attentional, arousal, and emotional responses are common to many situations, although not entirely amodal (we sense increased attention and alertness, and different kinds of emotions). We are thus primed by these alerting systems to respond to the specific properties of objects and situations. The parts are bound in the objects, objects are separated in holistic contexts, and organisms have evolved to perceive and respond to the parts or wholes. The neuroscience question is how the brain does its job in this multilevel interaction between the organism and its environment. A broader question is how organisms, including their brains and functional "minds," have evolved to adapt to the seemingly endless variety of complex environmental niches in which they are found. This moves us to the second major theme of this volume, the mind-evolution issue, for which I have tried to construct a theoretical foundation up to this point.

III

EVOLUTION OF THE DUAL CODING MIND

CHAPTER TEN

Basic Evolutionary Issues

This review of basic evolutionary concepts and issues provides a background for the dual coding interpretation of cognitive evolution in subsequent chapters. The general assumption is that, throughout most of its history, cognitive evolution was founded on the same Darwinian principles as biological evolution. However, the explosive development of human mind over the last 100,000 years is often attributed to cultural evolution and it is therefore important to consider how such evolution might depart from Darwinian evolutionary principles. The topics include the following: (a) a sketch of Darwinian evolution,[27] (b) the distinction between evolution of structure and of function, (c) ways in which environment and heredity interact, (d) the kinds of evidence on which speculations about evolution of mind are based, (e) cultural evolution, and finally, (f) the novel hypothesis that memory is the engine of cognitive evolution from its preverbal form through language and beyond.

DARWINIAN EVOLUTION

Darwin's theory of natural selection is the foundation of evolutionary biology. The essential concepts are inheritance, variation, and selection. It had long been known that species characteristics are inherited with variations, and humans capitalized on that knowledge by selective breeding to produce new varieties of plants and animals. Darwin developed the brilliant idea that such selection occurs in nature, so that small changes in characteristics that are advantageous to the

---

[27]Chapter 18 presents a further discussion of Darwin and his legacy. Detailed reviews of the history and current status of Darwinian ideas can be found in any number of recent volumes (e.g., Buss,1999; Dawkins, 1989; Dennett, 1985; Gruber, 1974; Jones, 2000). Four of the most influential works of Darwin are available in one volume, edited, with commentary, by Nobel Laureate James D, Watson (2005).

survival of individual members of a species in a particular environment are accentuated over generations. The modified traits are adaptive so that individuals having such traits to some degree are likely to survive longer and thereby reproduce more offspring (including some with more of the modified trait) than individuals without the adaptive modification.

Darwin assumed that there was a basic hereditary mechanism and even speculated (unfruitfully) about germcell "gemmules" as transmitters. He also assumed that hereditary variation was much more limited than it is now known to be. Gregor Mendel inferred from characteristics of successive generations of peas that there are functional hereditary units, later called genes. In 1953, Watson and Crick (popularly told by Watson, 1968) described the biochemical structure of the long DNA molecule in which the genetic information is stored. The gene is a segment of that molecule. Genetic mutations result in variant forms of genes known as alleles. They come in pairs, one allele inherited from one parent and the other, from the other parent. The pair of alleles at a given locus of the molecule could be identical (e.g., each pair member codes for blue eyes) or different (e.g., one codes for the brown eyes of one parent and the other, the blue eyes of the other parent). When the two alleles are identical at a given locus, the individual is said to be homozygous for that trait; when different, the individual is heterozygous for the trait. The existence of multiple heterozygous alleles in a population is necessary for evolution to occur. However, no aspect of cognition is similarly determined by a single gene or any number of genes, for reasons that are considered in the following sections.

Structure and Function in Evolution

Biological evolution entails changes in structure and function. For example, the eye evolved from a photosensitive pigmented spot to complex eyes that are sensitive to form, color, and so on. The structure-function distinction raises the chicken-and-egg problem of which came first. Darwin did not discuss the problem explicitly, presumably because he took for granted that natural selection operates on structural changes that are useful in the organism's (and hence the species's) struggle for existence in a given environment. "Nature cares nothing for appearances [forms], except in so far as they may be useful to any being" (Darwin, 1859/1998, p. 69). "Hence every detail of structure in every living creature ... may be viewed, either as having been of some special use to some ancestral form, or being now of special use to the descendants of this form ... (Darwin, 1859/1998, p. 163). The eye evolved in complexity because perception of form, color, and distance benefited species living in environments where vision is useful. Apparent exceptions have to be seen on the broad scale of dependence of a species on other species or on the physical environment. The "nature-made" bright colors of flowers, for example, are functional because they attract bees that pollinate other flowers. The wind carries the seeds in other cases. The colors of the flowers and the forms of the seeds are useless in themselves and would not have evolved independent of their relation to other environmental entities or forces. They are functionally useful in the same sense that a bolt is useful to a door's function only if there is a socket into which the bolt can be inserted.

So, too, in regard to the evolution of the cognitive skills that collectively define mind, including the complex adaptive functions of the nonverbal and verbal systems as described by DCT. The point is often missed or at least disputed. For example, the eminent biologist S. J. Gould (1997, cited in Buss, 1999, p. 39) suggested that such uniquely human qualities as language are merely byproducts of our large brains. The functional counterargument is that the brain is big because it has to contain language and other specialized mental organs (Bloom, 1998, p. 208). Neuroscientist William Calvin and linguist Derek Bickerton (2000) proposed that brain enlargement was the result of evolutionary pressures that favored intelligence and motor coordination for making tools and throwing weapons. Language evolution may have been an incidental byproduct of those intellectual selection pressures. The production of speech sounds also depends on the position of the larynx but that doesn't explain the functional advantages of speech as a communication system as compared to, say, a gestural language. which is a fully functional communication system for the deaf (hence not dependent on the larynx). Language and other cognitive functional tools evolved because of their adaptive advantages and their anatomical and physiological embodiments necessarily coevolved with them. Tooby and Cosmides (1995) neatly made the general case that brains evolved as functionally adaptive problem-solving devices.

HEREDITY AND ENVIRONMENT

This section deals with current views on the ancient nature-nurture issue already encountered in the contrast between Platonic innate ideas and Locke's empiricist view that the mind is a tabula rasa on which experience writes. The contrast in biology and psychology applies to all physical and behavioral characteristics of organism:What is innate and what acquired? Or, to what extent are traits one or the other, or both? The issue was relevant to Darwin because the most influential theory of evolution in his time was Lamarck's theory of acquired characteristics, namely, that bodily changes due to use and disuse are inherited. Darwin (1998 p. 110 ff) accepted the theory but was never comfortable with it and assumed that use and disuse played at most a small part as compared to heredity (Ward, 1927, pp. 332–345). Evidence did not support Lamarck, and his theory generally has been rejected. Modern genetics explains why it can't work (discussed further later). What persists is the question of how much of the form and behavior of organisms is due to heredity and how much to environment.

Hebb (1953) used evidence from animal studies to make the case that behavior can't be divided into learned and unlearned, or even into how much of a given piece of behavior is dependent on one or the other, for that is like asking how much the area of a field is due to its length and how much to its width. The only reasonable answer is that the two proportions are each 100% essential. It is more meaningful, Hebb suggested, to ask how much of the variance in behavior is determined by heredity and how much by environment. As is well known, this is the approach taken by psychologists who investigate the issue and come up with such answers as 50% of intelligence (IQ) is inherited and 50% acquired. The problem here is to know how much variability there is in the two sources of influence. The classical method is to compare identical twins and nontwin siblings raised in the same or different homes. But even this is tricky because of the multiplicity of factors that constitute environment, everything from the biochemical environment in which cells develop to external physical, nutritional, and social contexts of the developing individual.

Biologist Paul R. Ehrlich (2000) illustrated the point using identical Siamese twins who, despite being raised in as close to the same environment as possible, nonetheless differed in their natures. One twin dominated his brother, was quick tempered, eventually drank to excess, and became deaf in both ears. The brother was even tempered, usually submissive, sober, and in old age became deaf in only one ear. Thus, genetic identity does not necessarily produce identical natures even when combined with substantially identical environments. Ehrlich suggested that the slightest environmental differences, perhaps starting with different positions in the womb, could have led to escalating reinforcement of differences.

The conclusion from Hebb, Ehrlich, and other scientists is that nature and nurture are completely intertwined and interactive in their effects. Next we shall examine the nature of those interactive effects beginning with an analysis from the perspective of modern genetics and ending with my pragmatic position on the issue.

Genotype and Phenotype

Early in the 20th century, evolutionary biologists began to draw a general distinction between the genotype and phenotype of an individual organism. Genotype refers to heritable information transmitted from generation to generation, and it is now described in terms of an organism's genome, the unique sequence of four kinds of chemical elements (nucleotides) making up the DNA molecules that are the material basis of the gene. Phenotype describes the organism's phenome, its observable form, physiology, and (most important for us) its behavior. A phenotype is determined jointly by genotype and the environment, but it only changes over generations due to natural selection. This means that, contrary to Lamarck's theory, acquired characteristics are not inherited.

Environmental effects on a human phenotype are obvious in such cases as changes in athletic and academic prowess as a result of exercise and study. Even height, which is genetic in that it varies greatly across human population, is affected by nutrition so that children are taller than their parents who immigrated to a country where the food is more nutritious than in the parents' homeland. Phenotype is sometimes said to be the expression of a genotype, as if the latter is the defining essence of a person. This is implicit in common views of intelligence and talents as being inherited "gifts." As discussed earlier, researchers quantify the notion in terms of the heritability of traits, the percentage of population variance in a trait that can be explained by hereditary factors. The question remains challenging because of great uncertainty in every step of the developmental pathway from nucleotides to phenotypes, affected as they are by complex interactions of many kinds.

Richard Lewontin (2004), an evolutionary biologist and geneticist who is an expert in this domain, summarized the complexities. In humans, there are 3 million nucleotide differences between any two people taken at random. Even identical twins are not completely alike at the cellular level because spontaneous mutations occur during cell growth and development. Small variations in phenotype can occur because of interconnections of metabolic pathways from nucleotides of the DNA, pathways that carry the information that specifies the chemical structure of the proteins from which cells and organs are built. The relation between the DNA sequence and the amino acid content of the proteins is many-to-one, and it is impossible to specify all causal pathways of connections between genotype and phenotype even at this level.[28]

Uncertainty increases because "the actual correspondence between genotype and phenotype is a many-to-many relation in which any given genotype corresponds to many different phenotypes and there are different genotypes corresponding to a given phenotype" (Lewontin, 2004, p. 6). In addition to the DNA-protein relation just described, uncertainties arise from many-to-many relations between genes and between genes and environment, and from random variation in processes operating at the cellular level. The gene-environment mapping is most relevant to evolutionary issues in subsequent chapters.

Lewontin (2004) stated that the mapping of different genotypes into phenotypes in one environment is often completely unpredictable from their mapping in another environment. As evidence, he cited an experiment in which clones of immature plants were produced by cutting each into three pieces. Pieces of each plant were grown at low, medium, and high levels of a mountain. The result was that the relative heights of the growing plants were unpredictable from one environment to another. For example, the genotype that grew tallest at low elevation was shortest at medium elevation and second tallest at high elevation. Experiments on many different organisms where it has been possible to produce multiple individuals of the same genotype show the same result. Lewontin concluded that the outcome of the development of any genotype is a unique consequence of the interaction between the genotype and the environment.

The conclusion applies fully to the evolution of human traits that are our ultimate concern. Paul Ehrlich's (2000) article, cited earlier, is aptly titled *The Tangled Skeins of Nature and Nurture in Human Evolution*. In it we read that "Genes do not shout commands to us about our behavior. At the very most, they whisper suggestions, and the nature of those whispers is shaped by our internal environments (those within and between cells) during early development and later, and usually also by the external environments in which we find ourselves as adults" (Ehrlich, 2000, p. 88). The same point has been made by zoologist and science writer Matt Ridley (2003a, 2003b), who told us that "Genes are not static blueprints that dictate

---

[28]The carriers of the information are RNA "messenger" molecules, chemically-related to DNA molecules from which they are derived. RNA is then translated into amino acids and proteins by means of molecules related to RNA.

our destiny. How they are expressed—where and when they are turned on or off and for how long—is affected by changes in the womb, by the environment, and by other factors" (p. 34).

Punctuated Equilibrium

This concept refers to the sudden impact of global events on evolution over long periods of time. It is specifically relevant to us because it has been extended by some to the origin and evolution of language. Whereas Darwinism assumes that phyletic evolution is gradual, punctuated equilibrium, as proposed by Eldredge and Gould (1972), stated that evolution occurred in periodic spurts with long intervening periods of relative stability. Eldredge (1998) extended that idea with emphasis on the interaction between biological evolution and the physical world of "matter in motion," according to which evolution always takes place within changing ecosystems. Thus it occurs in the context of a changing earth, ranging from effects of (a) the global influence of sudden catastrophes such as meteor and comet collisions that wiped out the dinosaurs 65 million years ago and gradual global changes like continental drift (due to plate tectonics) that separated populations of plants and animals to evolve separately, to (b) local changes of varying extent due to regional climatic changes, drought, hurricanes, volcanic activity, and so forth, that affect local populations to the point of extinction of species. New species "move into" these niches—evolve in them or simply move in without evolving ("habitat tracking"). The result is long periods, perhaps millions of years, of stasis punctuated by sudden extinctions, and so forth, and emergence of new species.[29] The concept of punctuated equilibria is controversial because, among other reasons, gradual changes occurring during periods of apparent stasis might not be detectable. Although the controversy need not concern us, the concept is relevant to later chapters on language evolution because it has been used to justify the Chomskyan view that a "language module" emerged suddenly in the course of human evolution.

This sketchy account is enough to identify the bare bones of the genetic evolutionary mechanisms and the kinds of environmental influences that resulted in the changes, over millions of years, in the brain and other physical structures that must support the intellectual functions we call mind. Much of the evolution of mind has, however, occurred too recently and too quickly to be based on genes or gene-environment interactions as usually understood. The alternative interpretations have instead emphasized cultural evolution. The genetic sketch is nonetheless relevant here as well because aspects of cultural evolution have been interpreted by analogy with genetic evolution. It can even be argued that culture ultimately rests on biological mechanisms. For example, culture is learned and the capacity to learn is based on

---

[29]Note, however, that the ecosystem and evolutionary changes can be very fast, e.g., grey and white moths in Britain. Also, rapid changes occur because of human intervention, as in breeding new varieties of animals and plants, and direct modification of genes. The interventions reflect one of the impacts of cognitive evolution-a kind of bootstrapping in that we have evolved genetically and culturally so that we can affect the evolutionary process itself.

inherited biological structures whose adaptive strength is their plasticity; that is, their modifiability by experience. Nonetheless, biological changes are not the immediate causes of cultural evolution.

CULTURAL EVOLUTION

The basic mechanism of cultural evolution is individual learning under the guidance of parents and other members of social groups (I refer to humans and our hominid ancestors, although some cultural evolution has been observed in other animals as well). The learning mechanisms themselves are open to different theoretical interpretations (discussed in Chapter 11). The behaviorist B. F. Skinner proposed quite detailed analyses in terms of an analogy between operant conditioning and genetic evolution: behaviors that are successful in that they result in positive consequences, such as food, or escape from or avoidance of negative consequences, such as a painful event, are reinforced and are more likely to be repeated under the same or similar circumstances in the future. The reinforced behaviors are selected from a repertoire of alternative behaviors because of their adaptive consequences. At the social level, other individuals serve as reinforcers of socially desirable behaviors and those behaviors become the habits, mores, and customs of the society. Why particular social behaviors are reinforced is itself a function of their reinforcement history within the society. Society thus reinforces behaviors that serve both biological and social needs—that is, we are taught such survival skills as how to obtain food and shelter, as well as social manners.

Other learning theorists emphasize perceptual or observational learning in which the learner imitates the successful behavior of others (behaviorists would say that imitation is itself learned by operant conditioning, and some neuroscientists stress the role of mirror neurons as described in Chapter 7). For our purposes, we can accept the practical usefulness of different interpretations of learning—operant conditioning, classical conditioning (relevant to the analysis of emotions, as we have already seen), and imitation. The last mentioned is the basis of the following conceptualization of cultural evolution in terms of a comparison with genetic evolution.

Memetics

The idea is that cultural evolution is based on informational units analogous to the gene. The idea has been discussed for several decades under different labels. The label that has now become common currency among evolutionary sociobiologists and other scholars is *meme* (rhymes with cream), introduced by the ethologist Richard Dawkins (1976) and developed by psychologist Susan Blackmore (1999). The term shares the Latin and Greek roots of the words imitation and mimic, meaning to copy. Thus, like the gene, the meme is functionally a replicator, the basis whereby an individual idea (expressed in behavior or an invented product) is copied by others and then spreads like wildfire, or perhaps like molasses, among members of a wider community. The analogies include virtually all of the characteristics of genes and genetic evolution: memes have variant forms analogous to alleles, memetic evolution might spread over a small population and die out quickly or spread widely and survive over generations. New words, jokes, and songs are more or less popular memes of limited scope. Scientific ideas, works of literature and art, and technological inventions might be similarly limited or enormously successful memes. Darwin's theory is one of grandest memes in all of science, of great influence, durability, and variability (in terms of its extensions beyond its biological origins to microbiology, cultural biology, and the very origins and evolution of the universe). Gutenberg's invention, the printing press, is of comparable scope, copied quickly around the world and persisting and evolving into ever changing variants up to the computerized electronic versions of the present day. Just think of e-mail and the struggle for survival in the electronic Gutenberg niche! Finally, the most sweeping of all is the god meme, about which you can easily develop your own evolutionary scenario in all its scope and variety, but see Dennett (1995) for a detailed discussion.

Is the meme a useful scientific concept? At the very least it is a convenient metaphor for thinking about cultural evolution, and some have suggested that it goes beyond analogy or metaphor, so that the meme "exists" as a functional brain unit of some kind. In 1981, biologists Lumsden and Wilson (1981; further discussed by E. O. Wilson, 1998) proposed that the cultural-evolutionary unit is the same as the conceptual node of semantic memory with its brain correlates—labeled nodes that are organized in semantic memory in the way described in Chapter 3. Wilson conceded that this interpretation might be superceded by others as the relevant sciences progress.

Without waiting for such developments, I offer the following comments. First, the concept of semantic memory nodes in a "nodal network" is not in fashion among all memory theorists, myself included. The main objections have to do with the abstractness of the proposed memory representation. Like its variants, proposition and schema (also mentioned by Wilson), the semantic node must be instantiated in rich modality-specific forms before it can serve any explanatory purpose beyond labeling the "nodal complex." The general arguments have already been presented in the preceding chapters, but I concretize them here. Consider Einstein's theory of relativity. Adults everywhere know the theory by its name, and so, to that extent at least, it is a piece of semantic memory information that we share. Its status as a meme, however, depends on all of the scientific implications of the name of the theory—the verbal associations, mathematical equations, predictive implications for astronomical and cosmological phenomena, and so on. Furthermore, its success and survival as a meme depends on the copiers having all that knowledge about the theory and how to test it. We could argue that the Einsteinian meme-node is instantiated in all those ways, meaning either that the node contains all of that knowledge or is a pointer to the more specific instantiations.

The bottom line is as follows: From my dual coding perspective, I could interpret the meme as consisting of an identifying verbal label and its internal logogen representation, which is connected with varying strength to other logogens, some of which have connections to nonverbal referents (imagens) in the imagery system, with both classes of symbolic representations having connections to relevant verbal and nonverbal output systems. The different components vary in their activation probabilities depending on the context in which the meme label (e.g., theory of relativity) or some salient associate (e.g., Einstein, $E = mc^2$, atomic bomb) is used. The activation pattern consists of the expressed verbal associations, experienced images, and behaviors relevant to the associative domain of the meme. The domain varies in scope so that some individuals have only the meme label and a few associates, whereas others have a larger meme package, which can be realized behaviorally in various ways. A large Einsteinian relativity meme, for example, would include the behavioral skills for testing implications of the theory, perhaps even making a bomb (some may have that know-how without knowing much else about the theory!); a rich Shakespearian Hamlet meme might include the memory skill for reciting the entire play (a very long meme indeed, not easily replicated!), producing the play, and so on. Finally, whatever their scope, such memes persist and spread to the extent that their behavioral realization is valued or rewarding for individuals in a community.

The proponents of the meme concept describe such properties by analogy with genes and Darwinian evolutionary principles. That helps explain aspects of cultural evolution in an interesting and communicable way. The point of my interpretation is to show some of the complexities of the underlying cognitive representations and more particularly to emphasize that the meme cannot be a unitary node in a nodal (semantic memory) network, even if it is restricted to the meme label. The concept must include whatever modality-specific knowledge—narrow or broad, shallow or deep—that may be associated with it. My analysis is simply a domain-specific extension of the analysis of meaning and comprehension in Chapter 4: for different people, a given language segment can have narrow or broad meaning and be understood at a shallow or deep level, depending on the richness of its defining associative network. This comparison reveals the potentially unconstrained nature of the meme concept. The ultimate logical extension is that any concept (a word and its meanings) qualifies as a meme for a linguistic community, or communities. A word has an origin and evolution (etymology), it has its "alleles" (synonyms and translation equivalents across languages), it could become extinct, and so on. In principle, this is not a new analysis; Darwin himself recognized the parallels between evolutionary concepts and those used by philologists in their investigations of the geneology of languages. The argument is simply focused here—any language unit is an evolutionary meme. This may be what is intended by the proponents of the concept. If so, what unique value does it have as a scientific concept? (For another analysis of the shortcomings and strengths of the meme concept, see Dennett, 1995).

SOURCES OF EVIDENCE FOR SPECULATIONS

Evolution of mind is a speculative enterprise. It cannot be studied by the kinds of direct observational and experimental methods that have been used by students of biological evolution since Darwin and before. Darwin grounded his theory on detailed and extensive observations of variations among finches, barnacles, and many other species. Mendel observed and experimentally produced varieties of peas. Evolution is fast-tracked in the fruit fly, and so it has long been a favorite experimental model for studying and influencing evolutionary changes. Bacteria and viruses are on an even faster evolutionary track and so they are emerging as new experimental models. Moreover, specific genetic mutations can even be created using genetic engineering techniques. Perhaps some day we will have comparable empirical tools to study cognitive evolution, but for now we have to rely on indirect inferential methods. The following summarizes the general categories of evidence, and the subsequent chapters expand on relevant details.

Bones, Stones, and Molecular Fossils

Archeologists, paleoanthropologists, and other evolutionary scientists have long used fossil records as a basis for making guesses about the origin and evolution of language, consciousness, and other aspects of cognition (e.g., see Leakey & Lewin, 1978). The richest finds in regard to our primate ancestors have been in the Great Rift Valley in East Africa, where it stretches from Tanzania in the south through Kenya and Ethiopia to Israel in the north. The notable specific sites include the Olduvai Gorge in Tanzania, the shores of Lake Turkana in Kenya, and parts of Ethiopia. For example, the famous Lucy fossil was discovered in northern Ethiopia. The nature of the skeletal fossil remains and stone tools found in the same areas reveal something about the physical characteristics and habits of our early hominid ancestors—whether they walked upright, their brain size and shape as inferred from skull remains, and the size of social groups in which they lived. Dating of fossils and evolutionary changes in different specimens is done using the depth of the layers of rock and interlayered volcanic ash in which the specimens are found and by radioactive carbon dating. Such data are crudely informative about evolution of mind as inferred from correlations between changes in "bones and stones," changes in the complex organization of the brain and behavior, and the relation between those and cognitive functions as these are known from modern humans and related species. For example, the fossil record shows that Homo erectus, the immediate ancestor of Homo sapiens, moved out of Africa almost 2 million years ago and spread rapidly through Europe to Southeast Asia. This suggests that erectus had highly developed nonverbal congitive skills (for spatial orientation, hunting, and so on), despite lack of speech as far as one can tell from careful analyses of its fossilized bones (Walker & Shipman, 1996)

The quest for the origins of mind extends to fossil records of the ancestors of animals other than primates, including single-cell protozoans and their multicellular descendants. Developments in evolutionary molecular biology have extended the fossil record to molecular fossils discovered in shale beds that are 2.7 billion years old (e.g., Brocks, Logan, Buick, & Summons, 1999). Some extant protozoan descendants of the primitive life forms have sensory and memory capacities that suggest that mind first emerged in their ancestors hundreds of millions of years ago. We shall touch on the evidence later on but the relevant point for now is that inferences about mind from bones, stones, and molecular fossils must be grounded in evidence on the cognitive skills of living descendants of ancient species.

Animal Cognition and Communication

Much of the current research on cognitive evolution is based on extrapolations from comparative analyses of the cognitive abilities of other animals, especially the natural and human-taught communication systems of apes and monkeys. A central issue is whether similarities to human language and other cognitive abilities involve homologous or homoplastic (analogous) relations. Homologous traits have common functions and evolutionary origins whereas homoplasies have common functions but different origins. Both bats and birds can fly but but their wings have different evolutionary origins, so the relation is homoplastic. Parrots can be taught to speak like humans up to a point, but that relation, too, is homoplastic and not homologous. But what about the chimpanzee's ability to communicate using gestures or tokens (lexigrams) that stand for words? The quality of the gesture language of trained chimpanzees has been questioned, but their lexigram communication skills are quite remarkable. Even more striking is the ability of the pygmy chimpanzee, the bonobo, not only to communicate effectively using lexigrams and gestures, but also to understand human speech. Kanzi, the first of these bonobos, picked up such communicative skills just by observing psychologist Sue Savage-Rumbaugh trying to teach the skills to his mother, and Kanzi's younger sibling began to pick up the skills the same way. This suggests that bonobos and humans have homologous communicative abilities, at least up to a point. This has been a hotly debated issue and I return to it later (Chapter 13), along with other examples of animal communication that bear directly on dual coding interpretations of the origins and evolution of human language. I also discuss the human relevance of other cognitive skills among animals.

Extrapolations From Cognitive Development in Children

Shortly after Darwin's publication of *The origin of species* in 1859, Ernst Haekel proposed the theory that "ontogeny recapitulates phylogeny," that is, that anatomical and functional development during the early life of individual organisms go through the same stages as they do in phylogenetic evolution. The theory was generally discredited but is still accepted in the case of embryological development. Students of cognitive evolution rely heavily on a cognitive version of the theory by making guesses about the evolution of cognitive abilities, especially language, from their developmental sequence in children (see Chapter 12).

Historical Language Changes

Historical linguists have been able to track changes in language as far back as 6,000 years (Antilla, 1972). Remarkably, the historical records reveal probable changes in phonology (sound and pronunciation), as well as, with more certainty, changes in syntax. Contrary to the views of some linguists, this historical evidence suggests that languages have evolved gradually along Darwinian lines (see Chapter 13).

Logical Argument

This is not a class of empirical evidence, but rationality (logical and analogical reasoning) is part of the methodology of all science and was notably systematic in Darwin's theory construction, which we discuss in some detail later (Chapter 18). I draw attention to it here because the logical reasoning has to be truly Sherlockian when we are dealing with the evolution of mind. Thus, we often rely on analogical reasoning and the argument that unknown past X can be inferred from what we know about present Y, a weak version of the syllogism, X therefore Y. For example, mental rotation has been empirically demonstrated in the domestic pigeon using a procedure similar to that used in human experiments. There are, however, many breeds of domestic pigeons and still others in the wild. Is it reasonable to assume that most are capable of mental rotation? At least the question can be tested in principle. It is a pure logical argument to extend the hypothesis back thousands of years to times when humans began to domesticate pigeons. And what about wild pigeons even before recorded history? The most we can do is argue from other similarities in structures and behaviors of known species that mental rotation ability probably appeared long ago in pigeons. That sort of inferential bridging is applied to a variety of animal cognitive abilities in the next chapter.

MEMORY AS THE ENGINE OF COGNITIVE EVOLUTION

This hypothesis ties together all the past and present of human mind, an idea I support by argument and empirical evidence.In a general sense, all evolution is memory.Biological evolution involves changes in genes that are retained in the genetic structure and replicated if the changes are adaptive. This can be called biological or genetic memory and it has even been invoked to explain some universal psychological experiences such as the common fears of falling, dark places, and snakes, among others, and the so-called atavistic dreams related to them. Carl Jung used the term collective unconscious to refer to such racial memories, which are expressed symbolically in common art forms, dreams, and other "archetypes" of racial experience. Such experiences also are a theme of Carl Sagan's (1977) popular book, *The Dragons of Eden*. The claim here is that the potential for such collective experiences gets incorporated into the genetic code, not in the Lamarckian sense of direct inheritance of acquired characteristics, but rather as a genetically-based readiness to attend to and remember the kinds of emotion-arousing events that were significant for early hominid survival. It is a kind of bias in gene expression, a realization of memory potential given exposure to relevant events.

Cultural evolution involves memory in another sense, namely retention of the habits, customs, myths, and artifacts that are valued by social groups and essentially define them. They could be called social memories that are entrenched in the oral traditions and visual (eventually written) records of a people. But the ultimate basis of such memories is the individual. This view has been nicely captured by Tomasello (1999) in his analysis of sociogenesis and "cumulative cultural evolution," which he dubbed the "ratchet effect." Thus, newly invented artifacts and other creations entail faithful social transmission that prevents slippage backward, so that it is not necessary for each succeeding generation to start "re-inventing the wheel."He suggested, in addition, that "all types of cultural learning are made possible by a single very special form of social cognition, namely the ability of individual organisms to understand conspecifics as beings *like themselves* who have intentional and mental lives like their own" (p. 5).

At some stage of evolution, perhaps beginning with single-celled animals (Chapter 11), individual memory became a vital evolutionary adaptation. The development of sense organs permitted adaptive reactions to sensory stimuli, for example approach or withdrawal. Memory enabled organism to seek food and mates in their absence and to avoid predators before a fatal contact. It entailed an ability to recognize survival-significant objects and situations that the individual has encountered before and lived to see another day. It evolved into a capacity to respond appropriately to stimuli that had been associated with the significant objects—for example, to react to moving grass as a sign of a possible predator. The better the memory the greater its adaptive value, and so memory evolved: the relevant anatomical structures and physiological processes became more efficient at storing more and more complex information for longer periods of time. Memories of individual encounters, episodic memories (Chapter 3), somehow accumulate, get modified, and organized into more capacious long-term memories that form the knowledge base or representational base of cognition.

It is in the aforementioned sense that memory is the engine of cognitive evolution, the driving force that has led to more intelligent systems. It is a bootstrapping operation in that memory potential is itself genetically retained and evolves, pulls itself upward, by virtue of its adaptive success. All evolving systems do that, but memory is more far-reaching in its evolutionary consequences. Memory is of course biologically and psychologically complex, as we have already seen in Chapters 3 and 4, as well as subsequent chapters on the brain. It is linked to sensorimotor systems that capture information that is sent along to memory systems. The information comes from objects and events that are experienced in different modalities and contexts, including social contexts.The evolution of these capacities before language entered the scene is the topic of the next chapter.

CHAPTER ELEVEN

Animal Minds

This chapter uses the nonverbal side of DCT to interpret the evolution of the minds of nonverbal animals. Animal minds had eons of time to evolve before there was any glimmering of language.Over millions of years, evolutionary pressures favored developments in all of the component systems that collectively define cognition, permitting flexible adaptation to increasingly varied and complex environments, including social environments. The emerging skills necessarily included nonverbal communication systems and we touch on those here, postponing more detailed discussion to the subsequent chapters on language origins and evolution.

A comparative psychological approach is used to analyze the basic cognitive processes and their adaptive functions across species, which eventually came together in the collection of capacities that characterize human minds. The analytic approach is applied to creatures that differ enormously in their complexity and the evolutionary time periods at which they emerged. However, in describing relevant differences and changes, I only touch on taxonomic evolutionary descriptions of those changes, sufficient for the selective approach of this volume. More systematic taxonomies are available elsewhere; for example, Byrne (2000) in regard to primate cognition, Jerison (2000) in regard to animal intelligence across species, and a succinct overview of taxonomic classifications (cladograms) in the context of the evolution of brain and behavior (Kolb & Whishaw, 2001, pp. 14–32). A related caveat, already discussed earlier, is that I do not rely on inferences about mind based on bones, stones, and molecular fossils—the kinds of evidence that evolutionary archeologists, anthropologists, and molecular biologists emphasize. The ultimate benchmark for the cross-species comparisons is the nonverbal mind of modern humans as known from performance on nonverbal cognitive tasks that have clear adaptive significance in the ways described in Chapter 4.[30]

---

[30]Cognitive capacities and tasks have long been investigated by comparative psychologists and are the focus of numerous recent works on animal cognition and its evolution (e.g., Beckoff, Allen, & Burghardt, 2002; Jerison, 2000; Roberts, 1998; Shettleworth, 1998; Zentall, 2000). I have drawn on such sources in my search for the nonverbal precursors to dual coding mind.

We begin with a *tour d'horizon* of the kinds of changes that occurred, followed by developments in specific systems, including sensorimotor, emotional-motivational, learning, memory, and imagery systems. Then we deal with the processing capacities and adaptive functions of these systems using a particular inferential approach. Finally, we consider the social context in which they evolved. That context provided the basis for the cultural evolution of the representational substrate of mind, the kinds of memories that are acquired during the life times of individuals and are needed for improvements in shelters, hunting and food gathering, defensive weapons, mating skills, and opportunities for play.

THE BIG PICTURE

The evolution of nonverbal cognition entailed interdependent anatomical and physiological changes to an extraordinary degree. Interdependence means that a given genetic change could only occur if an accommodating change also occurred in another anatomically or functionally related part. To take an obvious example, increases in brain size (crucial to cognitive evolution) required proportionate increases in skull size. Conversely, however, evolutionary increases in skull size would not have occurred unless there were evolutionary pressures for increased brain size. Thus the changes were interdependent, involving a particular kind of variation and selection: Brain size varied, larger brains were advantageous, and were selected to the extent that their cranial environment had coincidentally increased in size. However, the increased head size required accommodating increases in the size of the female pelvis and the pelvic opening through which the head must pass during birth. The changes are limited by other factors—too large a female pelvis would compromise her walking gait, and increased head size would require stronger necks and other body parts that support the head (already heavy in humans compared to the body-proportionate head weight of other large mammals). The advantageous combinations of matching changes co-evolved, or a functional anatomical niche was already available to accommodate adaptive changes in another system later. Such interdependent evolutionary changes occurred in skeletal, muscular, behavioral, perceptual, and memory systems that collectively define cognitive evolution, to which cultural factors eventually contributed in what sociobiologists refer to as gene-culture co-evolution.

An arboreal lifestyle fostered the evolution of intelligence in our primate ancestors, although that style presumably evolved initially because trees protected small and vulnerable early monkeys (e.g., *Eosimias,* 45 million years ago) from many predators, as they do today. Other small animals, such as squirrels, move through trees using all four feet and the earliest primates presumably were squirrel-like in that respect. Brachial movement would favor larger body size, which in turn benefited from the development of prehensile hands with opposable thumbs useful for grasping larger branches. Longer arms facilitated swinging movement and hence travel through the trees (especially efficient in gibbons). The usefulness of such changes also depended on the development of stereoscopic vision and eye-hand coordination, so that secure branches could be quickly spotted and effectively grasped. These in turn required changes in head shape that moved the eyes to the front of the head, accompanied by changes in sensory-motor and brain systems that permitted visual focus on a target and coordinated reaching and grasping movements toward it. Those developments also had other benefits, such as detecting predators and arboreal fruit, which carried over to terrestrial forays as well.

A terrestrial lifestyle had advantages for our ancestors that required new adaptive changes. Food is available on the ground. Cooperative social interaction is easier on the ground than in the trees. The mobility of heavier primates would be compromised in the trees. Forests decreased and savannas increased in size. Such factors moved some arboreal primate species, including our direct ancestors, back to the ground. The long primate arms favored the knuckle-walking gait characteristic of chimpanzees and gorillas today. This evolved into bipedalism, the upright walking that is the hallmark of humanity, including early hominids going back as far as 6 million years ago, when australopithecus africanus (African southern ape) walked about using what probably was an imperfect bipedal gate.

Whatever its locomotive advantages, upright walking freed the hands for other purposes, including, especially, tool use, and eventually, tool making. Efficient manipulative use of the hands required anatomical changes in the wrists. Modern apes have stiff wrists that stabilize the arms for knuckle walking. Early hominids had such wrists as well. Interestingly, recent inspection of the fossil remains of Lucy, who lived in Africa some 3.5 million years ago, revealed that she had stiff wrists like chimpanzees (Richmond & Strait, 2000) but her hip and leg bones showed that she walked upright. Thus she was at a transitional evolutionary stage in that her hands were not used for walking but neither were they fully adapted for skillful manipulation of objects.

Tool use and manufacture also depended on evolution of the brain and perceptual-motor systems that control skilled movements. Here we have the structure-function issue—we could say that intelligent systems evolved first or that tool making promoted evolutionary selection of better brains and perceptual systems. Both interpretations entail the kind of reciprocal co-evolution we have already discussed. We turn next to more specific changes that are directly relevant to this theoretical approach.

SENSORIMOTOR SYSTEMS

These systems are generally categorized according to sensory modalities and the related receptors, but, as functional systems, they necessarily include motor processes. Indeed, it has been suggested that the sensory systems evolved to aid the motor system (P. Milner, 1999, pp. 3–4). The intimate involvement of response systems in perception was emphasized by James Gibson (1966). Among current perceptual theorists, Goodale (2000) insisted especially strongly on the importance of motor processes in perception.

How do the rich multimodal sensorimotor systems described in Chapters 3 and 7 compare individually and collectively with the systems of other animals? The sensory systems of all animals are limited in that each is specialized to respond to a very small range of information that is potentially available in the stimulus—for example, electromagnetic energy in the case of vision and the vibration of air molecules in the case of audition. Moreover, species vary greatly in the information their senses can process so that, individually, each of our senses is surpassed in at least some respects by those of other animals but all are useful and some are superbly adapted for the environments in which we evolved. My guess is that, collectively, our sensory capacities are unsurpassed by any other creature in that none has a combination of functionally interconnected perceptual systems as well suited as ours for living in complex and varied environments—such functional interconnectedness necessarily implicating memory, as we see later.

The aforementioned supposition follows logically from the fact that no other animal is adapted for survival under as wide a range of conditions as are modern humans. Much of that survival capacity is due to cultural evolution as already mentioned—the transmission over generations of the art of making tools and clothes, controlling and using fire, building shelters and means of travel, and all manner of "prosthetic" devices that extended our perceptual-motor abilities far beyond their unaided reach. Such artificial extensions could only have originated and evolved because the necessary perceptual systems had already evolved collectively to a more versatile level than those of other species. I do not know of any quantitative measure of the average strength of sensory-perceptual-motor systems that directly supports this logical argument, but let's see if we can get a subjective feel for the idea from a brief review of the individual sensorimotor systems.

Vision

Vision has generally been emphasized as our dominant sense and we have touched on its general adaptive advantages for life in the trees and on the ground, extending to life on savannas. The evolutionary result is a remarkably well-rounded visual system. Visual acuity is about as sharp as it can get, so that a healthy human eye can detect a line so thin that it stimulates only a micron-wide strip of retinal cells. Our visual motion detectors pick up comparably small movements of objects. Our color vision, like that of other primates, is well adapted for distinguishing variously colored edible fruits and leaves from their backgrounds, and likewise for detecting safe branches, perches, predators, and recognizing relatives (even their facial expressions). We are surpassed on individual visual sensitivities by other species. Such raptors as hawks and eagles have far better visual resolution, enabling them to see objects at greater distances than we can. Owls have proportionately more light-sensitive rods than we do, an adaptation for locating prey in the dark. Bees can respond to ultraviolet light and polarized light (pattern of vibration of light); we cannot. And so on for other species-specific visual adaptations on which we are evolutionary misfits, but on average our visual system is useful in a wider range of conditions than the visual systems of other animals. Except for ultraviolet, the color vision of bees is more limited than ours; for example, they can't see red. Birds distinguish moving prey against the relevant terrestrial, aquatic, or aerial contexts but they may not have the range of detailed pattern perception that we do. Our visual strength and versatility is reflected as well in our strong visual memory and imagery skills, discussed shortly.

Audition

Our auditory system is almost as efficient as our vision within the range of acoustic information it is specialized to process. A good ear can detect as sound movements of only a few air molecules at the ear drum. It has been said that if our hearing was any more sensitive, we would hear the sound of our blood moving through veins and arteries. Again, other creatures surpass us in some respects: dogs respond to auditory pitch too high for us to hear, bats use sonar to locate insects by emitting bursts of high pitched sounds that bounce off their tiny prey; we cannot do that or even hear the emitted sounds, which are so loud to bats that they have a feedback mechanism for shutting down their ears at the moment they emit the sound. Dolphins also receive information about the sizes and shapes of objects in the water from the pattern of echoes of exploratory sounds the dolphins make; and so on. Such sensitivities are beyond our auditory competence, although, within our acoustic range, we can use the temporal and spatial patterns of sound waves to locate the direction and distance of stationary or moving sound sources accurately enough to guide head movements that permit us to refine the judgments visually. We even receive some useful information about the nature of surfaces and enclosed spaces from the echoes made by our shoes when we walk, or the tapping of the walking canes used by the blind. Those sensitivities are, however, crude compared to the auditory specialists already mentioned, and crude compared to our peak areas of auditory competence.

Consider, for example, the enormous number of sounds we can differentiate and identify—sounds made by different birds and other animals, sounds of wind, rain, thunder, flowing water, crackling fire, rustling leaves, and all manner of natural sounds available to our primate ancestors and relatives as well as us; and then the sounds of telephones, sirens, whistles, and all manner of auditory gadgets we have invented. And most remarkable of all is our ability to process the complex sound patterns of music produced by different instruments and the even more complex patterns of speech sounds—learned and culturally transmitted skills for which we have the necessary genetic base as a species. Our specialized auditory capacities do not function in isolation, however, but cooperatively with other senses, among which vision is paramount, entailing parallel processing of auditory and visual stimuli and cross activation of imagery in the two modalities through interconnections between their memory representations (Chapter 7).

Haptics

Here we deal with the sensorimotor systems that pick up information by active touch (Gibson, 1966; Klatzky & Lederman, 1987)—the skin receptors stimulated, for example, by passing one's fingers over different grades of sandpaper; the feedback from skin, muscle, and joint receptors that permits us to identify any known feelable object (key, pencil, comb, eyeglasses, knife, spoon, needle, nail, ring, rubber band, toy animals, silk stockings, etc.) by palpating it with our hands, or, if it is small enough, even our mouths. Temperature sensitivity is a part of the haptic system as well. Our evolved hands make us superstars in this perceptual modality. The hands of monkeys, apes, racoons, and other animals with grasping paws, useful though they be, are clumsy by comparison and hence haptically inferior. The antennae of insects contain olfactory chemo receptors that are used as distance receptors (discussed later) as well as topochemical "feelers," so that passing them over the surfaces of objects provides spatial information analogous to that provided by haptic senses, but less usefully than ours. Again, as described in Chapter 7, haptic senses are adapted to cooperate with the visual sensory system, and visual imagery in particular.

Olfaction and Taste

Next, we discuss the chemical senses, olfaction and taste, the former involving distance chemo receptors and the latter, proximal (contact) chemo receptors. These are evolutionarily early and relatively simple systems as compared to the ones already considered. Identification of chemical stimuli is performed by the chemo receptors themselves, which have direct connections to the contractile molecules of the motor system, thereby facilitating such behaviors as engulfing food and escaping from bad environments (P. Milner, 1999). Many animals rely on them more than our primate relatives and we do, given the compensatory development of our other senses. Recall, too (Chapters 3 and 7), that these "chemo receptors" detect tasty and smelly objects or substances; their chemistry is complex.

Humans long ago recognized the prowess of dogs as sniffers and learned to use them as olfactory sensory aids.[31] The sense of smell receded in primates partly because they lack the rhinarium, an area of moist snout skin that helps fix odors wafted to the nose, and partly because their olfactory bulbs have been overtaken by parts of the brain concerned with other senses (Hewes, 1978, p. 2). Nonetheless, primate noses serve them well enough to distinguish rotten from ripe fruit, avoid rotten carcasses and fecal deposits, and help males determine the sexual receptivity of the female. Modern humans have learned to use their noses for distinguishing the bouquets of fine wines, perfumes, and flowers. But we cannot locate potential predators, prey, or sexual objects at a distance by their smell, however much we might "dream of Jeannie with the light brown hair, drifting like a vapor in the soft summer air."

The gustatory system is more than a chemoreceptive taste system in mammals. The taste buds of the tongue and mouth do respond to passive contact with sweet, sour, salty, and bitter liquids with appropriate effector responses, such as salivation, swallowing, or spitting out. In addition, however, it is a haptic system that is sensitive to the shape and texture of food and makes use of complex oral manipulations to perceive those qualities and chewing actions to refine the texture so that the food

---

[31]The differential olfactory sensitivity between humans and dogs is based on the number of olfactory receptor cells-about 40 million in the average human as compared to 2 billion in the German shepherd!

can be swallowed. Swishing wine around in the mouth also has haptic characteristics in that, like active touch, it enhances receptor contact with relevant stimuli.

Smell and taste are interactive in regard to eating behavior. We know that smell can make food more or less palatable. Both have connections to motivational systems so that, for example, hunger increases sensitivity to food odors and ensures that food oriented responses come under the control of food-sensitive receptors (P. Milner, 1999). They also have connections to representational information from the other senses. Thus, in modern humans, odors activate visual memories of their sources—lilacs, forest pine, fish frying, and so forth. We know this from subjective experience as expressed verbally using the names of the source objects. We can only surmise similar experiences in the case of our preverbal ancestors and other animals, although we see later that there are empirical and theoretical arguments that support such speculations. The analysis is similar in the case of tastes in that, for us, the liquid chemicals in orange and other juices can elicit images of oranges, and so on, unlikely imagery conditions for other animals and early humans who presumably ate fruit whole rather than as juice.

EMOTIONAL-MOTIVATIONAL SYSTEMS

Sensorimotor systems are closely linked to affective, emotional, and motivational systems in all complex animals, including us (Chapter 4). What we label as hunger, thirst, and fear are aspects of survival mechanisms that mediate behaviors intended to obtain food and safe places, and escape from or avoid dangerous ones. Sexual drive and pleasure are similarly associated with mate seeking and other reproductive behaviors that ensure transmission of genes. The physiological systems that underlie emotions and motives are wired-in genetically but their connections to relevant perceptual objects, situations, and behaviors require at least some learning. Evolutionary psychologists have long emphasized that some emotional reactions, such as fear of snakes, spiders, and high places, are more easily learned than fear of cars and electrical outlets because the former have a longer adaptive evolutionary history than the latter. Nonetheless, even neutral objects can acquire positive or negative valence given sufficient association with positive or negative consequences—much studied experimentally using both Pavlovian and operant conditioning methods (see Rolls, 1995). Social stimuli are particularly important in that regard, becoming sources of pleasurable emotions and approach behaviors or unpleasant emotions such as fear and anger and the avoidance or aggressive behaviors associated with them. A later section presents a detailed analysis of the complexities and adaptive functions of social perceptions, emotions, and behaviors.

LEARNING PROCESSES

Learning and memory (the topic of the next section) are intimately related. One concept implies the other—learning means that something has been retained from past experience; conversely, memory exists only for what has been learned. Nonetheless, the concepts became associated with somewhat separate research streams and theories, with learning traditionally studied using a wider range of species and with more attention to evolutionary issues than has been the case with its conceptual mate. Thus, here too we focus on evolution of learning. Theorists have generally assumed that learning processes evolved from simple to complex, with orientation mechanisms and imprinting at one end and classical and operant conditioning at the other. There has been considerable variation, however, in the number of different forms and the classification schemes that have been proposed. Bruce Moore (2004) recently offered the most comprehensive analysis to date, consisting of an evolutionary cladogram that links nearly 100 forms of learning and shows the paths through which they evolved. The hierarchical structure includes multiple forms of imprinting, Pavlovian conditioning, instrumental conditioning, mimicry, and imitation. Also included are "new" processes, such as abstract concept formation, percussive mimicry, cross-modal imitation (e.g., an infant's imitation of its mother's blinking), hybrid conditioning, and image-mediated learning. Imitation is one of Moore's research areas, and so, he gives considerable attention to its varieties—vocal mimicry in song learning by song birds and movement imitation in mammals as well as some birds. It may come as a surprise that, contrary to popular belief, there is no evidence that monkeys can imitate. Among primates, it has been seen thus far only in great apes and in humans at least 9 months old. Only humans and primates show "putting through," a form of skill learning in which the teacher guides the passive learner through the desired response. Combinations of different forms of learning are involved in the acquisition of complex skills (e.g., language). Examples are discussed later in relevant contexts.

A general implication of the analysis is that "Species capable of process n should be capable of process $n-1$, as should their immediate ancestors, and, in most cases, their nearest living relatives. The processes should therefore occur in nested phylogenetic taxa . . ." (Moore, 2004, p. 328). The hypothesis is compatible with an impressive body of comparative data, especially in the case of birds. Moore (2004) recognized that parts of the cladogram are clearly incomplete and others may simply be wrong.

One aspect that is strikingly wrong from this theoretical and empirical perspective is Moore's (2004) classification of image-mediated learning. He viewed it as a product of cultural evolution that is sometimes used to communicate complex movements. For example, a violinist might be taught a fingering technique by being told to release the string "as if testing a very hot iron," which works more quickly than any demonstration or detailed description of movement. The analysis is appropriate but incomplete and too restrictive phylogenetically. It refers only to language-evoked imagery and omits perceptually evoked memory imagery of the kind described in earlier chapters. More importantly in this context, it excludes the possibility that image-mediated learning goes far back in evolution and might subsume some other types of learning in the cladogram. The evidence is reviewed shortly.

MEMORY

Plants do not have living memories derived from learning experience. They have evolved to react to light, chemicals in water or soil, and physical contact. Plants with leaves"seek" the sunlight to promote photosynthesis, they stretch out their roots to obtain support and nourishment from the soil. Some insectivorous plants do capture prey. For example, the Venus flytrap reacts to contact by an insect or any other particle by closing its leaves. These are evolutionary adaptions that sustain life. They entail genetic memory as discussed in Chapter 10. It can be said that carnivorous plants have "learned" to prey on insects, a reversal of nature's norm that fascinated Darwin (he wrote a volume on the subject), but the learning is phylogenetic and not ontogenetic: however often the Venus flytrap is exposed to instances of both substances, it never remembers the difference between a fly and a piece of dirt so that it would eventually close its leaves and begin to digest only the fly.

Animals, however, have developed memory systems that enable them to modify their behavior adaptively during their life times. This was not the case in the beginning. In the primeval soup (or perhaps deep beneath the ocean floor) 3.5 billion years ago, simple single-celled animals without nuclei (bacteria and other prokaryotes) presumably drifted around like ungrounded plants, obtaining nourishment directly from the chemical environment or by cannibalizing each other. Judging from their extant descendants, they had orientation mechanisms that allowed them to detect concentration changes in their environment but no memories of what they had encountered. Memory arose instead in more complex eukaryotes, organisms made up of cells containing nuclei, a domain consisting of everything from unicellular protozoa to multcellular animals, including humans.

Protozoa evolved into creatures with rudimentary sensory and effector systems. For example, the Euglena is a single-celled aquatic animal that lives by photosynthesis. It has a red pigmented spot that is sensitive to light, the most primitive visual receptor or "eye" that controls the activity of a whip-like appendage that moves it into areas where the light intensity is optimal for photosynthesis. No learning or memory is involved; the Euglena has an adaptive trap mechanism that keeps it in light.

The paramecium is a more complex single-celled eukaryote that apparently has memory. Its bristles with cilia that beat so that it swims around like a spinning top seeking food (bacteria) and avoiding obstacles. Gelber (1958) trained "hungry" paramecia to go to a sterile platinum wire on which they had previously found bacteria. Significant retention was demonstrated 3 hr after training. To the extent that such results can be systematically replicated and extended (for difficulties encountered in such extensions, see Applewhite, 1979), they suggest that memory began to emerge 500 million years ago, or at some point thereafter when early species of paramecia had evolved to their modern complexity.

The paramecium has no neurons and its memory is presumably based on excitable properties of its cytoskeleton. Neurons evolved in multicellular animals, from invertebrates to vertebrates, with increasingly complex perceptual, motor, and memory systems that enabled them to find food, mates, and refuge in diverse environments. Planaria, free-living flatworms, are the simplest animals that have a true nervous system that includes a brain with a cortex of nerve cells, nerve fibers, and synapses. They have advanced sensory systems for detecting light, chemical gradients, and tactile stimulation, which control motor responses. It is viewed as an evolutionary ancestor of the vertebrate (including human) brain. It played a starring role in psychological memory research beginning in the 1950s, which led to failed attempts to demonstrate transfer of a "memory molecule" from trained to untrained planaria (see Rilling, 1996, for a review of this bizarre episode in memory research). The important point for our purposes is that carefully-controlled experiments showed that pairing a light with a shock produced a conditioned response to the light that lasted for 4 weeks. We can only surmise that this impressive memory capacity originated in ancestral planaria perhaps as long ago as 400 million years.

The evolutionary memory story holds for all types of invertebrates and vertebrates that have been studied in laboratories and in natural settings. Examples of different species and the ballpark times of their evolutionary origins, taken from Fig. 18. 2, (p. 397) are fish (400 million years ago), reptiles (325 million), insects (300 million), mammals (175 million), and birds (130 million). Memory evolved in these species continuously or independently, in varying degrees of complexity, so that different learning experiences could result in engrams that were adaptive because they benefited survival and reproductive success of the individual organisms, and the memory mechanism was passed on in a Darwinian fashion. The potential is embodied at the most fundamental level in evolutionary changes to neurons and the synaptic connections between them so that sets of neurons respond to a stimulus pattern after repeated exposures in a way that differs from the first time the pattern was encountered (the stimulus becomes "familiar").

Evolutionary elaboration of memory systems also created the potential for associative memories, which implies that component engrams can activate each other, thereby enabling organisms to respond in an appropriate anticipatory way to a stimulus in its absence. For example, a flight response to a fluttering leaf could be a simple reaction to movement or it could occur because engrams activated directly by the leaf in turn activate engrams previously formed to a predator. This is a jargony way of saying that the leaf reminds the fleeing animal of the predator. A more complete interpretation requires us to say that the perceptual memory engram activated by the leaf also arouses fear, which motivates flight as an appropriate avoidance response. This is a neuropsychological view of associative memory changes that presumably underlie learning as studied, for example, using perceptual learning, classical conditioning, and operant conditioning procedures.

The structural and biochemical modifications that constitute a memory trace or engram are yet to be fully understood. The evolution may have involved changes in single genes that affect sodium and potassium ion channels that conduct impulses along neuronal membranes, chemical neurotransmitters at synapses between neurons, neuronal branching processes, cell signalling, and so on. Multiple genetic mutations presumably affected the development of the brain structures that are involved in memory. The result is the evolutionary emergence of multiple memory systems that differ across species and within species.

As we saw in Chapter 3, just what constitutes a memory system is somewhat controversial among memory scientists. Sherry and Schacter (1987) discussed the issue in the evolutionary context. They especially defended functional incompatibility as the hallmark of distinct systems, elaborating on the idea that memory and learning abilities in animals are adaptive specializations that are shaped by natural selection to solve specific problems posed by an animal's environment. Sherry and Schacter suggested that functional incompatibility exists when a specialized adaptation that serves one function cannot effectively serve other functions. Their examples of such incompatibility included the distinction between memory for song and memory for spatial location in birds, and between habit formation and episodic memory in humans and other primates.

Functional incompatibility is an appropriate criterion of memory systems but I would broaden the definition to include functional independence based on structural distinctions. Sensory-motor modality is one distinction. Just as there are visual auditory, haptic, olfactory, and taste sensations, so too are there memories corresponding to these modalities and species differences in the availability and efficiency of the underlying systems. Moreover, multiple independent systems have evolved within complex species. Such systems are functionally independent according to criteria described in Chapter 4 for modern humans, such as additive memory effects of different sensory components (auditory and visual, olfactory and visual) of multimodal objects. Functional independence was especially emphasized for verbal and nonverbal memory systems even when the input modality was constant (e.g., pictures and printed words), which is beyond the nonverbal focus of this context but is nonetheless relevant to the general point of evolved multimodal systems within species. The inclusion of language in such systems was discussed in the chapters on the neuropsychology of (evolved) dual coding systems and comes up again in the next chapter.

Another example of specialized memory systems is the distinction between episodic memory and the representational long-term memory systems that are the storehouse of the perceptual, affective, and behavioral knowledge of all animals. Consider once again the memory involved in the simple case of perceptual recognition. Recognition requires that a neural representation corresponding to a stimulus is available and reexposure to the stimulus sets up a pattern of activity that somehow matches the corresponding memory representation. The nature of this matching process has usually been discussed in relation to visual recognition, but it must occur in other modalities as well. Ants, rats, and dogs rely on smells to find food, distinguish friend from stranger, recognize trails and landmarks, and so on. Newborn animals of many species learn to recognize the odor of their mothers or they would not survive. Odors are familiar because they match odors stored in longterm memory. Such matching also occurs when a sound is recognized as familiar. For example, males of territorial songbirds learn to recognize a large number of songs of their species members to defend their territory—they have a vast representational memory system for conspecific songs.

Representation systems entail development of connections between memory representations for different objects, environmental contexts, and their behavioral affordances, both within and between modalities. Different perceptual-motor systems can be brought into play cross-modally without recognition—for example, we can turn our heads toward a sound source so that we might be able to recognize it visually and even then not be successful. Or recognition can occur because of cross-modal activation of available representations. A dog can distinguish between a familiar person and a stranger by smell or vision. When I used to drive to my niecee's place near my summer cottage, her two dogs barked loudly and approached threateningly when they first saw my car, then stopped barking and ran toward it eagerly, finally wagging their tails as they sniffed and looked me over when I got out of the car. This sequence occurred after a year or more between visits, evidence that the dogs have representational memory systems in which I am an entry, in different modalities.

We have already noted, too,that eagles and hawks have marvelous visual systems that enable them to detect moving prey at great distances. This means that they must have representational memory systems that enable them to recognize a potential prey. They do not, however, spend much time looking for one that has vanished from view— perhaps a case of out of sight out of mind, relatively short-term episodic memory. Their representational memories also are efficient for spatial information, such as locations where they are likely to find prey. As a child growing up where I now have my summer place, I often saw a fish hawk appear at the outlet of our lake where fish collected to swim down stream. The hawk would hover high above, suddenly drop straight down into the water, and emerge with a fish in its talons. Its special-purpose representational memory system, which includes entries for classes of prey and their locations, increased the probability that it would find fish, and its acute vision ensured that it would recognize an available morsel when it was spotted.

Food-storing birds have a different pattern of abilities. They quickly detect locations where they can hide seeds or nuts and later they can find the same caches with a high degree of success. For example, chickadees, jays, and especially nutcrackers can store thousands of seeds in different locations and retrieve them days, weeks, or months later. This spatial memory capacity is related to the size of the hippocampus, a structure inside the temporal lobes (Chapter 6) that is crucial to memory in mammals and other species. Food-storing birds have a strikingly larger hippocampal complex than non-food-storing birds. Moreover, within the food-storing family, greater dependence on stored food means a larger hippocampus. For example, Clark's nutcracker, the mnemonic champion of the food-storing birds in field tests and laboratory tests of spatial memory (Kamil, Balda, & Olson, 1994), is the species most dependent on stored food and also has the largest hippocampus. Sherry (1990) suggested that their hippocampal complex has been adaptively modified in response to the cognitive demands of food storing. The perceptual-motor activity of food storing readily establishes representational structures that function also as episodic memory systems—cues associated with caches are recognized when the bird flies over the familiar terrain at a time dictated by subsequent motivational states.

Such special-purpose memory systems clearly are adaptive and they can be viewed as limited cognitive systems that are used for problem solving; limited, because they are genetically tuned to a narrow range of situations rather than being broad and flexible. Within their evolutionary niches, the systems evolve so that different species vary in their memory capacity—how many objects, locations, and so on, they can remember, in what modality, and for how long. Primates have the most complex multimodal representational memory systems adaptive for the environments in which they have evolved. Thus, monkeys and apes have better all around memories than other animals, and our memories are better still. The evolution is based on adaptive changes to the genes that are expressed in all of the biochemical and structural components of representational, episodic, and procedural memories. These are reflected in the complexity and overall size of the brain. Modern humans and our hominid ancestors developed the largest and most complex representational systems of all, marked especially by the development of the cortex, with concomitant functional memory superiority. We know this about modern humans and we can guess that early hominids pulled themselves upward by their memory bootstraps until they achieved a superior capacity for developing complex representational memories, useful in tool making and other cognitive tasks. This memory evolution story is summarized by the dual coding idea of memory as the engine of cognitive evolution. Which moves us to the evolution of cognition generally, with a focus next on imagery, imagination, and consciousness.

NONVERBAL COGNITION AND IMAGERY

Imagery had to happen because it is adaptive, for reasons that follow directly from the adaptiveness of perception and memory on which imagery is based. Imagery is the most direct way of representing the perceptual-behavioral world mentally so that animals can recognize, anticipate, and prepare to respond to objects and situations in specific adaptive ways even before encountering them. Its perceptual properties make imagery a more useful mode of representation than more abstract representations that do not directly provide information about the appearances and affordances of situations and things. Precisely for that reason, imagery was an inevitable evolutionary development from sensorimotor and memory systems, a kind of perceptual-motor memory system that had increasing survival value as it evolved. But how can we get at imagery as it might have functioned in the dim and distant past? Are we limited to the kinds of speculations that have been associated with imagery's twin, namely, the phenomenon of consciousness?

Consciousness and Imagery Revisited

The rapid increase in scholarly analyses of consciousness was documented in Chapters 3 and 7. Empirical studies have not led to a satisfactory scientific definition of the essence of the phenomenon, which therefore remains elusive and subject to speculation. Given that consciousness is so difficult to define and study, evolutionary ideas about it have been particularly speculative and diverse (see Blackmore, 2004, pp. 147–165). The evolution of imagery has been discussed less often, perhaps because it is usually equated with consciousness. For example, the following two scientists discussed both concepts in the same breath, so to speak, one a psychologist known for his research in the area and the other a biologist who speculated about the problem.

David Marks's (1999) psychological research and theory on consciousness and imagery were introduced in Chapter 3. His overriding assumption is that mental imagery is a basic building block of consciousness. He proposed an activity cycle theory of conscious imagery according to which "a primary function of consciousness is the mental rehearsal of adaptive, goal-directed action through the experimental manipulation of perceptual-motor imagery" (Marks, 1999, p. 567). The important functional attribute of conscious imagery is its vividness (clarity and liveliness), which, in the case of visual imagery, can be measured reliably and validly by his questionnaire on the vividness of visual imagery (VVIQ). Marks (1999) alluded briefly to evolution, first by emphasizing the adaptive function of imagery in preparing for action and coping with change, and second by suggesting that mental imagery was available earlier in evolution than was language. Related to that is his reference (p. 578) to Piaget and Inhelder's (1971) observation that conscious imagery is developmentally available before language.

Marks's (1999) emphasis on the forward-looking function of imagery is appropriate and I focus on it in my later analysis. Other aspects of his analysis, based largely on empirical findings using the VVIQ, contrast in some respects with my dual coding treatment. The main empirical inconsistency is that reported vividness does not correlate with memory tests whereas it correlates significantly with other cognitive and perceptual-motor tasks. This led Marks to de-emphasize the mnemonic function of imagery, which has been the centerpiece of dual coding research. Decades of research (Chapter 4) strongly supported the usefulness of imagery as a memory aid. Some of the support included participants' verbal reports that they used imagery to remember items, but the main evidence came from other indicators of imagery, including the powerful effects of instructions to learn by imaging. Thus, the discrepant findings are related to different measures of imagery, vividness as compared to the operational procedures that have shown predictive and explanatory success in the memory research. The different findings could mean that imagery vividness is important in the tasks with which it correlates, whereas "just having an image," however unclear, is sufficient as a memory aid. This suggestion merely restates the empirical findings, but at the moment it might be as far as we can go to resolve the puzzling discrepancies.

An even more important issue concerns the verbal report criterion for conscious imagery and its relations to other indicators of imagery and its origins. Thus Marks (1999) stated the following: "Without concurrent validation provided by verbal reports of conscious imagery content . . . the validity of any so-called "objective" indicators is inevitably uncertain and will always remain so" (p. 575) . . . "Mental imagery should never be assumed to be present in the consciousness of research participants without corroboration from their verbal reports. Behavioural or physiological indicators can never stand alone as evidence of mental imagery in human consciousness" (p. 576).

A conundrum here is that the verbal report criterion invalidates imagery interpretations of the results of all those studies that have used other indicators of imagery, such as mental rotation tasks. Marks (1999) escapes this bind by distinguishing between conscious imagery and "a cognitive ability and/or form of analogue representation that is different in kind and independent of conscious mental images" (p. 576). The distinction agrees in principle with my early position that the underlying nonverbal imagery system can be functional at an unconscious level as well as a conscious level. Marks specifies tasks that can be affected by each form of imagery. These are open to empirical investigation provided that we can agree on the measures of conscious and unconscious imagery.

A second problem with the verbal report criterion is that it precludes evolutionary and developmental statements about conscious imagery, including Marks's (1999) own assertions that such imagery preceded language phylogenetically as it does ontogenetically. Neither statement can be supported if the evidence must include corroboration from verbal reports, which (it goes without saying) can never be obtained from preverbal hominids or modern infants. This is precisely why, in my view, it is necessary to bypass the consciousness criterion and rely instead on behavioral evidence to justify statements about the adaptive functions and evolution of imagery.

Donald R. Griffin, an experimental biologist famous for his studies of bat sonar and bird migration among many other contributions, wrote the following in his 1976 book on animal awareness:

> The possession of mental images could well confer an important adaptive advantage on an animal by providing a reference pattern against which stimulus patterns can be compared; and it may well be an efficient form of pattern recognition . . . Even greater adaptive advantage results when such a mental image also includes time as one of its dimensions, that is, the relationships to past and future events. Mental images with a time dimension . . . would allow the animal to adapt its behavior appropriately to the probable flow of events . . . Anticipation of future enjoyment of food or mating or fear of injury could certainly be adaptive by leading to behavior that increases the likelihood of positive reinforcement and decreases the probability of pain or injury . . . the image of food within reach might well be coupled with an image of the act of grasping the food, another with swallowing it, or even the image of its pleasant taste. (p. 84)

We see that Griffin's (1976) speculations about imagery are consistent with behavioral evidence. However, he took the further step of postulating a linkage between imagery and the adaptive value of conscious awareness in animals. For reasons already discussed, I question whether the step has any explanatory value. The criterion for consciousness awareness is the verbal report and questions about its nature and functions apply as much to perception as to imagery. It is enough to say that imagery is functionally like perception in that animals behave as if they are responding to internal scenes, sounds, and so on, without adding that both perception and imagery might entail conscious awareness if only the animal could say so.

The conclusion from this analysis of Marks's (1999) and Griffin's (1976) statements concerning imagery-as-consciousness applies as well to the numerous writings on consciousness that do not emphasize its relation to imagery. An important example, already discussed in earlier chapters, is Tulving's (1985, 2005) revised concept of episodic memory, which he associates with personal awareness that an event occurred at a particular place and time. This definition is crucial to the later section on the evolution of the sense of time, for it excludes animals from having a time sense unless one can come up with a measure of consciousness that is independent of verbal reports. Until then, there is no scientific value in coupling consciousness with imagery or memory in the evolutionary context. This is not to deny the value of verbal reports as an additional criterion for these concepts in the case of language-competent humans. I include that criterion in the following empirical-inferential approach, which is based on extrapolations from the performance of humans on operationally defined imagery tasks to the performance of animals on similar tasks.

AN OPERATIONAL APPROACH TO IMAGERY EVOLUTION

It is reasonable to assume that there was a reciprocal relation between imagery and evolution: Imagery evolved as part of cognition because it was useful for survival and in turn influenced the evolution of other cognitive systems—another instance of the ratcheting effect of interactive evolutionary processes. The evidence supports speculations by many writers that imagery is widespread across animal species whose origins and stable forms go back millions of years. If we accept that evidence, then the conclusion is compelling that imagery began early in animal evolution and evolved along different paths to accommodate diverse and increasingly complex challenges arising from the physical and biological environment.

I evaluate the hypothesis in an indirect empirical fashion by extrapolating from evidence for human imagery to imagery in existing animals with a long evolutionary past. We can think of the method as a kind of scientific anthropomorphizing that I call operational-inferential bridging.[32] Recall from Chapter 3 that imagery was operationalized in terms of stimulus and task concreteness, relevant experimental manipulations, psychometric tests of nonverbal cognitive abilities that implicate imagery, and subjective reports of imagery experiences and strategies. Of these, tasks using concrete stimuli provide the most direct operational-inferential bridge from human imagery to animal imagery. Fortunately, this is a strong bridge because it has been buttressed on the human side by other convergent evidence that

---

[32]The approach is related to but different from the kind of anthropomorphism identified by Blumberg and Wasserman (1995) in their discussion of animal mind. The central issue concerned conscious awareness in animals, which arose historically in the 19th century. Thus, they quote Romanes's (1883, p. 6) conclusion that "the activities of organisms other than our own, when analogous to those activities of our own which we know to be accompanied by certain mental states, are in them accompanied by analogous mental states" (cited in Blumberg & Wasserman, 1995, p. 140). The analogy here is based on introspections about one's mental processes, which are subject to the criticisms already discussed above in relation to the concept of consciousness. A similar disclaimer applies to what Povinelli and his collaborators (e.g., Povinelli, Bering, & Giambrone. 2000; Povinelli & Vonk, 2003) describe as the flawed analogy of second-order mental states, that is, unjustifiably ascribing the human capacity to reason about mental states to primates and other animals. My analogical approach pertains instead to objective experimental procedures that have been used to define and measure cognitive abilities of humans, and which have been extended directly to other animals.

imagery mediates performance in many tasks involving concrete stimuli (Chapters 3 and 4). Performance on such tasks could even be used ultimately to measure individual and species differences in imagery abilities in the same way as, say, the Hebbs–Williams maze has been used to compare humans and animals on spatial intelligence (Shore, Stanford, MacInnes, Brown, & Klein, 2001). In addition, however, the broader the convergent evidence for imagery as a mediator of human performance on a given task, the more confident we can be that it also mediates animal performance on similar tasks.

A reminder about the status of brain activity as a source of evidence on imagery: like overt behavior, what goes on in the brain is a dependent variable and not an independent one. We cannot "locate" imagery in the brain until we know what to look for on the basis of evidence provided by one or more of the other operational procedures. Given such evidence, neuropsychological correlates of imagery (Chapter 7) are fascinating in their own right and become especially informative in the evolutionary context.

The following is a sample of evidence across species that operationally defined imagery is involved in overlapping classes of nonverbal cognitive skills of different levels of generality. Three involve relatively specific adaptive skills, namely recognition memory, anticipation, and mental transformations. These are implicated in the more complex problems of categorization, cognitive mapping, insightful problem solving, and evolution of the "sense" of time.

Imagery in Recognition Memory

We need not elaborate further on how important it is for animals to remember objects and situations that are dangerous, safe, edible, helpful, attractive, and so on. Animals indicate that they remember the positive or negative value of the objects by approach or avoidance responses, but here we are looking for evidence of recognition memory for specific objects and scenes. The human research comparison is picture memory. The relevant findings (Chapter 4) that justified imagery mediation were that (a) recognition memory decreased from pictures to concrete words to abstract words, (b) persons with high imagery ability were superior to low imagers in picture recognition, and (c) memory capacity for pictures was extraordinarily high.

Researchers have used various procedures to study recognition memory in different species of animals. The closest parallel to the human research is a discrimination-learning paradigm in which the animals learn to discriminate between positive and negative slides by being rewarded for choosing the positive ones (e.g., by pecking the appropriate key). They can then be tested for memory of the discriminatory response after different retention intervals. Vaughan and Greene (1984) used this procedure to study visual memory in pigeons. The birds learned to discriminate between 160 positive and 160 negative slides showing pictures of various objects and scenes. They showed above chance discrimination on a retention test after an interval of more than 2 years, an impressive performance for a species so different from humans. This inference is that they developed imagen-like memory representations during discrimination learning against which the test pictures could be matched relatively successfully. The representations necessarily included some kind of positive or negative "tag," perhaps the presence or absence of a food component in the picture imagen, corresponding functionally to the "right" and "wrong" verbal tags humans use in verbal discrimination learning experiments.

Recognition memory for pictures has been demonstrated in other animals using various procedures. However, because of its close procedural parallel to human studies, the pigeon experiment is sufficient to establish an inferential "imagery bridge" between evolutionarily diverse species, related to the formation of memory images of specific pictures shown repeatedly during the experimental trials.

Anticipating Objects and Events

The capacity to anticipate events before they occur has great survival value because it enables organisms to gear up for appropriate action before an event occurs. Anticipation is based either on long-term memory knowledge of where and when significant events are likely to occur, or episodic memories of recent occurrences. In either case, associations must be learned between the events and the situations in which they occur. The interest here is in the role of imagery as a mediator of those predictive associations in humans and other species. The evidence for such anticipatory imagery comes from studies of object permanence, Pavlovian conditioning, and expectancy.

Anticipatory Imagery and Object Permanence. We saw in Chapter 4 that research following Piaget's pioneering research on these concepts indicated that infants as young as 6 months have developed image-like representations that mediate anticipatory behavior. For example, 6-month-olds show surprise when they watch an object disappear behind a screen and then see a different object appear on the other side. Variants of the disappearing-object test have yielded evidence for anticipatory images in species ranging from dogs and cats to various non human primates. For example, tufted capuchin monkeys, chimpanzees, and gorillas search for objects hidden under covers and perform as well as human infants 15 to 18 months of age (Hauser & Carey, 1998; see also Call, 2001). The following behavioral criterion suggests even earlier evolutionary beginnings for anticipatory imagery.

Anticipatory Imagery and Pavlovian Conditioning. Imagery was linked decades ago to classical conditioning in adult humans. Leuba (1940) found that hypnotized individuals reported the smell of creosote when a bell was rung if the bell had previously been rung a number of times while they were actually smelling creosote. Ellson (1941) similarly found that, following paired presentation of a light and a tone, 80% of his participants reported hearing a tone when the light was presented alone. Such effects occurred even when the participants were simply asked to imagine the conditional stimulus (CS). The researchers interpreted such imagery as conditioned sensations and even hallucinations. The interpretation was extended later to conditioning in animals by learning theorist O. Hobart Mowrer (1960).

Since then, representational concepts, including imagery, have become increasingly accepted in conditioning theories. For example, psychologist Peter Holland (1990) wrote that, "Currently the display of Pavlovian CRs [conditioned responses] is almost universally described as mediated by internal representations of the CS and US" (p. 106). He suggested more specifically that "A CS-activated US representative with a large perceptual component is essentially an image of the absent US" (p. 127). This implies that, in the classical Pavlovian experiment, the conditioned salivary response to the tone is mediated by an image of food. Holland reported experiments with rats that support the imagery view in that a CS such as a tone came to control what appeared to be perceptual processing of the absent stimulus. In this context, the processing can be described as anticipatory imagery that prepares the animal for responding appropriately to the stimulus when it becomes available.[33]

The evolutionary adaptive significance of conditioned anticipatory responses was nicely illustrated experimentally by Karen Hollis (1984). She reasoned that "anticipatory conditioned responses function to optimize interactions with predators, rivals, mates, and food" (p. 414). She described the process as prefiguring, which is suggestive of anticipatory imagery, especially given psychometric definitions that link imagery to figural processing. She tested her hypothesis using male blue gourami fish, which defend their territory against rivals. Fish in a tank were exposed to a conditional stimulus (the front of the tank glowed red when lights were turned on behind it) that was associated with the appearance of a rival fish in an adjoining tank. The relevant general result was that the conditioned fish later showed much more aggressive reactions against the rival fish than did fish that only observed the rivals without the conditioning treatment. Moreover, during conditioning, the fish came to exhibit aspects of typical aggressive reactions toward the CS, as if the latter elicited conditioned images of the rival together with defensive reactions that later occurred more vigorously in the presence of the rival. Stretching things a bit, this could be viewed as a kind of evolutionary analogue of mental practice of game strategies used by athletes prior to a competitive match (Chapter 15).

Anticipatory Imagery and Expectancy.   Expectancy was the defining concept in Tolman's (1932) expectancy theory of learning. He interpreted expectancy in two ways: first, as learned associations between representations corresponding to stimuli (S-S associations), so that, for example, the sight of the refrigerator (S1) "reminds" us of food (S2), and second, as representations that also include a response component (SRS associations), so that we expect to see food if we open the refrigerator. Tolman predicted various phenomena from his theory. The most pertinent here is

---

[33]As an alternative to the traditional feedbackward ("law of effect") view of learning, Gardner and Gardner (1988) proposed a feedforward model based on anticipatory responses. They noted that the vocal and gestural responses of cross-fostered chimps to signed communication are, to some degree, anticipatory reactions previously associated with the taste or sight of food, emotional reactions evoke by the sight of a favorite human friend, and so on. It seems reasonable to interpret these as image-mediated anticipatory reactions, much as in Holland's (1990) interpretation of Pavlovian conditioning.

disruption of typical behavior when an expected stimulus is changed. Tinklepaugh (1928, 1932), a student of Tolman, investigated the problem using a variant of the delayed response experiment with monkeys and chimps. For example, a monkey observes its favorite food, a banana, being placed in a container and after a delay interval is allowed to find it. In the meantime, the experimenter surreptitiously substitutes less preferred lettuce for the banana. The monkey finds the container, and, on seeing the lettuce, behaves as if surprised and annoyed, dumps the lettuce out, looks around, and then walks away without eating the lettuce. This pattern was observed in a chimpanzee using 10 pairs of containers, under one of which it finds the lettuce instead of the expected banana. Watanabe (1996) repeated the study using a different task during which he recorded the animal's cortical activity. The surprise reactions occurred along with distinct patterns of brain activity corresponding to the monkeys' expectations of a variety of different rewards—apple, raisin, water, and so on.

Tinklepaugh's (1928, 1932) expectancy results can be seen as evidence of anticipatory imagery in primates, corresponding to experiences familiar to us all. We can easily see as well that expectancy is the most general term that can be used to describe the object permanence and conditioning phenomena already reviewed, and can be similarly interpreted as mediated by anticipatory imagery. It is relevant to note in passing that expectancy theory has also been used to explain sensitivity to risk in foraging behavior in terms of payoff probabilities associated with temporal patterns of rewards (Shettleworth, 1998). It is, of course, completely speculative to suggest that such behaviors might be mediated by probabilistic evocation of anticipatory images of predators on the one hand and food on the other.

Mental Transformation and Integration

Chapter 3 reviewed evidence that we can manipulate objects and scenes in our minds to help resolve disparities of information within and between senses, and also assemble parts to complete a whole. Such mechanisms are adaptive because perceptions are fickle—we see things from different angles or perspectives because they move or we move. Objects can also be camouflaged or glimpsed only fragmentarily. We deal with such problems behaviorally by rotating objects, changing our viewpoint, and trying to put pieces together. Dynamic imagery derived from such behaviors enables us to do these manipulations mentally.

Psychometric tests reviewed earlier in connection with the dual coding research program were designed to tap individual differences in the relevant mental abilities. Thurstone (1938) developed Space Relations to measure the ability to transform figural patterns mentally using imagery. Closure tests, which require completion of fragmented or incomplete objects to identify them, measure the ability to put pieces together mentally. The Minnesota Paper Form Board consists of items that require both mental transformation and integration of geometric patterns to come up with the appropriate combination. It has been used in many studies as a measure of imagery ability, often combined with Space Relations and imagery questionnaires. Transformation and integration abilities are related—for example, Carole Ernest

(1980) showed that spatial ability tests predicted closure speed for fragmented pictures and words. The following summarizes animal studies of mental transformation and integration, after reminders of the human paradigms.

Mental Rotation.   Recall from Chapter 3 that Shepard and Metzler (1971) measured the speed of mental rotations by asking participants to indicate whether line drawings of two geometric objects were the same or different (mirror images of each other). The two objects were shown as they would appear when rotated to different degrees relative to each other. Shepard and Metzler found that decision speed was related directly to the rotational difference—the larger the rotational disparity (up to 180°) the slower the decision time, suggesting that, to compare them, the participants juxtaposed the objects by rotating one of them using mental imagery. The interpretation has been supported in many subsequent studies using variants of the original task, some of which provided evidence that the motor system is involved in mental rotations (e.g., James, Humphery, & Goodale, 2001). This is relevant because it accords with the early dual coding assumption that motor processes contribute to transformational and integrative effects of imagery in memory and other cognitive tasks (Paivio, 1971b). Motor involvement also makes evolutionary sense of the evidence for mental rotations in species as diverse as the baboon (Hopkins, Fagot, & Vauclair, 1993), California sea lion (Mauck & Dehnhardt, 1997), and pigeon (Hamm, Matheson, & Honig, 1997).

The baboon and sea lion experiments used variants of the matching-to-sample procedure in which the animal sees a form on a central panel and is reinforced for choosing the correct rotated version from two other comparison panels. The baboon does so using its hands and the sea lion swims to the panels and pushes one panel with its snout. The successful pigeon experiment (earlier ones did not show the rotation effect) used a "go-no-go" procedure in which stimuli were presented one at a time in a list and the birds were rewarded if they pecked the positive stimulus but not its mirror image. Abstract geometric patterns, letters, and pictures of objects were used as stimuli in the different studies. The linear rotation effect was obtained for all three species, evidence that they used imagery to manipulate and compare perceptual objects mentally. For example, Hamm et al. (1997, p. 81) concluded specifically that pigeons use both imagery and mental rotation in the task.

Neiworth and Rilling (1987) used a dynamic variant of the mental rotation task to study imagery in pigeons. The pigeons observed a clock hand that rotated from upright (12:00) to different positions at a constant speed. On perceptual trials, the clock hand was always visible. Imagery trials were identical except that the hand disappeared at the 90° position (3:00) for a specific delay and then reappeared at another location as if it had rotated with constant speed during the delay. On trials in which velocity was violated, the clock hand disappeared at 90° but reappeared after a delay at a position inconsistent with constant velocity during the delay. The pigeons were reinforced for discriminating (by pecking a left key or a right key) between the constant and inconsistent velocity conditions whether or not the hand was always visible. They initially learned to discriminate between the two conditions at locations of 135° and 180° under conditions in which location and delay were counterbalanced so that the pigeons had to rely on both location and time information to discriminate between imagery and violation trials. On subsequent transfer tests, the pigeons showed immediate positive transfer to an intermediate location (158°) and to a novel location outside the boundaries trained (202°). This means that the pigeons relied on visual memory images of rotating clock hands during the delay, and that this gradually shifting visual memory "overshot" the objective location in a manner similar to "representational momentum" in humans—described in Chapter 4 as a preparatory function of imagery.

As a final example, recall from Chapter 7 that cortical activation rotated across populations of neurons in motor areas of monkey brains during a task in which the monkey learned to anticipate the rotated location of a stimulus, providing neuropsychological evidence of anticipatory mental rotation in that species.

Integration of Parts.   What is needed here are animal experiments that provide evidence of integrative use of imagery that would be comparable to human studies of, say, closure of fragmented pictures or associative learning of integrated pairs of pictured objects. The experiment by Baker et al. (2002), described in Chapter 7, yielded such evidence. Responses of single neurons in monkey brains were recorded when the monkeys learned a discriminative response to each of two parts of a figure. The brain cells learned to respond to each part. The cell response increased more than additively when both parts of the figure were shown together— evidence that the parts were integrated. Another example is integration (or synthesis) across modalities. The reference human experiment is one by Johnson, Paivio, and Clark (1989) on tactual-to-visual cross-modal transfer in children. The pertinent result was that children who were high in visual imagery ability matched feelable objects to visual forms more accurately than low imagers, especially under instructions to image during the task. This is strong convergent evidence that imagery can mediate transfer from touch to vision. In effect, imagery integrated the figural information from the two modalities.

The evolutionary extension of the interpretation is justified by observations of cross-modal transfer in preverbal infants as well as monkeys and chimpanzees (studies cited in Stolz-Loike & Bornstein, 1987). The inference is that imagery had evolved as a mechanism for cross-modal integration at some period in primate evolution and probably in other species as well. In fact, Clayton, Yu, and Dickinson (2001) reported that scrub jays formed integrated memories of the multiple features of caching episodes. This bears on the question of sensory-integration areas in the brain, with the implication that integration is achieved by cross-modal transformation rather than by some kind of amodal integrative code, consistent with the general interpretation of cross-modal integration (binding) in Chapter 9.

Categorization

Earlier we discussed the importance of recognition memory for the well-being and survival of individuals. However, all creatures must recognize the positive or negative value of whole classes of objects and situations—edible and inedible things, friends and enemies, and safe and dangerous places. Some of this general categorical behavior requires little learning. A dog needs only one close encounter with a skunk or porcupine to steer clear of all such beasts thereafter, but it takes more experience to learn to discriminate among complex categories of stimuli. The nature of such category representations has long been studied with animals as well as humans (the latter already discussed in earlier chapters). The animal studies use discrimination learning procedures in which animals learn to distinguish between categories of natural objects or artificial patterns that can be categorized according to common characteristics (for reviews, see Roberts, 1998; Shettleworth, 1998). For example, Bhatt, Wasserman, Reynolds, and Knauss (1988) taught pigeons to discriminate between pictures showing different exemplars of persons, flowers, cars, and chairs. The pigeons learned to do so even when individual members of a category were shown only once, although performance was better when specific exemplars were repeated. The results have been replicated and extended in numerous studies with birds and other species.

The traditional explanation of category learning is in terms of direct or mediated stimulus generalization and discrimination learning. Direct stimulus generalization applies to the extent that familiar and new exemplars are similar in some way—pigeons rewarded for pecking at a picture of a specific flower easily learn to peck at a picture of a similar flower. Mediated generalization (or transfer) is invoked as the explanation when unrelated stimuli are associated with each other in experience and a response learned to one now transfers to the other.

The simplest demonstration of mediated generalization was in a sensory preconditioning experiment by Brogden (1939), mentioned earlier. A light and a buzzer were presented together to a dog a number of times. The light was then used as the conditioned stimulus for an avoidance response (lifting a paw) to an electric shock. The buzzer was then presented and the dog lifted its paw. Because the sound had never been directly associated with the shock, the response must have been mediated by a memory representation (an image, we could say) of the light evoked by the buzzer. Rephrased in this context, the light and buzzer acquired stimulus equivalence or became members of the same category.

Additional explanatory processes, also familiar from previous discussions of adaptive functions of dual coding systems, are anticipation and "retrospection" (memory). Peter Urcuioli (2001) described the roles of these processes in categorization behavior in pigeons. Anticipation is illustrated by one experiment in which pigeons first learned to match red and circle samples to a vertical choice stimulus, and green and dot samples to a horizontal choice. They then learned to match a red sample to blue and a green sample to yellow. The pigeons could then match the circle sample to blue and the dot sample to yellow although these reactions had never been conditioned. The pigeons learned to anticipate vertical on seeing either the red or the circle sample and to anticipate horizontal on seeing the green or dot sample. Consequently, the blue-yellow choices generalized from the samples to which they had been explicitly conditioned (red and green) to samples to which they had not been conditioned (circle and dot) because each pair of samples produced common mediators, the anticipation of "vertical" and "horizontal."

Retrospection was introduced to account for the results of an experiment in which the training conditions were reversed so that the birds learned many-to-one associative matching of stimuli after they had learned to match two of the samples to comparisons that were not included in the new associative set. For example, some pigeons learned to match red-blue and red-circle, and green-yellow and green-dot. The birds were then required to match a circle sample to blue and a dot sample to yellow during transfer. They did so better than chance, as if the circle reminded them of "red" and the dot sample reminded them of "green," colors they had previously associated with blue and yellow, respectively.

Urcuioli (2001) viewed both anticipation and retrospection as speculative explanations of mediated stimulus equivalence. From this perspective, however, they accord with other evidence of anticipation in conditioning experiments and of retrospective cuing by remembered mediators in associative learning. Moreover, the human evidence suggests that the mediators could be images of the effective exemplars.

The comparison with humans can only go so far, however. Shepard, Hovland, and Jenkins (1961) found that human adults learned complex categories made up of sets of geometric forms that varied in size, shape, and color more rapidly than could be explained in terms of gradual conditioning and stimulus generalization processes. They concluded instead that the participants learned categories by testing hypotheses and using rules. Smith, Minda, and Washburn (2004) compared rhesus monkeys and humans on the same tasks. They performed similarly when the category consisted of a single relevant dimension. However, the monkeys performed poorly on a more complex task that required taking account of more than one dimension simultaneously, whereas humans learned the categorization quickly. The authors proposed that the monkeys' performance could be explained in terms of conditioning and stimulus generalization but the human performance was better explained by hypothesis-testing and rule-discovery processes, just as Shepard et al. suggested. As others have done, Smith et al. considered language as providing the rule-based system that gave humans the advantage, but they preferred an explanation in terms of an explicit categorization system probably mediated by frontal cortical structures with working memory and executive functions. Dual coding suggests a simpler interpretation that would emphasize the cooperative activity of verbal and nonverbal systems, of which only the latter is available to rhesus monkeys and other animals.

Spatial Representation ("Cognitive Mapping")

All animals have to find their way about to survive. How they do that has been much studied and theoretically debated. The role of environmental cues and conditioning mechanisms are reasonably well understood in the case of species-specific migratory behavior of fish (especially salmon) and birds. The spatial behavior of many animals can be similarly described in terms of relatively simple stimulus-response learning. We focus here on explanations that have a more cognitive flavor. Edward Tolman (1948) introduced the term *cognitive map* to refer to internal representations that are like field maps, enabling rats to take novel shortcuts to food locations in a maze. The animals presumably learn the spatial relations between paths and choice points rather than a chain of stimuli and responses leading to the goal box, as proposed by behaviorists. [34] O'Keefe and Nadel (1978) elaborated on the concept in an influential volume on the role of the hippocampus in cognitive mapping. Others have questioned the assumptions underlying the concept and accordingly prefer the more theoretically neutral term *spatial orientation* to refer to the same phenomenal domain.

Modern research on the problem has usually focused on memory for the spatial locations of objects and landmarks that enable animals to find their way to food and back home. The problem thus combines recognition memory for objects and their locations. Different species use various mechanisms to find their way around, including some kind of dead reckoning of a path direction, polarized rays of the sun, salient visual landmarks, response learning, and many other guidance systems (for reviews, see, e.g., Hazen, 1983; Roberts, 1998; Shettleworth, 1998). People are especially flexible in using different means for finding their way, including magnetic compasses, verbal coding of cardinal directions, verbal route maps describing distances and turns on the way to a place, marked trails, moss on trees, in short any natural or artifactual orienting information. A remarkable example is the navigational ability of natives of the Caroline Islands of Micronesia, who travel for days between islands with no land in sight and never get lost (e.g., see summary and references in Hazen, 1983).

Here I focus on evidence that humans and animals use image-like cognitive maps. The reference human experiments, described in Chapter 8, involved London taxi drivers who recalled the routes they would take to get to different destinations. The critical results were that the drivers gave detailed and accurate memory descriptions of the routes and locations of the London landmarks. and that the task activated a network of brain regions that notably included the right hippocampus. The control tasks activated separate and overlapping regions that did not include the hippocampus. We saw evidence, too, that the detailed route descriptions were mediated by memory imagery.

Chimpanzees have cognitive mapping abilities comparable to those of humans (Menzel, 1978). The question is, how far down the evolutionary scale can the concept be stretched and interpreted in terms of imagery? We have already noted the remarkable spatial memory of Clark's nutcracker, which can retrieve thousands of seeds from their caches months after they were hidden. The birds behave as if they have topographical images of storage sites and flight paths between them. The

---

[34]It is interesting that Tolman's concepts of cognitive maps and expectancy are theoretically connected in that, early on, he referred to cognitive maps as sign-gestalt expectations, alluding to the idea that a stimulus such as a choice point in a maze becomes associated with a stimulus configuration, such as the whole maze pattern. A further connection to anticipatory imagery is illustrated by the ecologically-relevant example of a primitive hunter who imagines game animals on the other side of a hill. That is, he expects to see game when he gets to the top of the hill.

similarities between the navigational behavior of the birds and the human memory navigation of real or virtual towns is the operational bridge to imagery as a common evolutionary mechanism for cognitive mapping. The inference is strengthened by the role played by the hippocampus in the spatial memories of both species.

The same argument can be extended to other species. Consider the bee. Since von Frisch's (1967) pioneering research on the communicative dances of bees, many studies have focused on the nature of the locational and food information that is remembered by foraging bees and communicated to other bees so that they can fly out of the hive and find the nectar-bearing flowers. The essentials are that a bee returns to the hive and begins a dance and other bees join in and eventually fly out to find the food. The communicated information includes an olfactory component (the odor of pollen carried by the forager), the energy of the dance (the farther the food the slower the dance), and its general pattern and orientation (for food sources farther than 50 m or so from the hive, the dance includes a tail-wagging component in which the bee's movement relative to the vertical corresponds to the direction of the food source from the hive, relative to the direction of the sun). A strong cognitive interpretation is that the foraging bees form cognitive maps of the terrain that includes all of the information just mentioned and that the dance somehow communicates an isomorph of the map to the bees in the hive. Biologist James L. Gould (e.g., 1990) has been a proponent of the cognitive mapping interpretation of the foraging ability and the communicative waggle dance of bees, even speculating that dancing bees may use imagination to create a mental map of the search terrain prior to flying out.

The interpretation of the bee's remarkable spatial memory and the communicative dance remain controversial. For example, Dyer (1991) concluded that his experimental results were better explained by the hypothesis that bees use landmarks associated with specific routes traveled previously. Bennett (1996) argued more generally that no animal has been shown conclusively to have a cognitive map as defined by Tolman and by O'Keefe and Nadel, because simpler explanations of novel short-cutting spatial behavior are invariably possible.

For our purposes, we need not pursue the controversy. I note simply that there has been enough inferential evidence to suggest to some that image-like cognitive maps have a very long evolutionary history that cuts across species ranging from the ancestors of modern humans to infrahuman primates, other mammals, birds, and perhaps even bees. Other researchers dispute such interpretations. It will be interesting to see how the debate plays out.

Imagery and Insight

Scientists began studying animal cognition more than 100 years ago by posing animals with problems they had to solve to obtain food, access to a mate, escape from unpleasant conditions, and so on. Some tests entailed trial-and-error learning, as in classical experiments in which cats learned by trial and error to escape from a box by pulling on a string, and variants of such problems suitable for the perceptual and behavioral repertoires of different species—frogs, snakes, insects, birds, rats, monkeys, and chimpanzees, to name a few. Interest quickly moved to problems that required use of symbolic processes for their solution, problems in which the necessary information is not perceptually present but must be supplied from memory and used successfully. In brief, they required a representational memory system that could be used insightfully, by "looking inside one's mind."

Insight is defined by subjective experience in humans as a relatively sudden awareness of a solution to a problem (see later in Chapter 17). The concept has been stretched to apply it to other animals by defining it in terms of behavioral criteria. The classical studies were the observations of insight in chimpanzees by the Gestalt psychologist, Wolfgang Köhler (1925). The animals learned to use sticks and boxes to obtain bananas that were out of reach. The implements could be separated from the banana, requiring the chimp to remember the stick or box and infer its potential use as a tool in this situation. The chimps even learned to use a short stick to pull in a longer one needed to reach the banana. The criterion for insight was the relative abruptness of the solution, seemingly a sudden awareness of how to put pieces together.

Köhler recognized that experience with sticks was necessary for the insightful behavior but did not systematically study the role of experience. For example, the chimps were exposed to sticks for hours on end without any observer being present. Birch (1945) corrected for this and other shortcomings by raising six chimps so that all but one had no experience with sticks. The chimps were then given a T-shaped stick and a banana out of reach. Only the chimp that had experience using a stick solved the problem within a half-hour test period. Then the chimps were given piles of sticks to play with. Among other things, they started prodding with the sticks but never used them as rakes to pull something in. Then they were given the banana problem. All the animals solved it within 20 sec, treating the rake as an extension of the arm. The important point is that they needed experience with sticks before they could display what seemed like insightful problem solving.

The insight experiments with chimps and other animals were criticized precisely on the grounds that experience was needed with elements of the problem before it could be solved insightfully (see Roberts, 1998), as if "true" insight does not require such experience. That might be too strict a criterion for insight. The fact is that experience with the elements of a problem is an important variable in human problem solving—the more frequent the experience, the faster a problem is solved. We can interpret that to mean that such experience establishes a representational substrate for the elements–engrams of sticks and their behavioral affordances, for example—which is quickly activated when the problem solver sees the elements.

Whatever the precise interpretation, insightful and other kinds of complex problem solving require use of specific representational processes already discussed. For example, Köhler's chimps might have transformed and integrated perceptual elements mentally, used anticipatory imagery to evaluate the outcomes, tried out available alternatives mentally if the initial attempts failed, and so on. This is sheer speculation in the absence of parallel human studies that included imagery measures and manipulations. Although many studies have considered the role of imagery in problem solving, none to my knowledge map nicely onto the animal insight studies so that the operational-inferential bridging approach could be applied in its entirety. Accordingly, we are left mostly with intriguing speculations.

Imagery and Evolution of the Sense of Time

Living things have to develop adaptive mechanisms for dealing with environmental changes over time—daily changes in light and dark, seasonal changes in temperature, the consequent changes in the availability of food, and a myriad of less predictable events that go on over shorter periods of time. Many of the adaptations involve biochemical and physiological reactions to changing environmental cues, such as internal "circadian oscillators" that rise and fall through daily cycles. Such temporal adaptations could be called an innate sense of time. Of more concern here is the psychological sense of time that has reached its highest level in modern humans because we can represent and think about time using language, clocks, and calendars (for a relevant discussion, see Friedman, 1989). The critical question for this chapter is how time can be marked using nonverbal devices, some of which might be available to other animals as well as us.

That animals have timing mechanisms is known from experiments and naturalistic observations. Rats learn to press levers and pigeons peck keys at regular or irregular time intervals, depending on the schedule of reinforcement that has been imposed on them. Snakes demonstrate time-place learning in that they will wait for long periods in front of a mouse hole, presumably because they have experienced the emergence of mice in the past. Birds and other animals hoard food for the future. The time-related behaviors suggest a kind of anticipation that could be based on imagery, perhaps recurrent images of the food itself, or, in the case of the experimental animals, of the discriminative stimulus (e.g., a lighted key) that signals the availability of food if the animal makes the appropriate operant response at the right time. Of course, we don't have more direct evidence of the role of imagery as a timing device in such cases, and students of the sense of time in animals generally do not invoke such an interpretation.

William Roberts (2002), an authority on animal cognition, reviewed the topic comprehensively in an article with the intriguing title, "Are Animals Stuck in Time?" The evidence shows that in some ways, animals are sensitive to the passage of time. Many animals are highly sensitive to the time of day in that they wait for the appearance of prey or food given by humans at the precise time of day it usually arrives in its usual location. As already mentioned, in interval-timing conditioning experiments, animals learn to withhold a response until just before food is scheduled to arrive. They learn to respond to different temporal sequences of distinctive cues to earn a reward. And so on, for a variety of experimental procedures that have been used to test animals' capacity to respond to time-related cues to maximize the amount or quality of the food they obtain.

By and large, however, the results do not support the idea that animals have our concept of time. Our time sense is tied to episodic memories of when and where we experienced particular events, on the basis of which we can anticipate similar future events, or imagine that they might occur, and thus prepare ourselves for them. We can freely project ourselves backward and forward in time. Animals can't do that. Their time sense is instead governed by strength of memory traces (cf. Staddon, 2001, p. 338 ff), circadian cues, motivational states conditioned to secondary cues in food locations, sequences of behaviors or internal events that mark a time interval, and so on. Where time tracking seems to occur, it is limited to brief time intervals or event sequences. Roberts (2002) concluded that the bulk of the evidence suggests that animals have a very limited sense of past and future time.

The hypothesis seems applicable even to our closest animal relatives. Köhler (1925) argued that ". . . besides in the lack of speech, it is in the extremely narrow limits [in the breadth of the time window] that the chief difference is to be found between anthropoids and even the most primitive human beings" (p. 238, cited in Roberts, 2002, p. 473). Roberts (2002) cited others who reached a similar conclusion more recently, but he left open the possibility of exceptions. For example, a cynomolgus monkey learned to forego an immediate small reward in favor of a larger delayed reward, an act of self control that rats and pigeons fail to show. We have already seen that food-storing birds remember the locations and contents of their caches. Clayton and Dickinson (1998) showed in addition that scrub jays remembered when food items were stored by allowing them to recover perishable wax-moth larvae (their favorite food) and nonperishable peanuts previously cached in distinct sites. The jays searched preferentially for the fresh larvae when allowed to recover them 4 hr after caching, but they quickly learned to go to the peanut locations after a longer time (124 hr), during which the larvae would have decayed. Clayton and Dickson concluded that jays demonstrated memory for what, when, and where, thus fulfilling the behavioral criteria for episodic-like memory. Roberts also asked whether such cognitively advanced animals as chimpanzees and bonobos could be taught a sense of time by being raised in the presence of animal equivalents of calendars and clocks that continually mark the occurrence of important events in their lives.

A critical issue here is the definition of episodic memory that is linked to the sense of time. We saw in Chapter 3 that Tulving (e.g., 2005) redefined episodic memory in terms of "autonoetic consciousness"—awareness of where and when one experienced specific events in the past and awareness of future possibilities—a subjective time sense not available to animals or young children. We are faced here with the same conundrum as already discussed in relation to the general issue of consciousness in animals, namely that, by Tulving's definition, animals cannot have "autonoetic" episodic memory unless it can be defined independently by some behavior other than verbal reports. Clayton and Dickinson (1998) noted similarly that the conscious experience that accompanies episodic recall has no obvious manifestation in nonlinguistic behavior and is probably undetectable in many species. Which is why they referred to the "what, when, and where" memory of scrub jays as episodic-like, only analogous to episodic memory as Tulving defined it. Other researchers in this domain also continue to find similar behavioral evidence that different species of animals have at least a limited sense of future as well as past time. For example, the journal *Learning and Motivation* recently published a special issue on cognitive time travel in people and animals, edited by Roberts (2005). Five of ten articles reported positive results for rats, pigeons, and a gorilla; two other articles reported failures to find evidence for cognitive time travel in rhesus monkeys and rats. The pattern of results obviously depends on particular test conditions as well as species differences.

Encouraged by the picture emerging from the animal research, I speculate about how our preverbal hominid ancestors might have acquired a concept of time simply on the basis of "ordinary" episodic memory and imagery. I assume that early in hominid evolution, at a time when they were cognitively more advanced than modern chimpanzees, our ancestors had a sufficient episodic memory base to remember repeated diurnal events, and eventually, seasonal events. They not only observed the sun's apparent movement across the sky but also remembered—could image—it rising in the "east" and disappearing in the "west." Associated with these would be memory images of what they were doing and what else was happening during those changes—images of food eaten at sunrise, setting out to hunt and gather, preparation of bed when the sun was descending, and so on. These images would become anticipatory—for example, awakening before dawn, the hominid might image the sun rising and soon have the image "confirmed" and eventually anticipate that occurrence. Motivational states such as hunger would also serve as cues for the anticipatory imagery. And so a sense of time evolved, marked by temporal sequences of memory images and anticipatory images covering increasing periods of time and increasing numbers of time-related events, including such perceptible biological changes as the increasing size of a pregnant woman's belly during gestation, which served as a continuously updated cue for anticipatory birth imagery, not only for the expectant mother, but also for the entire tribe. It is conceivable too that the sequences would eventually be marked in some external symbolic way even before language—nothing as sophisticated initially as, say, drawings of a series of circles to represent the sun moving across the sky, but something analogous although more fragmentary. That will suffice for my argument. I leave it to the reader's imagination to come up with more detailed scenarios about the evolution of a preverbal sense of time that exceeds the relatively limited time sense of other animals in both temporal directions.

THE SOCIAL CONTEXT OF COGNITIVE EVOLUTION

Humans and most other animals evolved in social contexts. The implications of that social evolutionary core are far-reaching and complex. Much has been written about the topic in terms of the evolution of such interpersonal behaviors as mating, cooperation, competition, dominance hierarchies, altruism, and so on (e.g., see Buss, 1999; Dawkins, 1989; Leakey & Lewin, 1978). Especially relevant is Leslie Brother's (1995) concept of the social situation/representation response, which she defined as neural "ensembles that simultaneously encode the sensory aspects of discrete social situations and set into motion the relevant responses . . . " (p. 1108). Also relevant is

Greenspan and Shanker's (2004) hypothesis that coregulated, emotional interactions between mother and infant are the basis of the growth of intellect over countless generations in our hominid ancestors. Here I can do no more than touch on the subject, approaching it via a scheme for categorizing and analyzing social influence and social behavior, including the cognitive and affective processes that mediate their occurrence. The scheme arises by direct analogy with significant classes of objects, situations, and events in the physical environment, all of which have already been mentioned in this chapter without categorizing them.[35]

The Physical Context of Behavioral Evolution

The physical environment of most animals contains four categories of objects and events that affect survival and call for different kinds of adaptive responses. The most important are food and shelter. Let us call these primary goal-objects or incentives, because without attaining them, the individual has no hope of survival (cf. Rolls, 1995). The adaptive responses directed toward the attainment of those goals can be called goal-oriented behaviors. Learning theorists also refer to the goals as reinforcers because they strengthen the behaviors that lead to their attainment. All food- and shelter-seeking actions are by definition primary goal-oriented behaviors, as is avoidance of predators and other dangers, from which shelter is sought.

A second category of objects functions as means to the achievement of primary goals. Examples are sticks, twigs, and stones that can be used as tools, instruments, or manipulanda. The bars that rats can press and the disks that pigeons can peck to get food in learning experiments, although not part of the natural environment, also belong in this category. Searching for and using such objects for reaching bananas, fishing for termites, cracking nuts, getting a food pellet, and building shelters can thus be called instrumental-oriented behaviors. These are mainly learned although some, like the beavers' search for and use of branches and mud to build houses and dams, are largely innate.

A third category includes objects or events that serve only as signs that inform the animal of the availability, or possible availability, of a primary goal or a useful instrument. Spoor on the ground, colors in the distance, and carrion birds hovering overhead are examples of informative signs, as is a lighted key that informs a pigeon in a learning experiment that pecking the key will result in a seed reward. Thus, sniffing, looking, and listening for such signs can be appropriately called information-oriented behaviors, which are primarily learned.

The fourth category comprises all objects and situations that are obstacles to the achievement of primary or secondary (instrumental or informative) goals. Obvious examples are obstructive trees, branches, hills, stones, rivers, and other barriers to

---

[35]I developed the categorization scheme around 1960 for organizing social psychology lectures during that phase of my academic career. The categories of adaptive behaviors can be viewed as broad functional systems and the analytic scheme thus fits into Timberlake's general behavior systems approach in which a basic assumption is that "the determinants of behavior are organized in functional systems" (Timberlake & Fanselow, 1994, p. 403).

perceived or remembered food, shelter, or tools. Such obstacles frustrate attempts to attain the goals, and the animals' attempts to remove, circumvent, or otherwise deal with them can be called obstacle-oriented or frustration-driven behaviors.

In addition to overt responses, the adaptive reactions to the four categories of objects and events would also include internal reactions such as emotions and images of the kind already described in this chapter, related in this case to positive or negative goals and incentives, instruments, informational cues, and obstacles.

The Social Evolutionary Context

The extension of the analytic scheme to the social context is straightforward. In social interaction, we are influenced by others functioning in ways that directly parallel the four functions of stimuli in the physical environment. Others first of all are primary goal objects (incentives, reinforcers) in that they are direct sources of reward and punishment and we accordingly seek or avoid contact and hope for their approval or fear their disapproval. Second, they are social instruments from whom or through whom we can get what we want. Third, they are sources of information who help us improve our goal-seeking skills by serving as models or teachers. And fourth, others can be obstacles who frustrate our attempts to achieve goals and we accordingly respond by seeking to remove, circumvent, or withdraw from them.

The four functional classes are inevitable consequences of social life, with one or more of the functional roles predominating under different circumstances and for different people, and with the influenced persons similarly reacting in different ways according to the situation and their own response predispositions. Some people tend to be reinforcer-oriented in that they are especially sensitive to others as potential sources of reward or punishment. Some people characteristically see others as instruments, to be used for their own ends. Some are information-oriented socially, constantly seeking instruction or advice from others. And finally, some individuals tend to perceive others as obstacles and sources of frustration, to be removed from their path, literally or figuratively. The categories of functional roles and reactions are universal in human societies. They must have emerged early in our evolution because many are shared by our primate relatives and other animals. The following are specific everyday and research examples of each functional category.

The Incentive-Reinforcer Function. Others become goal objects or incentives early in life as providers of food, comfort, and shelter. (Learning theorists refer to others in such roles as secondary reinforcers.) The mammalian mother gives milk; among birds, either parent might provide the worms or grubs; and some birds and members of other species regurgitate food for the young. The parents provide shelter directly with their own bodies and indirectly by building nests. The dependent young respond in ways that are partly instinctive as in seeking the nipple, opening the beak wide, and staying close to a parent (most dramatic in the case of imprinting, which can be misdirected to other species or even inanimate objects). Staying close to the source of comfort is an aspect of attachment behavior that can generalize into a kind of dependency on a sheltering parent because of exposure to social and environment threats

(Bowlby, 1969; for a review of alternative models, see Pederson & Moran, 1999): The mother herself disappears for a time or otherwise withholds comfort, other individuals may arouse fear (fear of strangers, especially strange men, beginning around the age of 6 months in human infants, is an example that seems to have a genetic component), and so on.

With sexual maturity, others become powerful incentives as sex objects, resulting in all of the varied and complex manifestations of mating behavior, together with the emotions and (certainly in humans) imagery associated with it. The potential mate is directly rewarding and the sexual behavior—courting and consummation— is genetically driven. Evolved physical and behavioral characteristics attract males and females to each other when the hormonal conditions are right (obviously this matters less to humans than other species). Peacock tail feathers, the red swollen belly of the female stickleback fish, the odor of a female dog in heat, male displays of prowess in one form or other, bird songs, and so on, and on. The examples are legion. There are enough displays of affection in primates and other animals that it is safe to assume that love was a potent factor in the social life of our preverbal hominid ancestors, as was jealousy (more about that later, for it entails another source of social influence). And might we assume as well that sexual fantasies were an important part of hominid imagery, as it is in our lives, motivating and guiding mating behavior in its broadest sense?

Also associated with the primary reinforcing function of others is the universal human emotion of grief at the death of loved ones, or permanent separation from them for other reasons. Everything has its cost, they say, and grief is the price that survivors pay for love. The emotion can be understood as a form of anxiety or fear akin to separation anxiety associated with attachment behavior, a negative emotion associated with the disappearance of a primary social reinforcer, complicated by the anticipatory imagery and fear of one's own death that becomes possible only with self-awareness. Grief is puzzling from the evolutionary perspective. What could be the survival value of grief? In the evolutionary context, grief and bereavement have been analyzed as reactions to the threat to group integrity when a member dies (Averill, 1968), a threat therefore to the replicative success of genes in the gene pool of related individuals (this would follow from the theory of inclusive fitness proposed in 1964 by William Hamilton.)[36] The memory images, memorial rituals, and memorial objects can all be interpreted as symbolic ways of keeping the missing person alive, motivated by the powerful contrasting emotions of love and grief aroused by the images and symbols. Whatever the detailed explanation, the evolutionary relevance of grief is supported by its universality in human societies as far back as there is any recorded evidence in art, oral histories, and myths. Moreover, such social animals as chimpanzees and elephants show clear signs of distress at the death of a baby or even an older animal.

---

[36]Inclusive fitness refers to the reproductive fitness of all those who share a common gene pool-the individual's reproductive success plus that of his or her genetic relatives. The theory particularly implies that altruistic acts will be directed more to close relatives than to more distant ones or unrelated individuals.

A final example of the influence of social reinforcers is the effect of observers on behavior. Recall from the discussion of social motivation in Chapter 4 that audience effects are due to the contingencies between observation, evaluation, and "approval" or "disapproval" of the behavior of the observed. We learn that we must be seen or heard to receive the approval or disapproval of others. The effect of this manifests itself clearly in positive and negative reactions to formal audiences—some people seek the limelight despite any stage fright they might experience, others primarily experience stage fright and avoid audience situations. We reviewed evidence that individual differences in these audience-oriented reactions are due at least in part to the individual's history of social rewards and punishments in the context of observation and evaluation of behavior (e.g., Paivio, 1965b). That is, parents, teachers, and peers must see what the child does and evaluate it as good or bad before they can approve or disapprove. The child learns to seek or avoid being seen and evaluated, depending on how often these have been followed by approval or disapproval. The reactions generalize in an exaggerated form to formal audiences with their many judging eyes and potential cheers or jeers. Stage frightened people typically refer their fear to all those eyes out there staring at them, but show offs just love those eyes!

Sensitivity to eyes and being looked at probably has an evolutionary basis because it appears early in human infancy and is widespread in other species (Hewes, 1978; Ristau, 1998). A nursing infant seeks eye contact with the mother but hides from the gaze of a stranger. Higher primates react to staring as a form of aggression: a stare from a subordinate male monkey will precipitate attack by a dominant male. A stare from a stranger will cause a female gorilla to run screaming. Chimpanzees will shift their gaze from each other to the ground to avoid an altercation. The gaze of a potential predator can cause the prey to engage in prolonged defensive behavior—for example, death feigning in the hognose snake and tonic immobility in chickens (Ristau, 1998, p. 142). Such reactions can be viewed as homologies and homoplasies of human audience oriented reactions. We see later that others' eyes also are an important source of information.

Instrumental Function of Others. The use of others and "willingness" to be used are means to goal attainment that also are ubiquitous among humans and other species. The mother's point of view shifts subtly from her role as reinforcer to that of an instrument when she changes the diaper of a fussing infant or gives it a nursing bottle or a toy, depending on how she reads the situation. Fussing, crying, and temper tantrums can be considered instrumental-oriented behaviors, ways of manipulating others to provide what the child wants. In cooperative behavior, group members play shared or reciprocal instrumental roles. Requests and commands are typical verbal means of soliciting cooperation, but nonverbal gestures (e.g., beckoning) can be used as well, by higher primates as well as humans. Because social animals are dependent on others for survival, cooperation and other forms of instrumental-oriented behaviors would be expected to emerge early in their evolution. Among social insects such as ants and bees, some members are born and bred to be workers or "warriors," thus playing an instrumental role. Chickadees emit a mobbing cry that attracts other chickadees for a cooperative defensive attack on a predatory bird. Some types of parasitic behavior clearly fit into this category. For example, the cuckoo uses nests of other species for its own eggs and leaves the chicks to be fed by the host. The term *parasite* is commonly used as well to describe people who live off others without contributing something useful in return, a doubtful qualification because parasitic behavior sometimes also benefits the host, at least in the short run, and thus even this behavior is cooperative in a broad sense.

In human societies, hunting and gathering are largely organized cooperative activities; slavery, recruitment of armies, employing others, and formation of political groups are examples of more formal ways of using others as instruments, where the use depends on the power of the users. Machiavellianism is a classical example of the manipulative use of power at the social level. Sociopathy is a pathological example of individuals who use others for their own ends. The instrumental role of others and the individual's instrumental-oriented reactions would have been important in the lives of our hominid ancestors as they are today, and the function would likely have been manifested in their mental lives in the form of imagery and emotions— as fantasies, imagined plans, pride, and fear, depending on where one stood in the hierarchy of social power and dominance.

Informational Function of Others.   We come next to others functioning as sources of information, as "discriminanda" rather than as "manipulanda. " They show the way rather than carry us to our desired goals. All forms of demonstration, modeling, and teaching are examples of others functioning as sources of information. Imitation and other ways of following gestured directions are nonverbal information-oriented reactions. Eyes, the direction of gaze, are subtly informative as well. Experiments have shown that humans become very sensitive to where others are looking at an early age, as do animals of other species (Ristau, 1998). They show this by looking for a salient object in the direction of the other's gaze. The information so received can be used to guide behavior vis-à-vis the target. The ability to follow directed gaze has also been interpreted by some as possible evidence for mind reading, the emergent understanding that others are seeing something, although this is a stretched interpretation in the absence of language to express such understanding. Facial expressions also are informative about the emotional and motivational states of others, and they have characteristic effects depending on whether the observer interprets them as signs of affection, anger, fear, or indifference. The evolutionary basis of facial expressions as informational cues can be seen in their unlearned occurrence in the form of grimaces, tooth baring, frowns, smiles, eyebrow raising, and so on—many of them in other species and more in humans. Humans also have evolved the most elaborate facial musculature that permits such a wide range of informative expressions. We learn to read them and actors learn to produce them to influence our interpretations and emotional reactions. Such information-oriented expressions and reactions have been extensively studied in psychological experiments.

Frustrative Function of Others.   This function is clearly defined by dictionaries: others are frustraters when they foil, thwart, oppose, or block individuals from achieving their aims; in brief, when they are obstacles to goal-oriented behavior. They may frustrate directly by physically standing in the way, or, more often, indirectly by constructing barriers (fences, walls, moats), or, at some point in the evolution of human societies, by creating laws, prohibitions, and "thou shalt not" commandments. The goals that are blocked by such means could be physical resources—food, shelter, and tools in the general sense—or resources intrinsic to other individuals, implicating the different functional roles they have in interpersonal relations. Thus, the frustrater could block access to others as sex objects, assistants (instrumental aids), or, sources of information. Whatever the blocked resources, the classes of adaptive reactions are the same: if possible, remove the frustrater; if not, find some way of getting around it; or if all such attempts fail, withdraw and seek the resources elsewhere. This analysis organizes a diverse range of universal social behaviors and emotions and helps us understand their evolutionary basis.

Aggression is the most obvious and most discussed form of the frustration-oriented reactions. Buss (1999) presented a comprehensive analysis of aggression as a solution to adaptive problems. The solutions and problems include using aggression to co-opt resources held by others, defend against attack, inflict costs on sexual rivals, increase one's status in power hierarchies, and deter long-term mates from sexual infidelity. The variety of problems means that "aggression is likely to be highly context specific, triggered only in contexts that resemble those in which our ancestors confronted certain adaptive problems and reaped particular benefits" (p. 284). Buss went on to discuss the contextual and evolutionary factors that lead to sex differences in aggression, homicide, and warfare. He also concluded that the current evolutionary psychological perspective on human aggression cannot account for the variety of forms that aggression can take—wife-beating, homicide, or drunkenness as alternative reactions to a wife's infidelity; male violence leading to status and power in some societies and reputational damage in others: and the high prevalence of homicidal fantasies to name a few.

This functional analysis suggests a common basis for the diversity of aggressive reactions in different contexts, and for alternatives to aggression. All of the adaptive problems discussed by Buss entail others as frustraters or obstacles to one's goal-oriented activities—they withhold resources, try to prevent our access to them by attacking us, thwart our access to a sexual partner, stand in our way to the use of others as means to ends (instruments or sources of information), and frustrate by withdrawing themselves as sexual partners, or, for that matter, as cooperative or informative partners. Aggressive acts are direct attempts to remove such obstacles—kill or otherwise disempower whoever stands in the way of material or social resources of whatever kind, block their attempts to withdraw themselves as goal objects (by such means as threats and beatings), and so on. If such attempts don't work, try to get around the problem by other means, such as begging and pleading or directly rewarding the frustrater for the resources, or getting out of the way of one's access to them. When nothing works, there is nothing left but to withdraw physically or psychologically. Drinking as a reaction to infidelity qualifies as a kind of psychological withdrawal when access to the sexual partner seems irrevocably blocked. Seeking another partner is a more positive way of dealing with the frustration.

Characteristic emotions accompany the diverse reactions to others as frustraters. Anger is an energizing component of aggression. Jealousy is a complex mix of fear and anger aroused by actual or perceived sexual rivals. The love–hate relation is understandable as contrasting reactions to a sexual partner who thwarts access to them by leaving or withholding sexual favors; love switches to hate and anger. Feelings of frustration that clients report to therapists are complex mixtures of emotions, anxiety and perhaps anger, aroused by recognized social impediments and thus easily labeled as frustration.

The fantasy imagery associated with frustration are understandable symbolic solutions to the impediments and emotions they arouse. They take the form of planned attacks or other ways of dealing with people who thwart access to any of the goals described earlier. Their content and frequency is determined by the nature and frequency of the actual frustrating events and how they affected the frustrated person at the time. The events and reactions are remembered, and possible solutions devised and rehearsed in one's imagination, and perhaps eventually carried out in reality. Frustrating social situations are ubiquitous and so too are the cognitive, emotional, and behavioral reactions to them.

The evolutionary basis of the frustrative function and reactions also is clear on rational and factual grounds. By its classical definition, evolution is a change in living things (species) that enable them to survive and reproduce. A big problem is posed by competitors for resources necessary for survival. The competitors include other species and conspecifics. They become obstacles to those resources and the most direct solution is to remove them. Thus aggression in all its forms was highly likely to evolve as a behavioral strategy for dealing with others as obstacles or anticipated obstacles. From this perspective, homicide and war were inevitable in human evolution, at least as one form of adaptive solution to frustrative competition. These are known from fossil evidence of homicide (a hominid skull evidently crushed by a club) and suspected from the disappearance of perhaps dozens of other hominid species over millions of years until only Homo sapiens remained (Tattersall, 2000). Aggression as an evolutionary strategy is also known from its prevalence in our primate relatives and other species, even in its extreme form of killing of conspecifics. I need not recount the innumerable familiar examples of "nature red in tooth and claw," except for the dramatic recent discovery of "kamakazi" sperms that attack and destroy "alien" sperms that are competing for an ovum.

But, however likely, aggression was not the only evolutionary strategy for dealing with others as potential competitors. Cooperation is the usual alternative emphasized by evolutionary psychologists, and it, too, was inevitable because it pays off for individuals to use each other as instruments for attaining mutually useful resources. We know this from cooperative behaviors that evolved in all social creatures from insects to humans. In its extreme form it is called reciprocal altruism (Dawkins, 1989), which may be partly genetic in origin as well as a product of social learning. Evolutionary optimists hope that biological and social evolution of cooperative behavior will lead to the extinction of war—eventually.

CHAPTER TWELVE

Evolution of Language: Words
to Associations

DCT implies that language emerged when a protoverbal code of some kind attached itself to an established (although still evolving) nonverbal cognitive system. The most recent evolutionary phase involved increasing functional autonomy of the verbal system, in keeping with the DCT assumption that evolved nonverbal and verbal cognitive systems are functionally independent but interconnected, so that one or other or both systems can be used in memory and other tasks. Normal language behavior entails a continual interplay between the two systems. However, the theory further implies that, initially, language development was completely dependent on the nonverbal cognitive base and gradually became capable of functioning independently for some purposes. The hypothesis is the main theme of this chapter and the subsequent one on syntax.

Why and How Did Language Originate?

The first important question is why language began. What adaptive functions were served by its emergence, persistence, and explosive growth? The question assumes that we can identify the crucial functions from our present understanding of the nature of language. That this is a non-trivial issue is suggested by Chomsky's assertion that, "If we hope to understand human language and the functional capacities on which it rests, we must first ask what it is, not how or for what purpose it is used" (1968, p. 62). From a functionalist perspective, however, what language is cannot be separated from what it does. In any case, enough is known that we can begin to ask the functional question in the evolutionary context. The emphasis on the priority of function also contrasts with traditional theories of the origins of language, which focused on the form and manner in which language began rather than why it began. One of the most enduring theories is that language evolved from gestures (e.g., see the collection of articles on the topic in Harnad, Steklis, & Lancaster,

279

1976; more recently, Corballis, 2003; Givón, 1998; Stokoe & Marschark, 1999; Volterra, Caselli, Capirci, & Pizzuto, 2005). Other ideas are that language arose from imitation of natural sounds (onomatopoeia), expressive sounds, or some abstract symbolic relation between vocal sounds and physical characteristics of the referents. Such views have been revitalized by the recent discovery of mirror neurons and their interpretation as an evolutionary mechanism for the emergence of language from gestures and imitation. I evaluate these ideas briefly and then develop a completely different functional hypothesis about why language began and evolved.

Gesture Theory.   The principle supporting arguments for gesture theory include the following: (a) the use of visual communication signals by other animals (e.g., threatening postures, submissive turning and bowing of the head), (b) its usefulness for communication between hunters in quiet pursuit of prey, (c) its early and widespread use in human communities such as North American Indians, and (d) the spontaneous invention of signing by deaf-mutes in the absence of formal instruction. Such examples are evidence of the adaptive value and universality of gestural communication systems. However, they are not useful in some situations. Darwin, for example, pointed out that gestures cannot be effectively used in the dark or when the hands are otherwise employed. And they cannot be used when the communicators can't see each other because of natural barriers such as trees and hills. None of these limitations apply to vocal languages and so the gesture proponents must explain how a gestural language evolved into a vocal one, or assume that vocal language emerged independently simply because it is so broadly adaptive.

Onomatopoeia.   The other traditional theories are attempts to account for the origin of the sound units of languages. The best known is the onomatopoeic theory, according to which words arose as imitations of natural sounds. This would account for such English words as the "hiss" of a snake, "bow wow" or "woof" of a dog, "rustling" of leaves, "buzz" of a bee, "gong" of a bell, "neigh" of a horse, and so on. The criticisms are that onomatopoeia can't explain the origin of the vast majority of words in any language or account for the abstract, symbolic character of language. Nevertheless, sound imitation might be one way that vocabulary got started and augmented. Phonetic symbolism is a related theory according to which certain sounds are meaningfully related to classes of referents so that, for example, the vowel sound [i] indicates something small, insignificant, dainty, or close by, whereas back vowels such as [a] and [u] "refer" to things that are larger, stronger, farther away, and so on. Such correspondences could arise from articulatory gestures, that is, differences in tongue position or the size of the oral cavity in the production of the sounds, among other possibilities. Phonetic symbolism continues to be an interesting research topic, but it, too, is limited in its potential to account for the origins of language. Even more limited is the interjectional or "pooh-pooh" theory according to which some words evolved from expressive sounds. I mention these theories again later along with other ideas about the origins and development of vocabulary.

Mirror Neurons.   Recall from Chapter 8 that mirror neurons discharge both when an object is manipulated and when similar actions are perceived in others

(Rizzolatti & Arbib, 1998). First discovered in the ventral premotor cortex of monkeys, mirror neurons were subsequently found in Broca's area and other left-hemisphere areas in humans. Rizzolatti and Arbib (1998) suggested that these neural mediators of imitation might be the missing evolutionary link between gestures and speech. Others have interpreted that idea, in different ways (summarized in a review by Holden, 2004). For example, Corballis (2003) suggested that the mirror system evolved first for manual control and later picked up vocal and facial control required for speech. Peter MacNeilage argued conversely that mirror neurons evolved to support imitation of oral behaviors (e.g., lip smacks, tongue smacks, teeth chatter) that are the precursors of speech according to his vocal-gesture theory of speech evolution (see MacNeilage & Davis 2003). David McNeill, drawing on relevant aspects of his research on getures and language (McNeill, Bertenthad, Coles & Gallaher 2005), proposed that the combination is the essential property, that neither gesture nor speech could have evolved without the other. The important point is that oral-vocal imitation and mirror neurons evolved in a codependent way at some stage. The addition of learning mechanisms to the mix would allow for generalization of imitative skills to imitation of sounds, as in onomatopoeia, musical humming, and so on.

However, mirror neurons are not a sufficient explanation of imitation or its possible role in language evolution. For example, crows and other birds are excellent imitators of the songs of other species—and speech of humans in the case of parrots—but no one to my knowledge has yet identified anything like a human mirror neuron system in birds. In a general review, Hurford (2004) noted that mirror neurons might help explain some aspects of language evolution (e.g., the role of speech imitation) but not others (e.g., learning the meanings of linguistic signs). He concluded that there is a long way to go from mirror neurons to language. In any case, mirror neurons and their role in imitation relate only to the question of how language evolved, but not why it began and evolved into the most salient hallmark of humanity. The answer is to be found in the adaptive functions served by language.

Much has been written about the usefulness of language for communicating information, intentions, requests for help, and other purposes that arise in the context of pressures for social cooperation (e.g., see Knight, Hurford, & Studdert-Kennedy, 2000). All such suggestions, however, depend on the implicit assumption that people already had nonlinguistic knowledge about the need for cooperation and that the emerging language tapped into that knowledge. Because all knowledge is memory (Chapter 3), we are brought back to the thematic idea of memory as the engine of cognitive evolution, in this case language evolution. Hence the following hypothesis.

Language Originated as a Mnemonic Device

This strong claim was first proposed in a text on the psychology of language (Paivio & Begg, 1981). It is a functional hypothesis in that it assumes that the crucial adaptive purpose of language is to serve memory. The hypothesis has a precedent in Hockett's (1963) inclusion of displacement as a design feature of language; that is, language can be used to communicate about what is not present as well as what is present. The design feature is accepted by all students of language as a statement of one of its functions. For example, in a chapter on the evolution of reference, Allen and Saidel (1998) mentioned almost in passing that "One of the advanced functions of language is to allow us to talk about people and things in their absence" (p. 190). This hypothesis is much stronger—the memory function is not just one of many functions but the primary reason why language began and continues to be its essential raison d'être. Paivio and Begg (1981) expressed the hypothesis as follows:

> . . . if everything that language was used for was always present, there would be no need for a language. This suggests the intriguing idea that language may actually have originated as a means of tapping the memories of people for social communication. If we were concerned only with the present, pointing would be the easiest way to draw attention to particular events. It is possible that visual language, such as cave paintings, was an early attempt to draw attention to absent, but thought about, events. Perhaps our ancestors were adept at tracing outlines in sand or mud before speech developed. Be that as it may, spoken language is a particularly flexible means of tapping . . . memories, cuing or prompting the listener to attend to memories of past events. In short, language is a very handy mnemonic system, in addition to its other virtues. (p. 171).[37]

To avoid any misunderstanding, I repeat that the mnemonic hypothesis is about why language began and not how it began. Everyone agrees that language requires a vocabulary and most would say that the initial vocabulary must have consisted of "names" (signs or symbols) for objects (e.g., Burling, 1999). The names arose as responses to the things themselves rather than to their memories. This perceptual-motor beginning is a general answer to how language began (more specific answers are the gestural and other theories already mentioned). The mnemonic hypothesis remains a proposal about why it began, with the understanding that a vocabulary is the minimal requirement for talking about things in their absence. A further clarification is that memory refers not only to episodic memory but also to the long-term memories that are the basis of nonverbal representations, and eventually, the verbal system. Given those clarifications, I spell out why the hypothesis is compelling from a dual coding perspective using evidence from human and animal studies. This is followed by dual coding analyses of language evolution beyond its origins.

The description follows a sequence corresponding to overlapping stages of human language development, and, as far as it goes, communication systems in animals. Adapted from Paivio and Begg (1981, pp. 247–248), the sequence begins with the development of nonverbal cognitive representation (imagens) for objects and events, as described in Chapter 3 and assumed in Chapter 11 on the evolution of nonverbal cognition. The second stage necessarily combines the development of verbal representations (logogens) and their referential connections to imagens, for meaningful language units cannot arise in a vacuum but only in connection with referent objects and events. The third stage is the development of associative structures, both verbal and nonverbal, during which the verbal system begins to develop some functional autonomy. Chapter 13 develops the further argument that syntax also evolved initially from a nonverbal cognitive base that included imagery. The hypothesis is generally consistent with theories that assume continuity in language evolution, as opposed to the discontinuity view that syntax is so unique that it required a rather abrupt emergence of a special language organ or module of some kind. The functional emphasis on memory is a theme that runs through the different levels of structures and processes.

IN THE BEGINNING WAS THE WORD

Language must have begun with the development of a meaningful vocabulary of signs. It is generally agreed that, as in the case of language development in the child, the initial human vocabulary was concrete and referential, consisting of "names" that refer to things, events, actions—anything that can be discretely labeled. In dual coding terms, this required the development of cognitive representations for the names and referents, as well as the referential interconnections and processing systems necessary for getting from one to the other to name and understand names. The vocabulary, the referents, and interconnections were internal. What were the first "words" in such referential structures and how did the construction get started?

Evolutionists say that there was a first human, and, on the basis of DNA evidence, that this human was a woman, "mitochondrial Eve" (for a review, see Dennett, 1995). Lacking similar evidence, we can at least argue logically that there must have been a first "word."[38] Speculating on what that word might have been is an interesting language game that I have played with family and friends. They generally agree that the word (grunt, scream, whatever) must have been related to primary survival needs and had to be communicated at a distance, hence implicating memory. Candidates include food, shelter, and predator (with "Over here!" implied). Predator is a likely first choice that is supported by recent animal studies.

Referential Signaling

Monkeys, apes, meerkats, domestic chickens, and members of many other species emit alarm calls when they see predators, and group members that hear the cries

---

[38]This speculation is consistent with, but goes beyond Darwin's view that evolutionary changes in language resembled the processes of biological evolution, beginning with inheritance from a common ancestor. The idea has been supported for evolution of vocabulary families from a common source by Gray and Jordan (2000). They constructed an evolutionary vocabulary tree for a large family of Austronesian languages which supports the idea that an ancestral language, probably in Taiwan, evolved and spread rapidly to Polynesia through colonization of the Pacific. The present suggestion is a speculative but logical extension to the idea that human languages began with a single "word."

take appropriate action to avoid the predator, or to drive it away as in the case of the chickadees' mobbing call mentioned earlier. Characteristic vocal sounds also occur to situations related to other survival needs; for example, chimpanzees grunt to "indicate" a food source. These are examples of what has come to be called referential signaling, communication systems with obvious adaptive value and evolutionary significance. Theorists who view language evolution as a continuous process might be willing to accept referential signaling as a possible model of how language began. Discontinuity theorists would argue that such signaling systems are unrelated to properties of human language in that they are involuntary, involve fixed repertoires that are linked to perceptually present objects, and lack combinatorial syntax (e.g., Chomsky, 1968, p. 61). Such criticisms have long been directed at naming in general as a possible basis of language origins, as demonstrated amusingly in the following poem by the philosopher Quine (1953, cited in Allen & Saidel, 1998, p. 183):

> The unrefined, untutored mind
> Of Homo *javanensis*
> Could only treat of things concrete
> And present to the senses.

The criticisms are not entirely valid even if they have some core of truth. For example, the well-known studies by Seyfarth and his colleagues (e.g., Seyfarth, Cheney, & Marler, 1980) showed that vervet monkeys emit three different alarm calls when they spot eagles, leopards, or snakes, and other monkeys in the group respond with appropriate evasive actions. Thus they have something like a mini vocabulary (albeit a fixed one) which, in the receiver, mediates avoidance responses to predators not present to the senses, and occur even in the absence of the sender (i.e., to recorded calls). Predication is implied in such signaling in that, for example, the eagle alarm means "There's an eagle! Hide under something!" and is so understood by at least one receiver whose actions might be imitated by others.

We can counter many of the objections simply by recognizing that the referential processes are internal. Thus, in dual coding terms, the production of referential signals involves recognition memory that requires activation of a representation (imagen)—one of many—that corresponds to a given predator class, and then activation of a vocal response generator (analogous to a motor logogen) via connecting (referential) pathways. This sequence is reversed for the receiver: first activation of a vocal representation, then referential activation of a predator imagen, which in turn activates situation-specific avoidance responses. Moreover, referential activity is not entirely fixed and involuntary. For example, young monkeys must learn to respond appropriately by narrowing the range of generalization to members of the predator species (Cheney & Seyfarth, 1986). Learned inappropriate responding was shown dramatically by the observation of an infant vervet that saw a herd of stampeding elephants, gave a leopard alarm call, and the alpha male saw a leopard and also gave the leopard call. The infant persisted for several months in giving leopard alarm calls to approaching elephants (Caro & Hauser, 1992, cited in Allen & Saidel, 1998, p. 195).

The internal character of referential signaling was more directly revealed by a study of diana monkeys by Zuberbühler, Cheney, and Seyfarth (1999). Males emit either of two different alarm calls to leopards and eagles, and females within earshot begin a chorus of different but appropriately differentiated sounds. This entails something like spreading activation within the vocal signal system, which increases the survival value of the signals presumably because more monkeys are likely to hear the warning. In any case, the investigators used a priming technique involving recorded alarm calls as well as eagle shrieks and leopard growls to show that females were responding to the semantics rather than the acoustic properties of the males' alarm calls. For example, the females increased appropriate response calls when the male's leopard alarm call was preceded by a leopard growl but not when it was preceded by an eagle shriek. The investigators concluded that monkeys perhaps responded to "mental representations [that] are not unlike those linked to the human linguistic concepts of *leopard* and *eagle* (Zuberbühler et al., 1999, p. 41). Thus, the representations are functionally equivalent to mental images.

Expansion of Closed Naming Systems

Referential signaling as just described is based on closed systems of a few apparently meaningful signals. It is reasonable to suppose that these evolved into larger vocabularies that were still fixed or closed before becoming the open and productive systems characteristic of modern humans. For example Homo erectus, although lacking complex speech, might have had a larger fixed referential "vocabulary" than, say, chimpanzees. Indeed, this is not entirely supposition because we know that other species can be taught large vocabularies. For example, an African grey parrot raised by Irene Pepperberg (e.g., 1999) learned to produce and comprehend more than 80 items, including names of objects, colors, shapes, actions, and numbers. Louis Herman and colleagues (e.g., Herman & Uyeyama, 1999) taught two female dolphins to understand and respond behaviorally to a language based on a vocabulary of about 40 items communicated by gestures or word-like clicks by the trainer. Among other categories, the "words" referred to objects in a swimming tank, related actions, and modifiers of object location. Most impressive of all are the bonobos (pygmy chimpanzees) studied by Sue Savage-Rumbaugh and colleagues (summarized by Savage-Rumbaugh, Shanker, & Taylor, 1998). Kanzi, the longest-studied of these animals, learned to produce and understand a large vocabulary of lexigrams (artificial abstract symbols activated by a computer keyboard, a communication system that the common chimpanzee had already used successfully) and gestures, as well as to understand human speech. The items covered the full range of categories of names and other words used by humans. The scientists are interested in understanding the syntactic and cognitive abilities of the different animals, about which more is said later. The point here is that the animals were able to learn substantial vocabularies taught to them by people (or, in the case of bonobos, by observing another bonobo interacting with a teacher), but, with some possible exceptions discussed later, they never learned to invent new words even given the head start they received from their trainers. They are stuck with human-taught closed vocabularies rather than productive systems with unlimited growth potential.

Productive Vocabulary Expansion

We have seen that the referential signals of different species show an expansion from a single all-purpose alarm call to two or more differentiated signals for different predators and other classes of referents, up to many different gestural signals in the case of wild chimpanzees. Presumably our hominid ancestors progressively extended the scope of their fixed vocabularies over generations (one new "word" every 10 generations would have resulted in a substantial vocabulary in only a few thousand years) before someone twigged to the idea that names can be invented. But that's moving far ahead in the generation process because deliberate invention implies reflexivity, the use of language to talk about language, which in this case requires the understanding that words are names (reflexivity is discussed further in Chapter 13).

Like closed vocabularies, early open vocabularies would have been names for concrete objects, actions, and qualities. To be understood, the heard or signed names would have to evoke images of the referent objects, actions, and so on, eventuating in the referential-processing capacity of the evolved, multimodal, dual coding mind described in Chapter 3. How might the expansion have occurred? We might suppose, as already suggested, that the initial closed "vocabulary" consisted of alarm calls and gestural referential signals related to predators and food sources. Thus, they would have had an innate basis but would also have been shaped up by experience, entailing conditioning mechanisms and observational learning, including especially imitation. I cannot insist too strongly that something like that must have occurred given (a) the existence of referential signaling and related signaling systems, such as bird songs and other modalities of mating signals in other species, (b) their instinctive (species-specific) character, and (c) their modulation by learning to the extent that, for example, song birds readily learn the songs of other bird species to which they are exposed.

The reasoning becomes more speculative when we ask how far such processes could have taken vocabulary growth in early hominids. Among other things, the rate of growth might have been linked to the evolution of the vocal tract. We can take such factors for granted and deal with the generative processes operating within the articulatory limits. Here the various old theories of the origins of language become relevant. Could imitation of natural sounds (onomatopoeia) gradually produce differentiated warning signals from an undifferentiated base? For example, could the different warning calls of diana monkeys in response to leopards and eagles have resulted from attempts to imitate leopard growls and eagle shrieks? There is no suggestion of such a sound resemblance in the differentiated alarm calls of diana monkeys as studied by Zuberbühler and colleagues, and so we would have to speculate that the acoustic structure of the alarms had evolved into a more abstract form from onomatopoeic beginnings. The speculation has some empirical support. For example, the anthropologist Franz Boas (1938) noted that the formation of new words by sound imitation is a live process in such languages as American Indian

Chinook and many South African Bantu dialects. Indeed it is so in modern English (consider "woofer" and "tweeter" amplifiers). The suggestion is, therefore, plausible although limited in how much of early hominid vocabulary it could explain. The possibilities increase somewhat if we add the expressive ("pooh-pooh") and phonetic symbolism theories into the generative mix. The gesture theory is even more plausible, but inasmuch as we are dealing here with the origins of a spoken vocabulary, the gestures would have to generalize to articulatory shapes and movements, which in fact is an entailment of phonetic symbolism (for example, smaller and larger oral shapes correspond to "small" [i] and "large" [u] sounds and referents). All three theories share an element of vocal or gestural imitation that generalizes within and across modalities.

Such generalization is apparent in some familiar modern words. It has been suggested that "mama" as the child's word for mother in many languages originated by imitation of the sound made when feeding at the breast, which generalizes to the person who is the feeder. The words mammary and mammal illustrate further generalization at least in the case of Indo-European languages. Another set of examples are related to the word "nose." The initial [n] is a nasal, produced by air coming out of the nose. Translation equivalents include nez (French), nariz (Spanish), and nena (Finnish). A disproportionate number of English words beginning with [n] or [sn] refer to nasal activity: sniffle, snuffle, sneeze, snooze, snore, neigh, snot, nag (from the Scandinavian nagga, to grumble), gnaw, and many metaphorical extensions such as nosy. Could the word "nose" have originated by generalization to the body part from the sound and activity associated with sniffing, snorting, and the like? Etymological studies cannot take us that far back, but they are consistent with the hypothesis that a core vocabulary could have begun that way. Human cultural evolution had a long time to expand that vocabulary bit by bit, although we don't know when and how the process became completely open, productive, and apparently non imitative so that any physical similarity between words and their meanings now are mostly arbitrary.

We can guess that the early invented vocabulary also consisted of names for things that were important for survival, as is the case with the fixed repertoires of referential signals of other animals. Thus, names for animate things would have had priority as they do in children's vocabulary development—they first learn names for things that move. They also attend preferentially to moving objects, especially animate ones, as do other animals (L. Bloom, 1976, pp. 170–171). The behaviors may echo ancient adaptive attentional and signaling priorities. We could go on to construct an expanded vocabulary sequence but that's unnecessary for our purposes, except to say that the early vocabulary was concrete, referring to objects, events, actions, and so forth, including socially relevant characteristics. The invented vocabulary units would likely have been holistic initially rather than constructed from parts as they later became, so that human vocabularies can expand componentially by combining and recombining a small number of phonemes to produce what is potentially an indefinitely large number of morphemes and words. This is the duality of patterning that characterizes human languages generally (Hockett, 1963).

While continuing to expand, concrete vocabulary development necessarily overlapped with the emergence of referentially distanced vocabulary, that is, general and abstract terms that refer to categories, properties, relations, inner states—anything abstracted out of concrete referents. Of course, abstractness is relative, so that even concrete terms other than proper names are general or abstract in that they refer to classes of referents. My suggestions for the first words were the equivalents of general terms for predators, edibles, mates, and shelters because this is a useful starting level, and these differentiated into more specific terms and images, which could mediate more specific adaptive responses. Modern early vocabularies are similarly rather general—woman, man, dog, house, talking, walking, wind, rain, whatever. The initial concrete terms in vocabulary evolution probably were of some middle level of generality, such as the basic level as defined by Rosch et al. (1975). The interest here is in the adaptive value of more abstract terms and how they might have entered evolving vocabulary. For example, it would have been adaptive for our ancestors to have terms for even broader classes of things that are dangerous, edible, living, hot, cold, dead, flying, terrestrial; spatial terms for near, far, up, down; modalities of sensation (it would make a difference whether a potential predator had been seen or only heard in the distance by a hunter scout); and emotional states such as anger and fear.

I suggested earlier that a less speculative list could be developed empirically, hopefully guided by a theory that suggests super ordinate categories and a method for filling in the categories. Charles Osgood (e.g., Osgood, Suci, & Tannenbaum, 1957) left us with one such approach—a theory of dimensions of meaning and the semantic differential rating scale method for identifying the dimensions. Factor analytic studies across many languages and cultures consistently turned up three dimensions of meaning: *evaluative*, defined by such bipolar scales as good–bad and pleasant–unpleasant; *activity*, defined by fast–slow, active–passive and related terms; and *potency*, defined by strong–weak, potent–impotent, and their synonyms. The three factors measure connotative meanings presumably derived from affective and behavioral responses to things. Osgood interpreted their universality as reflecting the importance of affect in human affairs, now and in the distant past. In this context, the theory and research suggest that general terms corresponding to good–bad, active–passive, and strong–weak emerged early in the evolution of vocabulary.

The functional categories of physical and social stimuli described in the last chapter map onto the adaptive categories of possible first words and also overlap with the semantic differential dimensions. For example, the terms *good* and *bad* are relevant for positive and negative goal objects (reinforcers, incentives), *strong* and *weak* are important properties of instrumental stimuli (tools and other means to goal attainment) as well as obstacles or frustraters (for which "fast–slow" would also be relevant in the case of competitors). The information function would be tapped by descriptive terms that are mainly denotative rather than connotative, such as words for appearances of things (color, shape, etc.), dynamic events such as growth (of plants, belly size of a pregnant woman), changing seasons, and the like.

The candidates for the putative protovocabulary list could be expanded by studying commonalities across the languages of different contemporary hunter-gatherer societies (Gray & Jordan, 2000, provided a precedent for such an analysis; see Footnote 37). Informants could even be asked to generate words in response to super-ordinate labels by a method that has been used to generate lists of basic vocabulary of modern languages. For example, Savard and Richards (1970) developed a list of more than 3,000 basic French words by having francophones write specific associates to such labels as kitchen utensils, foods, toys, and so on. They then used measures of frequency and other indexes to rank the same words according to their communicative usefulness (*utilité*). The same procedures could be used to develop a list of terms ranked according to their adaptive usefulness for hunter-gatherers, perhaps edited for their evolutionary significance by anthropological linguists.

Such a list could suggest answers to the more interesting question concerning processes that produced general and abstract terms. The processes by definition entail generalization based, for example, on visual similarity of referents. Use of appropriate general terms requires attention to differences and differential responding, presumably acquired through discrimination learning as discussed in the last chapter in regard to categorization in animals. Generalization occurs in referential signaling, as in the case of the young vervet that persisted in emitting a leopard warning at the sight of elephants. Domestic chickens provide another example; they give different alarm calls to aerial and terrestrial predators, and their aerial alarm will tend to occur to a terrestrial predator (racoon) shown on an overhead TV monitor, although less reliably than to a similarly-displayed raptor (Evans & Marler, 1995).

The emergence of increasingly general terms into a vocabulary means that responses are "permitted" to generalize over increasingly different stimuli. In language evolution as in current usage, the different levels presumably arose because they were useful for different purposes: "Animal!" is a sufficient and useful signal by a scouting hunter if he is uncertain whether a noise in the bush was made by a predator or a game animal. A wary response by other hunters would be appropriate; further information might elicit "Antelope!" or "Leopard!" triggering specific evasive responses.

Synonyms stay at the same level of generality and in modern languages they usually originate as borrowings (or impositions) from different languages. For example, stream is old English whereas river is from the French *rivière* (earlier, from Latin). A similar expansion of vocabulary could have occurred early in language evolution when hominid tribes with speech split into different groups, developed different dialects, again came into contact and began to learn each other's terms for the same referents. This would have been an advanced stage of language evolution, far beyond the beginnings and early expansion of a vocabulary.

The expansion of vocabularies by discoveries or inventions of new word units would have been slow and limited in communicative usefulness. It would be more productive to combine existing words or their parts to name newly discovered entities. This leads to associative structures and processes as the mechanism for generating literal and figurative words and expressions, as well as being a basis for productive use of language.

Verbal Associative Structures and Processes

Associative experience used to be thought of as the basis of language learning and behavior. It became the *bête noire* of Chomsky and the generative linguists who followed him, and was abandoned by most psycholinguists. Even during associationism's darkest hour, however, some brave souls defended it as one important process in language development and behavior. For example, George Kiss (1973) reasoned that verbal (associative) mediation theory could at least account for the acquisition of word classes from experience with a vocabulary. He developed a computer simulation model in which one component constructed a network of internal representations corresponding to an input vocabulary and a second component formed a representation for word classes based on word groups that are similar to each other. Tested using vocabulary from mothers talking to their children, the simulation program generated groupings corresponding to nouns, verbs, adjectives, and other classes. Thus the results supported a cognitive version of verbal association.

A more general revival of associationism emerged in the form of connectionist and (related) neural network theories. These are based on Hebb's 1949 proposal that associations form between neurons that are active at the same time. This Hebbian "synaptic rule" (discussed in Chapter 9) and connectionist models based on it can be seen as modern versions of the Aristotelian law of contiguity, one of his three laws concerning the formation of associations, the other two being similarity and contrast (Peter reminds us of Paul because we have experienced them together, or because they are similar, or because they are opposites in some way).

The aforementioned models accord with the dual coding position that association is a crucial process in the development of language structures and skills. That view stemmed from the compelling nature of the empirical evidence that associative variables have strong effects on memory and other cognitive tasks (Chapter 4). Syntax as viewed by transformational grammarians implicated additional creative principles, but they did not replace associative ones. More about that later; here I discuss the dual coding version of associationism as it might apply to the evolution of vocabulary and larger language structures, as well as language use.

The distinguishing feature of the dual coding approach in this context as elsewhere is its emphasis on both verbal and imagery systems; specifically, associations within the verbal system (between logogens) and within the nonverbal system (between imagens), with referential connections and processes continuing to be essential. On the basis of empirical evidence, contiguity and similarity are assumed to be the important determinants of association.

We have already considered the roles of similarity and contiguity in traditional theories of the origins of structural units of language. In onomatopoeia, for example, imitation of natural sounds is based on acoustic similarity. So too is the echolalic developmental stage in classical descriptions of language acquisition. Like song birds, we apparently have a built-in mechanism for imitating sounds, although the imitative response is shaped by the proximity of the sound we produced and the sound that we imitate, thereby implicating stimulus-response contiguity. The analysis extends to vocabulary expansion involving literal and metaphorical compound words, habitual phrases, and idioms.

Compound Words and Habitual Phrases. The chimpanzee Washoe reportedly signed "waterbird" the first time she saw a duck in the water. She thus created an appropriate compound name from component signs she already had in her reper-toire. The parrot Alex said "banacker" on being presented a banana and a cracker, thereby conflating the component words into a compound. The records of Alex and the bonobo Kanzi contain hundreds of examples of two-word "utterances," although these do not necessarily suggest the emergence of compound structures. The animal evidence in any case agrees with the hypothesis that, early in language evolution, vocabulary expanded by a combinatorial process in which new words were formed by linking existing words into compounds. The Washoe and Alex examples illustrate contiguity of referents—seeing a bird in water and a banana with a cracker. The components already had bases in referential connections between imagens and response logogens, so that the co-occurrence of the referents jointly activated corresponding imagens and then (given contextual support for naming) referentially related logogens.

Child language development also supports a cultural-evolutionary version of the ontogeny-recapitulates-phylogeny argument. After the one-word stage, children begin to combine words into two-word utterances that have been variously inter-preted as reflecting underlying syntax (e.g., pivot grammar; Braine, 1963) or seman-tics (structural meanings; Brown, 1970). These include noun–noun (baby book), adjective–noun (pretty boat), verb–noun (pull hat), and other productive combina-tions, some of which become fixed as compound words. That this has happened historically can be seen by perusing almost any page of a dictionary. One finds words formed from two nouns (longbow, oarlock, textbook, wallboard), adjective and noun (blueberry, redbird, wildflower), verb and noun (puffball, pushcart, row-boat), among others. These are literal compounds originating from contiguous experience with the referents. The components often originated from other lan-guages and the associative connection is not so transparent, as in *thermometer* and *telescope*. Many complex words that combine parts of root words as affixes derive from associative experience with referents of the (now-contracted) roots, as in *leop-ard* ("lion with spots"), *locomotion* (movement from place to place), and *malaria* ("bad air"). Longer habitual phrases such as back and forth, in and out, and now and then probably derive from verbal associative experiences for most of us, even if they once originated from things that move back and forth, and the like.

Figurative Compounds and Abstract Language.   Metaphorical extension is a particular kind of generalization process that has often been used to explain the his-torical development of abstract vocabulary (e.g., Givón, 1998; Lakoff & Johnson, 1980). The process is complex and many books and journals are devoted to its study as reflected in such varieties of figurative language as metaphor, irony, and proverbs. Figurative language has been studied from the dual coding perspective (e.g., Paivio & Walsh, 1994) and I draw on that background in the present context. It entails both verbal and imaginal associative processes. Associations are involved in metaphoric words as well as longer expressions, and therefore must be consid-ered when metaphoric extension is used to explain evolution of abstract vocabu-lary. This is because metaphor is based on underlying similarity relations, as is seen when we examine the concept.

Metaphoric expressions pervade even the most literal language, to the point where it is often claimed that existing languages consist mainly of words and expressions that had metaphoric origins. For example, the term *metaphor* itself originated from the Greek *metaphora,* meaning "transfer. " Metaphora in turn derives from *meta* ("over") and ("carry"), conveying the idea that meaning is carried over, transferred, or transported from one linguistic unit to another. The literal meaning survives in that metaphora is the identifying label on moving vans in Greece. The similarity relation is in the common aspect of meaning that is carried over from a literal source to the metaphorical term. The term metaphor is a rather complex example that anticipates a later discussion of the reflexive function of language— that is, metaphor is about language itself, although it has also been applied to non-linguistic visual situations, such as movement indicators in static pictures (Kennedy, 1976). Moreover, the referents are nonlinguistic in such familiar metaphorical extensions as "foot" (of a mountain), "leg" (of a table), "eye" (of a needle), and "mouth" (of a river). The similarity is between perceptual aspects of the referents of the literal terms: foot is the bottom part of bodies and mountains, and both parts protrude; the associative aspect is that, whenever the term was first use metaphorically, the mountain bottom reminded the inventor of a foot. The mountain was perceptually available whereas the referent of the literal term was available in memory as a foot imagen. Similarly, the eye of a needle has an eye-like shape located at one end of a longish object (functionally its top when one threads the needle), and so on.

Note that even literal terms are abstractions that could have originated by metaphorical extension from concrete acts. For example, the imitation involved in onomatopoeia is based on similarity—"bow wow" resembles the sound made by a dog. A child's use of the term to name the animal is a metaphoric extension of a vocal property of the object to the object as a whole, a kind of synecdoche analogous to using "redbreast" as a synonym for robin. The word mother could be similarly interpreted as metaphoric extension, a transfer to the nursing mother of an oral response pattern that produces the mouthing sounds made during breast-feeding. From this perspective, it can be argued that all initial "words" had a metaphoric origin, entailing transfer of acoustic properties and behavioral affordances of referents to the verbal responses themselves. The process then expanded to metaphorical extensions of existing vocabularies to generate more abstract usages, based on similarity of perceptual, motor, or affective reactions to specific and general terms.

The extensions are historical, known to etymologists. Most speakers learn metaphorically-derived words and idioms in the same way as they learn literal terms—the idiosyncratic meanings are assigned by convention. For example, a person learning the word "comprehension" does not ordinarily think of it as a frozen metaphor that translates directly into its metaphorical equivalent, grasping an idea. Similarly, in early language evolution, metaphoric extensions would soon have become conventionalized and their meanings assigned to them by the group.

Associative Processing.   Here we turn to the evolution of associative influences on language use. Such influences are ubiquitous in evolved language and have been studied by word association, sentence completion, cloze, and remote associates tests, among many others. They show up routinely in everyday speech, newspaper headlines, advertisements, and so forth. They differ from associative structures such as compound words and habitual phrases in that the associative processing is freer, less constrained, but still not random. In free association tests, for example, many different responses occur to "knife" but "fork" is by far the most likely. Nonetheless, knife and fork have not become integrated into a compound word that functions like a lexical unit, although we can think of circumstances under which this could occur—a utensil that functions as both would probably be called a "fork-knife."[39] The difference between association and integration once was a matter for theoretical debate (see p. 50, this volume), but for these purposes, it suffices to say that associative processing varies according to the number and strength of interconnections between units in associative networks. Given a cue, association spreads over a region of the total network in a non-random fashion so that lexical units (logogens in DCT) are activated according to past co-activation frequencies or similarity relations, as described in Chapter 3.

The influences on language use stem from the synchronous and hierarchical associative structure of the nonverbal imagery system as well as the sequentially organized verbal system. Thus, table knives and forks are often experienced together and form parts of an imagen structure such that imaging one part activates an image of the other, perhaps as part of an imagined table setting in an even larger kitchen scene. The point is that language associations, when they involve concrete words, could be based on imagery or the verbal systems or both, so that associative influences reflect a continuous interplay of referential processing between systems and associative processing within systems, depending on the context and prior associative experiences.

Research has established the power of associative influence in all aspects of language use involving anything from word pairs, to sentences, to text and connected discourse (Paivio & Begg, 1981). Associations benefit language comprehension and memory, and they are reflected as well in language production. The positive effects can be based on experiential contiguities (thus predictable from word association norms) or formal (phonemic or visual) similarity, so that sentences containing words that sound or look alike are easier to understand and remember than sentences with dissimilar words. Associations can also have negative effects if they cross functional units—in paired-associate memory experiments, for example, interference occurs if a stimulus word is associatively related to response words in different pairs. And we've all had the experience of making anticipatory errors in speech, the kind of slip of the tongue in which we prematurely utter a syllable or word that is related to a later word–asking for smoyked oysters, for example. It is important to emphasize that these associative effects occur independent of syntactic structure; that is, they occur when the grammatical pattern is held constant and the associative effects therefore cannot be explained in terms of syntactic variables.

---

[39]Mark Sadoski informed me that there is a new blended word for "spoon" and "fork," namely "spork," which refers to plastic spoons with short fork-like tines or teeth on the end.

It is relevant, too, that the associative effects are independent of the imagery value of the materials. Recall from Chapter 4, for example, that relatedness and concreteness (image-evoking value) of words have independent and additive effects on memory for noun–noun pairs, adjective–noun phrases, and sentences. Comprehension is similarly affected independently by relatedness and concreteness.

The important general point is that associative factors link up with the hypothesized importance of memory in language evolution. Associative processes contribute to the power of language as a mnemonic device. The associations involve the verbal system and the imagery system, separately and cooperatively, the latter via their optionally traversable interconnections.

How did such factors influence the cultural evolution of language? I will illustrate the principles by elaborating on an analysis of the evolution of poetry some 30 years ago. The argument began as follows:

> The intimate nature of the relation between poetry and memory is evidenced by the long educational tradition in which "memory work" has been associated with poetic recitation. Perhaps poetry itself evolved as a mnemonic system for preserving and transmitting valued traditions of early societies before writing was invented. To the extent that this is true, we might expect the useful mnemonic features of the speech sounds to be more characteristic of early rather than recent poetic forms. The latter, having developed in the context of writing, might have been freed to some extent from the need to preserve auditory mnemonics. (Paivio, 1971b, p. 471)

I then went on to analyze the various "poetic variables" (e.g., acoustic similarity) that have been shown to affect memorability in verbal memory experiments. Without going into the experimental details, I will illustrate their evolutionary significance.

One of the oldest epic poems in Europe is the Finnish *Kalevala*. Its meter and other poetic forms are imitated in Longfellow's poem, Hiawatha.[40] The Kalevala is composed of magical poems or "songs" (Finnish *runo*) about creation and other mystical themes. Many go back to antiquity and were recited over the centuries by "singers" (cf. bards) in various parts of Finland and neighboring countries. The same runo was recited with variations by different singers and by the same singer at different times, but always so that the poetic forms and themes were retained (Comparetti, 1898, p. 2). Each runo and the *Kalevala* as a whole are characterized by a rich use of alliteration, rhyme, rhythmical patterning, repetition, and high imagery content. All of these are known to enhance memory for language. They

---

[40]Longfellow discovered the Kalevala on a trip to the Scandinavian countries and was inspired by its poetic form and mythical content to write Hiawatha. More recently, Handwerk (2002) suggested that J. R. R. Tolkien's *Lord of the Rings* was inspired by the Kalevala, in two ways. First, Tolkien used the phonetic pattern and structure of Finnish as the model for the elfin language; and second, there are parallels between the Kalevala and Tolkien's saga in terms of the characters and the idea of the hero's journey.

would have aided the poets and their listeners. The evolutionary hypothesis is that, over time, memorable features were introduced by different runo-singers, and by the same singer as he repeated the same runo to different audiences. The less memorable characteristics would thus have been gradually extinguished and replaced by mnemonically "fitter" ones. Some of the changes could have been introduced consciously, with an intuitive understanding that they are more memorable, but this need not have been the case. The runo-singer would sometimes simply forget segments and replace them with other wording, some of which would be more memorable in the context of the rest of the runo and thus have a better chance of survival. Gradual modifications of that kind resulted in a "mature" *Kalevala*, packed with memorable acoustic patterns and imagery. This evolutionary process conformed to Darwinian principles: variation of linguistic forms and survival of the mnemonically fittest within a cultural context in which myths are valued.

I cannot cite direct evidence for the evolutionary hypothesis from scholarly works on the *Kalevala*. The observational base is the poem as put together by Elias Lönnrot in 1849 from the runes he collected and as analyzed by Comparetti (for a recent complete English translation of the poem, see Friberg, 1988). The runes incorporate all of the memorable poetic devices just described. The evolutionary hypothesis is based on the argument that evolved collective forms must have originated from simpler forms and were not created full-blown in all their poetic glory. Sadoski (2002) summarized work done on Homeric and other poems by linguistic historians that is consistent with the DCT hypothesis. It also has support from empirical studies by psychologist David Rubin (1995) on memory processes involved in the transmission of poetic forms, emphasizing in particular the importance of such factors as rhyme, rhythm, and imagery.

The mnemonic hypothesisis not a denial of the aesthetic value of poetry. The *Kalevela* and other myths and epic poems all over the world might have become more pleasing as their form and content became more memorable. Eventually, perhaps very early on, bards and poets created poems and songs just for fun, for their own enjoyment, and that of their audiences, or because they gained prestige or were otherwise reinforced for their poetry. In brief, poetry, like more prosaic forms of language, took on new functions while still tapping into and aiding memory through their evolving associative structures and processes, both verbal and imaginal.

The evolution of the *Kalevala* and other examples of traditional poetry could also have included systematic changes in syntactic variables, which I have not tried to evaluate. Others have done so in regard to languages more generally. We turn to that in the following chapter.

CHAPTER THIRTEEN

Evolution of Language: Syntax

This chapter deals with the cultural evolution of the ability to organize words in meaningful grammatical sequences. The argument is that syntactic skill evolved because it was necessary for communicating about perceptually absent (past, future, hidden, or possible) events that are or can be represented in the nonverbal imagery system, thereby enhancing the communicative usefulness of language in constantly changing contexts. This view contrasts with abstract computational theories of grammar that are designed to generate an infinite number of grammatical sentences using combinatorial rules that operate recursively on a set of linguistic symbols. Such grammars formalize the reflexivity design feature of language, that is, they use language rules to operate on language itself. This intriguing language game is limited as a model of real language because it does not include the situational uncertainties of language use. In this regard, formal grammars share the explanatory limitations of all formalisms as discussed in earlier chapters. Natural-language syntax is free of such constraints because it is driven by meaning and pragmatic demands. Such a system evolved in ways that can be described by DCT.

We begin by reviewing the main issues involved in current debates about the origins and evolution of syntax. Evidence from animal and human studies is used to analyze the issues and then justify the dual coding approach to them.

WHY THE EMPHASIS ON SYNTAX?

Syntax is the crucible of language evolution theories. The most challenging aspect of grammatical patterning is its hierarchical structuring in which smaller structures are recursively embedded within larger ones:The cat is sleeping, the cat that killed the mouse is sleeping, the cat that killed the mouse that ate the cheese is sleeping, and so on. Another crucial aspect is the use of grammatical items that consist of a closed class of words and morphemes with grammatical functions, such as (for English) articles, pronouns, relational terms, markers for plurality, tense, and possession. Grammatical rules define what kinds of structures are permissible in a given language. Psychologically, rules can be conceptualized as processing systems that enable the speaker to produce and understand novel, but grammatically

296

"correct," combinations. It is this creativity that Noam Chomsky considers to be the hallmark of human language, distinguishing it from the communication systems of all other animals.

The Discontinuity View of Language Evolution

Chomsky's view led him to conclude that human language is too complex and unique to have evolved gradually from earlier communication systems. This *discontinuity theory* of language evolution has been adopted by some of Chomsky's followers. They rest their case on the seemingly abrupt emergence and growth of language, analogous to the big-bang theory of the origin of the universe. Thus, discontinuity theorists have argued for rapid emergence of brain structures specialized for creating grammatical languages, a universal language acquisition device that Chomsky even described in biological terms as a language organ. It has been suggested that this syntactic organ resulted from a genetic mutation caused by some catastrophic event (Bickerton, 1990) or by a rapid cascade of small changes (Bickerton, 1995, p. 69) consistent with the theory of punctuated equilibrium (described in Chapter 10) that Eldredge and Gould (1972) had proposed as an alternative to neo-Darwinian gradualist views of evolution.

Discontinuity theorists could find comfort in recent evidence that a particular gene plays a role in language production, and moreover, that the gene might have resulted from a genetic mutation as recently as 100,000 years ago. This gene, FOXP2, is a member of a class of genes that promote the transcription of other genes from DNA to RNA, the "messenger" molecules involved in the chain of biochemical events that result in proteins. The human version of FOXP2 influences the development of brain structures (a region of the basal ganglia) that control facial movements involved in speech, among other motor functions. The putative language functions of the gene were identified through a disorder in a family in which half the members have severe articulation difficulties along with linguistics and grammatical impairments. It turned out that the affected members all have a mutated version of FOXP2 (Lai, Fisher, Hurst, Vargha-Khaden, & Monaco 2001).[41]

Other observations converge on the gene's language connection. Chimpanzees and other "dumb" primates, as well as mice, have variants of FOXP2 genes that differ from the human form by two or three critical amino acids out of a total of 715 (Enard et al., 2002). Thus the human variant emerged less than 200,000 years ago, when human and chimpanzee branches separated. Vocal-learning songbirds such as finches, canaries, song sparrows, and black capped chickadees, as well as parakeets, have FOXP2 genes that are almost identical (98%) with humans and expressed in the same brain area (the basal ganglia). A very different species thus shares a vocal "language" gene with humans (Haesler et al., 2004).

Such findings have fueled a continuing controversy concerning the genetic basis of language, with some scientists arguing that there are genes that control the

---

[41]The language connection and evolution of FOXP2 are conveniently reviewed in an internet article by Alec MacAndrew, May 29, 2004.

development of specialized grammar circuits in the brain, and others arguing for genetic control of general-purpose cognitive mechanisms, including ones important to language. All agree, however, that no single gene can be all-important in such a complex phenomenon as language. MacAndrew (2004) summarized the point as follows:

> No-one should imagine that the development of language relied exclusively on a single mutation in FOXP2. There are many other changes that enable speech [including the] profound anatomical changes that make the human supralaryngeal pathway entirely different from any other mammal. The larynx has descended so that it provides a resonant column for speech . . . Also, the nasal cavity can be closed thus preventing vowels from being nasalized and thus increasing their comprehensibility. These changes cannot have happened over such a short period as 100,000 years. Furthermore the genetic basis for language will be found to involve many more genes that influence both cognitive and motor skills. (p. 4)

My own views add to the aforementioned constraints on the genetic basis of language. First, human language is a communication system that does not depend exclusively on speech; sign language is an effective and complex communication system from which speech might have evolved, as discussed in the last chapter. Second, the genetic discussions generally neglect the essential role of nonverbal (environmental and cognitive) factors in the development and functioning of language as a communication system. The key to understanding the evolution of grammatical language is to identify the complex gene-environment interactions that account for the complex and flexible interplay of verbal and nonverbal systems in all human communication, between and within individuals, "within" referring to what we do when we think. That is another phrasing of my dual-coding refrain, on which I elaborate later.

What, then, might be the role of the FOXP2 gene as a part of the machinery of language? It is lies in the general motor-sequential basis of verbal processes emphasized throughout this volume. A recent study (Lai Gerrelli, Monaco, Fisher, & Copp, 2003) found a homologous pattern of expression in human and mouse variants of the FOXP2 gene that "argues for a role of this gene in development of motor-related circuits throughout mammalian species . . . [thus supporting] the hypothesis that impairments in sequencing of movement and procedural learning might be central to the FOXP2-related speech and language disorders" (Lai et al., 2003, p. 2455). That gets us to continuity theories of language evolution, where we find a similar emphasis on common cross-species mechanisms, ultimately converging on the importance of patterns of motor activity.

Continuity Theories of Language Evolution

Continuity theorists reject the idea that human language evolved discontinuously on the back of a brand new language organ. Givón (1998) found that the discussion of the evolution of language has brought together a bizarre version of neurological modularity [i.e., a newly-emerged left-cortical language organ] with an equally bizarre approach to discontinuous evolution. He instead proposed a specific version (described later in this chapter) of the general evolutionary-continuity view, applicable to language as well, that relatively small quantitative changes in several lower-level modules can produce a spectacular qualitative jump in the overall behavior. Even Stephen Pinker, whose 1994 volume, *The Language Instinct*, reflects his nativistic emphasis, was puzzled by Chomsky's argument that language is too complex to have emerged gradually along Darwinian lines. Like Givón, Pinker argued that evolutionary processes, operating over a long period of time, is the only reasonable explanation for the origins of complex biological systems, including those that underlie language.[42] Continuity theorists have looked for supporting evidence in communicative capacities of other species and from changes in human languages over time.

Let's be clear about what's at issue here. The origins of vocabulary and associative structures discussed in the last chapter are not the issue, although they need explaining. They belong to what Chomsky called the surface structure of language (later, external or E-language). Those characteristics vary across languages and everyone agrees that they are acquired gradually, both ontogenetically and phylogenetically. The descriptive and explanatory problems associated with E-language are simpler and less interesting to Chomsky and his followers than those associated with the deep structure of language (now internal or I-language). This inner language is characterized as being abstract, universal, and innate. Its core is a syntax machine that consists of abstract grammatical categories and rules that can generate an infinite number of grammatically acceptable sentences given a lexicon. Many such theories have been proposed since Chomsky's first attempt in 1957.

It is important to stress that the Chomsky-type syntax machine operates on abstract linguistic symbols to generate strings of such symbols, and that its relations to meaning and the nonverbal world are separate problems. Other theorists assume that such meaningful relations are what language is all about, and accordingly argue that Chomsky's theory is wrong, irrelevant, or at least incomplete. However brilliant, the theory is founded on an incorrect premise about natural language. Its realization as a brain module is also mysterious, as is its origin in the human species. Some alternative theories rely instead on different levels of associative structures, in which smaller structures are embedded in large ones, and different "permissible" arrangements are learned according to the language conventions of a society. Zelig Harris (1991), who was Chomsky's teacher, proposed such a theory, expressed in terms of mathematical information theory as a series of constraints on word combinations, each later constraint being defined on the resultants of a prior one: "This is not transitional probabilities between units such as words in sentences but rather dependence between word classes, or dependence on dependence because classes are defined by their dependence on other word classes" (p. 17). This is rather like

---

[42]Pinker and Jackendoff (2005) recently affirmed the continuity position in a thorough review of defining attributes of language. In particular, they disputed the hypothesis, proposed by Hauser, Chomsky, and Fitch (2002), that recursion is the only unique aspect of human language that appeared suddenly in human evolution.

continuous word associations where each succeeding word is determined probabilistically by all that has already been produced. Recursive center embedding
would still be a problem for such a theory, but it can be solved by including changing situational or imagery contexts as determining factors (discussed later). We turn
next to specific evidence on the different views of the evolution of syntatic skills.

SYNTACTIC SKILLS OF ANIMALS

Griffin (1976) found support for most of Hockett's design features of human language in the communicative systems of other species. These features include, for
example, use of the vocal-auditory channel, broadcast transmission, rapid fading,
and learning. At one time, chimpanzees showed the most promise of learning syntactic skills using sign language (e.g., Gardner & Gardner, 1975), but analyses of
the contexts in which the language was used suggested that the animals were
responding to subtle nonverbal cues inadvertently provided by the human teacher
rather than producing gestural sentences on the basis of syntactic skills (Terrace,
Petitto, Sanders, & Bever, 1979). The Gardners persuasively countered that critique
(e.g., Gardner & Gardner, 1985), but its negative impact nonetheless persisted, so
that interest in the possibility of teaching animals human language skills waned.
The interest has recently been rekindled by the success achieved with the three
species already mentioned in Chapter 12 in connection with vocabulary learning,
namely the grey African parrot, bottle-nose dolphin, and the bonobo (pygmy chimpanzee). The important general point is that all of these animals not only learned
substantial vocabularies but also learned to understand and produce complex syntactic patterns. The dolphins display comprehension by responding appropriately
to visual or auditory language patterns presented by their trainer, whereas the parrot and bonobo can produce as well as understand language.

Edward Kako (1999) evaluated the language skills of the animals in terms of four
"core properties" of syntax, including (a) use of discrete combinatorics, in which
parts are combined and recombined to produce new meaningful patterns; (b) category-based rules that specify how to combine classes of words to form phrases and
sentences; (c) argument structure—how many and what kinds of arguments or "participants" can be associated with different kinds of verbs; and (d) closed-class items
(grammatical terms as described earlier). Kako concluded that each of the three
species possesses at least some of the core properties. All have discrete combinatorial competence: they understand that the parts retain their identities in such combinations as *rose paper* (Alex), *pipe tail-touch* (the dolphins Ake and Phoenix interpret
this to mean "touch the pipe with your tail"), and hug + [gesture to person] (Kanzi's
expressed wish that the caretaker hug him). They have category-based rules that permit novel combinations, such as producing "rock corn" when given a dry kernel of
corn (Alex), carrying out novel commands to transport a frisbee through, over, or
under a hoop (Ake and Phoenix), and "Put the money in the mushroom" (Kanzi).
The dolphins and bonobo have some knowledge of argument structure: the dolphins

recognize that actions have two arguments (the dolphin and the object), whereas relations have three arguments (the dolphin, the transport object, and the destination object); Kanzi has an even richer knowledge of the relations between participants and actions. For example, "take the rock" and "get the rock" mean different things to him although rock has the same syntactic position in each. And he could respond correctly most of the time to reversed sentences such as "Take the potato outdoors" and "Go outdoors and get the potato," indicating that he understands both the meanings of the words and the relations between syntactic position and thematic role. Finally, the data suggested minimal, if any, knowledge of such closed-class items as articles, prepositions, tense markers, and plural markers.

What do the data have to say about the origins of such abilities? Kako (1999) concluded that "several of the core properties of human syntax lie within the grasp of other animals. Evolutionarily, this makes excellent sense: Modern human language could not have been created out of nothing, in a single massive mutation. Rather, it must have evolved in stages, each building on preexisting capacities" (p. 12). Thus, Kako favored a continuity position, which he interprets in terms of random mutations that integrated building blocks such as those displayed by the three species he reviewed and put them "collectively, to a new (and massively adaptive) purpose" (p. 12). He called for new studies to determine precisely which components of language are species specific.

The researchers whose work Kako (1999) reviewed responded in different ways. Pepperberg (1999) questioned the importance of determining whether any component of language is uniquely human, suggesting that specific ecological-evolutionary pressures determine whether a given species has or lacks human-like syntax. Herman and Uyeyama (1999) presented further evidence from their dolphin studies for the acquisition of concepts with closed-class functionality, and that such modeled subsets of human linguistic competence could derive from general cognitive mechanisms, rather than language-specific ones.

Shanker, Savage-Rumbaugh, and Taylor (1999) argued that ape language research has been marked by constantly shifting demands by those who feel that only humans can acquire language, and that Kako (1999) continues in this tradition in that, although he conceded that Kanzi has rudimentary syntactic skills, he nonetheless questioned whether he has morphosyntax. Shanker et al. suggested further that Kako's argument "proceeds from a generative preconception . . . that language is an autonomous, decontextualized. . . code" (p. 25), a preconception that inevitably led him to search for species-specific components of language and to enquire whether the non-human primate cortex has the neural structures to process the various subsystems of language. "But this way of framing the problem runs the risk of collapsing back into the modularity thesis. . . that the brain contains distinct language-processing centers and that language is a hierarchical system that is composed of distinct subsystems" (Shanker et al., 1999, p. 25). Their view instead is that language is always contextually embedded and that a child's or non-human primate's socioaffective, communicative, cognitive, and linguistic development depends on dyadic interaction. Accordingly, rather than asking about linguistic elements not yet mastered, it is more fruitful to focus on what exactly Kanzi can do and how this came about in the human environment in which he was raised.[43]

HISTORICAL EVIDENCE ON SYNTAX EVOLUTION

Bickerton (1990) proposed that syntactic language emerged rather suddenly (the discontinuity hypothesis) from an earlier protolanguage that lacked important syntactic characteristics. He found evidence for what such a protolanguage might have been like in the language of trained apes, children under 2, adults who have been deprived of language in their early years, and speakers of pidgin (a common language that develops when immigrants of different languages must communicate with each other). The mode of expression of all four groups is characterized by an absence of syntactic constraints on word order, omission of constituents from utterances, realization of the number and type of arguments of verbs, recursive mechanisms for expanding utterances, and infrequent and atypical use of grammatical items. This is a plausible description of early language but the evidence does not allow one to infer when and how it changed into syntactic language—the changes could have been piecemeal and cumulative over time rather than emerging together because they are controlled by an all-purpose syntactic language organ that suddenly loomed into existence. Pinker and Bloom (1990) also are advocates of innate grammars. Unlike Bickerton, however, they proposed that the biological correlates of Chomsky's Universal Grammar evolved gradually via Darwinian natural selection in a series of small steps—intermediate grammars that were useful to their possessors.

Linguist Bernard H. Bichakjian (1999) took a different approach from such nativistic views primarily because they are based on the popular linguistic assumption that all natural languages are equally complex, whether they belong to technologically advanced nations or to hunter-gatherer communities. Bichakjian distinguished between formal and functional complexity and presented historical evidence that linguistic features have consistently evolved by decreasing their complexity of form while increasing the complexity of their function.[44]

---

[43]There is an absence of abstract concepts in the records for Kanzi, that is, use of symbols for truth, justice, beauty, and so on. In response to my e-mail query about this, Stuart Shanker suggested that their absence may simply be a limitation of the lexigram board, which the investigators were in the process of modifying. I also wondered about the possibility of reflexive use of language. For example, could bonobos be taught to pick lexigrams that correspond to grammatical classes? Griffin (1976) had suggested that "we should ask ourselves whether, if it does occur in animals, any of our present methods of investigation would suffice to disclose it [reflectiveness]" (p. 37). Perhaps bonobos could serve as a test model given an appropriately-modified lexigram board.

[44]Bichakjian presumably took for granted that the hypothesis applies to a very recent period in language evolution. On logical grounds alone languages must have increased in complexity over eons of time, beginning with simple vocabulary and adding elements gradually, in the manner described in the last chapter. This would be analogous to biological evolution where more complex organs and organisms arise from simpler ones by modification or addition of parts, often in less than optimal ways.

A reduction in formal complexity is advantageous because simpler systems require less expenditure of neuromuscular resources and are learnable earlier in life, enabling children to get a head start in the development of social and mental skills. These advantages can only occur if functional capabilities are maintained at an equal or greater level as formal complexity decreases. The evidence for these changes comes from a study of linguistic developments in Indo-European languages, "which have the distinct advantage of having the greatest geographic spread [and] the best documented history . . ." (Bichakjian, 1999, p. 7). The data cover the linguistic range from phonology to syntax. I summarize the salient points, especially ones with implications for aspects of DCT addressed subsequently.

Phonological development of both consonants and vowels reflect the complexity-optimization process. The ancestral consonantal system included glottalized stops, and voiceless and voiced aspirates that do not have exact phonetic equivalents in modern French, but the total number of consonants is about the same. The number of consonant-vowel-consonant (CVC) roots that can be formed are much lower in the protolanguage, however, because of selection restrictions on how they can be combined (e.g., a root could not begin and end with a glottal consonant). In contrast, modern consonants can appear anywhere and be combined with any other in a CVC root and even with each other or after a vowel. Thus, the modern consonant system is much more functional than the ancestral one.

Similarly, the ancestral vowel system included a unique functional "e" combined with three different "h"-like sounds that did not change the vowel (this is known from modern Arabic, which retains the system). These also had distributional restrictions that disappeared when the ancestral laryngeals were replaced by modern vowels, which boosted the word building potential of the ancestral language. The modern consonants and vowels also entail a lower cost. For example, French toddlers can produce all their consonants before age 2, whereas Mayan children still have problems producing their glottal consonants past the age of 10, as do Arabic children in acquiring their equivalents of the ancestral laryngeal vowels.

Morphological development in the ancestral language eventually reached a state in which it had three genders and three numbers (singular, dual, and a more-than-two plural). These presumably served a useful purpose for our ancestors but have no linguistic function and are steadily disappearing from modern languages such as English. The retention of grammatical gender in some languages (e.g., the Romance languages, German, Russian) reflects conflicting psychological pressures that operate on other linguistic complexities as well, and are thus retained despite their less-than-optimal functionality.

The marking of grammatical distinctions also increased in efficiency as it evolved from vowel alternation to case suffixes to free particles—prepositions, articles, personal pronouns, and auxiliaries of time, voice, and mood. The free particles reduce complexity and increase organizational efficiency. Prepositions also are cost efficient in that they are learned earlier than the corresponding set of case endings of modern agglutinative languages, such as Hungarian and Finnish.

The most challenging examples of the form-function trade-off are syntactic developments involving temporal distinctions, the passive voice, and serial organization of speech. Historical scholars tell us that, in early protolanguage, only the active imperfect indicative had a past tense and that chronological distinctions were conveyed by aspectual distinctions of the verb. "The subject was always the 'present' author of an action either in progress or brought to an end, or the patient of a present state, but the action was never set in another time slot" (Bichakjian, 1999, p. 11); I suppose perhaps it was something like "I walking," "I walking yesterday (not today)," and "Walking yesterday I here". The development of the past tense, and later the future, enabled the mind to travel through time because the new verbal system was no longer compelled to force the account of events into a here and now presentation.

Note that this analysis of verb tense has startling implications for the sense of time that go beyond our discussion of that topic in Chapter 11. It implies that not only animals and preverbal hominids were locked in time, but so too were our verbal ancestors prior to the development of linguistic temporal distinctions. I presently evaluate that logical conclusion from Bichakjian's (1999) analysis and also address a related question that bears on the mnemonic function of language, namely how could a hominid scout have reported on what he remembers, using a language that has no verb tense? But first, back to Bichakjian's analysis of other aspects of syntax.

Early Indo-Europeans also did not have an active–passive syntactic opposition. Instead, action was viewed from two different perspectives of the agent, one that included an independent patient (e.g., I lay something down) and another in which the agent also was the seat of the action (I lie down, equivalent to I lay me down). This is understandable, said Bichakjian (1999), given that humans throughout their phylogenetic development beheld actions in terms of agent and patient. Thus only the agent could occupy the position that corresponds to subject of the verb. The development of a distinction between grammatical subject and grammatical object meant that any noun could serve as the subject, thereby greatly increasing the functionality of nouns and also enabling speakers to capture events from different vantage points. We see that this development, too, has implications for imagery and dual coding.

Finally, we consider two evolutionary changes in the serial organization of speech. One is the reordering of constituents in syntactic units and the other, a shift from free to fixed order. Protolanguage, Latin, and some modern languages use a head-last order in which an item that grammatically governs the other is typically placed after the item it governs (the modifier). Thus the Latin *victoriam reportavit* literally reads [a] victory [he] won. English and most modern Indo-European languages have reversed this to a head-first order: he won a victory. According to Bichakjian (1999), the change is important for perception and thought. The head-last order means that an utterance can only be interpreted globally, after the entire utterance has been heard, whereas the head-first order permits the interpretation to begin immediately and continue progressively as the modifiers unfold. The advantage of the head-first order increases with the length of the utterance because it taxes the working memory of speakers and listeners less than the head-last order. Consequently, it is argued, language evolution moves in the direction of the head-first order and becomes fixed in the subject-verb-object (SVO) order, the preferred sentence order in Indo-European languages.[45] The head-first model also gave rise to the technique of embedding subordinate clauses within sentences, which has enormous advantages in terms of minimizing memory load, increasing the potential for transmitting information, and eliminating the need to learn inflectional forms of verbs. This evolutionary picture is qualified by a variety of trade-offs, conflicting pressures, and "bushy patterns" that are common in biological evolution as well. One result is that there are as many head-last as head-first languages in the world today despite the overall advantages of the latter. In surviving, the head-last languages also have built on the adaptive potential within that pattern. For example, agglutination facilitates the processing of grammatical markers. I would speculate that the process of joining words (or words and suffixes) together is a kind of chunking technique that reduces memory load during sentence processing once the compounds and inflectional system have been learned, which entails a trade-off between learning time for mastering the system and possible memory advantages later.

In summary, Bichakjian (1999) rationalized the evolution of structural and functional aspects of the linguistic features of language. He also alluded to nonlinguistic perceptual influences on the origins and modifications of syntactic patterns and of the cognitive advantages of such changes. The final section of this chapter focuses directly on those nonlinguistic influences on the evolution of syntax.

MOTOR ACTIVITY, IMAGERY, AND SYNTAX

Many psychologists have proposed that the precursors to language development in the child are to be found in perceptual-motor skills (see Chapter 4). Paleoanthropologists and psychologists have extended this view to language evolution, including syntax (e.g., Greenfield, 1991; Leaky & Lewin, 1978, p. 218; Reynolds; 1976). Reynolds (1976) took the view that "a language is a phylogenetic derivative of the skilled motor system. It is a system of communication that requires the skilled motor system not only for its acquisition but for its ordinary expression" (p. 162). He used stratificational grammar (sentences are analyzed hierarchically in terms of constituents embedded within larger constituents) to describe the dyadic social play in rhesus monkeys, revealing among other things how the activity involves recursive embedding of activities within larger activity patterns. Patricia Greenfield (1991) argued that language and tool use share an underlying cognitive basis in the capacity to complete object manipulation tasks that involve the completion of subassemblies for combination into larger objects.

---

[45]Bichakjian presumably took for granted that the hypothesis applies to a very recent period in language evolution. On logical grounds alone languages must have increased in complexity over eons of time, beginning with simple vocabulary and adding elements gradually, in the manner described in the last chapter. This would be analogous to biological evolution where more complex organs and organisms arise from simpler ones by modification or addition of parts, often in less than optimal ways.

   Givón (1998) questioned whether manual tool-use routines are a crucial
evolutionary link to language. He pointed out that prehuman primates have equally
complex prelinguistic hierarchic activity routines in foraging, hunting, and so on but
which are more abstract than, tool-use and tool-making. He noted further that the
proto-grammatical skills that seem to be present in the human-taught linguistic
behavior of prehuman primates (Greenfield & Savage-Rumbaugh, 1991) are also
much more abstract than tool use. A possible response is that increasing abstraction
is part of behavioral evolution. For example, chimpanzees' use of twigs for termite
fishing entails hierarchical behavioral structuring that is less complex and less
abstract than play activity. Importantly, play is abstract in the sense that it entails
symbolic ("pretend") behavior, thus moving it closer to the fully symbolic nature of
language. Whether motor skills are crucial links to language evolution depends,
however, on whether we define those skills narrowly as motor only or more generally as part of internal perceptual-motor systems that guide action. My dual coding interpretation is that motor skills alone are a necessary but not a sufficient link
to syntax. The necessary and sufficient link is to be found in dynamic imagery.
   The role of imagery in the origins and development of language is occasionally
mentioned in the evolutionary literature. Leakey and Lewin (1978) wrote that " . . .
a complex of evolutionary pressures must have conspired to put words into the
mouths of our ancestors, but almost certainly one of them was the advantage of
being able to create better pictures in their heads" (p. 204). It isn't easy to interpret
this apparently simple statement but, loosely speaking, it implies that imagery preceded language and that language arose partly in the service of imagery. It says
nothing about the opposite possibility that imagery might have shaped up language
and put better words in our mouths. So too in the case of Bickerton's (1990) suggestion that images had to be organized by syntactic mechanisms. Byrne (1995) proposed that "The ability to imagine different viewpoints is a necessary precursor to
language, and it certainly evolved first" (p. 233). He was referring to a kind of mind
reading, the ability to interpret situations from another person's perspective, which
must have been a rather late development based on imagery. He does not otherwise
mention imagery in relation to language or other contexts. These and other brief statements recognize that imagery has some role in language evolution but the statements
are fragmentary or vague—understandably so, because they are not based on any general theory that deals with both imagery and language in a systematic and comprehensive way.

A Dual Coding Theory of Syntax Evolution

My theoretical analysis of how imagery and dual coding influenced the evolution
of syntax is an analogical extension of the DCT approach to language development
in children, reviewed earlier. As a reminder, the following are the main points:
(a) Language development depends initially on a substrate of imagery derived from
the child's observations and behaviors related to concrete objects and events, and
relations among them; (b) language builds on this foundation and remains interlocked

with it as referential connections are being formed, so that the child responds to object names in the presence or absence of the objects, and begins to name and describe them (even in their absence); (c) the events, relations, and behaviors are dynamically organized (repeated with variations) and thereby display natural syntax that gets incorporated into the imagery as well; (d) the natural syntax is enriched by motor components derived from the child's actions, which have their own patterning; (e) This basic stage becomes elaborated as function words are acquired and intra-verbal networks expand through usage; and (f) abstract verbal skills are eventually attained, so that language becomes relatively autonomous, free of dependence on situational contexts and imagery. In brief, "the grammars first learned by children will be 'tied to' the syntax of concrete objects and events . . . via the medium of imagery . . . and only later will more abstract grammars emerge" (Paivio, 1971b, pp. 437–438).

The relevant evidence (Chapter 4) came from research on the effects of referential contexts on learning foreign languages, miniature artificial languages, and language learning by children with learning difficulties. The hypothesis was most directly supported by Moeser and Bregman's (1973) experiment on a miniature artificial grammar that was learned with and without syntax-correlated referents. Participants who received different sentence exemplars presented only as "word" strings showed no learning after 3,200 trials. Those who saw the sentences along with syntax-correlated referent pictures showed rapid learning, and could subsequently learn new instances from verbal contexts alone. The authors noted that the results were consistent with predictions from my dual coding analysis of syntax learning.

The empirical evidence provides grounds for extending the developmental hypothesis to the evolution of syntax. The analysis assumes the background discussed in the last chapter, namely that our evolving speakers had referential and associative structures and processing capacities that enabled them to name objects and events, image to the names, and generate words as associates to other words. The imagery could be in any modality, dynamic as well as static, and mediated emotion and action. A system so complex can go a long way toward explaining how our ancestors acquired a meaningful protolanguage as described, for example, by Bickerton (1990), but it needs to be elaborated to accommodate syntax. Moreover, we need to consider the adaptive significance of syntactic features and their evolution.

Nowak, Plotkin, and Jansen (2000) proposed a mathematical model of the evolution of syntactic communication that is based on assumptions very similar to those of DCT. The general idea is that syntactic communication evolved because it led to higher adaptive fitness than nonsyntactic communication. It is useful for individuals to communicate about events in the world around them—correct communication confers a fitness advantage to the interacting individuals. Events are combinations of objects, places, times, and actions, simplified in the model to combinations of objects and actions. Nonsyntactic communication uses words for events, whereas syntactic communication uses words for objects and actions—nouns and verbs that combine into sentences. These arbitrary meanings of the words are acquired by interaction between people who already know the words and those who do not. It is relatively more difficult to learn syntactic signals because the relation to other signals (e.g., that words are nouns or verbs) must be learned along with the relation to events. However, the model shows that the maximum number of nonsyntactic signals is more limited than the number of syntactic signals because all words have to be learned, but syntactic signals enable the formulation of "new" sentences (new noun–verb combinations) that have not been learned beforehand. Thus, the model suggests that

> . . . the crucial step that guided the transition from non-syntactic to syntactic communication was an increase in the number of relevant events that could be referred to. "Relevant event" means there is a fitness contribution for communication about this event. As the number of such relevant communication topics increased, natural selection could begin to favour syntactic communication and therefore lead to a language design where messages could be formulated that were not learned beforehand, (Nowak et al., 2000, pp. 497–498)

Note that the model focuses on the creative power of syntax that Chomsky emphasized, but unlike in Chomsky, the model depends on an increase in communication topics—the number of relevant events—and not only recombinations of elements in an autonomous syntax for creativity to emerge in an evolving language. The model resembles DCT precisely in its emphasis on nonverbal influences on syntactic evolution. However, it does not have some of the specific features of the dual coding approach, especially the latter's emphasis on the internalization of perceptual events in an imagery system before meaningful words or syntax are acquired. Such details would be irrelevant in the mathematical model but are essential for a full understanding of the DCT approach to syntax evolution.

Bichakjian's (1999) analysis provided additional fuel for the dual coding approach through his emphasis on the early origins of agent-patient structures from observation of such relations in nature, beneficial effects of grammatical changes on cognition (e.g., of tense markers on the sense of time), energy savings (e.g., ease of learning) that result from simplification of syntax. Also relevant is Bickerton's (1990, p. 74) reference to "the vast increments in cognitive capacity" that result when thoughts come into being and are organized by the formal properties of syntax. Thus, Bichakjian and Bickerton seem to be at opposite poles on this issue in that Bichakjian alluded to origins of syntax and thought in the organization of natural events, whereas Bickerton saw the origins and evolution of "serious" thinking in linguistic syntax, which came into being autonomously and precipitously. Bickerton's view is a strong form of linguistic determinism in the evolutionary context, but it does not explain why or how syntax evolved; it simply happened.

I turn to a more detailed application of DCT to the evolutionary issues. The fitness of syntax must relate in some way to the mnemonic role of language that was our point of departure in the last chapter. In this context, syntactic properties became part of language because they can activate useful memories of relevant events in both listener and speaker in the absence of the perceptual events themselves. The selective pressures for syntactic language behavior came originally from natural events that were already internalized in the nonverbal representational structures of the interlocutors. According to this analysis, meaning came before syntax in that memory images, actions, and emotions are the meaningful residues of experience that must already exist in the mind if they are to be captured by language. The nonverbal meanings include event structures that reflect the affordances (uses) of things, which eventually become correlated with the evolving syntax of language because it helps activate memories of those affordances. Syntactic language can also guide the reorganization and transformation of nonverbal memories, as in the case of interactive imagery instructions. These linguistic powers were an intrinsic part of language syntax as it evolved to accommodate the variable states and affordances of perceptual objects and their nonverbal memory representations. Thus, syntax evolution was a bootstrapping process that reflected the effects of the interplay of verbal and nonverbal representational systems as they expanded through the cumulative experiences of successive generations. This analysis is consistent with Bichakjian (1999) and the Nowack et al. (2000) model, but goes beyond them in psychological details.

The concept of attention also becomes important in the dual coding analysis. An observer attends preferentially to some aspect of a scene or soundscape. The focus of attention is determined by salient features of perceptual objects and events. We saw earlier that infants and animals first attend to things that move, especially animate objects. We notice flickering lights, new sounds, and any other kind of change from a steady state, including figures that "stand out" from their backgrounds (the figure-ground relation so dear to Gestalt psychologists). If we have been attending to something, our attention shifts readily to any novel event. Attention is also determined by what is important to the observer: a mother wakes up to the tiniest cry of her baby while the father sleeps on; similarly, at a cocktail party, we readily hear our name against the background of noise. The salient changes often involve memory—we notice what is different from a moment ago or from yesterday. And, importantly for us, we focus on different aspects of our mental images just as we do in perception.

The concept of attention has also been prominent in analyses of language processing under such labels as the focus, topic, and perspective, which relate particularly to factors that determine the starting point and sequential order of processing. MacWhinney (1977) proposed a general perspective hypothesis, according to which both the choice of a starting point in production and the use of a starting point in comprehension are determined by processes involved in the active construction of a perspective. The preferred starting points are based on the persons' interactions with the world and they include the kinds of attentional factors summarized earlier—figures (rather than grounds), entities that are active and potent as opposed to passive and less potent, earlier events in a causal chain of events, and (sometimes) starting points that are high in imagery value, among others. The starting point is also influenced by linguistic contextual factors, such as order of mention in a description or what is emphasized in questions that elicit an utterance.

Here, attentional focus, movement, and perspective are especially relevant to sequential order effects that are defined as syntactic, namely active versus passive and hierarchically embedded structures; or, in terms of transformational grammars, passivization and recursion. The dual coding view is that these order effects originated and evolved from a nonverbal base of perception, action, and imagery, interacting along the way with their verbal correlates as they emerged. We must work backward again from our understanding of these syntactic effects in contemporary language processing. Much research has been done on variables that influence comprehension and production of actives and passives. The active order is normally preferred because it is based on the tendency for perceptual attention to move preferentially from potent agents to the objects (patients) affected by the agent's actions. The passive order is induced by factors that focus attention initially on the patient, so that, in production,the logical object becomes the grammatical subject. In comprehension, passives should elicit imagery that begins sequentially with the logical object.

The predicted effect has been observed in comprehension. Sheila Jones (1982) asked adults to draw pictures that would best represent the information in sentences. The fact that half the sentences were active and half passive was not mentioned to the participants. As predicted from a perceptual hypothesis, she found a significant preference for placing the logical object to the left of logical subjects in passive sentences, such as "The wine is being served by the waiter." There was no positional preference in drawings to active sentences, such as "The waiter is serving the wine." She interpreted the differences to mean that active sentences serve as a neutral (directionally "unmarked") base by reference to which the directionally-marked passive takes on its significance. Be that as it may, the directional bias in passive-induced drawings supports an imagery-focus or perspective interpretation in that, according to DCT, drawing is mediated by perceptual-motor information in the imagery system. MacWhinney (1977, p. 153) also noted that informants often report images that reflect the different perspectives induced by the different starting points in actives and passives.

The perceptual hypothesis has not been clearly supported in production studies in that manipulations of perceptual contexts in ways designed to elicit passives have failed to do so. However, the effect has been obtained when a linguistic context accompanies the perceptual one. For example, showing children a picture of a snake and then a turtle did not get them to produce a passive like "A snake is followed by a turtle." Passives were produced only when the eliciting pictures were preceded by a model picture and passive model sentence (Turner & Rommetveit, 1967, cited in MacWhinney, 1977, p. 160). MacWhinney (1977) concluded that the normal human perspective is active rather than passive and that passivization seems to require linguistic contextual effects.

The production results seem problematic for the hypothesis that passives evolved from a nonverbal perceptual base. They suggest instead a linguistic origin for passives which, once developed, could influence attentional focus in perception and imagery. However, an alternative interpretation follows directly from DCT and the hypothesized importance of memory in language evolution.

The argument is as follows. Assume first of all that the perceptual processing of our early ancestors was influenced by the factors that are now known to affect focus of attention and point of view. Thus, they would have focused first on active and potent agents in event sequence that also involved, say, an instrument and patient. However, either of the last two could be processed first if they have salient perceptual properties in a given context. Suppose that an observer wanted to describe an event to another person in her best protolanguage. The mnemonic hypothesis implies that such a description is communicatively more useful in the absence of the event than in its presence. Thus, the speaker could describe the event while observing it or from memory, but in either case, the listener can't see the event. Assume further that the speaker's utterances are order-free, much as in early Latin. Suppose, for example, that she describes a remembered event in which a man hit a bear with a club. The description could be "Man club bear" (the verbalized instrument is familiar in contemporary speech), "Club man bear, or Bear club [by] man". The listener's imagery could be similarly variable and her comprehension uncertain because she did not observe the original events. Her signs of puzzlement ("questions") cause the speaker to try different sequences accompanied by appropriate gestures (cf. McNeill, 1992). Let's say that "Man club bear" accompanied by a hitting gesture is the most effective sequence in that the listener vigorously nods her understanding. The successful sequence (perhaps the gestural cues, too) would tend to be repeated by the speaker when describing similar events from similar perspectives in the future. Active constructions would thus be reinforced and become favored in speech.

The same analysis is applicable to descriptions of event sequences that the observer originally perceived so that her attention was on the patient (the bear) and she then wanted to describe the events from that perspective. By the same trial and error process just described, the passive construction might be communicatively most successful, and accordingly, would tend to be used again under analogous circumstances in the future.

In summary up to this point, the evolutionary mechanisms consist of reinforced learning at the individual level and Darwinian cultural evolution over generations. Memory is the engine that drives the changes because the adaptive value of syntactic devices lies especially in what they do for the efficiency of communicating about events in their absence, or at least not observable by the listener, who must accordingly rely on memory images evoked by the speaker. (This fanciful interpretation can easily be extended to take account of situations in which speaker and listener both observe an event, and the speaker might say, "[Look] man hit bear!"). Once started, the successful communicative forms generalize to new instances, mediated analogically by similarities of perceptual-motor events as well as the verbal patterns that describe those events, as in the second phase of the Moeser and Bregman (1973) experiment described earlier (110–111). The analysis also explains the role of verbal context on syntactic choice—in this case, the listener shapes up the speaker's use of the active or passive voice. The speaker, too, might begin to modify her internal verbalization to the perceived events so as to emphasize what is perceptually salient, thereby affecting her later description of the scene.

The same analysis is applicable in principle to embedded and recursivae structures. We have seen that scenes, events, and skilled behaviors have hierarchical structures. One can focus on different objects or their parts and move around so as to view them from different perspectives. The hierarchical structure can be described beginning with any object from any viewpoint, but changing the sequence midstream to enhance descriptive clarity. An event sequence also has hierarchical structure, which can be described so as to focus on different aspects of the same dynamic scene. Suppose you see a boy across the street. He has red hair, he is carrying a puppy, and he is walking. The descriptive sequence would depend on what aspect you want to emphasize to your listener—red hair, puppy, or walking— which would be determined by prior events and the situational context. In this example, the description serves to discriminate among perceptual alternatives, but the events could be entirely in memory. At a conference I might say to a colleague, "The psychologist we met yesterday—remember, the one with the grey beard?—is speaking today." My colleague might reply, "Oh yes, that's Professor Smith from X university." My recursive description is based on hierarchically organized imagery and focuses on aspects that are designed to evoke relevant imagery in my colleague, and he replies according to the aroused imagery.

It is reasonable to suppose that the recursive language skills of our ancestors evolved because they were similarly useful to them. Speakers focused on aspects of complex perceived or remembered events that were relevant to them and other members of the community. Gradually, over generations, those aspects were coded linguistically by building on existing vocabulary along with existing expressive and comprehension skills. The grammar could thus have begun as minimal embedded structures such as red berry,[46] in which redness is a part of berry (note in this example how associations merge into grammar) and saying red berry serves to distinguish the referent from, say, blue berry. Further similar structures could develop by analogy, and extended to include more embedded elements, such as red mountain berry as distinguished from, say, red forest berry. Some optimal level might have been reached at which an embedded expression most effectively evokes an organized "gestalt" image for the listener, as compared to what can be evoked by stringing out the parts sequentially. Presumably, the mechanisms again entailed reinforcement of hierarchical organization of speech by feedback in the form of "comprehension" cues from individual listeners, and cultural evolution of such language structures over generations.

Most other syntactic variables entail grammatical morphemes and words (in addition to word order changes in the case of questions). I comment on these generally and then deal with one variable in more depth. The important general point is that all of the grammatical markers could have been learned only because they were based on existing, nonverbal, perceptual-motor knowledge. Thus linguistic plurality, possession, negation, and relational terms have nonverbal correlates. Questions have correlates in uncertainties involved in identifying, locating, and remembering

---

[46]The plausibility of this conjecture for early humans is shown by the fact that, in a vocabulary test, even a cross-fostered chimpanzee (Tatu) spontaneously signed "red berry" for a picture of cherries (Gardner & Gardner, 1985, p. 168).

useful information about things or situations, and, as already discussed, the uncertainties might have been expressed originally as signs of puzzlement, which evolved into grammatical questions. Even the variants of the subjunctive mood have correlates in the imagined outcomes associated with wishes, suggestions, possibilities, uncertainties, conditionals, and so on. Animals readily learn to respond conditionally. For example, rats learn to press a lever for food only when a light is on, behavior that we have already discussed as mediated by food-imagery elicited by the light. Partial reinforcement schedules ensure that food is only a possible outcome of the response, equivalent to, "If I do this now, I might get what I want." The imagined possibilities and uncertainties eventually developed linguistic correlates. The evolutionary point simply extends what has often been written about language learning in the child (e.g., Hebb et al., 1971; Macnamara, 1972; Snow, 1977), the ontogeny-phylogeny recapitulation argument coupled with what is logically compelling.

I turn now to grammatical tense and its implications for the dual coding interpretation of the psychological sense of time. Recall Bichakjian's (1999) historical analysis of language evolution in which he proposed that the development of the past and future tenses allowed the mind to travel back and forth in time. The strong implication is that cognitive time travel depended on the emergence of grammatical tense. But that is unlikely because our ancestors must already have had the concepts of past, present, and future in a useful form prior to acquiring linguistic markers for them. This was discussed in Chapter 11 in terms of memory images of repeated past events, which also has become anticipatory images of future events that could mediate adaptive preparatory behaviors. The time sense became greatly extended and refined with the invention of devices for recording and measuring time, and of linguistic means for describing the natural and artefactual variables that define psychological time. The instruments and vocabulary enriched our sense of time, building on a more rudimentary but useful time sense based on environmental and biological changes to which all living things must adapt to survive, and, in which imagery plays a crucial role. In a nutshell, time-related imagery was a necessary precursor to grammatical tense—without imagery, there would be no past or future tense.

Finally, I touch on reflexivity as a design feature that appears to be unique to human language. When and how did this begin? Perhaps it began early in vocabulary development when our superstitious ancestors equated words and things, a confusion that still plagues our thinking according to general semanticists (e.g., Hayakawa, 1949; Korzybski, 1933). If so, using language to talk about thing-words was a simple extension of talking about things. Two other, perhaps more important, influences were the invention of writing and grammatical analysis. It is easy to treat visual symbols as referents and thus to talk (or write) about them. And parsing and all later forms of grammatical analysis are reflexive by definition and associated with, if not entirely dependent on, written language. That is, abstract labels are needed for grammatical units, classes, structures, and processes to talk about language, and it is easier to have those when language is written and not only spoken. This would explain why reflexivity is unique to humans, and it also suggests that Kanzi and his bonobo kin might acquire that design feature given experience with lexigrams for grammatical descriptors.

The next chapter begins a less speculative final section of the volume, which deals with culturally evolved "peak mind" as manifested in expert skills, creativity, and "genius" in all its splendid forms. The analyses are a further extension of DCT, but speculation is minimized because the evidence is currently available in the results of empirical studies and biographical analyses of recent or living "specimens."

IV

PEAK EVOLVED MIND AND PERFORMANCE

CHAPTER FOURTEEN

Introduction to Expertise: A Dual Coding Perspective

At the turn of the millenium, Time/Life published lists of the 100 most eminent people and 100 most influential events during the previous 1,000 years. The eminent people included inventor Thomas Edison who lighted the world; scientists Galileo, Newton, Darwin, Einstein, Madame Curie, and Freud who changed our conceptions of the universe and our place in it; writers like Shakespeare and Dante who entertained us and stimulated our imagination; and artists and musicians such as Michaelangelo, Picasso, and Beethoven who gave us beauty that continues to leave us speechless. The achievers' list also includes Roger Bannister, who for the first time in human history ran the mile in under 4 min. It did not change our lives but it did forever lift what was long thought to be a ceiling on human performance in athleticism. The influential achievements included Gutenberg's invention of the printing press and other notable events that broadened our horizons and enriched our lives in countless ways.

These acknowledged "geniuses" and discoveries exemplify the summit of what evolution has enabled our species to achieve. They are benchmarks of what is humanly possible without a commitment to the nativistic connotations of "genius." The genetic base of mind has not changed much over the brief period since the beginning of the big intellectual bang. What has changed dramatically is human culture, which evolved from the genetic base and provided the niches that protected and nourished the individuals who made further growth possible. We admire such individuals and perhaps envy them for their fame and fortune. And so we want to know more about what they are like and how they got that way. Perhaps at the end of the day we will conclude, as many do, that it's all just natural talent—some people have it and the rest of us don't. But that's a refuge of ignorance that is not acceptable to all students of human intellect and performance. I draw on their expertise in my analyses of the frontiers of cognition and performance.

DCT continues to serve as the lens through which we examine and interpret expert skills, intelligence, and creativity. Studying the skills involved in playing a musical instrument or game is interesting in its own right and potentially relevant to the understanding of more complex intellectual domains such as science because the latter can be interpreted as involving collections of specific skills (Fischer, 1978; Wood 1983). As for intelligence, everyone has some rough and ready operational definition in terms of general measures such as school grades and IQ test scores, although, as we see later, the scientific definitions vary greatly. It suffices for now to think of intelligence as a collection of cognitive skills or abilities. Creativity implies further that the skillful behavior and intelligence, or their products, have a degree of originality that is valued by others and tend to generate advances in their domains—new artistic styles, inventions, scientific theories, and so on. The dual coding framework is used to analyze the various skills and abilities that character- ize high achievers, however defined. Before turning to those topics, however, I put them in the context of background issues that run thematically through all them.

OPERATIONAL DEFINITIONS AND EVIDENCE

The benchmark of advanced skill, intelligence, and creativity is the performance of elite achievers—individuals publicly recognized as being outstanding in sports, sci- ence, technology, arts, and skilled activities of all kinds. The operational definition of achievement is completely objective when it can be quantified by direct mea- sures of accuracy, speed, or quantity. Typing skill is a familiar example. Others are based on a combination of objective performance (e.g., completion of targeted jumps in figure skating) and subjective evaluation by expert judges (who judge the artistic merit of the skating routine as a whole). The criteria are mostly subjective in the case of music, painting, and other performance arts. There is a subjective ele- ment even in the definition of scientific achievement in that editorial referees judge the quality of contributed papers, committees decide who gets a Nobel prize, and so on. Even original discoveries can languish unnoticed until someone judges them to be important to the solution of a larger puzzle. Ultimately, eminence is defined by the cumulative impact of the work of the high achievers on the work and lives of others.

The sources of evidence for analyses of causes and correlates of peak achieve- ment are biographies, psychometric tests, experiments, and combinations of these. Achievers and skill domains have been analyzed using informed interpre- tations of individual biographies, quantitative historical methods (historiometrics; e.g., Simonton, 1997), historical-philosophical treatises on advances in science (e.g., Miller, 1984, on physics), and questionnaire and interview studies of the experiential backgrounds of high achievers. Psychometric instruments have probed their cogni- tive abilities and personality traits. Neuropsychologists have considered brain struc- tures and processes that might differentiate them from ordinary achievers. And there is an increasing use of experimental methods to study creative skills. This analytic approach draws on all such sources of published evidence.

BASIC ISSUES

Three general issues run thematically through the subsequent topics as they did in the preceding evolutionary chapters. These center on the roles of nature versus nurture, memory, and motivation in the climb to peak levels of achievement.

Nature Versus Nurture

Over the years, I often debated the origins of genius with colleagues who argued that the achievements of the Mozarts, Shakespeares, and Einsteins of the world are due to some mysterious factor X that is largely inborn and that experience is a necessary but not a sufficient condition to account for the large gap between their achievements and those of the rest of us. How would you know, I asked, given that their genes are completely confounded with their stimulating environments? This debate is familiar to everyone, and most debaters would agree that some talents are largely genetic in origin.

The most influential modern source of that belief was Sir Francis Galton's 1869 book, *Hereditary Genius*. Using biographical data, Galton (a cousin of Charles Darwin) showed statistically that eminent people have more eminent relatives in various fields than is the proportion in the British population at large. Galton recognized that this could be interpreted to mean only that eminence runs in families, but he concluded instead that the differences are due mainly to hereditary dispositions that included natural ability, zeal, and the capacity to work hard. Exercise, study, and education are necessary for high achievement but nature sets a rigid limit on the maximum level of performance that can be attained. The superstars rise higher because nature gave them more of the right stuff.

This remains the popular societal view of the wellspring of peak achievement and it is usually based on the same kind of ambiguous evidence, especially child prodigies who come from families that provided early opportunities to develop the skills for which the children came to be noted. Experience and heredity are thoroughly confounded in such cases, although analysts have tried to disentangle the two sources by contrasting the meteoric rise of some high achievers with those whose achievements remain modest despite lofty aspirations and hard work. The interpretive uncertainties are not resolved by such selective anecdotal comparisons.

Scientific studies have compared identical twins with fraternal twins and nontwin siblings, raised in the same or different homes, yielding heritability estimates which suggest that about 50% of the variability in intellectual skills can be accounted for by genetic factors. The meaning of such estimates is uncertain, however, especially in light of recent evidence on the origins of expert skills, which I review after restating my empiricist views on the general issue.

Earlier chapters emphasized that the representations and processes that are the basis of cognition and performance derive from modality-specific perceptual-motor experience. It follows that advanced cognitive and performance skills depend on a rich representational foundation in the relevant areas of expertise, which in turn depends directly on the amount of relevant perceptual-motor experience. This is conventional wisdom for learning theorists and some students of cognitive abilities. For example, in the classical model of creativity proposed by Wallas (1926), the preparatory phase of the creative process entails the development of a broad knowledge base in the creative domain. DCT puts more weight on experiential than hereditary factors in the growth of intellect because its contents must be learned.

The argument that "geniuses" are born and not made can only be interpreted to mean, as Galton intended, that some people have the genetic potential to acquire intellectual and performance skills faster or with less relevant experience than others, but experience is necessary nonetheless. The question is how much and what kind of experience is needed for peak achievement.

Transfer of Learning.   George Ferguson (1954, 1956) proposed a flexible version of the traditional approach together with a theory of how different abilities arise through transfer of learning. He defined abilities as patterns of behavior which, through overlearning, have reached a crude limit of performance in adults and show considerable stability over shorter time periods in children. Biological factors fix limiting conditions but learning has a substantial influence within those limits. Cultural factors determine what will be learned at what age, and variations in those factors lead to different patterns of ability. Abilities emerge through transfer of learning that has different effects in different situations and at different stages of learning. Thus, positive transfer of specific skills across similar situations produces the high correlations between tests that define abilities of some level of generality. Ferguson elaborated on the concept of transfer, problems associated with the definition of similarity, and other issues that need not detain us here. As evidence for the theory, Ferguson (1956, pp. 127–129) cited experiments showing substantial and systematic changes in the factor structure of a learning task with continued practice, so that abilities involved at one stage differ from those involved at another. Other studies showed markedly different ability patterns for children reared in relatively isolated regions as compared to urban communities. Ferguson's theory has been favorably received by other students of cognitive abilities (e.g., Carroll, 1993; Guilford, 1967; Hunt, 1961), and it is especially compatible with this approach when qualified by recent evidence.

Scientific advances in the area of expert skills, reviewed in the next chapter, has lifted the implicit ceiling on the degree to which abilities can be changed through deliberate practice. The "crude limit" suggested by Ferguson implies that intensive learning could refine or polish the rough edges of performance, but it now appears that abilities at their highest level are much more than mere refinements of relatively stable limits in the population at large. Instead, they entail cumulative changes that build up gradually from undistinguished beginnings to performance levels that ultimately reach the seemingly "unreachable stars." Ferguson (1956) perhaps anticipated that possibility in a general way in concluding that, "Although it is conceded that biological factors fix certain boundaries, all the evidence seems to suggest that the range of variation that results from learning is, indeed, very great" (p. 130).

Ferguson's (1956) emphasis on the importance of cultural values on abilities also has a parallel in the expert skills literature. For example, the kind of music that is taught at a given period shapes the musical skills acquired by the experts at that time. Whereas Ferguson emphasized qualitative differences in patterns of abilities, the skills literature emphasizes both qualitative and quantitative changes in expert skills over generations, which result from technical advances, expansion of settings in which skilled activities (e.g., music, sports) can be performed, opportunities for being rewarded for surpassing standards set by others, and so on. The net effect has been a ratcheting upward of skills so that, today, amateur musicians routinely perform pieces once considered too difficult for all but the most elite performers, and amateur athletes easily surpass the records set by Olympic gold medalists a century ago. All reflect cultural evolution, changes in social factors that determine the kinds of skills learned, how well they are learned, and even the manner in which they are learned. Let us turn to that literature.

Deliberate Practice.   The relevant research was sparked by a collaborative study of chess expertise by Nobel laureate Herbert Simon and his colleague William Chase (Simon & Chase, 1973).[47] They concluded from their study that 10 years of intense preparation is necessary to reach the level of an international chess master, and suggested further that similar requirements might apply to other domains. That suggestion has been amply confirmed.

K. Anders Ericsson and his colleagues (e.g., Ericsson & Charness, 1994; Ericsson, Krampe, & Tesch-Römer, 1993) investigated implications of the experiential hypothesis. The question they asked was, how did elite performers in a variety of fields get to the top? The samples included professional musicians, chess players, and athletes from several sports. Background information was obtained on starting age, parental and teacher influences, practice habits, and so forth. Detailed information was obtained in two studies of piano and violin performers. Typically, these experts started early in life under the encouragement and guidance of one parent, usually the mother, then professional teachers, and eventually enrolment in prestigious music schools. Throughout, the developing musician devoted much time to deliberate practice of skill routines recommended by the teachers. Ericsson et al. (1993) compared the experiential histories and progress of these aspiring professionals with less skilled professional musicians and dedicated amateurs.

The results showed that the progress and eventual achievement level was a direct function of time spent at practicing skills under the guidance of teachers and alone. The researchers referred to this background experience collectively as deliberate practice, as compared to time spent simply playing as amateurs typically do. Ten or more years of deliberate practice was required to attain peak expertise. This means that the earlier the start the better the results as long as practice continued.

The developmental picture was the same for other areas of expertise. Chess is particularly informative because achievement levels can be precisely quantified from competition records kept worldwide. As in the case of musicians, the levels

---

[47]Simon, a psychologist, was awarded the Nobel prize for his contribution to the area of economics.

attained are a monotonic function of cumulative deliberate practice, so that late starters do not catch up with early starters. The same conclusion emerged from studies of high achievers in sports, mathematics, science, the arts, and other fields (Ericsson, 1996).

What were the contribution from other sources, including possible hereditary factors? Essentially none, in the sense that almost all of the variance in level of achievement was accounted for by experiential variables that converged on opportunities for and implementation of deliberate practice. Even absolute pitch, often cited as a prototypical innate ability, is acquired relatively easily by young children given musical training. This is the most surprising general conclusion, one that has been disputed (e.g., Gardner, 1995). Ericsson and Charness (1995) responded by saying in effect, show us the evidence. They pointed out that physical height (more generally, long-bone length) is the only characteristic for which heredity is a major determinant. Other characteristics such as anatomical and physiological properties of muscles, hands, and brain are strongly shaped by the amount of experience in relevant skill domains. The constraints on achievement other than environmental opportunities are those that limit individual practice time—fatigue or injury to crucial body parts, and maintaining motivation during long stretches of solo practice. Elite performers have routines that minimize fatigue and injury. Maintaining motivation is a greater puzzle, for which DCT offers a specific solution, as we see later.[48]

The nature-nurture issue comes up again in Chapter 16, on theories of general intelligence. What is most notable at this point is the overriding effect of the amount and quality of experience, including deliberate practice, related specifically to a given area of expertise—experience necessary for the development of perceptual-motor systems used in music, chess, mathematics, sciences, sports, and other domains; systems that include all of the functional structures that make up multimodal verbal and nonverbal representations. All are long-term memory structures that result from domain-specific "memory work." It is especially fitting, therefore, that memory itself has been studied as a skill domain in which expertise can be acquired through deliberate practice (more about that in Chapter 15), which raises once again the question of the nature and adaptive role of memory.

---

[48]Over the years, critics have argued that Ericsson and his colleagues have not sufficiently considered the overwhelming evidence for the influence of heredity on talent differences. Ericsson, Nandagopal, and Roring (2005) have responded by presenting reasons why expert performance may not be mediated by heritable talents. The most important general point is that the mechanisms that mediate skilled performance change dramatically with deliberate practice, to the point where ability variables that predict performance early in practice are unrelated to performance later on, and heritabilities for even moderately skilled performance are low. Ericsson and his colleagues conclude that the evidence that innate capacities limit people's ability to attain expert performance is essentially non-existent, although they do not preclude the possibility that genetic endowment may some day emerge as a useful predictor.

Memory: Nature or Nurture?

Memory continues to be the engine of cognitive evolution at this advanced stage as it was throughout cognitive evolution because the attainment of peak intellectual and performance skills is mediated by progressive changes in long-term memory structures and processes. Memory viewed in the mythical guise of the ancient Greek goddess, Mnemosyne, might seem to be an especially suitable metaphor in this context because she was the mother of the nine Muses who were the inspirational sources of creativity in the arts and sciences, the funnels for memories from which aspiring mortals could build their dreams. This metaphor, however, has the same misleading implications as the traditional views of talent already discussed, namely that memory and its creative consequences are innate gifts from the gods. This view is not supported by modern evidence.

Clearly, memory like other endowments is biologically based and we are fortunate to have especially good "mnemonic organs" relative to other species (Chapter 11). What is important to appreciate here is the extent to which memory is an acquired set of skills. We saw this in the effectiveness of mnemonic techniques that originated with Simonides's method of loci. The early Greek and Roman scholars described this as artificial memory in contrast to natural memory, which is appropriate in the sense that average memory performance is augmented by learned mnemonic techniques. As pointed out earlier, however, the technique and its variants simply capitalize on variables on which "natural" memory performance is dependent, namely organization, distinctiveness, retrieval cues, and the rest. The ancients recognized this, for they taught that "nature herself tells us what to do" when selecting effective loci, although they assumed nevertheless that some people were additionally endowed with superior "natural" memories. We see later that these natural memory skills are as elusive as the other kinds of "talents" and are as profoundly affected by deliberate practice (e.g., Ericsson, 1985, 2003b). We also see, however, that memory skills differ from all the others in that memory is implicated in all domains of expertise, ranging from such specific ones as typing, chess, and music to such general ones as science, including the creative aspects of those activities. Additionally, memory metaskills can be acquired that are applicable to any domain of skilled knowledge.

Motivation for Peak Achievement

In 1983, Tak Wah Mak discovered a vital part of the body's defense system called the T-cell receptor. His view of what motivates scientists in their competitive race is that, in a domain where people will never be paid enough for what they do and failure and disappointment are endemic, the thirst for fame is the only real engine that can drive scientists hard enough (Strauss, 1987, p. 77). Social recognition is indeed a powerful reinforcer, but reinforcement is a more general mechanism that shapes and maintains performance of all organisms. In Chapter 11, we discussed such primary reinforcers as food, sex, and shelter, which satisfy biological needs. We also considered the secondary rewards and negative consequences that emerged in the social context of evolution. Both kinds of reinforcers spark and sustain the activities that lead to peak behavioral and cognitive skills. Studies of future elite performers and their parents (e.g., Bloom, 1985), showed that parents typically expose their children to the skill domain under playful conditions. When a child has "caught the bug" and shows promise, the parents enthusiastically encourage practice and participation. They might provide material rewards, including subsidizing study and practice time, as the performer advances. Performance itself pays off in time. A critical feature here is what behavioral scientists call the schedule of reinforcement: The payoffs can become increasingly infrequent and irregular and still do their motivational work. B. F. Skinner, the scientist who did more than anyone to advance our understanding of the power of reinforcement, was asked late in life how he could bear the strain of being so misunderstood for his behaviorism. His answer was that he needed to be understood but three or four times a year (Salzinger, 1990).

Additionally, however, Skinner found ways to reinforce important personal activities. For example, he kept a cumulative daily record of his writing productivity. His writing schedule was reinforced by seeing the plotted line moving upward regularly. Elite performers in other fields similarly keep track of practice hours, which provides feedback that helps them to stick to their schedules. Anecdotal and research evidence also suggest that imagery and talking to oneself about one's goals and goal-related activities can energize, direct, and sustain the hard climb to the summit of achievement. The details are described later (Chapter 15) in the context of a dual coding model of imagery and language in human performance.

The Dual Coding Approach

DCT provides an integrated framework for describing and explaining the diverse phenomena that comprise expert knowledge and performance skills, intelligence, and creativity—a way of understanding their nature and nurture. The basic principles of the theory remain unchanged. They are simply qualified to accommodate the unusual characteristics of expert systems. The representational systems of experts and "ordinary" people can be described at the most general level as a Herbartian apperceptive mass (Chapter 3) that is differentiated into specific regions or domains, each composed of structural entities, connecting pathways, and dynamic processes. All derive from perceptual-motor experience and retain the modality-specific characteristics of that experience. The domains vary in size and complexity, and the degree to which their content can be defined as cognitive or noncognitive and verbal or nonverbal. What sets expert systems apart are (a) the exceptional richness and organizational coherence of the structural content of a given domain; (b) the precision of the processes that activate, organize, and transform the representational content; and (c) the efficiency of the input and output systems that mediate its commerce with the external world. These salient characteristics result from the intensity and richness of the domain-specific perceptual-motor experiences, including especially deliberate practice.

The general description needs only to be appropriately rephrased and instantiated in more precise DCT terms as domain-specific imagens and logogens, referential and associative interconnections and processes; synchronous and sequential processing constraints; memory and other functions of the systems; and so forth. This rephrasing begins in the next chapter in the context of different areas of expertise and a specific analytic model.

CHAPTER FIFTEEN

Expert Performance and Knowledge

This chapter analyzes expertise using a model originally applied to sports performance (Paivio, 1985), and extended here to other domains. The original model focused on cognitive and motivational effects of imagery on performance skills and game strategies, guided by verbal cues and instructions. It was depicted as a 2 × 2 orthogonal model consisting of cognitive versus motivational and specific versus general as its dimensions. The extended model, shown in Fig. 15.1, retains the cognitive-motivational and specific-general dimensions, gives equal weight to verbal and nonverbal processes, and distinguishes between performance and knowledge domains. Thus, the model is about *cognitive and motivational effects of verbal and nonverbal stimuli and dual coding processes on specific and general aspects of human performance and expert knowledge.*

The effects are cognitive if they are mediated by dual coding processes that directly affect performance efficiency, even if the target domain is not intrinsically cognitive. Observing or imagining a perfect tennis serve in the hope that it might improve one's own serve is cognitive activity related to a specific motor skill. Observing or imaging a chess match is similarly cognitive, but the target activity also is cognitive, focused on problem solving rather than motor skill. The core content in both examples is nonverbal. If it were verbal, then the performance domains would necessarily be classed as cognitive, as are most practices designed to improve verbal skills. Of course there are exceptions—for example, learning to produce a French uvular "r" by holding down the front of the tongue with a spoon while trying to articulate the "r," is a motor rather than a cognitive practice aid.

The general cognitive functions relate primarily to strategies rather than specific skills. They include training and study strategies as well as performance strategies. Teachers tell students when and how long to practice a skill, and how to study school subjects. Students and experts develop their own training and study strategies, and plan how to implement them by imaging and talking to themselves.

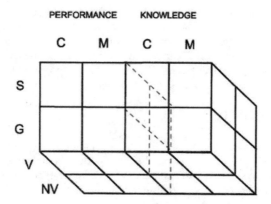

FIGURE 15.1. Dual coding model of factors used in the analysis of expert performance and knowledge: cognitive-motivational (C, M), specific-general (S, G), and verbal-nonverbal (V, NV).

The planning takes account of the context of performance and brings in the anticipatory function of imagery. For example, skilled actors plan different strategies according to the acoustics and design of a theater, anticipated characteristics of the audience, and so on. Strategies impinge on execution of skills but are not directly designed to improve performances.

The motivational-specific function refers to variables that focus and maintain the performer's practice efforts on relevant goal-oriented activities. Being reminded of a possible gold medal if one continues practicing is explicit encouragement to do just that. Even without explicit reminders, we all imagine the fruits of our labors and are thereby motivated to practice and study harder to achieve those anticipated rewards. Such goal-oriented imagery must be distinguished from idle fantasies like those of Thurber's hero, Walter Mitty, who imagined himself as a renowned person in one field or another—surgeon, ship's captain, and so on—but he was not moved by such daydreams to do what was necessary to achieve the laudatory expertise.

The motivational-general cell of the model includes cues and activities designed to optimize the level of physiological arousal. Verbal prodding or "stroking" have their metaphorical origins in physical beating or gentle patting to move people to more effort or to calm their frazzled nerves. Such hypnotic suggestions as "You are feeling very strong and energetic" or "You are very calm and relaxed" are dramatic examples of the motivational power attributed to words. Arousing or relaxing music is often intended to have similar physiological effects. Again, it is especially interesting that performers use imagery and self-talk to move themselves in either direction. They try to "psych themselves up" by imagining themselves behaving energetically, as if in a speeded-up film, or simmer down by imagining themselves in a quiet place or doing a progressive mental relaxation procedure.

Although the dimensions of the model are shown as discrete categories, each is a weighted mix of variables that define the labeled endpoints. Thus, tasks involve more or less emphasis on performance and knowledge, cognitive and motivational demands, verbal and nonverbal processing, and breadth of focus. Applications of the model to specific domains clarify its assumptions and provide information on its explanatory and practical value. We begin with performance.

EXPERT PERFORMANCE

Jack of all trades and master of none is a useful starting point because it applies to all domains of expertise. It implies that there is a trade-off between breadth and level of expertise in the components of complex skills. Consider expertise in track and field sports. The decathlon is a mosaic of 10 individual events, a broad domain of expertise measured by a kind of averaging of world rankings of performance in the different events. Thus, the decathlon champion has the highest average score over all events relative to other decathlon athletes, and might be the very best in one or more of the individual events. However, no decathlon champion can match the performance of the specialist in any of the component events—sprint, pole vault, shot put, and all the others. This is a physiological limitation on what can be achieved through deliberate practice—decathlon athletes have to divide their practice time and energy between the different events. The pole vault specialist can focus deliberate practice on that single event and thus excel in it.

The analysis applies to all domains in which skill components can be arranged hierarchically and evaluated within different levels of the hierarchy. This is typically done in all complex sports. Performance in team sports is ranked at the level of the entire team as well as between offensive and defensive teams, different positions, and so on; gymnasts win on the basis of overall performance but also are scored on individual events; golfers vary in driving, short game, and putting skills; pool players vary in potting, positional play, and defense strategies. Musical, language, memory, and other complex skills are made up of components that can be evaluated individually or collectively.

The following are examples of performance domains that vary in breadth and complexity as well as the dominance of the coding and processing modalities they entail. Sports expertise is the broadest and most noncognitive of the domains, but is nonetheless strongly influenced by cognitive variables. Chess is entirely cognitive and very specific. Music performance is cognitive and broad, similar to language in some ways and different in others. Dancing is a skilled motor activity that maps onto music. Under language we consider a performance consequence of expert knowledge and a specific perceptual-motor skill. Finally, we touch on expert memory as a skill that is the foundation of all of the others; we consider it again in a broader sense under domains of knowledge expertise.

Sports Skills

We have seen that deliberate practice accounts for the attainment of expertise in a wide range of specific sports. DCT identifies the representational basis of such skills. The motor skills in sports are nonverbal by definition, and so the primary cognitive representational base is nonverbal, as it is in instrumental musical performance, dance, and all other nonverbal performance skills. Imagery is strongly implicated in practice and performance. Verbal processing also gets involved as an omnibus "executive," an all-purpose instructional and performance guide. These features stand out in analyses of sports in terms of the DCT model.

The model has been tested in a number of studies by sports psychologist Craig Hall and his colleagues. One study (Hall, Mack, Paivio, & Hausenblas, 1998) involved the development and evaluation of a Sports Imagery Questionnaire (SIQ), now published (Hall, Stevens, & Paivio, 2005), in which specific items were designed to tap each of the four cells of the model that are relevant to sports performance. Examples are as follows:

Cognitive Specific:	When learning a new skill, I imagine myself performing it perfectly.
Cognitive General:	I image alternative strategies in case an event or game plan fails.
Motivational Specific:	I image the audience applauding my performance.
Motivational General:	When I image a competition, I feel myself getting emotionally excited.

The questionnaire was administered to elite university athletes from different sports who, among other things, rated them on frequency of use. Factor analyses of their responses showed that the items separated into distinct factors that corresponded well with functions expected from the model, with the one qualification that the general motivational function emerged as two factors, one reflecting arousal imagery and the other, mastery (focus, mental toughness, self-confidence).

A further experiment tested the predictive validity of the SIQ using competitive athletes in track and field events and ice hockey. The athletes varied in experience and skill levels from high school to national level competitors. The results showed that greater imagery use was associated with successful performance, with different functional categories emerging as the best predictors depending on type of sport, skill level, and sex of the participant. For example, frequency of motivational imagery was the best predictor for the most elite athletes, perhaps because at the time tested they were concerned with performing well and achieving their goals, rather than thinking about getting better (the primary reason for cognitive imagery).

Aspects of the model have also been supported by experimental research. Many studies (reviewed, e.g., by Denis, 1985; Feltz & Landers, 1983; Hall, 2001) have shown that mental practice of skills in diverse sports improves performance relative to no practice, although never as much as equivalent physical practice. A study bearing on the motivational functions of imagery (Hall, Toews, & Rogers, 1990) found that athletes who were instructed to image a successful performance of a simple motor task in a laboratory environment voluntarily practiced harder and longer than a control group. They found in addition, however, that skill-oriented instructions were just as motivating as the goal-oriented instructions. Other studies have demonstrated motivational effects of different mixes of performance and goal-oriented imagery (e.g., Cumming, Hall, Harward, & Gammage, 2002).

Whatever further qualifications might result from future studies, the results to date establish the relevance of a model derived from DCT for analysis of elite performance in sports. Athletes report deliberate mental practice in the form of imagery to help them improve performance and achieve success. The model has been extended to dance expertise (Fish, Hall, & Cumming, 2004) and new research is addressing the problem of maximizing the efficiency of deliberate imagery practice as a supplement to deliberate physical practice, with promising results (Cumming & Hall, 2002). Such studies have not yet been done in other skill domains and we must rely on anecdotal evidence and analogical extensions of the dual coding model to those domains.

Chess Expertise

Chess is entirely a cognitive skill in which performance doesn't depend on the precision with which pieces are moved to locations. It is based on a domain-specific apperceptive mass of long-term memory representations and processes of which the essential core is the visual-spatial imagery system. This was established by the finding that positional problem-solving in chess is depressed by a concurrent visual-spatial.interference task but is not similarly affected by a concurrent articulatory task (e.g., Saariluoma, 1991).

The representational base is nonverbal and visual even when the game is played using auditory or written input in which chess pieces, positions, and moves are described in a kind of algebraic code, but in addition, this requires verbal-referential encoding from the description into imagery. Chess in whatever form also entails continual verbal-associative and referential activity in the anticipatory planning and evaluation of chess moves. Chess therefore involves complex dual coding processing skills that operate on entities in a game played on a visual-spatial map, which may be available perceptually or only in imagery, and which chess masters can play nearly as well blindfolded as when they see the chessboard (Ericsson & Kintsch, 2000, p. 580).

It was mentioned earlier that chess expertise requires 10 years or more of study and deliberate practice. To my knowledge, there are no direct studies of mental practice in chess. It is simply a compelling inference that aspiring experts engage in a great deal of private verbal and imagery activity when studying books that describe championship matches, and perceptual-motor activity and anticipatory imagery when trying out chess positions and moves on an actual board, or only in imagery. The general point is supported by the finding that the time spent on solitary study and analysis of published games between chess masters is closely related to chess players' tournament performance (Charness, Krampe, & Mayr, 1996).

Musical Expertise

Musical performance skill, like chess, is essentially cognitive and nonverbal, but unlike chess, it requires fine-tuned motor skills that share characteristics with verbal skills. In particular, both music and language consist of sequentially organized changes in motor patterns that produce correlated changes in sound. Beyond that, however, the defining characteristics are fundamentally different. Music consists of temporal segments of sound (notes) that vary only in relative frequency and length. The notes can be relatively discrete, especially when produced by a keyboard instrument, and length is then represented by pauses or sound repetitions. The segments become complex in orchestral music when the acoustic characteristics (fundamenal frequency, timbre, loudness, etc.) of different instruments are combined.

However complex, the musical segments and their temporal patterning are not meaningful in the same sense as language. Music has aesthetic or emotional meaning, but it has no referential meaning. The changing patterns in music are like prosodic changes in speech unaccompanied by meaningful phonemic changes. Albert Bregman (1990) initially described the patterning of sound, including music, as auditory streaming, but later changed the metaphor to auditory scene analysis, which yields auditory analogues of Gestalt principles for vision (for a recent summary of the principles of the theory, see Bregman, 2005). This is particularly appropriate for orchestral music in which the qualitative differences between different instruments are heard in parallel but can be distinguished from each other by skilled musicians and conductors.

We have already discussed the acquisition of musical expertise through early reinforced experience and increasing commitment to deliberate practice whereby the aspiring musician builds up an expanding repertoire of perceptual-motor skills. Analyzed in terms of the DCT model, explicit causal variables would include a teacher's instructions to focus specifically on, say, the tempo of piano playing, which the student tries to execute and practice. Acoustic feedback from the playing and "that's better" comments from the teacher help fix the improvements. Part of the effect is specific and cognitive in that it is mediated by improvements in the cognitive structures and processes that control performance. The effect is also motivational, encouraging practice of the specific skill. More general effects relate to practice strategies, how often and how long to practice, guided by recommendations by the teacher and changes in feelings of alertness, fatigue, and efficiency associated with different practice patterns. Explicit rewards (winning competitions, scholarships, getting applause) would be powerful incentives to stick with music as a career goal (a specific motivational effect) and to continue working hard toward that end (a general motivational effect).

All of those combinations of variables also operate at the internal level in the form of mental imagery and inner speech. Musicians might engage in motivational imagery—imagining themselves getting applause and winning rewards—or motivational self-talk to practice harder on particular skills. The practice might include imagery rehearsal in which auditory imagery is generated by covert activity of the vocal system (e.g., silent humming, cf. Smith, Wilson, & Reisberg, 1995), along with rhythmical activity in the form of, say, tapping. These musical surrogates presumably originated as extramusical behaviors that accompany playing. This was especially apparent in the case of the famous pianist Glen Gould, who always mouthed along as he played (among other behavioral peculiarities). A TV special on his life showed him strolling in a park, arms extended and fingers moving rhythmically in imitation of piano playing, simultaneously mouthing in correlated rhythm. This suggests mental practice that spilled over into overt activity.

The analysis implies that the long-term memory representations for instrumental music are primarily motor rather than auditory. We might call them motor "melogens," paralleling the DCT concept of motor logogens that vary in length. Consistent with this view, John Sloboda (1996), who studies musical expertise, contended that

> what bootstraps the process of representing expressive devices in music is the existence of extramusical functions and formulas that act as ready-made templates onto which musical expression can be mapped . . . These templates arise from a number of domains, the most plausible being those of bodily and physical motion, gesture, speech and vocal intonation, and expression of emotion (p. 119)

Musical expertise also involves a kind of reading skill when the performer follows a written score. It entails nonverbal sensorimotor recoding in which a visual pattern is transposed into instrumental (or vocal) motor production. The mapping is primarily analog in that, for example, the ups and downs on the score sheet correspond to changes in pitch. Except for some verbal cues, the score sheet contains no words that correspond to discrete sounds and meanings. Presumably musicians can generate a visual mental image of a score while imaging or actually playing music, but we don't know whether such visualization is helpful in acquiring musical expertise.

Singing can be similarly analyzed, with the vocal system as the musical instrument, tightly linked to the memorized lyrics. Thus, auditory streaming and verbal sequential processing go on in parallel, rather like the joint activation of prosodic patterns and long motor logogens. The acquisition of expert singing skill demands the same kind of deliberate practice as other musical skills. There is evidence that peak levels of singing expertise may have been reached much earlier historically than instrumental performance (Lehmann & Ericsson, 1998), perhaps because systematic training of singers has a longer tradition than training of instrumentalists. Development of playing skills depended on improvements over recent centuries in instrument design, new teaching techniques, and increased instrument specialization of the performer.

Overall musical expertise includes subskills, the most notable of which is the recognition and production of pitch segments. At the highest level, this is known as absolute pitch (for a succinct review, see Deutsch, 2002), which can be described in DCT terms as a referential processing skill that requires correct naming of the 64 tones (or producing the tones to their names) and therefore depends on very specific connections between nonverbal auditory representations (melogens?) and their corresponding letter-name logogens. As already mentioned, it is now known that this is not a genetic gift. Instead, individuals with absolute pitch started musical training early, before ages 5 or 6, and "ordinary" children 3 to 6 years of age can be taught the skill (Ericsson & Charness, 1994, p. 728). It is subject to the same principles of deliberate practice as the rest of musical expertise but it also depends on early experience with sound systems independent of musical training. For example, Deutsch, Henthorn, Marvin, and Xu (2004) reported a large-scale study in which speakers of Chinese Mandarin and of English were compared on a test for absolute pitch. Unlike English, Mandarin is a tone language in which the meaning of a word depends on the pitch and contour in which it is spoken (e.g., *ma* can mean "mother" or "hemp" when spoken in different tones). The groups were students enrolled in prestigious music schools in China and in the United States. They varied comparably in the age at which they had started music training. Absolute pitch scores for students in both groups were higher the earlier they had begun training. The more striking finding was that the Mandarin speakers were greatly superior to the English speakers at all starting ages. For example, among those who started between ages 4 and 5, 60% of the Chinese and only 14% of the English speakers met the criterion for absolute pitch. By starting at ages 8 to 9 years, the percentages dropped to 42 for the Chinese and zero for the English speakers. The researchers hypothesized that, for speakers of tone languages, acquiring absolute pitch during musical training is analogous to learning the tones of a second language. Speakers of monotone languages like English are at a disadvantage because they have not had the same opportunity to associate pitches with meaningful words in infancy.

Verbal Expert Skills: Reading and Typing

Language is a very broad and complex domain that has been analyzed into more than a dozen factorially distinct abilities (Carroll, 1993). Here, we focus on reading and typing because both have been investigated as expert skills and entail interesting similarities and differences.

Reading requires familiarity with print and understanding what it means. In DCT terms, it depends on availability and activation of visual logogens, connections to corresponding auditory-motor logogens, and referential connections to imagens and the affective and motor systems associated with them. All levels must be activated in meaningful reading (a general DCT interpretation of reading is given in Sadoski & Paivio, 2001). Reading expertise accordingly depends on experiences that result in a rich representational region within the broader language domain. We focus most directly on the verbal representational level.

The beneficial effect of familiarity on word recognition presumably reflects the availability of visual logogens (and their connection to auditory-motor logogens if the test requires a spoken response). Familiarity is related to frequency of experience with print. For example, familiarity ratings of meaningless words increase in a negatively accelerated fashion as a function of exposure frequency (reviewed in Paivio, 1971b, pp. 194–196). Specifically relevant to reading expertise are findings that individuals with more exposure to print through reading are faster and more accurate on measures of word and pseudoword recognition skill than are those with less exposure (Chateau & Jared, 2000; for qualifications, see Wagner & Stanovitch, 1996, pp. 213–217). In DCT terms, these findings reveal the effect of reading experience on availability and use of visual logogens. The experience does not necessarily qualify as deliberate practice unless the interested reader also has the habit of looking up unfamiliar words in a dictionary to improve vocabulary knowledge, but the benefit of exposure to print on word recognition skill is nonetheless a cumulative practice effect.

Typing is a more specific language-related skill than reading, although still formidable in its complexity. It entails visual-haptic processing in which a few dozen letter and function keys are referentially linked to finger activity. Touch typing is intended to become independent of visual control, except for a complication on the stimulus side when typing from copy. There we have a pathway from print to visual logogens and from those to haptic motor logogens ("haptogens", "dactylogens"), thus a specialized domain of reading and machine-writing skill in which experts reach extraordinary levels of performance speed and accuracy. Interestingly, typists report that they work faster from copy if they do not try to read for meaning. When composing freely, however, as when describing a remembered event in a letter to a friend, typing is driven fully by meaningful inner speech and imagery.

Attaining typing expertise requires learning experiences, including deliberate practice, similar to those described for piano, especially in that both require learning sequences of finger movements. They differ in that, ideally, the ultimate goal in deliberate typing practice is to type with guidance only from haptic-proprioceptive feedback whereas piano practice is normally guided by auditory feedback. Reading skill can accompany both, with typing based on processing of discrete units and music on processing of visual "scenes" in sheet music. (The simpler analog nature of the latter might explain why some children from musical families learn to read music before they learn to read print.) Judging from reports by typists, the practice can include deliberate mental practice—imaging fingers moving over a keyboard or simply typing words in the air, much as described earlier for mental piano practice.

Both typing and music implicate sequential procedural memory with differences in the sensory components just described. In addition, they differ in the size of their respective representational memory base or apperceptive mass. The skilled typist develops sequential chunks ("haptogens") for words and familiar phrases, but longer sequences are generated by recoding print or inner speech and imagery into typing movements. Skilled musical performers develop large auditory-motor representational memories corresponding to the size of their musical repertoire (playing unfamiliar music from a sheet is also a skill, but the quality of the production can never match that for expertly memorized performance), which connects us seamlessly to the next domain.

Memory Expertise

We have dealt all along with memory in that expert performance in all domains is based on long-term motor and procedural memory, as well as semantic memory in such cognitive domains as chess and reading. The research on memory expertise differs in that the target domain is performance in episodic memory tasks, memory for items or events experienced at a particular time and place. We see, however, that episodic memory performance sometimes includes procedural memory and is influenced by meaning. We also ask whether there is some general memory factor that influences performance regardless of memory content or whether memory is always task-specific.

Ericsson (1985) reviewed the research on memory skills of experts and trained participants. The review focused especially on memory span for digits. The digits are typically presented in random order and the memorizer tries to recall them in that order. In its standard form, the test is intended to tap short-term sequential memory. The average digit span for untrained people is less than seven digits. This capacity is far exceeded by established experts and trained participants, so that the best performers can memorize 100 or more digits in correct order and even remember the spatial positions of the digits presented in a matrix. The champion in this mnemonic domain memorized a list of more than 2,000 digits in about 6 hr and recalled all of them with only seven errors within 2 hr.

There are several notable aspects to such mnemonic expertise. One is that it changes from a test of short-term memory to one that incorporates use of long-term memory knowledge. The general technique used by the experts is to recode the number sequences into meaningful groupings or chunks (a term introduced by George Miller in 1956 to describe such encodings)—significant dates, running times for races, and the like. These chunks are used as mediators for retrieving the digit sequence. Finding and using such mediators as memory aids takes time, so that, if the digits are presented at a fast rate of, say, a half second per digit, the digit span of experts falls back sharply to a level close to average (more about that in a moment).

A second important aspect is that expert memory turns out to be very task specific. Digit span experts are no better than average when tested on letters, syllables, or colors. They neither "naturally" possess nor acquire superior all-purpose memories. The established experts come to the test situations with coding strategies acquired before the tests. Laboratory participants discover or are taught such techniques over repeated trials and become memory experts with the type of material and task on which they practiced the technique, in this case, sequential memory for lists of digits.

A third point is that experts become faster at finding and using mediators with increased practice. Ericsson (1985) interpreted this as faster encoding into and retrieval from long-term memory structures. Thus the superior immediate memory span of the experts and of some untrained individuals reflects an acquired semantic memory skill that enables them to recall digit sequences presented at fast rates.

These generalizations apply to specific domains that involve other kinds of memory materials and organizational structures. For example, experts in chess, bridge, medicine, music, electronics, computer programming, dance, and various sports activities show superior memory for organized but not for random arrangements of stimuli from their own domains, and they do not profit from organization of stimuli from other domains (Ericsson & Kintsch, 1995).

The important theoretical conclusion is that memory experts are skilled at incorporating new domain-specific information into long-term memory structures from which they can quickly retrieve the relevant information. Such structures in effect become long-term working memory systems. In a broader sense, the memory systems are representational knowledge structures that can be used for problem solving and reasoning in the specific domain. For example, the expert chess player deals with familiar chess positions as organized spatial chunks to decide on the next strategic move, and can do so from memory. However, because these representations are acquired to meet specific demands for reasoning in a domain, their transfer across domains is quite limited (Ericsson, 2001, 2003a, 2003b).

We turn next to expert knowledge in domains that vary in breadth and content. The memory theme continues in that knowledge consists of long-term memories of all kinds, an apperceptive mass of facts and fictional information. We conclude the section by once again coming round full circle to the domain of memory itself, in this case memory as a higher order system comprised of skills that can be applied deliberately to any specific domain of expertise.

EXPERT KNOWLEDGE

Some people are knowledgeable in a performance domain without being expert performers in it. Such experts are found among critics, teachers, and ordinary fans of sports, visual arts, music, theater, cinema, literature—whatever. Like performance domains, the knowledge domains vary in breadth, verbal and nonverbal content, and memory or other cognitive demands. The following is a sample of such domains analyzed from the DCT perspective.

General Knowledge Experts

The Renaissance was a period when some people strove to become knowledgeable in all areas of learning. The Time-life millenium list described the 17th-century English poet, John Milton, as the last Renaissance man. Women generally did not have the independent means or encouragement to become similarly knowledgeable, but the first Queen Elizabeth did that and could be described as a Renaissance woman. The explosion of knowledge since then has made it impractical for modern generalists to have all-encompassing expert knowledge of everything that is known. This is not even possible within specific domains in the arts and sciences. For example, Steve Jones (2000) told us that "Darwin was the last biologist who could claim [such broad knowledge] . . . Nobody could do that now. So great is today's knowledge that there are no Miltons even of biology . . ." (p. xxiii). Everything is relative, however, and some people have pretty broad domains of expertise.

Movie Knowledge

The following anecdote illustrates broad expertise in a domain that especially implicates the visual imagery system. Chapter 3 described the mind metaphorically as a vast audiovisual film library, which is an incomplete dual coding characterization, but the metaphor nonetheless has an interesting parallel in movie expertise. Elwy Yost was captivated by movies as a young boy and eventually turned his pastime into a

25-year career as host of a "TVOntario" program called Saturday Night At the Movies. The format included the introduction and presentation of two famous movies of whatever vintage, each followed by interviews with movie producers, actors, and critics. Yost became increasingly knowledgeable over the years, often remembering details about the films and people associated with them that had been forgotten by the interviewees. His expertise was acquired through repeated viewing, study, and evaluation of the films—the kind of deliberate study and practice required for the development of expertise in any domain.

Yost's area of expertise is notable here for its breadth, dual coding relevance, and the fact that it is embedded in an apperceptive mass of general knowledge. It includes fictional (or fictionalized-factual) knowledge about people, places, and events dating back to the earliest historical times covered by the films, supplemented by knowledge directly acquired through Yost's interviews with real people, locations, and events related to the film industry (interviews themselves filmed and shown on the Saturday Night episodes). Note especially that Yost's rich knowledge necessarily engages dual coding systems in the fullest sense, dynamic multimodal memories of verbal and non-verbal events based not only on films, but also his real-life contacts with Hollywood and its personalities. Beyond this broad domain are all the memories and skills derived from the rest of his private life, much of it colored as well by his passion for movies—an infectious passion as shown, for the example, by the fact that his son Graham wrote the script for the blockbuster movie, "Speed."

Others have expert knowledge about more specific film domains, which focus on a particular movie star or film genre. Michel Denis, psychological scientist with the Centre Nationale de la Recherche Scientifique in Paris, is one of the world's leading imagery researchers (e.g., Denis, 1991). His expertise in that domain developed from an earlier period of interest in cinema and cinematography during which he became an expert on the life and movie career of comedian Buster Keaton. It culminated in a book on Keaton (Denis, 1971). The cinema-science connection could lead us to speculate about the long evolutionary reach of the Keaton "meme" but . . . je m'en passe.

Literary Knowledge

Others have expertise in verbal domains of varying breadth. For example, some university professors teach 20th-century American literature. Their expert knowledge would necessarily include nonverbal content derived from imagery activated during reading, or more directly from seeing movie versions of the literary works, but proportionately more of the multimodal core would be verbal than is the case with Yost's film expertise. And, of course, such domains of literary expertise, like film expertise, could be narrow in scope, focused on the writings of a single author.

Sports Knowledge

This domain nicely connects with related performance skills. Some sports journalists are knowledgeable about every sport and others are more specialized in their knowledge, focusing on, say, baseball. The expertise of the journalist is exceeded by some fans, who can recount what teams won every world series, the names of players, their batting and pitching records, and statistics of all kinds. Much of their knowledge was acquired through reading and watching TV, but also from seeing games (some fans follow teams around the circuit) and perhaps even from having played the game. Thus, the expert knowledge in that domain, too, consists of organized, verbal and nonverbal representational structures and processes, all of which is manifested in the ability to retrieve, manipulate, and talk about baseball lore.

Mnemonic Expertise

Memory can become a metaskill that escapes the limitations of the domain-specific memory skills considered earlier, although it is a collection of these. Mnemonic techniques function as all-purpose memory knowledge and performance systems that depend on a large and complex apperceptive mass. The metaskill is not quite equivalent to the familiar concept of metamemory, which refers to knowledge about the nature of memory without necessarily including the performance skills that define mnemonic expertise. Moreover, as the following anecdote clearly shows, the expertise draws on the full power of dual coding mechanisms.

The students' society at my university once invited a professional mnemonist as a guest speaker. As people entered the auditorium, the mnemonist greeted them individually, asked for their names, and handed each one a page torn from a weekly news magazine, up to a total of 100 pages (50 sheets). He began his performance by asking someone—anyone—to call out his or her page number. He first identified the person by name and then proceeded to describe the contents of the page—the topic of a news item, advertisement, salient numbers, dates, anything. He did this repeatedly in response to randomly presented page numbers until it was apparent that he could similarly recall information on all 100 pages if time permitted. He went on to describe how he did it, emphasizing that no "magic" was involved and that everyone in the audience could learn to do the same.

He had picked up the magazine in an airport in Florida and memorized the main points during the flight to London, Ontario, which took about 3 hr in all, given connecting flights. The methods he used were elaborations of imagery-based mnemonics as described in Chapters 2 and 4. The principal method was a peg-word or hook mnemonic that is the standby of all modern mnemonists (e.g., Lorayne, 1974). In it, the numbers 1 to 100 are recoded into letters, words, and images, to which images that code new information can be attached. Thus the first hook becomes "t" as in tea, which is imaged as, say, a tea pot; 2 becomes "n", recoded as a bearded Noah; 3 to "m" to a moa image, and so forth, through double digits in which zero becomes "s" (thus the 20th hook becomes n+s, "nose," and the 100th becomes t+s+s, as in "thesis"). The mnemonist decided on some salient item on a page as the first associate—an interactive image of, say, a bank and a teapot as a reminder of an article on banking on the first page. Other imagery methods served to elaborate on the theme, for example, imagery chains constructed pairwise to remember some details of the banking story. Numerical information such as a telephone number in an ad was coded into consonants in words that can be imaged, and so forth.

This extraordinary memory demonstration is noteworthy, for several reasons. First, it is an elaborate variant of the ancient memory tradition that began with Simonides. The earliest memory peg system may have been developed by Metrodorus of Scepsis a century or so BCE (see references in Yates, 1966), who used the signs of the Zodiac as loci, dividing the 12 basic signs into "decans" to yield a total of 360 numbered images that served as pegs. Retrieval was thereby possible from number cues presented in any order, just as in the case of our modern mnemonist. In addition to memory for "things," Metrodorus also used some kind of shorthand notational system that allowed him to remember the exact wording of speeches, all of which led to his reputation as having a memory that was "almost divine." Other orators and mnemonists over the centuries used similar systems to remember vast amounts of various kinds of information. Some (e.g., Fenaigle in the late 18th century) showed how the techniques could be used to memorize such school subjects as history and geography, just as memory improvement books do today. The elaborate combinations of spatial loci and different kinds of numbered pegs were progressively simplified to the peg-word systems used by modern mnemonists.

A second important point is that, although the principles of the mnemonic techniques are easy to understand, it takes time to learn its various components and how to use them to remember a large amount of complex information. Professional mnemonists become memory experts through long study and deliberate practice of mnemonic performance skills. The skills are elaborations of what goes into acquiring memory skill in specific domains. Moreover, experiments have shown that novices can easily learn to use the basic peg-word systems effectively (see Chapter 2), and, with sufficient practice, they presumably could extend them to the level of expertise of the professional mnemonist.

The third point is perhaps the most important from a practical perspective: the expert mnemonic systems are fundamentally different from the domain-specific memory skills reviewed earlier precisely because the mnemonics are not material or task specific. They are instead applicable to any domain, any content area, and even more than one domain at the same time. Of course, as mentioned at the outset, they are composed of some domain-specific skills, so that, for example, the method for remembering numbers involves recoding them into meaningful chunks much as in the case of the digit-span experts. Even then, however, there is a difference in that the specific components entail use of the same basic word-image associative technique, or variants that rely entirely on imagery, such as the chaining method in which a long list of concrete items is stored by constructing overlapping, pairwise, interactive images. Thus the series *book, lamp, shoe, gate* becomes images of book-lamp, lamp-shoe, and shoe-gate. The mnemonist develops expertise in using different component methods that are especially suited for remembering different kinds of complex information, such as the diverse contents of a news magazine. The mnemonist's tool kit is completely flexible as to the memory task and contents to which it is applied, although each memory tool is self-made and not divine.

The vast memory capacity and unlimited flexibility of the omnibus mnemonic techniques give them powerful potential as educational tools. In that regard, they face two formidable barriers, one being the time and practice it takes to really master them (the barrier to the mastery of any skill), and the other, the persistent medieval negative attitudes toward mnemonics as being at best mere artifacts rather than the "real thing," or at worst, practices of unnatural black magic (cf. Chapter 2). We consider such impediments in more detail in Chapter 19 in connection with the educational implications of what is known scientifically about nurturing expertise. Before that, however, we deal in three chapters with the expertise involved in general intellectual skills, creativity, and the culmination of both of those in the achievements of "geniuses" in various domains.

CHAPTER SIXTEEN

Intelligence: Toward a Dual Coding Theory

Intelligence is generally viewed as the crowning attribute of mind. It follows that multimodal DCT, being a theory of mind, is also a theory of intelligence. All of its structural, processing, and functional principles are directly applicable to the mental capacities that define intelligence. What is required in addition is a switch in emphasis from the general properties of dual coding systems to individual differences in such properties. Individual differences have long been part of the DCT research program as one of the classes of operations used to define and test DCT constructs and hypotheses. This aspect is systematically applied here to the phenomenal domain covered by traditional approaches to intelligence. We see that the emphasis arises quite naturally from the historical distinction between verbal and nonverbal factors in psychometric tests of intelligence, and DCT has even been compared to an influential testing approach to intelligence. I describe those "natural" dual coding connections to psychometric and other traditional approaches to intelligence, and also identify what they lack when viewed from the DCT perspective. A long-term research program would be required to fill that gap and thereby develop a complete dual coding theory of intelligence. All I can do here is present a prolegomenon to such an enterprise.

I first discuss the concept of intelligence and key issues associated with it. Then I sketch the history of intelligence testing with an emphasis on aspects most relevant to DCT. Finally, I present a detailed analysis of prominent psychometric and other theories of intelligence, relating them to DCT and concluding with suggestions about how a complete, multimodal, DCT of intelligence could be constructed.

WHAT IS INTELLIGENCE?

The concept of intelligence is "an inexact, unanalyzed popular concept that has no scientific status unless it is restated to refer to the abilities that compose it" (Carroll,

1993, p. 627). As in expert skills, research and theory concerning intelligence have focused on individual differences in whatever abilities are used to define the construct operationally. The abilities are learned in specific situations, and so the influence of situational factors must be taken into account in definitions of intelligence. Earlier we saw Ferguson's (1954) approach to such influences in terms of transfer of learning across different situations, so that individuals can respond adaptively to them. But adaptation often requires the ability to change the environment to suit the individual. Robert J. Sternberg (1997) takes account of the reciprocal influences of the learning environment and mental abilities on each other in the following:

> Intelligence comprises the mental abilities necessary for adaptation to, as well as shaping and selection of, any environmental context . . . Intelligence is not just reactive to the environment but also active in forming it. It offers people an opportunity to respond flexibly to challenging situations. Because the landscape of an environmental context changes over time, adequate adaptation, shaping, and selection involve a process of life-long learning . . . . (p. 1030)

Sternberg (1997) implied that the abilities that define intelligence can change over the life span with expanded learning experiences, rather than remaining stable as standard IQ tests imply. The preceding chapter showed as well that expert skills and knowledge are heavily dependent on extensive experience (deliberate practice) in the relevant domains. However, the history of intelligence testing led to an interpretation of intelligence as a general component of all specific intellectual abilities, one mainly biological in origin.

General intelligence became identified with the concept of IQ after intelligence testing began. It is closely associated with a common factor introduced by Charles Spearman in 1904 to account for the intercorrelations among tests of school subjects (e.g., English, math) as well as measures of pitch discrimination and music ability. He symbolized this general factor by the letter "g" and developed his factor analytic methods and theory in an influential volume (Spearman, 1927). It is especially noteworthy that Spearman was initially interested in the relations between tests of sensory acuity (e.g., pitch discrimination) and abilities usually viewed as more intellectual. The question was influenced by Galton's similar interest in identifying the biological basis of intelligence in such characteristics as head (brain) size and sensory processing speed. Because such factors were thought to be largely hereditary, their emphasis specifically implied that the biological basis of general intelligence is genetic, as distinguished from environmental and learning determinants just discussed.

Biological Correlates of Intelligence

Over the years, there have been many studies of the biological correlates of intelligence as measured by IQ tests and more specific tests (e.g., verbal ability) related to IQ and thus general intelligence. Philip A. Vernon and other major investigators (Vernon, Wickett, Bazana, & Stelmack, 2000) summarized studies from 1906 to 1998 on the relations between IQ and four biological measures of particular theoretical interest. These are (a) head size and brain volume, (b) ERPs as measured by EEG activity patterns to stimulus presentations (the ERP was described in Chapter 8, pp. 194–195), (c) nerve conduction velocity, and (d) the rate at which the brain metabolizes glucose. These measures purportedly tap overall brain power and the speed or efficiency with which neurons can process stimulus information, characteristics thought to be related to general intelligence. It turns out that all but nerve conduction velocity correlated reliably with IQ.

Head size shows an average correlation of .19 with intelligence over 35 studies involving child and adult participants. For example, a study by Rushton (1997) with 7-year-old children yielded a correlation of .21. Brain volume as measured by brain scans shows a higher correlation with IQ, averaging .35 over 16 experiments. The latency of a particular ERP wave form (P300), known to be related to the speed of stimulus classification and decision making, typically correlated with IQ in the −.25 to −.45 range across different decision tasks. The interpretation is that higher IQs are associated with faster neural processing in cognitive tasks. Finally, the brain-scan studies of glucose metabolic rate (an index of brain activity level) show relations with intelligence that vary from positive to negative, depending on the participants involved (e.g., Alzheimer's patients have lower metabolic levels than normal controls) and whether metabolism is measured at rest or during a cognitive task (e.g., participants with higher IQ scores have lower metabolic rates during such tasks than do lower IQ participants). Vernon et al. (2000) interpreted the pattern of relations to mean that "at rest, when subjects can engage in any mental activity they wish, those subjects with higher IQs demonstrate increased brain activity but, when they are required to perform an assigned cognitive task, subjects with higher IQs are able to accomplish the task with lower consumption of energy" (p. 258), suggesting that they have relatively more "brain power" at their disposal, to be used in greater or lesser amounts as necessary.

Vernon et al. (2000) discussed biological theories that have been proposed to account for such results, which emhasize the relation between general intelligence (e.g., Spearman's g) and mental energy or neural efficiency. They concluded however, that theory lags behind empirical demonstrations of relations between intelligence and biological measures. Their hope is that, eventually, such measures can be integrated into a cohesive explanatory framework that goes beyond correlations to causal relations between "compelling" biological mechanisms and measures of intelligence.

Biological Correlates and the Nature-Nurture Issue

The question of biological causality brings us back to the general nature-nurture issue already discussed in relation to evolution (Chapter 10) and evolved peak mind (Chapter 14), but focused in this case on IQ. Two kinds of puzzles arise. One involves discrepancies in estimates of the possible contribution of genetic factors to IQ based on biological correlates on the one hand and estimates of heritability on the other. The different biological measures just reviewed correlate in the range of

.20 to .50 with IQ. Given various attenuating factors, let us take a maximum value of .50 as the correlation of biological measures with IQ. This means that 25% of the variability in IQ can be explained by biological factors that are deemed to be relevant to intelligence and likely highly genetic in origin.[49] This compares with heritability estimates of about .50 from studies of correlations between IQ scores of pairs of individuals that range in genetic relatedness from identical twins to unrelated people. Thus biological factors account for half as much of the variance in intelligence as do genetic ties. This means that the selected biological factors underestimate genetic contributions, or genetic relatedness overestimate them, or both. What is important to notice here is that, taking both kinds of studies into account, at least 50% of the variability in intelligence scores across a population of individuals must be due to environmental factors, including the kinds of learning experiences discussed earlier.

The second puzzle is the discrepancy between the 50/50 contribution of nature and nurture (including experience) to IQ test scores and the much higher contribution of deliberate practice to performance in a wide range of cognitive and motor skills in the studies by Ericsson and others, reviewed in the last chapter. With respect to music and chess, for example, the data suggested that all of the variance in performance could be accounted for by the amount of time (from childhood on) spent at deliberate practice guided by teachers and by self study. Nothing was left over to be explained by hereditary or other factors.

The two kinds of puzzles could be explained by a combination of incomplete data and confounding of variables—important biological determinants remain to be identified, everyday learning experiences vary enormously and are spread over many domains as compared to the specialized deliberate practice of experts, and so on. Such factors are similar to those discussed by analysts of the heredity–environment research in general. Their writings are readily available and I would be going too far afield to review them here.[50] However, three relevant conclusions arise from the literature and my review of the issues. First, nature and nurture are completely intertwined in their effect on intelligence in the manner described in Chapter 10 for evolutionary phenomena generally. Second, we are not in the business of eugenics except for eventual genetic engineering to correct for missing or faulty genes that contribute to specific intellectual deficiencies. The general viable alternative is to improve nutritional, educational, and other environmental factors that are already known to contribute to intellectual functioning. The third conclusion, related to the second, is that DCT focuses on experiential determinants of mind, which remains an implicit guide even as we consider approaches to the study

---

[49]The percentage of variance in a dependent variable, in this case IQ test scores, that is accounted for by its correlate is calculated as the square of the correlation coefficient.

[50]For those interested in more details, any introductory psychology text would provide a good overview of the general topic of intelligence. Carroll (1993, Chapter 17) gives excellent brief reviews of nature versus nurture and other relevant issues. Mackintosh (1998) presents in-depth analyses of historical background and critical issues concerning IQ and human intelligence.

of intelligence that began with a strong hereditary bias and which, in weaker forms, continue to influence conceptual distinctions in this domain.

A BRIEF HISTORY OF IQ TESTING: FROM ONE TO MANY SOLITUDES

The psychometric approach began a century ago with Alfred Binet's development (Binet & Simon, 1905) of an intelligence test designed to identify children likely to have learning difficulties in Parisian schools.[51] The school system in France and other Western countries emphasized language skills and this was reflected in the verbal bias in Binet's test and Lewis Terman's American adaptation of it, the Stanford–Binet Intelligence Scale (Terman, 1916). The bias could have originated in two historical sources that also influenced the development of DCT. One possible source was the iconoclastic rejection of imagery mnemonics in education and its replacement by verbal-logical teaching methods advocated by Ramus during the Renaissance (see Chapters 2 and 19, this book). The other is the language-dominance view of cognition that prevailed at that time and long after (Chapter 1). Be that as it may, Binet and Simon (1905) developed tests that suited the verbally biased educational system for which they were targeted. Intelligence testing thus began as a verbal solitude.

Other settings demanded nonverbal performance skills and these were incorporated into aptitude and intelligence tests. During World War I, the United States military developed both verbal and nonverbal tests (the Army Alpha and Army Beta, respectively) to help place military recruits in positions that suit their skills (Yerkes, 1921). The practical goals subsequently extended to work and clinical settings. A particularly relevant example was Hebb's interest in tests for use with brain damaged patients when he worked with neurosurgeon Wilder Penfield at the Montreal Neurological Institute. The interest stemmed from his observation that loss of large amounts of brain tissue that did not affect language also did not affect the patients' IQ scores as tested by the Stanford–Binet Intelligence Scale (Hebb, 1949, pp. 277–281), although diminished capacities were obvious to family members. Hebb accordingly undertook the construction of conceptually related verbal and nonverbal (performance) tests of intelligence (e.g., Hebb & Morton, 1943). There is no evidence that those tests had any broad influence on intelligence testing (for example, Hebb is not cited in Carroll's 1993 reviews). Nonetheless, that aspect of Hebb's background is relevant because it helped motivate the development of his influential cell assembly theory and his theoretical views on intelligence already discussed in earlier chapters and later in Chapter 18. The tests are specifically relevant here because of their emphasis on the importance of nonverbal as well as verbal abilities in intelligence, abilities that came to be systematically measured by psychometric tests of intelligence.

David Wechsler pioneered in the development of tests that were explicitly designed to measure verbal and nonverbal abilities. This began with the Wechsler-Bellevue

---

[51]Binet and Simon did not use the term IQ (Intelligence Quotient), which was introduce later and refers to the ratio of mental age as measured by the test and chronological age.

Intelligence Scale (Wechsler, 1939), later known as the Wechsler Adult Intelligence Scale (WAIS), which incorporated items from earlier tests and underwent revisions and expanded into children's forms. All stressed the verbal–nonverbal performance distinction. For example, the Wechsler (1981) revised WAIS for adults (the general description holds for the most recent version, WAIS–III) includes tests designated as Verbal (information, comprehension, arithmetic, similarities, digit span, and vocabulary), and tests designated as Performance (digit symbol, picture completion, block design, picture arrangement, and object assembly). Factor analyses of the items revealed subcategories that partition the basic verbal–nonverbal dichotomy into more specific aptitudes without adding new elements.

The same argument holds for the hierarchical model proposed by P. E. Vernon (1961, see Carroll, 1993, pp. 60–61) in which, as in a branching tree, a general intelligence factor, *g*, dominates (sits on the top of) verbal-educational and spatial-mechanical factors, which in turn dominate other more specific (lower order) factors. The higher order factors reflect correlations between lower order ones and the major distinction here, too, is verbal versus nonverbal, but their slight correlation defines a shared general component. Another dichotomy appears under the labels crystallized and fluid intelligence in a theory developed by Horn and Cattell (1966), for which the tests also correspond largely to the verbal–nonverbal distinction. We see that the fluid-crystallized terminology became popular in other models, which, like Horn and Cattell's, link the distinction to general intelligence, *g*.

L. L. Thurstone's (1938) theory of mental abilities and his factor-analytic test methods set a trend that evolved into differential aptitude testing, "a practice that goes well beyond the simple differentiation of verbal and nonverbal scoring" (Guilford, 1967, p. 10). Thurstone developed the method of multiple factor analysis to reveal the independent factors (uncorrelated clusters of test items) present in a matrix of correlations between all tests. His 1938 study yielded seven factors, which he called "primary mental abilities;" (a) verbal comprehension, (b) verbal fluency, (c) inductive reasoning, (d) spatial visualization, (e) number, (f) memory, and (g) perceptual speed. Factors a, b, c, and perhaps e are defined mainly by verbal tests, whereas factor d is clearly nonverbal, and factors f and g are defined by a mix of the two (e.g., pictures and words). Thus, the verbal–nonverbal distinction shows up clearly in the analysis, and spatial visualization adds the first specific factorial link to DCT in that it was measured by spatial rotation tests. Moreover, Thurstone defined the factor as facility with spatial and visual imagery. That factor was the main initial source of imagery ability tests in DCT research (see Chapter 4). The verbal–nonverbal and imagery connections continued to emerge from subsequent factor-analytic approaches to intelligence testing, which is analyzed in detail from the dual coding perspective after two further bridging points.

First, dual coding variables are often involved implicitly rather than explicitly in test performance. For example, the verbal–nonverbal distinction is completely implicit in the following: To meet the needs of non-English speaking immigrants to the United States and children with limited hearing and language abilities, McCallum and Bracken (1997) developed the Universal Nonverbal Intelligence Test (UNIT), in which the item content is nonverbal and which also is administered completely nonverbally using gestures and modeling by the examiner. However, the nonverbal content does not necessarily mean that test processing is nonverbal. Foreign language children are likely to verbalize in their own language if it helps, which makes the test language-fair but not necessarily language-free. For example, an analogic reasoning test uses pictures of common objects (e.g., hand/glove, foot/____?) that the examinee is highly likely to name silently. Such dual coding is less likely in other tests, such as Object Memory, which uses pictures along with a recognition memory procedure that does not require naming. The test developers surely are aware of potential influences from such processes but the point is that they are not taken into account systematically in the way suggested by DCT and the operational procedures that are used to test it.

The aforementioned point has been explicitly supported by research. The Raven Progressive Matrices Test is the most widely used nonverbal test of general intelligence. Zaidel and Sperry (1973) administered a version of the Raven to participants with "split brains" (cerebral commissurotomy). The matrices with missing parts were viewed in free vision but the answer to each matrix (the missing item) had to be sought among a choice array of raised metal-etched patterns presented to the right or left hand separately, thus to the left or right hemisphere. The important findings were that performance showed a consistent left hand (right hemisphere) superiority but scores for the left hemisphere nonetheless were well above chance. The left and right hemispheres apparently solved the problems using different strategies: "Performance with the left hemisphere was accompanied by verbal comments and seemed to involve verbal reasoning, while that with the right hemisphere, by contrast, was usually silent and more rapid and direct" (Zaidel & Sperry, 1973, p. 38). In brief, the test implicates dual coding processes.

The dual coding interpretation of the Raven test is directly supported as well by psychometric research. P. A. Vernon (1983) included an advanced version of the Raven along with the WAIS and other tests to university students. The pertinent results in this context were that the matrices had their highest correlations with the WAIS performance subtests, Block Design (.62) and Object Assembly (.52), but also correlated significantly with WAIS Vocabulary (.44) and Arithmetic (.52). Thus, the putatively nonverbal Raven Matrices test involves both nonverbal and verbal skills, and we are on safe ground in assuming that this is true as well of other nonverbal tests, such as the UNIT described earlier. A more general point is that the Raven is widely regarded as the single best measure of g ever devised. For example, in Vernon's (1983) study, it had by far the highest "g loading" (.80) of all tests, followed by Block Design at .69. These results are extraordinarily significant for a DCT analysis of intelligence, to which I return after this brief review of the history of intelligence tests and theories.[52]

The second bridging comment is that the psychometric history moved from one to two or more conceptual solitudes in that the tests were designed to identify

---

[52]I am indebted to Tony Vernon for pointing out these features of his data in a personal communication.

separate abilities and not their functional interactions. Thus, first, there was the verbal solitude, then the two solitudes of verbal and nonverbal factors, and finally, the many solitudes of multiple abilities emerging from factor analytic studies. They are solitudes because the abilities are viewed as separate "entities" that do not interact, or at least their dynamic interplay is not revealed by the factor analytic methods. This is so even in the case of the hierarchical structures that emerge from methods in which factors are somewhat correlated rather than independent, simply because the structure itself does not tell us how the underlying abilities interact to affect behavior. To put it plainly in the dual coding context, the identification of verbal and nonverbal factors defines independent dual coding systems but not their cooperative interplay as the nuclear power source of intellect. The following elaborates on this general point.

DUAL CODING THEORY AND PSYCHOMETRIC AND OTHER APPROACHES TO INTELLIGENCE

I begin explaining the DCT approach to intelligence by mapping it onto psychometric and functional approaches to the domain covered by the concept of intelligence. The starting point for the psychometric analysis was the historical relation already described between the verbal–nonverbal distinction in DCT and its status in psychometric approaches to assessment of intelligence. However, DCT includes much more than that basic distinction, namely sensorimotor modalities within each system, different kinds of representational connections and processes, and the many adaptive functions of multimodal dual coding systems acting independently and jointly. In brief, all the basic principles and adaptive functions of the theory described in earlier chapters can be used in the analyses. We first consider a series of relevant psychometric models and then several theories that emphasize intellectual processes and functions rather than ability structures.

The Structure-of-Intellect (SI) Model

Guilford's (1967) SI model is the best place to begin, for several reasons. First, it was the first truly comprehensive model of intellectual abilities. Second, it was a rich source of tests for other models. Third, counterparts of many of the factors appear in more recent psychometric theories. Finally, the model maps onto DCT concepts most completely, as I showed more than 30 years ago (Paivio, 1971b). I elaborate on my earlier analyses here with full awareness of the fact that the SI model has been criticized for its complexity and exclusive reliance on orthogonal factor analyses (which yield independent factors) rather than hierarchical factor analyses, which permit correlated factors to emerge and thereby yielding multilevel factor structures already mentioned. For the moment, that doesn't matter because my aim is to highlight similarities and differences in the SI and DCT categories.

The SI model consists of a three-way classification of intellectual factors into content, operation, and product categories. Content includes figural, symbolic, semantic, and behavioral types. Operations include evaluation, convergent production,

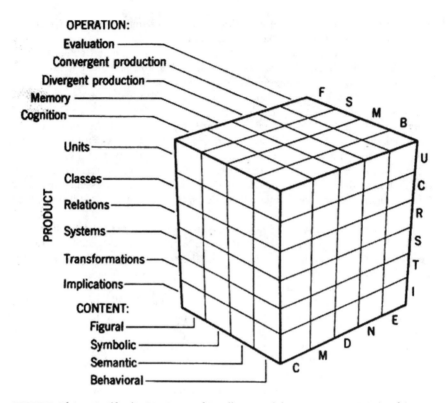

FIGURE 16.1.   Guilford's Structure of Intellect model. From Figure 3.9 (p. 63) in J. P. Guilford (1967). The nature of human intelligence. Copyright 1967 McGraw-Hill, Inc. Reprinted by permission of McGraw Hill Companies.

divergent production, memory, and cognition. The product categories are units, classes, relations, systems, transformations, and implications. Thus, the original model, shown in Fig. 16.1, can be seen as a $4 \times 5 \times 6$ cubic structure whose inter-secting cells define a total of 120 identified or potential factors. Subsequent modifi-cations added to that number; for example, the figural category was expanded to include auditory and kinesthetic sensory modalities.

Dual coding categories generally map onto two or more SI categories, and vice versa, especially because the SI model does not draw a major distinction between verbal and nonverbal content categories or processes. It turns out, however, that the SI figural content category is defined as "Pertaining to information in concrete form, as perceived or as recalled in the form of images" (Guilford & Hoepfner, 1971, p. 20), for which the marker tests are nonverbal. Accordingly, here we find clear corres-pondences between SI and DCT categories. For example, cognition of visual-figural transformations is measured by spatial ability tests that have been used as tests of imagery ability in dual coding experiments (e.g., see Chapter 4 in this volume).

Memory for figural units is measured by tests of recognition memory for forms, faces, and objects—materials that were prominent in dual coding studies of concreteness effects on memory, and so on, for many other SI figural content factors and dual coding processing categories. Some figural ability tests in SI are, however, "contaminated" by verbal components. A pertinent example already encountered in Chapter 3 is Block Visualization, an SI test of cognition of figural transformations in which a colored block of wood is described verbally with instructions about cutting it into smaller cubes. The content is presented entirely verbally but the test loads on a figural category, along with mental rotation and other tests that use only nonverbal material. This means that the cube visualization task involves a great deal of referential processing, from the description to imagery, imagery to internal counting, and so forth. If enough other tasks that require similar processing were used, a referential processing factor might emerge, especially from an analysis that allows for correlated factors.

The SI symbolic category refers to "denotative signs that have no significance in and of themselves, such as letters, numbers, musical notations, codes, and words (as ordered letter combinations)" (Guilford & Hoepfner, 1971, p. 20). Many of the examples qualify as verbal units in DCT but they also are ambiguous psychologically because they can be treated as verbal or nonverbal (figural) units or structures, depending on context. Recall, for example, that individual letters behave like printed words in perceptual recognition tests and as geometric forms when their inner and outer corners are counted. The ambiguity shows up similarly in the SI context in that identification (completion) of Mutilated Words shares its variance with (is equally good as a test of) visual symbolic and visual figural units because both letter units and words must be recognized.

Semantic content is defined entirely by vocabulary tests in which knowledge of word meaning is tapped by production or recognition of definitions, analogies, and synonyms. Dual coding "contamination" is explicitly implicated only in a few tests in which pictures are named (e.g., free verbal recall of pictures as a test of memory for semantic units). Dual coding is implicit in semantic content tests using verbal material to the extent that nonverbal imagery might be required for the response. For example, a Word Matrix test item includes the pairs *ground:air, street:route,* and the test word *automobile:?,* for which the correct relational choice is *airplane.* My guess is that, if asked, many examinees would report using imagery with such items.

The SI operation and product categories have comparable conceptual distinctions in DCT. For example, convergent and divergent production operations correspond to particular kinds of associative processing. In convergent production, multiple stimuli converge on a unique answer corresponding to any product type. Word-Group and Picture-Group Naming are strong tests for convergent production of semantic units, but in DCT, the former would be classed as convergent verbal associative processing and the latter, convergent referential processing. Divergent production entails generation of multiple verbal or nonverbal associative responses to a given stimulus (e.g., words rhyming with a given word, names of round things). The tasks and factorial descriptions are complex in the case of relations, systems, and transformations as products, all of which have operational parallels in DCT. However, the DCT analysis of structures and processes in terms of direct, cross-system (referential), and within-system (associative) levels has no direct counterpart in SI.

Evaluation and memory abilities in the SI operation category and implications in the product category correspond to classes of adaptive functions in DCT. Evaluation is defined in SI as "Comparison of items of information in terms of variables and making judgments concerning criterion satisfaction (correctness, identity, consistency, etc.)" (Guilford & Hoepfner, 1971, p. 20). Most of the nonverbal tests in this category require direct perceptual judgments, so they differ from DCT evaluative comparisons on such memory attributes as size, pleasantness, and value (Chapter 4). The SI tests for evaluation of figural transformations are exceptions in that they implicate mental rotation or rearrangement of given figures, suggesting that imagery could be used. The SI evaluation category also is broader and requires more complex inferential processing than the DCT applications of the concept.

Many DCT correspondences show up in the SI memory factors. A relevant nonverbal factor is memory for visual systems as defined by such tests as Position Recall and Space Memory, both of which involve memory for the locations of figures or objects previously seen on study sheets. Verbal memory is tapped by tests of memory for symbolic units, systems, and so forth. The strongest test for memory for symbolic units is a free recall test of Memory for Nonsense Words, which involves episodic memory but not for meaningful units. Memory span tests (consonants, digits, nonsense words) also loaded on the units factor as well as on memory for symbolic systems, presumably because sequential order is characteristic of symbolic structures and processes. The obvious conceptual link here is to the sequential structures and processes of the verbal system in DCT. Some SI memory tests for semantic information also implicate dual coding. For example, a strong test for memory for semantic units was a free verbal recall test of Picture Memory. Guilford (1967) commented that we can't tell how much the examinee might have depended on visual memory in such tests, as opposed to "the generally strong preference for memorizing material semantically" (p. 119). The comment reveals the difference between Guilford's unitary view of semantic content and the dual coding relational definition, in this case, the referential relation between the object and its name, or, theoretically, between their internal representations.

A notable difference between SI and DCT memory categories is that SI does not include tests that tap the ability to use nonverbal imagery as a memory aid. This contrasts sharply with the attention given in DCT research to imagery mediators in associative memory for pairs of pictures or words. Such research has occasionally focused on individual differences in imagery-mediated memory, but not in relation to SI memory tests (e.g., Paivio, 1971b, pp. 505–513).

The SI implications product category is related to anticipation as a functional category in DCT. Thus, Guilford (1967) defined implication as "something expected, anticipated, or predicted from given information" (p. 64). He suggested, too, that it is close to the concept of association, thereby linking it to conditioning as discussed in Chapters 3 and 11. The SI concept also is related to inference and elaboration, which stretches it beyond its connection to anticipation in DCT. The more direct parallels can be seen in various factors and tests. Foresight and planning are measured by nonverbal tests of cognition of figural implications, such as Planning a Circuit, in which the problem is to find, in a line drawing, a pair of terminals on which a battery should be placed to complete an electrical circuit. Performance presumably could benefit from use of anticipatory imagery. Divergent production of figural implications is measured by Figural Productions in which lines are added to one or two lines to make a meaningful figure. Again, anticipatory imagery could come into play. Contingencies is a test of semantic implications in which the examinee states conditions that might require the use of specified objects in a described situation. Thus, although verbal in content and response mode, the test would seem to require referential processing and imagery.

Finally, the SI model contains no category specifically labeled as emotion or motivation. However, such relevant variables as needs, desires, moods, and intentions appear in the definition of behavioral content (Guilford & Hoepfner, 1971, p. 21), which refers generally to the use of nonverbal figural information in human interactions. Judgment of expressions in pictured faces is a test of cognition of behavioral units that makes contact with research on judgments of emotions from facial expressions, as discussed earlier.

The aforementioned suffices to show the overlap and discrepancies between the SI model and DCT as it relates to individual differences. We now turn to psychometric theories that overlap with other aspects of DCT, beginning with a critique of DCT by the authors of one of the theories.

The Das–Kirby–Jarman Model

Most specifically relevant to DCT is a theory of cognitive abilities first introduced by Das, Kirby, and Jarman (1975). The theory is based on Luria's (1973) distinction between simultaneous and successive syntheses, familiar to us from Chapter 7. Theoretical contact stemmed from comments on DCT in the 1975 article and a more pointed critique by Kirby and Das (1976), in which they focused on the dual coding linkage of the simultaneous-successive processing distinction to imagery and verbal systems. My response (Paivio, 1976a) emphasized misinterpretations of DCT and evidence that the battery of tests Das et al. used to measure simultaneous and successive processing was almost completely confounded with the verbal–nonverbal distinction. Here I address only the confounding issue. Inspection of the factor analytic data that Das et al. used as evidence for their model suggested that almost all of the tests that loaded highly on their simultaneous-synthesis factor involved nonverbal visual-spatial processing, whereas successive processing was defined by serial-verbal recall of short lists of words presented auditorily.

To lend more objectivity to the analysis, I asked two independent judges to categorize eight tests used in one study in terms of the degree to which they required imaginal or verbal processing. The results were clear for seven of the tests: All those that loaded highly on the simultaneous factor were rated as predominating in image processing whereas the successive tests were rated as verbal. One test in the simultaneous factor was rated as verbal but the judges noted that some of the items may predominate in imagery and others in verbal processing.

The foregoing interpretation was subsequently confirmed by intelligence test experts who were unaware of my analysis. In a volume on neurological foundations of intelligence, Hynd and Willis (1985, pp. 119–157, cited in Carroll, 1983, pp. 660–661) favored Luria's distinction particularly as interpreted by Das et al. (1975), relating it to studies that have "suggested that successive (or analytic) processing is primarily a function of the left cerebral hemisphere and simultaneous (or holistic) processing is primarily a function of the right cerebral hemisphere" (p. 146). Carroll (1983) noted additionally that Hynd and Willis pointed out a possible confound of processing style and response modality in this research, in that "successively processed tasks are more often presented and responded to verbally, and simultaneously processed tasks are more often presented and responded to nonverbally" (p. 147).[53] Carroll conclude similarly in regard to the mental processing scales of Kaufman's Assessment Battery for Children (more about the Kaufman tests later), which incorporate the Das et al. (and Luria) simultaneous-successive distinction: "The simultaneous processing tests can be interpreted in more traditional terms as tests of . . . Visualization; the successive processing tests are tests of language processing . . . and short term memory . . ." (Carroll, 1993, p. 703).

The main point here is that the preceding critiques completely support a DCT interpretation of an influential psychometric model of intelligence. The explanatory and practical value of the Das et al. (1975) model and its successors is a separate matter that can be judged only in the context of wide-scale comparative analyses, such as Carroll's in 1993. The value of a more complete theory of intelligence based on DCT also does not rest on the simultaneous-successive contrast, although it would form part of such a theory, the elements of which I will sketch out after reviewing further developments in psychometric and other recent approaches. I now continue with analyses of successors to the Das et al. (1975) model.

The PASS-CAS Theory and Assessment of Intelligence

Das, Naglieri, and Kirby (1994) presented a revision of the Das et al. (1975) model that adds planning and attentional processes to the earlier simultaneous-successive processing distinction, hence PASS theory. A subsequent Cognitive Assessment System (CAS; Naglieri & Das, 1997) is based on PASS. My analysis draws on Alan Kaufman's (2000) summary. Planning is defined as a mental process by which the individual determines, selects, applies, and evaluates solutions to problems. Attention refers to stimulus selection processes. All processes continue to be founded on Luria's (1973) analyses of functions of different brain areas. Confirmatory factor-analytic studies

---

[53]Carroll (1993, p. 661) noted further that Hynd and Willis warned against accepting the assumption made by many educators that teaching to preferred modalities (left brain vs. right brain) is worthwhile, since research has not supported such an assumption-a conclusion emphasized as well in the next chapter of this book.

using the 12 subtests of CAS showed that four PASS-defined factors were the best fit to the data.

Now for the DCT correspondences. As before, simultaneous and successive processes map onto the fundamental distinction between synchronous and sequential organizational processes in DCT. A seeming discrepancy is that simultaneous processing in PASS applies to both nonverbal spatial and imagery tasks as well as language tasks involving logical-grammatical relations. The resolution is that even the latter can be based on spatial imagery,. For example, research cited in Chapter 4 suggests that some individuals use imagery to solve three-term series problems (e.g., Tom is taller than Sam. John is shorter than Sam. Who is tallest?), whereas others use a linguistic strategy. Moreover, performance improves when people are instructed to use imagery. Finally, different dual coding strategies and abilities correlated with activity in different brain areas in language processing (e.g., Reichle et al., 2000).

In PASS as in DCT, successive processing applies to sequential ordering of speech sounds and responses. It also extends to syntactic aspects of narrative speech, which Luria (1973) viewed as being organized into a successive series of meaningful elements. In DCT, too, syntactic behavior includes a substantial component based on associative habits as well as grammatical rules that entail higher order sequential habits that constrain syntactic order. Nonverbal perception and imagery also come into play in DCT as contextual factors that determine the choice of different grammatical constructions (e.g., active versus passive), resulting in different permissible verbal sequences. These aspects of the DCT approach to grammar were described in the earliest versions of the theory and are summarized in Chapter 4.

Planning includes anticipatory and evaluative functions attributed to both verbal and nonverbal processes in DCT, along with their complex cooperative activity in other aspects of problem solving and reasoning discussed in Chapter 4. Attentional processes and their neural correlates also were analyzed earlier and they need no special emphasis here because they are an important part of all psychological and neuropsychological theories. The PASS contribution is in suggesting tests that defined an attention factor.

This was not intended as a critique of PASS or its empirical realization in the CAS tests. Both have been favorably reviewed (Kaufman, 2000, pp. 469–470) and further improvements will depend on research designed especially to clarify the construct measured by the Planning Scale. My purpose was to show that DCT provides an alternative description of the psychometric domain covered by PASS, with differences suggested by the joint involvement of both verbal and nonverbal processes in all aspects of that domain. I postpone the salient details of that argument until later.

The Kaufman Adolescent and Adult Intelligence Test (KAIT)

Kaufman and Kaufman (1993) launched a new intelligence test in which they abandoned their earlier emphasis on the simultaneous-successive processing distinction derived from Luria (1973) and Das et al. (1975). They were still guided by Luria's view of planning ability, coupled with Piaget's concept of formal operations, because both stress the ability to deal with abstractions. The firmest foundation for the new test, however, was the Horn-Cattell (1966) distinction between crystallized (Gc) and fluid (Gf) intelligence, with the difference that the Kaufmans sought to measure broader versions of Gc and Gf than were identified in traditional studies of the two factors. A related aim was to distinguish the new approach from Wechsler's (1981) verbal–nonverbal test dichotomy, long thought to be the empirical correlate of the Gc-Gf distinction.

All of the aformentioned motivated a close look at the relations between the Kaufman approach and DCT. We begin with an analysis of the tests and rationale for KAIT as summarized by Kaufman (2000) and Kaufman and Kaufman (1997). In KAIT, Gc "measures acquisition of facts and problem solving ability using stimuli that are dependent on formal schooling, cultural experience, and verbal conceptual development . . . [whereas Gf] "measures a person's adaptability and flexibility when faced with new problems, using both verbal and nonverbal stimuli" (Kaufman & Kaufman, 1997, p. 210).

Each scale includes three "core" subtests plus one alternate test each for Gc and Gf. The Gc tests are Definitions (of words), Auditory Comprehension (of news stories), Double Meanings (generating such words), and Famous Faces. The Gf tests are Rebus Learning, Logical Steps, Mystery Codes, and Memory for Block Designs. There also are supplementary delayed recall tests of memory for Rebus learning and the Auditory Comprehension stories. I first summarize the empirical case for the KAIT and then describe its correspondences with DCT categories.

The construct validity of the KAIT was supported by factor analytic studies that consistently yielded two factors that correspond to the Gc and Gf scales (Kaufman & Kaufman, 1997). There was some "spillover" of subtest loadings across factors, in agreement with the Kaufmans' (1997) aim of identifying broad Gc and Gf factors that would reflect the complexity of reasoning processes. The validity of the scales was further supported by age-related differences which showed, as did previous studies, that Gc abilities increased or were maintained until age 75 and older, whereas Gf peaked in the early 20s and then leveled off before declining after the mid-50s.

Further studies also showed that Wechsler and KAIT tests measure overlapping but distinct abilities. The analyses yielded three factors, one composed of both Wechsler Verbal and KAIT Crystallized subtests, one composed only of KAIT Fluid subtests, and a third composed only of Wechsler nonverbal Performance subtests (which require organization of nonverbal stimuli). These results particularly inform the following DCT analysis.

A DCT Interpretation of KAIT. We can see at once that, at the most general level, crystallized intelligence as defined in KAIT (and other models) corresponds to experientially determined knowledge in DCT. We could say that the Gc tests sample regions of the apperceptive mass that individuals accumulate through their shared and distinctive experiences. The Fluid Intelligence tests, on the other hand, reflect adaptive functions of the knowledge base that are largely distinct from those tapped by the Gc subtests. A detailed analysis shows that the preceding is not simply a paraphrase of the KAIT definitions and subtests.

The intellectual functions described in DCT involve cooperative activity of verbal and nonverbal systems. The verbal system predominates in some tasks, the nonverbal system in others, and both systems are fully required in many more. The interplay entails cross-system activation via referential connections in both directions. Examples of such cooperative activity abound throughout this volume and can be detected in the KAIT tests.

The DCT analysis of the KAIT subtests is uncomplicated in principle. The first obvious connection is that all of the Crystallized Scale tests involve verbal material and all of the Fluid Scale tests involve nonverbal pictorial material. Initially, therefore, the test materials differentially activate verbal and nonverbal systems. Subsequent processing demands are mainly verbal only in the Definitions subtest, which requires completion of fragmented words given a verbal clue about its meaning (e.g., "-NT-Q—" completes to ANTIQUE, given "It's awfully old" as the clue). Thus, a logogen unit is activated (redintegrated) by components and by verbal associative information. Imagery could be evoked as well but would be useful (confirmatory) only after word completion. On the Fluid side, only Memory for Block Designs mainly requires nonverbal processing, entailing study of a briefly exposed abstract design and then its reproduction from memory using six cubes and a formboard. Idiosyncratic verbalization during study could also be useful as a retrieval cue during reproduction of the design, provided that the verbalization is remembered at that time. There is some support for this analysis from the factor-analytic results in that Definitions has the highest pure loading on the Gc factor, and Memory for Block Designs has the highest on Gf.

From the DCT perspective, all of the other subtests involve repeated cross-system activation, with a bias toward the verbal–nonverbal direction in the Gc tests because their content is verbal, and the nonverbal–verbal direction in the Gf tests because their content is nonverbal. Take the Gc subtests: Auditory Comprehension of news stories benefits from imagery because the stories are about concrete events, and imagery is especially useful (perhaps necessary) for answering inferential questions. Double Meanings implicates both dual coding and verbal associative processing. For example,"BAT" goes with animal and vampire as well as with baseball and stick because of verbal connections and imaged contexts.

On the Gf side, Rebus Learning requires naming of the pictured objects and then use of the decoded verbal-acoustic trace to read sentences composed of the rebuses. Logical Steps compels dual coding because premises are presented both visually (nonverbally) and aurally (verbally), but imagery would be evoked even if the test items were presented only verbally (e.g., "Here is a staircase with seven steps," as the pictured setting for the premise might become "Think of a staircase . . ."). Mystery Codes involves study of verbal codes associated with pictures and then using deductive reasoning to figure out the codes for novel pictures—the latter requiring complex interplay between verbal and nonverbal systems.

This DCT interpretation is not intended to invalidate the KAIT theory or tests. The approaches are at different levels. KAIT is intended as a clinical diagnostic instrument based on the crystallized-fluid model of intelligence that replaces the narrower verbal–nonverbal dichotomy that defines other models. The DCT analysis is a more microscopic description of the mental representations and processes presumed to underlie the dichotomies. The balance of dual coding processes will always depend on the nature of the tests. For example, use of more abstract

Piaget-type logical reasoning tests would tip the dual coding balance strongly to the verbal side, but DCT could still serve as the basis for analyzing reasoning. I return to that point in my final DCT summary.

Carroll's Three-Stratum Theory of Cognitive Abilities

Carroll's theory is a tour de force, the pinnacle of psychometric approaches to intelligence developed by re-analyses of more than 460 factor-analytic datasets obtained from the most prominent investigators of cognitive abilities (Carroll, 1993, 1997). Collectively, the datasets included hundreds of different ability tests. For example, factorial research motivated by Guilford's SI model was a particularly rich dataset for Carroll (more than 500 SI tests are listed in Guilford & Hoepfner, 1971, Appendix B). The re-analyses entailed hierarchical factor analyses that yielded different levels of factors, or strata, that differed in the variety and diversity of the variables covered by a factor. For example, factor analysis of the items of a vocabulary test would yield a very narrow or specific factor (three-stratum theory does not mention such narrow factors, interesting though they might be in some contexts). Analysis of variables more diverse in their content would result in a broader factor, such as fluid intelligence in the theories already described.

Carroll's (1993) analysis generated three factorial strata. The first is a narrow stratum consisting of first-order factors resulting from analysis of typical sets of psychological tests, essentially a distillation of salient first-order factors identified by other theorists in relation to specific models. For example, the Structure of Intellect factors described earlier are all first-order factors (Guilford, 1967 did not use hierarchical analyses to go beyond the first level). Carroll 's second stratum is broader, consisting of second-order factors from such datasets, where the analyzed "scores" are loadings of the tests on first-order factors. Technically, they result from factor analysis of correlations among loadings of tests on first-order factors. The third stratum is a single general factor resulting from analysis of test loadings on second-order factors. I describe these factors with particular emphasis on how they relate to other psychometric models and DCT.

The factor structure is outlined in Fig. 16. 2 and the ability "domains" that make up the structure are described in detail in Carroll (1993). Note especially how Carroll's hierarchical factor structure contrasts with Guilford's orthogonal factor structure in Figure 16. 1. The general (stratum III) factor corresponds to what has traditionally been called general intelligence. This factor dominates (consists of) eight second-order factors that define stratum II, which in turn consists of subsets of 65 first-level factors at stratum I. It is convenient for our purposes to begin with a breakdown of the 8 second-order factors, which Carroll identified as Fluid intelligence, Crystallized intelligence, General memory and learning, Broad visual perception, Broad auditory perception, Broad retrieval ability, Broad cognitive speediness, and Processing speed.

Fluid intelligence was defined by four reasoning tests. Crystallized intelligence was defined by 16 language tests of two different "flavors," one made up of 8 tests primarily related to written language skills (e.g., reading, writing, spelling); the

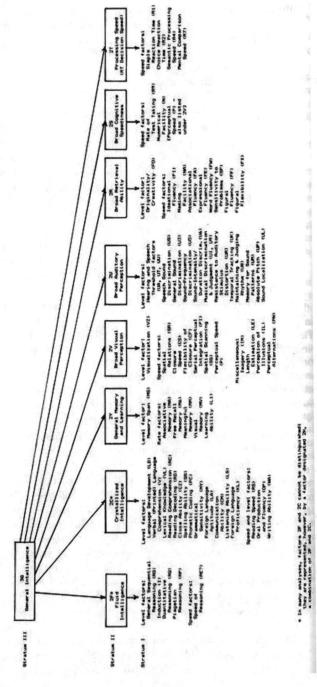

FIGURE 16.2. Hierarchical factorial structure of Carroll's three-stratum theory of intelligence. From J. B. Carroll (1993). *Human cognitive abilities: A survey of factor analytic studies*, p. 626. Copyright 1993 Cambridge University Press. Reprinted by permission.

other, 8 tests related mainly to spoken language (language development, listening ability, phonetic coding, verbal language comprehension, oral language production and fluency, etc.). These two general factors correspond nicely to the traditional Fluid-Crystallized dichotomy. In DCT terms, the Fluid factor reflects adaptive reasoning functions of dual coding systems. For example, it includes sequential reasoning tests that "emphasize the ability to draw conclusions from given conditions or premises, often in a series of two or more sequential steps . . . [using] literal, verbal (semantic), numerical, pictorial, or figurative" stimuli (Carroll, 1993, p. 234). The Crystallized factor is verbal in test content but some tests (e.g., Comprehension) clearly implicate the interplay of dual coding processes, as already discussed.

The general Memory and learning factor includes the kinds of tasks described earlier under adaptive memory functions of dual coding systems. A Memory span factor derives from a large number of datasets because memory span tests have been included in numerous intelligence scales and memory span has often been regarded as a measure of general intelligence. The standard task in that context is digit span, involving immediate repetition of a series of orally presented digits. Many variations include letters, sentences with the words repeated in the same order, visual and/or auditory presentation, and many more. Carroll (1993) concluded that there is little evidence that the variations make any difference in the factorial composition of such tasks.[54] He noted, too, that much research is still needed to identify and describe the basic dimensions of individual differences in memory span and related performances. For example, factorial studies have thus far failed to differentiate possible processes involved in memory for items and memory for order, a distinction that seems to have been drawn more clearly in experimental memory research. The distinction has been important in the DCT analysis of the sequential memory capacity of the verbal system and motor processes generally (discussed earlier in several chapters).

The Associative memory factor is defined by paired associate recall of pairs of unrelated items of various kinds—number–number, word–number, picture–number, first and last names, and so on. The nature and content of the paired stimuli mattered little in the factor loadings, so we could think of the factor as tapping rote (mostly verbal) associative learning. At any rate, Carroll (1993) found no studies of possible correlations between tests of this factor and the degree to which participants used natural language mediators or mnemonic strategies (p. 271). Carroll raised the question, relevant here, as to whether this dimension is important in the sense of predicting performance in real-life learning situations. In brief, does it have any functional significance?

Meaningful memory as part of the general memory factor differs from associative memory in that there is a meaningful relation between paired stimuli, or the material consists of meaningful stories or connected discourse. Representative tests of this factor (Carroll, 1993, pp. 278–280) clearly implicate dual coding: memory for

---

[54]Note that this conclusion contrasts with experimental data, reviewed in the last chapter, which showed that there is no transfer from digits to letters in training on mnemonics. Apparently this experimental independence was not revealed by factor analysis.

ideas in a one-paragraph story, selection of a picture to complete a picture sequence, (named) object-attribute paired associates, films of actors followed by true–false questions about the depicted actions and interactions, and the like. Carroll (1993) defined a more tentative Visual memory factor as "performance on tasks in which the subject must form and retain a mental image or representation of a visual configuration that is not readily encodable in some other modality" (p. 284) Test candidates include reproduction of visual designs, recognition and reproduction tests of map memory, and a recognition memory test for pictures of persons or objects shown in the same position as in the study phase (the distractor pictures showed different positions, hence verbal coding is difficult). Therefore, this factor corresponds to nonverbal visual memory in DCT, entailing mnemonic functions of visual imagens.

A Free Recall memory factor was derived from studies that used the classical free recall paradigm, mostly using word lists or other language materials (e.g., letters, nonsense syllables). Among the few nonverbal tasks were recall of objects that appeared in a film sequence and recall of aspects of figural matrices and designs. These tests reflect only a small contribution of direct dual coding to the factor. Implicit dual coding contributions would have come from studies (generally unspecified by Carroll) that used lists of "common words," which surely would have included image-evoking concrete words.

The final first-order factor that contributed to General Memory at stratum II was Learning Abilities (Carroll 1993, pp. 284–303). The salient characteristics of contributing tests is that all measured rate of learning over multiple trials, and a few also investigated forgetting rates. The studies used a variety of learning tasks and materials, both verbal and nonverbal. Examples from different datasets are as follows: learning and recalling words, objects, nonsense syllables, or picture-number pairs; verbal and spatial conceptual learning; and mechanical-motor learning. One relevant observation is that the factor reflects contributions from verbal, nonverbal, and dual coding processes in unknown proportions. Another is that general learning ability correlated substantially with performance on tests of cognitive abilities, particularly ones that define fluid and crystallized intelligence.

The Broad visual perception factor at stratum II is "involved in any task that requires the perception of visual forms . . . [and] is involved only minimally, if at all, in the perception of printed language forms" (Carroll, 1993, p. 625). It dominates a variety of first-order factors that fall into two sets, each rather heterogeneous in test content. For example, one set includes tests of visual imagery, perceptual illusions, and length estimation; the other, visualization as defined by such tests as Form Board and Paper Folding, which require "the ability to manipulate or transform the image of spatial patterns into other visual arrangements" (Carroll, 1993, p. 316), along with spatial relations, closure speed, spatial scanning, and so forth. In brief, this broad factor entails visual-perceptual and imagery skills involving nonverbal stimuli, hence implicating direct activation and manipulation of imagens.

Broad auditory perception at stratum II also consists of two sets of first-order factors, one set related primarily to psychophysical measures of sensory discrimination (e.g., sound intensity and duration thresholds, absolute pitch, frequency discrimination); the other, to more complex properties of sound (speech sound discrimination, temporal tracking, music discrimination, etc.). Theoretically, this broad factor encompasses nonverbal and verbal auditory-motor representations and processes.

Carroll (1993) defined the stratum II Broad retrieval ability factor as "a capacity to call up concepts, ideas, and names from long-term memory" (p. 612). It also is made up of two kinds of first-order factors, one more verbal and the other more nonverbal in test content, although both involve some mix of content as well. Moreover, both types include tests that require cross-system processing. Examples of the first-order factors are Word fluency (e.g., generate words given first and last letters), Ideational fluency (e.g.,generate names of round things), Associational fluency (e.g., producing controlled word associations to words or word pairs), Naming facility (e.g., naming colors, generating first names), tests that define Originality and Creativity (discussed in more detail in the next chapter), Figural fluency ("the ability to draw quickly a number of examples, elaborations, or restructuring based on a given visual or descriptive stimulus," Carroll, 1993, p. 432), and Sensitivity to problems associated with common (named) objects and described plans or actions. From the DCT perspective, this broad factor is loaded with tests that require cross-system activation as well as tests involving direct verbal or nonverbal associations.

Two other stratum II factors are Broad cognitive speediness and Processing speed-Decision speed, which are measured by rate of processing (e.g., of test taking) and simple or choice reaction time. Again, we have a mix of nonverbal tasks (e.g., RT to a tone or a flashed light, rate of cube construction), verbal tasks (e.g., finding letters in words, decisions concerning physical or name identity of letters), and tasks requiring code-crossover (e, g., deciding whether a named object is a living or nonliving thing). Both factors are designated as broad because each is defined by tests that include the different mixes of codes as well as sensory modalities. The dual coding distinctions of verbal, nonverbal, and referential processing are differentially involved in different tests but the differences merge at this higher factorial level.

I turn finally to General Intelligence (G), the stratum III factor that reflects what processes are common to the tasks that define the lower-order factors. As Carroll (1993) put it, the most important criterion for classifying a factor as measuring general intelligence "was the variety of its lower-order factors or variables. On the supposition that a general factor should show great generality of application over the total domain of cognitive abilities, it should have substantial loadings for lower-order factors or variables in several different domains; the more domains covered, the greater the generality" (p. 591). What lower- order factors contributed most to G?

The second-order factors at stratum II contributed roughly in the order in which they are described earlier, with Fluid and Crystallized intelligence ranking highest and Processing-Decision speed lowest in terms of their factorial loadings on G. However, the ranking does not necessarily reveal the relative contribution of lower-level factors or individual ability tests because tests generally have significant loadings on more than one factor at the same level or different levels. Carroll (1993,

p. 597, Table 15. 5) listed the average loadings of first-order factors on third-order factors in a number of datasets that contributed strongly to G. It is especially notable that Visualization ranks along with Induction as the factors loading most highly (.57, median loading) on G, followed closely by Quantitative Reasoning (.51) and Verbal Ability (.49). Then come the other first-order factors described earlier in relation to second-order factors, especially those that define the stratum II factors, Fluid and Crystallized Intelligence (the highest loading Stratum I factors are listed in Carroll, 1993, pp. 598–599).

Carroll (1993) recognized that his general factor G is close to former conceptions of intelligence and IQ. He argued, however, that his three-statum theory departs from traditional theories in putting much greater emphasis on the mulitfactorial nature of abilities that constitute intelligence, and that the "eventual interpretation of factor G must resort to the analysis of what processes are common to the tasks used in the measurement of such factors as Induction, Vizualization, Quantitative Reasoning, and Verbal Ability, and to the analysis of what attributes of such tasks are associated with their difficulties" (p. 597). It can be inferred from those tests and others listed by Carroll that test-defined, dual coding processes contribute saliently to intellectual performance at the most general level, although their cooperative contributions are not revealed here any more than they are at the lower levels already described. I elaborate on that statement in my summary after reviewing theories that stress adaptive processes and systems that go beyond those identified in most psychometric approaches. I focus on Gardner's and Sternberg's theories and then touch on recent theories of emotional intelligence.

Gardner's Theory of Multiple Intelligences

The 1993 version of Howard Gardner's (Gardner, 1993b) popular theory includes the following types of intelligences, defined here by illustrative activities: linguistic (reading, writing, understanding speech), logical-mathematical (solving mathematical problems, logical reasoning), spatial (reading a map, finding one's way around), musical (singing, playing an instrument), bodily-kinesthetic (dancing, sports activities), interpersonal (understanding others' behaviors, motives, emotions), intrapersonal (understanding oneself), and naturalist (understanding the natural world). In his review, Carroll (1993, pp. 641–642) noted that most of the intelligences show a fairly close correspondence with the broad domains of ability (or sub factors) found at stratum II of his theory. Bodily-kinesthetic ability and intrapersonal intelligence in particular have no parallels in Carroll's or traditional psychometric theories, except for Guilford's (1967) SI theory, which leaves room for a kinesthetic modality under figural content. A debatable point is that Gardner rejects a hierarchical approach to intellectual abilities despite the psychometric evidence for its usefulness. His justification is that all types of intelligence are adaptive in different cultural settings and different situations in which we find ourselves.

The theory has a neuropsychological foundation in that Gardner (1993b) viewed its classes of abilities as reflecting the activities of separate but interactive modules in the brain. He defined the modules and their adaptive functions operationally by patterns of effects from localized brain damage, developmental changes across the life span, and performance of individuals with exceptionally high or low skills in the different domains. He also used evolutionary arguments to support the theory. What is needed is specific evidence that supports the categories of intelligence in the model, especially those that depart so far from the kinds of abilities that are usually included under intelligence. Carroll (1993) suggested that Gardner's research provides a useful source for further studies of cognitive abilities that could be conducted within the framework of his three-stratum theory. The most general connection to DCT is Gardner's emphasis on the adaptive functions of intelligence, about which I have more to say.

Sternberg's Triarchic Theory

In Robert Sternberg's theory (e.g., 1985), intelligence is a complex system in which information processing components work together at different levels of generality to solve problems of all kinds. High-level metacomponents ("executives") are used to plan, monitor, and evaluate problem solving; lower order performance components implement the commands of the metacomponents; and knowledge acquisition components are used to learn how to solve the problems in the first place. The three kinds of components contribute to analytic, creative, and practical abilities. Analytic abilities compare, evaluate, and manipulate elements or relationships involved in a problem. A planning component, for example, might be used analytically for solving a geometry problem. Creative abilities are used to create, invent, discover, and imagine ways to solve a new problem (e.g., planning a new experiment) by comparing and manipulating its elements in new ways. Practical abilities implement ideas in the real world, enabling us to adapt to our existing environments (e.g., mapping a travel route to a destination), shaping them to create new environments (e.g., planning, building, and landscaping a new home), and selecting a new environment (e.g., a university at which to study). According to the theory, people are intelligent in different ways, and they capitalize on their strengths by applying them to many different kinds of problems.

Triarchic theory has been used to analyze intelligence in relation to other concepts. For example, Sternberg and O'Hara (2000) discussed the different ways in which theorists view the relation between intelligence and creativity, the topic of the next two chapters in this volume. Some see creativity as a subset of intelligence (e.g., Guilford and Gardner). Sternberg and others see intelligence as a subset of creativity in that intelligence as defined by conventional tests is one of many elements that make up the concept of creativity. (We see examples of such tests in Chapter 17; moreover, creative intelligence is usually considered to be the hallmark of creative individuals such as those described in Chapter 18). Still others view intelligence and creativity as overlapping sets such that the two are similar in some ways and different in others—in brief, that they are largely independent. This interpretation is supported by data from subjective estimates of IQ and rank order of eminence among historically recognized "geniuses," and more objective contemporary studies of leaders in various fields. Overall, the correlations between IQ and creativity measures ranged from moderately positive to low negative, perhaps reflecting variation in motivational factors and abilities that are relevant to different domains of intellectual and creative performance (Sternberg & O'Hara, 2000, pp. 618–621).

In a similar vein, Sternberg (2000) discussed interpretations of the relation between intelligence and wisdom, ending with his own view from the triarchic theoretical perspective. From that standpoint, wisdom is quite distinct from both intelligence and creativity as these are traditionally defined: wisdom derives primarily from practical intelligence, traditional intelligence primarily from analytic intelligence, and creativity from creative intelligence.

The emphasis on adaptive functions of intellectual abilities is the most obvious general connection between triarchic and dual coding theories. This can be seen in the repeated references to planning in different settings (implicating anticipatory functions of verbal and nonverbal systems), evaluation of outcomes as in problem solving, and so on. A specific difference is the explicit inclusion of practical intelligence in Sternberg's (1985) theory and not in DCT, although the latter has practical implications in relation to education and other applied domains (see later in Chapter 19). Thus, DCT separates the basic theory from its practical applications. A more general difference is that triarchic theory includes a high-level "executive" whereas such functions fall out of the operation of verbal and imagery processes on their own output in DCT (Chapter 3). There is no separate, mysterious, metacomponent.

Theories of Emotional Intelligence

Emotional intelligence is an aspect of interpersonal intelligence in Gardner's (1993) theory. It is an old concept that has recently been given special attention by numerous investigators (e.g., Epstein, 1998; Mayer, Salovey, & Caruso, 2000). Mayer et al. (2000) defined it as

> the set of abilities that accounts for how people's emotional reports vary in their accuracy and how the more accurate understanding of emotion leads to better problem solving in an individual's emotional life . . . More formally . . . the ability to perceive and express emotion, assimilate emotion in thought, understand and reason with emotion, and regulate emotion in the self and others. (p. 396).

It can be seen immediately that the emphasis here is on the adaptive functions of emotions, which relates it to the role of emotion in DCT (Chapters 4 and 8). Mayer et al. described different models and measures of emotional intelligence as well as alternative concepts. Emotional intelligence is not a specific concept in DCT, but the defining phenomena and measures are relevant. For example, naming emotional experiences or facial expressions of emotion were discussed as special kinds of referential reactions (e.g., Chapter 3), on which individuals differ. Autistics in particular are viewed as deficient in "reading" emotions. More generally, alexythymia, which means "no words for feelings, " has been characterized as a deficit in emotional intelligence (Taylor, Bagby, & Parker, 1997). I touch further on some of the dual coding connections to this concept in my general conclusions.

CONCLUSIONS FROM THE DCT PERSPECTIVE

What can we conclude in regard to the place of DCT in the lofty world of theories and tests of intelligence? The boldest conclusion is that the psychometric and processing approaches have missed an essential contribution to human intellect because their conceptual foundations and empirical tests have not systematically taken into account the cooperative interplay of verbal and nonverbal cognitive systems. This implies reciprocally that the full explanatory potential of DCT has not been tested in this domain. The history of intelligence testing and theory tells us why.

We saw at the outset that Binet and Simon's intelligence test was mainly verbal because it sought to predict performance of children in schools that emphasized language skills, perhaps reflecting a historical verbal bias in education. The practical demands of World War I recruiting added nonverbal performance tests and this carried over into subsequent psychometric approaches so that IQ was divided into verbal and nonverbal components. Guided by that history, factor analytic theorists looked for tests that would fit neatly into the two categories or the more general crystallized versus fluid dichotomy, which corresponded in part with the verbal–nonverbal split. The factors thus provided general support for the two sides of DCT and some specific support in the form of spatial ability tests loading on the nonverbal side and vocabulary tests on the verbal side. What could not emerge from the analyses was a separate factor (or factors) composed of tests that clearly reflect the interplay of verbal and nonverbal systems. Some tests, such as picture-naming and comprehension of concrete stories, require direct and cross-over (referential) activation of representations that engage both systems according to the experimental evidence reviewed in this volume. In my view, however, there never were enough of such tests to cohere into a factor because investigators looked for test items that fit into their dichotomies, including ones dominated by a general factor.

The same conclusion applies to the multifactorial models from Thurstone (1938) to Carroll (1993). Thurstone's primary mental abilities were tested by nonverbal perceptual recognition and spatial manipulations tasks, and a mix of verbal and numerical tasks, some of which incidentally require dual coding (verbal comprehension, word fluency, reasoning). Guilford's (1967) SI tests included many nonverbal tests of figural ability and many verbal tests in his semantic content category. Tests implicating dual coding fall into SI cells throughout the cubic model. Clear examples are Block visualization, a verbal test of cognition of figural transformations, and Picture-Group Naming, a strong test for convergent production of semantic units. Many others are listed in my detailed review (pp. 348–352) of the DCT correspondences found in SI categories and defining tests. We have seen that a similar mix of nonverbal, verbal, and cross-system tasks show up in different factors at different levels (strata) in Carroll's theory. Nowhere do the tests cluster together into factors in which cooperative dual coding is the defining theme.

The Das et al. PASS theory and its predecessors are a bit of an exception in that, both conceptually and empirically, the simultaneous-successive processing distinction maps directly onto the organizational capacities that distinguish nonverbal and verbal systems in DCT. Moreover, the planning aspect of PASS entails anticipatory and evaluative cognitive activities that also are adaptive functions of dual coding systems. However, the interplay of the two systems has not been described let alone measured in any aspect of the PASS program.

It seems, therefore, that the great intellectual potential that DCT attributes to the cooperative activities of verbal and nonverbal systems does not and cannot show up in psychometric theories of intelligence because their investigators have not included enough relevant marker tests to reveal dual coding factors that can be so labeled. Cooperative dual coding remains a maverick in search of its own factorially branded herd.

A different interpretation is that the scattered presence of dual coding tests across the broad factorial landscape of intellectual abilities faithfully reflects their ubiquitous contribution to all regions of the domain. Dual coding systems cooperate in different ways in different tasks, with one system or other dominating, depending on task demands. What is needed from this perspective are tests that would reveal the degree and nature of the contribution from each system along with any novel insight that might result from joint activity—precisely the same kinds of tests that would be needed to evaluate the preceding interpretation of dual coding as a factorial maverick in psychometric models of intelligence.

Sternberg's (1985) and Gardner's (1993b) complex theories have not been unpacked systematically into specific abilities that might map factorially onto their broad categories, although some relations to psychometric theories are obvious. For example, Sternberg's analytic and practical abilities correspond generally to fluid and crystallized intelligence; and, as already mentioned, several of Gardner's types of intelligence (e.g., linguistic, logical-mathematical, spatial) have direct psychometric equivalents. Relations to dual coding processes are completely implicit in the category names and descriptions rather than explicit in tests that are operationally related to DCT. It is relevant in that connection to note that Gardner's bodily-kinesthetic intelligence finds a ready home in the dual coding framework, specifically in the model of cognitive and motivational functions of imagery (and guiding verbal processes) in sports, dance, and other activities that require high motor skills (Chapter 15).

DCT similarly accommodates theories of emotional intelligence because emotion (coupled with motivation) is a major adaptive function of dual coding systems. As a specific example of the connection, recall from Chapter 4 that actors could produce facial expressions corresponding to more than 400 named emotions, and judges could name those expressions reliably—dual coding abilities that would qualify as examples of emotional intelligence. Moreover, Baron-Cohen's (2003) purpose in developing software programs for teaching the expressions and names was to help autistic children to recognize emotions, an important social skill they typically lack.

RETROSPECTIVE SUMMARY AND PROSPECTS FOR A
DUAL CODING THEORY OF INTELLIGENCE

I suggested at the outset that what is required to transform DCT into a theory of intelligence "like the others" is to switch the emphasis from general properties of rhe representations and processes that define DCT to individual differences in such properties. Individual differences have long been part of the DCT research program as one of the classes of operations that define and permit empirical tests of DCT constructs and hypotheses. The aim was to relate nonverbal and verbal abilities and thinking styles to performance in memory and other cognitive tasks. The individual difference measures were selected from standard psychometric batteries. A new test was an Individual Difference Questionnaire (IDQ), developed in the 1960s to measure self-reported imagery and verbal modes of thinking, which turned out to be factorially independent (Paivio & Harshman, 1983). A broader study (Paivio, 1971b, pp. 495–197) turned up no fewer than four imagery-spatial and two verbal factors. Similar complexity emerged from a psychometric investigation of children's eidetic imagery and cognitive abilities (Paivio & Cohen, 1979).

The relations between the individual difference tests and performance in other cognitive tasks also varied. For example, positive correlations between imagery ability and memory performance on relevant tasks appeared and vanished like a will-o'-the-wisp over different studies. Even the reputed picture-perfect memory of eidetic imagers did not live up to expectations in that Cohen and I (Paivio & Cohen, 1979) found only a slight correlation between a factor defined by eidetic imagery as a subjective experience and a factor defined by memory test items. In retrospect, the inconsistent results for memory are not surprising, given that memory and learning are factorially distinct from other cognitive abilities in the psychometric studies summarized in Carroll's 1993 three-stratum theory. From the DCT perspective, too, memory as an adaptive function of dual coding systems should be independent of problem solving and other functions except when the defining tasks depend on episodic memory for their components.

The results were more consistently positive when the target tasks entailed use of representations in long-term memory. Consider the symbolic comparison task already familiar from Chapter 4, in which participants decide which of two named or pictured concepts have more or less of some quality, such as size (which is larger, a cat or a toaster?) or pleasantness (which is more pleasant, a cactus or a scorpion?): On a number of concrete dimensions as well as more abstract dimensions, participants who scored high on an imagery test battery made the decisions faster than low-scoring participants. The imagery tests presumably predicted performance on such a variety of tasks because all require the participant to access long-term memory representations that contain the information in question (even pleasantness, although abstract, is a property of the named objects). Persons with high imagery ability apparently access or process the representations especially quickly. Other examples are that (a) participants high in imagery ability recognized briefly flashed pictures more readily than low imagery participants (Paivio & Ernest, 1971), (b) scores on the imagery scale of the IDQ correlate positively with geography and geometry school grades (Paivio & Harshman, 1983), and (c) scores on the Sports Imagery Questionnaire predict performance of athletes in several different sports (Hall et al., 1998; summarized on pp. 329–330 of this volume).

The list could be expanded, but even so, the successful predictions from abilities relevant to DCT are sparse and spread over many domains. The findings do not give a coherent picture of the factorial structure of dual coding abilities and their relation to the broad range of tasks that define the main dimensions of intelligence as they appear in the various models we have discussed. And they were not intended to do so. Instead, the tests were selected as potential predictors of performance in targeted experimental tasks that implicate dual coding processes.

Constructing a Theory

Two kinds of empirical approaches could be used to develop a dual coding theory of intelligence, broadly conceived. The two approaches are mirror images of each other. One is to use the basic principles of multimodal DCT as a framework for selecting relevant tests from all those that were used in the development of other intelligence tests, and to add new tests to cover dual coding gaps in the standard repertoire. This strategy is the same in principle as the one Guilford used to develop and test his SI model, with the difference that the model is theoretically eclectic and intuitive whereas DCT is an established cognitive theory. Tests would be sought that map onto the structural and processing assumptions as well as the adaptive functions of the theoretical systems as described in Chapters 3 and 4. Experimental support for the assumptions would be an important selection criterion, with the caveat that the implications of the assumptions have only begun to be tested experimentally, despite the progress made in the last several decades.[55]

The reciprocal strategy would be to construct a dual coding quilt by patching up an existing theory, such as Carroll's (1993) three-stratum theory, which is a kind of metatheory that incorporates the best tests and factors from other psychometric studies and theories. We have seen that the psychometric and processing theories all include the same kinds of verbal and nonverbal structures, processes, and adaptive functions as DCT, but organized differently and with unsystematic representation of some cognitive abilities that define DCT. I particularly singled out the shortage of tests that tap the interplay of verbal and nonverbal systems. Such activity is required in a variety of naming tests and a few that require generating pictures or images to language, but not enough tests were included to emerge as a factor distinct from a nonverbal factor such as visualization or a verbal one such as fluency.

A supplemental strategy that could be combined with either of the aforementioned approaches would be to systematically question participants on their problem solving strategies after having answered test questions. Precedents include the use of verbal protocol analysis in the study of cognitive processes involved in problem solving (Ericsson & Simon, 1984) and postexperimental questionnaires to tap participants use of imagery and verbal strategies in dual coding memory experiments (comprehensively reviewed in Paivio, 1971b, pp. 355–366, and summarized in Chapter 4, this volume). To appreciate how dual coding questionnaires could be

---

[55]It goes without saying that theories in all domains of science are empirically incomplete in varying degrees in terms of their coverage of their known phenomenal territory, with their frontiers always bordering on the unknown. In science as in other adventures, ". . .all experience is an arch wherethrough gleams that untravelled world whose margin fades forever and forever when I move" (Tennyson's Ulysses).

used in the intelligence testing context, consider the Raven Progressive Matrices results reviewed earlier in this chapter. Recall first of all that the Raven is widely accepted as the single best test of general intelligence. For example, it had the highest g loading (.80) of the tests in Vernon's (1983) factor analytic study. Thus it would be a good marker test for trying out a posttest strategy questionnaire. Second, the results of the study with split-brain individuals (Zaidel & Sperry, 1973) and Vernon's psychometric study indicated that the test involves both verbal and nonverbal processes. Thus it has strong empirical validity as a dual coding intelligence test. Moreover, the split-brain individuals tested with their right hands (hence using their "verbal" left-hemispheres) reported using verbal strategies to select the missing parts. The systematic extension would be to question normal participants on their use of verbal and nonverbal (imagery) strategies after they had answered the test items. An important emphasis would be to try to identify any cooperative, back and forth use of verbal and nonverbal strategies, including the balance of each, and then to relate differences in dual coding strategy patterns to performance differences.

It is an empirical question whether a recognizable dual coding "intelligence quilt" would result from such approaches. Hopefully they would at least reveal broad verbal, nonverbal, and dual coding factors in a multidimensional framework. The quilter would need much material, time, and tolerance for uncertainty because the end product might turn out to be elusive. To the extent that the project works, however, it would further buttress DCT and its implications for individual differences in creative achievement, the topic to which we now turn.

CHAPTER SEVENTEEN

Dual Coding Theory and Creativity

All of the dual coding theoretical principles and adaptive functions are implicated in the set of cognitive abilities related to individual differences in creativity, which consist of domain-specific knowledge and innovative skills that have been hard to pin down scientifically. The emphasis here is on general processes and principles that cut across domains and individuals, analyzed in terms of DCT, with the expectation that the general principles will help explain the achievements of individual "geniuses" in their respective domains as reviewed in the next chapter. Once again the analyses reflect the constructive empiricism of the DCT approach, which relies on linking hypothetical creative processes as directly as possible to observables. This contrasts with reliance on such nonexplanatory notions as intuition and insight, which are refuges of ignorance unless they are themselves defined.

WHAT IS CREATIVITY?

Earlier we defined creativity as skilled activity that results in novel outcomes that are valued by others and set trends for them to follow in the various skill domains—scientific theories, artistic styles, and so forth. The skill involved is not precision, adroitness, or any other characteristic we considered under expert skills. Most of those can be scaled on some quantitative dimension (even musical performance requires accuracy in "hitting the right notes") whereas the criteria for creativity are qualitative, not just measurable differences but differences judged to be more useful or aesthetically pleasing than the norm. Creative activity above all requires expert knowledge but even that is not enough. The "skills" involved are related to noticing and deliberately seeking something new, which depends on knowing a lot about a creative domain to recognize a valued difference when it is discovered or produced. The valued difference is motivationally based, related to a practical, aesthetic, or theoretical need to be fulfilled or problem to be solved. The attempts to do so require exploration of the problem domain, going beyond the beaten path, to find or invent a solution. Necessity, as they say, is the mother of invention. Creative skills are

370

domain specific because they are based on expert knowledge about a specific domain, or domains, for there are the Princes of Serendip (from the book by Horace Walpole) who have the "habit" of making new discoveries and the Edisons who specialize in inventing many things for many purposes. Even so, the creative generalist requires some expert knowledge in each domain, much as the decathlon athlete requires expert performance skills in many events. Creative generality resides especially in the general applicability of a specific discovery or invention—most notably, a theoretical principle that applies to many phenomena. Thus, metaphorically speaking, the most general level of creative genius would be the ability "To see a world in a grain of sand . . ." (William Blake).

The terms *discovery* and *invention*, although often used interchangeably, are conceptually distinct and are so treated in science and technology. Thus, dictionaries tell us that discovery is finding out about something that exists but is unknown (e.g., Madame Curie discovered radium), whereas invention is making or working out something that did not previously exist (e.g., Alexander Graham Bell invented the telephone). Some novel advances in science can be seen as discoveries and others as inventions and still others are ambiguous as to that distinction. For example, was Archimedes's formulation of the hydrostatic principle a discovery or an invention? The principle describes a common feature of all floating objects, hence something to be discovered (a Platonic Idea?), but it is a generalization that did not previously exist and was therefore invented. Be that as it may, science and technology are founded on both discoveries and inventions—often serendipitous ones, as already mentioned. Both concepts, moreover, fall under the more general concept of problem solving.

Innovations in the arts are stylistic inventions that are evaluated on the basis of aesthetic criteria, the degree to which the creative products are pleasing as well as novel. They could be called discoveries only when the artist stumbles on an unfamiliar style of, say, painting or music from another time or place and then incorporates it into his or her artistic work. It is not exactly artistic creativity in the usual sense.

THE DUAL CODING THEORETICAL APPROACH TO CREATIVITY

The most general requirement for creative achievements from the dual coding perspective is the development of expert knowledge in a creative domain, coupled with the motivation to seek solutions to unsolved problems in the domain (and even looking for such problems in the first place). Thus, the foundation is in the background of domain-specific experience that results in a broad and organized apperceptive mass in the area. Biographical data provide the most consistent evidence for this requirement (Chapter 18). Students of creativity, however, also explore the idea that there is a general creative trait which can be measured by psychometric tests (e.g., Torrance, 1966; Wallach & Kogan, 1965). Jackson's (1974) Personality Research Form includes a test for a general innovative style of thinking. It is also thought that creativity can be taught by appropriate methods. We shall review both approaches in the context of dual coding principles.

At the outset, it is important to address the role of imagery in creativity because, aside from its relevance to DCT in this problem area as in others, there is a large and varied literature on the topic. It has been the most frequent concept in analyses of creative individuals and often a focus of psychological research and theory. Unfortunately, that research has not produced a systematic body of reliable findings that we would like for our analyses. In a broad review of the area, Houtz and Patricola (1999) offered the following caveat:

> While studies have demonstrated positive relationships among imagery ability, imagery use, and creative problem solving performance, the reader is cautioned that the literature is large. Many studies have shown conditional, neutral, or even negative results. Imagery is not a guarantee of creative success. It may not even be one of the main predictors of of creative performance. (p. 8)

A meta-analysis of the literature on imagery and creativity illustrates the point. LeBoutillier and Marks (2003) analyzed nine studies (1,494 participants) in which correlations were computed between self-report measures of individual differences in imagery control or vividness and scores on verbal and figural tests of divergent thinking as the measures of creativity (more about the latter tests shortly). The overall correlation was .15, highly significant statistically but accounting for only 3% of the variance in the data sets and thus showing "minimal support for the claim that mental imagery is an important associate of creativity" (p. 37).

The authors of the foregoing reports discuss various problems that might account for the "disappointing" results. For the moment, I note only that the fuzzy picture is due partly to the many ways that imagery has been defined in the literature, and especially the reliance on self-reports in the meta-analytic study. As pointed out earlier in this volume, imagery is a multidimensional process that shows up as a number of factors in correlational studies, in which verbal report measures consistently separate from more object tests such as spatial ability. Perhaps no single study has used enough different imagery tests to reveal more robust correlations with creativity. On the other hand, creativity is at least as complex and hard to pin down; we thus have double-trouble in finding the much sought-after relationship. Or the problem could be with the individual difference approach and it might be more profitable to invest more resources in experimental creativity tests deemed to require imagery resources (e.g., Finke, 1990).

A more important point from the DCT perspective is that creativity cannot depend on imagery alone any more than on verbal processes alone, but depends instead on the cooperative interplay of verbal and nonverbal systems interacting with the nature of the task. Unfortunately, there is a paucity of systematic research on dual coding contributions to creativity and I mainly propose interpretive extensions of dual coding principles based analogically on empirical results in other problem areas already reviewed.

Contributions of Independent Dual Coding Systems

Recall that the functional independence of the verbal and nonverbal systems was demonstrated by additive effects of dual coding on memory for items in episodic memory tasks (Chapter 4). The principle extends here to the long-term memory substrate of creative behavior. All creative activities depend on resources of the verbal and nonverbal systems to different degrees, benefitting from one or the other or both, depending on the demands of the creative problem. The effects are not additive in the same statistical sense as in episodic memory performance because it is hard to say how much of a novel discovery or invention is due to language and how much to imagery even when the evidence suggests that both were essential. The joint effects depend on functional differences between the systems, each contributing according to its particular strengths.

Conceptually similar distinctions appear in the creativity literature. Some explicitly contrast imagery with a verbal-conceptual system. The contrast is implicit in the so-called hemisphericity hypothesis, which capitalized on the growing evidence of differences in the cognitive functioning of the two cerebral hemispheres (reviewed in Chapters 7 and 8). It became increasingly popular to talk about the right hemisphere as the more fluid, intuitive, and creative side, and the language-dominant left hemisphere as the more linear, logical, and analytical side. This simplistic distinction was replaced by the view that both hemispheres contribute to creative thinking but in different ways (e.g., Katz, 1997). Psychometric approaches have tried to capture the essential differences, and interestingly, it turns out that that the so-called left-hemisphere tests are mainly verbal ability tests and the right-hemisphere tests are mainly nonverbal, thus operationally linking the hemispheric distinction to the two general representational systems of DCT.

Recent neuropsychological evidence suggests, however, that the hemisphericity hypothesis cannot be tied neatly to the verbal–nonverbal distinction. Jung-Beeman et al. (2004) investigated neural correlates of creative insight using both fMRI and EEG recordings. The participants were presented compound remote associates adapted from Mednick (1962). For example, they saw the words PINE, CRAB, SAUCE, and indicated whether the correct solution (APPLE) occurred with or without a "sudden flash" of insight. The neural scans showed increased activity in right anterior superior temporal gyrus. The EEG response showed up as a sudden burst of activity 300 msec prior to the insight solution, suggesting unconscious cognitive processing prior to the conscious solution. The study operationalizes the concept of insight, but the test problem was verbal and the insightful connections occurred in the right hemisphere, rather than the left as would be expected from the hemisphericity hypothesis. The study adds to the language processing capacities of the right hemisphere as discussed in Chapters 7 and 8, perhaps because the test items consisted mainly of concrete words.[56]

Synchronous and Sequential Processing

This functional distinction implicates imagery and verbal systems and is especially important theoretically to creativity. The imagery system is not only a rich storehouse

---

[56]The Jung-Beeman et al. (2004) article includes a useful review of the concept of insight and psychological research on it. Further evidence on the hemisphericity hypothesis will be reviewed in the next chapter in the context of studies of creative individuals and domains. The point here is that neither the hemisphericity research nor others in the literature clearly revealed the joint contributions of dual coding processes to creative performance.

of interconnected imagens, but it also makes large chunks of that information simultaneously available for parallel processing, which should contribute to the speed and flexibility of creative thinking because it is free from sequential constraints. The verbal system, a storehouse of its own kind of information (interconnected logogens), is specialized for sequential processing, which entails sequential constraints operating at every level of language structure. Therefore, verbal processes should help keep imagery on track, focused on the creative task rather than wandering off into unconstrained flights of fantasy in a typical Walter Mitty fashion. This is an aspect of its function as a control system that operates on imagens through referential interconnections, and reflexively on its own verbal output through associative interconnections.

Associative and Referential Processing

The two concepts most often associated with creativity in psychometric studies are divergent thinking and originality (e.g., see Carroll, 1993, pp. 423–431), which are usually measured by association tests of different kinds—divergence, by the number of different responses produced to a given stimulus (associative variety), and originality, by the relative number of unusual responses produced. Their priority as measures of creativity is especially interesting because they can be viewed as particular kinds of exploratory behavior or symbolic activity that take the associative side roads instead of the well-traveled highways of the mind (cf. Berlyne, 1965).

Verbal association tests, such as the Mednick's Remote Associates Test just mentioned, are most often used but referential processing tests would also qualify if they were scored so as to take account of the variety and novelty of naming responses to pictures or of images to words. Many marker tests for creativity, such as Alternate Uses, require thinking of novel uses for named objects (e.g., a newspaper), so that referential processing is presumably involved. The stimuli and responses are both verbal, however, so they are not direct referential processing tests.

Wilma Bucci's (1984) color naming measure of referential activity (conceptually similar to DCT verbal referential processing) could be investigated as a potential creativity test because she found that high scorers characteristically used metaphorical expressions to distinguish closely related colors—lime green, burnt orange, flesh, forest green, and so forth, whereas low scorers preferred more conventional combinations of basic color names and adjectival modifiers to categorize the same colors—dull green, reddish brown, greenish yellow, and the like. Persons high in referential ability thus used more unusual color names that seemed to be mediated by imagery. In a study of the reciprocity of the two directions of referential processing (Paivio et al., 1989), we found that the number of different images to words and of names to pictures were among the variables that distinguished imaginal and verbal referential processing factors, suggesting that they might be relevant predictors of creativity. More complex tests can be found in the creativity literature. For example, Form Completion requires the participant to name objects that could be made by adding lines to given figures (Carroll, 1993, p. 434). Thus, it includes a nonverbal associative component in the referential task.

Creative Conceptual Pegs

This DCT metaphorical workhorse is stretched here in various ways. Used originally to refer to the evocative power of concrete stimuli as retrieval cues for associated responses in episodic memory tasks, the idea extends readily to perceptual events, images, and words that play a key role in retrieval and organization of information from long-term or semantic memory—the apperceptive mass that constitutes the creative cognitive domain. The conceptual peg could be a specific event that prompts an analogical leap to a more general application. Famous examples of such leaps include Archimedes's sudden discovery ("Eureka!") of the hydrostatic principle when he felt himself bobbing up and down in his bathtub, and Newton's generalization from a falling apple to the idea of a falling moon, and eventually, to the laws of gravitation. Alternatively, the conceptual peg might be deliberately invented as the scientist or writer tries out different models or verbal summaries that somehow capture the essence of a theory or play. A scientific example is the tree-of-life metaphor that Darwin developed as a heuristic model of how species evolved (discussed further in Chapter 18). A literary example is the image of the shooting of the albatross in Coleridge's "Rime of the Ancient Mariner", which "carried in its train the ground plan of the poem and the thronging images which that released. . ." (Lowes, 1927, p. 228). I have also referred to specific experimental procedures as scientific conceptual pegs when they are perceived to be applicable to the study of new phenomena, thereby expanding the empirical domain of a theory (Paivio, 1991b, Chapter 1).

The following characteristics of creatively effective conceptual pegs are based on Paivio (1983b). First of all, symbolic images, such as the albatross in Coleridge's poem, somehow "stand for" general ideas. They can be thought of as exemplars that capture the common features of general categories of things or ideas, which vary in the breadth of what they encompass. Eleanor Rosch (1975) studied narrow categories such as birds. She showed experimentally that some birds are better category exemplars than others—a robin is a better bird than is a turkey. She also found that people evaluate the category membership of other exemplars by comparing them with the prototypical exemplars, which serve as reference points or standards against which other exemplars are compared.

The relevant extension here is that specific images can have general symbolic value because they are good prototypes within the range of ideas that comprise a theory or literary work. Moreover, such symbolic images are good conceptual pegs precisely because they are effective retrieval cues for related exemplars and associated ideas. As Lowes (1927) put it in his analysis of Coleridge, the symbolic image is a good hook for retrieving relevant ideas from the memory well—for the reader as well as the poet. This is the evocative function of symbolic images as conceptual pegs. They also function as organizers for the range of ideas they evoke—metaphorically, the ideas hang on the same peg.

The analysis implicates relational processing and comparisons between conceptual pegs and the ideas they evoke. The comparisons are based on some form of similarity, typically analogical, as in the case of Archimedes and the other examples mentioned earlier. Analogical processes have received much attention in relation to creativity and other forms of reasoning (e.g., Gentner et al., 1997; Gentner & Markman, 1997; Holyoak & Thagard, 1997; Kolodner, 1997). Especially relevant here is Kolodner's (1997) analysis of case-based reasoning, which entails applying knowledge from specific experiences to solving new problems. In dual coding terms, such cases function as conceptual pegs that activate analogous components when thinking about the new problem. This was one way in which DCT was extended to new domains (Paivio, 1991b). For example, knowledge about the general effect of spacing of repetitions on memory suggested how the same paradigm could be modified to test the hypothesis that verbal and nonverbal codes are functionally independent (pp., 72–73 x–y, this volume). The repetition effect was the conceptual peg for new experiments. The general point is that such experiences are frequent in everyday creative thinking just as they are in the arts and sciences.

Evaluative Processes in Creative Thinking

We have already seen that evaluation is a primary function of thought—humans and other animals try to determine whether objects and situations are dangerous, safe, or useful in some way. Evaluation often requires comparison of different objects in the mind's eye, which in turn might require that they be rotated or otherwise transformed mentally so that their salient properties are brought into focus. Such processes are relevant here as high-level intellectual skills used by innovators in science, technology, and the arts when they try out different solutions to theoretical or practical problems. Their ability to do so is a product of their perceptual-motor experience with relevant objects and the language that describes them. Recall, for example, that objects can be evaluated and compared mentally on any of the perceptual dimensions of the objects themselves, with the speed of doing so being a function of the real-life perceptual-motor difference and how often the referent objects have been experienced together (Paivio, 1986, p. 190). Such evaluative comparisons are ubiquitous in the thinking of artists and scientists, and they can be based directly on the objects themselves or on their memory images, or both. For example, as is detailed later, Darwin's comparisons of similarities and differences among varieties of finches, barnacles, and other species played an important role in the development of his theory of evolution.

For purposes of evaluation, objects can be rotated mentally on any plane and otherwise transformed on any dimension. An example of the role such manipulations play in scientific creativity is Kekulé's (see Beveridge, 1957) dream of a snake-like row of atoms swallowing its own tail, which led by analogy to his working out the structure of the benzene ring, an idea that revolutionized organic chemistry. Whether the dream really occurred isn't important here because such anecdotes can only be illustrative at best and not hard evidence. The possibility of such an effect is supported by the finding that mental rotations can be performed on complex holistic patterns, provided that they have become sufficiently familiar (Bethel-Fox & Shepard, 1988).

The evaluated pieces of information might need to be pulled together mentally before they can converge on the solution to a problem. We considered this kind of process under such terms as integration and synthesis of information, both within and between sensorimotor modalities. Convergent thinking as discussed earlier is generally relevant to creativity, although the associative tasks used to measure it do not necessarily involve combining parts into an integrated whole. More directly relevant is Rothenberg's (1986) concept of homospatial processing, especially in the form of combined-composite visual images, which has been shown to be related to measures of artistic creativity.

Motivational-Emotional Functions of Dual Coding Theoretical Systems in Creativity

These functions parallel those discussed in connection with the DCT expert performance model in Chapter 14. Motivational and emotional processes determine what we select from our perceptual environment and memories as being relevant to the creation of a novel product or to the solution of a theoretical or practical problem. Thus we are moved and guided by images that are awakened by our "predominant passions" (Coleridge). What becomes a symbolic image for the scientist or artist serves those motivational functions as well as the cognitive function of standing for a more general idea, as discussed earlier. The good symbolic image must be pleasing as well as useful. Moreover, this relation between imagery and emotion is a two-way street: specific images can arouse emotions, and conversely, emotions can activate specific images, memory images of joyful or sad occasions, or anticipatory images of attainable goals (Chapter 4).

As in the expert performance model, the emotional-motivational function of imagery has both general and specific aspects. The general aspect entails emotions that motivate effort and action in relation to a creative product, such as when a scientist imagines getting accolades for solving a scientific puzzle. The specific aspect entails goal-directed imagery—for example, images of the training and study required for attaining the skills involved in scientific problem solving.

Evaluation is intimately involved in the motivational aspects of creative thinking. This is implicit in the definition of creativity as socially valued originality, which has implications for the development and maintenance of creative behavior. Creativity is founded on a felicitous experiential history, circumstances that encourage productive variety without evaluation in the early years and stimulate valued productivity later. Parents might praise random and unconventional artistic scribbles of young children much as we all marvel at the "paintings" of chimpanzees, but gradually adults comment on realistic aspects of children's art. Consequently, children tend to become more goal-oriented and organized in tests of drawing production as they become aware of the kinds of products that are socially accepted and rewarded (Urban, 1991, cited in Runco & Charles, 1997, p. 119).

Runco (1991) suggested that evaluative processes are necessary for creativity and account for developmental changes in creative productivity. Children become more conventional and realistic about their creative products because they develop evaluative skills. This is reflected in a slump in performance on tests of creativity, which is reversed later among creative adolescents who learn to evaluate their productions in terms of what is valued in their cultural setting. The motivational basis for the changes can be interpreted in terms of conflicting tendencies to seek recognition and avoid criticism, both of which are contingent on being observed and evaluated by others—inevitable contingencies, according to our analysis of the social context of cognitive evolution in Chapter 11.

The principles just discussed are used in the analysis of creative individuals and their domains in the following chapter. The analysis highlights the historical, philosophical, scientific, and experiential antecedents of processes that are pertinent to the development of individual genius and differences between domains.

CHAPTER EIGHTEEN

Creative Geniuses and Their Domains

Individual differences and imagery have been especially emphasized in psychological and biographical analyses of creative geniuses in virtually all domains of arts and sciences. As in psychometric studies of creativity, the emphasis reflects the "giftedness" interpretation of exceptional achievers, which motivates the search for characteristics that set them apart. Here we focus instead on domain-specific experiential factors and modes of thought that come together in different ways in creative individuals in various fields. Imagery remains important in the analyses but verbal processes and dual coding take on more prominent roles than in the traditional literature.

BACKGROUND

Psychological studies of genius began with Galton's "inquiries" in 1883. Historical and biographical analyses began systematically in 1937 with Caroline Spurgeon's monumental analysis of Shakespeare's imagery. From the 1960s to the present we saw an explosion of historical studies of imagery, visualization, and pictorial representation in geology, chemistry, biology, medicine, mathematics, physics, sociology, and specific fields within these (see references in Cambrosio, Jacobi, & Keating, 1993).

Sir Francis Galton (1883) set the stage with his famous "breakfast table" questionnaire on imagery vividness, which he sent to "100 men, at least half of whom [were] distinguished in science or other fields of intellectual work" (p. 61). He was astonished to find that many individuals reported little or no use of visual imagery. This was especially true of scientists, whose thinking tended to be predominantly abstract and verbal. Persons "in the general society," however, reported more use of imagery.

Psychologist Ann Roe (1951) pursued the developmental implications of Galton's work. She studied 64 scientists from various fields, from whom she obtained interview data on life history, work habits, modes of thought, and several kinds of test data. She found significant relations between habitual type of symbolic activity and scientific field, with biologists and experimental physicists predominating in visual imagery whereas theoretical physicists, psychologists, and anthropologists reported more use of verbal symbolization. She also found that the fathers of the verbalizers tended to be in "verbal" professions, whereas the fathers of the visualizer were primarily in nonverbal professions. Roe could not decide whether the relations reflected heredity or training and experience.

Galton (1883) and Roe (1951) both contrasted visual imagery with verbal habits of thought, implying a kind of dual coding. However, neither considered differences in the functional properties of the two codes and how they might operate jointly and separately in creative work in the different fields. More recent studies across individuals and domains have distinguished different modes of thought using a variety of tests of creativity. Particularly relevant here are the "new age" studies that linked performance on such tests to hemisphericity, already introduced in the last chapter—that is, functional differences in the two sides of the brain thought to be important to creativity.

Psychologist Albert Katz (1997) comprehensively reviewed the research, including his own large-scale study (Katz, 1983), in which he measured hemisphericity and creativity in 100 individuals using a wide range of tests. It turned out that, knowing only the scores on several hemisphericity tests, about 75% of the sample could be correctly classified as high or low creative according to their scores on the creativity tests. The two groups differed in the pattern of lateralized brain functions, which suggested that "the highly creative individual may be better able to both recruit and use the right hemisphere processes often associated with inspirational aspects of creativity and be more efficient at accessing the left hemispheric processes required for elaboration" (Katz, 1997, p. 212). Another study by Katz (1986) focused on creativity processes across domains as well as individuals. He computed a right hemisphere–left hemispheric functional ratio using archival data on eminent creative architects, scientists, and mathematicians. He found that hemisphericity was related to indexes of creativity, especially objective measures such as the number of patents held by the creator, and subjective ones such as ratings given by an expert panel of peers, but not to scores on psychometric measure tests of creative abilities. Additionally, the data did not support the simplistic right-hemisphere dominance view of creativity. Instead, creative achievement was related to left-hemisphere dominance for architects and right-hemisphere dominance for scientists and mathematicians. Katz concluded that both hemispheres support creative performance, with different professions demanding a specific cognitive mode that is best served by the complementary cerebral hemisphere.

Katz (1997, p. 214) concluded as follows from the large number of psychometric studies he reviewed: (a) the hemisphericity relations are usually found with only a few of the creativity measures that are included in test batteries; (b) for those measures, the evidence suggests a privileged role for right-hemisphere mediated processes; and (c) when the relation is observed, it appears to emerge with nonverbal tests of creativity and is less likely to be found with verbal tests of creativity. The review thus confirms the already-noted elusiveness of creativity as defined by psychometric tests, and extends it to include hemispheric correlates. From the dual coding perspective, moreover, the data indicate that creativity is mediated by both nonverbal and verbal cognitive modes operating in some proportion. The trick, of course, is to be able to say what that proportion is for different domains. For the most part, the best we can do is to extend the empirical–theoretical approaches already considered and show how dual coding principles apply to creative people, processes, and products in different domains.

THE DUAL CODING THEORETICAL APPROACH

We have seen that biographers found anecdotal evidence that imagery played a significant role in specific discoveries, theoretical ideas, and creative products of eminent achievers. Psychologists have interpreted the processes that can be inferred from such evidence (e.g., Gardner, 1993a; Paivio, 1983b; Sadoski & Paivio, 2001; Shepard, 1978). I analyze some of the same cases and others from two related perspectives. One involves application of DCT principles to the analysis of the creative process in individuals from different domains. The other is the analysis of the creative products or achievements, in particular, theoretical concepts and theories, at which point DCT becomes a metatheory, a theory about theories. The analysis of the creative process is patterned after Ann Roe's (1951) study of scientists from different fields, but this analysis includes a broader range of creative domains and is guided by a specific theory.

Like domains of expertise reviewed in Chapter 15, the creative domains vary on the relative nonverbal or verbal content of their target phenomena and cognitive representations. The target domains of the physical and biological sciences are nonverbal whereas those of linguistics and computer science are verbal or language-like, and the social sciences deal with a mix of both. Similarly, visual art and musical composition are nonverbal whereas the literary arts are verbal by definition. Creative thinking in all of the domains, however, relies on dual coding. Theoretical and conceptual work depend on the verbal system, including its externalization in writing and the language-like symbol system of mathematics. Even at that abstract level, however, the thought processes make use of the resources of the nonverbal imagery system—internal and external concrete symbols, models, and heuristics.

I first address general philosophical and scientific issues concerning the nature of theory and its relation to the phenomena theories seek to explain. DCT provides a natural framework for the discussion.

GENERAL CONCEPTUAL ISSUES

The aim of all sciences is to understand observable phenomena. Scientific understanding entails observation, cognitive representation of the observations in the form of descriptions and images, and interpretations that are general enough to capture a range of specific observations and predict new ones. The interpretations are called theories, hypotheses, axioms, conceptual schemes, and so on. This enterprise is essentially old-fashioned "normal" science as described by Conant 1947 (xxxx) and partly by the logical positivists. Here I present a general DCT analysis of the scientific creative enterprise and then apply it to specific domains and individuals. Largely because theories are the main products of the creative process in science, I begin with the nature of theories and how they incorporate the phenomena they seek to explain in the theoretical framework. The analysis is based on a review article by Clark and Paivio (1989).

Observational Versus Theoretical Terms in Science

This issue was at the heart of debates between proponents and opponents of logical positivism as a philosophy of science. Logical positivism was founded on the conceptual distinctions between observable phenomena, descriptive observational language, and theoretical language that captures the postulates of a scientific theory. The proponents aimed to develop an axiomatic system in which observable phenomena would map onto observational (O) terms and these in turn onto theoretical (T) terms by conversion rules. Rationalist opponents directed their attack on the O/T distinction, arguing that it is fuzzy because O and T terms are equally inferential and that the classification can change. For example, T concepts can get connected to observables when appropriate measuring instruments (e.g., the electron microscope) are invented. Each side sought to defend its position by proposing criteria that do or do not distinguish O and T terms. The rationalists seemed to win out so that logical positivism essentially faded from the scene, although other forms of philosophical empiricism emerged from its ashes (e.g., constructive empiricism as described in Chapter 2).

Jim Clark and I (Clark & Paivio, 1989) explored the O/T issue as a problem in cognitive psychology. Rather than being motivated by the logical positivist goal of developing a formal (axiomatic) theory of science, we were interested in the O/T distinction because it seemed to be a special case of the concreteness dimension as studied in dual coding research. Observable phenomena map directly (referentially) onto concrete terms and the latter map associatively onto abstract terms. If so, the rationalist objection to the O/'T distinction implies that the concrete–abstract distinction might similarly have no special functional significance. Hence its relevance in this context.

We investigated the relations between concreteness–abstractness and the observational-theoretical status of scientific terms, as well as other criterial attributes that may or may not distinguish the two classes of terms—their inferential level, consistency of meaning, distinctiveness, and difficulty. We used definitions and ratings obtained from experts: philosophers of science selected and defined the distinguishing criteria, scientists provided a pool of scientific terms, and other scientists from the same field rated the terms on the different dimensions. The participating scientists were psychologists and the terms were psychological.

The first important result was that the observational-theoretical ratings of terms correlated very highly (.89) with their concreteness–abstractness. For example, *ego, image, instinct,* and *delusion* were judged to be highly theoretical and abstract, whereas *test score, bar press, eye movement,* and *heart rate* were highly observable and concrete.

The second important outcome was that these dimensions correlated almost as highly with their putative criterial attributes as they did with each other, so that the higher the concreteness and observational level of the terms, the higher their semantic consistency and distinctiveness and the lower their inferential status and difficulty.

Note that the scientists in our study made judgments similar to those made by individual philosophers engaged in the O/T debates. It is interesting, therefore, that our results contradict statements by some opponents of the distinction, who argued that the defining features of observational and theoretical terms do not permit unambiguous classification, and that observability is entirely separate from the theoretical status of scientific terms rather than the opposite pole of a continuum. More important, however, was the close relation between the observational-theoretical distinction (together with its criterial correlates) and the concreteness–abstractness dimension that runs thematically through this volume.

We also extended our research directly to the availability of perceptual and linguistic knowledge associated with the scientific terms by measuring the time it took psychology graduate students to think of a mental image or a word related to each of the psychological terms. As can be seen in Fig. 18. 1, imagery reaction times became progressively faster as the terms increased in observability, ranging from more than 6 sec for the most theoretical terms to about 2 sec for the most observable terms. Word association time, however, remained constant at about 2 sec. As further evidence of the expected relation between observability and ease of imagery, reports of spontaneous imagery increased directly with the observability level of the stimulus words during the word association task (also shown in Fig. 18.1). Thus, observational and theoretical psychological terms differ primarily in how easily they arouse mental images of observable referents. These results closely parallel the speed of imagery and verbal associative reactions to everyday concrete and abstract words.

Our results and their interpretation go beyond the scope of the operationists' view of the O/T distinction, in which observables are linked to O-terms and these in turn are mapped onto T-terms. The DCT interpretation links O-terms in a probabilistic fashion to images of observables and to verbal associates that include T-terms. What this means in this context is that the intellectual work of scientists likely includes a large component of nonverbal imagery when they are thinking about procedures to test theoretical ideas and relatively more verbal associations when they are theorizing.

We did not extend our research to other disciplines, although it would be easy to do so in principle. The same pattern of results would not be expected across different intellectual domains that vary in the degree to which they deal with natural phenomena (e.g., physics, biology) or equally concrete human artifacts (e.g., architecture, painting) as compared to fields in which the intellectual activity is largely intraverbal and abstract (e.g., philosophy, linguistics, poetry). Nevertheless, all areas deal with phenomena that vary in concreteness–abstractness and implicate imagery as well as verbal processing. What varies is the nature of the referents and the verbal–nonverbal ratio of the thought processes they require. For example, in contrast to the psychologists in our study, descriptive linguists use the articulatory and acoustic patterns of speech as referents in phonetic analysis of a language—the observable phenomena and the medium of analysis are both largely verbal.

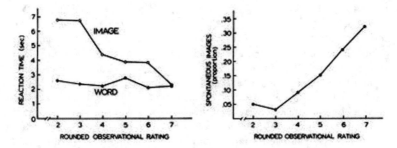

FIGURE 18.1   Imagery and word association reaction times (left panel) and
spontaneous imagery reported by word association subjects (right panel)
for psychological terms varying in rated observational value. Adapted from
Figures 2 & 3 (page 506) in J. M. Clark and A. Paivio (1989), Observational and
theoretical terms in psychology. *American Psychologist, 44,* p. 500–512.
Reproduced by permission of the American Psychological Association.

That some disciplines are more or less verbal or nonverbal is familiar enough.
DCT provides a systematic way of analyzing the differences and their implications
for the nature of higher order thinking in those disciplines. Importantly, the creative
thinking benefits (indeed requires) externalization of its processes and products,
which also implicates the O/T distinction in ways that lead directly to the expanded
DCT interpretation of theory itself.

Externalization of Thought in Sketching and Writing

Drawing and writing were discussed in Chapter 3 as externalization of imagery and
language, hence response analogs of pictorial and verbal stimuli used so extensively
in dual coding memory research. The internal–external connection was explicitly
assumed in studies (e.g., Paivio & Foth, 1970; Paivio & Lambert, 1981) in which participants were asked to image to words and to show that they "had" the image by
quickly sketching it on paper or in the air, paralleling similar written externalizations of their verbal mediators. Sketching (or the construction of concrete models
by computer or other means) has been viewed as a heuristic externalization of
memory images by other students of intellectual skills (e.g., Arnheim, Piaget), and
has played a vital role in scientific discoveries and inventions, as we see later.

Writing has been essential to the development of theories for related reasons. I
alluded to this in Chapter 13 in connection with the role of writing in the development of a metalanguage necessary for grammatical analysis—general terms for grammatical classes, structures, and processes. Linguistic science could not have emerged
without a writing system that externalized language into durable objects that can be
described and analyzed using an even more abstract metalanguage. This is true as
well of mathematics, which could not have developed without the invention of

written symbols for quantities, relations, and the rest. Educational psychologist David R. Olson (1976) suggested more generally that abstraction as defined by superordinate categories was a simple consequence of the invention of writing systems. He extended the causal connection between writing and abstraction to rationality, and hence, intelligence. From our perspective, however, intelligent behavior is equally dependent on concrete aspects of thought, and hence, sketching as just discussed. As externalizations of memory knowledge, both sketching and writing function as durable mnemonic artifacts that further exemplify the bootstrapping or ratcheting effect of memory on its own evolution and beyond, as it elevates associated cognitive accoutrements to new heights in creative acts. The peak attainments include scientific theories.

What is a Theory?

Theories are conventionally defined as interpretations or explanations of phenomena. They are based on observation and reasoning and are necessarily expressed in abstract or general terms because theoretical statements are generalizations about what they are intended to explain. However, the generalizations become meaningful only when they are unpacked into representations of the phenomena themselves and include entailments of the interpretive statement. A meaningful theory thus includes abstract "theoretical" terms, concrete "observational" terms, and a representation of some salient or prototypical aspect of the nonverbal referent of the concretized statement in the form of a picture, image, or procedure. By this definition, the essential cognitive kernel of a theory is the juxtaposition of a verbal statement (verbal generalization and concretized interpretation) and its nonverbal referent (picture, image, action pattern). A "simple" example (I elaborate later) is the concept of the gene defined biochemically in terms of DNA. At a bare minimum, the meaningful kernel is the verbal label deoxyribonucleic acid, a verbal description of the shape of the molecule and of its nucleotide components, together with a picture of the double helix (most directly, the image projected by an electron microscope and indirectly as a drawing or 3D model). This is a dual coding representation of the DNA concept even when the picture is excluded because the chemical description is about the referent molecule and evokes its mental image. A more meaningful theoretical statement would say something about its function as the unit of reproduction and evolution, the properties by which it carries out these functions, and so on.

In DCT terms, the core of the DNA concept consists of a theory logogen (the DNA verbal statement) referentially connected to the theory imagen (the double helix image). The concept expands by associative connections to other logogens and imagens. The associations fill out the theory by specifying assumptions, implications, and experimental and measurement procedures associated with the conceptual domain, procedures that would have had high priority in the theoretical statement when they were called operational definitions. The connections vary in number and strength so that the activation pattern is probabilistic and dependent on experience with the conceptual domain. In brief, DNA and its theoretical entailments is a region in an individual's dual coding representational structure or apperceptive mass, a region that is large and well-organized in the case of experts and small and fragmentary in the case of ordinary folk.

Abstract Representational Concepts Revisited

Most approaches to the study of scientific creativity are empiricist in their emphasis, for they generally do not rely on abstract concepts such as propositions or on computational modeling. The exceptions are hand-waving contrasts between images and propositions in historical analyses of advances in various specific domains and I address the contrasts in those contexts. There is, however, one persuasive rationalist approach that merits special consideration here because it implies that the creative thought processes that were responsible for the great technological and theoretical advances in biology, physics, and other sciences (and presumably the innovative products in the humanities and arts as well) could be explained and modeled in computational terms. The modeling was applied to known facts and theories and so it is a metatheoretical approach, an alternative to the dual coding approach just outlined.

Proposed by Langley, Simon, Bradshaw, and Zytkow (1987), the approach involves use of artificial intelligence programs to simulate human thought processes and discover scientific laws. The programs rely on abstract list-processing computer languages that are applicable to any domain because the domain-specific content is translated into the programming language by human programmers. The programs are production systems with two main components, a set of condition-action rules or productions and a dynamic working memory. Conditions are the system's goals and data patterns; actions are the computational rules that set the goals, formulate laws, define terms, and so forth. The resulting products are matched against the state of the computer's working memory, which consists of continuously updated information relevant to the problem to be simulated.

The results were impressive. The program "discovered" laws in data from physics and chemistry, and integrated the results. The outcomes suggested that the approach could be extended to find research problems, devise new instruments, and invent appropriate ways of representing problems, all of the ingredients essential to scientific and technological creativity, or so it would seem.

The authors added a relevant caveat to their agenda:

> We have striven for generality in BACON [the principle program] because we wish to explore the role in scientific discovery of heuristics that may be relevant over a wide range of scientific disciplines and hence may contribute to our understanding of discovery wherever it might occur. *In adopting this strategy, it is not our intention to deny the important role that discipline-specific knowledge and heuristics play in the work of science; rather, we want to see how far we can go initially with data-driven, semantically impoverished processes* (Langley et al., 1987, p. 65, italics added).

Later (pp. 319–336), they specifically identified difficulties that list structures have in handling complex imagery, especially imagery that involves continuous geometry. They nonetheless went on to suggest how imagery might be represented as computational symbol structures, such as a raster of discrete pixels on which certain operations can be performed.

The implication is that the computer-generated images would serve heuristic functions. For example, an image of the DNA molecule could be computationally examined for useful details. But we are left wondering why that would be necessary, because the images would have no information that is not already in the computational program that generates them. The images would be additionally useful only if they have new emergent properties, which they cannot have in an internally consistent logical system. This is quite unlike DCT, in which imagery derives from nonverbal experience and is functionally independent of the descriptive verbal system that can activate imagens and guide image transformations, and so forth, but not generate them *de novo* from the verbal structures themselves.[57] I identify other specific shortcomings of such formal computational approaches later in the context of particular creative domains.

We turn now to those domains, beginning with a systematic study of invention in applied science and technology because it provides the most solid empirical foundation we have for more speculative theoretical interpretations of creative processes and products in other scientific and artistic domains. The general strategy is to sample domains that vary in the degree to which they involve nonverbal and verbal phenomena and conceptual processes. Thus, following technology, I focus in turn on biology, physics, mathematics, psychology, linguistics, literary arts, and performance arts.

TECHNICAL CREATIVITY IN INVENTION

Invention has often been used to study creativity because the creative product is so concrete. The literature is rich in anecdotal evidence concerning factors that contribute to inventive skills. Thomas Edison's famous quotation, "Invention is one percent inspiration and ninety-nine percent perspiration," attests to the importance of extensive experience in the creative domain. Experience is the sine qua non for the development of the representational base for creative processes and products, especially the kind of focused experience described in Ericsson's (e.g., 2001) deliberate practice theory of expertise discussed earlier. Moreover, relevant imagery stimulated by the practice of one's craft has been emphasized as a major contributor to technical creativity. For example, its role in the work of the inventive genius, Nikola

---

[57]An appropriate verbal analogy to a raster of discrete pixels is concrete poetry in which imagery is depicted in the spatial printed pattern of the poem itself. For example, a poem about snails might be visually represented in a form that is analogous to the action of a snail (Paivio, 1971, p. 473).

Tesla, who served for a time as Edison's employee, has been described in detail by Shepard (1978, pp. 141–142).

More generally, Eugene Ferguson (1977) reviewed the important role of drawings and pictures in technological development beginning in the 15th century. He concluded that "Much of the creative thought of the designers of our technological world is nonverbal . . . It is out of this kind of thinking that the clock, printing press, and snowmobile have arisen" (p. 835). He went on to decry the abandonment of nonverbal knowledge in engineering colleges, predicting that "engineers in charge of projects will lose their flexibility of approach to solving problems as they adhere to the doctrine that every problem must be treated as an exercise in numerical systems analysis" (p. 835).

The aforementioned sources appropriately emphasize the crucial role of visual imagery in this domain, but not the part played by verbal processes. Accordingly, I present a detailed summary of a systematic analytic approach that highlights imagery and also reveals the interplay of imagery and verbal processes in technological invention.

Theodore H. Krueger (1976) worked directly with groups of applied scientists ro discover their mode of thinking during creative invention and problem solving. One study used a reconstructive approach to analyze the flow of thought leading up to the point of synthesis of the inventive process, the point at which the technological fragments or threads came together as a unified solution to a technical problem. His inventors were 15 applied scientists with strong records of creative work, each of whom verbally reconstructed one of his inventions, and in some cases sketched the reconstructions.

The results suggested that visual imagery was most often used as the mode by which technical fragments were brought together in a new synthesis, which was the cognitive basis of the invention. The exceptions included one inventor who didn't recall the mode of synthesis and one whose synthesis came about when observing an accident in the laboratory. The other cases generally involved active manipulation of component images, accompanied by hand movements, drawings of possible configurations, analogical leaps from earlier experiences to the problem situation, and so on. Krueger (1976) noted that five of the cases also involved verbal reasoning and system analysis at some point during the synthesis. However, the following examination of his interview data indicates that dual coding was at work in every case.

The invention of magnetic tape smoothing by Marcel Vogel illustrates several of those processes:

> People call me on the phone . . . and want a magnetic tape. They want it to be . . . smooth . . . The moment they said the question, I saw, as a child, a piece of wood being put over a plane . . . rough wood on this side and as it went halfway through the plane, the finished side of the wood being smooth and completely different in appearance . . . I took that experience and just put it into the problem . . . I machined the surface of the tape, and they got . . . exactly what they wanted. Now that is still being used to every speck of [IBM] tape" (Vogel, quoted in Krueger, 1976, p. 12).

The essential verbal component here was the question about smooth magnetic tape. It presumably evoked an image of tape, from which there was an analogical leap to the memory imagery of wood being planed and from that to a similar procedure being tried with tape.

Dual coding at different stages of the synthesis are revealed by other examples from Krueger's (1976) interview data such as the (a) invention of radar pulse tracking by Barney Oliver: "... I was ... visualizing the pulse [wave] as seen on the scope. . . . and said, 'now this is what we got to work with here;" (p. 11) (b) invention of the induction plasma torch by Thomas Reed: "I think probably in the image I just had a tube and a coil around it, and then I said to myself, how on earth am I going to get it started?" (p. 17) (c) invention of the solid state TV tube by Dr. Georg Szisklai: ". . . I essentially *looked at my hands*; and I said that . . . there was a word, complementarity . . . These two hands are complementary. *If I'm going to hand things over from one transistor to the other* . . . then Im going to have this complementary operation in a sense;" (p. 19) and (d) invention of HP-35 pocket calculator circuitry by Dr. David Cochran: "Some of it falls into place by talking about it [in order to keep my mind on the right track]; most of it falls into place by . . . imagery." (p. 173).

In a second study, Krueger (1976) gave each of eight scientists four invention problems (e.g., an artificial iris, a fan without moving parts), to which they responded with a solution viewpoint or approach. They did so using a method of *isomorphic reporting*, in which the participants reported verbal thinking in words (tape recorded) and images by drawings. Krueger also recorded gestures and movements, which he saw as being "closely tied up with visual imagery" (cf. my reference to McNeill's (1992) theory of gestures in Chapter 4, p. 159). This phase of Kreuger's research is especially important because it captured expert performance under standardized conditions that allow it to be recorded and measured, a recommended procedure in the scientific study of expertise (Ericsson, 2003a, p. 50 ff).

The evidence for imagery was clear in the detailed protocols. As summarized by Krueger (pp. 30–31), all of the scientists "used visualizing heavily" in the following ways: (a) images representing or combining with the task environment, (b) image elements combined into larger technical images, (c) holistic movement of images, (d) visual analogy, (e) single images that led to a solution format, (f) image-gesture interaction, (g) images simulating physical effects and properties, (h) hierarchical shifts in imagery from specific to general and general to specific, (i) substitution of image equivalents for each other, and (j) image elaboration. These reflect the creative functions of imagery described earlier: conceptual pegs or other problem-related imagery, analogical shifts, image associations, image integration, and image transformation.

Dual coding was equally evident in the protocols. In DCT terms, the most frequently reported thinking operations entailed referential processing, in both directions: (a) verbal-imaginal ("words elicit images which represent technical building blocks and effects"), (b) imagery-verbal ("judgments about images stated in words," "imagery elicits verbal reporting of imagery"), and (c) an interplay of the two ("back and forth shifts between images and words").

Krueger's (1976) extensive discussions, although focused on holistic (Gestalt) imagery, cover points that are completely consistent with dual coding analyses of creativity in scientific domains. The following commonalities are especially pertinent.

Krueger asked whether the creative problem and solution falls under an axiomatic system as in set theory, geometry, mathematical analysis, logic, Boolean algebra, and so forth. He concluded that "Creative science is, by definition, not subsumed by an axiomatic system. . . Instead, solutions are configurational in nature, structural, spatial" (p. 94). This bears on the limitations of formalism discussed earlier and again in later sections of this chapter, especially in relation to physics and (more surprisingly) mathematics.

Krueger (1976) suggested that the significant processes of translation between imagery and verbal modes in the contexted of problem solving "appear to be (1) the narrowing down of imagery properties by verbal (or felt) definition constraints, so as to satisfy specialized property criteria, often of a type unusual in the physical world, and (2) the back and forth building process in which elicited image is judged, and the judgment elicits further (judgment-satisfying) imagery" (p. 78). The first statement refers to the guidance function in which verbal processes keep imagery focused on the target problem. The second refers to the evaluative functions of both codes, presumably involving comparisons between past and present images relevant to progressive stages of the creative process.

Krueger (1976) stressed the creative importance of externalizing imagery in the form of drawings, especially cumulative collections of fragments that are relevant to the problem. Studies of major inventions "showed that in most cases the technical fragments (needed for the new combination) were available and known years before the invention was made" (p. 102). "A collection of [such] problem fragments, each translated into diagram, constructs a situation which greatly increases likelihood of perception. Solution insights are derived from an overview of elements and patterns of relationships between elements, the very essence of holistic representation" (p. 99). Such externalized image fragments are evident in the protocols of his samples of inventors and in biographies of such famous innovators as Edison, Polya, and Darwin (discussed further in the next section).

An important aspect of image collections is that they reach a "critical mass" that accelerates "psychological collisions [so that] elements collide in the mind, due to their proximity in time and space" (Krueger, 1976 p. 99). There is a limit to how many diagrams or other externalized images can be viewed at one time, so the reference here must be to a cumulative memory record of such images, which can be externalized as drawings given appropriate retrieval cues (including salient conceptual pegs). The primary source for such collections is "the visual free association of the problem solver" (Krueger, 1976, p. 100), supplemented by deliberate searches of external sources, such as patent diagrams in the problem area. The obvious parallel is the more general DCT idea of long-term growth of a domain-specific apperceptive mass of verbal and nonverbal representations and their connecting pathways, which can be selectively activated by external cues so that the components come together in an integrated solution to a problem. That problem is itself part of the apperceptive mass, a verbal question and its associated image fragments waiting for closure.

Krueger's (1976) systematic studies of creative thinking in applied scientists justify more confidence than we might otherwise have in similar interpretations of creative processes of the major movers of the sciences and arts together with analyses of their creative products. The spotlight turns first on Darwin because his conceptual scheme is at once the running theme of this volume and an object of study from the dual coding perspective.

DARWIN AND HIS LEGACY IN BIOLOGY

This is a trilogy in which the first part is a dual coding interpretation of Darwin's creation of his theory of evolution and a metatheoretical analysis of the theory itself. The second part describes his legacy in immunology, a subdomain of the Darwinian struggle for survival. The third part presents similar analyses of the discovery of the structure and function of DNA, the unit of heredity and evolution that was unknown to Darwin but now is the culmination of what he started.

My analysis of Darwin's creative thinking and the final theoretical product draw on general biographical works (e.g., Ward, 1927) and more specifically on Howard Gruber's (1974) psychological study of Darwin. I first describe the rich experiential foundation for the apperceptive mass that was necessary for Darwin's creativity. I then present evidence for cooperative dual coding during all phases of the development of the theory, including (a) his observations of varieties of life forms as the source of imagery, and his reading of works on evolution that prompted verbal expressions of his theory; (b) the tree-of-life model and accompanying commentaries; and (c) Darwin's views on imagery as a mechanism of thought.

Experiential Foundations

The experiences that led to Darwin's theory began early in life. As a boy he was more interested in observing worms, beetles, and plants than attending school, presumably because of the naturalist bent of his father and other relatives and acquaintances. Moreover, the concept of evolution was in the air, for his grandfather Erasmus had published an evolutionary theory that was elaborated on by the French naturalist, Lamarck. Their ideas must have been familiar to Darwin through family conversations and his reading. He was directly influenced as well by the great geological evolutionist, Sir Charles Lyell, and by John Stevens Henslow, Professor of Botany at Cambridge, who was so impressed by Darwin that he recommended him as the natural historian for the 5-year exploratory voyage of H. M. S. Beagle to the South Seas from 1831 to 1836. Thus, at that time, Darwin already had considerable expertise in biology and an interest in evolutionary ideas, which formed a background against which he could compare the new species of plants, birds, fish, and reptiles he saw during that famous voyage.

Such experiences created an expanding domain-specific apperceptive mass that was associatively organized across and within species. For example, finches formed a specific subdomain by virtue of generalization based on perceptual similarity and verbal classification, a set of referentially-connected finch imagens and logogens. The finches varied systematically on such perceptual characteristics as beak size and shape, constituting a differentiated series within a larger finch domain. Add other species and we have a massive, hierarchically organized representational structure corresponding to different levels of biological classes.

Darwin's study of barnacles after his return from the Beagle voyage provided his most penetrating insights into the nature of species. The work, published in four volumes, was so thorough and meticulous that 100 years later a zoologist was able to say that Darwin's example was still to be followed, for few animals had received such comprehensive and world-wide treatment (source cited in Gruber, 1974, p. 26).

Darwin's knowledge derived as well from his voracious reading. His autobiography and working papers refer to hundreds of books and papers on biology, geology, geography, gardening, breeding, and other domains. Together, the concrete observations and his reading laid the nonverbal and verbal foundations of his theory of evolution by natural selection. This apperceptive mass became increasingly organized around the evolutionary theme that motivated and guided his observations and thinking, both of which were externalized in his writing and sketching.

Dual Coding Processes in Darwin's Creativity

The argument here is that Darwin's theory emerged from the cooperative interplay between evolving, domain-specific nonverbal imagery and verbal processing systems. The evidence must show clearly that both systems were involved and that they fulfilled specific creative functions as described earlier. Because imagery is so important in the DCT analysis, I first try to resolve an ambiguity concerning Darwin's own introspections about the role of imagery in his thinking.

On one hand, Darwin favored an imagery theory of thought and described himself as someone with fairly strong visual imagery (Gruber, 1974, pp. 236–237). On the other hand, "it should follow [from his imagistic theory] that abstract ideas are harder to think about than concrete objects. He sees immediately that this is not so: love and pain are as easy as scarlet. Another difficulty: lightning calculators must have strong visual imagery, but they are 'not clever people, ' so the essence of inventive thought may not lie in imagery" (Gruber, 1974 p. 319).

From the DCT perspective, however, there is no necessary contradiction in Darwin's statements about imagery. His introspective analysis suggests that he often experienced visual imagery. His deductions about the limitations of imagery in thinking also were appropriate given his assumptions, but they do not follow from DCT. Concrete and abstract concepts alike are understood using both imagery and verbal processes, and intelligence is defined by a combination of verbal and nonverbal skills. Furthermore, we now know that abstract ideas are harder to think about than concrete ones in many tasks, although typical differences might not show up for Darwin's examples because the abstract words "pain" and "love" arouse imagery almost as easily as the word "scarlet" according to our imagery ratings (Clark & Paivio, 2004). The ratings on a 7-point scale are 6. 37, 5. 43, and 5. 60 for scarlet, agony (pain is not on our list), and love, respectively. The ratings for agony and love are in the ballpark of the imagery ratings for many familiar concrete words (e.g., apron, 5.88; cabbage, 5.75; country, 5.47).

Darwin's ambivalent self-analysis alerts us once again to the limitations of introspective reports as evidence for specific cognitive processes and how they affect performance. More objective clues to the role of imagery in thinking can be found in the style and content of the origin of species and his notebooks, especially the concreteness level of his writing and the theoretically-relevant images and verbal processes suggested by key text passages and his "*tree of Life* sketches.

Darwin's biographers routinely refer to the factual richness, specificity, and vividness of his writing. Steve Jones told us that "*The Origin* is the high point of the literature of fact" and then went on to compare Darwin's and Herman Melville's descriptions of the Galapagos: "Darwin is vivid and direct. . . Melville is, in contrast, feeble" (Jones, 1999, xxi). Alison Jolly alluded to metaphors derived from observation: "[Darwin] led a life of perpetual fascination with natural forms and behaviors; earthworms, barnacles, orchids, pigeons, peoples. His metaphors inspired the great literary minds of his time, and Darwin's image of the entangled bank remains with us today" (Jolly, 1999, p. 25).

The Galapagos–Malthus Connection to Dual Coding

The most direct sources of Darwin's productive imagery were the concrete observations of "natural forms" throughout his life, but especially on the Galapagos; and the most obvious sources for verbal theorizing were his readings. Both sources are revealed by his autobiographical description of how reading Malthus's (1798) *Essay on Population* illuminated for him the idea of natural selection.

> In October 1838, that is fifteen months after I had begun my systematic enquiry, I happened to read for amusement Malthus on *Population*, and being well prepared to appreciate the struggle for existence which everywhere goes on from long-continued observation of the habits of animals and plants, it at once struck me that under these circumstances favourable variations would tend to be preserved, and unfavourable ones to be destroyed. The result of this would be the formation of new species. Here, then, I had at last got a theory by which to work . . . (cited in Gruber, 1974, p. 173)

The main point is that reading Malthus triggered memory images of animals and plants as well as relevant verbal associations, culminating in the critical theoretical insight. Darwin also emphasized how his earlier observations prepared him for the theoretical deduction. Moreover, the idea of natural selection appears in his notebooks much earlier in various forms including, importantly, awareness of the analogy between artificial selection by breeders and selection by nature. What Malthus helped him see was the significance of natural selection for evolutionary theory (Gruber, 1974, p. 119).

The same confluence of nonverbal and verbal processes can be seen in the following example, in which imagery now elicits the verbal theoretical association:

. . . in the summer of 1838 Darwin was studying biological variation, and he was searching for a mechanism of selection. Neither process alone would generate a workable theory of evolution. As it happened, on September 23 he wrote in his notebook: "Saw in Lodigges garden 1279 varieties of roses!!! proof of capability of variation." On September 28 he recorded his reading of Malthus and his insight about superfecundity and natural selection: "until the one sentence of Malthus no one clearly perceived the great check among men." (Gruber, 1974, p. 251)

The Tree-of-Life Image and Dual Coding

It could be argued that Darwin's famous visual metaphor as expressed in his tree sketches simply illustrated ideas already arising from his observations and his reading, rather than being essential to the creative process. His notebooks show, however, that the model served as "one guiding image. . . depicting the theoretical model of branching evolution referred to repeatedly throughout the *Origin*" (Gruber, 1974, p. 141), a model that went through progressive modifications as his theoretical ideas evolved.

The sketches also provide clear evidence of dual coding processes operating in the creation of the theory. Each sketch and the accompanying text include written notes that explain the theoretical intent of the drawing. Thus, "From the notes immediately following [the first sketch], it is apparent that Darwin was able to use even his first crude version of the tree schema to produce further deductions. He sees immediately that the branching model accounts for certain observed discontinuities . . . between relatively similar forms" (Gruber, 1974, pp. 142–143).

The more elaborate second sketch (reproduced here as Fig. 18. 2) is headed by the introspective note, "I think," which reinforces the interpretation that this was creative work in progress. It shows labeled branches and descriptions of extinct and living forms, with further notes commenting on the "great gap between birds and mammalia, still greater between vertebrate and articulata, still greater between animals and plants'. . . all to be accounted for in the branching model" (Gruber, 1974 p. 144). The final sketch (Gruber, 1974, p. 197) "reformulates the branching model in terms of human survival and descent [in relation to other primates], as though the ordinary form of a genealogical family tree were inherent in his idea from its conception" (Gruber, 1974, p. 144).

The generation and functions of the sketches are intertwined in the dual coding interpretation. They were generated from internal images and verbal cues, perhaps by analogy with labeled genealogical family trees seen against the background of rich imagery, verbal descriptions, and (more or less) inchoate interpretations of relations among the varieties of natural forms already part of Darwin's mental repertoire. In turn, the acts of drawing and writing, together with feedback from the completed sketches and notes, modified and added to the representational base in specific ways that coalesced around the verbal concept "theory of evolution," which increasingly dominated Darwin's thinking during his Galapagos voyage.

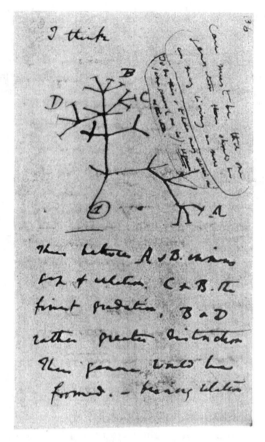

FIGURE 18.2 The second annotated tree-of-life sketch in Darwin's notebooks clearly showing the role of verbal and nonverbal (sketching) processes in his creative thinking. Reproduced by permission of the Syndics of Cambridge University Library.

The sketches served two related creative functions. First, they helped concretize and integrate separate pieces of cognitive information, which consisted of evolution-relevant imagens and logogens that converged on the different versions of the branching tree diagram. Second, the sketches functioned as conceptual pegs to which the related specific images and verbal concepts in long-term memory could be attached. Reciprocally, the externalized conceptual pegs served as especially effective retrieval cues for the growing collection of images and verbal representations, exemplifying the redintegrative power of pictures, which, in this case, was reinforced by the accompanying verbal cues.

The Missing Genetic Link

Darwin recognized that his theory needed a satisfactory mechanism of variation and it troubled him that he could not come up with one. Mendel worked out the fundamental laws of heredity based on discrete hereditary units just after the mid-19th century, and even after that the nature of genetic "mutations" remained poorly understood for a long time. Today it is linked to the interpretation of the gene as a replicator—it produces copies of itself. No copy machine, however perfect, can produce exact copies. There is always a slight change and copies made from copies accumulate changes until the result is noticeably different—genetically, a new variety or species. Gruber (1974) suggested that Darwin is to be appreciated all the more because he persisted with the development of his theory despite being troubled all along by a missing piece of the puzzle, a piece that he assumed must exist for the theory to work.

A Metatheoretical Summary

I propose that the theory of evolution by natural selection is understandable as a dually coded representation consisting of a verbal description coupled with a representation of the phenomenal domain to which the description applies. No one has presented the verbal description more vividly and succinctly than Darwin himself in the final paragraph of *The origin of species* (1998 reprint) The description evokes imagery that illustrates the phenomenal domain but does not capture it in an integrated way that corresponds to the description. The closest we can come to such a dual coding portait of Darwin's theory is to juxtapose a branching tree-of-life model with his verbal statement. Figure 18.3 from Attenborough, 1979, pp. 310–311) concretizes the branching tree with pictures of salient species members. Darwin's verbal summary was as follows:

> It is interesting to contemplate an entangled bank, clothed with many plants of many kinds, with birds singing in the bushes, with various insects flitting about, and with worms crawling through the damp earth, and to reflect that these elaborately constructed forms, so different from each other, and dependent on each other in so complex a manner, have all been produced by the same laws acting around us. These laws, taken in the largest sense, being Growth with Reproduction; inheritance which is almost implied by reproduction; Variability from the indirect and direct action of the external conditions of life, and from use and disuse; a Ratio of Increase so high as to lead to a Struggle for Life, and as a consequence to Natural Selection, entailing Divergence of Character and the Extinction of less-improved forms. Thus, from the war of nature, from famine and death, the most exalted object which we are capable of conceiving, namely, the production of higher animals, directly follows. There is grandeur in this view of life, with its several powers, having been originally breathed into a few forms or into one; and that, whilst this planet has gone cycling along according to the fixed law of gravity, from so simple a beginning endless forms most beautiful and most wonderful have been, and are being, evolved (Darwin, 1859, pp. 488–490).

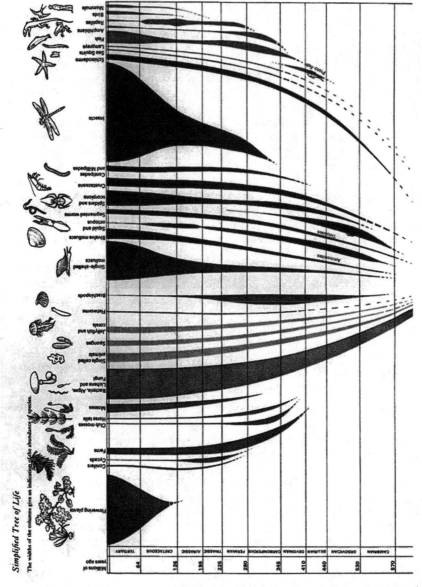

FIGURE 18.3. Simplified tree of life. Adapted from D. Attenborough (1979). *Life on earth*, p. 310–311.

Immunology: A Darwinian Microcosm

I now trace the origin and controversial history of the role of imagery in the pioneering work of the German immunologist Paul Ehrlich around the turn of the 20th century. I intend to show how the issues can be understood and resolved in dual coding terms. The topic has a direct evolutionary connection that is well-understood today but not when immunology emerged as a branch of medical science. The following sketch provides a retrospective bridge between Darwin and Ehrlich.

Immunology is a medical subdomain of biology and chemistry that entails a microcosm of the Darwinian struggle for life. The battle takes place within our bodies—the bodies of all living things. The invaders are bacteria, viruses, and other pathogens. The territorial defenders are cellular antibodies and other components of the immune system. Joining forces with the latter are nutrients and drugs that boost the immune system or directly attack the pathogens. It is a war in which the winner takes all: If the pathogens win, we get sick and die; if the immune system wins, the pathogens die. The interesting—and frightening—aspect of the struggle is the speed with which natural selection operates to modify the pathogens so that they are resistant to the drug-reinforced defenders and thus take over their territory and move to others when the resources of one are used up. The battle against the AIDS virus is a dramatic current example of Darwinian evolutionary laws acting around (and within) us (e.g., see Jones, 1999).

Ehrlich sought to understand the nature of the defense mechanisms. The entities and their weapons were invisible and they had to be inferred from experimental results, and imagined if one wanted to "see" the action. Ehrlich did both and the imagery side in particular embroiled him in the same kinds of controversial scientific and epistemological issues that are familiar to us from earlier contexts. Ehrlich's case has been comprehensively presented in an article by Cambrosio et al. (1993). I rely on that source as the basis of my summary of the theory and the evidence for my DCT interpretations.

Erlich's Side-Chain Theory

Ehrlich developed a theory of antibody formation based on side chains (receptors) attached to cells. Normally responsible for anchoring nutrients among other functions, these side chains can be blocked by toxins. The cell reacts by overproducing receptors, which are then shed into the bloodstream to become antitoxins by combining with toxins in a lock-and-key manner and neutralizing them by hemolysis. Ehrlich illustrated the theory in a lecture in 1900 using a series of eight pictures (reproduced in Cambrosio et al., 1993, p. 664), which are still taken to be direct ancestors of the geometric shapes that are used by immunologists to represent antibody-antigen reactions. For example, the picture shown in Fig. 18.4 serves as the logo of the journal, *Immunobiology*.

The pictures were intended to represent both static and dynamic mechanisms of the immune reactions. Thus, in the first six illustrations

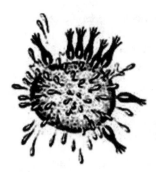

FIGURE 18.4   Ehrlich's model of an immune system antitoxin combining with toxins in a lock-and-key manner. From A. Cambrosio, D. Jacobi, & P. Keating (1993). Ehrlich's "beautiful pictures" and the controversial beginnings of immunological imagery. *Isis*, 84, p. 664. Original source: Paul Ehrlich, "On Immunity with Special Reference to Cell Life," Proceedings of the Royal Society of London, 1900, 66, 424–448.

The perfect geometrical fit between the corresponding toxins and antitoxins shows the specificity of their union and illustrates a static understanding of the immune reaction. The dynamic understanding is introduced by the detailed ["comic strip"] narrative of how an organism is able first to recognize specific toxins and then to react by producing antitoxins that will protect it from further damage. (Cambrioso et al., 1993, p. 680].

How did Ehrlich develop the theory and why was it controversial?

Creative Processes in the Development of the Theory

Ehrlich apparently had a penchant for imagery as evidenced by his "extensive—nay, obsessive—resort to graphic images in the most bizarre situations, including the drawing of diagrams on tablecloths, stacks of postcards, shoe soles, or the floor" (Cambrosio et al., 1993, Footnote 54, p. 689). This externalization of his imagery presumably reflected visualization as a style of thought His theoretical use of imagery was based on a series of analogies derived from chemistry and biology. The chemist August Kekulé used the term *side-chains* to refer to the chains of atoms attached to the hexagonal shape with which he represented the benzene molecule (recall that Kekulé claimed to have worked out the structure by analogy with his dream of snakes swallowing their own tails). Emil Fisher used the lock-and-key metaphor in 1894 to describe the stereo chemical interaction between enzymes and their glucoside substrate. Ehrlich acknowledged these sources of the metaphors when he presented his "beautiful pictures."

The biological source is evident from the resemblance of the pictures to animal shapes and actions, characterized in one example as "hungry polywogs biting eagerly at inviting bits of protruding protoplasm of just the right size to make a mouthful" (source cited in Cambrosio et al., 1993, p. 676). Ehrlich himself spoke of the "tentacular" apparatus exercising a digestive function analogous to insectivorous plants: "it has been known since the famous researches of Darwin that the tentacles of Drosera secrete a protein digesting fluid" (Cambrosio et al., 1993, p. 677). The biological imagery might have been motivated partly in an attempt to reconcile his humeral (hemolytic) theory with Metchnikoff's phagocytic theory of immunity (Cambrosio et al., 1993, p. 277), which, by his own account, originated analogically from observation of the mobile cells of starfish larva.[58]

The historical assessment is that Ehrlich's theory was both chemical and biological. "He resorted simultaneously to chemical (benzene rings) and biological (insectivorous plants) analogies, not to speak of his borrowings from cellular pathology . . . by edging his way between the two [disciplines], he constructed a new disciplinary form" (Cambrosio, et al., 1993, p. 679).

The Controversies

The debates engendered by Ehrlich's immunological imagery involved a set of related issues concerning scientific explanation. They implicated (a) the explanatory as compared to expository status of theoretical concepts; (b) the problem of reification and circularity of the latter, thus implicating operational definitions and the distinction between observational and theoretical terms; and (c) an opposition between imagery ("visual") and verbal ("textual") explanations. It is evident that these are the same general issues that later characterized the imagery/verbal/propositional debates in cognitive psychology and the dual coding response to it.

Some immunologists thought that Ehrlich's pictures were expository rather than explanatory, at best facilitating "clearness of explanation" or serving as a "good mnemo technical device for immunological theory," and at worst as "puerile graphic representations." Ehrlich himself was initially ambivalent about the purpose of his pictures, referring to them as "merely a pictorial method " of presenting his views, and a "convenient pedagogical resource" (Cambrioso et al., 1993, pp. 666–681). Others, however, saw them as an important heuristic tool for subsequent experiments, and were in fact so used by Ehrlich and his coworkers (Cambrosio et al., 1993, p. 694). Beyond that, there was a gradual conceptual shift in which the pictures

---

[58]"One day when the whole family had gone to the circus to see some extraordinary performing apes, I remained alone with my microscope, observing the life of the mobile cells of a transparent starfish larva, when a new thought suddenly flashed across my brain. It struck me that similar cells might serve in the defence of the organism against intruders. Feeling that there was in this something of surpassing interest, I felt so excited that I began striding up and down the room and even went to the seashore to collect my thoughts' (Metchnikoff, cited in Beveridge, 1957, p. 94)

became explanatory in the sense that they served as symbolic representations for "real" antibodies and their functions.

The conceptual shift raised the specter of reification and explanatory circularity because, in Ehrlich's time and long after, antibodies were invisible and hypothetical. There was "absolutely no knowledge of what these antibodies might be, or even that they exist as physical objects . . . we recognize them by what they do without discovering just what they are" (Wells, cited in Cambrosio et al., 1993, p. 670). Thus the concept was entirely theoretical and not observational. In the normative science of the time, it could only be defined operationally by chemical procedures and such reactions as agglutination of blood in test tubes. No wonder, then, that the scientific status of Ehrlich's "beautiful pictures" of invisible antibodies was suspect: such "images ought to be discarded because they bear the inherent danger of slippage from model to reality" (Cambrosio et al., 1993, p. 684).

That situation was radically altered by technological advances in the 1920s, especially X-ray analysis, which transformed antibodies into real substances with physicochemical properties that had potential explanatory power. The "proper" nature of the explanation, however, remained an issue.

The issue can be characterized in terms of interactive relations between the observable phenomena, their symbolic representation, and their theoretical (explanatory and predictive) interpretations. The observables included the manifestations of disease and immunity, the diagnostic procedures by which they were identified or defined, and eventually (when sophisticated equipment became available), aspects of the structural-chemical substrate of the immune system in action. All of the observational steps were, however, guided by tentative symbolic representations and interpretive conceptual schemes, constituting normal empirical science as defined by Conant (1947, Chapter 2, this volume). Debates about these relations concerned the scientifically appropriate "language" or format of representation and interpretation.

Cambrosio and his colleagues (1993) saw the debates as involving, implicitly or explicitly, an opposition between Ehrlich's visual iconography and a textual propositional analysis of experimental facts favored by his critics. The latter approach could, for example, include the use of letter symbols to represent toxin and antitoxin molecules, and textual accounts of processes such as hemolysis. Thus, the debate can be described in dual coding terms as an opposition between nonverbal and verbal approaches to the conceptualization of immunological phenomena.

A Dual Coding Theoretical Resolution

The dual coding resolution of the issues is straightforward: At all stages, immunological theory and research advanced on the basis of an interplay between imagery and verbal systems, and immunological theory itself is the domain-specific legacy of that interplay. The drama never was and could not be just a silent film or radio script, it was live theater that began as science fiction and evolved into a documentary about mini creatures in action.

Ehrlich's side-chain theory was based on prior contributions from chemists and biologists—stereo chemical iconography and formulas about invisible molecular structures together with images and descriptions of insectivores and other biological creatures. Whether in a Eureka moment, the entities were stretched, shrunk, and reshaped in Ehrlich's imagery and expressed verbally and graphically. The nonverbal– verbal interplay was first documented in a 1898 letter to a cousin which included sketches of a side chain reacting with a toxin, accompanied by handwritten descriptions of the entities and reactions (Cambrosio et al., 1993, p. 678). This is the same kind of annotated pictorial presentation of a theoretical idea that we saw in Darwin's notebook sketches. By 1900, Ehrlich's pictures had become more precise and systematic, presented in his lecture as an unannotated visual model of of the theory accompanied by an oral interpretation. Could the pictures have stood alone as a theoretical "statement?" Not from the perspective of DCT: the static pictures of structural entities and interactions are open to different readings—different referential and associative reactions— the nature of which would have depended, in this case, on the experiential background and theoretical biases of the scientific audience. The resulting controversy about the scientific status of the pictures was an inevitable consequence of their interpretive uncertainty. For the textually biased critics, Ehrlich's verbal interpretation would have sufficed.

But we have seen that verbal statements, too, are uncertain in meaning, especially if they are as general and abstract as theoretical statements must be. Ehrlich narrowed down the interpretation by painting metaphorical word-pictures and pairing those with his visual models. The theory was still tentative and in need of empirical support, but at least it was clearer as a theory because its verbal and pictorial-imaginal expressions were mapped onto each other. The term *expression* is misleading, however, because it implies that there is an underlying abstract theory that is simply expressed in the two forms. Not so according to dual coding metatheory. Instead, Ehrlich's immunological theory consisted *of* interconnected verbal and nonverbal representations and their activation by the "beautiful pictures," the verbal statements, or the evocative name of the theory.

Ehrlich's creation has evolved into a much more elaborate theory in terms of the number of agents and modes of action of the immune system. The theory retains its pictorial and verbal character, enriched by images and notational descriptions of chemical structures and processes, all of which can be symbolically represented in its dynamic richness by modern audiovisual technology. Following Ehrlich, the great Linus Pauling contributed to such advances in pictorial models of the immune system (Cambrosio, Jacobi, & Keating, 2005), just as he pioneered in biochemical modeling techniques that helped reveal the structure of DNA.

The DNA Molecule

James D. Watson, Francis Crick, and Maurice Wilkins shared the 1962 Nobel Prize for their discovery of the structure of the DNA molecule. An unrecognized collaborator was molecular biologist Rosalind Franklin, whose expertise in X-ray crystallograhy led to the discovery of the double helix structure of DNA (Maddox, 2002). This is the unit of heredity that was unknown to Darwin and even Gregor Mendel, although Mendel came close to the idea of a functional genetic unit. Today, Darwin's theory and Mendel's "laws" of heredity have been transformed into a DNA-based conceptualization of reproduction and evolution.

Watson and Crick were spurred on in their effort to crack the DNA code by the prize that surely awaited the discoverer and their awareness that Nobel laureate Linus Pauling was hot on the trail of the elusive entity. Watson (1968) described how they relied on a method of visualization and concrete modeling that had been used successfully by Pauling: "The main working tools were a set of molecular models superficially resembling the toys of pre-school children" (p. 38). Psychological accounts of their creative thinking have typically emphasized the nonverbal analogical modeling and spatial imagery (e.g., Paivio, 1983b; Shepard, 1976, p. 146). Here I insist once again that the process necessarily involved dual coding—that is, simultaneous and successive verbal and nonverbal processing. The interpretation is based on Watson's account, but there is a missing aspect to the story that reinforces the dual coding interpretation while enhancing the human drama. I begin with the more familiar imagery story as told by Watson.

The model construction involved cardboard parts that could easily be tried out and finally put together in metal. The model had to satisfy chemical rules and X-ray evidence concerning plausible forms of the DNA molecule. The modelers arrived at a configuration in which two sugar-phosphate "backbones" twisted in opposite directions on the outside of base pairs of hydrogen bonded to the backbones, forming a double helix resembling a twisted ladder. The base pairs were known to consist of the nucleotides adenine, cystosine, guanine, and thymine. Watson (1968) first guessed that they were paired like-with-like, adenine with adenine, and so on. "If DNA was like this," he wrote, "each adenine residue would form two hydrogen bonds to an adenine residue related to it by a 180-degree rotation" (p. 116), and similarly for the other nucleotide pairs. Watson continued as follows: "For two hours [after midnight] I happily lay awake with pairs of adenine residues whirling in front of my closed eyes" (p. 118).

However, by noon the following day, through feedback from an expert on hydrogen bonding and Crick's recent "fiddling with the model, " Watson (1968) realized that like-with-like base pairs would not work. A day later, Watson began trying out different base pairings and suddenly "became aware that an adenosine-thymine pair held together by two hydrogen bonds was identical in shape to a guanine-cytosine pair [similarly bonded]. All the hydrogen bonds seemed to form naturally; no fudging was required to make the types of base pairs identical in shape" (p. 123). This turned out to be the solution to DNA structure that satisfied all chemical criteria. Its published description included the sentence, "It has not escaped our notice that the specific pairings we have postulated immediately suggests a possible copying mechanism for the genetic mechanism" (cited in Watson, 1968, p. 139). This is an understatement of the explosive realization of the implications of the model. The copying mechanism is schematized in Fig. 18.5.

The standard imagery interpretation of the creative achievement rests on the trial-and-error model building and anticipatory imagery of such outcomes as the

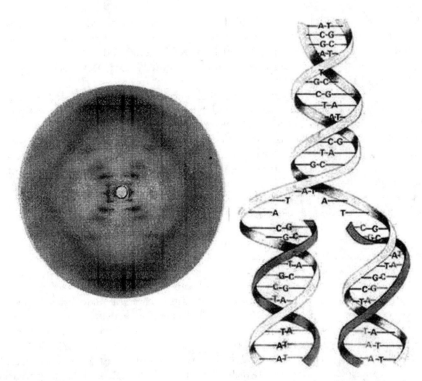

FIGURE 18.5   Left side: x-ray photo 51 of the DNA molecule taken on May 2, 1952, by Rosalind E. Franklin and R. G. Gosling. On the right, the molecule envisaged as replicating. Adapted from the photographic insert of the x-ray photo and the DNA model on p. 135 in J. D. Watson (1968), *The double helix*. New York: Atheneum Publishers. Used with permission of J. D. Watson.

DNA structure resulting from mental rotation of a helical shape. However, there is more to the story. First, prior to the final model construction, Rosalind Franklin's fellow crystallographer Maurice Wilkins had shown Watson Franklin's X-ray photograph of DNA that revealed an X-shaped pattern that was conclusive evidence of the double helix structure of the molecule. The photograph is reproduced here in Fig. 18. 5 alongside the familiar DNA model. Watson said as follows: "The instant I saw the picture my mouth fell open and my pulse began to race. The pattern was unbelievably simpler than those obtained previously . . . Moreover, the black cross of reflections which dominated the picture could arise only from a helical structure" (p. 107). Thus, the decisive event for the final problem-solving imagery and model manipulations was a picture of the sought-after molecular structure. In DCT terms, the picture was the conceptual peg that integrated all the rest of the chemical information known up to that time. Sadly, Franklin, DNA's unsung hero died without knowing that she had been edged out by Watson and Crick (Maddox, 2002) and it is unknown whether she would have shared the Nobel prize inasmuch as it is awarded only to the living.

A second point about the creative thinking that culminated in the DNA revelation was the covert and overt verbalization that accompanied every stage of the process, the blind alleys as well as the advances. In a general sense the point is obvious, for scientists talk and write about their ideas and research as part of the science game. That misses the important point that imagery has been the focus of interpretive attention in the DNA breakthrough as in the other cases reviewed here. It's as if imagery did the creative work on its own. Crucial as imagery is because of its spatial properties, freedom from sequential constraints, and so forth, its content comes from the concrete experiential background of the scientist and is evoked and guided by contextual cues, including especially referentially related language. In this case, the names of the relevant chemicals and processes are combined with the nonverbal base in the DCT analysis.

Dual Coding Metatheoretical Analysis

As with Darwin's and Ehrlich's theories, DNA as the molecular theoretical foundation of heredity and evolution can be analyzed in terms of dual coding metatheory. The microentities and their structural interrelations can be symbolized stereochemically as three-dimensional models on the one hand and verbal descriptions on the other. The latter includes letter notations for names of chemical elements and structures, descriptions as in the codon sequence of DNA molecules, and so on. The structures and letter symbols are combined in the DNA picture in which the chemical molecular entities are presented in their alphabetic guises, with their single- or double-bond interconnections symbolized by lines. The meaning of the theoretical representation is the juxtaposition of its verbal description or equation and its explicit or implicit nonverbal depiction, together with the functional implications of the dually coded representation, namely its role in heredity represented as an expanding set of verbal associations and images.

EINSTEIN AND PHYSICAL SCIENCE

It is passing strange that physics deals with phenomena that are so distant from psychology and yet the creators of the domain have been deeply immersed in psychological issues. This is especially true of the central issues here, the nature of the creative processes, and the resulting physical theories. Odder still, imagery was at the center of debates among 20th-century physicists, according to physics historian and philosopher Arthur I. Miller (1984). Quoting from the dust jacket of his volume:

> Miller focuses on Niels Bohr, Ludwig Boltzmann, Albert Einstein, Werner Heisenberg, and Henri Poincaré because the depth of their research led them to consider the problem of thinking itself. To a large degree, these philosopher

scientists set the intellectual milieu of the 20th century. The historical case studies reveal that fundamental advances in science are closely coupled to, and affected by, changing notions of mental imagery.

Imagery was important in the creative work of Einstein and other influential physicists, and thus they discussed its role in relation to concepts, concept formation, and their own creative thinking. Visualizability also had high priority as a criterion of the relevance and truth-value of theories, but, as the physical phenomena became increasingly invisible and elusive, visualizability gave way to abstract, quantitative interpretations of theoretical truth.

Miller (1984) described this conflict in physics as analogous to the imagery-proposition debate in cognitive science. Although he did not discuss the debate in dual coding terms, he nevertheless concluded with the "hope that the interplay that has been demonstrated here *between language and imagery* . . . will provide the stimulus for further investigations in this fascinating realm of thought" (p. 312, italics added). Miller in fact described the conceptual interplay among the physicists themselves in terms of language (not propositions) and imagery. It comes as no surprise that I take the analysis a step further and explicitly propose DCT as a way of conceptualizing and potentially resolving the issues in this area as it did in its own domain. The application of the theory is direct in the case of the creative process, and in its guise as a metatheory for the analysis of imagery and language in physical theories.

As others have done, I use Albert Einstein for developing the analysis because of his dominance in shaping 20th-century physics and because imagery apparently played such a prominent role in his creative leaps. He analyzed the nature of thought in general and described his own thought processes in detail. His biographers have traced his predilection for imagistic thinking to early difficulties with language. Physics provided a comfortable climate for his imagery because visualizability was a criterion of good theory.

I elaborate on (a) relevant aspects of Einstein's experiential background, (b) his views on imagery and thought, (c) the role of imagery and verbal processes in his development of the special theory of relativity, and (d) the derivation of his earth-shaking equation, $E = mc^2$, which also serves as the focus of my metatheoretical dual coding analysis.

Experiential Background

Einstein's difficulties with language have been well-documented (e.g., Patten, 1973). He didn't begin speaking until age 3 and his verbal problems persisted into adult life; he was a poor speller; he found writing difficult. At some point he would have been diagnosed as dyslexic in today's terminology. Equally notable, however, were his nonverbal interests and abilities. He liked telling the story of how impressed he was by the magnetic compass he saw when he was 4 or 5. The needle's invariable northward swing convinced him that there had to be "something behind things, something deeply hidden." He was known for his construction of intricate and colossal playing-card houses. He often completed large jigsaw puzzles and assembled buildings from toy blocks. He enjoyed extracurricular study of geometry, and, when introduced to the Pythagorean Theorem, Einstein thought that it was obviously true and needed no proof. Before age 10 he nonetheless proved it using his own method based on similarities of triangles.

He had good grades generally and excelled in mathematics in the first high school he attended in Munich. However, he hated the school because it was authoritarian, word oriented, and emphasized rote learning. He was rescued when, at age 15, he enrolled in a school founded by Johann Heinrich Pestalozzi, the Swiss educational reformer who based his approach on the view that "conceptual thinking is built on visual understanding; visual understanding is the basis of all knowledge." The teaching method focused on the object lesson, in which real objects are observed and described. It also included a discussion that moved from sense impressions to abstract principles, verbal definition, and concept formation (Sadoski & Paivio, 2001, p. 30). From our analytic perspective, the method entailed a combination of nonverbal and verbal experiences that would fully engage dual coding processes.

Einstein's domain-specific experience began early with home study of books on mathematics, physics, and philosophy. It continued through to doctoral education at the University of Zurich. He became familiar with the problems, experiments, and theories that engaged physicist-mathematicians from Galileo and Newton through to his immediate intellectual ancestors and contemporaries, including especially those covered in Miller's story of the role of imagery in the creation of 20th-century physics. Thus, Einstein's unprecedented theoretical contributions were founded on a rich experiential background.

Imagery in Einstein's Thinking

Einstein's biographers have attributed unusual importance to the role of imagery in his creative thinking. The emphasis is based mostly on Einstein's statements coupled with the analysts' desire to explain his mysterious creative leaps. The anecdotal evidence fully justifies the imagery emphasis, but in the final analysis, it does not explain the last step in the creative process.

The evidence includes Einstein's description of his own thought processes, his analysis of the nature of the thinking, and his recollections of his Gedanken experiments. Einstein's self assessment, according to Hadamard (1945, p. 142), already quoted in Chapter 1, is an example of his imagery-dominance view of thought: "Words or language, as they are written or spoken, do not seem to play any role in my mechanism of thought. " He went on to refer to "certain signs and more or less clear images which can be voluntarily reproduced and combined" as the first stage of thought, with "words or other [communicable] signs" coming laboriously in a second stage. We know, however, that such introspections should be interpreted cautiously. Evidence reviewed in Chapter 4 suggests that subjective reports can be valid indicators of a person's preference for nonverbal imagery as compared to verbal modes of thought. They are more suspect when it comes to the modus operandi of imagery and how it relates to language processes in cognitive tasks. Those relations have been gradually revealed by combining experimental methods with self-reports and other indicators of imagery and verbal thinking. The general picture now is that both processes are involved in different ways and amounts in different tasks. The best we can do here is extend the analysis by analogy to Einstein's creative thinking.

The following is his view of the nature of thinking, which presumably reflects his introspections of his own thought processes as well as other sources:

> What, precisely, is "thinking"? When, at the reception of sense-impressions, memory- pictures emerge, this is not yet "thinking." And when such pictures form series, each member of which calls forth another, this too is not yet "thinking. " When, however, a certain picture turns up in many such series, then . . . it becomes an ordering element for such series, in that it connects series which in themselves are unconnected. Such an element becomes an instrument, a concept . . . the transition from free association or "dreaming" to thinking is characterized by the more or less dominating role which the "concept" plays in it. It is by no means necessary that a concept must be connected with a sensorily cognizable and reproducible sign (word); but when this is the case thinking becomes by means of that fact communicable. (Einstein, 1949, p. 7)

Einstein obviously did not intend to cover all of the complex phenomena that define thinking in the widest psychological sense. Instead, he emphasized an aspect I have described as the conceptual peg function of symbolic images—images that remind us of associates in memory and provide an integrative link for them. Einstein referred to the recurrent organizing image as a concept. For him, words are not part of a concept, they only make it communicable. DCT, however, defines concept more broadly (Chapter 3). Images and words can be viewed as minimal conceptual units, but their conceptual status derives from their connections to each other, and associatively, to other units (e.g., different kinds of imaged or named dogs). Words serve the communication function stressed by Einstein only if they also are concepts in that sense.

Imagery and the Creation of Special Relativity Theory

Einstein's description of his Gedanken experiments are most often cited as evidence of the creative power of his imagery. Especially relevant is the "experiment" that led eventually to the special theory of relativity. Einstein's biographers have relied on his own description of the experience in his 1949 Autobiographical Notes. I refer to those presently in the context of my own analysis of problems associated with drawing inferences from the Gedanken experiment en route to my dual coding interpretations. For now, I cite Roger Shepard's (1978) concise description of the thought experiment because it particularly highlights the role of visual imagery:

> . . . the paradox that eventually led [Einstein] to develop the special theory of relativity first came to him when, at age 16, he imagined himself traveling along beside a beam of light (at the velocity of some 186, 000 miles per second). It then struck him that the stationary spatial oscillation that he mentally "saw" corresponded neither to anything that could be perceptually experienced as light nor to anything described by Maxwell's equations for the propagation of

electromagnetic waves. . . The elimination of the paradox required a revolutionary restructuring of the spatiotemporal configuration visualized in his thought experiment. However the translation of this restructuring into the verbal and mathematical symbols necessary for communication to others was, for Einstein, a very uncongenial and difficult business that he could undertake only when he had worked out his conceptualization of the physical situation by "more or less clear images that can be 'voluntarily' reproduced and combined". (pp. 134–135).

Here we run into two problems, first, the acceptance of Einstein's recollection at face value, and second, how he worked out his imagery-based conceptualization of the "physical situation" so that it could be reconstructed in verbal-mathematical terms. The first problem arises because Einstein first described the crucial Gedanken experiment in his Autobiograhical Notes in 1946, roughly 50 years after he conceived the thought experiment. This is a very long time for autobiographical memories to remain intact even for episodes we have seen and all the more so for ones we have only experienced in our thoughts. We know from experimental studies that recollections of recently witnessed events can be distorted by subtle verbal cues and misleading imagery instructions (Ceci, 2003, pp. 861–862). Perhaps Einstein often recounted and ruminated on his Gedanken experiment over the years, thereby reinforcing the memory, but we have no objective evidence on that possibility.

The memory problem seems to have gone unnoticed by Einstein's biographers. For example, Max Wertheimer (1945, as described by Miller, 1984, Chapter 5) apparently accepted the accuracy of Einstein's recollections when he used them to reconstruct the development of special relativity theory in terms of his Gestalt psychological view of thinking. The memory problem is compounded in that case because Wertheimer based his interpretations on his own recollections, years later, of conversations he had with Einstein beginning in 1916 (there is no evidence that he used notes taken at the time of the conversations; Miller, 1984, p. 190). Wertheimer's account raises other uncertainties that I address later.

The second problem, related to the aforementioned, is that Einstein left no workbooks comparable to Darwin's that give clues to the crucial imagery steps that he might have taken during the 10-year period between the Gedanken experiment in 1895, which revealed a puzzle but not its solution, and the publication of the theory that did resolve it 10 years later. He left us instead with mysterious intuition to explain the creative leaps. Miller (1984, pp. 123–124) stated this conclusion specifically in regard to the Gedanken experiment: "According to contemporaneous physics the Gedanken experimenter should be able to catch up with a point on the light wave. According to Einstein's 'intuition' the laws of optics should be independent of the observer's motion . . ." so that the velocity of light is c, always. More generally, Einstein asserted that "There is no logical way to the discovery of these elemental laws. There is only the way of intuition, which is helped by a feeling for the order lying behind the appearance" (source cited in Shepard, 1978, p. 135). However, with intuition and feeling for order unexplained, so too is the creative leap.

I encounter the same informational gaps in trying to interpret Einstein's theory development in dual coding terms. I accept at the outset his stated predilection for imaginal thinking because it is also consistent with his preferred activities as a child. Beyond that I rely on specific experiences that might have influenced Einstein's imagery and verbal thinking. According to Miller (1984, pp. 113–124), who used Einstein's writings to reconstruct his thinking "toward this momentous invention" (special relativity theory), Einstein was influenced generally by inconsistencies in theoretical physics that arose from the basic assumptions that space, time, and mass are fixed properties of physical systems. Einstein resolved the paradoxes by assuming that these properties can only be described relative to each other in ways that went far beyond more specific relativity principles proposed by Newton and Poincaré.

Einstein's solution drew on what was known or hypothesized prior to 1905 about relevant physical phenomena (e.g., the special importance of the nature of light, the effect of velocity on the mass of an electron, the properties of radiation) and controversies related to them. On the verbal-mathematical side, he capitalized on a series of transformational equations developed by the great Dutch physicist, H. A. Lorentz, in which the velocity of light is a universal constant but all measurements of time and distance are modified according to the velocity of the reference system.[59] In effect, "clocks" slow down as velocity increases and "yard sticks" shrink in the direction of motion, with the contraction effects becoming very large when velocity approaches that of light. Einstein saw in these transformations formal expression of the concept of the relativity of simultaneity, a specific variant of the relativity of time and distance. Einstein dramatized his insight by another railway analogy described as follows by Barnett (1948, pp. 56–60). An observer sitting on an embankment sees two lightning bolts simultaneously strike the tracks at each end of a moving train just as he is opposite the middle of the train. Another observer perched on top of the middle car of the train sees the flashes through mirrors that enable him to see both ends of the train at the same time, just as he is opposite the stationary observer on the bank. Will the flashes be simultaneous to the moving observer? The answer based on the traditional Newtonian idea of additivity of velocities is that they will not: the flash at the rear of the train will be seen a moment later than the one at the front because the observer is moving away from the flash, so the light from the rear needs extra time to catch up to him. By this account, if the train were moving at the speed of light, the light beam would never reach the moving observer and he would see only the flash in front. Einstein saw that the Lorentz transformations could resolve the simultaneity paradox on the principle that time and distance are variable quantities that nonetheless remain constant throughout the universe when their measurement takes account of moving as well as stationary reference contexts.

---

[59]Apparently Einstein discovered the transformations independently but referred to them as Lorentz equations because they were already known by that name. Subsequently they have generally been referred to as Lorentz-Einstein transformations (French, 1968, p. 63ff).

Special relativity theory incorporated all of the foregoing assumptions in regard to relativity of time, distance, and velocity. The theory generated remarkable explanations and predictions about physical phenomena. Before moving on to those, however, we must pause to reconsider the issues concerning the role of memory and intuition in relation to Einstein's development of the theory and its predictions.

By 1895 (the date of Einstein's Gedanken experiment concerning light as perceived by a moving observer), Lorentz had already used his transformations to account for the constant speed of light as measured against the earth's movement by Michelson and Morley in 1887. According to Lorentz, the dimensions of the measuring rod in the direction of the earth's motion contracted just enough to compensate for the movement speed. Lorentz later extended the hypothesis to account for other experiments and Einstein generalized it further in the context of his theory. In contrast with his recognition and use of Lorentz's equations and the contraction hypothesis, Einstein was uncertain whether he had even known about the Michelson–Morley experiment. Max Wertheimer, who wrote a Gestalt analysis of Einstein's thinking (see Miller, 1984, Chapter 5), apparently assumed that Einstein knew about the experiment because he asserted that it played a key role in Einstein's discovery of the relativity of simultaneity. This has been widely assumed by other historians as well. Einstein, however, wrote that the experiment played no decisive role in his development of the theory (Miller, 1984, p. 215), although he later cited it as important empirical confirmation. However, only some vagary of memory could explain his uncertainty about an experimental result that was common knowledge in physics by 1895 and encountered by him, if only incidentally, when he used the Lorentz equations to help develop his theory 10 years later.

There was no similar empirical precedent for one of the most striking predictions from the theory concerning time relativity. H. E. Ives and G. Stillwell (1938) confirmed that time slows up at high velocities using the frequency of vibration of hydrogen atoms as the clock: the frequency of the atoms moving at high speeds was reduced relative to stationary atoms, exactly as expected from Einstein's interpretation of the Lorentz equations. Even more momentous predictions arose from the following implicit aspect of the theory.

$E = mc^2$. Einstein viewed this equation as the most important deduction from special relativity theory. He described different derivations of the equation in 1905 and 1935. I focus here on Einstein's (1935) "elementary derivation" as analysed by science philosopher Francisco Flores (1998) because it provides explicit information concerning the interplay of imagery and verbal-mathematical processes in Einstein's reasoning. The goal of the derivations was to show formally that energy and mass are equivalent, that one can be transformed into the other. (The use of c as a constant in the equation was due to the special importance of the nature of light in Einstein's thinking prior to 1905.) The specific mathematical proofs are not relevant here, which is a good thing because I would be out of my depth if I needed to evaluate the mathematics to make my case.

Both derivations began with thought experiments. Motivated by the fact that special relativity theory grew out of Maxwell's electromagnetic equations, the first imagined situation traced consequences of the movement of two equally energetic particles of light. In 1935, however, Einstein argued that special relativity itself was independent of Maxwell's theory and that $E = mc^2$ as an implication of the equation is likewise independent of Maxwell. This was important because it wasn't certain that Maxwell's energy concepts would hold up in the face of the data of molecular physics. Accordingly, Einstein sought a formal proof of the equivalence of mass and energy that depends only on the core principles of special relativity. The proof assumes that the classical laws of conservation of energy and momentum (mass times velocity) are true. One thought experiment focused on the relation between mass and kinetic energy. Einstein imagined an elastic collision of two particles of equal mass and equal but opposite velocities. The particles bounce off in different directions but their velocities will be the same before and after the collision provided that the principles of conservation of momentum and energy hold true. By the same reasoning, the masses of the particles will also remain the same before and after the collision. Application of Lorentz transformations and "a little algebra" provide definitions for relativistic momentum and kinetic energy from which the equivalence of mass and energy can be derived in a straightforward way.

Einstein then considered the case in which rest-energy changes (e.g., when a particle emits energy in the form of electromagnetic radiation) without any change in translational velocity. His argument now is that any change in rest-energy of the particle results in a proportional change to its inertial mass, and vice versa. The proof begins with an inelastic collision of two particles of equal rest-energy moving with equal but opposite velocities. Einstein assumed that any internal changes the particles might suffer as a result of the collision, including changes in energy and mass, are equal in the particle pair. Again using Lorentz transformations, Einstein derived an equation from which he concluded that rest-energy changes additively like the mass. It follows from this that rest-energy will vanish if mass does, and the equivalence of energy and mass is thereby proved. Add c to the recipe and we have the Einstein cocktail, aka $E = mc^2$.[60]

The predictive power of the equation has been empirically confirmed, in both directions. The relevant implication of the equation is that when a particle splits into two or more particles and releases energy, or when we combine masses by any method that releases energy, the classical law of conservation of mass will no longer hold. John Cockcraft and E. T. S. Walton (1932) demonstrated release of a great amount of energy when an atom was split, leaving fragments with slightly less total mass than the intact atom (part of its mass was released as energy), as predicted. At about the same time, Irene and Frederic Joliot-Curie (1933) confirmed the empirical reality of the equation in the reverse direction by showing the energy of a quantum of light changing into particles of matter.

---

[60]Einstein illustrated energy-mass equivalence in an expository way in a popular article (Einstein, 1954, pp. 337–338) using changes in the mass of a swinging pendulum-at the highest points the mass is greatest but velocity is lowest whereas mass is lowest and velocity greatest at the bottom of the swing. It is as though the lifting height (mass) could be converted entirely into velocity and vice versa. What remains constant throughout is energy, the potential energy of position and the kinetic energy of motion. This analogy, though an aid to understanding, would have been out of tune in the elementary-particle context of Einstein's equation.

Dual Coding Summary

The important question from a DCT perspective is whether particle imagery was necessary for the derivation or simply expository. It can be reasonably argued that something like the particle imagery example was essential to Einstein's reasoning. All of the key concepts—mass, energy, velocity—have referents (instantiations) in physical reality. Derivation of the equation isn't a numbers game with internal consistency among abstract quantities and relations as its only goal. It is about entities that move, push, collide, and have static and dynamic properties that are quantifiable, at least in principle. If not yet seen, they can be imagined in some form and relation to each other. Recall that precisely this kind of imagery was associated with Ehrlich's "beautiful pictures" of antibodies. Such imagery was at the center of the visualization-visualizability debates in physics. Einstein used imagery effectively in that context because it had paid off for him even as a child. For him, concretization of a problem was essential for its solution.

Once again it goes without saying that abstract verbal-mathematical reasoning was also essential for the derivation (formal proof) of the equation. In analyzing his thought processes, however, Einstein said that formal solutions were possible only after he understood the physical situation by manipulating "more or less clear images." Nonetheless, verbal thinking was essential even at that creative stage. The names of physical entities, relations, and properties were common coinage in physics. They were the cues that evoked images of their referents and controlled their dynamic transformations and interactions. Finally, there was Einstein's mathematical knowledge of physical laws, Lorentz transformations, and other theoretical ideas that made up the verbal side of his scientific apperceptive mass.

In sum, $E = mc^2$ emerged from the same experiences and thought processes as its parent theory. These include the early and continuous background that produced the knowledge about mathematics, physical problems and attempted solutions, and the imagery and verbal thinking habits and skills that he used to solve problems. The details of how all of this came together at decisive stages of theory construction are unknown. Einstein did not record those crucial moments and we can only guess what they might have been like and thereby reduce the mystery of intuition, Einstein's ultimate explanation of his theoretical inventions.

Metatheoretical Dual Coding Analysis

We conclude with a metatheoretical resumé of Einstein's famous equation and its context in 20th century physics. The equation, $E = mc^2$, is the verbal-mathematical side of a dual coding relation. The nonverbal side consists of the physical phenomena that can be observed, measured, manipulated, and imaged in their instantiated forms—most dramatically, the image of a rising mushroom cloud. The equation is meaningful only when it is coupled with mental representations of its concrete referents and other associations. With it, Einstein redefined energy in terms of the equation and its elemental referents. This was convenient because, by then, he saw light speed as a universal constant and cast the definition in a ballpark that accommodated even the smallest physical units of mass that could be affected by light energy. To understand that this is a redefinition, contrast it with how the energy released by an exploding stick of dynamite is described.

The dual coding account applies as well to the history of imagery in physics as described by Miller (1984). The waxing and waning of visualizability as a criterion of theory had to do with difficulties associated with pinning down the slippery empirical phenomena and inconsistencies on the verbal-mathematical side. Visualizability faded as a criterion when Heisenberg and others tried to formalize physics so that it becomes an internally consistent theoretical statement. However, that goal couldn't be reached because the phenomena insisted on being considered in their own right within the theories. This was done by portraying them as abstract pictures accompanied by verbal descriptions—for example, Gregor Wentzel's depiction of beta-decay (Miller, 1984 p. 166) with labeled entities and arrows for the processes in which they are involved, and Nobel Prize winner Feynman's diagram of repulsion between two electrons (Miller, 1984 p. 171).

Miller (1984) described the conceptual shift in terms of the "startling contrast" between pictures constructed from objects and phenomena actually perceived, and vizualizability according to quantum mechanics (pp. 256–257). As I see it, the latter abstracts out some essential characteristics of the phenomena and allows for "minimalist" constructed images which have some of the characteristics of concrete poetry (patterns of labeled entities). It seems likely that, in physicists' thinking, the abstract depictions "spill over" into more concrete images made possible by techniques developed for seeing the tracks of interacting and decaying particles—the operational procedures for identifying their properties.

According to this view, past and present physical theories are conjunctions of verbal-mathematical descriptions and the phenomena to which they refer (their meaning), and theoretical progress has entailed changes in the descriptions on the one side and depictions (images) on the other. Any given theory is a slice of this continuing verbal-imaginal interplay—perhaps forever continuing, so that the unified field theory envisaged by Einstein is impossible because his goal had become the development of "logically perfect" theories (Miller, 1984, pp. 47–48). Which leads us naturally to mathematics and the limitations of formalism according to dual coding metatheory.

MATHEMATICS

The analysis of creative processes and products in mathematics follows seamlessly from physics and biology. Geometry was the bridge. The great mathematician and scientist, Henri Poincaré, used biological arguments to support the privileged position of three-dimensional Euclidean geometry in physical theory. Simply put, a practical knowledge of geometry evolved because it is necessary for the survival of organisms in our world. Einstein suggested that Euclidian geometry validated (gave meaning to) the concepts of classical physics and the special theory of relativity: "Geometry thus completed is evidently a natural science; we may in fact regard it as the most ancient branch of physics. I attach special importance to the view of geometry which I have just set forth, because without it I would have been unable to formulate the theory of relativity" (Einstein, cited in Miller, 1984, p. 42). Einstein and others went on to use non-Euclidean geometry as the conception of objects in space and time became more complex. Mathematics itself went its own way as an evolving formal discipline concerned with numbers, relations, and mathematical operations that have no necessary relation to referents in the natural world. Even geometry was viewed as completely formal, transformable in principle into axioms, theorems, and algebraic expressions. We see, however, that complete formalization has not been achieved even in this most formal of all creative domains.

Dual Coding in Mathematical Skill and Creativity

Given the abstractness of the phenomenal domain, imagery has received a surprising amount of attention in relation to mathematical cognition. Creative mathematicians have reported relying on nonverbal imagery in mathematical thinking involving problems ranging from numerical relations to non-Euclidian (e.g., four-dimensional) geometry. Poincaré characterized the creative mathematician as one who thinks in "sensual" images, which he defined as "the ability to see the whole of the argument at a glance" (cited in Miller, 1984, p. 233). How it did that and the nature of sensual imagery remained unexplained, but the point here is that mathematical creativity was attributed to nonverbal imagery even by mathematicians themselves. Moreover, empirical support has been obtained for the role of imagery in mathematical thinking and performance (e.g., Hayes, 1973).

What, then, is the nature of mathematically relevant imagery? In the case of geometry, it obviously entails spatial imagery, as in mental manipulations of visual forms, and by sketching (interestingly, Poincaré was an inveterate doodler; Miller, 1984, pp. 236–238). More abstract images, generally called number forms, are experienced by one in four people (Paivio, 1971b, 482–483) and many can image and rotate numerals mentally (Chapter 4, this volume).

DCT accommodates such imagery but goes far beyond it in dealing with mathematical skills and creativity. Mathematics is interpreted as a dual coding domain in that mathematically educated people in Western culture have learned names and shorthand visual symbols for geometric forms, numbers, relations, operators, and computational procedures. They have also learned how to use the symbols and procedures. Other cultures include visual-haptic representations and procedures, such as those associated with the Chinese abacus and Japanese soroban. This implies that mathematical skills are based entirely on experientially-derived, modality-specific representations and processes.

A contrasting view, more compelling in this case than in other cognitive domains, is that mathematical representations and activities are abstract, logical, and propositional, and that creative mathematicians seek to capture more and more mathematical species in their formal net—not a hypothetical goal, for it was in fact what Whitehead and Russell (1910–1913) attempted to achieve in their monumental *Principia Mathematica*. I deal with the formalism issue after the following summary of evidence on the contrasting psychological views of mathematics.

James Clark and Jamie Campbell (1991) compared two theories of number skills that exemplify the aforementioned contrasts. Their specific-integrated theory of number processing (Campbell & Clark, 1988) assumes that

> calculation and related processes are based on modality-specific number codes. Specific verbal codes include articulatory, auditory, orthographic, and motor codes for various spoken and written number words, as well as unique codes for special populations (e.g., sign language). The nonverbal codes . . . include visual and motor codes for digits, imaginal and other analogue codes for magnitude (e.g., number lines), and combined visual-motor representation for various number-related activities (e.g., finger counting, using an abacus). Because they are associatively connected, specific codes can activate one another to produce a multi component pattern of activation that we call an encoding complex (Clark & Campbell, 1991, pp. 205–206). Overlapping processes and shared underlying representations contribute in different ways to number comprehension, calculation, and production tasks.

A contrasting abstract-modular theory (McCloskey, Caramazza, & Basili, 1985) assumes that different surface forms of numbers (e.g., digits and number words) are derived from or translated into a single type of abstract quantity code, which underlies different numerical operations. The theory assumes further that comprehension, calculation, and production are controlled by independent subsystems or "modules" that use and communicate via the abstract code.

Clark and Campbell (1991) argued that abstract codes entail such conceptual inadequacies as arbitrariness and circularity of abstract notations, which can be avoided by assuming that the underlying representations are modality specific. They also reviewed evidence that is consistent with their theory and problematic for abstract code theories. The most direct evidence is that stimulus format (e.g., digits versus number words) influences performance in tasks requiring calculation or judgments of magnitude, odd-even status, and so on. Mental comparisons of numbers differing in magnitude produce symbolic distance functions and other effects similar to those obtained in such tasks as symbolic size comparisons of objects, and are thus consistent with the interpretation that the number comparisons, too, are based on visuospatial analogue codes. Presentation format for odd–even judgments interacts with visual field so that judgments are faster in the right-visual field (suggesting a left hemisphere advantage) for number words, but faster in the left field (right hemisphere) for digits. Calculation performance can differ for different surface forms of numbers. Finally, studies with aphasics and individuals with specific number-processing deficits (acalculia) show that brain injury can selectively disrupt comprehension and calculation performance for a specific format. All such findings are consistent with modality-specific (including dual coding) theoretical interpretations of number skills.[61]

---

[61]Gallistel and Gelman (1992) described a more abstract dual-coding number processing mechanism that consists of (a) a preverbal computational system in which numerosities are represented by magnitudes, and (b) a verbal counting system acquired on the basis of the preverbal system. The preverbal and verbal systems operate in parallel in number processing tasks.

Mathematical Theories: A Dual Coding Metatheoretical Analysis

Despite the aforementioned evidence, can innovative mathematicians create theories that are completely internally consistent and formal, and thus independent of representational format? The basic issue has a long history in mathematics and logic. The following account (taken from an earlier review (Paivio, 1986, pp. 6–9) illustrates a possible limitation of mathematical formalism and what it means for dual coding metatheory.

The example concerns problems in the methodology of mathematics that arose from clashes between formal and informal philosophies of mathematics. Told by Lakatos (1963–64), the story recapitulates the history of proofs and refutations applied to a theorem concerning the number of vertices (V), number of edges (E), and number of faces (F) of three-dimensional forms (polyhedra). The 18th-century mathematician L. Euler was attempting to classify polyhedra when he noticed that $V - E + F = 2$. He and others sought a proof for the theorem. One approach was to imagine a hollow polyhedron with a surface made of thin rubber. By cutting one of the faces, the remaining surface could be stretched out flat without tearing it. A procedure applied to the surface appeared to prove the theorem. The refutation of this and other proofs was by means of counter examples that showed some subconjecture or lemma to be false, or global counter examples that refuted the theorem itself. The counter examples consisted of solid figures that satisfy the definition of polyhedra but do not conform to Euler's theorem in that $V - E + F \neq 2$. Thus, for a crested cube (a large cube with a smaller cube sitting on top of it), $V - E + F = 3$. Such counter examples were met by redefinitions of polyhedron or its defining terms so as to rule out the nonconforming exceptions to the theorem. At each turn, however, new counter examples were discovered that satisfied the "improved" definition and yet did not conform to Euler's theorem. Moreover, there was no reason to hope that the cycle would come to an end with any particular redefinition or refutation because each new version of the conjecture (theorem) was merely an ad hoc elimination of a counter example that cropped up, and one could never be sure that all exceptions had been enumerated.

The dialogue reveals the psychological nature of the informal processes in mathematical logic, including the use of concrete examples and conceptual shifts in proofs and refutations. Thought experiments using concrete examples is an ancient method of mathematical proof. The point is that the discovery and use of such examples lie outside of formal logic because the process does not rely on conceptual entities with fixed meanings and rule-determined arguments applied to those entities. It depends instead on informal psychological processes of perception, imagery, language, and creative discovery. Logicians over the ages consistently relied on informal processes and especially spatial analogues in their work. Our analysis suggests that they had no alternative.

The conceptual shifts included both concept contraction and concept stretching. The former redefined polehedra so as to eliminate counter examples to Euler's theorem. Concept stretching consisted of expansions designed to include increasingly complex forms. The process evolved so that more and more concepts were stretched, and consequently, the number of (as-yet) unstretched terms was reduced. The process slowed down in the 1930s so that the demarcation between unstretchable (logical) and stretchable (descriptive) terms seemed to become stable. The former were viewed as logical constraints deemed to be essential to rational discussion. Lakatos (1963–1964) concluded, however, that mathematicians eventually accepted unlimited concept stretching in mathematical criticism and that their acceptance marked a turning point in the history of mathematics. The conclusions have held up in subsequent evaluations of the issues (Davis & Hersh, 1981, pp. 345–359).

A major conclusion from Lakatos (1963–1964) is that formalism is limited in its applicability, "that no conjecture is generally valid, but only valid in a certain restricted domain that excludes the *exceptions*" (p. 26). Thus all theoretical general-alizations in mathematics and science have boundary conditions. An important additional point is that tests of theorems require empirical procedures that are not formal, and that the pressure for changes in formal, theories is a result of discover-ies due to such procedures. Finally, Euler's theorem itself fits the dual coding metatheoretical analysis in that it entails a probabilistic relation between an abstract verbal-mathematical statement and implicit representations of the nonverbal phe-nomena the theorem is intended to explain.

PSYCHOLOGY

It is difficult to identify a single creative individual that influenced the course of psy-chology in the way that Darwin influenced biology and Einstein 20th-century physics. One reason is that, historically, psychology has branched into an unusually broad and varied range of subdisciplines. There is, however, some consensus about three indi-viduals whose contributions have impacted major branches of psychology. These are Sigmund Freud, B. F. Skinner, and D. O. Hebb. The evidence on their creative think-ing varies as much as their approaches to psychological issues, but the role of analogy stands out as a common theme as it does among creative individuals in other domains.

Sigmund Freud

Freud ranks high on the Time/Life list of millenium movers. He is notable more for the broad appeal of his conceptual schemes than as a shaper of psychological sci-ence or even the applied field of clinical psychology. His most general and endur-ing contribution is the distinction between conscious and unconscious mind. The distinction goes back at least as far as Plato, but Freud was the first to emphasize the scope and power of motivational and cognitive processes operating below the level of conscious awareness. The Freudian unconscious is particularly identified with phenomena related to repressed memories of unpleasant experiences and inhi-bition of socially unacceptable behaviors, especially sexual behaviors. The memo-ries and behaviors supposedly manifest themselves indirectly in nervous disorders, slips of the tongue, symbolic dreams, and various other forms of "psychopathology of everyday life." Freudian theory and psychoanalysis as a method of psychother-apy have been subjected to the most intense scrutiny of any psychological approach. I do not review that history but focus instead on a dual coding analysis of Freudian creative processes and products.

Freud's contributions issued from long experience with psychopathology and its treatment, most notably the use of hypnosis by psychiatrists Jean-Martin Charcot and Joseph Breuer to treat hysteria. His collaboration with Breuer revealed that patients under hypnotic procedure sometimes spontaneously fell into a state of reverie that brought back old memories as effectively as hypnosis. From this Freud developed his famous free association method in which patients narrate their lives. He noticed, too, that he could use dreams to initiate free associations, which yielded clues that dreams were expressions of wishes, including socially unacceptable sexual wishes. This led to the idea of an unconscious mind in which repressed impulses and memories reside, from which they emerge as bizarre dreams, slips of the tongue, forgetting, and other disguised manifestations of unconscious influences on behavior.

Notable here is the interplay that Freud saw between nonverbal imagery and language in the thinking and behavior of patients. The same interplay presumably took place in Freud's own creative thinking in the sense that his theoretical ideas about mind were analogical extensions of what he observed with patients, cast in the form of psychic entities and forces (primal impulses of the id controlled by the ego and superego).

Psychoanalytic Theory and Dual Coding

Psychologist Wilma Bucci (1985) proposed that "The psychoanalytic account of the mental apparatus is inherently a dual coding approach. The basis for the division of the mental apparatus and the characteristics associated with each part has shifted with the evolution of the theory; however, the premise of dual representation remains inherent throughout" (pp. 597–598). The Freudian position differed from DCT in its emphasis on verbal processes as the basis of conscious thought: "On the one hand, the mental representation of material which has never been verbalized, or where the links to words have been lost, is a fundamental tenet of psychoanalytic theory, present in all its forms . . . On the other hand, verbalization is viewed as a necessary condition for rational, productive thought. This view may be traced throughout Freud's writings" (p. 598).

Bucci went on to propose a reinterpretation of psychoanalytic theory that is completely consistent with DCT: a "system of private, symbolic, imagistic representations . . . which have functional significance in thought [associated with] machinery for "the operation of referential relations linking the two symbolic systems" (p. 599). This dual coding view of psychoanalysis can be illustrated using the classical Freudian context. Anxiety-provoking images, wishes, and impulses are represented in the nonverbal system. Retrieval of threatening representations is blocked by active inattention, and becomes possible only when the emotional structures are altered. This is achieved by changing the verbal interpretations of the nonverbal representations through the psychoanalytic process, namely the verbal interaction between patient and analyst. The goal is "to have verbal input reach the underlying imagistic and emotional material, which has not previously been linked to words, or which has been wrongly named" (p. 595). The interaction results in the formation of referential connections from the imagistic-emotional representations to the verbal system so that the patient can express the changed interpretations of past experiences and their emotional consequences. Without such bidirectional referential activity, the patient would be restricted to repeating and paraphrasing the analyst's interpretations of his or her problem.

B. F. Skinner

Skinner is viewed as one of the greatest psychological scientists of the 20th century, even by those who disagree with his radical behavioristic account of "mind" in terms of private events that are part of a causal chain that begins with selective environmental influences. In that regard, Skinner is similar to Darwin, emphasizing selection of responses whereas Darwin emphasized selection of species. A closer connection is that survival and evolution of all organisms depend on changes in response systems for obtaining nutrients and protecting themselves from toxins and predators.

Skinner discovered intermittent reinforcement and worked out its "laws" in a series of experiments that showed how behavior can be shaped by reinforcing successive approximations to the desired new response (Salzinger, 1990). He and his followers applied his ideas to education, behavior modification, and raising children with the aim of improving the human conditions. He applied the principles to the analysis of language in his book *Verbal Behavior* (Skinner, 1957; for a summary, see Paivio & Begg, 1981), which he considered his most important contribution to psychology. Technical inventions were inspired by his theory, and, although they worked in principle, some were as controversial as the theory itself (an example is given later).

Experiential Background for Creativity

Skinner's career began with early domain-specific experiences with technology, invention, exploration, and reading. As summarized by his biographer Daniel Bjork (1993, Chapter 1), he was always building things: scooters, steerable wagons, sleds, rafts, seesaws, merry-go-rounds, sling shots, bows and arrows, blow guns, tops, a workable telegraph, musical instruments, magical devices (inspired by observing a magician), new games, and so forth. "Fred's childhood inventions and activities were enough to turn has mother's head gray with worry and distress, not to mention the mess and the complaints from neighbors" (p. 18). From countryside explorations, he learned first-hand about plants and animals. Reading dominated his intellectual activities and was pursued eventually in "a box to hide in," (p. 2) constructed from packing cases and containing shelves for books, writing materials, and so on. Skinner summed up his background by insisting that he "was not born with a character called curiosity or with an inquisitive spirit or an inquiring mind" but gravitated instead toward a world that "richly reinforced looking, searching, investigating, uncovering." (cited in Bjork, 1993, p. 18).

The reinforced exploratory and perceptual behaviors, however, could not have resulted in new gadgets or analytic schemes without a cumulative apperceptive mass against which new experiences could be compared. Skinner analyzed such comparisons in terms of stimulus and response generalization, but this requires memory for previous instances and analogical thinking that could be based on the "covert processes" of imagery and language, as suggested by a personal experience that led to his notable invention (summarized by Bjork, 1993, p. 122 ff). On a train trip to a convention in 1940, Skinner wondered whether a technology could be created to stop bombers before they delivered their deadly cargo. "I was looking out the window as I speculated about these possibilities and saw a flock of birds lifting and wheeling as they flew alongside the train. Suddenly I saw them as 'devices' with excellent vision and extraordinary maneuverability. Could they not guide a missile?" (Skinner, cited in Bjork, 1993, p. 122) The idea was that birds might be trained as navigator-bombardiers during WW2. This idea eventuated in a workable guidance system. Pigeons were first reinforced to peck at a visual target in the nose cone. The behavior controlled a guidance system that kept the missile on target. Use of two pigeons corrected for errors made by either one. Laboratory experiments showed that the system was successful and practical but the defense department found the idea bizarre and it was never implemented. In any case, it was made obsolete by newer electronic guidance systems. The relevant point, however, is that Skinner engaged in analogical thinking based on imagery triggered jointly by his verbal speculations and the birds he saw—in brief, dual coding activity.

Skinner on Creativity

Skinner (1984) wrote the following:

> Creativity was one of the shabbiest of explanatory fictions, and it tended to be used by the least creative people. It was said to be out of the reach of the behaviorists, and would, indeed, have been so if behavior were simply a response to stimuli. But, as Darwin has shown, selection as a causal mode dispensed with a creator, and that was true of operant conditioning. Just as contingencies of survival replaced an explicit act of creation in the origin of species, so contingencies of reinforcement replaced the supposed creative acts of artist, composer, writer, or scientist. Artists could be taught to increase the likelihood that new forms of behavior would occur by generating variations which would be selected when they prove to have reinforcing consequences (p. 304).

If that were the end of the argument, there would be no point in a dual coding or any other cognitive analysis of creativity, but it is not the end even for Skinner. Recall from Chapter 4 (p. 153), Skinner's description of a task in which one imagines a cube cut into smaller ones and answers questions about the latter. Skinner attributed causal power to these images ("private responses") in that they "may produce discriminative stimuli which prove useful in executing further behavior of either a public or private nature" (Skinner, 1953, p. 273). We saw proof of such causality in the results of numerous imagery experiments (Chapter 4). For example, people remember twice as many words from a list when they are asked to image to each word than when they are asked to pronounce the words to themselves. Thus, trivial differences in instructional cues result in dramatic differences in recall. Skinner would want to look for the ultimate explanation in reinforcement histories associated with the words "image" and "pronounce, " even as he agreed that private events (images) are a crucial link in the causal chain.

Metatheoretical Analysis

Skinner's analytic scheme can be conceptualized as follows. His general theory consists of the verbally expressed laws of reinforcement effects on learning and production of classes of operants. These explain and predict effects of situational variables on response classes ("acts") as depicted graphically in cumulative records. A prototypical representation might be an image of a Skinner box with all its instantiations of stimulus conditions that control responding—a light (discriminandum), response bar (manipulandum), and food in a tray (reinforcer). Elaborations might include conditions for terminating or avoiding negative events. A more complete understanding of the theory would require further imaginal and verbal associations that represent real-life behavioral situations for which the Skinner box is the conceptual peg.

Skinner's interpretive theory of verbal behavior (Skinner, 1957; summarized in Paivio & Begg, 1981) would require a more complex analysis of verbal operants and how they relate to the phenomenal domain of verbal behavior in nonverbal and verbal stimulus contexts. This is all much more complex than behavioristic explanations often are assumed to be and I won't try to capture it in a theoretical "equation" or model.

D. O. Hebb

Hebb's singular creative contribution was the cell assembly theory presented in his 1949 volume, *The Organization of Behavior*. It has been said by many that it began the era of cognitive neuropsychology. It resulted in this evaluation: "If there had been a Nobel prize in psychology, Donald Hebb would surely have been one of our most distinguished laureates" (Bruner, 1982, p. 6). Hebb's emphasis on central control of behavior was the antithesis of Skinner's emphasis on the environment, although Hebb fully recognized the importance of environmental influences—early experience in particular—in shaping the organized neuronal systems that mediate stimulus effects.

His neuropsychological thinking was motivated on one hand by the puzzling observation that widespread brain lesions may have little effect on intelligent behavior. For example, IQ remained high in a human patient who had an entire cerebral hemisphere surgically removed. On the other hand, individuals born blind with cataracts that were later removed required a prolonged learning period before they could see the world in the way that normal people do. Thus, early visual experience seemed to be essential for the development of normal perception, a conjecture supported by visual deprivation experiments with animals. Hebb explained these and other findings in terms of his theory of experientially developed neuronal cell-assemblies (described earlier in Chapter 9, pp. 220–221) that presumably are the basis of meaningful perception and thought. The conceptual scheme was an analogical extension of closed neuronal loops in the brain (discovered by Lorente de Nó), which included the idea that such loops can be formed through experience, that they are not narrowly localized, and that a period of reverberating cell assembly activity is necessary for the establishment of long-term representational systems. We have seen (Chapter 9) that the precise nature of such neuronal systems remains elusive but the general idea continues to be appealing and the "Hebb neuron" in particular is the basis of modern connectionist theories.

The analogical nature of Hebb's creative thinking includes the visual metaphor of the cell assembly pictured as a three dimensional latticework. Moreover, imagery was salient in Hebb's theorizing, conceptualized in terms of the activity of higher order assemblies, as were linguistic ideas. Metatheoretically, his theory maps verbal descriptions of cell assembly structure and activity onto schematic pictorial representations of reverberatory circuits and how they function in such phenomena as pattern perception, set, and selective attention. The theory generated predictions about effects of such factors as early experience, perceptual deprivation, and brain lesions on perception, cognition, and emotion. The results have been a mixture of successes and failures, the latter coming as no surprise to Hebb, who maintained that a good theory leads to its own destruction by making better theories possible. It is a tribute to his theory that there have been many attempts to modify his ideas to accommodate troublesome neurological and neuropsychological observations.

LINGUISTIC SCIENCE

By definition, linguistics is the most verbal of scientific disciplines. Its phenomenal domain is language and its traditional focus has been on description and explanation of syntactic structures and processes. Over the past several decades, however, some linguists have turned the spotlight on semantic and pragmatic aspects of language and how these impinge on language use, including grammatical behavior. From the DCT perspective, the syntactic approaches have sought explanations entirely within the units, structures, and processes of the verbal system whereas the semantic approaches have taken into account nonverbal processes, including imagery. Here, we look at creativity within both approaches.

Noam Chomsky

Chomsky is the acknowledged creative genius in the syntactic theoretical approach to language. He is considered one of the most influential intellectuals of the 20th century partly because of his revolutionary approach to linguistics (the other source of influence being his political writings), and some linguists regard him as the Newton of their field (Bickerton, 1990, p. 5). His revolutionary insight was that traditional structural linguistics could not explain our ability to produce and understand an infinite variety of novel sentences. From 1957 to the 1990s, he proposed different versions of generative syntactic theories designed to explain that productive competence. His approach entailed analogical extensions of everyday language skills described in terms of the meta language of structural linguistics and computer programs. All of that became internalized as mental linguistic structures and processes.[62]

The early theories from 1957 to 1965 took the hierarchical grammatical structures associated with sentence parsing and reversed the procedure so that larger structures were built up from smaller units and structures by generative rules. The structures could be systematically modified by transformational rules that add, delete, or transpose morphemes and phrases to produce active, passive, interrogative, negative, and other variants of any given sentence type. Recursive application of the rules allowed for unlimited language productivity. Other rules instantiated these internal structures as externalized speech. The process was reversed in comprehension so that language input activated cognitive mechanisms that generated suitably transformed abstract internal language structures. The latest version (Chomsky, 1995) simplified the theory by the assumption that all of the syntactic and other language information is part of the subjective lexicon, the speaker's internal dictionary.

Chomsky's theories formalize our informal knowledge of what must occur in speech production and comprehension. Chomsky's creative trick was to invent computional devices that could in principle carry out such operations, on the assumption that the generated structures together with equally abstract interpretive mechanisms explained language competence. The process appears to be purely intralinguistic. The only hint of nonverbal processes and imagery is in Chomsky's reliance on concrete sentences to illustrate the underlying abstract syntactic structures. Even the anomalous string "Colorless green ideas sleep furiously", so often used to illustrate the independence of syntax from meaning, seems to be about concrete entities, but these are generalized as labeled tree diagrams and abstract-notational strings with transformational symbols.

A major criticism of Chomsky's approach has been that it is based on his personal observations and intuitions about language rather than objective scientific evidence. Thus it has been characterized as philosophy rather than psychology despite his own assertion that linguistics is a branch of cognitive psychology. It follows in this context that Chomsky's linguistic theory is not a scientifically based theory of mind. At best it might be considered a speculative theory of verbal mind, in the category of linguistic dominance approaches already evaluated in Chapter 1 and elsewhere throughout this volume. Accepted as such, Chomsky's theory was a creative analogical leap that connects language to formal computational devices.

---

[62]In reviewing Chomsky's contributions I will not deal again with his nativistic views concerning the origin and acquisition of language, already discussed in Chapters 12 and 13.

We have already reviewed alternative theories that emphasize the semantic and nonverbal perceptual-motor basis of language. Collectively, they form the basis of a lasting science of language that is embedded within a general theory of mind. Charles Osgood (1953) deserves special mention as one of the early proponents of such a theory. It began with his research on synesthesia, an unusual cross-modal sensory experience (e.g., seeing colors when hearing music), which he extended analogically to such sensory metaphors as *bright sound, sharp taste,* and *dull pain,* presumably reflecting synesthetic cross-overs from sensations to language. Osgood devised the semantic differential to measure the salient metaphorical meanings of concepts using bipolar adjectival scales—the degree to which *mother,* for example, is warm or cold, dull or bright, active or passive. Osgood's emphasis shifted to affective and connotative meaning because three general dimensions kept emerging from cross-cultural and cross-language studies—concepts were reliably evaluated as having some degree of pleasantness, activity, and potency. These were further interpreted as reflecting covert response tendencies of approach or avoidance, excitement, and tension evoked by the concepts. Thus the meanings emerged from and reflected behaviors toward things.

The neobehaviorist emphasis might have impeded Osgood from developing a more complete theory that incorporated perceptual attributes and imagery along with the affective-connotative meanings. His early factor analytic studies included tangible–intangible and substantial–insubstantial scales but not enough such scales were included to permit a general concreteness-imagery factor to emerge. This occurred later in our own research (Paivio, 1968b) and was confirmed by others. Osgood's semantic factors remain relevant, however, even in an evolutionary context, as we saw in Chapter 11.

THE ARTS

This final section deals with creative individuals and their products in the domains of literature, music, and visual art. We focus mainly on one acknowledged creative genius from each domain, namely Shakespeare, Beethoven, and Picasso. They did not create theories, and so, there can be no metatheoretical analyses here, only dual coding interpretations of their creativity.

Shakespeare and Writing

William Shakespeare demonstrated "a facility for wordplay unrivaled by any writer before or since. Shakespeare's ubiquity on world stages, on film, in textbooks and in our everyday vernacular is a testament to his achievement" (Millenium Top 100, 2001). The influences on his creativity are more uncertain than those of the other "geniuses" we have analyzed because he left no autobiography or notebooks about his work. We're not even sure what he looked like, judging from the interest in the recent discovery of a portrait painted during his lifetime and purported to be of him at age 39 (Nolan, 2002). (The sculpture and picture familiar to every schoolchild were done after his death by journeyman artists.) There is considerable information on his personal life (the Nolan 2002, volume is a good source), but what we know about the wellspring of his creativity comes from analyses of his writings and contemporary events and people he probably knew. I have already mentioned Caroline Spurgeon's (1935) monumental work, *Shakespeare's Imagery and What it Tells Us* and I draw on that again.

Spurgeon (1935) counted and classified all of the metaphors, analogies, and other imaginative word pictures in all of Shakespeare's plays. She showed that Shakespeare produced a greater range and variety of word pictures than his contemporaries, Bacon and Marlowe, particularly in relation to nature and everyday life. Sports imagery was especially abundant, and, within that category, falconry was one of the richest sources of metaphorical meanings in the early plays (Morrow, 1988). Spurgeon inferred that the word-imagery derived from direct personal experience in those domains. She also drew special attention to the recurrent symbolic images that ran thematically through passages and entire plays–growth in gardens and orchards in the early historical plays; swift and soaring movement as seen in the flight of birds in Henry V; the sense of sound throughout The Tempest; the images of sun, moon, and stars reflecting the light of beauty and love in Romeo and Juliet; metaphors of darkness and evil in Macbeth. Such recurrent symbolic images are common in literature, but Spurgeon said that they are especially characteristic of Shakespeare. She suggested, too, that the recurrent images probably existed as conscious mental pictures but perhaps without awareness of how they revealed his symbolic vision.

In our terms, the recurrent images functioned as conceptual pegs that organized the plays' themes for the audience as well as for Shakespeare. Other examples identified by literary biographers include the symbolic organizing roles of the white whale in Melville's *Moby Dick*, the shooting of the albatross in Coleridge's *Rime of the Ancient Mariner,* and the image of a shark's fin in Virginia Woolf's *The Waves*. These and other examples of literary images with organizing and memory functions are analyzed in detail elsewhere (Paivio, 1983b; Sadoski & Paivio, 2001, pp. 152–159).

Current experimental evidence on the role of imagery in the generation of concrete text (Chapter 4) gives us confidence that Shakespeare and other creative writers experienced and used imagery in their work. This is indirectly supported in Shakespeare's case by his Sonnet 27 "Weary with toil, I haste me to my bed, The dear repose for limbs with travel tired; But then begins a journey in my head, To work my mind, when body's work's expired" (Nolan, 2002, p. 16). More direct anecdotal support comes from writers who have described how they have relied on imagery to create stories. C. S. Forester, author of the Captain Horatio Hornblower novels and *The African Queen,* had no doubt that he wrote from a series of visualizations of scenes he witnessed as if he were an invisible ghost walking about on stage observing actors from all sides, hearing their speeches and aware of their emotions as well (Forester, 1964, p. 77). Others report similar generative effects of "unbidden" or self-prompted imagery in initiating and guiding their writing (e.g., Blake, Coleridge, Faulkner, Shelly, C. S. Lewis, Joyce Carole Oates, and Marquez; for details, see Sadoski & Paivio, 2001).

Fictional and poetic writing especially highlight the creative and aesthetic functions of imagery in composition. However, imagery also plays a necessary if more mundane role in technical and other nonfictional writing (Sadoski & Paivio, 2001, p. 155). I have already referred to this in the case of Darwin's (anything but mundane) closing summary of his theory. We saw it in the use of metaphors and analogies by other creative scientists. And imagery is strikingly evident in the popular scientific writings of such hard-nosed scientists as Dawkins, Gamow, and Sagan.

Although seemingly less dramatic, the creative and aesthetic functions of the verbal system must not be forgotten. Sadoski and I (Sadoski and Paivio, 2001, p. 158) cited evidence that verbal associations can set the stage for a novel, and that abstract language can serve as a thematic organizer. An example of the latter is how Shakespeare effected an irony throughout *King Lear* by the repeated use, in many variations, of the abstract words "nature" and "nothing. " Notice as well that poetry is admired for the aesthetic appeal of the wording itself—for example, rhyming, alliteration, verbal associations, and telling repetitions of the same word. In Chapter 12, I described the possible role of such verbal devices in the evolution of poetry itself.

As in the other domains, the dual coding analysis of literary creativity and its products stresses the continual interplay of verbal and imagery systems. The phenomenal domain is written language and the verbal system must, therefore, guide the selection, sequential organization, and output of words and sentences that best tell the story. The writer's skill in telling the story depends on experience with language itself through listening, reading, and writing—internalized as a rich, multimodal apperceptive mass in the verbal system. The nonverbal imagery system (the richness of its apperceptive mass) is similarly dependent on experiences that relate the language to real-life referents and contexts, especially ones laden with emotion (Opdahl, 2002), which represent the meaning of the message to the writer and audience alike. In disagreement in this case with Marshall McLuhan, the medium is not the message—at least not all of it.

Beethoven

Ludwig van Beethoven is generally regarded as Western music's greatest composer. Was he a born musical genius if ever there was one? Perhaps, but a review of his life reveals that his creativity fits right into the deliberate-practice model of expertise. I review that experiential background as summarized by William Lane in his 2003 Web site on Beethoven (his sources are listed there) and then speculate briefly on the role of auditory imagery and dual coding processes in his creative work. Many great composers have described their auditory imagery,[63] but such imagery assumes unusual importance in the case of Beethoven because, as everyone knows, some of his best musical compositions were created after he became deaf.

Music lessons were first "beat" into Beethoven's young head by his drunken father, a court musician and singer who wanted to show him off as a child prodigy. Despite the brutal teaching methods, Ludwig showed promise and other teachers

---

[63]According to a review by Agnew (1922), Tchaikovsky couldn't sleep as a child because the music in his head wouldn't stop. Wagner intensely imaged scenes and music at the same time for his operas. Schumann said his inner music was more beautiful and heartbreaking than his performed music.

were called in. He played violin in public at age 7. He progressed rapidly in piano performance and composition under the tutelage of a composer who introduced him to the works of Bach and Mozart. In 1787, at age 17, he took leave from work as a musician in Bonn to study under Mozart who, having heard him play, reported, "Watch this lad. Some day he will force the world to talk about him." Beethoven later studied music under the prestigious musicians Haydn and Albrechtsberger.

Compositions poured from him during his 20s, but his main recognition in Vienna and other parts of Europe at that time came from his innovative virtuosity as a pianist. He launched his first symphony in 1800 at age 30. One year later, deafness began to hit him and he plunged into composing—a precarious living for a time because his compositions were in advance of popular taste. Although he was totally deaf for the last 10 years of his life, he continued to compose until his death in 1827.

Dedication was evident in Beethoven's work habits when he was creating a composition. As described by Anton Schindler (cited in Lane, 2003), he rose at daybreak and went at once to his work-table, where he worked until 2.00 or 3.00, when he took his midday meal. In the interim, he usually ran outside two or three times, where he also "worked while walking" for perhaps an hour. Such excursions, which resembled the swarming out of the bee to gather honey, never varied with the seasons. He spent the afternoons at other activities and his winter evenings at home reading. He went to bed at 10.00 at the latest.

I conclude with the following speculative dual coding analysis. Beethoven's deafness as a middle-aged man means that by then he had acquired the long-term musical memories that would continue to serve as the basis of musical imagery. He was no longer able to perform well because he had no auditory feedback to guide his playing, but the imagery would suffice for composing mentally and expressing it as a score. The musical notations would activate motor and auditory components of the imagery and these would guide unhurried corrections, although not finely-tuned performance. Verbal processes (writing, talking to oneself) could participate in the composition process as well. The evidence is the following Beethoven Web site account of "the possessed genius as he worked upon his last string quartet: At 5:30 A.M. he was at his table, beating time with his hands and feet, humming and writing. After breakfast he hurried outside to wander in the fields, calling, waving his arms about, moving slowly, then very abruptly stopping to scribble something in his notebook" (Lane, 2003). (Recall my earlier description of pianist Glenn Gould strolling in the park.) It would be nice if, in addition, we had an Einstein-like report from Beethoven describing his imagery experience, but the musical behavior (nonverbal and verbal-notational) just as directly suggests guidance by imagery. How else can we explain its occurrence in an open field, unprompted by musical hearing?[64]

---

[64]Mozart, who would have served just as well as the creative musical genius in this section, explicitly described his auditory imagery of a new and as-yet unwritten composition as not of the "parts successively" but "all at once" (Miller, 1984, pp. 233–269). This is a mysterious idea, given the sequential nature of music. Had the composition already been written, one could interpret it as a "melogen" that was available all at once in Mozart's memory but nonetheless accessible to him only sequentially, paralleling the earlier analysis (Chapter 3) of

Picasso

"In the beginning the canvas was without form, and void, and the brush of Pablo Picasso moved upon the surface, and he created women, but not in the image of humankind, nor in the image of any creatures who ever existed" (Prideaux, 1968, p. 51). Thus began Tom Prideaux's article on cubism in a special double issue of Life Magazine devoted to Picasso and his works. From the new and shocking cubist style, Picasso went on to dominate 20th-century art with his innovations in a career that spanned 70 years and an influence that spread across generations and cultures (Life's Millenium citation). His preeminence is supported specifically by the fact that his 1905 painting, "Boy With a Pipe", sold at an auction on May 5, 2004, for $104 million, an all-time record for an auction painting. As in other cases, I review the experiential roots of Picasso's skill and productivity (he left us with an astounding 22,000 pieces of art), and then speculate about his creativity in dual coding terms.

Life Magazine's informative articles clearly reveal the early influence of the home, outside teachers and models, and intense personal effort on Picasso's artistic development. He drew before he could talk. He was fascinated by the brush handling and painting of his father, a professional painter who was his first teacher. By 9, he was painting pictures of his own. In school, he remembered numbers by making little human figures of them. At age 14 in Barcelona, he was admitted into an advance class in an art college by tossing off in a day a detailed drawing from life that other candidates were given a month to complete. The following year a painting of his won a place in a national exhibition in the city. He left school at 16 to go study the great Spanish masters in Madrid. Back in Barcelona at age 18, he joined other bohemian artists and eked out a living hawking sketches of streets, markets, cafes, dance halls, and brothels in styles ranging from El Greco to Daumier. Later, in Paris, there followed a flurry of cabaret pictures in the manner of Toulouse-Lautrec, whose work he especially admired. He already had more than the minimum of 10 years of deliberate practice needed to develop peak expertise.

Over the years, he studied and practiced the styles of all of the major artists, using them as springboards to launch himself into the unique styles that shook the art world. "Les Demoiselle d'Avignon", the painting that began cubism in 1907, was influenced particularly by Cezanne but also incorporated styles derived from primitive Iberian sculpture, El Greco paintings, Congolese masks and figures, and more—all emerging as almost shadeless figures that Prideaux (1968, p. 52) described as "broad flat planes—Or might we say plain flat broads?" A year later, Picasso and his friend Georges Braques combined their talents to promote cubism as an evolutionary style. Picasso's cubist period came to a close in 1924 with another spectacular work, his *"Mandolin and Guitar,"* although cubist elements persisted in his many great works to come.

---

memorized plays as long motor logogens. In any case, one cannot give scientific credence to Mozart's introspective analysis of the precise nature of his auditory imagery. His description is acceptable, however, as evidence that he experienced such imagery.

How do we account for Picasso's dramatic artistic innovations? His rich artistic experience obviously laid down the domain-specific knowledge and skill that were the internal sources of his art. "What I create in painting is what comes from my interior world, " he said to Françoise Gilot (Gilot & Lake, 1964, p. 123). However, artistic skills begin with perception of objects, learning to copy these with corrective feedback from others, and comparisons of drawing and model by the artist. At some point, the skill expands to drawing from memory, which means that it is now based on visual imagery guided by feedback from the developing drawing (try sketching a face with your eyes closed). Neuropsychological evidence (Chapter 7) tells us that copying and drawing from memory are controlled by separate subsystems (brain damage can wipe out copying skill while sparing the ability to image and draw objects from memory, or vice versa). Thus, both need to be practiced.

Picasso obviously developed high level skills of both kinds, but often preferred to work from memory. Gilot's recollections (Gilot & Lake, 1964, pp. 115–119) of how he painted a nude portrait of her reveal the complex interplay of sketching and related processes in his creative activity. First he draw nude poses of her while looking at her. He tore these up and then looked at her for an hour or more, tense and remote, without sketching pad or pencil, and finally said, "I see what I need to do. . . . You won't have to pose again" The following day, he made, from memory, a series of drawings of her in that pose along with 11 lithographs of her head, and began a portrait that came to be called "La Femme-Fleur"

For the next month, Gilot watched Picasso work on the portrait, alternating with other still lifes because he couldn't carry the "plastic idea" any further that day. The painting started in a realistic manner and then he began to alter the figure, saying that, "A realistic portrait wouldn't represent you at all" he elongated her figure and said he would compensate for her long oval face by "making it a cold color— blue . . . like a little blue moon". He then cut out oval shapes varying in degree and size, drawing on each of them little signs for eyes, nose, and mouth. He then arranged them on the canvas in slight variations until he could say, "Now it's your portrait". He marked the contours on the canvas, took off the paper, then carefully painted in the forms. He modified body parts and commented on the reasons— for example, that a circle painted in the right hand "Rhymes with the circular form of the breast". At other times, he commented on the need for a change before executing it: Remarking that the head was so well balanced it annoyed him, he proceeded to change it by cutting out the skull shape from paper and moving it around the canvas until he found the spot where "the balance hung by a thread". Now satisfied, he painted out the portrait head and painted the new one in its new location.

The example reveals Picasso's incessant search for novelty in what he created. Verbal guidance was involved but the dominant process was nonverbal visual-motor. He once said the following to Gilot:

Painting is poetry and is always written with plastic rhymes, never prose. . . Plastic rhymes are forms that rhyme with one another or supply assonances with other forms or with the space that surrounds them. . . When you compose a painting, you build around lines of force that guide you in your construction . . . one graphic sketch evokes the idea of a table. . . another, movement behind the table. . . that leads you to where you are going (Gilot & Lake, 1964, p. 120).

We would say that the finished composition is created by elaborating on a partial or inchoate image, which is initiated by a perceived form or verbal cue and guided by feedback from what has been drawn or painted. The nonverbal ("plastic") processes dominate but the verbal ("symbolic") system puts in a good word now and then.

But whence came the bizarre elements that define Picasso's style? The anecdotal evidence suggests that they, too, began with unusual perceptions and images that were incorporated into the developing composition. Recall that "Les Desmoiselles" initially consisted entirely of five unusual but "plain flat broads, " which he modified by repainting the heads of two figures to look as if they had African masks. The revision "invested the Demoiselles with a savage power that up to then was unmatched in Western art" (Prideaux, 1968, pp. 50–53). The whole process proceeded through 30 preliminary versions of the painting plus numerous sketches of each nude. Preceding the painting, Picasso was inspired by assemblages of nudes in Titian's 16th-century realistic painting, "Diana and Her nymphs", and in Matisse's "Joy of life". He transformed the memory images of these stages into novel "plastic" forms with bizarre elements, always with feedback from the transitional product until he achieved a gestalt that pleased him,

The same processes were at work in the creation of "Guernica", Picasso's anguished memorial to the innocent dead when, in 1937, German bombers flying for Franco annihilated the defenseless town:

> The figures in *Guernica* rage across the canvas in a rush of terror. Heads everywhere are flung high and mouths forced open in frozen outcries that reverberate across surfaces as bleak as an echo chamber. Even a shattered statue adds its shouting to the din . . . [the mural] virtually sums up the insights of a lifetime. Its style combines the jumbled surfaces of cubism, notably in the horse, with the pure lines of Picasso's neoclassic drawings and the troubled distortions of recent "psychological" paintings. Its figures rise from a pool of images, invented or assimilated from the distant past. . . (Kern, 1968, pp. 90–92)

The initial sketches and paintings appear at first sight to be "a sequence of erratic leaps from comprehensive views and back, a restless play of combining the constituents in ever new ways, and many changes of style and subject matter. Yet the final painting is a synthesis of tested acquisitions, a statement whose completeness and necessity defies further modifications" (Arnheim, 1969, p. 134).

I mention finally that dreams might have been an early source of Picasso's style. He said the following to Gilot: "When I was a child, I often had a dream that used to frighten me greatly. I dreamed that my legs and arms grew to an enormous size and then shrank back just as much in the other direction. And all around me, in my dream, I saw other people going through the same transformations, getting huge or very tiny" (Gilot & Lake, 1964, p. 119; cf. the analysis of REM sleep and dream transformations in Chapter 7, p. 175, this volume). Gilot suggested that many of Picasso's paintings in the1920s started through recollections of those dreams and were carried on as a means of breaking the monotony of classical body forms. This concurs with autobiographical reports of dream images as the source of scientific discoveries and literary themes as reviewed in the last chapter. Recent research suggests, too, that the idiosyncratic imagery in dreams models the free association or "brainstorming" that precedes actual creation (DeAngelis, 2003).

This concludes our analysis of a sample of acknowledged creative geniuses and their domains. A running theme was the innovators' rich experiential background, including its motivational elements, which resulted in the domain-specific apperceptive mass of expert knowledge and skills from which new ideas and products emerged under the influence of stimulating environments. Another theme was the DCT analysis of the nature of the apperceptive mass and the interplay of the two coding systems working together in different ways and proportions according to the requirements of the creative enterprise. From this analysis of the background and nature of creative genius, we turn in the final chapter to the age-old practical problem of how to nurture the mind so that all people have the chance to fulfil their dreams.

CHAPTER NINETEEN

Nurturing the Mind: Applications of Dual Coding Theory

This concluding chapter extends DCT to the practical problems in education and remedial education as related not only to school topics, but also to problems of mental and physical health. Dual coding variables have a long history in traditional education, where imagery in particular was both advocated and repeatedly suppressed to the point that at least one zealot was burned at the stake for promoting it. As an applied theory, DCT is in a position to go beyond the earlier related practices because it provides scientific understanding of how its defining variables operate to augment practical skills and knowledge. We review in turn the broad domains of education, psychotherapy, and health. Unimodal verbal and schema alternatives also are revisited, for they are as popular and problematic in applied contexts as we found them to be in empirical–theoretical settings.

EDUCATION

DCT has its roots in controversies that began 2,000 years ago (Chapter 2) and concerned the effectiveness and morality of imagery as compared to verbal methods of learning and remembering. The positions are less extreme today but the beat goes on. I first summarize the history of educational practices related to imagery and verbal methods. Then I make the case for the integration of these methods in a DCT approach to education, building on Clark and Paivio (1991), who presented a roadmap for a general DCT of educational science, and Sadoski and Paivio (2001), who applied the theory more specifically to problems of literacy.

Historical Background of the Approach

From the dual coding perspective, the goal of education is to foster the development of verbal and nonverbal systems that can cooperate in useful ways in all spheres of

433

human activity. Most important here are the reciprocal principles of concretizing abstract verbal information on the one hand and verbalizing to concrete information on the other. Concretization was the main emphasis of the imagery-based learning and memory techniques that were prominent in Western education for 2,000 years. With the rise of Christianity, people were bombarded with images of heaven and hell as an aid to learning the virtues and vices. Annotated educational picture books grew out of the imagery tradition.

The apex of the tradition was Giordano Bruno's 16th-century occult memory system (Yates, 1966), which aimed to unify earthly knowledge and the supercelestial world of ideas using the traditional imagery mnemonics and prevalent astrological notions. The two levels were linked by magical star-images organized according to the associative structure of astrology, so that the multiplicity of earthly phenomena were brought together in memory through a hierarchical system of images that derived magical power from the stars. For example, one Brunian method combined a square architectural system with a round celestial system. The former consisted of rooms subdivided into places for images of everything in the physical world. The round celestial system was based on a Lullian memory device (Yates, 1966, pp. 173–198), in which moveable concentric wheels were used like a slide ruler to combine different subjects and predicates to generate new propositions. Bruno's version of the round system contained the celestial figures and images that were to animate, organize, and unify the earthly images contained in the memory rooms.

The direct route from Bruno to educational picture books was Tommaso Campanella's (1602) philosophical utopia, *The City of the Sun*. It describes a theocratic society inspired by Plato's Republic and imbued with influences from a mixture of Christianity and Hermetic religious astrology that originated in Egypt. In the Solarian educational system, the city itself serves as the basis for the classical mnemonic system. The city is surrounded by seven concentric walls within which are housed a central magical temple, large palaces, arches, and galleries. The Brunian influence on the mnemonic use of the city is evident everywhere. The earth and other heavenly bodies are painted on globes over an altar in the dome. In the dome's vault "can be discerned representations of all the stars of heaven . . . with their proper names and power to influence terrestrial things marked with three little verses for each . . . [The temple's] seven golden lamps hang always burning, and these bear the names of the seven planets" (p. 3). Here one sees astral magic ready to be used to influence earthly images.

Earthly knowledge is represented in innumerable pictures and explanations that adorn the walls of the city. There are mathematical figures; pictures of the seas and rivers; specimens of minerals, trees, herbs, wines, and animals of all kinds; representations of weather phenomena; depictions of mechanical arts and historically important people. Teachers provide verbal instruction by reading aloud explanatory verses that accompany the pictures and by reading from one great book. All is guided by a supreme ruler, aided by three princes (each with their magistrates and doctors) who presided over the liberal arts, science, and mechanics (one is reminded here of Mnemosyne, mother of the nine Muses of Greek mythology). It is not much of a conceptual stretch to translate Campanella's pictorial-verbal educational system into dual coding theoretical terms.

The great Moravian educator Jan Amos Comenius took the further step of concretizing Campanella's instructional system in actual pictures and descriptions. His volume, *Orbis Sensualium Pictus* ("The visible world in pictures"), was the mother of all children's picture textbooks (see Sadoski & Paivio, 2001, pp. 25–27). Since it was first published in Nuremburg in 1658, it has been used as the model for more than 200 editions in 26 languages.[65] The *Orbis* was intended as a visual textbook for learning Latin and other languages. It contains none of the occult elements of its imagery ancestors but is instead a straightforward summary of the world in 150 pictures with titles. The objects in the pictures are numbered and accompanied by parallel columns of labels and short sentences describing the numbered objects. About 2,000 words and their meanings are thus concretized and explained. The pictures and vocabulary are organized into domains that include the world, the sun, the heavens, eclipses, fire, birds, cattle, cooking, printing, and so forth, and abstract notions such as Prudence. For example, a section entitled "The Barbers-Shop" shows Renaissance barbers trimming the hair and beards of customers (Sadoski & Paivio, 2001, p. 26) along with numbered objects, labels, and descriptions of the the barber, hair, beard, scissors, and other objects typically seen in barbershops of the day. The *Orbis* also includes a picture alphabet intended to cue phonetic associations, for example, a picture of a growling dog for the sound of "*r*".

The *Orbis* reflected Comenius's commitment to concretization as an educational method. The teacher, he argued in the great Didactic (1896), must enable children to have direct experience with things, for "things are essential, words only accidental; things are the body, words but the garment; things are the kernel, words the shell and husk. Both should be presented to the intellect at the same time, but particularly the things, since they are as much objects of understanding as are language" (p. 267, cited in Piaget, 1993 p. 5).

The educational applications of DCT parallel the historical emphasis on concretization of knowledge through imagery and pictures. However, the justification for the dual coding emphasis rests on the scientific evidence that has only recently become available. The mnemonists who were one source of inspiration for Comenius learned about the effectiveness of imagery from their own experiences and historical anecdotes. They did not know whether it worked better than the verbal methods advocated by Quintilian and the Ramists over the centuries. Although Comenius may have been the first to conceive of a full-scale science of education, he did not develop that science even as applied to the concretization principle he espoused. Today we have ample scientific evidence and a more explicit theoretical framework in which the facts can be embedded. Some of the key findings from Chapter 4 are reviewed next, followed by educational research extensions.

---

[65]A revision of the Orbis was developed in Amsterdam by van Tijen and Vojtechovsky (1996) in the form of an interactive computerized exhibition that provides access to the original pictures and vocabulary in several languages, as well as progressive updating of the vocabulary from the 17th century to the present.

Relevant Findings From Basic Research

The most important findings are those related to concreteness and imagery effects on learning and memory. Recall that pictures are remembered better than concrete words by as much as a 2:1 ratio. Concrete words enjoy a similar advantage over abstract words, which extends to sentences and beyond. The concreteness effect is especially striking in associative memory tasks in which recall is prompted by pictures or concrete words that serve as reminders for the rest of the studied material (the conceptual peg effect in DCT). Diagnostic studies suggested that these effects are due to additive contributions of verbal and nonverbal memory codes, with the nonverbal (pictorial or image) memory component contributing more than the verbal component to their combined effect. Imagery also reduces memory load by making it easy to combine separate components into an integrated memory representation. Using concrete materials and encouraging imagery in educational settings should therefore help learners build up the long-term memories that constitute knowledge.

The dual coding evidence also supports the traditional emphasis on the importance of language in the growth of knowledge. Naming increases recall of pictures, especially with young children who are less likely than adults to name them spontaneously. Verbal relatedness increases memory for abstract as well as concrete word pairs and sentences. Integrative memory for sentences as measured by cued recall is better when subjects and objects are connected by meaningful relational terms such as verbs or prepositions as compared to simple conjunctions. Presenting words in a logical hierarchical pattern, as in a Ramist epitomy, results in better recall than random arrangement of the same words in the same visual pattern (Bower, Clark, Lesgold, & Winzenz, 1969).

Language comprehension and production also benefit from concreteness, imagery, and verbal relatedness. Whether measured by memory tests or simply by asking people whether statements are true or false, language is easier to understand the more concrete and verbally coherent it is. Sentences, definitions, and compositions are produced more easily to concrete than abstract words. Selective dual coding is implicated in that, for example, participants report using imagery when they define concrete words and verbal strategies when they define abstract words. Sentences are even generated more easily to object pictures than to concrete words, further implicating imagery. The direct practical implication is that language reception and production skills will develop best in concrete contexts that encourage use of imagery as a mediator.

The dual coding processes are similarly implicated in experimental problem solving, concept formation, and reasoning skills. They are prominent as well in tests of intelligence, with visualization ability consistently loading highly on a general intelligence factor along with verbal abilities. Moreover, we saw biographical evidence of the importance of these dual coding variables in the creative work of inventors, scientists, and artists in different domains. Systematic instruction that encourages dual coding should thus benefit the development of higher level intellectual and creative abilities.

School Education

The aforementioned evidence bears on the usefulness of already-established dual coding systems in memory and other cognitive tasks. The question here is whether dual coding variables can be similarly helpful in initial learning of language and other skills in school settings. Early educators certainly thought so because they developed visual alphabets in which letters look like objects, taught letter sounds using pictures of animals and things that make similar sounds, and used pictures and imagery to learn the meanings of words. The object lesson mentioned earlier grew out of that tradition. Similar concretization methods abound in modern education and are justified by research evidence. The following examples are from a comprehensive review by Sadoski and Paivio (2001, Chapter. 8).

Reading Skills. Pictures in which letters are shown as integrated parts of objects (e.g., the letter "f" depicted as the stem of a flower with a drooping head and the crossbar as leaves) were twice as effective as control conditions in teaching pre-readers to learn the relations between letters and their sounds. Kindergartners learned to read concrete words by sight 80% faster when the words were accompanied by referent pictures than when paired only with their pronunciations. The acquisition of meaningful vocabulary is aided by a keyword method in which the learner forms an interactive image between the definition of an unfamiliar word and a familiar concrete word that shares the same sound. For example, the word *carlin* ("old woman") can be learned using the keyword "car" and imagining an old woman driving a car. Later, the word *carlin* reminds the learner of "car" through the acoustic association, which evokes the car-woman image that yields the meaning of carlin. Concrete material enhances reading comprehension and recall in children and adults. Concrete advance organizers (e.g., brief written texts read prior to other texts) result in better comprehension and recall of text about astronomy or linguistics than abstract or no advance organizers. Such results presumably reflect the various contributions of concreteness-evoked imagery and dual coding to the meaningfulness, memorability, and retrievability of the main ideas and theme of the text.

A minor downside is that imagery can also increase errors (miscues) when reading aloud because of modality-specific interference—that is, visual imaging interferes to some extent with visual perception of print. Moreover, in memory tests of comprehension, semantically related words such as synonyms might be substituted for the text items (e.g., "lady" recalled as "woman;" Kuiper & Paivio, 1977). Such intrusions could also reflect both imagery and verbal associations to presented material (e.g., Rhodes & Anastasi, 2000). These negative effects are small and do not override the general positive effects of concreteness.

Instructing learners to form images during reading further enhances reading comprehension and recall. With beginning readers, however, the burden of verbal processing of printed words can interfere with image formations. This is the mirror image of the modality-specific interference explanation just discussed. For the same reason, imagery instructions can slow up reading even in some adults (Denis, 1982). It has been shown, moreover, that reading can interfere with image-mediated recall. De

Beni and Moè (2003) found that adults given imagery instructions recalled more from orally presented than from written passages, whereas participants given rehearsal instructions recalled more from written than oral passages. The effect could be even more pronounced for young readers. The solution might be to have them read and form images successively (Pressley, 1976).

Combining pictures, mental imagery, and verbal elaboration assists understanding and learning from text. This has been demonstrated with learners ranging from grade school to university level. For example, Purnell and Solman (1991) directly tested for additive effects of text and illustrations on the comprehension of technical material by high school students. Some students read text alone, some saw illustrations of the text content, and others received both text and illustrations. When text and illustrations were presented alone, they were repeated to control for the repetition experienced by those who received both. One set of materials consisted of explanations of such phenomena as the water cycle of condensation and precipitation, either as text or as labeled illustrations of clouds, rain, and so forth. Comprehension measured by multiple choice questions was superior for the group that received both text and illustrations as compared to those who received either form alone either once or repeated. This additive dual coding effect is shown in Fig. 19.1. The authors noted that their results are completely consistent with DCT.

On the basis of the combined results of such studies, Mayer (1999) made the following recommendations about multimedia learning: (a) use words and pictures rather than words alone, (b) present pictures and corresponding words or narrations close together in space or time, (c) minimize extraneous (irrelevant) details, and (d) present words as speech rather than on-screen text in animations (presumably to minimize modality-specific interference). These recommendations generally accord with the practical implications of multimodal dual coding theory.

Written Composition. The use of concreteness, imagery, and dual coding makes writing more readable and memorable. Studies show that use of concrete language improves ratings of comprehensibility, interest, recall, and writing quality of text. In a meta-analysis of 73 experimental interventions, Hillocks (1986) found that techniques that focused on concrete data were the most robust in improving writing quality. Sadoski et al. (1997) found even larger effects in their study of written definitions of words (reviewed earlier, Chapter 4)—quality ratings of concrete as compared to abstract definitions was greater than the concreteness effect size in Hillocks's meta-analysis.

Imagery and verbal-associative instructional techniques also improve the quality of writing. For example, training gifted students on use of imagery resulted in subsequent written compositions judged to be more original than those written by control participants. An instructional approach (Schultz, 1982) that uses both verbal and imagery techniques based on DCT produces improvements in composition length, concrete expression, and fluency of high school remedial students. Finally, such verbal associative techniques as listing relevant words that might be used in writing about a topic and practice combining sentences improves such features as organization and syntactic fluency of writing.

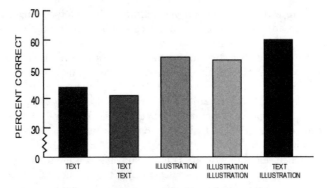

FIGURE 19.1 Additive dual coding effects of text and illustrations on the comprehension of geographic material. Figure (p. 293) from Purnell, Kenneth N., & Solman, Robert T. (1991). The influence of technical illustrations on students' comprehension of geography. *Reading Research Quarterly, 26(3),* 277–299. Reprinted with permission of Kenneth N. Purnell and the International Reading Association. All rights reserved.

In sum, applications consistent with DCT principles have been shown to benefit literacy education. Concreteness, referentially related pictorial accompaniments, and imagery processing facilitate comprehension of text. Concreteness, imagery, and verbal- associative processing similarly enhance the quality of written compositions.

Such literacy skills are increasingly perfected in the context of learning new facts and skills. Reading educators sometimes refer to the overlapping stages as learning to read and reading to learn. We focus next on the latter from the dual coding perspective. Factual content areas such as geography, history, botany, and zoology require no special emphasis because the applications of dual coding principles are straightforward. The teacher need only take advantage of the powerful effects of concretization, imagery, dual coding, and verbal-associative organization in instructions, discussions, and tasks assigned to learners. The applications are somewhat trickier in the case of mathematics and second-language learning.

Mathematics.   Chapter 18 presented a detailed summary of how Clark and Campbell (1991) used dual coding mechanisms to develop a general theory of number processing. The theory emphasizes the concrete basis of number concepts and the roles of associative mechanisms and imagery in performing numerical operations. The basic dual coding processes have long been used in teaching arithmetic. Children first learn to name numer als and then their meanings by associating them with groups of objects or their pictures, They learn addition, subtraction, and multiplication concretely by adding marbles to a pile or taking them from it. They literally calculate, which derives from the Latin root that refers to small stones used in reckoning on an abacus. They learn corresponding verbal number associations by rote memorization of addition, subtraction, and multiplication tables: two and two are four, five take away two leaves three, two times three is six; or $2 + 2 = 4$, $5 - 2 = 3$, $2 \times 3 = 6$. Productive extensions to large numbers and columns of numbers require the further operation of carrying products, and so on. Learning fractions builds on an understanding of division, similarly acquired by concrete examples translated into verbal-numerical operations. All of these skills entail development of increasingly long and varied logogens for number names and operators (rapid production of "two times three equals six" implies activation of a corresponding sentence- length logogen) as well as imagens of numerals and operators.

Rudolph Arnheim (1960, Chapter. 12), one of the staunchest advocates of the power of visual thinking, pointed out that teaching arithmetic by concrete examples is double-edged. One side charges students with discovering the numbers hidden in life situations while ignoring abstractions; the other side distracts from the abstractions to be learned, especially when pictures of objects and numerical operators are thrown together. His preference was to use pure shapes such as Cuisenaire rods of different lengths and colors for teaching addition, subtraction, fractions, and so forth, because they represent abstract relations and yet can be easily manipulated and imaged by children.[66] Arnheim also showed how algebga is made easier by transforming equations into geometric shapes. Like generations of students, I learned the binomial expression, $(a + b)^2 = a^2 + b^2 + 2ab$, entirely by rote. A simple figure (Arnheim, 1960, p. 221) shows immediately why the algebraic expression is true. This is a clear example of dual coding representations in algebra in that the geometric shape is a labeled nonverbal referent of the verbal binomial expression.

Effective mathematical education relies on appropriate concretization of abstract symbols and relations (Skemp, 1987). This recapitulates the origin of mathematical abstractions from concrete situations. For example, Leibnitz's invention of the calculus independent of Newton grew out of his interest in the classic method of loci and his search for a universal language that would contain abstract memorable symbols for things in general (Rossi 2000, Chapter VIII; Yates, 1966, pp. 382–383). This topic is continued in a later section on remedial education, where we look at an astonishingly successful teaching program for "nurturing mathematical talent."

Second-Language Learning.   Second-(or foreign-) language learning has been important to social adaptation from the time that diverging human groups came in contact after having developed different languages. In historical times, conquest and enterprise have been powerful motives for learning other languages. Migration for whatever reason has meant that learning two or more languages is the norm in most

---

[66]Belgian teacher George Cuisenaire introduced the colored rods for teaching arithmetic in 1952. Caleb Gattegno, his early collaborator (Cuisenaire & Gattegno, 1954), continued to popularized the approach in a series of mathematics textbooks and also advocated the use of Cuisenaire rods in foreign language teaching.

modern countries, and educational systems accommodate to that norm. For adult learners, learning a foreign language is a special problem because it takes much time to learn enough to say what they want to say in the new language. Successful adult learners focus especially on vocabulary learning (Ramsey, 1980, p. 88), and educational systems in the past emphasized that aspect more than they do today. Rote translation has long been the favored study method, but we see that it is inferior to the use of pictorial aids and imagery mnemonics.

Pictures have been used as learning aids as far back as 2,500 years ago (Kelly, 1969). We saw that Comenius's *Orbis Pictus* was intended for teaching Latin in the context of pictorial and vernacular equivalents for Latin vocabulary. The long-untested implication is that pictures enhance learning relative to traditional translation practice. A simple prediction is that foreign language responses will be learned faster when paired with pictures rather than words (the native language translations) as stimuli—for example, a picture of a head as compared to the word "head" as stimuli for *caput*. Many experiments have confirmed this prediction (summarized in Paivio, 1986, p. 253). The results are explainable in terms of bilingual DCT: learners covertly pronounce the names of the pictures in their native language, and the names and the pictures converge on the foreign language responses, increasing the probability of recall relative to the word-stimulus condition. The *Orbis* must have been especially successful because it explicitly provided both translations and pictures during study. Methods designed to encourage imagery should have similar benefits.

We saw earlier that the keyword imagery technique is superior to rote study of word pairs for learning the meanings of unfamiliar native or foreign-language words as measured by the ability to translate them into familiar words (e.g., carlin = old woman). The technique by itself, however, does not help one to recall the unfamiliar word given the familiar word as the stimulus (old woman = carlin), although it does so when imagery is combined with verbal-associative coding (Rodriguez & Sadoski, 2000).

Years ago (Paivio, 1978c) I used the hook (or pegword) technique to increase my productive French vocabulary. I kept the learning context in the target language by constructing and memorizing a 100-item French pegword list (Table 19.1 shows examples). I could then associate new vocabulary items with the pegwords by means of interactive images. For example, take *chaise* ("chair"), *arbre* ("tree"), *camion* ("truck"), and *maison* ("house") as the first words to be learned. The respective images might be a teapot on a chair, a tree with a knotted rope hanging from it, a truck on top of a ship's mast, and a king building a house. On recall trials, one starts with the numbers and runs through the associated mnemonic chain in French (e.g., "*un–thé* [teapot + chair image]–*chaise*"). With practice, the mediating chain shortens so that saying "un" covertly generates the integrated teapot-chair image. The image facilitates recall of the target word chaise, presumably for the same reason that picture stimuli speed up learning of new vocabulary relative to translation practice.

I used the technique to study written lists of French words and idioms, up to 100 items at a time. I practiced recalling the target words during otherwise mindless activities such as jogging or walking to work. I checked my recall later against the study list and corrected errors. A second mental run through the list the next day was

TABLE 19.1

Examples of French Mnemonic Peg-Words and Translations With
the *Critical* (Pronounced) Consonants Italicized

Number	Peg-Word	Number	Peg-Word
1	*th*é ("tea")	11	*t*ê*t*e ("head")
2	*n*oeud ("knot">	12	*n*o*c*e ("wedding")
3	*m*ât ("mast")	30	*m*ou*ss*e ("moss," "foam")
4	*r*oi ("king")	41	*r*â*t*eau ("rake")
5	*l*oi ("law")	52	*l*ai*n*e ("wool")
6	*ch*ou ("cabbage")	63	*ch*a*m*eau ("camel")
7	*c*amp ("camp")	74	*c*a*rr*é ("square")
8	*f*eu ("fire")	85	*f*i*l* ("thread")
9	*p*ain ("bread")	96	*p*o*ch*e ("pocket")
10	*t*a*ss*e ("cup")	100	*d*i*s*eu*s*e ("fortune teller")

usually error free. Then I moved on to a new list. The method was enjoyable and it seemed effective in that I generally recalled about 90% of the studied list on the first trial and I could later use the words in conversation. There was, however, no research literature to confirm my impressions. In fact, I knew of no instructional literature on the second-language "immersion" use of the hook technique—and so, Alain Desrochers and I (Paivio & Desrochers, 1979) conducted the following experiment.

English-speaking university students with some French knowledge first learned a 96-item pegword list and were also tested for their knowledge of the English meanings of 96 French vocabulary targets. Half of the targets were concrete and half abstract, and, within each level of concreteness, equal numbers were high, medium, or low in preexperimental familiarity. The participants attempted to translate the words into English and also rated them on familiarity. Later, they were taught the imagery mnemonic technique and then had one learning and number-cued recall trial with four blocks of 24 words. Sequences of imagery and repetition instructions were alternated over blocks so that each participant learned half the blocks using imagery and half using repetition. A day later, they had unexpected translation and familiarity rating tests on the experimental items and an equal number of items they had previously translated and rated but had not seen during the experiment.

The most striking result (Fig. 19. 2) was the superiority of imagery mnemonics over the rote condition across all levels of familiarity and concreteness of the French vocabulary. Overall recall was 3 times higher under the imagery mnemonic than the control condition. In addition, recall was generally higher for concrete than abstract words and increased with familiarity, especially under the imagery condition. The translation tests showed further that an increase in correct translations for the initially unfamiliar words was twice as high in the imagery than in the repetition

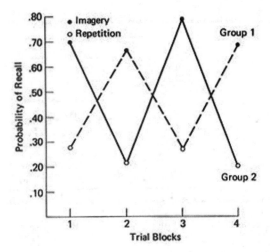

FIGURE 19.2 Probability of recall under imagery and repetition instructions for four blocks of items, with the imagery condition occurring on blocks 2 and 4 for Group 1 and on blocks 1 and 3 for Group 2. From Figure 3 (p.24) in Paivio, A., & Desrochers, A. (1979). Effects of an imagery mnemonic on second language recall and comprehension. *Canadian Journal of Psychology, 33*, 17–28. Copyright 1979 Canadian Psychological Association. Reprinted with permission.

condition. Finally, rated familiarity of initially unfamiliar words increased more under imagery than repetition conditions. The hook technique thus facilitated both recall and comprehension of second-language vocabulary.

The hook technique fits into the bilingual dual coding model (Chapter 4) in that the language learning experience requires use of imagery as well as intraverbal associative connections between pegwords and new target items. It thereby encourages the formation of verbal associative and referential connections within the second language system, and also promotes direct verbal connections between translation equivalents in the two languages. It can be extended to idioms and sentences that vary in syntax using translation equivalents and imagery in which the context provides clues to tense, number, and so on. For example, Desrochers (1983) applied the technique to the learning of French grammatical gender, with promising results. The technique can be elaborated in other ways suggested by DCT (e.g., see Paivio, 1986, p. 255).

The keyword and hook mnemonic techniques have shown enough promise that they could be added to foreign-language learning kits along with other augmentative techniques, such as *Orbis*-type picture books, audiovisual video programs, use of Cuisenaire rods for construction or description of referent objects and relations, and physical responses to commands (such techniques are reviewed in Paivio,

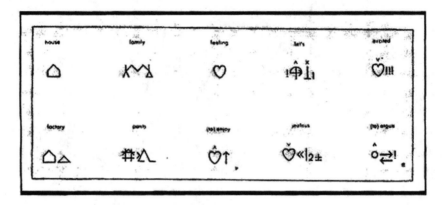

FIGURE 19.3.   Examples of Blissymbols.

1983c). The methods vary in their potential benefits for different language skills and ease of implementation in different contexts.

REMEDIAL EDUCATION

Methods that implicate dual coding principles have been used in remedial education for learning difficulties related to communication skills, reading, spelling, and mathematics, among others. The methods can all be classed as augmentative aids in that they supplement traditional classroom teaching methods. All make use of nonverbal stimuli and some encourage use of imagery.

Communicative Disorders and Blissymbolics

Blissymbolics is a logographic symbol system invented by Charles Bliss (1965) as a universal communication system modeled after Chinese ideograms. Blissymbols have been used to help people with severe speech problems to communicate effectively. William Yovetich (1985), a researcher and clinician in communicative disorders, investigated the scientific validity of Blissymbols by studying their memory effects from the dual coding perspective.

The experiments were patterned after the bilingual coding experiment (Paivio & Lambert, 1981; this volume, p. 113) in which image-verbal dual coding resulted in higher recall than bilingual dual coding, which in turn exceeded recall of words that were simply copied. Yovetich (1985) used synonyms and Blissymbols that represent concrete words and abstract concepts, as in the examples shown in Fig. 19.3. The design tested the overall memorability of Blissymbols and the specific effects of stimuli that concretize abstract concepts. The synonym condition substituted for the bilingual coding condition of the Paivio and Lambert (1981) experiment. The experimental participants were teachers who had used Blissymbols as teaching aids. They

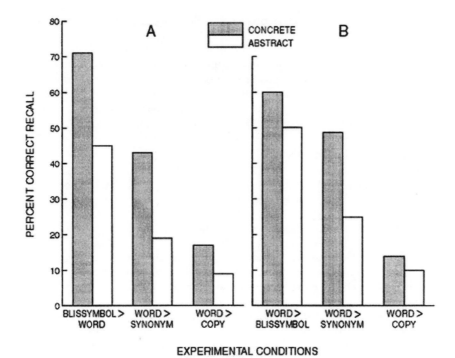

FIGURE 19.4.   Free recall of words that Blissymbol experts had generated by writing the names of Blissymbols, writing the synonym equivalents of words, or copying them (panel A), and presented words that experts had coded by drawing Blissymbol equivalents, writing synonyms, or just copying (panel B). Based on data from Yovetich (1985).

were shown a list of Blissymbols and printed words one item at a time. In one condition, they wrote down the names of Blissymbols, the synonym equivalents for some words, and simply copied others. Then they tried to recall the words they had written. In the reverse condition, they were presented only words, some of which they coded by drawing Blissymbol equivalents, others by writing synonyms, and the remainder by just copying the words. They then recalled the words they had been presented.

The results are shown in Fig. 19.4. The general pattern of recall closely paralleled the bilingual memory results described earlier in that recall was best for the Blissymbol conditions, intermediate for synonym coding, and lowest for the copy condition. Notably, the same pattern occurred with both abstract and concrete concepts, with the expected difference that recall was generally lower for the abstract concepts. The results supported the additivity hypothesis for synonym dual coding as well as image-verbal dual coding. They showed further that abstract words were functionally concretized by their association with Blissymbols, although concrete words benefited additionally from their superior preexperimental capacity to evoke images. The combination of Blissymbol and synonym results thus went beyond earlier studies in the memory literature that also have demonstrated functional concretization of abstract language using pictorial and imagery procedures, but without simultaneously revealing memory enhancement by verbal dual coding. The results and interpretations justify the use of Blissymbols and other similar augmentative methods to enhance learning in other areas of remedial education.

Reading and Spelling Remediation

Language reading problems used to be lumped together under the term *dyslexia* without any specific implication regarding the causes of the problems, but now the term generally implies a neural malfunction (e.g., Eden, et al., 2004). Here I discuss remedial programs for language problems without reference to the causes (relevant brain information is included in Chapter 7).

Reading problems are usually classified into difficulties with decoding or comprehension, or both. Remediation has traditionally focused on decoding because readers must be able to recognize printed words before they can get their meaning. Decoding ability is measured by tests that require reading words or naming letters aloud. Comprehension tests require understanding what words and text mean. It turns out that decoding and comprehension are not highly correlated. Statistically, the respective tests load on different factors (with subcategories within each). A striking example of dissociation of the two abilities is that some high-functional autistic people (those with Asperger's syndrome) are "superlexics" who can read aloud extraordinarily well and yet not understand what they are reading.

Lindamood-Bell Learning Processes, a private remedial education company, developed reading programs that fit well with DCT (Bell, 1991a; Lindamood, Bell, & Lindamood, 1997). As a remedy for decoding problems, phonemic awareness is taught by associating phonemes with motor acts and pictures of the mouth. Bilabial plosives ("p" and "b") are taught as "lip poppers," lingual alveolar plosives such as "t" and "d" are (tongue) "tip tappers," and so on. The positions of the phonemes in words and longer sequences are taught using colored blocks.

Comprehension is taught through a program of visualizing and verbalizing that is explicitly related to DCT (Bell, 1991b). Instruction entails progressive buildup of imagery to larger and larger text segments—words, phrases, sentences, texts—with learners being encouraged to describe their images in increasing detail. Higher order comprehension involved in inference, prediction, and evaluation is dealt with through imagination and verbal elaboration. This instructional technique clearly was designed to teach learners how to concretize text using imagery and dual coding as they read. Lindamood et al. (1997) provided clinical evidence of the effectiveness of their programs with reading disabled individuals of various ages. Much evidence has accumulated since then, including the results of a multi school augmentative intervention program that dramatically raised the reading performance of students in Grades 3, 4, and 5 of schools with low reading achievement in the Pueblo School

District in the State of Colorado, so that the schools eventually outperformed other comparable Colorado schools in tests of reading (Sadoski & Willson, in press). Fig. 19.5 shows the improvement over years for students who started in grade 3.

Johnson-Glenberg (2000) experimentally compared the effects of visualization-verbalization with a verbal strategy called reciprocal teaching (Palincsar & Brown, 1984) on improvement in comprehension of narrative stories by poor comprehenders. Both procedures resulted in greater gains on 10 different measures of comprehension than a control condition. The effect sizes favored the reciprocal teaching group on several measures of explicit, factual learning whereas the visualization-verbalization group was favored on several visually mediated measures. Johnson-Glenberg suggested that a combination of the two methods may be very powerful. From the DCT perspective, both methods involve dual coding, with differences in the degree to which they engage verbal or imagery processes. Their relative contributions might be revealed more clearly by varying the concreteness of the narratives, questioning participants on their use of verbal and visual strategies, and other procedures that have been used informatively in dual coding research.

Mathematics

Mathematician John Mighton is also an award-winning playwright and actor. He appeared in the Academy-Award-winning film *Good Will Hunting,* which is about a working class math genius whose ability seemingly emerged out of the blue. Contrary to that "giftedness" premise, Mighton's character said the following: "Most people never get to see how brilliant they are. They don't find teachers who believe in them. They get convinced they're stupid." The lines reflect his own struggles with mathematics as a child and his reaction to his experiences. While completing a doctorate in mathematics in 1998, he started an educational charity called JUMP (Junior Undiscovered Math Prodigies), which provided free tutoring for elementary school students in his Toronto neighborhood. The program was so successful that from its inception with 8 tutors and 15 students, JUMP grew exponentially so that, by 2003, it was established in 12 inner-city schools in Toronto, with over 200 volunteers and 1,500 students.

The approach is described in a volume (Mighton, 2003). It merits detailed consideration here because it is a systematic application of concretization of mathematical concepts and operations compatible with DCT. It also has the essential characteristics of deliberate practice as described in Ericsson's approach to the attainment of expertise, comparable, say, to the Suzuki method of teaching violin to children.

Mighton (2003) wrote the following:

> In teaching mathematics I often use simple diagrams or concrete materials. A finite state automaton can be "built" using a penny, a piece of paper, and a pencil. The notion of fractional equivalence can be taught using coloured block. . ., and objects in sets may be represented by lines inside boxes . . . In abstract mathematics, the ability to draw a picture or create a model in which only the essential features of a problem are represented is an essential skill. (p. 59).

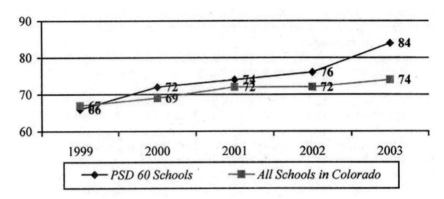

FIGURE 19.5   Reading performance test scores over four years for students in Pueblo School District 60 in the State of Colorado who, in grade 3, started a multischool augmentative reading intervention program using the Lindamood-Bell Learning Processes programs. Their growth curve significantly exceeds that of students in other comparable Colorado schools (Sadoski & Willson, 2006). Based on data that are publicly available from the State of Colorado and Pueblo School District 60.

The approach is founded on the premise that understanding of mathematical rules and concepts emerges from mastery of basic operations. Virtually all mathematical concepts can be reduced to the basic operation of counting and grouping objects into sets, which most children can do before they enter kindergarten. Their application to fractions, multiplication, division, and so on, is taught using "pie" diagrams and other concrete methods. A child must first demonstrate or be taught how to count by twos, threes, and fives on the fingers. Then the operations are applied to fractions, multiplication, division, ratios, and percentages using "pie" charts or box diagrams along with the corresponding numerical manipulations.

Such methods are familiar to all teachers. What is different in the JUMP program is that they are used systematically so that every student masters the operations as applied to one problem before moving to a more complex one. The skills are taught bit by bit, with more time devoted to children who need it. Mastery of problems is tested using questions stated in terms of objects ("How many apples and oranges . . .?)" or only numbers ("What number is 3/4 of 20?"). Progress sometimes seems slow and then there might be a sudden leap to a new level of operational ability and understanding, explainable by a property of natural systems that tiny changes of condition can have dramatic and often unpredictable effects—formalized in chaos theory and illustrated by the familiar saying, if a butterfly flaps its wings over the ocean, it can change the weather in New York City.

The evidence for the success of JUMP currently is anecdotal, the accumulation of case after case of dramatic progress of children written off by teachers, parents, and the children themselves as just not having the right stuff to succeed in mathematics.

Quoting from the back cover of Mighton's (2003) volume: "A student in a remedial class who couldn't count by twos is now in an academic program a year ahead of her level. An entire Grade 3 class, including so-called slow learners, scores over 90% on a Grade 6–7 math test. A boy who nearly failed Grade 8 math is now completing a PhD in math on scholarship." More formal studies of the program are presently in the works.

In addition to its remedial reading programs already described, Lindamood-Bell Learning Processes has developed a remedial mathematics program (Tuley & Bell, 1997). The program is similar to JUMP in its emphasis on concretization of mathematical operations and concepts. It differs from JUMP in that it teaches children how to use visualization (mental imagery) to represent numbers and operations. The program proceeds from (a) concrete experience using number lines, cubes, and the like; to (b) imaging the entities and operations; to (c) computation. The steps are depicted as a "math-ladder" with imaging numerals at the lowest rung and fractions at the top. Learners climb step by step at their own pace. As in the case of JUMP, much anecdotal evidence supports the effectiveness of the Tuley and Bell (1997) math program.

Cognitive Remediation for the Aging Mind

Cognitive decline with aging is more than a remedial education issue when it is associated with disease processes such as Alzheimer's. Even in such cases, however, cognitive interventions are helpful at least in slowing down the decline, and they are even more so in "normal" aging. In any case, age-related changes, especially in memory, are disturbing enough that many people seek remedial help. Thus it is not surprising that there is a large scientific and applied literature in the area. Here we touch on aspects of aging and cognition that are amenable to dual coding analyses and possible interventions.

Many studies have investigated effects of variables that have been typically used to test DCT. These include cognitive and memory tasks that compare pictures and words, concrete and abstract words, imagery and verbal strategies, cued and noncued retrieval, and semantic versus episodic memory. In general, older adults are slower and make more errors than young adults; performance across ages is affected by the same variables (e.g., task complexity, concreteness of materials); and age interacts with task so that older people show smaller benefits of some variables and greater negative effects of others. The following are relevant examples.

Dror and Kosslyn (1994) compared old and young adults on four imagery tasks that test Kosslyn's imagery theory. Older participants were slower overall and made more errors than the young. Interactions occurred so that the aged showed more slowing and errors in image generation and rotation as the complexity of the images increased, but image maintenance and scanning were unaffected by complexity. The tasks involved memory images directly evoked by matrices with novel patterns of black and white squares, and it is uncertain whether the results would be the same when imagery is evoked indirectly by words.

Dirkx and Craik (1992) compared free recall of abstract and concrete words by young and older adults. The words were learned by rote repetition, forming an image to each word, or by organizing the words in sentences or stories. Recall was generally better for concrete than abstract words, and the young benefited most from imagery whereas the older participants benefited most from language-based organization.

The imagery results suggest that the older participants either had more difficulty generating images to words (referential processing) or that they profited relatively less from imagery or dual coding. The referential processing interpretation is supported by the consistent observation that older people also have particular difficulty naming pictures, suggesting that aging results in loss of referential processing ability in both directions (more about that shortly). The language organization effect, on the other hand, suggests that verbal associative processing is relatively intact in the elderly, consistent with their performance on vocabulary and other verbal tests of crystallized intelligence (described in Chapter 16). That interpretation remains uncertain, however, because putting the target words in sentences or stories evokes imagery as well as verbal associative processing.

The effects of classical imagery mnemonic techniques also vary with age. For example, Lindberger, Kliegl, and Baltes (1992) reported that expertise in mnemonic techniques did not eliminate a general aging decrement in imagery-based memory performance. However, others have found that the learning gap with aging is reduced by instruction on mnemonic strategies (e.g., Gruneberg & Pascoe, 1996; Roberston-Tchabo, Hausman, & Arenberg, 1976). The results are also affected by individual differences in imagery and verbal cognitive styles. Neils-Strunjas, Krikorian, Shidler, and Likoy (2001) found that older adults who scored high on the imagery scale of the Paivio and Harshman (1983) Individual Difference Questionnaire recalled more names and faces than those who scored low on imagery, whereas verbal style showed no relation to recall.

We can conclude that the effects of imagery and dual coding variables with aging depend on differences in experimental and subject variables. Practical applications thus hinge on theoretical understanding of the general effects and specific inconsistencies. Craik's (1986) environmental-support theory of age-related memory decline is immediately relevant because of its emphasis on the importance of concrete contexts as an aid to memory retrieval in the aged. When environment support is weak, the memorizer must rely on internal resources ("self-initiated operations") to prompt recall. Those internal processing resources decline with age, hence the decline in some memory tasks and not in others. For example, differences between old and young memorizers are small in recognition memory because support comes from the items themselves, but older people suffer in free recall because task performance depends heavily on internal resources. Cued recall is intermediate in difficulty for the aged because the cue provides some environmental support. DCT offers similar predictions and explanations, couched specifically in terms of the variables that affect the cooperative activity of dual coding systems, as shown by the following studies.

Sharps, Foster, Martin, and Nunes (1999) investigated the effects of visuospatial and relational contexts on verbal free recall of common objects by young and older adults. The spatial context consisted of an abstract "map" of multiple shapes in various locations of a black-and-white diagram, or presented as three-dimensional reliefs in a wooden array. The recall items were relatively unrelated common objects placed in the various locations. The relational context used recall items that were derived from 10 readily identifiable categories (e.g., animals, utensils, tools) presented in the same spatial contexts as the unrelated items. Results were compared against free recall of the items. The interesting results were that (a) free recall of unrelated items was lower for older than younger adults (a common finding), and (b) both spatial and relational contexts raised recall of the older participants to the same level as that of the younger participants. There also was a suggestion that the effects of the two contexts were somewhat additive ("synergistic") at short retention intervals. Sharps et al. interpreted the spatial context effects in terms of Craik's (1986) environmental support theory and the relational context effects as consistent with an observation that relational processing is generally well preserved with aging.

The Sharps et al. (1999) results can also be interpreted in DCT terms, with the proviso that the relational benefit might apply particularly to verbal relations. Thus, the aged benefited independently from spatial imagery organization and verbal-sequential organization, much as in the independent and additive effects of pair concreteness and verbal relatedness in dual coding recall experiments (e.g., Paivio et al., 1994) described in Chapter 4.

Dual coding processes were explicitly implicated in a picture–word memory experiment by Rissenberg and Glanzer (1986). They found that elderly participants displayed the typical picture superiority effect in free recall only when they had to name overtly the pictured objects as they were presented. This effect was interpreted as being due to dual coding. Younger adults showed the effect willy nilly because they were more likely to name the depicted objects spontaneously even without naming instructions. Note that the same patterns of results and interpretations were described earlier in regard to differences between children and adults in picture–word effects on recall (Chapter 4). The picture-superiority effect appeared with children only when they were required to name pictures as well as words during input. Thus, the dual coding additivity hypothesis holds up across the life span for picture recall but for different reasons: children and elderly people alike need to be prompted before they can take advantage of dual coding; children have not yet learned to do so spontaneously whereas the elderly have lost the tendency, perhaps through disuse.

A final example supports a similar interpretation of word concreteness effects and brings in brain processes to boot. Logan, Saunders, Snyder, Morris, and Buckner (2002) used fMRI to determine what brain areas were used by older and younger adults when they memorized words or nonverbal materials such as faces. They found that the older adults underutilized anterior ventral regions of the frontal cortex that are typically used in difficult tasks that require careful attention. The participants were then asked to think about the meanings of words by deciding whether a word was concrete or abstract. Now, the frontal brain areas of the older adults suddenly "lit up" when they used the "trick." The researchers noted the relation between this simple technique and imagery mnemonic techniques advocated as memory aids since ancient times. In addition, the older adults recruited multiple frontal regions in a nonselective manner that was not reversed by the semantic task. Logan et al. concluded that the underrecruited frontal areas are potentially amenable to cognitive training that would reverse the deficit.

The concreteness effect in the Logan et al. (2002) study raises the intriguing possibility that the same reversible brain processes are involved under conditions in which dual coding variables such as concreteness, picture versus words, and imagery mnemonic benefit the elderly. A common feature of the tasks that reverse age-related decrements is that they are designed to encourage referential processing, namely, imaging to words and naming pictures. Would the helpful tasks recruit a common frontal area more than, say, tasks that require verbal associative processing, which seem to be less affected by aging? Such questions and others suggested by DCT have not been systematically explored despite the attention that has already been paid to individual dual coding variables.

PSYCHOTHERAPY AND HEALTH

Psychotherapy refers to psychological treatment of maladaptive thoughts, behaviors, and emotions. DCT is directly relevant because emotions are associated with affective situations and verbal labels as described in several chapters. Especially pertinent here are the emotionally charged flash-bulb memories of people who suffer from posttraumatic stress disorder (PTSD). As described in Chapter 8, brain scan research (Lanius et al., 2004) showed that the memory reports of PTSD clients correlated with activation of right hemisphere regions typically associated with nonverbal processing whereas control participants, who had experienced similar traumatic events but without subsequent stress, show activation in left hemisphere sites associated with verbal processing. The authors commented on the relation of this pattern to DCT.

Dual coding processes also are directly or indirectly implicated in most psychotherapies for psychological disorders. Behavioral psychotherapy seems an exception in that it aims to treat phobias and other disorders by means of direct re-conditioning procedures. Fear of snakes, for example, would be treated by increasingly-intimate exposure to snakes. The procedures nonetheless include talking to the client in ways that are likely to evoke relevant imagery, and verbally guided imagery was explicitly incorporated by Wolpe (1958) into an imagery-based counterconditioning procedure called systematic desensitization, in which increasing exposure to the feared situation is experienced in the form of imagery. I return shortly to a fuller description. Numerous other cognitive and cognitive-behavioral therapies that incorporate imagery evolved from behavioral, Gestalt, and other sources (for a comprehensive review, see Sheikh, 2002). I touch on a few examples that illustrate the role of dual coding processes in different therapies.

We saw in the last chapter that Wilma Bucci (1985) interpreted Freud's psychoanalytic theory and therapeutic procedures in DCT terms. The client's free associations are not completely "free" but are instead elicited by the analyst's request and are related to the client's problem. The associations are mediated by imaginal memories and dreams that also are related to the problem, or so Freud assumed. Research support, however, is stronger for other (briefer) therapies that implicate dual coding. Perhaps the clearest example is systematic desensitization.

Wolpe (1958) developed the technique especially to deal with phobias. It entails increasingly intimate exposure to the feared situations or objects (e.g., snakes) by means of verbally guided imagery. The therapist and client first construct a hierarchy of feared situations from the most to the least feared. Therapy begins with instructions to imagine the least feared situation, and, when able to do so without fear, move up the hierarchy gradually to more feared ones, backtracking if the fear becomes too intense, until the client is able to tolerate the most feared situation. The technique has been shown to transfer successfully to real-life situations. For example, systematic desensitization was more effective than psychoanalysis and control conditions in treating fear of public speaking (Paul, 1966). The technique is similarly effective 80% of the time for circumscribed fears and phobias (Rachman & Wilson, 1980).

Despite its effectiveness, there was a sudden and lasting decline of interest in systematic desensitization among academics and researchers after 1970 (McGlynn, Smitherman, & Gothard (2004). The decline followed criticisms of methodological problems in the early studies, most of which were corrected within a decade. McGlynn et al. (2004) accordingly suggested that the decline may have been premature and that a period of renewed interest might be beneficial. They concluded, however, that this is unlikely to occur because the neobehavioristic lineage and language of systematic desensitization placed it outside the growing cognitive behavior therapy movement. Some psychotherapists nonetheless retain systematic desensitization as a therapeutic treatment for specific problems, and many of the prime movers of cognitive psychotherapy have emphasized other imagery-based techniques at some point in their careers (e.g., Horowitz, 1968; Meichenbaum, 1977; Singer, 1974).

Imagery techniques have also come under attack especially when used in the treatment of childhood sexual abuse (Arbuthnott, Arbuthnott, & Rossiter, 2001). The reason is that guided imagery can lead to false memories that offset the acknowleged positive effects of imagery on memory, a double-edged imagery effect already familiar to us from earlier contexts including education. As a consequence, some therapists have concluded that guided imagery is a risky procedure that should not be used to treat people with "uncertain memories." Arbuthnott et al. (2001) discussed strategies for using guided imagery that would reduce the risk of memory distortions, but research is lacking on such alternatives. The problem is difficult because other variables besides imagery (e.g., verbal associations, response habits) can create memory confusions.

The role of imagery has become more implicit or embedded in therapeutic procedures that emphasize language, emotions, and schema. Current experiential or emotion-focused psychotherapy is one approach that includes imagery as a main component. I first learned about it from my daughter, Sandra, who does outcome research on its effectiveness. The treatment model (e.g., Greenberg & S. Paivio, 1997) derives from gestalt therapy, in which imaginative techniques are used to help the client become aware of the whole background of feelings, wishes, and thoughts associated with a specific psychological problem. The problems involve "unfinished business" related to traumatic incidents, grief or loss, and otherwise disrupted interpersonal relations. The goal is to have clients reprocess traumatic memories by imaginal-confrontation intervention, (S. Paivio & Nieuwenhuis, 2001 in which they imagine the perpetrator of abuse or neglect and express previously restricted feelings and needs to this imagined other. The aim is to change maladaptive feelings, and perception of self and other, that develop as a result of the trauma.

The participants in one study (S. Paivio & Nieuwenhuis, 2001) were adult survivors of emotional, physical, or sexual abuse. They completed questionnaires and interviews that measure frequency of the childhood trauma, severity of pretreatment symptoms, and assess changes in symptoms after 20 weeks of individual, emotion-focused therapy. Twenty-two clients began therapy at the outset and 24 others began after a variable delay. The immediate therapy group achieved significant improvements in multiple domains of disturbance. Clients in the delayed treatment condition showed minimal improvements over the wait interval but after treatment showed improvements comparable to the immediate therapy group. Importantly, the gains were maintained at 9-months follow-up. The results replicated and extended previous findings on the efficacy of experiential therapy, reviewed in that study. A follow-up study (S. Paivio, Hall, Halowaty, Jellis, & Tran, 2001) using observer ratings of video tapes of the therapy sessions showed that client engagement in the imagery confrontation procedure specifically contributed to client improvement in that, with other factors controlled, high engagers achieved significantly greater resolution of issues than low engagers.

The relevant aspects of this intervention from the DCT perspective are that it entails (a) verbal guidance by the therapist, (b) nonverbal cues (e.g., an empty chair) for enactment and imagery confrontation with the abuser, and (c) relevant verbalization on the part of the client in response to the imagery and the therapist's verbal cues. The intervention is notable in its demonstrated success, thus joining a growing number of imagery-based therapies that are supported by research evidence (e.g., see Arbuthnott et al., 2001; Sheikh, 2002, pp. 82–83).

A final example links DCT directly to the analysis and treatment of generalized anxiety disorder (GAD). The disorder is characterized by chronic worry about personal problems. A reduced-concreteness theory of GAD worry (Stöber & Borkovec, 2002) assumes that worry consists mainly of verbal thoughts that reduce the amount of aversive imagery and consequent somatic anxiety associated with threatening problems. In the long run, however, the reduced imagery impedes the process of finding concrete solutions to the problems. Therapy designed to increase concrete imagery should reduce pathological worry. Stöber and Borkovec (2002) tested the theory by having GAD clients describe problems they worried about before and after they received cognitive-behavior therapy. The descriptions were rated for concreteness and compared with those of untreated clients and normal controls. The results were that untreated clients provided less concrete descriptions of their major worries relative to controls. After successful therapy, the problem descriptions by GAD clients showed the same level of concreteness as the controls. The authors concluded that concretization of worries may play a prominent role in the reduction of pathological worry. The further (untested) implication is that the concretization of thinking is likely to lead to concrete problem solutions.

It is pertinent to the reduced concretization theory of GAD that Destun and Kuiper (1999) found that recollective descriptions of real or imagined stressful events contained much less sensory detail and information about location and time than descriptions of pleasant events. Destun and Kuiper commented that aversive emotions associated with the memories of the real stressful events may "function to hinder any substantive embellishment or elaboration of these negative experiences, limiting further [stressful] rehearsal" (p. 183).

Interestingly, the low concreteness and imagery of memory descriptions associated with stressful and worrisome events contrasts with what Lanius et al. (2004) observed in the case of patients with PTSD (Chapter 8). That is, PTSD patients described their traumatic events in high imagery terms, whereas non-PTSD controls recalled their traumatic events in more neutral terms. The brain scans showed correspondingly contrasting patterns of activation in areas typically associated with imagery and verbal thinking. The memory descriptions in the different studies are not necessarily contradictory, however, because PTSD may result from more stressful experiences than the worries and unpleasant memories of GAD participants (in fact, by definition, GAD excludes PTSD and other specific anxiety disorders). One conciliatory interpretation is that both GAD worriers and stress-free trauma victims have learned to reduce anxiety by thinking verbally about their problems. Another is that both groups always were habitual verbal thinkers whereas PTSD sufferers were habitual imagers even before their traumatic experiences. Tests of such hypotheses would require measures of thinking habits or styles that are independent of the current worries and anxieties of participants using, for example, a retrospective version of the Individual Difference Questionnaire on imaginal and verbal thinking habits (Paivio & Harshman, 1983).

Physical Health

We deal next with the use of imagery and language processes to promote physical health. The procedures are indistinguishable from psychotherapy in such cases as psychosomatic health problems and fear caused by heart disease or cancer. They are also similar in relation to problems such as weight management and smoking, where the goal is behavior change.

Imagery has long been used to promote health and healing in both Western and Eastern cultures (Sheikh, Kunzendorf & Sheikh, 2003). The use has been justified by anecdotal evidence and basic scientific research on imagery. Direct research on the outcome of imagery approaches has only recently begun (Sheikh, Kunzendorf, & Sheikh, 2003, p. 22) and the support for many popular approaches remains anecdotal. A few of the better supported procedures illlustrate the interplay of imagery and verbal processes.

Edmund Jacobson was an important pioneer in this field. He developed the method of progressive relaxation and electrophysiological methods for measuring minute muscular contractions during mental activity. The two contributions are closely related (Jacobson, 1973). In the 1920s, Jacobson began to record electrical activity of muscles (in microvolts, millionths of volts) when participants imagined bending an arm or moving other body parts. This required training the participants to relax because muscles normally are doing something all the time and subtle electromyographic (EMG) changes would not stand out from that noisy background. Recordings from relaxed participants revealed EMG activity in arms or legs when they imagined moving those parts; activity of the tongue, lips, and jaw when they imagined saying letters of the alphabet; and so on. Among the methods for teaching relaxation, Jacobson used what later came to be called biofeedback: the participants observed oscilloscope tracings of their muscle activity as they learned to relax. Progressive relaxation therapy emerged from that context.

The electrophysiogical research and progressive relaxation therapy necessarily implicate dual coding. For example, the participant is instructed to imagine bending an arm. In DCT terms, this entails activation of motor imagens via referential pathways from logogens activated by the instructions. Measurements of electrical activity of eye muscles show that people tend to look in the direction of the arm they were asked to imagine, suggesting that visual imagery of the arm occurs as they imagine bending the arm. In progressive relaxation therapy, the patient is induced by instructions to tense and relax specific body parts beginning with the feet or head and moving up or down part by part. That, too, requires referential processing and implicates imagery related to the target body area. The procedure was first used by Jacobson and subsequently by others (e.g., Benson, 1976) to treat such stress-related disorders as insomnia, anxiety, gastrointestinal problems, and cardiovascular disorders. The effectiveness of relaxation techniques is supported by clinical observations but controlled studies are wanting.

Biofeedback treatment as an offshoot of Jacobson's relaxation procedure has been shown to influence numerous physiological processes, such as heart rate, gastrointestinal motility, brain rhythms, and immune system functioning (Sheikh, Kunzendorf, Sheikh, & Baer, 2003). Research suggests that biofeedback with imagery instructions is more effective than biofeedback alone, and imaging may be more effective than biofeedback (Sheikh Kunzendorf, Sheikh, & Baer, 2003, p. 39). The physiological results indirectly support the reported success of biofeedback therapies in treating migraine headaches, neurodermatitis, asthma, arrhythmia, ulcers, irritable bowel syndrome, and many others.

The other broad class of verbally guided imagery techniques focus treatment on specific clinical problems such as smoking, weight reduction, cancer, and heart disease. The techniques originate in Western and Eastern traditions (e.g., Achterberg, 1985). The verbal guidance of imagery may be more or less scripted but the procedures share the following stages: (a) imagery and breathing exercises for relaxation, (b) focusing imagery on healing the diseased organ or correcting an unhealthy condition, and (c) visualizing a successful outcome. The patient might describe his or her images and the therapist might provide further guidance.

An experiment by Manyande, et al. (1995) revealed positive effects of imagery rehearsal on coping with the stress of abdominal surgery. Twenty-six imagery patients were given brief relaxation instructions followed by instructions to imagine specific preoperative and postoperative discomforts, with suggestions that they would overcome the discomforts by imagining themselves coping with them. Twenty-five control patients received only background information about the hospital. Hormonal stress indicators and questionnaire responses were used to measure the effects. The results showed that hormonal levels did not differ for the two groups before preparation for the surgery, but cortisol levels in particular were lower in imagery patients than in controls immediately before and after surgery. In addition, imagery patients experienced relatively less postoperative pain, were less distressed by it, felt that they coped with it better, and requested less analgesia. Taking all factors into account, the preferred interpretation was that the preparatory imagery increased the patients' perception that they will be able to cope with the stress.

Note once again that the imagery procedure in the aforementioned study clearly engaged dual coding. It was initiated by the imagery script that was intended to induce anticipatory imagery associated with an expectancy of being able to cope with the surgery. The results demonstrated the adaptive function of dual coding processes under real-life stress.

Health care workers also use dual coding to improve their practical skills. Starting from a dual coding theoretical perspective, Edwards, Sadoski, and Burdenski (2005) investigated physicians' reported use of nonverbal images and language in examining and treating patients. The data consisted of rating-scale questionnaire responses from more than 150 surgeons and family physicians. The questions asked about the frequency and usefulness of (a) mental imagery in different modalities (visual, auditory, etc.); (b) remembered visuals such as medical photographs, x-rays, or CT scans; and (c) language descriptions remembered from textbooks, journals, and lectures. Physicians from both specialties reported that language and different types of imagery were common and useful in examining, treating, or operating on patients. The authors also summarized experimental research supporting the view that language and imagery are different and useful in combination, both contributing to diagnostic accuracy.

VERBAL AND SCHEMA APPROACHES

Theoretical approaches that emphasize monistic verbal or abstract conceptual representations are as popular in applied areas as they are in the cognitive sciences. Prominent examples of such theories in the areas of education and psychotherapy follow, with commentaries from the dual coding perspective.

Verbal and Schema Approaches to Education

Pristine verbal coding approaches to education are rarer today than they once were. Currently popular verbal remedial approaches to reading focus on development of phonemic awareness (learning to pay attention to articulatory processes) and fluency training. Both are intended to benefit decoding skills as well as comprehension on the assumption that comprehension is automatic for most children once they learn to recognize and pronounce words quickly. However, as already noted, decoding and comprehension entail different skills. Decoding is necessary for comprehension but does not guarantee it. Thus, phonics and phonemic awareness training can improve decoding performance without any marked effect on comprehension. Similarly, fluency instruction and repeated reading improve reading speed but have less consistent effects on comprehension (Kuhn & Stahl, 2003) when compared against standard classroom reading experience. From the DCT perspective, any technique that focuses primarily on verbal processes cannot be expected to benefit reading comprehension beyond what is contributed simply by recoding print into the auditory-motor code used in listening.

Schema alternatives to DCT have been evaluated systematically in relation to reading (Sadoski & Paivio, 2001). The basic assumptions of such theories are unchanged in updated versions presented in several chapters in Ruddell and Unrau (2004). In reading, text information is assumed to interact with background knowledge to create abstract propositional and schematic structures of different levels of generality. The schemas are "slots" to be instantiated with specific information during comprehension and use of text for learning. The nature of the schematic slots, how instances get transformed into schemas during input, and how they are transformed back (instantiated) to yield full understanding remain mysterious. The theoretical explanations and applications can be easily translated into the more tractable language and operational procedures of DCT (Sadoski & Paivio, 2001, pp. 117–136). Because schema theories are so abstract, one might expect them to be applicable to a wider range of phenomena than DCT, but the opposite seems to be the case for they have nothing to say about the ubiquitous and powerful effects of concreteness and dual coding variables, or the universal experience and use of imagery in thinking, memory, problem solving, and so on.

The situational model in Kintsch's (2004) theory is intended to account for the same phenomenal domain as imagery but the representational base of the model is entirely propositional. He conceded the following: "Situation models may be imagery based, in which case the propositional formalism currently used by most models fails us" (p. 1284). He nonetheless argued for their feasibility and future research success. However, propositional situation models have not explained the concreteness effects to which they should be most applicable and they are unlikely to do so as long as they remain linked only to an abstract propositional code.

Applications to education are similarly limited. Richard Anderson, one of the prime movers of schema theory, proposed five implications of the theory for the design of texts and classroom instruction: (a) include teaching suggestions that would help children activate relevant personal knowledge before reading, (b) include suggestions for building prerequisite knowledge when it cannot be presupposed, (c) feature lesson activities that will lead children to integrate what they know with what is presented on the printed page, (d) highlight the structure of text by using advance organizers or structured overviews, and (e) through research and publications, address the problem of matching instructional materials to the schemata of minority groups, which may differ from those of the majority culture (Anderson, 2004, pp. 604–605). These are all laudable suggestions, but they do not hinge on any schema theory of the child's background knowledge, text content, integration processes, guides to text structure, or minority group differences in background knowledge. The suggestions can easily be rephrased in terms of verbal and nonverbal knowledge organized in different associatively related domains, concrete advance organizers (conceptual pegs) for accessing the domains, subgroup experiential differences, and so on. The schema concept plays no useful role in that practical mix. I leave it to the interested reader to consider whether any of the specific schema theories have something more indispensable to offer the educational community.

Verbal and Schema Approaches to Psychotherapy

Similar monistic conceptual approaches have been applied to the treatment of physical and mental health problems. The clearest example of a verbal approach is the "Pennebaker paradigm," in which participants are instructed to write or talk about a stressful event in their lives. Interest has centered on the effects of the procedure on emotional arousal and thoughts during the verbalization sessions and on subsequent measures related to health. Initially, Pennebaker and Beall (1986) had college students (unselected in regard to stress experiences) write about a stressful incident on four consecutive days. Different groups were asked to write only about factual information, only about feelings, or both facts and feelings. A control group wrote about trivial matters. The pertinent results were that the participants who wrote about facts and feelings experienced more emotional discomfort immediately after the writing, but later they apparently experienced health benefits in that they made fewer visits to the health center in the 6 months following the writing procedure than did the other three groups. Subsequent studies investigated the procedure in other stress and health situations, and sought to determine the mediators of any salubrious effects that were observed. The issues and results have been comprehensively reviewed by Jill Littrell (1998). The following summarizes the facts and conclusions most pertinent to this context: (a) A rise and fall of emotional arousal at different stages of the writing procedure has been confirmed by a psychophysiogical indicator of arousal, the galvanic skin response; (b) the health benefits of trauma verbalization has been confirmed by reduced presession and post session concentrations of the Epstein-Barr virus in the blood, suggesting that the procedure enhanced immune system surveillance of the virus; (c) the benefits arise from a combination of emotional arousal and changes in thinking about the self and the painful events during the writing procedure; (d) cognitive behavior therapy in which negative thought patterns were challenged by the therapist surpassed the Pennebaker procedure on some outcome measures (e.g., feeling better about oneself as a result of the experience) but both procedures improved the clients' perspectives about the trauma; (e) trauma verbalization has been studied only with normally functioning individuals, so its effect on people needing treatment for stress-related or other health problems is unknown; (f) and finally the health benefits of learning new responses to the emotion-evoking material are comparable to the cognitive restructuring of emotional events in such treatment models as systematic desensitization and emotion-focused experiential psychotherapy.

Littrell (1998) concluded with the admonition that useful cognitions for the recasting of specific trauma situations should be identified. DCT offers obvious suggestions.

Writing or talking about stressful events is bound to arouse memory images of the events together with the associated emotions, as suggested by the Lanius et al. (2004) brain scan study of PTSD reviewed earlier. We could say that imagery mediates the effects of the Pennebaker procedure. The trick is to identify the nature of the imagery associated with various outcomes. Curiously, imagery is not mentioned in Littrell's review despite its prominence in psychotherapy and healing literature.

Turning now to the schema concept, we have already seen that it is incorporated into many approaches to psychotherapy. For example, the goal of Aaron Beck's cognitive therapy (its history is summarized in Beck, 1991) was to get people to change maladaptive cognitive schemas that led people to believe that they are incompetent and worthless. Horowitz (e.g., 1998) similarly tried to help people live better lives by improving their personal schemas. The concept has been most systematically exploited by Jeffrey Young (e.g., see Young, Klosko, & Wishaar, 2003) as the mainstay of an integrated conceptual framework and treatment guide for psychotherapy. The concept provides common terminology for analyses and recommendations. The problems with it are the same as those in education, relating generally to (a) reification of an abstract concept that is used in different levels of analysis, (b) how such reified schemas are constructed from concrete experiences, and (c) how they are instantiated by therapist and client. Some examples follow.

Young et al. (2003) defined schema as any organizing principle for making sense of one's life experience. It consists of a set of memories, emotions, bodily, sensations, and cognitions organized in the therapy context into maladaptive schemas, such as Abandonment-Instability, Mistrust-Abuse, Emotional Deprivation, Defectiveness-Shame, Dependence-Incompetence, and Negativity-Pessimism. These in turn are associated with different classes of maladaptive coping responses—surrender, avoidance, overcompensation, and so on. The schemas are instantiated into imagery and dialogue for both assessment and strategies for change. Clients are told "that the purpose of doing imagery is to enable them to feel their schemas and to understand how their schemas began in childhood" (p. 111). The imagery is initiated by instructions and guided by general questions that encourage the client to image and describe their own experiences, for example, "picture yourself in a safe place . . . tell me what it is an image of. . .can you see yourself? . . . How old are you?" The goal is to elicit core images associated with such emotions as fear, rage, and shame that are linked to the client's early maladaptive schemas. The clients are encouraged to conceptualize their imagery in schema terms, already familiar to them through a Schema Questionnaire they had answered. For example, a client describes an experience related to her Defectiveness Schema and the therapist reinforces the interpretation by saying "that's the schema talking" and the client replies, "Yeah, I realize that . . . " (note the reification here).

Imagery is similarly used in strategies for changing maladaptive schemas. For example, a primary strategy consists of imagery dialogues with people who caused their schemas, much as in confrontation imagery used to treat abuse-related traumas. Other strategies include imagery of traumatic memories, writing letters as homework assignments, and imagery for changing maladaptive patterns of behavior and feelings into positive ones, all comparable to what might be going on implicitly in the Pennebaker paradigm.

The important conclusion here is that schema therapy could be recast entirely in DCT terms that are already implicit in the therapy model and its applications, but elevated to schema abstractions of different levels. Maladaptive schemas could simply be described as behaviors, interpretations, and emotions related to classes of situations. Therapy could be conceptualized in terms of the imagery and verbalization that go on during the sessions, questionnaires could be purged of the redundant schema labels, and so on. As it stands, the schema therapy model is a variant of the triple-code hybrid models described in Chapter 5—modality specific verbal and nonverbal systems connected to a schema system comparable to the common conceptual system of the cognitive models. Schema practitioners could respond that the approach works, but what they need to do in addition is demonstrate that the schema concept is essential to the clinical successes. That it might not be essential is suggested by the fact that Piagetian theory has been evaluated (Siegel & Brainerd, 1978) without any reference to the overarching Piagetian concept of schema by examining effects of objective variables that define specific theoretical constructs.

SUMMARY

Dual coding as an applied theory for nurturing mind can be summarized in terms of a few general precepts that would guide practice: encourage optimal dual coding in all tasks by concretizing their abstract elements, verbalizing to the concrete, and engaging in deliberate overt and mental practice of dual coding skills. The aim is to take advantage of the power of cooperative verbal and nonverbal processing in due proportion to the demands of the task. Some tasks are inherently more verbal and others more nonverbal, as illustrated by the domains of expertise in the preceding chapters. The role of concretization is especially relevant to education because it contrasts so clearly with the traditional emphasis on verbal teaching methods. Concretization calls for instructional use of objects, pictures, and concrete language for teaching the content of a target domain, coupled with concrete conceptual pegs for organizing and retrieving the content. It also calls for teaching students how to use imagery strategies to concretize verbal material during study. Concretization by teacher and student makes verbal abstractions more comprehensible and memorable. Similar systematic use of verbalization increases memorability of concrete educational materials and ensures sequential-logical processing of the components of any task. Effective verbalization requires matching descriptive language to referent objects, situations, and actions as well as taking advantage of verbal associations to elaborate productively on a task.

Ericsson's concept of deliberate practice can be incorporated into the precepts, thereby going beyond the old adage that practice makes perfect by focusing on empirically based methods to make practice more effective, including practice of dual coding skills. The same principles apply to psychotherapy for problems related to physical health, mental health, and cognitive changes with aging, where the aim is to reeducate people by teaching them how to alleviate painful memories, aid failing memories, and cope with physical symptoms. We saw that even the applied schema models ultimately instantiate their abstract concepts into concrete language and into procedures that engage multimodal imagery and verbal processes.

Epilogue: A Graphical Summary

The accompanying graph and its notes summarize the dual coding theory of evolution of mind from its primeval nonverbal base to the emergence of the multimodal dual coding system that was characterized in Chapter 1 as the power source of human intellect and achievement. The graphic model is justified by the evidence that supports its narrative version. The evidence is direct and mainly experimental in the case of the DCT model on the right-hand side of the graph. It is indirect and inferential in the case of the evolution model on the left. The explosive recent increase in hominid cognitive power corresponds to what has come to be called "mind's big bang," as inferred from archeological and paleoanthropological evidence for the early phase, and increasingly from written records and direct psychological evidence for its more recent phase.

Although it seems reasonable to describe hominid cognitive growth as an exponential function, its exact shape cannot be estimated from present evidence. The traces of early mind left in bones, stones, and artifacts that have been used as evidence are sparse and limited in variety as compared to what later became available. Some common objective indicator of increasing cognitive power would be desirable. Human settlements come to mind as one possibility. Settlements increased in size, complexity, and number as humans moved from caves to cities. Thus, we could hypothesize that an index of settlement evolution based on such variables as size, number, and complexity would increase exponentially over time, empirically defining the cultural evolution of cognitive power. The ideal solution would be to sample artifacts of settlement regions from different time periods around the world, a daunting task indeed. Hopefully, someone will come up with a simpler measure. In the meantime, the empirical case for the dual coding evolutionary model is more inchoate than the case for the experimentally-based DCT model.

I draw attention to two specific aspects of the evolutionary model. First, why is the nonverbal part of the hominid cognitive power band portrayed as broader than the verbal part even for modern language-competent humans? The answer is that the difference is empirically justified. Given the assumption that memory is the engine of cognitive evolution, the most direct support comes from the fact that we generally remember nonverbal information better than verbal information. The nonverbal memory component of cognition is generally "stronger" than the verbal one, by as much as a two-fold margin in some tasks. Second, why is there an increasing

462

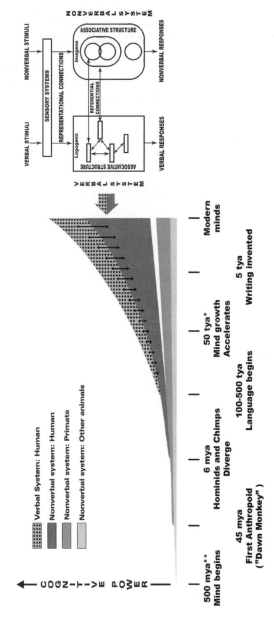

DUAL CODING MODEL OF MIND EVOLUTION

DUAL CODING MODEL OF MODERN HUMAN MIND

Verbal System: Human
Nonverbal system: Human
Nonverbal system: Primate
Nonverbal system: Other animals

500 mya**
Mind begins

45 mya
First Anthropoid
("Dawn Monkey")

6 mya
Hominids and Chimps
Diverge

100-500 tya
Language begins

50 tya*
Mind growth
Accelerates

5 tya
Writing invented

Modern
minds

*thousands of years ago; ** millions of years ago

DUAL CODING THEORY (DCT): A cognitive theory of evolved modern human mind postulating independent but interconnected nonverbal and verbal mental codes derived from multimodal sensorimotor experience.

MODERN HUMAN MIND: The functional interplay of the multimodal nonverbal and verbal mental codes.

COGNITIVE POWER (MIND): Knowledge, skill, products (artifacts, technology, etc.), and its adaptive functions (memory, anticipation, communication, etc.).

MIND EVOLUTION: (1) A long period of genetic evolution across animal species, (2) a recent period of accelerated human cultural evolution based on dual coding.

463

gap between cognitive power curves for humans and other animals? This signifies that the human intellectual advantage eventually became so great that it seems to reflect a leap to another level rather than a continuous change. The human species advantage similarly reflects the cumulative effects of social learning over generations, so that each generation starts off with a higher knowledge base from which it can build and store more cognitive power, viewed here as founded on dual coding machinery. Whatever proportions are true, there can be little doubt of the joint dual coding contributions made by nonverbal and verbal cognition to the evolution of the human mind and its incredible accomplishments.

References

Abeles, M. (1982). *Local cortical circuits: An electrophysiological study*. Berlin: Springer-Verlag.

Achterberg, J. (1985). *Imagery in healing: Shamanism and modern medecine*. Boston: Shambhala.

Agnew, M. (1922). The auditory imagery of the great composers. *Psychological Monographs, 31*, 278–287.

Alba, J. W., & Hasher, L. (1983). Is memory schematic? *Psychological Bulletin, 2*, 203–231.

Allen, C., & Saidel, E. (1998). The evolution of reference. In D. D. Cummins & C. Allen (Eds.), *The evolution of mind* (pp. 183–203). New York: Oxford University press.

Amedi, A., Malach, R., Hendler, T., Peled, S., & Zohary, E. (2001). Visual-haptic object-related activation in the ventral visual pathway. *Nature Neuroscience, 4*, 324–330.

Anderson, J. R. (1978). Arguments concerning representations for mental imagery. *Psychological Review, 85*, 249–277.

Anderson, J. R. (1983). *The architecture of cognition*. Cambridge, MA: Harvard University Press.

Anderson, J. R., & Bower, G. H. (1973). *Human associative memory*. Washington, DC: Winston.

Anderson, R. C. (2004). Schema in comprehension, learning, and memory. In R. B. Ruddell & N. J. Unrau (eds.) *Theoretical models and processes of reading* (5th ed., pp. 594–606). Newark, DE: International Reading Association.

Anderson, R. C., Goetz, E. T., Pichert, J. W., & Halff, H. M. (1977). Two faces of the conceptual peg hypothesis. *Journal of Experimental Psychology: Human Learning and Memory, 3*, 142–149.

Andrews, T. J., Schluppeck, D., Homfray, D., Matthews, P., & Blakemore, C. (2002). Activity in the fusiform gyrus predicts conscious perception of Rubin's vase-face illusion. *NeuroImage, 17*, 890–901.

Anglin. J. M. (1977). *Word, object, and conceptual development*. New York: Norton.

Antilla, R. (1972). *An introduction to historical and comparative linguistics*. New York: Macmillan.

Applewhite, P. B. (1979). Learning in protozoa. In M. Levandowski & S. H. Hunter (eds.)., *Biochemistry and Physiology of Protozoa* (2nd edition, Vol. 1), pp. 341–355. New York: Academic Press,

Arbib, M. A., & Érdi, P. (2000). Précis of *Neural organization: Structure, function, and dynamics. Behavioral and Brain Sciences, 23*, 513–571.

Arbuthnott, K. D., Arbuthnott, D. W., & Rossiter, L. (2001). Guided imagery and memory: Implications for psychotherapists. *Journal of Counseling Psychology, 48*, 123–132.

Arnheim, R. (1969). *Visual thinking*. Berkeley: University of California Press.

Arnold, M. B. (1960). *Emotion and personality: Vol. 2. Neurological and physiological aspects*. New York: Columbia University Press.

Aserinsky, E., & Kleitman, N. (1953). Regularly occurring periods of ocular motility and concomitant phenomena during sleep. *Science, 118*, 361–375.

Attenborough, D. (1979). *Life on earth*. Toronto, Canada: Little, Brown.

Attneave, F. (1974). How do you know? *American Psychologist, 29*, 493–499.

Averill, J. (1968). Grief. Its nature and significance. *Psychological Bulletin, 70*, 721–748.

Baddeley, A. D. (1986). *Working memory.* New York: Oxford University Press.

Badgaiyan, R. D., & Posner, M. I. (1998). Mapping the cingulate cortex in response selection and monitoring. *Neuroimage, 7*, 255–260.

Bahrick, H. P. (1984). Semantic memory content in permastore: Fifty years of memory for Spanish learned in school. *Journal of Experimental Psychology: General, 113*, 12–29.

Baker, C. I., Behrmann, M., & Olson, C. R. (2002). Impact of visual discrimination training on the representation of parts and wholes in monkey inferotemporal cortex. *Nature Neuroscience, 5*, 1210–1216.

Baker, R. K., & Poulin-Dubois, D. (1998). Infant's expectations about object-label reference. *Canadian Journal of Experimental Psychology, 52*, 103–112.

Bandura, A. (1986). *Social foundations of thought and action: A social cognitive theory.* Englewood Cliffs, NJ: Prentice Hall.

Barlow, H. (1995). The neuron doctrine in perception. In Michael S. Gazzaniga (ed.), *The cognitive neurosciences* (pp. 415–435). Cambridge, MA.: MIT Press.

Barnett, L. (1948). *The universe and Dr. Einstein.* New York: Harper & Brothers.

Baron-Cohen, S. (2003, March). *Mind reading: The interactive guide to emotion.* Paper presented at the 11th international Conference, Lindamood-Bell Learning Processes, Anaheim, CA.

Barsalou, L. W. (1999). Perceptual symbol systems. *Behavioral and Brain Sciences, 22*, 577–660.

Bartlett, F. C. (1932). *Remembering.* Cambridge, England: Cambridge University Press.

Basso, A., Bisiach, E., & Luzzatti, C. (1980). Loss of imagery: A case study. *Neuropsychologia, 18*, 435–442.

Beauchamp, M. S., Lee, K. E., Haxby, J. V. & Martin, A. (2003). fMRI responses to video and point-light displays of moving humans and manipulable objects. *Journal of Cognitive Neuroscience, 15*, 991–1001.

Beck, A. T. (1991). Cognitive therapy: A thirty-year retrospective. *American Psychologist, 46*, 368–375.

Becker, M. W., Pashler, H., & Anstis, S. M. (2000). The role of iconic memory in change-detection tasks. *Perception, 29*, 273–286.

Beckoff, M., Allen, C., & Burghardt, G. M. (2002). The cognitive animal: Empirical and Theoretical perspectives on animal cognition. Cambridge, MA: The MIT Press.

Begg, I. (1972). Recall of meaningful phrases. *Journal of Verbal Learning and Verbal Behavior, 11*, 431–439.

Begg, I. (1973). Imagery and integration in recall of words. *Canadian Journal of Psychology, 27*, 159–167.

Begg, I. (1982). Imagery, organization, and discriminative processes. *Canadian Journal of Psychology, 36*, 273–290.

Begg, I., & Clark, J. M. (1975). Contextual imagery in meaning and memory. *Memory & Cognition, 3*, 117–122.

Begg, I., & Paivio, A. (1969). Concreteness and imagery in sentence meaning. *Journal of Verbal Learning and Verbal Behavior, 8*, 821–827.

Behrmann, M., & Kimchi, R. (2003). What does visual agnosia tell us about perceptual organization relationship to object perception? *Journal of Experimental Psychology: Human Perception and Performance, 29*, 19–42.

Behrmann, M., Nelson, J., & Sekuler, E. B. (1998). Visual complexity in letter-by-letter reading: "Pure" alexia is not pure. *Neuropsychologia, 36*, 1115–1132.

Behrmann, M., Plaut, D. C., & Nelson, J. (1998). A literature review and new data supporting an interactive account of letter-by-letter reading. *Cognitive Neuropsychogy, 15*, 7–51.

Behrmann, M., Winocur, G., & Moscovitch, M. (1992). Dissociation between mental imagery and object recognition in a brain-damaged patient. *Nature, 359*, 636–637.

Bell, N. (1991a). Gestalt imagery: A critical factor in language comprehension. *Annals of Dyslexia, 41,* 246–260.

Bell, N. (1991b). *Visualizing and verbalizing for language comprehension and thinking.* Paso Robles, CA: NBI Publications.

Ben-Shachar, M., Palti, D., & Grodzinsky, Y. (2004). Neural correlates of syntactic movement: Converging evidence from two fMRI experiments. *NeuroImage, 21,*1320–1336.

Bennett, A. T. D. (1996). Do animals have cognitive maps? *The Journal of Experimental Biology, 199,* 219–224.

Benson, H. (1976). *The relaxation response.* New York: Avon Books.

Beretta, A., Schmitt, C., Halliwell, J., Munn, A., Cuetos, F., & Kim, S. (2001). The effects of scrambling on Spanish and Korean agrammatic interpretation: Why linear models fail and structural models survive. *Brain and Language, 79,* 407–425.

Berlyne, D. E. (1965). *Structure and direction in thinking.* New York: Wiley.

Bethel-Fox, C. E., & Shepard, R. N. (1988). Mental rotation: Effects of stimulus complexity and familiarity. *Journal of Experimental Psychology: Human Perception and Performance, 14,* 12–23.

Beveridge, W. I. B. (1957). *The art of scientific investigation.* New York: Random House.

Bhatt, R. S., Wasserman, E. A., Reynolds, W. F. Jr., & Knauss, K. S. (1988). Conceptual behavior in pigeons: Categorization of both familiar and novel examples from four classes of natural and artificial stimuli. *Journal of Experimental Psychology: Animal Behavior Processes, 14,* 219–234.

Bialystok, E., Craik, F. I. M., Grady, C., Chau, W., Ishii, R., Gunji, A., et al. (2005). Effect of bilingualism on cognitive control in the Simon task: Evidence from MEG. *NeuroImage, 24,* 40–49.

Bialystok, E., Craik, F. I. M., Klein, R., & Viswanathan, M. (2004). Bilingualism, aging, and cognitive control: Evidence from the Simon task. *Psychology and Aging, 19,* 290–303.

Bichakjian, B. H. (1999). Language evolution and the complexity criterion. Retrieved April 7, 2000 from http://www.cogsci.soton.ac.uk/psyc-bin/Newpsy?article=10.033&submit=View+Article

Bickerton, D. (1990). *Language and species.* Chicago: University of Chicago Press.

Bickerton, D. (1995). *Language and human behavior.* Seattle: University of Washington Press.

Biederman, I. (1987). Recognition-by-components: A theory of human image understanding. *Psychological Review, 94,* 115–147.

Biletzki, A., & Matar, A. (2003, Winter). Ludwig Wittgenstein. In E. N. Zalta (Ed.), *The Stanford Encyclopedia of Philosophy.* Retrieved January 14, 2005, from http:/plato.stanford.edu/archives/win2003/entries/wittgenstein

Binder, J. R., Westbury, C. F., McKiernan, K. A., Possing, E. T., & Medler, D. A. (2005). Distinct brain systems for processing concrete and abstract language. *Journal of Cognitive Neuroscience, 17,* 905–917.

Binet, A., & Simon, T. (1905). Méthodes nouvelles pour le diagnostic du niveau intellectuel des anormaux. [New methods for diagnosing the intellectual level of normals.] *L'Année Psychologique, 11,* 191–244.

Birch, H. G. (1945). The relation of previous experience to insightful problem solving. *Journal of Comparative Psychology, 38,* 367–383.

Bisiach, E., & Berti, A. (1989). Unilateral misrepresentation of distributed information: Paradoxes and puzzles. In J. W. Brown (Ed.), *Neuropsychology of visual perception,* (pp. 145–161). Hillsdale, NJ: Lawrence Erlbaum Associates, Inc.

Bjork, D. W. (1993). *B. F. Skinner: A life.* New York: Basic Books.

Black, C. A. (1998). *A step-by-step introduction to the government and binding theory of syntax.* http://www.sil.org/americas/mexico/ling/E002–IntroGB.pdf [February 1999]

Blackmore, S. J. (1999). *The meme machine.* Oxford, UK: Oxford University Press.

Blackmore, S. J. (2004). *Consciousness: An introduction.* New York: Oxford University Press.

Bleasdale, F. (1987). Concreteness-dependent associative priming: Separate lexical organization for concrete and abstract words. *Journal of Experimental Psychology: Learning, Memory, and Cognition, 13*, 582–594.

Bliss, C. K. (1965). *Semantography—Blissymbolics* (2nd ed.). Sydney, Australia: Semantography.

Bloom, B. S. (1985). Generalizations about talent development. In B. S. Bloom (Ed.), *Developing talent in young people* (pp. 507–549). New York: Ballantine.

Bloom, F. E. (1995). Cellular mechanisms active in emotion. In Michael S. Gazzaniga (ed.), *The cognitive neurosciences* (pp. 1063–1070). Cambridge, MA.: MIT Press.

Bloom, L. (1976). Discussion paper: Child language and the origins of language. In S. Harnad, H. D. Steklis, & J. Lancaster (Eds.), *Origins and evolution of language and speech* (pp. 170–172). New York: The New York Academy of Sciences.

Bloom, P. (1998). Some issues in the evolution of language and thought. In D. D. Cummins & C. Allen (Eds.), *The evolution of mind* (pp. 204–223). New York: Oxford University Press.

Blumberg, M. S., & Wasserman, E. A. (1995). Animal mind and the argument from design. *American Psychologist, 50*, 133–144.

Blumstein, S. E. (1995). The neurobiology of the sound structure of language. In M. S. Gazzaniga (Ed.), *The cognitive neurosciences* (pp. 915–929). Cambridge, MA.: MIT Press.

Boas, F. (1938). *The mind of primitive man.* New York: Macmillan.

Bontempi, B., Laurent-Demir, C., Destrade, C., & Jaffard, R. (1999). Time-dependent reorganization of brain circuitry underlying long-term memory storage. *Nature, 400*, 671–675.

Borod, J. C., Andelman, F., Obler, L. K., Tweedy, J. R., & Welkowitz, J. (1992). Right hemisphere specialization for the identification of emotional words and sentences: Evidence from stroke patients. *Neuropsychologia, 30*, 827–844.

Botvinick, M., & Cohen, J. (1998). Rubber hands "feel" touch that eyes see. *Nature, 391*, 756.

Bousfield, W. A., & Samborski, G. (1955). The relationship between strength of values and the meaningfulness of value words. *Journal of Personality, 23*, 375–380.

Bower, B. (2003, April 19). Words get in the way. *Science News, 163*, 250.

Bower, G. H. (1970). Imagery as a relational organizer in associative learning. *Journal of Verbal Learning and Verbal Behavior, 9*, 529–533.

Bower, G. H., Clark, M. C., Lesgold, A. M., & Winzenz, D. (1969). Hierarchical retrieval schemes in recall of categorized word lists. *Journal of Verbal Learning and Verbal Behavior, 8*, 323–343.

Bowlby, J. (1969). *Attachment and loss. Vol. I. Attachment.* New York: Basic Books.

Braine, M. D. S. (1963). On learning the grammatical order of words. *Psychological Review, 70*, 323–348.

Breedin, S. D., Saffran, E. M., & Coslett, H. B. (1994). Reversal of the concreteness effect in a patient with semantic dementia. *Cognitive Neuropsychology, 11*, 617–660.

Brener, L. R. (1940). An experimental investigation of memory span. *Journal of Experimental Psychology, 26*, 467–482.

Bregman, A. S. (1990). *Auditory scene analysis: The perceptual organization of sound.* Cambridge, MA: MIT Press.

Bregman, A. S. (2005). Auditory scene analysis and the role of phenomenology in experimental psychology. *Canadian Psychology, 46*, 32–40.

Brewer, J. B., Zhao, Z., Desmond, J. E., Glover, G. H., & Gabrieli, J. D. E. (1998). Making memories: Brain activity that predicts how well visual experience will be remembered. *Science, 281*, 1185–1187.

Brocks, J. J., Logan, G. A. Buick, R., & Summons, R. E. (1999). Archean molecular fossils and the early rise of Eukaryotes. *Science, 285*, 1033–1036.

Brogden, W. J. (1939). Sensory preconditioning. *Journal of Experimental Psychology, 25*, 323–332.

Bronowski, J. (1997). The reach of imagination. *A sense of the future: Essays in natural philosophy* (pp. 22–31). Cambridge, MA: MIT Press.

Brooks, L. R., & Vokey, J. R. (1991). Abstract analogies and abstract grammars: Comments on Reber (1989) and Matthews et al. (1989). *Journal of Experimental Psychology: General, 120,* 316–323.

Brothers, L. (1995). Neurophysiology of the perception of intentions by primates. In M. S. Gazzaniga (Ed.), *The cognitive neurosciences* (pp. 1107–1116.). Cambridge, MA: MIT Press.

Brown, R. W. (1970). *Psycholinguistics.* New York: Free Press.

Bruner, J. (1982). A brain on the mind. Review of D. O. Hebb (1980). *Essay on mind.* Hillsdale, NJ: Lawrence Erlbaum Associates, Inc. *Contemporary Psychology, 27,* 5–6.

Bryden, M. P. (1982). *Laterality: Functional asymmetry in the intact brain.* New York: Academic.

Bucci, W. (1984). Linking words and things: Basic processes and individual variations. *Cognition, 17,* 137–153.

Bucci, W. (1985). Dual coding: A cognitive model for psychoanalytic research. *Journal of the American Psychoanalytic Association, 33,* 571–607.

Buckley, K. W. (1989). *Mechanical man: John Broadus Watson and the beginnings of behaviorism.* New York: Guilford.

Bunzeck, N., Weustenberg, T., Lutz, K., Heinze, H-J., & Jancke, L. (2005). Scanning silence: Mental imagery of complex sounds. *NeuroImage, 26,* 1119–1127.

Burling, R. (1999). The cognitive prerequisites for language. *Psycoloquy 10.* Retrieved June 11, 2003 from http://psycprints.ecs.soton.ac.uk/archive/00000667/

Buss, D. M. (1999). *Evolutionary psychology: The* new *science of the mind.* Needham Heights, MA: Allyn & Bacon.

Byrne, R. W. (1995). *The thinking ape: Evolutionary origins of intelligence.* Oxford, England: Oxford University Press.

Byrne, R. W. (2000). Evolution of primate cognition. *Cognitive Science, 24,* 543–570.

Call, J. (2001). Object permanence in orangutans (*Pongo pygmaeus*), chimpanzees (*Pan troglodytes*), and children (*Homo sapiens*). *Journal of Comparative Psychology, 115,* 159–171.

Calvin, W. H., & Bickerton, D. (2000). *Lingua ex machina: Reconciling Darwin and Chomsky with the human brain.* Cambridge, MA: MIT Press.

Cambrosio, A., Jacobi, D., & Keating, P. (1993). Ehrlich's "beautiful pictures" and the controversial beginnings of immunological imagery. *Isis, 84,* 662–699.

Cambrosio, A., Jacobi, D., & Keating, P. (2005). Arguing with images: Pauling's theory of antibody formation. *Representations, 89,* 94–130.

Campanella, T. (1602). *The city of the sun.* Retrieved February 22, 2004 from http://www.levity.com/alchemy/citysun.html

Campbell, J. I. D., & Clark, J. M. (1988). An encoding-complex view of cognitive number processing: Comment on McCloskey, Sokol, and Goodman (1986). *Journal of Experimental Psychology: General, 117,* 204–214.

Caramazza, A., & Zurif, E. B. (1976). Dissociation of algorithmic and heuristic processes in sentence comprehension: Evidence from aphasia. *Brain and Language, 3,* 572–582.

Caro, T. M., & Hauser, M. D. (1992). Is there teaching in nonhuman animals? *Quarterly Review of Biology, 67,* 151–174.

Carroll, J. B. (1993). *Human cognitive abilities: A survey of factor-analytic studies.* New York: Cambridge University Press.

Carroll, J. B. (1997). The three-stratum theory of cognitive abilities. In D. P. Flanagan, J. L. Genshaft, & P. L. Harrison (Eds.), *Contemporary intellectual assessment: Theories, tests, and issues* (pp. 122–130). New York: Guilford.

Ceci, S. J. (2003). Cast in six ponds and you'll reel in something: Looking back on 25 years of research. *American Psychologist, 58,* 855–864.

Chafe, W. L. (1970). *Meaning and the structure of language.* Chicago: University of Chicago Press.

Charcot, J. M. (1883). Un cas de suppression brusque et isolée de la vision mentale des signes et des objets (formes et couleurs). [An abrupt and localized loss of visual images of signs and objects (forms and colors)]. *Progrès Médical, 11,* 568–571.

Charness, N., Krampe, R.Th., & Mayr, U. (1996). The role of practice and coaching in entrepreneurial skill domains: An international comparison of life-span chess skill acquisition. In K. Anders Ericsson (Ed.) *The road to excellence: The acquisition of expert performance in the arts and sciences, sports and games* (pp. 51–80). Mahwah NJ: Lawrence Erlbaum Associates, Inc.

Chateau, D., & Jared, D. (2000). Exposure to print and word recognition processes. *Memory & Cognition, 28,* 143–153.

Cheney, D. L., & Seyfarth, R. M. (1986). Vocal development in vervet monkeys. *Animal Behavior, 34,* 1640–1658.

Chomsky, N. (1957). *Syntactic structures.* The Hague, Netherland: Mouton.

Chomsky, N. (1959). Review of *verbal behavior* by B. F. Skinner. *Language, 35,* 26–58.

Chomsky, N. (1968). *Language and mind.* New York: Harcourt, Brace, and World.

Chomsky, N. (1982). *Some concepts and consequences of the theory of government and binding.* Cambridge, MA: MIT Press.

Chomsky, N. (1995). *The minimalist program.* Cambridge, MA: MIT Press.

Christiansen, M. H., & Kirby, S. (2003). Language evolution: consensus and controversies. *Trends in Cognitive Sciences, 7,* 300–307.

Clark, A. (2000) Cognitive incrementalism: The big issue. *Behavioral and Brain Sciences, 23,* 536–537.

Clark, J. M., & Campbell, J. I. D. (1991). Integrated versus modular theories of number skills and acalculia. *Brain and Cognition, 17,* 204–239.

Clark, J. M., & Paivio, A. (1989). Observational and theoretical terms in psychology: A cognitive perspective on scientific language. *American Psychologist, 44,* 500–512.

Clark, J. M., & Paivio, A. (1991). Dual coding theory and education. *Educational Psychology Review, 3,* 149–210.

Clark, J. M., & Paivio, A. (2004). Extensions of the Paivio, Yuille, and Madigan (1968) norms. *Behavior Research Methods, Instruments, & Computers, 36,* 371–383.

Clayton, N. S., & Dickinson, A. (1998). Episodic-like memory during cache recovery by scrub jays. *Nature, 395,* 272–274.

Clayton, N. S., Yu, K. S., & Dickinson, A. (2001). Scrub jays (*Aphelocoma coerulescens*) form integrated memories of the multiple features of caching episodes. *Journal of Experimental Psychology: Animal Behavior Processes, 113,* 403–416.

Cockfort, J., & Walton, E. T. S. (1932). Disintegration of lithium by swift protons. *Nature, 129,* 242.

Cohen, L., Lehericy, S., Chochon, F., Lemer, C., Rivard, S., & Dehaene, S. (2002). Language-specific tuning of visual cortex? Functional properties of the visual word form area. *Brain, 125,* 1054–1069.

Cole, M., Frankel, F., & Sharp, D. (1971). Development of free recall learning in children. *Developmental Psychology, 4,* 109–123.

Collins, A. M., & Loftus, E. F. (1975). A spreading-activation theory of semantic processing. *Psychological Review, 82,* 407–428.

Coltheart, M. (2004). Are there lexicons? *The Quarterly Journal of Experimental Psychology, 57A,* 1153–1171.

Comenius, J. A. (1896). *The great didactic.* London: Adam & Charles Black.

Comparetti, D. (1898). *The traditional poetry of the Finns* (I. M. Anderton, trans.) London: Longmans (Original work published 1891).

Conant, J. B. (1947). *On understanding science: An historical approach*. New Haven, CT: Yale University Press.

Conlin, D., & Paivio, A. (1975). The associative learning of the deaf: The effects of word imagery and signability. *Memory & Cognition, 3,* 335–340.

Cooper, L. A., & Shepard, R. N. (1973). Chronometric studies of the rotation of mental images. In. W. G. Chase (ed.), Visual Information Processing. New York: Academic Press.

Corballis, M. (1982). Mental rotation: Anatomy of a paradigm. In M. Potegal (Ed.), *Spatial abilities: Development and physiological foundations* (pp. 173–198). New York: Academic Press.

Corballis, M. C. (2003). From hand to mouth—Gesture, speech, and the evolution of right-handedness. *Behavioral and Brain Sciences, 26,* 199–208.

Corkill, A. J., Glover, J. A., & Bruning, R. H. (1988). Advance organizers: Concrete vs. abstract. *Journal of Educational Research, 82,* 76–81.

Cornell, E. H. (1978). Learning to find things: A reinterpretation of object permanence studies. In L. S. Siegel & C. J. Brainerd (Eds.), *Alternatives to Piaget: Critical essays on the theory* (pp. 1–27). New York: Academic.

Cornoldi, C., Bertuccelli, B., Rocchi, P., & Shrana, B. (1993). Processing capacity limitations in pictorial and spatial representations in the totally congenitally blind. *Cortex, 29,* 675–689.

Coslett, H. B., & Saffran, E. (1991). Simultanagnosia. To see but not two see. *Brain, 113,* 475–486.

Coslett, H. B., & Saffran, E. (1994). Mechanisms of implicit reading in alexia. In M. J. Farah & G. Ratcliff (Eds.), *The neuropsychology of high-level vision* (pp. 299–330). Hillsdale, NJ: Lawrence Erlbaum Associates, Inc.

Craik, F. I. M. (1986). A functional account of age differences in memory. In F. Klix & H. Hagendorf (Eds.), *Human memory and cognitive capabilities, mechanisms, and performances* (pp. 409–422). Amsterdam: Elsevier.

Craik, F. I. M., & Lockhart, R. S. (1972). Levels of processing: A framework for memory research. *Journal of Verbal Learning and Verbal Behavior, 11,* 671–684.

Craik, F. I. M., & Tulving, E. (1975). Depth of processing and retention of words in episodic memory. *Journal of Experimental Psychology: General, 104,* 268–294.

Cree, G. S., & McRae, K. (2003). Analyzing the factors underlying the structure and computation of the meaning of chipmunk, cherry, chisel, cheese, and cello (and many other such concrete nouns). *Journal of Experimental Psychology: General, 132,* 163–201.

Crerar, M. A., Ellis, A. W., & Dean, E. C. (1996). Remediation of sentence processing deficits in aphasia using a computer-based microworld. *Brain and Language, 52,* 229–275.

Crick, F. (1994). *The astonishing hypothesis*. New York: Scribner's.

Crick, F., & Koch, C. (1995). Are we aware of neural activity in primary visual cortex? *Nature, 375,* 121–123.

Crick, F., & Koch, C. (2000). The unconscious homunculus. In T. Metzinger (Ed.), *Neural correlates of consciousness* (pp. 103–110). Cambridge, MA: MIT Press.

Cruciani, F. (1971). *Marcel Proust*. Paris: Editions Pierre Charron.

Cuisenaive, G. & Gattegno, C. (1954). Numbers in colour. London: Hememann.

Cumming, J., & Hall, C. R. (2002). Deliberate imagery practice: The development of imagery skills in competitive athletes. *Journal of Sports Sciences, 20,* 137–145.

Cumming, J., Hall, C., Harwood, C., & Gammage, K. (2002). Motivational orientations and imagery use: A goal profiling analysis. *Journal of Sports Sciences, 20,* 127–136.

Cummins, D. D., & Allen, C. (Eds.), (1998). *The evolution of mind*. New York: Oxford University Press.

D'Agostino, P. R., O'Neill, B. J., & Paivio, A. (1977). Memory for pictures and words as a function of level of processing: Depth or dual coding? *Memory & Cognition, 5,* 252–256.

Damasio, A. R. (1999). *The feeling of what happens: Body and emotion in the making of consciousness*. New York: Harcourt Brace.

Damasio, A. R., Grabowski, T. J., Bechara, A., Damasio, H., Ponto, L. L. B., Parvizi, J., et al. (2000). Subcortical and cortical brain activity during the feeling of self-generated emotions. *Nature Neuroscience, 3*, 1049–1056.

Darwin, C. (1859). *On the origin of species by means of natural selection*. London: Murray. (Oxford University Press reprint edition, 1998.)

Darwin, C. R. (1873). *The expression of the emotions in man and animals*. New York: Appleton-Century-Crofts.

Darwin, C. R. (1982).*The descent of man and selection in relation to sex*. London, UK: John Murray.

Das, J. P., Kirby, J. R., & Jarman, R. F. (1975). Simultaneous and successive syntheses: An alternative model for cognitive abilities. *Psychological Bulletin, 82*, 87–103.

Das, J. P., Naglieri, J., & Kirby, J. R. (1994). *Assessment of cognitive processes: The PASS theory of intelligence*. Boston: Allyn & Bacon.

Davis, J. L. (1994). *Mother tongue*. New York: Carol Publishing Group.

Davis, P. J., & Hersh, R. (1981). *The mathematical experience*. Boston: Houghton Mifflin.

Dawkins, R. (1976). *The selfish gene*. Oxford, England: Oxford University Press.

Day, J. C., & Bellezza, F. S. (1983). The relation between visual imagery mediators and recall. *Memory & Cognition, 11*, 251–257.

DeAngelis, T. (2003). The dream canvas. *Monitor on Psychology, 34*, 44–46.

De Beni, R., & Moè, A. (2003). Presentation modality effects in studying passages with imagery or rehearsal. *Psychonomic Bulletin & Review, 10*, 975–980.

Dejerine, J. (1892). Contribution à l'étude anatomo-pathologique et clinique des differentes variétés de cécité-verbale [A contribution to the anatomical-pathalogical and clininal study of different varieties of word blindness]. *Mémoires Societé Biolique, 4*, 61–90.

Della Sala, S., Logie, R. H., Beschin, N., & Denis. M. (2004). Preserved visuo-spatial transformations in representational neglect. *Neuropsychologia, 42*, 1358–1364.

Denis, M. (1971). *Buster Keaton*. Paris: Editions de l'Avant-Scène.

Denis, M. (1982). Imaging while reading text: A study of individual differences. *Memory & Cognition, 10*, 540–545.

Denis, M. (1985). Visual imagery and the use of mental practice in the development of motor skills. *Canadian Journal of Applied Sport Sciences, 10*, 4S–16S.

Denis, M. (1991). *Image and cognition*. Sussex, England: Harvester. (M. Denis & C. Greenbaum, Trans.). Original work published 1989.

Denis, M., Beschin, N., Logie, R. H., & Della Sala, S. (2002). Visual perception and verbal description as sources for generating mental representations: Evidence from representational neglect. *Cognitive Neuropsychology, 19*, 97–112.

Denis, M., & Carfantan, M. (1985). People's knowledge about images. *Cognition, 20*, 49–60. New

Denis, M., Pazzaglia, F., Cornoldi, C., & Bertolo, L. (1999). Spatial discourse and navigation: an anlaysis of route directions in the city of Venice. *Applied Cognitive Psychology, 13*, 145–174.

Denis, M., & Zimmer, H. D. (1992). Analog properties of cognitive maps constructed from verbal descriptions. *Psychological Research, 54*, 286–298.

Dennett, D. C. (1995). *Darwin's dangerous idea: Evolution and the meanings of life*. New York: Simon & Schuster.

Desrochers, A. (1983). Effect of instructions and retrieval cues on the recall of French article-noun pairs. *Human Learning, 2*, 295–311.

Destun, L. M., & Kuiper, N. A. (1999). Phenomenal characteristics associated with real and imagined events: The effects of event valence and absorption. *Applied Cognitive Psychology, 13*, 175–186.

Deutsch, D. (2002). The puzzle of absolute pitch. *Current Directions in Psychological Science, 11*, 200–204.

Deutsch, D., Henthorn, T., Marvin, E., & Xu, H. S. (2004). *Perfect pitch in tone language speakers carries over to music.* Paper presented at the meeting of the Acoustical Society of America. Retrieved December 9, 2004, from http://www.aip.org/148th/ deutsch.html

Dick, F., Dronkers, N. F., Pizzamiglio, L., Saygin, A. P., Small, S. L., & Wilson, S. (2005). Langage and the brain. In M. Tomasello & D. I. Slobin (Eds.), *Beyond nature-nurture: Essays in honor of Elizabeth Bates* (pp. 237–260). Mahwah, NJ: Lawrence Erlbaum Associates, Inc.

Digdon, N. L. (1986). *Conditional and biconditional interpretations of if-then sentences: The role of content and context.* Unpublished doctoral disseration, University of Western Ontario, London, Canada.

Dilley, M. G., & Paivio, A. (1968). Pictures and words as stimulus and response items in paired-associate learning in young children. *Journal of Experimental Child Psychology, 6,* 231–240.

Dirkx, E., & Craik, F. I. M. (1992). Age differences in memory as a function of imagery processing. *Psychology and Aging, 7,* 352–358.

Donald, M. (1991). *Origins of modern mind.* Cambridge, MA: Harvard University Press.

Donald, M., Mithen, S., Reply by Gardner, H. (1998, May 28). The Prehistory of Mind: An Exchange. *The New York Review of Books, 45,* No. 9. Retrieved April 27, 2004 from http://www.nybooks.com/articles/844

Dror, I. E., & Kosslyn, S. M. (1994). Mental imagery and aging. *Psychology and Aging, 9,* 90–102.

Ducharme, R., & Fraisse, P. (1965). Etude génétique de la mémorization de mots et d'image. [A developmental study of memory for words and pictures.] *Canadian Journal of Psychology, 19,* 253–261.

Durant, W. (1953). *The story of philosophy.* New York: Pocket Books, Inc. Reprinted from Durant, W. (1926). *The story of philosophy.* New York: Simon & Schuster.

Dyer F. C. (1991). Bees acquire route-based memories but not cognitive maps in a familiar landscape. *Animal Behavior, 41,* 239–246.

Easton, R. D., Greene, A. J., & Srinivas, K. (1997). Transfer between vision and haptics: memory for 2-D patterns and 3-D objects, *Psychonomic Bulletin and Review, 4,* 403–410.

Ebbinghaus, H. (1964). *Memory: A contribution to experimental psychology.* New York: Dover. (Original work published 1885).

Edelman, S. (2000). Brahe, looking for Kepler. *Behavioral and Brain Sciences, 23,* 538–540.

Eden, G. F., Jones, K., Cappell, K., Gareau, L., Wood, F. B., Zeffiro, T., et al. (2004). Neuro-physiological recovery and compensation after remediation in adult developmental dyslexia. *Neuron, 44,* 411–422.

Edwards, J. C., Sadoski, M., & Burdenski, T. K., Jr. (2005). Physicians' reported use of mental images and language in clinical reasoning. *Imagination, Cognition, and Personality, 24,* 41–49.

Efron, R. (1969). What is perception? *Boston Studies in Philosophy of Science, 4,* 137–173.

Ehri, L. C., & Wilce, L. S. (1978). The mnemonic value of orthography among beginning readers. *Journal of Educational Psychology, 71,* 26–40.

Ehrlich, P. (1900). On immunity with special reference to cell life. Proceedings of the Royal Society of London, 66, 424–448.

Ehrlich, P. R. (2000, September 22). The tangled skeins of nature and nurture in human evolution. *The Chronicle of Higher Education.*

Ehrsson, H. H., Spence, C., & Passingham, R. E. (2004, July 1). That's my hand! Activity in premotor cortex reflects feeling of ownership. *Science, 10,* 1126.

Einstein, A. (1935). Elementary derivation of the equivalence of mass and energy. *American Mathematical Society Bulletin, 41,* 223–230.

Einstein, A. (1949). Autobiographical notes. In P. A. Schilpp (Ed.), *Albert Einstein: Philosopher-scientist. The Library of Living Philosophers, Vol. VII,* (pp. 2–94). La Salle, IL: Open Court.

Einstein, A. (1954). *Ideas and opinions.* New York: Crown [S. Bargmann trans].

Ekman, P. (1973). *Darwin and facial expressions: A century of research in Review.* New York: Academic.

Ekman, P. (1976). *Pictures of facial affect*. San Francisco: Consulting Psychologists Press.

Eldredge, N. (1998). *Patterns of evolution*. New York: Freeman.

Eldredge, N., & Gould, S. J. (1972). Punctuated equilibria: An alternative to phyletic gradualism. In T. J. M. Schopf (Ed.), *Models in paleontology* (pp. 82–115). San Francisco: Freeman.

Ellson, D. G. (1941). Hallucinations produced by sensory conditioning. *Journal of Experimental Psychology, 28*, 1–20.

Enard, W., Przeworski, M., Fisher, S. E., Lai, C. S. L., Wiebe, V., Kitano, T., et al. (2002). Molecular evolution of FOXP2, a gene involved in speech and language. *Nature, 418*, 869–872.

Epstein, S. (1998). *Constructive thinking: The key to emotional intelligence*. Westport, CT: Praeger.

Epstein, W., Rock, I., & Zuckerman, C. B. (1960). Meaning and familiarity in associative learning. *Psychological Monographs, 74*, (No. 491).

Erdfelder, E. (1993). Markov modeling of imagery and verbal processes in human memory. In R. Steyer, K. F. Wender, & K. F. Widaman (Eds.), *Psychometric methodology. Proceedings of the 7th European Meeting of the Psychometric Society in Trier* (pp. 135–140). New York: Gustav Fischer Verlag.

Ericsson, K. A. (1985). Memory skill. *Canadian Journal of Psychology, 39*, 188–231.

Ericsson, K. A. (Ed.). (1996). *The road to excellence: The acquisition of expert performance in the arts and sciences, sports and games*. Mahwah, NJ: Lawrence Erlbaum Associates, Inc.

Ericsson, K. A. (2001). Attaining excellence through deliberate practice: Insights from the study of expert performance. In M. Ferrari (Ed.), *The pursuit of excellence in education* (pp. 21–55). Mahwah, NJ: Lawrence Erlbaum Associates, Inc.

Ericsson, K. A. (2003a). The acquisition of expert performance in problem solving: Construction and modification of mediating mechanisms through deliberate practice. In J. E. Davidson & R. J. Sternberg (Eds.), *The psychology of problem solving* pp. 31–83. Cambridge, England: Cambridge University Press.

Ericsson, K. A. (2003b). Exceptional memories: Made, not born. *Trends in Cognitive Sciences, 7*, 233–235.

Ericsson, K. A., & Charness, N. (1994). Expert performance: It's structure and acquisition. *American Psychologist, 49*, 725–747.

Ericsson, K. A., & Charness, N. (1995). Abilities: Evidence for talent or characteristics acquired through engagement in relevant activities. *American Psychologist, 50*, 803–804.

Ericsson, K. A., & Kintsch, W. (1995). Long-term working memory. *Psychological Review, 107*, 211–245.

Ericsson, K. A. & Kintsch, W. (2000). Shortcomings of generic retrieval structures with slots of the type that Gobet (1993) proposed and modelled. *British Journal of Psychology, 91*, 571–590.

Ericsson, K. A., Krampe, R. T., & Tesch-Römer, C. (1993). The role of deliberate practice in the acquisition of expert performance. *Psychological Review, 100*, 363–406.

Ericsson, K. A., Nandagopal, K., & Roring, R. W. (2005). Giftedness viewed from the expert-performance perspective. *Journal for the Education of the Gifted, 28*, 287–311.

Ericson, K. A., & Simon, H. A. (1984). Protocol analysis: Verbal reports as data. Cambridge, MA: MIT Press.

Ernest, C. H. (1980). Imagery ability and the identification of fragmented pictures and words. *Acta Psychologica, 44*, 51–57.

Estes, W. K. (2002). Traps in the route to models of memory and decision. *Psychonomic Bulletin & Review, 9*, 3–25.

Etard, O., Mellet, E., Papathanassiou, D., Benali, K., Houde, O., Mazoyer, B., et al. (2000). Picture naming without Broca's and Wernicke's area. *NeuroReport, 11*, 617–622.

Evans, C., & Marler, P. (1995). Language and animal communication: Parallels and contrasts. In J. A. Meyer & H. L. Roitblat (Eds.), *Comparative approaches to cognitive science* (pp. 341–383). Cambridge, MA: MIT Press.

Farah, M. J. (1990). *Visual agnosia: Disorders of object recognition and what they tell us about normal vision*. Cambridge, MA: MIT Press.

Farah, M. J. (1995). The neural basis of mental imagery. In M. S. Gazzaniga Ed., *The cognitive neurosciences*. Cambridge, Mass.: MIT Press, (pp. 963–975).

Fauconnier, G. (1997). *Mappings in thought and language*. Cambridge England: Cambridge University Press.

Feltz, D. L., & Landers, D. M. (1983). The effects of mental practice on motor skill learning and performance: A meta-analysis. *Journal of Sport Psychology, 5,* 25–57.

Ferber, S., Humphrey, G. K., & Vilis, T. (2004). Segregation andn persistence of form in the lateral occipital complex. *Neuropsychologia, 43,* 41–51.

Ferguson, E. S. (1977). The mind's eye: Nonverbal thought in technology. *Science, 137,* 827–836.

Ferguson, G. A. (1954). On learning and human ability. *Canadian Journal of Psychology, 8,* 95–112.

Ferguson, G. A. (1956). On transfer and the abilities of man. *Canadian Journal of Psychology, 10,* 121–131.

Fillmore, C. J. (1977). The case for case reopened. In P. Cale & J. Sadock (Eds.), *Syntax and semantics*. (pp. 59–81) New York: Academic.

Finke, R. A. (1990). *Imagery and creative imagination*. Buffalo, NY: Bearly Ltd.

Fischer, K. W. (1978). A theory of cognitive development: The control and construction of hierarchies of skills. *Psychological Review, 87,* 477–531.

Fish, L., Hall, C. R., & Cumming, J. (2004). Investigating the use of imagery by elite ballet dancers. *Avante, 10,* 1–11.

Flores, F. (1998). Einstein's 1935 derivation of $E = mc^2$. *Studies in History and Philosophy of Modern Physics, 29,* 223–243.

Forester, C. S. (1964). *The hornblower companion*. London: Michael Joseph Ltd.

Fraser, C., Bellugi, U., & Brown, R. W. (1963). Control of grammar in imitation, comprehension and production. *Journal of Verbal Learning and Verbal Behavior, 2,* 121–135.

French, A. P. (1968). *Special relativity*. New York: Norton.

Freyd, J. J. (1987). Dynamic mental representations. *Psychological Review, 94,* 427–438.

Friberg, E. (1988). *The Kalevala: Epic of the Finnish people*. Helsinki, Finland: Otava Publishing Co.

Frick, R. W. (1984). Using both an auditory and a visual short term store to increase digit span. *Memory & Cognition, 12,* 507–514.

Friedman, W. J. (1989). The representation of temporal structure in children, adolescents and adults. In I. Levin & D. Zakay (Eds.), *Time and human cognition: A life-span perspective* (pp. 259–304). Amsterdam: Elsevier.

Frymiare, J. L., McCrae, K., Angelakis, E., Stathopoulou, S., Paivio, A., & Kounios, J. *Concreteness effects and the right hemisphere: Evidence from event-related potentials*. Unpublished manuscript.

Gallistel, C. T., & Gellman, R. (1992). Preverbal and verbal counting and computation. *Cognition, 44,* 43–74.

Galton, F. (1869). *Hereditary genius: An inquiry into its laws and consequences*. London: Macmillan.

Galton, F. (1883). *Inquiries into human faculty and its development* (1st ed.) London: Macmillan.

Gardner, B. T., & Gardner, R. A. (1975). Evidence for sentence constituents in the early utterances of child and chimpanzee. *Journal of Experimental Psychology: General, 104,* 244–267.

Gardner, B. T., & Gardner, R. A. (1985). Signs of intelligence in cross-fostered chimpanzees. *Philosophical Transactions of the Royal Society of London, B308,* 159–176.

Gardner, H. (1993a). *Creating minds: An anatomy of creativity seen through the lives of Freud, Einstein, Picasso, Stravinsky, Eliot, Graham, and Gandhi*. New York: Basic Books.

Gardner, H. (1993b). *Frames of mind: The theory of multiple intelligences* (10th anniversary ed.). New York: Basic Books.

Gardner, H. (1995). Expert performance: Its structure and acquisition. Comment. *American Psychologist, 50,* 802–803.

Gardner, R. A., & Gardner, B. T. (1988). Feedforward vs feedbackward: An ethological alternative to the law of effect. *Behavioral and Brain Sciences, 11,* 429–403.

Gardner, R. C., & Lambert, W. E. (1972). Attitudes and motivation in second language learning. Rowley, MA: Newbury House.

Gardner, R. C., Tremblay, P. F., & Masgoret, A. M. (1997). Towards a full model of second language learning: An empirical investigation. *The Modern Language Journal, 87,* 344–362.

Gazzaniga, M. (Ed.). (1995). *The cognitive neurosciences.* Cambridge, MA: MIT Press.

Gazzaniga, M. (Ed.). (2000). *The New cognitive neurosciences.* Cambridge, MA: MIT Press.

Gelber, B. (1958). Retention in *Paramecium aurelia. Journal of Comparative and Physiological Psychology, 51,* 110–115.

Gentner, D., Brem, S., Ferguson, R. W., Markam, A. B., Levidow, B. B., Wolff, P., et al. (1997). Analogical reasoning and conceptual change: A case study of Johannes Kepler. *The Journal of the Learning Sciences, 6,* 3–40.

Gentner, D., & Markman, A. B. (1997). Structural-mapping in analogy and similarity. *American Psychologist, 52,* 45–56.

Georgopoulos, A. P., Lurito, J. T., Petrides, M., Schwarts, A. B., & Massey, J. T. (1989). Mental rotation of the neuronal population vector. *Science, 243,* 234–236.

Geschwind, N. (1965). Disconnexion syndromes in animals and man. *Brain, 88,* 237–294 and 585–644.

Geschwind, N. (1972). Language and the brain. *Scientific American, 226,* 78–83.

Geschwind, N., & Kaplan, E. (1962). A human cerebral deconnection syndrome—a preliminary report. *Neurology, 12,* 675–685.

Ghaëm, O., Mellet, E., Crivello, F., Tzourio, N., Mazoyer, B.,Berthoz, A., et al. (1997). Mental navigation along memorized routes activates the hippocampus, precuneous, and insula. *NeuroReport, 8,* 739–744.

Gibson, J. J. (1966). *The senses considered as perceptual systems.* Boston: Houghton Mifflin.

Gilot, F., & Lake, C. (1964). *Life with Picasso.* New York: McGraw–Hill.

Givón, T. (1989). *Mind, code, and context: Essays in pragmatics.* Hillsdale NJ: Lawrence Erlbaum Associates, Inc.

Givón, T. (1998). On the co-evolution of language, mind and brain. *Evolution of Communication, 2,* 45–116.

Glenberg, A. M. (1997). What memory is for. *Brain and Behavioral Sciences, 20,* 1–55.

Glucksberg, S. (1998). Understanding metaphors. *Current Directions in Psychological Science, 7,* 39–43.

Goldenberg, G. (1993). The neural basis of mental imagery. *Balliere's Clinical Neurology, 2,* 265–286.

Gonsalves, B., Reber, P. J., Gitelman, D. R., Parrish, T. B., Mesulman, M.-M., & Paller, K. A. (2004). Neural evidence that vivid imaging can lead to false remembering. *Psychological Science, 15,* 655–660.

Goodale, M. (2000). Perception and action in the human visual system. In M. S. Gazzaniga (Ed.), *The new cognitive neurosciences* (pp. 365–377). Cambridge, MA: MIT Press.

Goodale, M. A., & Milner, A, D. (1992). Separate visual pathways for perception and action. *Trends in Neuroscience, 15,* 20–25.

Goodale, M., A., & Westwood, D. A. (2004). An evolving view of duplex vision: Separate but interacting cortical pathways for perception and action. *Current Opinion in Neurobiology, 14,* 203–211.

Gould, J. L. (1990). Honey bee cognition. *Cognition, 37,* 83–103.

Gould, S. J. (1997, October 9). Evolutionary psychology. *New York Review of Books, XLIV* 53–58.

Gould, S. J. (1999). Foreword: The joy and necessity of illustration. In Carter, A. A. (1999) *The art of National Geographic* (pp. 6–9). Washington, DC: National Geographic Society.

Grandin, T. (1995). *Thinking in pictures.* New York: Doubleday.

Gray, R. D., & Jordan, F. M. (2000). Language trees support the express-train sequence of Austronesian expansion. *Nature, 405,* 1052–1055.

Graziano, M. S. A., & Gross, C. G. (1995). The representation of extrapersonal space: A possible role for bimodal, visual-tactile neurons. In M. Gazzaniga (ed.), *The cognitive neurosciences* (pp. 1021–1034). Cambridge, MA: MIT Press.

Greenberg, D. L., & Rubin, D. C. (2003). The neuropsychology of autobiographical memory. *Cortex, 39,* 687–728.

Greenberg, L., & Paivio, S. C. (1997). *Working with emotions in psychotherapy.* New York: Guilford.

Greenfield, P. (1991). Language, tools and the brain: The ontogeny and phylogeny of hierarchically organized sequential behavior. *Behavioral and Brain Sciences, 14,* 513–595.

Greenfield, P., & Savage-Rumbaugh, E. S. (1991). Imitation, grammatical development, and the invention of protogrammar by an ape. In. N. A. Krasnegor, D. M. Rumbaugh, R. L. Schiefelbusch, & M. Studdert-Kennedy (Eds.), *Biological and behavioral determinants of language development* (pp. 235–258). Hillsdale, NJ: Lawrence Erlbaum Associates Inc.

Greenspan, S. I., & Shanker, S. G. (2004). *The first idea: How symbols, language, and intelligence evolved from our primate ancestors.* Cambridge, MA: Da Capo Press.

Griffin, D. R. (1976). *The question of animal awareness: Evolutionary continuity of conscious experience.* New York: The Rockefeller University Press.

Grodzinsky, Y. (2000). The neurology of syntax: Language use without Broca's area. *Behavioral and Brain Sciences, 23,* 1–71.

Gruber, H. E. (1974). *Darwin on man: A psychological study of creativity* (Together with Darwin's early and unpublished notes transcribed and annotated by Paul H. Barrett). New York: Dutton.

Gruneberg, M. M., & Pascoe, K. (1996). The effectiveness of the keyword method for receptive and productive foreign vocabulary learning in the elderly. *Contemporary Educational Psychology, 21,* 102–109.

Guilford, J. P. (1967). *The nature of human intelligence.* New York: McGraw-Hill.

Guilford, J. P., & Hoepfner, R. (1971). *The analysis of intelligence.* New York: McGraw-Hill.

Hadamard, J. (1945). *The psychology of invention in the mathematical field.* Princeton, NJ: Dover.

Haesler, S., Wada, K., Nshdejan, A., Morrisey, E. E., Lints, T., Jarvis, E. D., et al. (2004). FOXP2 expression in avian vocal learners and non-learners. *Journal of Neuroscience, 24,* 3164–3175.

Halgren, E., & Marinkovic, K. (1995). Neurophysiological networks integrating human emotions. In M. S. Gazzaniga (Ed.), *The cognitive neurosciences* (pp. 1137–1151). Cambridge, MA: MIT Press.

Hall, C. R. (2001). Imagery in sport and exercise. In. R. Singer, H. Hausenblas, & C. Janelle (Eds.), *Handbook of sport psychology* (pp. 529–549). New York: Wiley.

Hall, C. R., Mack, D., Paivio, A., & Hausenblas, H. A. (1998). Imagery use by athletes: Development of the Sport Imagery Questionnaire. *International Journal of Sport Psychology, 29,* 73–89.

Hall, C. R., Stevens, D. E., & Paivio, A. (2005). *Sports Imagery Questionnaire.* Fitness Information Technology, International Center for Performance Excellence, West Virginia University.

Hall, C. R., Toews, J., & Rogers, W. (1990). Les aspects motivationnels de l'imagerie en activités motrices [Motivational aspects of imagery in motor activities.] *Revue des Sciences et Techniques des Activités Physiques et Sportives, 11,* 27–32.

Hamilton, W. D. (1964). The genetical evolution of social behavior. I and II. *Journal of Theoretical Biology, 7,* 1–52.

Hamm, J., Matheson, W. R., & Honig, W. K. (1997). Mental rotation in the pigeon (Columba livia)? *Journal of Comparative Psychology, 111,* 76–81.

Handwerk, B. (2002, December 18). *Lord of the Rings* inspired by an ancient epic. *National Geographic News.*

Hariri, A. R., Bookheimer, S. Y., & Mazziotta, J. C. (2000). Modulating emotional responses: Effects of a neocortical network on the limbic system. *NeuroReport, 11,* 43–48.

Harman, K. L., Humphrey, G. K., & Goodale, M. A. (1999). Active manual control of object views facilitates visual recognition. *Current Biology, 9,* 1315–1318.

Harnad, S., Steklis, H. D., & Lancaster, J. (Eds.), (1976). *Origins and evolution of language and speech.* New York: The New York Academy of Sciences.

Harris, Z. (1991). *A theory of language and information: A mathematical approach.* New York: Oxford University Press.

Hauser, M., & Carey, S. (1998). Building a cognitive creature from a set of primitives: Evolutionary and developmental insights. In D. L. Cummins & C. Allen (Eds.), *The evolution of mind* (pp. 51–106). New York: Oxford University Press.

Hauser, M. D., Chomsky, N., & Fitch, W. T. (2002). The faculty of language: What is it, who has it, and how did it evolve? *Science, 298,* 1569–1579.

Hayakawa, S. I. (1949). *Language in thought and action.* New York: Harcourt Brace

Hayes, J. R. (1973). On the function of imagery in elementary mathematics. In. W. G. Chase (Ed.), *Visual information processing* (pp. 177–214). New York: Academic.

Hazen, N. L. (1983). Spatial orientation: A comparative approach. In (pp. 3–37). Pick, Jr. & L. P. Acredolo, (Eds), *Spatial orientation: Theory, research, and application* New York: Plenum.

Hebb, D. O. (1949). *The organization of behavior.* New York: Wiley. (Reprinted 2003 by Lawrence Erlbaum Associates, Inc., Mahwah, NJ.)

Hebb, D. O. (1953). Heredity and environment in mammalian behavior. *The British Journal of Animal Behaviour, 1,* 43–47.

Hebb, D. O. (1968). *Concerning imagery.* Psychological Review, 75, 466–477.

Hebb, D. O. (1972). *A textbook of psychology.* Toronto, ON: Saunders.

Hebb, D. O. (1980). *Essay on mind.* Hillsdale, NJ: Lawrence Erlbaum Associates, Inc.

Hebb, D. O., Lambert, W. E., & Tucker, G. R. (1971). Language, thought and experience. *Modern Language Journal, 55,* 212–222.

Hebb, D. O., & Morton, N. W. (1943). The McGill Adult Comprehension Examination: "Verbal situation" and "picture anomaly" series. *Journal of Educational Psychology, 34,* 16–25.

Herbart, J. F. (1891). *A text-book in psychology.* New York: Appleton.

Herman, L. M., & Uyeyama, R. K. (1999). The dolphin's grammatical competency: Comments on Kako (1999). *Animal Learning & Behavior, 27,* 18–23.

Hershenson, M., & Haber, R. N. (1965). The role of meaning in the perception of briefly presented words. *Canadian Journal of Psychology, 19,* 42–46.

Hewes, G. W. (1978). Visual learning, thinking, and communication in human biosocial evolution. In B. S. Randhawa & W. E. Coffman (Eds.), *Visual learning, thinking, and communication* (pp. 1–19). New York: Academic press.

Hillocks, G., Jr. (1986). *Research on written composition: New directions for teaching.* Urbana, IL: ERIC Clearinghouse on Reading and Communication Skills and the National Conference on Research in English.

Hilts, P. J. (1995). *Memory's ghost: The strange tale of Mr. M. and the nature of memory.* New York: Simon & Schuster.

Hinton, G. (2003). The ups and downs of Hebb synapses. *Canadian Psychology, 44,* 10, 13.

Hintzman, D. H. (1984). Episodic versus semantic memory: A distinction whose time has come—and gone? *Behavioral and Brain Sciences, 7,* 240–241.

Hobson, J. A., & Stickgold, R. (1995). The conscious state paradigm A neurocognitive approach to waking, sleeping, and dreaming. In M. S. Gazzaniga (Ed.), *The cognitive neurosciences* (pp. 1373–1390). Cambridge, MA: MIT Press

Hockett, C. F. (1963). The problem of universals in language. In J. H. Greenberg (Ed.), *Universals of language* (pp. 1–21). Cambridge, MA: MIT Press.

Holcomb, P. J., Kounios, J., Anderson, J. E., & West, W. C. (1999). Dual-coding, context-availability, and concreteness effects in sentence comprehension: An electrophysiological investigation. *Journal of Experimental Psychology: Learning, Memory, and Cognition, 25,* 721–742.

Holden, C. (2004). The origin of speech. *Science, 303,* 1316–1319.

Holland, P. C. (1990). Event representation in Pavlovian conditioning: Image and action. *Cognition, 37,* 105–131.

Hollis, K. L. (1984). The biological function of Pavlovian conditioning: The best defense is a good offense. *Journal of Experimental Psychology: Animal Behavior Processes, 10,* 413–425.

Holyoak, K. J., & Thagard, (1997). The analogical mind. *American Psychologist, 52,* 35–44

Hopkins, W. D., Fagot, J. & Vauclair, J. (1993). Mirror image matching and mental rotation problem solving in baboons (Papio papio): Unilateral input enhances performance. *Journal of Experimental Psychology: General, 122,* 61–72.

Horn, J. L., & Cattell, R. B. (1966). Refinement and test of the theory of fluid and crystallized intelligence. *Journal of Educational Psychology, 57,* 253–270.

Horowitz, M. J. (1968). Visual thought images in psychotherapy. *American Journal of Psychotherapy, 22,* 55–75.

Horowitz, M. J. (1998). *Cognitive psychodynamics: From conflict to character.* New York: Wiley.

Houtz, J. C., & Patricola, C. (1999). Imagery. In M. A. Runco & S. R. Pritzker (Eds.), *Encyclopedia of creativity* (Vol. 2 pp. 1–11). San Diego, CA: Academic

Hull, R., & Vaid, J. (2005). Clearling the cobwebs from the study of the bilingual brain: Converging evidence from laterality and electrophysiological research. In J. Kroll & A. M. B. de Groot (Eds.), *Handbook of Bilingualism: Psycholinguistic Approaches* (pp. 480–496). Oxford, England: Oxford University Press.

Humphreys, G. W., & Riddoch, M. J. (1993). Interaction between object and space-system revealed through neuropsychology. In D. E, Myers & *Attention and performance XIV,* S. Kornblum (Eds.), (pp. 183–218). Cambridge, MA: MIT Press.

Hundtofte, C. S., Hager, G. D., & Okamura, A. M. (2002). Building a task language for segmentation and recognition of user input to cooperative manipulation systems. *10th Symposium on Haptic Interfaces for Virtual Environment and Teleoperator Systems,* Orlando, FL.

Hunt, J. McV. (1961). *Intelligence and experience.* New York: Ronald.

Hurford, J. R. (2004). Language beyond our grasp: What mirror neurons can, and cannot, do for language evolution. In D. Kimbrough Oller, U. Griebel, K. Plunkett (Eds), *Evolution of communication systems: A comparative approach* (pp. 297–313). Cambridge, MA: MIT Press.

Hynd, G. W., &Willis, W. G. (1985). Neurological foundations of intelligence. In B. B., Wolman (Ed.), *Handbook of intelligence: Theories, measurements, and applications* (pp. 119–157). New York: Wiley.

Imamizu, H., Miyauchi, S., Tamada. T., Sasaki, Y., Takino, R., Pütz, B., et al. (2000). Human cerebellar activity reflecting an acquired internal model of a new tool. *Nature, 403,* 192–195.

Indefrey, P., Brown, C. M., Hellwig, F., Amunts, K., Herzog, H., Seitz, R. J., et al. (2001). A neural correlate of syntactic encoding during speech production. *Proceedings of the National Academy of Sciences, USA, 98,* 5933–5936.

Intons-Peterson, M. J., & Roskos-Ewoldsen, B. B. (1989). Sensory-perceptual qualities of images. *Journal of Experimental Psychology: Learning, Memory, and Cognition, 15,* 188–199.

Intraub, H. (2004). Anticipatory spatial representation of 3D regions explored by sighted observers and a deaf-and-blind-observer. *Cognition, 94,* 19–37.

Intraub, H., Gottesman, C. V., & Bills, A. J. (1998). Effects of perceiving and imagining scenes on memory for pictures. *Journal of Experimental Psychology: Learning, Memory, and Cognition, 24,* 186–201.

Intraub, H., & Richardson, M. (1989). Wide-angle memories of close-up scenes. *Journal of Experimental Psychology: Learning, Memory, and Cognition, 15,* 179–187.

Ito, M. (2000). Internal model visualized. *Nature, 403,* 153–154.

Ives, H., & Stillwell, G. (1938). An experimental study of the rate of a moving clock. *Journal of the Optical Society of America, 28,* 215–226.

Jackendoff, R, (1992). *Languages of the mind: Essays on mental representation.* Cambridge, MA: MIT Press.

Jackendoff, R, (1987). *Consciousness and the computational mind.* Cambridge, MA: MIT Press.

Jackson, D. N. (1974). *Personality Research Form, manual.* Goshen, NY: Research Psychologists Press.

Jacobson, E. (1973). Electrophysiology of mental activities and introduction to the psychological process of thinking. In F. J. McGuigan & R. A. Schooner (Eds.), *The psychophysiology of thinking* (pp. 3–31). New York. Academic

James, K. H., Humphrey, G. K., & Goodale, M. A. (2001). Manipulating and recognizing virtual objects: Where the action is. *Canadian Journal of Experimental Psychology, 55,* 111–120.

James, T. W., Humphrey, G. K., Gati, J. S., Servos, P., et al. (2002). Haptic study of three-dimensional objects activates extrastriate visual areas. *Neuropsychologia, 40,* 1706–1714.

Jeannerod, M. (1994). The representing brain: Neural correlates of motor intention and imagery. *Behavioral and Brain Sciences, 17,* 187–245.

Jeannerod, M., & Jacob, P. (2005) Visual cognition: a New look at the two-visual systems model. *Neuropsychologia, 43,* 301–312.

Jerison, H. J. (2000). The evolution of intelligence. In R. J. Sternberg (Ed.), *Handbook of intelligence* England (pp. 216–244). Cambridge, England: Cambridge University Press.

Johanssen, G. (1973).Visual perception of biological motion and a model for its analysis. *Perception and Psychophysics, 14,* 201–211.

John, E. R. (2003). A theory of consciousness. *Current Directions in Psychological Science, 12,* 244–250.

Johnson, C. J., Paivio, A. U., & Clark, J. M. (1989). Spatial and verbal abilities in children's cross-modal recognition: A dual coding approach. *Canadian Journal of Psychology, 43,* 397–412.

Johnson, C. J., Paivio, A., & Clark, J. M. (1996). Cognitive components of picture naming. *Psychological Bulletin, 120,* 113–139.

Johnson, K. O., Hsiao, S. S., & Twombly, I. A. (1995). Neural mechanisms of tactile form recognition. In M. S. Gazzaniga (Ed.), *The cognitive neurosciences* (pp. 253–267). Cambridge, MA: MIT Press.

Johnson, M. K., Hashtroudi, S., & Lindsey, D. S. (1993). Source monitoring. *Psychological Bulletin, 114,* 3–28.

Johnson, M. K., & Raye, C. I. (1981). Reality monitoring. *Psychological Review, 88,* 67–85.

Johnson-Glenberg, M. C. (2000). Training reading comprehension in adequate decoders/poor comprehenders: Verbal versus visual strategies. *Journal of Educational Psychology, 92,* 772–782.

Johnson-Laird, P. N., Herrmann, D. J., & Chaffin, R. (1984). Only connections: A critique of semantic networks. *Psychological Bulletin, 96,* 292–315.

Johnson-Laird, P. N. (1983). *Mental models: Towards a cognitive science of language, inference, and consciousness.* Cambridge, England: Cambridge University Press.

Johnson-Laird, P. N. (1995). Mental models, deductive reasoning, and the brain. In M. S. Gazzaniga (Ed.), *The cognitive neurosciences* (pp. 999–1008). Cambridge, MA: MIT Press.

Joliot-Curie, I., & Joliot-Curie, F. (1933). Mass of the neutron. *Compte Rendu, 197,* 237.

Jolly, A. (1999). *Lucy's legacy: Sex and intelligence in human evolution.* Cambridge, MA: Harvard University Press.

Jones, S. (1982). Syntax in pictures. *Quarterly Journal of Experimental Psychology, 34A,* 235–243.

Jones, S. (2000). *Darwin's ghost: The Origin of Species updated.* Toronto, Canada: Doubleday.

Jones-Gotman, M., & Milner, B. (1978). Right temporal lobe contribution to image-mediated memory. *Neuropsychologia, 16,* 61–71.

Jung-Beeman, M., Bowden, E. M., Haberman, J., Frymiare, J. L., Arambel-Liu, S., Greenblatt, R., et al. (2004). Neural activity when people solve problems with insight. *PLoS Biology, 4,* 0500–0509.

Just, M. A., Newman, S. D., Keller, T. A., McKelney, A., & Carpenter, P. A. (2004). Imagery in sentence comprehension: An f MRI study. *NeuroImage, 21,* 112–124.

Kako, E. (1999). Elements of syntax in three language- trained animals. *Animal Learning and Behavior, 27,* 1–14.

Kamil, A. C., Balda, R. P., & Olson, D. J. (1994). Performance of four seed-caching corvid species in the radial-arm maze analog. *Journal of Comparative Psychology, 108,* 385–393.

Katz, A. N. (1983). Creativity and individual differences in asymmetric hemispheric functioning. *Empirical Studies of the Arts, 1,* 3–16.

Katz, A. N. (1986). The relationship between creativity and cerebral hemisphericity for creative architects, scientists, and mathematicians. *Empirical Studies of the Arts, 4,* 97–98.

Katz, A. N. (1997). Creativity and the cerebral hemispheres. In M. A. Runco (Ed.), *The creativity research handbook* (Vol. 1, pp. 203–226). Cresskill, NJ: Hampton

Katz, A. N., & Paivio, A. (1975). Imagery variables in concept identification. *Journal of Verbal Learning & Verbal Behavior, 14,* 284–293.

Kaufman, A. S. (2000). Tests of intelligence. In R. J. Sternberg (Ed.), *Handbook of intelligence* (pp. 445–476). Cambridge, MA: xxxx.

Kaufman, A. S., & Kaufman, N. L. (1993). *Manual for Kaufman Adolescent & Adult Intelligence Test (KAIT).* Circle Pines, MN: American Guidance Service.

Kaufman, A. S., & Kaufman, N. L. (1997). The Kaufman Adolescent and Adult Intelligence Test. In D. P Flanagan, J. L Genshaft, & P. L. Harrison (Eds.), *Contemporary intellectual assessment: Theories, tests, and issues* (pp. 209–225). New York: Guilford,

Kelly, L. G. (1969). *Twenty-five centuries of language teaching.* Rowley, MA: Newbury House.

Kennedy, J. M. (1976, xxxx). *Pictorial metaphor: A theory of movement indicators in static pictures.* Paper presented at the Information Through Pictures Symposium, Swarthmore College, Swarthmore, PA.

Kern, E. (1968, December). Guernica. *Life, 65,* 90–92.

Khan, M., & Paivio, A. (1988). Memory for schematic and categorical information: A replication and extension of Rabinowitz and Mandler (1983). *Journal of Experimental Psychology: Learning, Memory, and Cognition, 14,* 558–561.

Kimura, D. (1982). Left-hemisphere control of oral and brachial movements and their relation to communication. *Philosophical Transactions of the Royal Society of London, 298,* 135–149.

Kimura, D. (1993). *Neuromotor mechanisms in human communication.* New York: Oxford University Press.

Kinsbourne, M. (1995). Models of consciousness: Serial or parallel in the brain? In Michael S. Gazzaniga (ed.), *The cognitive neurosciences* (pp. 1321–1330). Cambridge, MA.: MIT Press.

Kintsch, W. (1998). *Comprehension: A paradigm for cognition.* Cambridge, UK: Cambridge University Press.

Kintsch, W. (2000). Metaphor comprehension: A computational theory. *Psychonomic Bulletin & Review, 7,* 257–266.

Kintsch, W. (2004). The construction-integration model of text comprehension and its implications for instruction. In R. B. Ruddell & N. J. Unrau (Eds.), *Theoretical models and processes of reading* (5th ed., (pp. 1270–1328). Newark, DE: International Reading Association.

Kirby, J. R., & Das, J. P. (1976). Comments on Paivio's imagery theory. *Canadian Psychologica Review, 17,* 66–68.

Kirsch, I. (1985). Response expectancy as a determinant of experience and behavior. *American Psychologist, 40,* 1189–1202.

Kiss, G. R. (1973). Grammatical word classes: A learning process and its simulation. In G. H. Bower (Ed.), *The psychology of learning and motivation* (Vol. 7). New York: Academic Press.

Kiss, G. R. (1975). An associative thesaurus of English: Structural analysis of a large relevance network. In A. Kennedy & A. Wilkes (Eds.), *Studies in long term memory.* (pp. 103–121). New York: Wiley.

Klatzky, R. L., & Lederman, S. J. (1987). The intelligent hand. In G. H. Bower (Ed.), *the psychology of learning and motivation* (Vol. 21, pp. 121–151). San Diego, CA: Academic.

Klein, I., Dubois, J., Mangin, J-G., Kherif, F., et al. (2004. Retinotopic organization of visual mental images as Revealed by functional magnetic resonance imaging. *Cognitive Brain Research, 22,* 26–31.

Knight, C., Hurford, J. R., & Studdert-Kennedy, M. (Eds.). (2000). *The evolutionary emergence of language: Social functions and the origins of linguistic form.* Cambridge, England Cambridge University Press.

Köhler, S., Moscovitch, M., Winocur, G., & McIntosh, A. R. (2000). Episodic encoding and recognition of pictures and words: role of the human medial temporal lobes. *Acta Psychologica, 105,* 159–179.

Köhler, W. (1925). *The mentality of apes.* New York: Harcourt Brace.

Kolb, B. (2003). The impact of the Hebbian learning rule on research in behavioural neuroscience. *Canadian Psychology, 44,* 14–16.

Kolb., B., & Whishaw, I. Q. (2001). *An introduction to brain and behavior.* New York: Worth.

Kolodner, J. L. (1997). Educational implications of analogy: A view from case-based reasoning. *American Psychologist, 52,* 57–66.

Korzybski, A. (1933). *Science and sanity: An introduction to non-Aristotelian systems and general semantics.* Lancaster, PA: Science Press.

Kosslyn, S. M. (1980). *Image and mind.* Cambridge, MA: Harvard University Press.

Kosslyn, S. M. (1994). *Image and brain: The resolution of the imagery debate.* Cambridge, MA: MIT Press.

Kosslyn, S. M., Ganis, G., & Thompson, W. L. (2005). *The case for mental imagery.* New York: Oxford University Press.

Kosslyn, S. M., Pascual-Leone, A., Felicien, O., Camposano, S., Keenan, J. P., Thompson, W. L., et al. (1999). The role of area 17 in visual imagery: Convergent evidence from PET and rTMS. *Science, 284,* 167–170.

Kounios, J., & Holcomb, P. J. (1994). Concreteness effects in semantic processing: ERP evidence supporting dual-coding theory. *Journal of Experimental Psychology: Learning, Memory, and Cognition, 20,* 804–823.

Kreiman, G., Koch, C., & Fried, I. (2000). Imagery neurons in the human brain. *Nature, 408,* 357–361.

Krueger, T. H. (1976). *Visual imagery in problem-solving and scientific creativity.* Derby, CT: Seal Press.

Kuhn, M. R., & Stahl, S. A. (2003). Fluency: A Review of developmental and remedial practices. *Journal of Educational Psychology, 95,* 3–21.

Kuiper, N. A., & Paivio, A. (1977). Incidental recognition memory for concrete and abstract sentences equated for comprehensibility. *Bulletin of the Psychonomic Society, 9,* 247–249.

Lai, C. S. L., Fisher, S. E., Hurst, J. A., Vargha-Khadem, F., &, Monaco, A. P. (2001). A fork-head-domain gene is mutated in severe speech language disorders. *Nature, 413,* 519–523.

Lai, C. S. L.,Gerrelli, D., Monaco, A. P., Fisher, S. E., & Copp, A. J. (2003). *FOXP2* expression during brain development coincides with adult sites of pathology in a severe language and speech disorder. *Brain, 126,* 2455–2462.

Lakatos, I. (1963–1964). Proofs and refutations. *The British Journal for the Philosophy of Science, 14,* 1–25, 120–139, 221–245, 296–342.

Lakoff, G. (1977, April). Linguistic gestalts. In Beach, W. A., Fox, S. E., & Philosoph S. (Eds.), *Papers from the thirteenth regional meeting,* Chicago Linguistic Society (pp. 236–287). Chicago, IL: University of Chicago.

Lakoff, G. (1990). The invariance hypothesis: Is abstract reason based on image-schemas? *Cognitive Linguistics, 1,* 39–74.

Lakoff, G., & Johnson, M. (1980). *Metaphors we live by* Chicago, IL: University of Chicago Press.

Lambert, S., Sampaio, E., Mauss, Y., & Scheiber, C. (2004). Blindness and brain plasticity: con-tribution of mental imagery? An fMRI study. *Cognitive Brain Research, 20,* 1–11.

Lambert, W. E., & Paivio, A. (1956). The influence of noun-adjective order on learning. *Canadian Journal of Psychology, 10,* 9–12.

Lambon Ralph, M. A., Graham, K. S., Patterson, K., & Hodges, J. R. (1999). Is a picture worth a thousand words? Evidence from concept definitions by patients with semantic dementia. *Brain and Language, 70,* 309–335.

Landauer, T. K. (1999). Latent semantic analysis (LSA), a disembodied learning machine, acquires human word meaning vicariously from language alone. *Behavioral and Brain Sciences, 22,* 624–625.

Landauer, T. K., & Dumais, S. T. (1997). A solution to Plato's problem: The latent semantic analysis theory of acquisition, induction and representation of knowledge. *Psychological Review, 104,* 211–240.

Lane, W. (2003). Beethoven: The immortal. Re-retrieved as January 2006 version July 16, 2006 from http://lucare.com/immortal.

Langacker, R. W. (1990). *Concept, image, and symbol: The cognitive basis of grammar.* Mouton The Hague, Netherlands:

Langley, P., Simon, H. A., Bradshaw, G. I., & Zytkow, J. M. (1987). *Scientific discovery: Computational explorations of the creative Processes.* Cambridge, MA: MIT Press.

Lanius, R. A., Williamson, O. C., Densmore, M., Boksman, K., Neufeld, R. W., Gati, J. S., et al. (2004). The nature of traumatic memories: A 4.0 Tesla fMRI functional connectivity analysis. *American Journal of Psychiatry, 161,* 36–44.

Large, M.-E., Aldcroft, A., & Vilis, T. (2005). Perceptual continuity and the emergence of per-ceptual persistence in the ventral visual pathway. *Neuropsychologia, 43,* 41–51.

Laubach, M., Wessberg, J., & Nicolelis, M. A. L. (2000). Corticle ensemble activity increasingly predicts behaviour outcomes during learning of a motor task. *Nature, 405,* 567–571.

Lazarus, R. S. (1982). Thoughts on the relations between emotion and cognition. *American Psychologist, 37,* 1019–1024.

Leakey, R. E., & Lewin, R. (1978). *People of the lake: Mankind and its beginnings.* Garden City, NY: Doubleday.

Le Boutillier, N., & Marks, D. F. (2003). Mental imagery and creativity: A meta-analytic review study. *British Journal of Psychology, 94,* 29–44.

Leff, A. P., Crewes, H., Plant, G. T., Scott, S. K., Kennard, C., & Wise, R. J. S. (2001). The func-tional anatomy of single-word reading in patients with hemianopic and pure alexia. *Brain, 124,* 510–521.

Lehmann, A. C., & Ericsson, K. A. (1998). The historical development of domains of expertise: Performance standards and innovations in music. In A. Steptoe (ed.), *Genius and the mind:*

Studies of creativity and temperament in the historical record (pp. 67–94). New York: Oxford University Press.

Lenneberg, E. H. (1967). *Biological foundations of language.* New York: Wiley.

Leuba, C. (1940). Images as conditioned sensations. *Journal of Experimental Psychology, 26,* 345–351.

Levine, D. N., Warach, J., & Farah, M. (1985). Two visual systems in mental imagery: Dissociation of "what" and "where" in imagery disorders due to bilateral posterior cerebral lesions. *Neurology, 35,* 1010–1018.

Levy, J. (1985, May). Right brain, left brain: Fact and fiction. *Psychology Today. 38–44.*

Lewontin, R. (2004). The genotype/phenotype distinction. *The Stanford Encyclopedia of Philosophy (Spring 2004 Edition),* Edward N. Zalta (ed.). Retrieved April 8, 2004 from <http://plato.stanford.edu/archives/spr2004/entries/genotype-phenotype.

Ley, R. G., & Bryden, M. P. (1983). Right hemisphere involvement in imagery and affect. In E. Perceman & J. Brown (Eds.), *Cognitive processing in the right hemisphere* (pp. xxx–xxx). New York: Academic

Lieberman, P. (2002). On the nature and evolution of the neural basis of human language. *Yearbook of Physical Anthropology, 45,* 36–62.

Lindamood, P., Bell, N., & Lindamood, P. (1997). Sensory-cognitive factors in the controversy over reading instruction. *Journal of Developmental Disorders, 1,* 143–182.

Lindberger, U., Kliegl, R., & Baltes, P. B. (1992). Professional expertise does not eliminate age differences in imagery-based memory performance during adulthood. *Psychology and Aging, 7,* 585–593.

Linebarger, M. C. (1995). Agrammatism as evidence about grammar. *Brain and Language, 50,* 52–91.

Linebarger, M. C., Schwartz, M., & Saffran, E. (1983). Sensitivity to grammatical structure in so-called agrammatic aphasics. *Cognition, 13,* 361–393.

Lissauer, H. (1890). Ein Fall von Seelenblindheit nebst einem Beitrag zur Theorie derselben (A case of visual agnosia with a contribution to theory.) *Archives of Psychiatry and Neurology, 21,* 222–270.

Littrell, J. (1998). Is the reexperience of painful emotion therapeutic? *Clinical Psychology Review, 18,* 71–102.

Locke, J. L. (1997). A theory of neurolinguistic development. *Brain and Language, 58,* 265–326.

Lockhart, R. S. (1987). Code duelling. *Canadian Journal of Psychology, 41,* 387–389.

Logan, J. M., Saunders, A. L., Snyder, A. Z., Morris, J. C., & Buckner, R. L. (2002). Under-recruitment and nonselective recruitment dissociable neural mechanisms with aging. *Neuron, 33,* 827–840.

Lorayne, H. (1974). *How to develop a super-power memory.* New York: New American Library.

Lowes, J. L. (1927). *The road to Xanadu.* London: Constable.

Lu, Z.-L., Williamson, S. J., & Kaufman, L. (1992). Behavioral lifetime of human auditorysensory memory predicted by physiological measures. *Science, 258,* 1668–1670.

Lumsden, C. J., & Wilson, E. O. (1981). *Genes, mind, and culture: The coevolutionary process.* Cambridge, MA: Harvard University Press.

Luria, A. R. (1973). *The working brain: An introduction to neuropsychology.* New York: Penguin.

Lyman, B. J., & McDaniel, M. A. (1990). Memory for odors and odor names: Modalities of elaboration and imagery. *Journal of Experimental Psychology: Learning, Memory, & Cognition, 16,* 656–664.

MacAndrew, A. (2004). FOXP2 and the evolution of language. Retrieved May 29, 2004 from http://www.evolutionpages.com/FOXP2_language.htm

Mackintosh, N. J. (1998). *IQ and human intelligence.* New York: Oxford University Press.

MacLeod, C. M. (1991). Half a century of research on the Stroop effect: An integrative Review. *Psychological Bulletin, 109,* 163–203.

Macnamara, J. (1972). Cognitive basis of language learning in infants. *Psychological Review, 79,* 1–13.

MacNeilage, P. F. (1998). The frame/content theory of evolution of speech production. *Behavioral and Brain Sciences, 21,* 499–546.

MacNeilage, P. F., & Davis, B. L. (2005). The frame/content theory of evolution of speech: A comparison with a gestural-origins alternative. *Interaction Studies, 6,* 173–199.

MacWhinney, B. (1977). Starting points. *Language, 53,* 152–168.

Maddox, B. (2002). *Rosalind Franklin: The dark lady of DNA.* New York: HarperCollins.

Magnussen, S., Greenlee, M. W., Aslaksen, P. M., & Kildebo, O. Ø. (2003). High-fidelity perceptual long-term memory revisited—and confirmed. *Psychological Science, 14,* 74–76.

Maguire, E. A., Frackowiak, R. S., & Frith, C. D. (1997). Recalling routes around London: activation of the right hippocampus in taxi drivers. *Journal of Neuroscience, 17,* 7103–7110.

Matthus, T. R. (1798). *Essay on the principle of population.*

Mandler, J. M., & Mandler, G. (1964). *Thinking: From association to Gestalt.* New York: Wiley.

Manyande, A., Berg, S., Gettins, D., Stanford, S. C., Mazhero, S.,Marks, D. F., et al. (1995). Preoperative rehearsal of active coping imagery influences subjective and hormonal responses to abdominal surgery. *Psychosomatic Medicine, 57,* 177–182.

Marks, D. F. (1973). Visual imagery differences in recall of pictures. *British Journal of Psychology, 64,* 17–24.

Marks, D. F. (1999). Consciousness, mental imagery and action. *British Journal of Psychology, 90,* 567–585.

Marschark, M. (2005). Metaphors in sign language and sign language users: A window into relations between language and thought. In H. L. Colston & A. N. Katz (Eds.), *Figurative language comprehension* (pp. 309–334). Mahwah, NJ: Lawrence Erlbaum Associates, Inc.

Marschark, M., & Hunt, R. R. (1989). A reexamination of the role of imagery in learning and memory. *Journal of Experimental Psychology: Learning, Memory, and Cognition, 15,* 710–720.

Marschark, M., & Paivio, A. (1977). Integrative processing of concrete and abstract sentences. *Journal of Verbal Learning and Verbal Behavior, 16,* 217–231.

Martin, A., Ungerleider, L. G., & Haxby, J. V. (2000). Category specificity and the brain: The sensory/motor model of semantic representation of objects. In M. Gazzaniga (Ed.), *The New cognitive neurosciences* (pp. 1023–1035) Cambridge, MA: MIT Press.

Martin, R. A. Berry, G. E., Dobranski, T., & Horne, M. (1996). Emotion perception threshold: Individual differences in emotional sensitivity. *Journal of Research on Personality, 30,* 290–305.

Martin, S. (2002, December 14). You just get on with it. *Globe and Mail,* p. R13.

Maslow, A. H. (1954). *Motivation and personality.* New York: Harper.

Matsumoto, R., Nair, D. R., La Presto, E., Najm, I., Bingaman, W., Shibasaki, H., et al. (2004). Functional connectivity in the human language system: A cortico-cortical evoked potential study. *Brain, 127,* 2316–2330.

Mauck, B., & Dehnhardtt, G. (1997). Mental rotation in a California sealion (Zalophus Californianus). *Journal of Experimental Biology, 200,* 1309–1316.

Mauner, G., Fromkin, V. A., & Cornell, T. L. (1993). Comprehension and acceptabililty judgments in agrammatism: Disruption in the syntax of referential dependency. *Brain and Language, 45,* 340–370.

Mayer, J. D., Salovey, P., & Caruso, D. (2000). Models of emotional intelligence. In R. J. Sternberg (Ed.), *Handbook of intelligence* (pp. 396–420). Cambridge, England: Cambridge University Press.

Mayer, R. E. (1999). Research-based principles for the design of instructional messages: The case for multimedia explanations. *Document Design, 1,* 7–20.

McCallum, R. S., & Bracken, B. A. (1997). The universal nonverbal intelligence test. In D. P. Flanagan, J. L. Genshaft, & P. L. Harrison (Eds.), *Contemporary intellectual assessment: Theories, tests, and issues* (pp. 268–280). New York: Guilford.

McClelland, D. C., Atkinson, J. W., Clark, R. W., & Lowell, E. L. (1953). *The achievement motive*. New York: Appleton-Century-Crofts.

McCloskey, M., Caramazza, A., & Basili, A. (1985). Cognitive mechanisms in number processing and calculation: Evidence from dyscalculia. *Brain and Cognition, 4*, 171–196.

McElree, B., Dolan, P. O., & Jacoby, L. L. (1999). Isolating the contributions of familiarity and source information to item recognition: A time course analysis. *Journal of Experimental Psychology: Learning, Memory, and Cognition, 25*, 563–582.

McGlynn, E. D., Smitherman, T. A., & Gothard, K. D. (2004). Comment on the status of systematic desensitization. *Behavior Modification, 28*(2), 194–205.

McKelvie, S. J. (1995). The VVIQ as a psychometric test of individual differences in visual imagery vividness: A critical quantitative review and plea for direction. *Journal of Mental Imagery, 19*, 1–106.

McKinney, J. P. (1963). Disappearance of luminous designs. *Science, 140*, 403–404.

McKoon, G., Ratcliff, R., & Dell, G. S. (1986). A critical evaluation of the semantic episodic distinction. *Journal of Experimental Psychology: Learning, Memory, and Cognition, 12*, 295–306.

McNeill, D. (1992). *Hand and mind: What gestures reveal about thought*. Chicago: University of Chicago Press.

McNeill, D., Bertenthal, B., Cole., J., & Gallagher, S. (2005). Gesture-first, but no gestures? Commenary on Michael S. Arbib. *Behavioral and Brain Sciences, 28*, 138–139.

Mead, G. H. (1934). *Mind, self, and society*. Chicago, IL: University of Chicago Press.

Mednick, S. A. (1962). The associative basis of the creative process. *Psychological Review, 69*, 220–232.

Meichenbaum, D. H. (1977). *Cognitive behavior modification*. New York: Plenum.

Mellet, E., Bricogne, S., Crivello, F., Mazoyer, B., Denis, M., & Tzourio-Mazoyer, N. (2002). Neural basis of mental scanning of a topographic representation built from a text. *Cerebral Cortex, 12*, 1322–1330.

Mellet, E., Tzourio-Mazoyer, N., Bricogne, S., Mazoyer, B., Kosslyn, S. M., & Denis, M. (2000). Functional anatomy of high-resolution visual imagery. *Journal of Cognitive Neuroscience, 12*, 98–109.

Mellet, E., Tzourio, N. Denis, M., & Mazoyer, B. (1998). Cortical anatomy of mental imagery of concrete nouns based on their dictionary definition. *NeuroReport, 9*, 803–809.

Melzack, R. (1975). The McGill pain questionnaire: Major properties and scoring methods. *Pain, 3*, 277–299.

Melzack, R. (1992). Phantom limbs. *Scientific American, 266*, 90–96.

Menzel, E. W. (1978). Cognitive mapping in chimpanzees. In S. H. Hulse, H. Fowler, & W. H. Honig (Eds.), *Cognitive aspects of animal behavior* (pp. 375–422). Hillsdale NJ: Lawrence Erlbaum Associates, Inc.

Metzinger, T. (Ed.). (2000). *Neural correlates of consciousness*. Cambridge, MA: MIT Press.

Michelon, P., & Biederman, I. (2003). Less impairment in face imagery than face perception in early prosopagnosia. *Neuropsychologia, 41*, 421–441.

Michelon, P., & Zachs, J. M. (2003). What is primed in priming from imagery? *Psychological Research, 67*, 71–79.

Mighton, J. (2003). *The myth of ability: Nurturing mathematical talent in every child*. Toronto, Canada: House of Anansi Press.

Miller, A. I. (1984). *Imagery in scientific thought: Creating 20th century physics*. Boston: Birkhauser.

Miller, G. (2001). *The mating mind*. New York: Anchor.

Miller, G. A. (1956). The magic number seven, plus or minus two: Some limits of our capacity for processing information. *Psychological Review, 63*, 81–97.

Milner, A. D., & Goodale, M. A. (1995). *The visual brain in action*. New York: Oxford University Press.

Milner, P. M. (1999). *The autonomous brain: A neural theory of attention and learning.* Mahwah, NJ. Lawrence Erlbaum Associates, Inc.

Milner, P. (2003). A brief history of the Hebbian learning rule. *Canadian Psychology, 44,* 5–9.

Mistler-Lachman, J. L. (1975). Queer sentences, ambiguity, and levels of processing. *Memory & Cognition, 3,* 395–400.

Mithen, S. (1996). *The prehistory of mind.* London: Thames & Hudson.

Moerman, D. E. (2002). *Meaning, medicine, and "the placebo effect."* Cambridge, England: Cambridge University Press.

Moeser, S. D., & Bregman, A. S. (1973). Imagery and language acquisition. *Journal of Verbal Learning and Verbal Behavior, 12,* 91–98.

Montgomery, G., & Kirsch, I. (1996). Mechanisms of placebo pain reductions: An empirical investigation. *Psychological Science, 7,* 174–176.

Moore, B. R. (2004). The evolution of learning. *Biological Reviews, 79,* 301–335.

Morrow, D. (1988). Sport as metaphor: Shakespeare's use of falconry in the early plays. *Aethlon, 2,* 119–129.

Morton, J. (1969). Interaction of information in word recognition. *Psychological Review, 76,* 165–178.

Morton, J. (1979). Facilitation in word recognition: Experiments causing change in the logogen model. In P. A. Kolers, M. Wrolstead, & H. Bouma (Eds.), *Processing of visible language* (Vol. 1, pp. 259–268). New York: Plenum.

Moscovitch, M., & Nadel, L. (1999). Multiple-trace theory and semantic dementia: Response to K. S. Graham (1999). *Trends in Cognitive Science, 3,* 87–89.

Mowrer, O. H. (1960). *Learning theory and the symbolic processes.* New York: Wiley.

Moyer, R. S. (1973). Comparing objects in memory: Evidence suggesting an internal psychophysics. *Perception & Psychophysics, 13,* 180–184.

Müller, M. (1892). *Lectures on the science of language.* New York: Scribner's.

Murphy, G. (1950). *Historical introduction to modern psychology.* New York: Harcourt Brace

Nadel, L., & Moscovitch, M. (2001). The hippocampal complex and long-term memory revisited. *Trends in Cognitive Sciences, 5,* 228–230.

Naglieri, J. A., & Das, J. P. (1997). *Das-Naglieri Cognitive Assessment System.* Chicago: Riverside.

Neils-Strunjas, J., Krikorian, R., Shidler, M., & Likoy, S. (2001). The influence of learning style and cognitive ability on recall of names and faces in an older population. *Journal of General Psychology, 128,* 433–435.

Neisser, U. (1967). Cognitive psychology. New York: Appleton-Century-Crofts.

Neiworth, J. J., & Rilling, M. E. (1987). A method for studying imagery in animals. *Journal of Experimental Psychology: Animal Behavior Processes, 13,* 203–214.

Nelson, K. (2005). Emerging levels of consciousness in human development. In H. Terrace & J. Metcalfe (Eds.), *The missing link in cognition: Evolution of self-knowing consciousness* (pp. 116–141). New York: Oxford University Press

Noble, A., Arnold, R. A., Buechsenstein, J., Leach, E. J., Schmidt, J. O., & Stern, P. M. (1987). Modification of a standardized system of wine aroma terminology. *American Journal of Enology and Viticulture, 38,* 143–146.

Nolan, S. with contribution by Bate, J., Cooper, T., Garler, M., Gurr, A., Leggatt, A., Titler, R., & Wells. S. (2002). *Shakespeare's face.* Toronto Canada: Knopf.

Nowak, M. A., Plotkin, J. B., & Jansen, V. A. A. (2000). The evolution of syntactic communication. *Nature, 404,* 495–498.

O'Doherty, J., Rolls, E. T., Francis, S., Bowtell, R., & McGlone, F. M. (2001). Representation of pleasant and aversive taste in the human brain. *Neurophysiology, 85,* 1315–1321.

Ogden, J. A. (1993). Visual object agnosia, prosapagnosia, achromatopsia, loss of visual imagery, and autobiographical amnesia following recovery from cortical blindness: case M. H. *Neuropsychologia, 31,* 571–589.

O'Keefe, J., & Nadel, L. (1978). *The hippocampus as a cognitive map*. Oxford England: Clarendon

Olson, D. R. (1970). Language and thought: Aspects of a cognitive theory of semantics. *Psychological Review, 77*, 257–273.

Olson, D. R. (1976). Culture, technology, and the intellect. In L. Resnick (Ed.), *The nature of intelligence*. (pp. 189–202) Hillsdale, NJ: Lawrence Erlbaum Associates, Inc.

Olson, D. R., & Filby, N. (1972). On comprehension of active and passive sentences. *Cognitive Psychology, 3*, 361–381.

O'Neill, B. J., & Paivio, A. (1978). Some consequences of violating selection restrictions in concrete and abstract sentences. *Canadian Journal of Psychology, 32*, 1–18.

Opdahl, K. M. (2002). *Emotion as meaning: The literary case for how we imagine*. Lewisburg, PA: Bucknell University Press.

Osgood, C. E. (1953). *Method and theory in experimental psychology*. New York: Oxford University Press.

Osgood, C. E., Suci, G. J., & Tannenbaum, P. H. (1957). *The measurement of meaning*. Urbana: University of Illinois Press.

Paivio, A. (1964). Childrearing antecedents of audience sensitivity. *Child Development, 35*, 397–416.

Paivio, A. (1965a). Abstractness, imagery, and meaningfulness in paired-associate learning. *Journal of Verbal Learning and Verbal Behavior, 4*, 32–38.

Paivio, A. (1965b). Personality and audience influence. In B. A. Maher (Ed.), *Progress in experimental personality research, Vol. 2*. (pp. 127–178) New York: Academic

Paivio, A. (1967). Paired-associate learning and free recall of nouns as a function of concreteness, specificity, imagery, and meaningfulness. *Psychological Reports, 20*, 239–245.

Paivio, A. (1968a). Effects of imagery instructions and concreteness of memory pegs in a mnemonic system. *Proceedings of the 76th Convention, American Psychological Association*, 77–78.

Paivio, A. (1968b). A factor-analytic study of word attributes and verbal learning. *Journal of Verbal Learning and Verbal Behavior, 7*, 41–49.

Paivio, A. (1969). Mental imagery in associative learning and memory. *Psychological Review, 76*, 241–263.

Paivio, A. (1971a). Imagery and deep structure in the recall of English nominalizations. *Journal of Verbal Learning and Verbal Behavior, 10*, 1–21.

Paivio, A. (1971b). *Imagery and verbal processes*. New York: Holt, Rinehart & Winston. Reprinted 1979, Hillsdale, NJ: Lawrence Erlbaum Associates

Paivio, A (1972). Symbolic and sensory modalities of memory. In M. E. Meyer (Ed.), *The third Western symposium on learning: Cognitive learning*. Bellingham, WA: Western Washington State College.

Paivio, A. (1973). Psychophysiological correlates of imagery. In F. J. McGuigan & R. Schoonover (Eds.), *The psychophysiology of thinking* (pp. 263–295). New York: Academic.

Paivio, A. (1975a). Coding distinctions and repetition effects in memory. In G. H. Bower (Ed.), *The psychology of learning and motivation, Vol. 9* (pp. 179–214). New York: Academic.

Paivio, A. (1975b). Perceptual comparisons through the mind's eye. *Memory & Cognition, 3*, 635–47.

Paivio, A. (1976a). Concerning imagery and simultaneous-successive processing. *Canadian Psychological Review, 17*, 69–72.

Paivio, A. (1976b). Imagery in recall and recognition. In J. Brown (Ed.), *Recall and recognition*. New York: Wiley, (pp. 104–129).

Paivio, A. (1977). Images, propositions, and knowledge. In J. M. Nicholas(Ed.), *Images, perception, and knowledge. The Western Ontario series in the philosophy of Science* (pp. 47–71). Dordrecht: Reidel, The Netherlands.

Paivio, A. (1978a). Comparison of mental clocks. *Journal of Experimental Psychology: Human Perception and Performance, 4*, 61–71.

Paivio, A. (1978b). Mental comparisons involving abstract attributes. *Memory & Cognition, 6*, 199–208.

Paivio, A. (1978c). On exploring visual knowledge. In B. S. Randhawa & W. E. Coffman (Eds.), *Visual learning, thinking, and communication* (pp. 113–132). New York: Academic.

Paivio, A. (1978d). The relationship between verbal and perceptual codes. In E. C. Carterette & M. P. Friedman (Eds.), *Handbook of perception. Vol. IX: Perceptual processing* (pp. 113–131). New York: Academic.

Paivio, A. (1980). On weighing things in your mind. In P. W. Jusezyk & T. W. Klein (Eds.), *The nature of thought: Essays in honor of D. O. Hebb* (pp. 133–159). Hillsdale, N.J.: Lawrence Erlbaum Associates, Inc.

Paivio, A. (1983a). The empirical case for dual coding. In J. C. Yuille (Ed.), *Imagery, memory and cognition: Essays in honor of Allan Paivio* (pp. 307–332). Hillsdale, N. J.: Lawrence Erlbaum Associates, Inc.

Paivio, A. (1983b). The mind's eye in arts and science. *Poetics, 12,* 1–18.

Paivio, A. (1983c). Strategies in language learning. In M. Pressley & J. R. Levin (Eds.), *Cognitive strategies research: Educational applications* (pp. 189–210). New York: Springer-Verlag.

Paivio, A. (1985). Cognitive and motivational functions of imagery in human performance. *Canadian Journal of Applied Sport Sciences, 10,* 22S–28S.

Paivio, A. (1986). *Mental representations: A dual coding approach.* New York: Oxford University press.

Paivio, A. (1989). A dual coding perspective on imagery and the brain. In J. W. Brown (Ed.), *Neuropsychology of visual perception* (pp. 203–216). Hillsdale, NJ: Lawrence Erlbaum Associates Inc.

Paivio, A. (1991a).Dual coding theory: Retrospect and current status. *Canadian Journal of Psychology, 45,* 255–287.

Paivio, A. (1991b). *Images in mind: The evolution of a theory.* Sussex, England: Harvester.

Paivio. A. (1991c). Mental representation in bilinguals. In A. G. Reynolds (Ed.), *Bilingualism, multiculturalism, and second language learning: The McGill conference in honor of Wallace E. Lambert* (pp. 713–126). Hillsdale, NJ: Lawrence Erlbaum Associates Inc.

Paivio, A., & Begg, I. (1971). Imagery and comprehension latencies as a function of sentence concreteness and structure. *Perception & Psychophysics, 10,* 408–412.

Paivio, A., & Begg, I. (1974). Pictures and words in visual search. *Memory & Cognition, 2,* 515–521.

Paivio, A., & Begg, I. (1981). *The psychology of language.* Englewood Cliffs, NJ: PrenticeHall.

Paivio, A., Clark, J. M., Digdon, N., & Bons, T. (1989). Referential processing: Correlates of naming pictures and imaging to words. *Memory & Cognition, 17,* 163–174.

Paivio, A., Clark, J. M., & Khan, M. (1988). Effects of concreteness and semantic relatedness on compound imagery ratings and cued recall. *Memory & Cognition, 16,* 422–430.

Paivio, A., Clark, J. M., & Lambert, W. E. (1988). Bilingual dual coding theory and semantic repetition effects on recall. *Journal of Experimental Psychology: Learning, Memory, and Cognition, 14,* 163–172.

Paivio, A., & Cohen, M. (1979). Eidetic imagery and cognitive abilities. *Journal of Mental Imagery, 3,* 53–64.

Paivio, A., & Csapo, K. (1969). Concrete-image and verbal memory codes. *Journal of Experimental Psychology, 80,* 279–285.

Paivio, A., & Csapo, K. (1973). Picture superiority in free recall: Imagery or dual coding? *Cognitive Psychology, 5,* 176–206.

Paivio, A., & Desrochers, A. (1979). Effects of an imagery mnemonic on second language recall and comprehension. *Canadian Journal of Psychology, 33,* 17–28.

Paivio, A., & Desrochers, A. (1980). A dual-coding approach to bilingual memory. *Canadian Journal of Psychology, 34,* 390–401.

Paivio, A., & Ernest, C. (1971). Imagery ability and visual perception of verbal and nonverbal stimuli. *Perception & Psychophysics, 10,* 429–432.

Paivio, A., & Foth, D. (1970). Imaginal and verbal mediators and noun concreteness in paired-associate learning: The elusive interaction. *Journal of Verbal Leaning and Verbal Behavior, 9,* 384–290.

Paivio, A., & Harshman, R. A. (1983). Factor analysis of a questionnaire on imagery and verbal habits and skills. *Canadian Journal of Psychology, 37,* 461–483.

Paivio, A., Khan, M., & Begg, I. M. (2000). Concreteness and relational effects on recall of adjective-noun pairs. *Canadian Journal of Experimental Psychology, 54,* 149–159.

Paivio, A., & Lambert, W. E. (1959). Measures and correlates of audience anxiety ("stage fright"). *Journal of Personality, 27,* 1–17.

Paivio, A., & Lambert, W. (1981). Dual coding and bilingual memory. *Journal of Verbal Learning and Verbal Behavior, 20,* 532–539.

Paivio, A., & Madigan, S. A. (1968). Imagery and association value in paired-associate learning. *Journal of Experimental Psychology, 76,* 35–39.

Paivio, A., & Okovita, H. W. (1971). Word imagery modalities and associative learning in blind and sighted subjects. *Journal of Verbal Learning and Verbal Behavior, 10,* 506–510.

Paivio, A., & O'Neill, B. J. (1970). Visual recognition thresholds and dimensions of word meaning. *Perception & Psychophysics, 8,* 273–275.

Paivio, A., Philipchalk, R., & Rowe, E. J. (1975). Free and serial recall of pictures, sounds, and words. *Memory & Cognition, 3,* 586–590.

Paivio, A., & Rowe, E. J. (1971). Intrapair imagery effects in verbal discrimination and incidental associative learning. *Canadian Journal of Psychology, 25,* 302–312.

Paivio, A., & Simpson, H. M. (1968). Magnitude and latency of the pupillary response during an imagery task as a function of stimulus abstractness and imagery ability. *Psychonomic Science, 12,* 45–46.

Paivio, A., Smythe, P. C., & Yuille, J. C. (1968). Imagery versus meaningfulness of nouns in paired associate learning. *Canadian Journal of Psychology, 22,* 427–441.

Paivio, A., & Steeves, R. (1967). Relations between personal values and the imagery and meaningfulness of value words. *Perceptual and Motor Skills, 24,* 357–358.

Paivio, A., & te Linde, J. (1980). Symbolic comparisions of objects on color attributes. *Journal of Experimental Psychology: Human Perception & Performance, 6,* 652–661.

Paivio, A., & te Linde, J. (1982). Imagery, memory, and the brain. *Canadian Journal of Psychology, 36,* 243–272.

Paivio, A., & Walsh, M. (1994). Psychological processes in metaphor comprehension and memory. In A. Ortony (Ed.), *Metaphor and thought* (2nd ed., pp. 307–328). New York: Cambridge University Press.

Paivio, A., Walsh, M., & Bons, T. (1994). Concreteness and memory: When and Why? *Journal of Experimental Psychology: Learning, Memory, and Cognition, 20,* 1196–1204.

Paivio, A., & Yuille, J. C. (1969). Changes in associative strategies and paired-associate learning over trials as a function of word imagery and type of learning set. *Journal of Experimental Psychology, 79,* 458–463.

Paivio, A., Yuille, J. C., & Madigan, S. A. (1968). Concreteness, imagery, and meaningfulness values for 925 nouns. *Journal of Experimental Psychology, 76,* 1–25.

Paivio, S. C., Hall, I. E., Halowaty, K. A. M., Jellis, J. B., & Tran, N. (2001). Imaginal confrontation for resolving childhood abuse issues. *Psychotherapy Research, 11,* 433–453.

Paivio, S. C., & Nieuwenhuis, J. A. (2001). Efficacy of emotion focused therapy for adult survivors of child abuse: A preliminary study. *Journal of Traumatic Stress, 14,* 115–133.

Patten, B. M. (1973). Visually mediated thinking: A report of the case of Albert Einstein. *Journal of Learning Disabilities, 6,* 415–420.

Patterson, K., & Hodges, J. R. (2000). Semantic dementia: One window on the structure and organization of semantic memory. In F. Boller & J. Grafman (Eds.), *Handbook of Neuropsychology* 2nd ed. Vol. 2 (pp. 313–333). Amsterdam: Elsevier.

Paul, G. L. (1966). *Insight versus desensitization in psychotherapy: An experiment in anxiety reduction*. Stanford, CA: Stanford University Press.

Pederson, D. R., & Moran, G. (1999). The relationship imperative: Arguments for a broad definition of attachment. *Journal of Family Psychology, 13,* 496–500.

Pennebaker, J. W., & Beall, S. K. (1986). Confronting a traumatic event: Toward an understanding of inhibition and disease. *Journal of Abnormal Psychology, 95,* 274–281.

Pepperberg, I. M. (1999). Rethinking syntax: A commentary on E. Kako's "Elements of syntax in the systems of three language-trained animals." *Animal Learning & Behavior, 27,* 15–17.

Perky, C. W. (1910). An experimental study of imagination. *American Journal of Psychology, 21,* 422–452.

Piaget, J. (1952). *The origins of intelligence in children*. New York: International Universities Press.

Piaget, J. (1993). *John Amos Comenius*. Retrieved Feb. 29, 2004 from http/www.ibe.unesco.org/publications/Thinkerspdf/comeniuse.pdf.

Piaget, J., & Inhelder, B. (1971). *Mental imagery in the child: A study in the development of imaginal representations*. London: Routledge & Kegan Paul.

Pinker, S. (1994). *The language instinct*. New York: Morrow.

Pinker, S., & Bloom, P. (1990). Natural language and natural selection. *Behavioral and brain sciences, 13,* 13, 585–642.

Pinker, S., & Jackendoff, R. (2005). The faculty of language: What's special about it? *Cognition, 95,* 201–236.

Platt, J. R. (1964). Strong inference. *Science, 146,* 347–353.

Plant, D. C. (2002). Graded modality-specific specialization in semantics: A computational account of optic aphasia. *Cognitive Neuropsychology, 19,* 603–639.

Posner, M. I., Boies, S. J., Eichelman, W. H., & Taylor, R. L. (1969). Retention of visual and name codes of single letters. *Journal of Experimental Psychology Monographs, 79*(1, Pt. 2).

Posner, M. I., & Rothbart, M. K. (2004). Hebb's neural networks support the integration of psychological science. *Canadian Psychology, 45,* 265–278.

Povinelli, D. J., Bering, J. M., Giambrone, S. (2000). Toward a science of other minds: Escaping the argument by analogy. *Cognitive Science, 24,* 509–541.

Povinelli, D. J., & Vonk, J. (2003). Chimpanzee minds: suspiciously human? *Trends in Cognitive Science, 7,* 157–160.

Prabhakaran, V., Narayanan, K., Zhao. Z., &. Gabrieli, J. D. (2000). Integration of diverse information in working memory within the frontal lobe. *Nature Neuroscience, 3,* 85–90.

Pressley, G. M. (1976). Mental imagery helps eight-year- olds remember what they read. *Journal of Educational Psychology, 68,* 355–359.

Price, C. J., & Devlin, J. T. (2003). The myth of visual word form area. *NeuroImage, 19,* 471–481.

Pritchard, R. M., Heron, W., & Hebb, D. O. (1960). Visual perception approached by the method of stabilized images. *Canadian Journal of Psychology, 14,* 67–77.

Prideaux, T. (1968, December). Cubism. *Life, 65,* 49–51

Purnell, K. N., & Solman, R. T (1991). The influence of technical illustrations on students' comprehension of geography. *Reading Research Quarterly, 26,* 277–299.

Pylyshyn, Z. (1973). What the mind's eye tells the mind's brain: A critique of mental imagery. *Psychological Bulletin, 80,* 1–24.

Pylyshyn. Z. (1981). The imagery debate: Analogue media versus tacit knowledge. *Psychological Review, 88,* 16–45.

Pylyshyn, Z. (2003). *Seeing and visualizing: It's not what you think*. Cambridge, MA: The MIT Press.

Quine, W. V. O. (1953). *From a logical point of view*. Cambridge, MA: Harvard University Press.

Rachman, S. J., & Wilson, G. T. (1980). *The effects of psychological therapy* (2nd ed.). New York: Pergamon.

Rado, A., & Scott, A. (1996). *Is* there a binding problem? Retrieved April 4, 2003 from: http://www.math.arizona.edu/~rado/bp4-New/bp4.html

Rafal, R. T., & Robertson, L. (1995) The neurology of visual attention. In M. Gazzaniga (Ed.), *The cognitive neurosciences*. (pp. 625–648). Cambridge, MA: MIT Press,

Ramachandran, V. S., & Blakeslee, S. (1998). *Phantoms in the brain*. London: Fourth Estate.

Ramsey, R. M. G. (1980). Language-learning approach styles of adult multilinguals and successful language learners. In V. Teller & S. J. White (Eds.), Studies in child language and multilingualism. (pp.73–96). New York: New York Academy of Sciences.

Rapp, B. C., & Caramazza, A. (1995). Disorders of lexical processing and the lexicon. In M. S. Gazzaniga (ed.), *The cognitive neurosciences* (pp. 901–914). Cambridge, MA: MIT Press.

Reddy, M. J. (1993). The conduit metaphor: A case of frame conflict in our language about language. In A. Ortony (Ed.), *Metaphor and thought* (2nd ed., pp. 164–201). Cambridge England: Cambridge University Press.

Reese, H. W. (1970). Introduction to imagery in children's learning: Symposium. *Psychological Bulletin, 73,* 383–384.

Reichle, E. D., Carpenter, P. A., & Just, M. A. (2000). The neural basis of strategy and skill in sentence-picture verification.*Cognitive Psychology, 40,* 261–295.

Reynolds, P. C. (1976). Language and skilled activity. In S. Harnad, H. D. Steklis, & J. Lancaster (Eds.), *Origins and evolution of language and speech* (pp. 150–166). New York: The New York Academy of Sciences.

Reynolds, A., & Paivio, A. (1968). Cognitive and emotional determinants of speech. *Canadian Journal of Psychology, 22,* 164–175.

Reynolds, S. T., & Glucksberg, S. (in press). The language specificity of discourse models. *Language and Cognition.*

Rhodes, M. G., & Anastasi, J. S. (2000). The effects of a levels-of-processing manipulation on false recall. *Psychonomic Bulletin & Review, 7,* 158–162.

Richardson, J. T. E. (2003). Dual coding versus relational processing in memory for concrete and abstract words. *European Journal of Cognitive Psychology, 15,* 481–50l.

Richardson, J. T. E., & Barry, C. (1985). The effects of minor closed head injury upon human memory: Further evidence on the role of mental imagery. *Cognitive Neuropsychology, 2,* 149–168.

Richardson, J. T. E., & Vecchi, T. (2002). A jigsaw-puzzle imagery task for assessing visuospatial processes in young and old people. *Behavioral Research Methods, Instruments, and Computers, 34,* 69–82.

Richmond, B. G., & Strait, D. S. (2000). Evidence that humans evolved from a knuckle-walking ancestor. *Nature, 404,* 382–385.

Riddoch, M. J. (1990). Loss of visual mental imagery: a generation deficit. *Cognitive Neuropsychology, 7,* 249–273.

Riddoch, M. J., & Humphreys, G. W. (1987). A case of integrative agnosia. *Brain, 110,* 1431–1462.

Ridley, M. (2003a). *Nature via nurture: Genes, experience, and what makes us human.* New York: HarperCollins.

Ridley, M. (2003b, June 2). What makes you who you are. *Time* (Canadian Edition), *161,* 32–39.

Rilling, M. (1996). The mystery of the vanished citations: James McConnel's forgotten 1960s quest for planarian learning, a biochemical engram, and celebrity. *American Psychologist, 51,* 589–598.

Rissenberg, M., & Glanzer, M. (1986). Picture superiority in free recall: The effects of normal aging and primary degenerative dementia. *Journal of Geronotology, 41,* 64–71.

Ristau, C. A. (1998). Cognitive ethology: The minds of children and animals. In D. L. Cummins & C. Allen (Eds.), *The evolution of mind* (pp. 127–161). New York: Oxford University Press.

Rizzolatti, G., & Arbib, M. A. (1998). Language within our grasp. *Trends in Neurosciences, 21,* 188–194,

Robbins, T. W., & Everitt, B. J. (1995). Arousal systems and attention. In M. Gazzaniga (Ed.), *The cognitive neurosciences* (pp. 703–720). Cambridge, MA: MIT Press.

Roberston-Tchabo, E. A., Hausman, C. P., & Arenberg, D. (1976). A classic mnemonic for older learners: A trip that works. *Educational Gerontology, 1,* 102–109.

Roberts, W. A. (1998). *Principles of animal cognition.* Boston: McGraw-Hill.

Roberts, W. A. (2002). Are animals stuck in time? *Psychological Bulletin, 125,* 473–489.

Roberts, W. A. (Ed.). (2005). Special issue on cognitive time travel in people and animals. *Learning and Motivation, 36,* 107–278.

Rodriguez, M., & Sadoski, M. (2000). Effects of rote, context, keyword, and context/keyword methods on retention of vocabulary in EFL classrooms. *Language Learning, 50,* 385–412.

Roe, A. (1951). A study of imagery in research scientists. *Journal of Personality, 19,* 459–470.

Roelops, A. (2004). Seriality of phonological encoding in naming objects and reading their names. *Memory & Cognition, 32,* 212–222.

Rolls, E. (1995). A theory of emotion and consciousness, and its application to understanding the neural basis of emotion. In M. S. Gazzaniga (Ed.), *The cognitive neurosciences* Cambridge, MA: MIT Press. (pp. 1091–1106).

Rosch, E. (1975). Cognitive reference points. *Cognitive Psychology, 7,* 523–547.

Rosch, E., Mervis, C. B., Gray, W., Johnston, D., & Boyes-Braem, P. (1975). Basic objects in natural categories. *Cognitive Psychology, 8,* 382–439.

Rosenbaum, R. S., Köhler, S., Schacter, D. L., Moscovitch, M., Westmacott, R., Black, S. E., et al. (2005). The case of K. C.: Contributions of a memory-impaired person to memory theory. *Neuropsychologia, 43,* 989–1021.

Rosenbaum, R. S., McKinnon, M. C., Levine, B., & Moscovitch, M. (2004). Visual imagery deficits, impaired strategic retrieval, or memory loss: Disentangling the nature of an amnesic person's autobiographical memory deficit. *Neuropsychologia, 42,* 1619–1635.

Roskies, A. L. (1999). The binding problem. *Neuron, 24,* 7–9.

Rossi, P. (2000, S. Clucas Trans.). *Logic and the art of memory: The quest for a universal language.* Chicago: University of Chicago Press.

Rothenberg, A. (1986). Artistic creation as stimulated by superimposed versus combined-composite visual images. *Journal of Personality and Social Psychology, 50,* 370–381.

Rubin, D. C. (1995). *Memory in oral traditions: The cognitive psychology of epic, ballads, and counting out rhymes.* New York: Oxford University Press.

Ruddell, R. B.. & Unrau, N. J. (eds) (2004). *Theoretical models and processes of reading* (5th ed.). Newark, DE: International Reading Association.

Runco, M. A. (1991). The evaluative, valuative, and divergent thinking of children. *Journal of Creative Behavior, 25,* 311–319.

Runco, M. A., & Charles, R. E. (1997). Developmental trends in creative potential and creative performance. In M. A. Runco (Ed.), *The creativity research handbook* (Vol. 1, pp. 115–152).

Rushton, J. P. (1997). Cranial size and IQ in Asian Americans from birth to age seven. *Intelligence, 25,* 7–20.

Russell, B. (1940). *An inquiry into meaning and truth.* London: Allen & Unwin. Whitehead, A. H. & Russell, B. (1910–1913). principle–mathematican. Cambridge, England: University Press.

Ryle, G. (1949). *The concept of mind.* London: Hutchison & Company.

Saariluoma, P. (1991). Visuo-spatial interference and apperception in chess. In R. H. Logie & M. Denis (Eds.), *Mental images in human cognition* (pp. 83–94). Amsterdam: Elsevier.

Sachs, J. S. (1967). Recognition memory for semantic and syntactic aspects of connected discourse. *Perception & Psychophysics, 2,* 437–442.

Sacks, O. (1985). *The man who mistook his wife for a hat.* New York: Summit.

Sadoski, M. (1983). An exploratory study of the relationship between reported imagery and the comprehension and recall of a story. *Reading Research Quarterly, 19,* 110–123.

Sadoski, M. (1999). Comprehending comprehension [Essay Review of the book *Comprehension: A paradigm for cognition*]. *Reading Research Quarterly, 34,* 493–500.

Sadoski, M. (2002). Dual coding theory and reading poetic text. *The Journal of the Imagination in Language Learning and Teaching, 7,* 78–83.

Sadoski, M., Goetz, E. T., & Avila, E. (1995). Context effects in text recall: Dual coding or context availability? *Reading Research Quarterly, 30,* 278–288.

Sadoski, M., Goetz, E. T., & Fritz, J. B. (1993). The impact of concreteness on comprehensibility, interest, and memory for text: Implications for dual coding theory and text design. *Journal of Educational Psychology, 85,* 291–304.

Sadoski, M., Goetz, E. T., & Rodriguez, M. (2000). Engaging texts: Effects of concreteness on comprehensibility, interest, and recall in four text types. *Journal of Educational Psychology, 92,* 85–95.

Sadoski, M., Kealy, W. A., Goetz, E. T., Paivio, A. (1997). Concreteness and imagery effects in the written composition of definitions. *Journal of Educational Psychology, 89,* 518–526.

Sadoski, M., & Paivio, A. (2001). *Imagery and text: A dual coding theory of reading and writing.* Mahwah, NJ: Lawrence Erlbaum Associates, Inc.

Sadoski, M., & Paivio, A. (2004). A dual coding theoretical model of reading. In R. B. Ruddell & N. J. Unrau (Eds.), *Theoretical models and processes of reading* (5th ed., pp. 1329–1362). Newark, DE: International Reading Association.

Sadoski, M., Paivio, A., & Goetz, E. T. (1991). A critique of schema theory in reading and a dual coding alternative. *Reading Research Quarterly, 26,* 463–484.

Sadoski, M., & Willson, V. L. (In press). Effects of a theoretically-based large scale reading intervention in a multicultural urban school district. *American Educational Research Journal*

Sagan, C. (1977). *The dragons of Eden: Speculations on the evolution of human intelligence.* New York: Ballantine.

Sagan, C. (1980). *Cosmos.* New York: Random House.

Salzinger, K. (1990, September). B. F. Skinner. *APS Observer, 3,* 1–4.

Savage-Rumbaugh, S., Shanker, S. G., & Taylor, T. J. (1998). *Apes, language and the human mind.* New York: Oxford University Press.

Savard, J-G., & Richards, J. (1970). *Les indices d'utilité du vocabulaire fondamental français* [xxxx]. Quebec, PQ: Les Presses de L'Université Lavale.

Schachter, S., & Singer, J. (1962). Cognitive, social, and physiological determinants of emotional state. *Psychological Review, 69,* 379–399.

Schacter, D. L. (1996). *Searching for memory: The brain, the mind, and the past.* New York: Basic Books.

Schacter, D. L., & Tulving, E. (1994). What are the memory systems of 1994? In D. L. Schacter & E. Tulving (Eds.), *Memory systems* (pp. 1–38). Cambridge, MA: MIT Press.

Schooler, J. W., & Engstler-Schooler, T. Y. (1990). Verbal overshadowing of visual memories: Some things are better left unsaid. *Cognitive Psychology, 22,* 36–71.

Schultz, J. (1982). *Writing from start to finish.* Upper Montclair, NJ: Boynton/Cook.

Schwanenflugel, P. J., Akin, C., & Luh, W. M. (1992). Context availability and the recall of abstract and concrete sentences. *Memory & Cognition, 20,* 96–104.

Schwartz, G. E., Fair, P. L, Salt, P., Mandel, M. R., & Klerman, G. L. (1976). Facial muscle patterning to affective imagery in depressed and nondepressed patients. *Science, 192,* 489–491.

Schwartz, M. F., Saffran, E. M., Fink, R. B., Myers, J. L., & Martin, N. (1994). Mapping therapy: a treatment programme for agrammatism. *Aphasiology, 8,* 19–54.

Segal, S. J., & Fusella, V. (1970). Influence of imaged pictures and sounds on detection of visual and auditory signals. *Journal of Experimental Psychology, 83,* 458–464.

Sejnowski, T. J. (2003). The once and future Hebb synapse. *Canadian Psychology, 44,* 17–20.

Seyfarth, R. M., Cheney, D. L., & Marler, P. (1980). Monkey responses to three different alarm calls: Evidence of predator classification and semantic communication. *Science, 210,* 801–903.

Seymour, P. H. K. (1973). A model for reading, naming, and comparison. *British Journal of Psychology, 64,* 35–49.

Shallice, T., & Jackson, M. (1988). Lissauer on agnosia. *Cognitive Neuropsychology, 5,* 153–192.

Shanker, S. G., Savage-Rumbaugh, E. S., & Taylor, T. J. (1999). Kanzi: A new beginning. *Animal Learning & Behavior, 27,* 24–25.

Shankweiler, D., Crain, S., Gorrell, P., & Tuller. B. (1989). Reception of language in Broca's aphasia. *Language and Cognitive Processes, 4,* 1–35.

Sharma, J., Angelucci, A., & Sur, M. (2000). Induction of visual orientation modules in auditory cortex. *Nature, 404,* 841–847.

Sharps, M. J., Foster, B. T., Martin, S. S., & Nunes, M. A. (1999). Spatial and relational frameworks for free recall in young and older adults. *Current Psychology, 18,* 241–253.

Sheffield, F. D. (1961). Theoretical considerations in the learning of complex sequential tasks from demonstration and practice. In A. A. Lumsdaine (ed.), *Student response in programmed instruction.* (NAS-NRS Publication No. 943) Washington, DC: National Academy of Sciences-National Research Council.

Sheikh, A. A. (Ed.). (2002). *Therapeutic imagery techniques.* Amytyville, NY: Baywood.

Sheikh, A. A., Kunzendorf, R. G., & Sheikh, K. S. (2003). Healing images: Historical perspective. In A. A. Sheikh (Ed.), *Healing images: The role of imagination in health* (pp. 8–26). Amityville, NY: Baywood.

Sheikh, A. A., Kunzendorf, R. G., Sheikh, K. S., & Baer, S. M. (2003). Physiological consequences of imagery and related approaches. In A. A. Sheikh (Ed.), *Healing images: The role of imagination in health* (pp. 27–52). Amityville, NY: Baywood.

Shepard, R. N. (1967). Recognition memory for words, sentences, and pictures. *Journal of Verbal Learning and Verbal Behavior, 6,* 156–163.

Shepard, R. N. (1978). Externalization of mental images and the act of creation. In B. S. Randhawa & W. E. Coffman (Eds.), *Visual learning, thinking, and communication* (pp. 133–190). New York: Academic Press.

Shepard, R. N. (1984). Ecological constraints on mental representation: Resonant kinematics of perceiving, imagining, thinking and dreaming. *Psychological Review, 91,* 417–447.

Shepard, R. N., & Cooper, L. A. (1982). *Mental images and their transformations.* Cambridge, MA: MIT Press.

Shepard, R. N., Hovland, C. I., & Jenkins, H. M. (1961). Learning and memorization of categorizations. *Psychological Monographs, 75*(13, Whole No. 517).

Shepard, R. N., & Metzler, J. (1971). Mental rotation of three-dimensional objects. *Science, 171,* 701–703.

Sherry, D. F. (1990). Evolutionary modification of memory and the hippocampus. In L. R. Squire & E. Lindenlaub (Eds.), *The biology of memory symposia Medica Hoechst 23* (pp. 401–421). Stuttgart: Schattauer Verlag,.

Sherry, D. F., & Schacter, D. L. (1987). The evolution of multiple memory systems. *Psychological Review, 94,* 439–454.

Shettleworth, S. J. (1998). *Cognition, evolution, and behavior.* New York: Oxford University Press.

Shore, D. I., Stanford, W., MacInnes, J. W., Brown, R. E., & Klein, R. M. (2001). Of mice and men: Virtual Hebb-Williams mazes permit comparison of spatial learning across species. *Cognitive, Affective, and Behavioural Neuroscience, 1,* 83–89.

Siegel, L. S., & Brainerd, C. J. (Eds.). (1978). *Alternatives to Piaget: Critical essays on the theory.* New York: Academic.

Simon, H. A., & Chase, W. G. (1973). Skill in chess. *American Scientist, 61,* 394–403.

Simonton, D. K. (1997). Historiometric studies of creative genius. In M. A. Runco (Ed.), *The creativity handbook* (Vol. 1, pp. 3–28). Cresskill, NJ: Hampton.

Singer, J. L. (1974). *Imagery and daydream methods in psychotherapy and behavior modification.* New York: Academic.

Skemp, R. R. (1987). *The psychology of learning mathematics.* Hillsdale, NJ: Lawrence Erlbaum Associates, Inc.

Skinner, B. F. (1953). *Science and human behavior.* New York: Macmillan.

Skinner, B. F. (1957). *Verbal behavior.* New York: Appleton-Century-Crofts.

Skinner, B. F. (1974). *About behaviorism.* New York: Knopf.

Skinner, B. F. (1984). *A matter of consequences: Part Three of an autobiography.* New York: New York University Press.

Sloboda. J. A. (1996). The acquisition of musical performance expertise: Deconstructing the "talent" account of individual differences in musical expressivity. In K. Anders Ericsson (Ed.), *The road to excellence: The acquisition of expert performance in the arts and sciences, sports and games* (pp. 107–126). Mahwah NJ: Lawrence Erlbaum Associates, Inc.

Smith, J. D., Minda, J. P., & Washburn, D. A. (2004). Category learning in Rhesus monkeys: A study of the Shepard, Hovland, and Jenkins (1961) tasks. *Journal of Experimental Psychology: General, 133,* 398–414.

Smith, J. D., Wilson, M., & Reisberg, D. (1995). The role of subvocalization in auditory imagery. *Neuropsychologia, 33,* 1433–1454.

Snodgrass, J. G. (1984). Concepts and their surface representations. *Journal of Verbal Learning and Verbal Behavior. 23,* 3–22.

Snow, C. (1977). Mother's speech research: From input to interaction. In C. Snow & C. Ferguson (Eds.), *Talking to children* (pp. 31–49). Cambridge, England: Cambridge University Press.

Spearman, C. (1927). *The abilities of man: Their nature and measurement.* New York: Macmillan.

Sperling, G. (1960). The information available in brief visual presentations. *Psychological Monographs, 74* (Whole No. 498).

Spurgeon, C. F. E. (1935). *Shakespeare's imagery and what it tells us.* New York: Cambridge University Press.

Staddon, J. E. R. (2001). *Adaptive dynamics: The theoretical analysis of behavior.* Cambridge, MA: MIT Press.

Stamenov, M. L. (2002). Some features that make mirror neurons and human language faculty unique. In M. L. Stamenov & V. Gallese (Eds.), *Mirror neurons and the evolution of brain and language* (pp. 249–271). Amsterdam: Benjamins.

Standing, L. (1973). Learning 10,000 pictures. *Quarterly Journal of Experimental Psychology, 25,* 207–222.

Standing, L., & Smith, P. (1975). Verbal-pictorial transformations in recognition memory. *Canadian Journal of Psychology, 29,* 316–326.

Stein, B. E., Wallace, M. T., & Meredith, M. A. (1995). Neural mechanisms mediating attention and orientation to multisensory cues. In M. S. Gazzaniga (ed.), *The cognitive neurosciences* (pp. 683–702). Cambridge, MA: MIT Press.

Sternberg, R. J. (1985). Beyond IQ: *Atriarchic theory of intelligence.* Cambridge: Cambridge University Press.

Sternberg, R. J. (1997). The concept of intelligence and its role in lifelong learning and success. *American Psychologist, 52*, 1030–1037.

Sternberg, R. J. (2000). Intelligence and wisdom. In R. J. Sternberg (Ed.), *Handbook of intelligence* (pp. 631–649). Cambridge, England: Cambridge University Press,

Sternberg, R. J., & O'Hara, L. A. (2000). Intelligence and creativity. In R. J. Sternberg (Ed.), *Handbook of intelligence* (pp. 611–630). Cambridge, England: Cambridge University Press.

Stöber, J., & Borkovec, T. D. (2002). Reduced concreteness of worry in generalized anxiety disorder: Findings from a therapy study. *Cognitive Therapy and Research, 26*, 89–96.

Stokoe, W. C., & Marschark, M. (1999). Signs, gestures, and signs. In L. S. Messing & R. Campbell (Eds.), *Gesture, speech, and sign* (pp. 161–181). New York: Oxford University Press.

Stoltz-Loike, M., & Bornstein, M. H. (1987). The roles of imagery, language, and metamemory in cross-modal transfer in children. *Psychological Research, 49*, 63–68.

Strauss, S. (1987, October). A scientist's triumph. *Report on Business Magazine*, 69–77.

Strømnes, F. J. (1974a). No universality of cognitive structures? Two experiments with almost perfect one-trialo learning of translatable operators in a Ural-Altaic and an Indo-European Language. *Scandinavian Journal of Psychology. 15*, 300–309.

Strømnes, F. J. (1974b). To be is not always to be: The hypothesis of cognitive universality in the light of studies on elliptic language behaviour. *Scandinavian Journal of Psychology, 15*, 89–98.

Strømnes, F. J. (2006). *The fall of the word and the rise of the mental model: A reinterpretation of the recent research on the use of language and spatial cognition.* Frankfurt-am Main, Germany: Peter Lang Publishing.

Strømnes, F. J., & Iivonen, L. (1985). The teaching of the syntax written language to deaf children knowing no syntax. *Human Learning, 4*, 251–265.

Tattersal, I. (2000, January). Once we were not alone. *Scientific American, 282*, 56–62.

Taub, S. E. (2001). *Language from the body: Iconicity and metaphor in Americal Sign Language.* New York: Cambridge University Press.

Taura, H. (1996). *A test on a bilingual dual coding hypothesis in Japanese–English bilinguals.* Unpublished master's thesis, Macquarie University, Sydney, Australia.

Taylor, G., Bagby, M., & Parker, J. (1997). *Disorders of affect regulation: Alexythymia in medical and psychiatric illness.* Cambridge, England: Cambridge University Press.

Tees, R. C., & More, L. K. (1967). Effect of amount of perceptual learning upon disappearances observed under reduced stimulation conditions. *Perception and Psychophysics, 2*, 564–568.

te Linde, J., & Paivio, A. (1979). Symbolic comparisons of color similarity. *Memory & Cognition, 3*, 635–647.

Teng, E., & Squire, L. R. (1999). Memory for places learned long ago is intact after hippocampal damage. *Nature, 400*, 675–677.

Terman, L. (1916). *The measurement of intelligence.* Boston: Houghton Mifflin.

Ternes,W., & Yuille, J. C. (1972). Words and pictures in an STM task. *Journal of Experimental Psychology, 96*, 78–86.

Terrace, H. S., Petitto, L. A., Sanders, R. J., & Bever, T. G. (1979). Can an ape create a sentence? *Science, 206*, 891–902.

Thom, R. (1980). The genesis of representational space according to Piaget. In M. Piattelli-Palmarini (Ed.), *Language and learning: The debate between Jean Piaget and Noam Chomsky* (pp. 361–368). Cambridge, MA: Harvard University Press.

Thomas, N. J. T. (1989). Experience and theory as determinants of attitudes toward mental representation: The case of Knight Dunlap and the vanishing images of J. B. Watson. *American Journal of Psychology, 102*, 395–412.

Thompson, C. P., Hermann, D. J., Bruce, D., Reed, J. D., Payne, D. G., & Toglia, M. P. (eds). (1998). *Autobiographical memory: Theoretical and applied perspectives.* Mahwah, NJ: Lawrence Erlbaum Associates.

Thompson, V., & Paivio, A. (1994). Memory for pictures and sounds: Independence of auditory and visual codes. *Canadian Journal of Experimental Psychology, 48,* 380–398.

Thompson, W. L., & Kosslyn, S. M. (2000). Neural systems activated during visual mental imagery: A review and a meta-analysis. In A. W. Toga & J. C. Mazziota (Eds.), *Brain mapping III. The systems* (pp. 535–560). San Diego, CA: Academic.

Thurstone, L. L. (1938). *Primary mental abilities.* Chicago: Education Industry Service.

Timberlake, W., & Faneslow, M. S. (1994). Introduction to symposium on behavior systems. *Psychonomic Bulletin & Review, 1,* 403–404.

Tinklepaugh, O. L. (1928). An experimental study of representative factors in monkeys. *Journal of Comparative Psychology, 8,* 197–236.

Tinklepaugh, O. L. (1932). Multiple delayed reaction with chimpanzees and monkeys. *Journal of Comparative Psychology, 13,* 207–243.

Tolman, E. C. (1932). *Purposive behavior in animals and men.* New York: Century.

Tolman, E. C. (1948). Cognitive maps in rats and men. *Psychological Review, 55,* 189–208.

Tomasello, M. (1999). *The cultural origins of human evolution.* Cambridge, MA: Harvard University Press.

Tooby, J., & Cosmides, L. (1995). Mapping the evolved functional organization of mind and brain. In M. S. Gazzaniga (Ed.), *The cognitive neurosciences* (pp. 1185–1197). Cambridge, MA: MIT Press.

Torrance, E. P. (1966). *Torrance Tests of Creative Thinking, research edition.* Princeton, NJ: Personnel Press.

Tuley, K., & Bell, N. (1997). *On cloud nine: visualizing and verbalizing for math.* San Luis Obispo, CA: Gander Publishing.

Tulving, E. (1983). *Elements of episodic memory.* New York: Oxford University Press.

Tulving, E. (1985). Memory and consciousness, *Canadian Psychology, 26,* 1–12.

Tulving, E. (2005). Episodic memory amd autonoesis: Uniquely human? In H. Terrace & J. Metcalfe (Eds.), *The missing link in cognition: Evolution of self-knowing consciousness* (pp. 3–56). New York: Oxford University Press.

Tulving, A., & Thomson, D. M. (1973). Encoding specificity and retrieval processes in episodic memory. *Psychological review, 80,* 352–373.

Turner, E. A., & Rommetveit, R. (1967). Experimental manipulation of active and passive voice in children. *Language and Speech, 10,* 169–180.

Tyson, N. deG., & Goldsmith, D. (2004). *Origins: fourteen billion years of cosmic evolution.* New York: Norton.

Ullmann, S. (1962). *Semantics: An introduction to the science of meaning.* Oxford, England: Blackwell.

Underwood, B. J., & Schulz, R. W. (1960). *Meaningfulness and verbal learning.* Chicago: Lippincott.

Ungerleider, I. G., & Mishkin, M. (1982). Two cortical visual systems. In D. J. Ingle, M. A. Goodale, & R. J. W. Mansfield (Eds.), *Analysis of visual behavior* (pp. 549–586). Cambridge, MA: MIT Press.

Urban, K. K. (1991). On the development of creativity in children. *Creativity Research Journal, 4,* 177–191.

Urcuioli, P. J. (2001). Categorization and acquired equivalence. In R. Cook (Ed.), *Avian visual cognition.* Retrieved November 26, 2004 from http://www.pigeon.psy.tufts.edu/avc/urcuioli/

Uttal, W. R. (2005). *Neural theories of mind: Why the mind-brain problem may never be solved.* Mahwah, NJ: Lawrence Erlbaum Associates, Inc.

Vaid, J. (1988). Bilingual memory representation: A further test of dual coding theory. *Canadian Journal of Psychology, 42,* 84–90.

Vaid, J., & Hall, D. G. (1991). Neuropsychological perspectives on bilingualism. In A. G. Reynolds (Ed.), *Bilingualism, multiculturalism, and second language learning: The McGill conference in honor of Wallace E. Lambert* (pp. 81–112). Hillsdale, NJ: Lawrence Erlbaum Associates, Inc.

Van Fraassen, B. C. (1980). *The scientific image.* New York: Oxford University Press.

van Tijen, T., & Vojtechovsky, M. (1996). Orbis pictus Revised: an interactive exhibition. Retrieved February 22, 2004 http://imaginarymuseum.org/OPR/OPRWAAGE.HTM

Vanderwolf, C. H., & Cain, D. P. (1994). The behavioral neurobiology of learning and memory: A conceptual reorientation. *Brain Research reviews, 19,* 264–297.

Vaughan, W., Jr., & Greene, S. L. (1984). Pigeon visual memory capacity. *Journal of Experimental Psychology, Animal Behavior Processes, 14,* 256–271.

Vernon, P. A. (1983). Speed of information processing and general intelligence. *Intelligence, 7,* 53–70.

Vernon, P. A., Wickett, J. C., Bazana, P. G., & Stelmack, R. M. (2000). The neuropsychology and psychophysiology of intelligence. In R. J. Sternberg (Ed.), *Handbook of intelligence* (pp. 245–264). Cambridge, England: Cambridge University Press.

Vernon, P. E. (1961). *The structure of human abilities* (2nd ed.). London: Methuen.

Vokey, J. R., & Higham, P. A. (2005). Abstract analogies and positive transfer in artificial grammar learning. *Canadian Journal of Experimental Psychology, 59,* 54–61.

Volterra, V., Caselli, M. C., Capirci, O., & Pizzuto, E. (2005). Gesture and the emergence and development of language. In M. Tomasello & D. I. Slobin (Eds.), *Beyond nature and nurture: Essays in honor of Elizabeth Bates* (pp. 3–40). Mahwah, NJ: Lawrence Erlbaum Associates, Inc.

von Frisch, K. (1967). *The dance language and orientation of bees.* Cambridge, MA: Harvard University Press.

Wagner, A. D., Schacter, D. L., Rotte, M., Koutstaal, W., Maril, A., Dale., A. M., et al. (1998). Building memories: Remembering and forgetting of verbal experiences as predicted by brain activity. *Science, 281,* 1188–1191.

Wagner, R. K., & Stanovitch, K. E. (1996). Expertise in reading. In K. A. Ericsson (Ed.), *The road to excellence: The acquisition of expert performance in the arts and sciences, sports and games* (pp. 189–225). Mahwah, NJ: Lawrence Erlbaum Associates, Inc.

Walker, A., & Shipman, P. (1996). *The wisdom of the bones: In search of human origins.* New York: Alfred A. Knopf.

Wallach, M. A., & Kogan, N. (1965). *Modes of thinking in young children: A study of the creativity-intelligence distinction.* New York: Holt, Rinehart & Winston.

Wallas, G. (1926). *The art of thought.* New York: Harcourt Brace.

Ward, H. (1927). *Charles Darwin and the theory of evolution.* NewYork: Bobbs-Merrill.

Watanabe, S. (1996). Reward expectancy in primate prefrontal neurons, *Nature, 382,* 629–632.

Watson, J. B. (1930). *Behaviorism.* Chicago: University of Chicago Press.

Watson, J. D. (1968). *The double helix.* New York: Atheneum.

Watson, J. D., (ed). (2005). *Darwin: The indelible stamp.* Philadelphia, PA: Running Press.

Weber, R. J., & Harnish, R. (1974). Visual imagery for words: The Hebb test. *Journal of Experimental Psychology, 102,* 409–414.

Wechsler, D. (1939). *Measurement of adult intelligence.* Baltimore, MD: Williams & Wilkins.

Wechsler, D. (1981). *Manual for the Wechsler Adult Intelligence Scale–Revised.* San Antonio, TX: Psychological Corporation.

Weiskrantz, L., Barbur, J. L., & Sahraie, A. (1995). Parameters affecting conscious versus unconscious visual discrimination with damage to the visual cortex (V1). *Proceedings of the National Academy of Sciences, USA, 92,* 6122–6126.

Weldon, M. S., & Roediger, H. L. (1987). Altering retrieval demands reverses the picture superiority effect. *Memory and Cognition, 15,* 269–280.

Werner, H., & Kaplan, B. (1963). *Symbol formation: An organismic-developmental approach to the psychology of language and the expression of thought.* New York: Wiley.

Wertheimer, M. (1945). *Productive thinking.* New York: Harper.

West, W. C., O'Rourke, T. B., & Holcomb, P. J. (1998). Event related brain potentials and language comprehension: A cognitive neuroscience approach to the study of intellectual functioning. In S. Soraci & W. J.McIlvane (Eds.), *Perspectives on fundamental processes in intellectual functioning* (pp. 133–168). Stamford, CT: Ablex.

Whitehead, A. N., & Russell, B. (1910–1913). *Principia mathematica.* Cambridge, England: University Press.

Whitehouse, P. J. (1981). Imagery and verbal encoding in left and right hemisphere damaged patients. *Brain and Language, 14,* 315–332.

Whorf, B. L. (1956). *Language, thought, and reality.* Cambridge, MA: MIT Press.

Wilson, E. O. (1998). *Consilience: The unity of knowledge.* New York: Knopf.

Wilson, M. (2002). Six views of embodied cognition. *Psychonomic Bulletin & Review, 9,* 625–636.

Wolpe, J. (1958). *Psychotherapy by reciprocal inhibition.* Stanford, CA: Stanford University Press.

Wood, G. (1983). *Cognitive psychology: A skills approach.* Monterey, CA: Brooks/Cole.

Yarmey, A. D. (2003). Eyewitness identification: Guidlines and recommendations for identification procedures in the United States and Canada. *Canadian Psychology, 44,* 181–189.

Yates, F. A., (1966). *The art of memory.* London: Routledge & Kegan Paul.

Yerkes, R. M. (Ed.). (1921). Psychological examining in the United States Army. *Memoirs of the National Academy of Sciences,* No. 15.

Yovetich, W. S. (1985). *Cognitive processing of blissymbols by normal adults.* Unpublished doctoral dissertation, University of Western Ontario, London, Canada.

Young, J. E., Klosko, J. S., & Weishaar, M. E. (2003). *Schema therapy: A practitioner's guide.* New York: Guilford.

Zaidel, D., & Sperry, R. W. (1973). Performance on the Raven's Colored Progressive Matrices Test by subjects with cerebral commissurotomy. *Cortex, 9,* 34–39.

Zaidel, E. (1978). Lexical organization in the right hemisphere. P. Buser & A. Rougel-Buser (Eds.), *Cerebral correlates of conscious experience, INSERM Symposium No. 6* (pp. 177–197). Elsevier.

Zajonc, R. B. (1984). On the primacy of affect. *American Psychologist, 39,* 117–123.

Zajonc, R. B. (1985). Emotion and facial efference : A theory reclaimed. *Science, 228,* 15–21.

Zentall, T. R. (2000). Animal intelligence. In R. J. Sternberg (Ed.), *Handbook of intelligence* (pp. 197–215). New York: Cambridge University Press.

Zhang, M., Weisser, V. D., Stilla, R., Prather, S. C., & Sathian, K. (2004). Multisensory processing of object shape and its relation to mental imagery. *Cognitive, Affective, & Behavioral Neuroscience, 4,* 251–259.

Zuberbühler, K., Cheney, D. L., & Seyfarth, R. M. (1999). Conceptual semantics in a nonhuman primate. *Journal of Comparative Psychology, 113,* 33–42.

Author Index

Subject Index